A HISTORY OF NORTHERN RHODESIA

Early Days to 1953

A HISTORY OF
NORTHERN RHODESIA

Early Days to 1953

by L. H. Gann

LONDON

CHATTO & WINDUS

1964

Printed in Great Britain by
Robert MacLehose and Company Limited
The University Press, Glasgow

PREFACE

Africa is on the move. A whole Continent is in the throes of transformation and as many ancient landmarks disappear, Rhodesians require a better understanding of their past to help them to map out the future. The present volume, the first in a series on the history of the Federation, aims at filling a serious gap in historical literature, thereby making the people of this country more conscious of the complicated forces that have helped to shape the present. The project began with a request from the Northern Rhodesian Government for a history of Northern Rhodesia, and the Federal Government subsequently decided to expand the scheme into a larger undertaking which would comprise a volume on each of the Federation's constituent territories, as well as a fourth, dealing with the Federal State as a whole.

This work largely confines itself to the story of Northern Rhodesia under British governance. This limitation has been set because far more work still remains to be done on Central Africa's remoter past, a vital task which calls for co-operation from people as varied as archaeologists, ethnographers, linguists, anthropologists, tribal historians and ecologists, each of whom has a major role to perform in elucidating events of the more distant days. Many questions also remain to be answered on the Portuguese pioneers of Central Africa, but historians will not be able to do full justice to this period until all the projected volumes of documents on South-East Africa, now being prepared as a joint Portuguese-Rhodesian venture, will have appeared in print.

The author of this present work also accepted a second limitation. In compiling this history, he has concentrated on events along the Copper Belt and the Railway Strip to a much greater extent than outlying rural areas. This choice again was dictated by necessity, for a general work must not be too long; and however important tribal politics may have been locally the major decisions affecting the country in more recent days were made in cities and townships rather than scattered villages. At the same time the writer has put Northern Rhodesian history into the wider setting which it requires, and has therefore devoted some space to events south of the Zambezi and overseas. This approach will necessarily make for some duplication when subsequent volumes appear in print, for subjects like the partition of Africa or the Federation campaign will have to be treated once more, albeit with a different emphasis. This, however, is unavoidable, for each book is intended to be a complete work, capable of being read on its own, without reference to its companion volumes.

The work is a general survey which should be of interest to specialists and general readers alike; the writer having made use of a large body of unpublished

sources. No history can of course ever be 'definitive', for fashions in historio-
graphy change as much as the fluctuating patterns of events which form their
subject matter. The present book will nevertheless provide a standard work as
well as an indispensable introduction for experts interested in more specialized
subjects, the work gaining by the topical nature of its contents.

In accepting responsibility for the present project, the National Archives
appointed their Editor, Mr L. H. Gann, to carry out this task. The choice was
justified by the fact that Mr Gann had already previously worked on Northern
Rhodesian history, and that he possessed some knowledge of anthropology as
well as the more orthodox background of a historian; in addition he has had
practical experience with archives, the raw material of history, and familiarity
with current administrative and political problems. The writer was given considerable liberty, on the assumption that in an age of impersonal institutions
there is much to be said for works written by individuals, by identifiable persons
with their own feelings, whose work is bound to make a greater impact than the
colourless compendia of committees which all too often hide their prejudices
behind a cloak of anonymity! The judgements on men and events expressed in
the present work are therefore Mr Gann's own, and do not in any way commit
either the Northern Rhodesian or the Federal Government or indeed any
person on whose knowledge the author has drawn.

In compiling this work Mr Gann was given access to closed records in the
Colonial Office and on Northern Rhodesia. He was also allowed to make use of
papers in the private collections of Lord Malvern and Sir Roy Welensky though
the authorship of confidential despatches, letters or minutes has not been quoted.
The writer has also consulted private manuscripts in the custody of the National
Archives, and has made extensive use of 'oral history', having discussed his
problems with a large number of people of all races and many professions,
political figures, clergymen and farmers, traders, civil servants and artisans, who
took part in building the country, and to whose kind co-operation the author is
deeply indebted. There finally remains the pleasant task of thanking all those
who have been instrumental in bringing this valuable work to its fruition,
including the Government of Northern Rhodesia, the Anglo American Corporation, the Rhodesian Selection Trust, the British South Africa Company and
the Rhodesia Printing and Publishing Company Limited, whose financial
generosity helped to make its publication possible.

T. W. BAXTER
Director
National Archives of Rhodesia and Nyasaland

CONTENTS

INTRODUCTION

Rhodesia is the land of limitless horizons, and nothing moves the stranger more than the sheer immensity of the veld. The bush stretches into the distance like a never-ending sea of brown and russet, that changes into green after the rains, and sweeps on against a background of translucent blue. During the brief spells of dawn and sunset the land is plunged into gold and purple, but becomes grim and oppresive under the white glare of the midday sun. At first sight the veld frightens by its monotony, but as the traveller finds his feet, the country acquires sharper definition. The greater part of Northern Rhodesia forms a plateau, some 3,000 to 5,000 feet above sea level, a flat surface broken by kopjes, the result of countless ages of erosion which wore away the underlying crystalline rocks containing the bulk of Northern Rhodesia's mineral wealth. Southward from the Congo-Zambezi divide, the plateau is broken by the valleys of the Upper Zambezi and its tributaries. In the mountainous north-eastern corner the land rises in places to over 7,000 feet, overlooking the western edge of the Great Rift valley, but these highlands are isolated by the low-lying, hot and unhealthy Luangwa valley. West of the Muchinga Mountains, which flank the Luangwa rift, there lies a plateau containing the shallow Lake Bangweulu and its vast swamplands. Geographers describe the country's vegetation as of the savannah type. In the drier areas of the south thick thornbush and coarse grass cover the ground, but as the visitor makes his way northwards, the rains get heavier and longer, and parkland savannah merges into forest.

On the little inset maps that newspapers print of foreign trouble spots, Northern Rhodesia looks a small country, where Lusaka, the capital seems practically next door to Nairobi in Kenya, but it is a city further away than London is from Algiers in North Africa. The country is geographically isolated, and more than 500 miles as the crow flies separate Lusaka from Beira, the nearest port on the African East Coast, whilst a train from the Northern Rhodesian Copper Belt has nearly 1,400 miles to travel till it arrives at Beira, or alternatively some 1,200 miles until it gets to Lobito, the nearest port on the West Coast on the other side of Africa. A traveller going up to Lusaka from Cape Town in the south has a long and weary journey before him, which takes him as far as London is to Kiev in Russia, or to the northern tip of distant Iceland; and yet this is as nothing compared to a trip from Lusaka to the Mediterranean Coast which is as far as England is from the Persian Gulf or Canada, with the difference that communications are infinitely worse, and lead across savannah, jungles and desolate desert. Northern Rhodesia itself occupies an area of some 290,587 square miles, a region bigger than Great Britain, Germany, Denmark, Switzerland,

Holland and Belgium put together. The territory's population, on the other hand, now only numbers some 2,510,000 people, a good deal less than the number of inhabitants that live in just one European capital like Paris. The country's vast mineral resources have only barely been scratched, and there are great potentials of minerals, hydro-electric power and agricultural wealth still awaiting future development.

Northern Rhodesia lies within the Tropics, and the lower reaches of the Zambezi, Luangwa and Kafue Rivers are hot and damp; but height tempers heat and the country despite its summer rains is spared that high degree of humidity and exhausting heat that can turn the Tropics into purgatory. Water of course is one of the territory's main problems. A student poring over a map might imagine a land full of rivers, but many of the smaller water-courses in the south and west dry up in summer, so that Rhodesians will jokingly tell visitors from overseas to get out and dust themselves whenever they fall into a river! Once the rains start pouring down between November and March, some of these empty streams become raging torrents that will sweep everything out of their way; but most of this water is lost, and this, together with evaporation and transpiration has led experts to calculate that hardly as much as fifteen per cent remains available in rivers and streams for man's use. The larger rivers nevertheless flow all the year round; and Northern Rhodesia boasts that two African giants, the Congo and the Zambezi, both have their origins within the territory. The headwaters of the Congo rise in the hills north of Isoka and run south-west under the name of Chambeshi to the vast Bangweulu Swamps and Lake. The effluent from this great expanse of water—called Luapula—runs in a wide semi-circle, forming part of the boundary of the Congo state, before joining Lake Mweru. This Lake is drained by the Luvua River which eventually becomes the Congo in the south. The Zambezi winds its way from North-Western Rhodesia to the Indian Ocean over a distance of some 1,700 miles. The river's course is broken by vast gorges and rapids, the greatest drop of all being formed by the Victoria Falls, one of the Wonders of the World, and perhaps the most imposing sight in the Southern Hemisphere. The Zambezi's strength has now been harnessed by the Kariba Dam, where engineers have created the world's greatest man-made lake, and where hydro-electricity is being produced on a vast scale. But natural obstacles render the river almost useless for purposes of navigation, the lack of good natural communications forming one of the country's greatest problems. Another great river, the Kafue, has its origins in the hill range between Solwezi and Chingola; it then flows through swamp land to reach the Copper Belt, the country's great mining centre, where its waters are used for sundry industrial and agricultural purposes. The river then swings south and west through tsetse fly country and past the uninhabited Lukanga Swamps, which may one day be transformed into an enormous flood-regulation basin. Then the river flows south to the Meshi Teshi gap, and abruptly turns east to meander some 200 miles through the vast Flats, where indigenous tribes raise large herds of cattle; finally it rushes through the famous Kafue Gorge, a great potential source of hydro-electric power, to merge its waters with the Zambezi. Another great Zambezi tributary is the Luangwa which rises in the mountains bordering Nyasaland, and runs south-west through forest and fly country, its lower reaches forming the boundary between Northern Rhodesia and Portuguese East Africa. Much of this country is little inhabited, the dreaded 'fly' having greatly limited the area where cattle can be kept, and this influenced both tribal migration routes and the areas of European settlement. Agriculturists can only breed stock within certain areas, including the Upper Zambezi valley and the Mazabuka Plateau, as well as parts of North-Eastern Rhodesia; and elsewhere people must rely on hunting or fishing to supplement their crops.

The frontiers of this huge and half-empty territory is marked by the Zambezi to the south, and by the Luapula and the Luangwa along parts of the northern and eastern borders respectively. Elsewhere the boundaries mostly consist of artificial lines drawn across the map in European Chancelleries some two generations ago, so that Northern Rhodesia comprises a multitude of African peoples, speaking different languages and observing different customs. Many Northern Rhodesians even object to the name of their country itself which they say puts them on a par with Southern Rhodesia on the other side of the Zambezi. In the past some Europeans, wishing to emphasize their country's separate identity suggested terms like 'Zambeziland' or even stranger words like 'Windsoria' or 'Cecilia', whilst most Africans nowadays prefer the newly-coined name of 'Zambia', which itself resembles 'Zambezia' a word used during the early stages of the country's career. But whether Zambia or Northern Rhodesia, the territory has won some administrative cohesion during its two generations of British rule, and become a well-defined, internationally-recognized political unit.

The vexed question of names also arises when talking of the country's white, brown and black inhabitants, whose national designation has tended to change in accordance with shifts in political attitudes. Throughout the earlier part of the last century the dark-skinned, Bantu-speaking peoples of South and South East Africa were commonly called 'kaffirs', an Arab term customary amongst geographers as well as European settlers. But as time went on, the term acquired a disparaging meaning, and towards the end of the last century 'native' came into use as a polite substitute. Then the word 'native' in turn dropped in prestige, and educated black men insisted on being called 'Africans', a term which came into official use in Northern Rhodesia at the end of the thirties. The expressions used to describe the Europeans underwent similar changes. In the nineteenth century Europeans born in countries like South Africa and Australia were known as 'Colonials', but this word (like 'Dutchmen' for Afrikaans-speaking South Africans) in time acquired an uncomplimentary colouring. The Europeans preferred to call themselves 'settlers', an honourable term; but now the word 'white settler' has again acquired an unpleasant ring for some, and whites in the Federation want to be known as Europeans or just Rhodesians. Indians face a similar problem. In the olden days the polite term used in governmental publications used to be 'Asiatics'; but in a country where status sharply fluctuated the customary word became offensive, and the acceptable word is now 'Asian'. In choosing his terminology the writer has adopted the words customary at the time so that Europeans are sometimes called colonists, whites, or settlers, whereas Bantu-speakers are variously described as natives, blacks or Africans, no pejorative meaning being intended in any of these cases. A similar rule had been adopted with reference to the indigenous tribal communities. The writer has always tried to use the word most widely used, rather than the term which is linguistically correct, even if this has led to some inconsistencies. The 'Ndebele' figures as 'Matabele' and the 'Lozi' as 'Barotse', whereas the tribes referred to as 'Awemba' or 'Batoka' in old travel-books now appear as 'Bemba' or 'Tonga' following the now customary usage. But names are only a secondary affair, and what matters is not phraseology but achievement. All these different people have played their part in building a country, and the record of their deeds forms the history of Northern Rhodesia.

L. H. GANN

Salisbury
Southern Rhodesia
1963

AUTHOR'S ACKNOWLEDGEMENTS

Many people, in Rhodesia as well as overseas, have helped me to write this book. I thank them all for their advice and assistance. I have learnt a great deal from people of all races, particularly those who were in Northern Rhodesia in the early days; they have been generous in putting their knowledge and experience at my disposal. Unfortunately it is not possible to mention them all by name; to do so would mean making lists that would extend over several pages. I must, however, specially include the following who have either discussed various problems with me, or helped me with information and criticism, or made private papers available for my scrutiny: the late Mr G. H. Baxter, C.M.G., C.I.E.; Mr G. C. R. Clay; Mr J. N. Clothier; Professor E. Colson; Mr E. C. Duff, C.B.E.; Commander T. S. L. Fox-Pitt, O.B.E.; Professor M. Gelfand, C.B.E.; Lieutenant Colonel Sir Stewart Gore-Brown, D.S.O., O.B.E., T.D.; Professor M. Gluckman to whom I owe my interest in Northern Rhodesia and its peoples; Mr R. S. Hudson, C.M.G.; Professor K. Kirkwood; Viscount Malvern, P.C., C.H., K.C.M.G.; Professor J. C. Mitchell; Mr V. D. Mistry; Sir John Moffat, O.B.E.; Mr H. M. Nkumbula; Rev. E. G. Nightingale; Mr W. R. Reeve, F.G.S.; Sir Gilbert Rennie, G.B.E., K.C.M.G.; Mr H. J. Roberts, J.P.; Rev. J. R. Shaw; Mr T. L. C. Symmes; Sir Roy Welensky, P.C., K.C.M.G. and Mr T. Williams, O.B.E., E.D.

I received unfailing kindness while perusing books or papers at the Anti-Slavery and Aborigines Protection Society, London, the Library and Registry of the Colonial Office, the Fabian Society, the London Missionary Society and the Methodist Missionary Society, London, the Library at Rhodes House, Oxford and the Southern Rhodesian Legislative Assembly Library, Salisbury. I owe a debt of gratitude to my colleagues at the National Archives of Rhodesia and Nyasaland, both at Salisbury and Lusaka, particularly to Mr T. W. Baxter, the Director, Mr E. E. Burke and to Mr R. W. S. Turner. All the views expressed in this book are, however, purely my own, and so are any errors that may have crept into it.

Chapter One

The stage is set

I

The beginnings; Bantu invaders, and Portuguese explorers

The history of man in Northern Rhodesia dates back to ancient days and some scholars indeed consider Central Africa to be one of the cradles of the human race. Ape men once roamed through the Zambezi valley and along the Kalomo river, and from these lowly beginnings here and elsewhere, man gradually evolved, learning how to make improved stone implements. The earliest of these aboriginal craftsmen probably preferred the narrow belts of forest fringing streams and rivers, where they found some protection against wild animals, where fresh water was available, and the woodland gave them cover for stalking their prey in the surrounding savannah country.[1] For a period of something like 400,000 years, early Stone Age man lived by killing game, scavenging for meat left over by savage beasts, and gathering roots and berries. His only dwellings were rude shelters made of branches, and pits hollowed out of the ground and covered by grass and brushwood. A great step forward came with the use of fire, which enabled man to control his environment to infinitely greater effect, and a very early site has been discovered at Kalombo Falls near the Northern Rhodesia-Tanganyika boundary, where the presence of charcoal and ashes indicates the presence of age-old camp fires.

Over the millenia tools and hunting equipment improved; different Stone Age culture slowly succeeded upon one another, and the simple cleavers, pebble and flake tools of old were gradually replaced by more efficient types. It seems fairly probable that a major change occurred in the techniques of tool-making some time about 10,000 to 12,000 years ago, when primitive artisans discovered that greatly superior tools could be fashioned by hafting a number of small and finely made stone blades or flakes into wood. These formed more effective spearheads and knives, and the new technique enabled man to use more suitable stones, for all he now needed was a collection of very small pieces. During the latter Stone Age bows and arrows became the hunter's main weapons. Early man made another important step forward with the introduction of the barb, for a barbed point smeared with poison will stick in a wound much longer and make certain that the toxin will disperse in the body of the prey. Arrows with a lighter and finer head possess greater range and striking force so that more food became available to these bands. This aboriginal culture reached its highest point during

[1] See Clark, J. D. *The prehistory of Southern Africa*. Penguin Books Ltd, 1959

B

what has become known as the Later Stone Age, which may have begun some 7,000 or 8,000 years ago. This was a period of regional specialization *par excellence* and in Rhodesia there were two major types. North of the Zambezi there flourished a culture which has been named after the Nachikufu Caves in the Muchinga Mountains, inhabited by a hunting people who roamed through woodland and forests, searched for the fruits of the field and produced all kinds of grindstones, pestles and mortars to prepare their food. Their hunters stalked zebras, hartebeests and wild pigs, their main weapon being the bow and arrow with poisoned arrow heads. Probably they also possessed baskets made of bark, whilst paintings found on the walls of inhabited rock-shelters reveal them to have been fine artists who decorated their dwellings with semi-naturalistic and geometric paintings which probably served magical purposes. A second culture has been named from a rock shelter on Wilton Farm west of Grahamstown; this spread through much of Southern Rhodesia and along the upper and middle Zambezi valley, producing a naturalistic rock art of high order, which still records to this day what life was like amongst these hunting and food gathering communities. Archaeologists have also found an important site in the Mumbwa Caves of Northern Rhodesia where quartz was used and where an extensive blade industry must have once been in existence.

The folk who developed these cultures were themselves probably of mixed ancestry, for Southern Africa had by then become a great racial melting-pot. Some of the hunters' ancestors were Bushmen and others belonged to the 'Boskop' type, distinguished by prominent, bulging foreheads and big broad faces, fairly tall in stature, with well-developed limbs. Pygmies north of the Zambezi also seem to have blended with the 'Bush-Boskopoids'. In some areas another strain may have gone into this mixture, known as the 'Erythriotes', a long-faced, robustly built people, resembling the Hamitic races of Southern Somalia. These Stone Age people probably lived in roving bands of up to 200 people who hunted and collected over areas of up to 3,000 miles in extent. The different groups may have come together from time to time for rain-making and marriage ceremonies, barter, or for the ritual burying of important personages. There was a strict division of labour between the sexes, the men being responsible for hunting, whilst the women collected edible roots and grasses, ants' eggs and locusts being considered a special delicacy.

These Stone Age communities probably never managed to acquire the art of cultivating crops. They lived a hand-to-mouth existence and when a rhinoceros was caught in a pit-trap, it had to be eaten before the carcass rotted; life in the Stone Ages must therefore have alternated between ravenous feasts when the hunters had been lucky, and long periods of hunger when no rain fell, the game perished, and famine stalked the land. The population accordingly remained infinitesimally small, and when new immigrants made their appearance from the north, the aborigines were helpless against the more highly civilized invaders.

No one knows exactly when this great migration started or what exactly set it in motion. Some authorities believe that it may have had its beginnings as early as 300 B.C., but it does seem fairly probable that the newcomers came originally from the Great Lakes of East Africa and were of negroid stock, the modern term 'Bantu' merely referring to a group of related languages spoken by the invaders. Presumably they made their way down south in small groups, mixing with the indigenous Bush-Hottentot breeds on the way, and seeking out the kinds of soil and bush land best suited to their differing ways of making a living. They drifted across the high plateau of Central Africa which became one of the main migration routes, traversed over and over again by new immigrants from the North.

The date of their arrival in Northern Rhodesia is not clear, but by A.D. 90 when the legionaries of Imperial Rome were marching against the Caledonians, a Bantu people, distinguished by a characteristic kind of 'Channel Ware' pottery, were probably already settled north of the Zambezi.

Some time in the period between the birth of Christ and A.D. 500 other Bantu groups recognizable by their manufacture of pots of a 'Stamped Ware' type, moved south from Lake Nyasa and down the Shire River. Then they are thought to have split up into several sections, one of which moved south to Mozambique, another pushing westwards into Northern Rhodesia, where they established various agricultural communities whose members perhaps traced their descent through the mother's line. A further group of immigrants made their way into what is now Mashonaland where they became the ancestors of the Kalanga and the Karanga people.[1] At some period before the year 1,000 a new group of Shona-speaking invaders travelled down the old migration route via Lake Nyasa, making their way into Southern Rhodesia and beyond. These were patrilineal herdsmen, able to build structures in stone, and probably comprised amongst them the ancestors of the Zezuru, Duma, Mari, Korekore and other groups who may originally have come from the highlands of Abyssinia. Not very much is known about these early immigrants and the way they lived, but Semitic influences may perhaps have influenced their religious concepts and material culture; and there seems little doubt that the coming of the Shona (or Mashona) brought a major social and economic revolution in its train. The invaders could build in stone, and there were skilled craftsmen amongst them who knew how to smelt iron; the technique of working this metal possibly having spread to East Africa and Rhodesia from the kingdom of Meroe via the Horn of Africa some time before the birth of Christ. Vast areas of Africa south of the Sahara entered the Iron Age without the intermediate steps of bronze and copper as in Europe. The use of metal was a tremendous step forward; the quality of weapons, of agricultural implements and other tools vastly improved and society could accumulate some kind of visible 'capital'. The new invaders also possessed herds of long-horned cattle and sheep; where there was enough water

[1] Summers, R. 'The Iron Age cultures and early Bantu movements' (in Brelsford, W. V., ed., *Handbook to the Federation of Rhodesia and Nyasaland*. Salisbury, Government Printer, 1960, p. 30–56)

and the country was free from the dreaded tsetse fly, hunting and food gathering thus gave way to stock farming. Where the country was densely wooded or where cattle diseases struck down the herds, the settlers grew crops; mixed arable and pastoral agriculture prevailed in open bush and savannah country free from 'fly'. The newcomers used hoes to cultivate millet, edible roots, pea crops and cucurbits, farming being based on the 'slash-and-burn' method of agriculture familiar to the ancient Teutons at the time of Tacitus, and indeed to most early peoples. The bush was cleared and the branches were then stacked in piles and set alight, the ashes enriching the soil for planting; when the old ground had been exhausted the tribesmen moved on, so that their farming entailed a shifting mode of life. The farmers' ways underwent considerable changes, a major innovation being brought about by the introduction of maize. In a few favoured regions, especially along the fertile valleys of the Luapula and the Upper Zambezi, Bantu people evolved more stable methods of agriculture; but slash-and-burn cultivation—often skilfully adapted to the peculiarities of differing soils and crops—remained the characteristic method of most Bantu-speaking people on both sides of the Zambezi, their agricultural practices in turn affecting the tribesmen's ecological environment.

Farming, or the herding of cattle, sheep and goats, supplemented by hunting and fishing, constituted a vast improvement on the old ways of life; more food became available; society could afford to give employment to a few 'specialists' such as smiths and magicians. Political units grew bigger as small bands coalesced into village communities, some of which merged into more powerful principalities and kingdoms. A few chiefs became powerful rulers, assisted by councillors, subordinate chiefs and village headmen. Next in rank came the free villagers, the lowest class of society being formed by bondsmen who had been taken in war or deprived of their freedom for some other reason. Bantu society was by no means an egalitarian one; but despite differences of status the tribesmen, broadly speaking, all lived in a similar fashion. Their diet was simple. 'The general food in Kaffraria is a paste of millet badly ground or pounded in their mortars,' wrote a sixteenth-century Portuguese priest; 'they have also a large quantity of palm-oil which is a penance to those who are not accustomed to its use.' This was supplemented by chicken, and occasionally by venison or goat's meat, their favourite drink being 'a wine made of millet or more generally of macqueny, a vegetable resembling mustard'. Neither was there any grandeur in their houses, 'small straw huts plastered with clay, resembling round dovecotes'.[1]

In such flimsy constructions it was difficult to store up much food, which would only have become spoilt or fallen victim to rats or weevils. Under these conditions there was no point for ordinary people in trying to accumulate large food-reserves; great distinctions of wealth became impossible, except for the aristocracy in a well-organized empire like Monomotapa's. No commoner could

[1] Monclaro, Fr. 'Account of the journey made ... with Francisco Barreto in the conquest of Monomotapa in the year 1569' (in Theal, G. M., ed., *Records of south-eastern Africa*. ... Cape Town, The Government of the Cape Colony, 1896–1905, v. 3, p. 230)

produce much more than his neighbour; neither was there any incentive to engage in more intensive methods of cultivating the soil. The supply of land was unlimited, so there was not much point in thinking of new ways of working it; even if a surplus had been produced, there were neither markets nor means of transporting it. A man could accordingly do little with his spare millet but give it away; he certainly could not invest his surplus in land, for the vast rolling veld which stretched endlessly from the village to the horizon was looked upon as something open to all, rather like the sea. Villagers received gardens for their own use and were allowed to keep the crops they cultivated; but there were no private land owners. Important men gained power and standing in the tribe by giving food and other benefits to kinsmen or strangers. The more followers a man had, the stronger became his position within the tribe, kinships, politics and rank becoming inextricably intertwined. There were many leaders, great and small; but whatever his rank, a lord—to the Bantu as to the Saxon of old—was above all expected to be a 'hlaford', a 'loaf-ward' or bread-giver who would deal generously with his dependents and feed the hungry.

Social life in the African village underwent considerable changes, but it is possible to arrive at certain generalizations which in some form held true for all Bantu societies. A man's entire life was bound up with that of his village which was itself largely composed of kinsmen, so that an African relied on his relatives in a way that Europeans now find hard to understand. Tribal organization itself varied, but broadly speaking there were two major patterns. After a long series of migrations, the people south of the Zambezi mostly came to consist of cattle-keeping tribes who traced their descent through their fathers and grandfathers. Their village consisted of kinsmen related to some common ancestor. A man and his several wives lived in one homestead; close to him might be the huts of his full and half brothers, and those of his paternal uncles; these groups helped each other both in peace and war; they worshipped the same ancestral spirits and accepted some responsibility for each others' acts. Intermarriage within such a descent group was forbidden for fear of terrible supernatural consequences. If a man wanted to seek a wife, he had to bring her in from outside. Traditionally there were two ways of doing this; a powerful and warlike tribe might acquire them as the Romans had got the Sabine women—by abduction; the other (and the more customary one) was by means of paying a 'bride price' to her kinsmen, who then agreed to let their female relative leave their village. Amongst pastoral peoples payment was normally made by means of handing over cattle, whilst those tribes who kept no stock paid by means of hoes, axes and by ornaments. There were also some groups where a man could acquire a wife by working for her, as Jacob had done for Leah and Rachel in Biblical days. Once the bride-price had been paid, the husband's kinsfolk could lay claim to his wife's children and to her labour. At first the newcomer did not count very much amongst her in-laws, but the more babies she produced the more highly respected she became, and a Bantu matron, whose sons had grown up and married in turn, was a person of great consequence.

In addition to this form of social organization, there was a second, known as the 'matrilineal' kind, most widely found north of the Zambezi, though some traces of it also remained among Shona political institutions. The matrilineal tribes traced their descent, not through men, but through women, villages being composed mainly of people who had sprung from a common ancestress. In some villages wives came in from other communities to live in their husband's homestead, but their children returned to their mother's village as soon as they became of age. There were also tribes where women formed the core of the village-settlement and husbands had to leave *their* homes in order to live with their wives. This did not mean that these societies were run by women; power still rested with the men, but it was not the husband who disciplined his children but his wife's elder brother. In such a society bride-wealth was unnecessary. A woman's reproductive powers remained, as it were, the property of her own kind; fatherhood was relatively unimportant; the marriage bond remained weak, and sexual morals, as understood in our Western society, or by the members of cattle-keeping 'patrilineal' tribes, like the Zulu or the ancient Hebrews, were extremely loose.

But whether a people was matrilineal or patrilineal, their ways of life remained broadly similar. There was, for instance, always a clear-cut division of labour between the sexes. The woman did the usual domestic chores, looked after the small children and performed many jobs in the gardens, such as hoeing and weeding. The men went out hunting, deliberated on public affairs, and fought as members of their tribal levies. Wherever it was possible to keep stock the men looked after the cattle, whilst in agricultural societies they were expected to perform tasks demanding greater physical strength like felling trees or lopping off big branches for the purpose of making ash-beds. Men associated with men in their work, and women with women. Children were looked after not merely by their mothers, but by a host of aunts, cousins and other relatives; and the tribesmen felt themselves as members of a closely-knit community that supported its members in sickness or health, peace or war, through a complicated net of kinship obligations.

Every Bantu tribe valued children, and a woman's standing rose the more offspring she produced. The reason for this was not merely that the Bantu liked children, which of course they did. Equally important was the fact that their society appears to have suffered from a permanent manpower shortage. There were very few labour-saving devices; neither horses, wagons nor ploughs, and everything had to be done with human muscles. This meant that there could never be too many workers and warriors to sustain the future of the tribe; even amongst the most advanced Bantu societies life was always insecure. No tribal community possessed sufficient resources to tide itself over prolonged periods of want, and famine was an ever-present danger. The rains might fail; locusts, disease or cattle plagues might make their appearance; or hostile war parties would descend on the land to loot the cattle, carry off the women and empty the granaries; any one of these contingencies was liable to lead to disaster capable of destroying a whole community. Life was accordingly infinitely more precarious than it is amongst modern Western societies which can accumulate vast capital reserves, control their natural environment, and possess sufficient resources to ensure economic co-operation on a world-wide scale.

The dangers of the material world were moreover imagined to be duplicated by threats of a supernatural order which, like the material ones, could only be resisted by co-operative means. The tribesmen knew no privacy; everyone knew everyone else, and magical or religious problems were simply viewed in personal terms. At one time or another every man and every society must answer Job's question of why misfortunes happen to the Just. Some explain this moral predicament by the workings of an inscrutable Providence; others talk of the statistical laws of chance. The Bantu, however, saw this question in a purely personal way. If—say—an unskilful hunter was trampled to death by an elephant, his friends would mourn him, but they did not talk of witchcraft; the victim's death had obviously been due to his lack of knowledge. But if an elephant killed a veteran with many tuskers to his credit no such simple explanation would suffice. The hunter's lack of experience could not be blamed; his death was accordingly put down to some occult evil-doing; somebody must have caused his death by magical means. The public malefactor had to be found, exiled or killed, the work of detection being entrusted to a diviner, one of the most important people in the community. The diviners used various incantations but the popular way of going to work was by means of throwing engraved slats of wood or bone which supposedly allowed their owners to peer into the unknown. A great variety of brews and concoctions were also used for medical purposes; most of these had no specific therapeutical value but depended on the spells cast which alone gave them powers.

Tribal life was also thought to be influenced by the ancestral spirits who might either help their descendants or punish them for their sins, keeping up a never-ending interest in the affairs of the community. There was moreover a whole pantheon of regional and tribal deities who had to be conciliated, the chief of a tribe sometimes acting as the High Priest of his people as well as their secular leader. Bantu thinkers also came to conceive of a Supreme Being who transcended the Universe, but the High God was generally believed to be so far removed from the world of man that there was no point in praying to him in person; neither was his will thought to be directly linked to the dictates of morality or the course of human history.

Bantu religious thought as a whole upheld a society in which tribal cohesion was the supreme good; woe to the man who 'got on' by means other than those sanctioned by custom. Thus if an African's crop was noticeably better than his neighbour's it must be by some illegitimate means: '. . . . if there is one among them who is more diligent and a better husbandman, and therefore reaps a fresh crop of millet and has a larger store of provisions' wrote Father Monclaro four centuries ago, 'they immediately falsely accuse him of all kinds of crimes, as an excuse to take it from him and eat it, saying why should he have more millet than another. . . . It is the same with cattle, and this is the cause of the scarcity. They are not provident but quickly waste and consume the new crops in feasts and drinking.'[1] Bantu religion provided no incentive for individual economic enterprise and so, the writer concluded, 'since they have inhabited this country, which must have been thousands of years, they have never used or invented any other article of food . . . or varied their dress or custom. . . .'

The good Father's view, echoed many thousands of times in later centuries by other Whites, was of course grossly over-simplified. Bantu society did change, and so did Bantu thought. But all the Africans' intellectual efforts had to be transmitted from one generation to the next by memory and word of mouth; the Bantu never acquired the art of writing. Storing information accurately over long periods was as difficult for them as storing grain; intellectual capital was as hard to accumulate as physical capital; and the tribesmen could never avail themselves of that artificial memory, inscribed on stone and papyri, which forms one of the pillars of civilization.

Within these limits, the Iron Age culture of the Bantu produced some considerable achievements. The earliest invaders lived very simple lives. They knew how to make pots of high quality; they had a few ornaments of copper and shell beads; they fashioned spears and hoes, and built themselves huts made of pole and mud-plaster. Sometimes they also constructed simple walls by piling up stones between big rocks to form cattle kraals. The next step forward took place south of the Zambezi where a great Bantu state, the empire of Monomotapa, came into being some time in the fourteenth century. The term 'Monomotapa' was a title like 'Caesar' or 'Kaiser', and the emergence of this state may possibly be associated with the arrival of a new group of immigrants manufacturing a characteristic kind of 'Ruin Ware' pottery, the development of gold-mining probably being linked to an increasing demand for precious metals from overseas.

Monomotapa's kingdom probably saw the period of its greatest prosperity during the fourteenth and fifteenth centuries when it extended over much of what is now Southern Rhodesia. The Monomotapas appear to have developed quite a complex state-organization, based like early mediaeval states, on the royal household. The kings maintained a considerable revenue around their person and Portuguese chroniclers relate that the youthful nobles were not allowed to marry as long as they were in the king's personal service; at the age of twenty they were moved outside the palace as the king's retinue, being subsequently appointed to offices in the state when their period of training was over. Monomotapa's kingdom was wealthy enough to maintain an administrative organization, which enabled him to rule over a very extended confederacy of tribes, his kingdom having access to the lower Zambezi, an important trade route. In addition he controlled a valuable group of gold mines, the most important of

[1] Monclaro, Fr. 'Account of the journey made . . . with Francisco Barreto in the conquest of Monomotapa in the year 1569' (in Theal, G. M., ed., *Records of south-eastern Africa*. . . . Cape Town, The Government of the Cape Colony, 1896–1905, v. 3, p. 231)

which probably lay south and west of the Hunyani River where to-day's main gold belt is still found in Southern Rhodesia.

It seems likely that Monomotapa's kingdom, like many other Bantu states, was based on a complex system of exchange through gifts, tributes and services to the king, who in turn gave away much of his surplus wealth to his vassals. The phenomenon of the 'distributor-king' was ably analysed amongst the Barotse (Lozi) of North-Western Rhodesia, whose kingdom flourished many centuries later,[1] but other Bantu states seem to have worked in a similar way, and so probably did Monomotapa's. The Monomotapas attempted to enforce rigid control over gold-mining in their country, but 'whenever the Monomotapa wants gold he sends cattle to his men, which are divided amongst the diggers according to their labour and the days worked'. Militarily, however, Monomotapa's kingdom was not greatly superior to its less civilized neighbours for 'the Mokaranga nation . . . are a feeble people, and have no weapons of defence, fortresses or walled cities. Their weapons of offence were bows, arrows and assegais', which equipment gave them no advantage over savage intruders, a weakness that probably went a long way to explain the weakness of their Empire, which began to show serious cracks after the turn of the fifteenth century.

Some areas north of the Zambezi appear to have passed under Monomotapa's influence, though they were never formally incorporated into his Kingdom.[2] The country now comprised within Northern Rhodesia probably went through another period of invasions, which were set off by disturbances in the Southern Congo basin. It was perhaps during the fourteenth and fifteenth centuries that a group of peoples, known collectively as the 'Maravi', made their way into Northern Rhodesia. Most of the remainder moved southward to Nyasaland, where they split into several groups now known as the Nyanja, Chewa and other tribes. Another invasion was that of the Kaonde who moved southwards into North-Western Rhodesia, where they met Lenje settlers who were then pushed to the south in turn. Little is known about these migrations, however; and the economic developments that took place south of the Zambezi do not appear to have been parallelled to the north. Traders would not brave the interior, with its enormous distances, the vagaries of a tropical climate and the ever-present danger of disease, unless a good profit could be made. North of the Zambezi there was little to attract foreign merchants; there was some copper, but no easily workable deposits of gold; neither were there diamond or silver mines, and only goods of such a kind, of small bulk and great value, would have stood the high cost of transport from inland.

This continued to hold true when, at the beginning of the sixteenth century, Arab power declined and the Portuguese, with their better armed vessels, broke

---

[1] Gluckman, M. 'Economy of the Central Barotse plain' (*Rhodes-Livingstone papers* no. 7, 1941), and 'Essays on Lozi land and royal property' (*Rhodes-Livingstone papers* no. 10, 1943)

[2] Information from P. D. Abraham, Senior Research Fellow in Ethno-History at the University College of Rhodesia and Nyasaland, who also advised on other sections.

into the Indian Ocean. The Portuguese were out to extend the Christian faith against competition from Islam, which at this time formed a religious and military threat to Southern Europe. In addition there were powerful economic motives for expansion. The Portuguese were anxious to outflank the Moorish gold trade through the Sahara by directly contacting African producers on the West Coast; as a long term project, they also thought of finding a sea-route round Africa to the Indies, enabling them to buy directly from the Orient instead of having to do business through Muslim middlemen in the Near East. This was an important consideration at a time when fine cloth, spices and many other kinds of luxuries were still derived from the East.

The Portuguese succeeded brilliantly in their venture. In 1482 Diogo Cão arrived at the mouth of the River Zaire or Congo, and friendly relations were established with the Congo kings, who for a time nominally adopted Christianity and tried to copy Portuguese institutions of government and European crafts—though without any permanent success. In 1498 the Treaty of Tordesilhas was concluded between Portugal and Spain, whereby the two greatest maritime powers of Europe agreed on the allocation of their spheres of influence. The agreement, though never strictly enforced, made it possible for the Iberian powers to expand overseas without coming into serious conflict with each other, and each of them was now free to pursue a monopolistic policy in its own chosen sphere.

The Spaniards concentrated their efforts in the New World; the Portuguese rounded the Cape of Good Hope, and in 1498 Vasco da Gama, the great Portuguese navigator, arrived at Calicut in India. 'What the devil brought you here?' an enraged Moorish merchant shouted at them when he saw their vessels lying in Calicut harbour. 'Christians and spices' roared back a Portuguese sailor, his answer being as sound as it was concise. The Portuguese had come to extend the Catholic religion and the European trade in Eastern goods. In both respects, however, they were faced with desperate hostility from the Arabs who were determined to defend both Islam and their monopoly of the Indian trade. Superior gunnery, navigation and fighting stamina at first gave victory to the Portuguese, who then embarked on the great strategic enterprise of controlling the entire Indian Ocean; Goa became the centre of their power, the settlement being proclaimed in 1518 as 'a royal city never to be separated from the Portuguese Crown'. Other ports were also seized, including Mombasa, Kilwa and Moçambique. As far as South East Africa was concerned the Portuguese were mainly interested in the area as a commercial and strategic appendage to their dominions in India. Sofala, just south of the modern port of Beira fell into Portuguese hands in 1505, and became the main Christian base in the area, some of the local Arabs along the East Coast, including the 'King' of Malindi, agreeing to collaborate with the White strangers against their local rivals.

The Portuguese then issued a series of *regimentos* which enjoined the captain of Sofala to treat the indigenous people well, whilst Muslims were not to be 'ill-treated', that is to say their hostility was not to be provoked without reason.[1] The Portuguese were enjoined to convert the local people to Catholicism, and those who adopted the True Religion were to be admitted to the same social status as Europeans. Practice of course often differed from theory, for the Portuguese were by no means free from race prejudice. But the invaders had for long been accustomed to deal with civilized, though darker-skinned, Moors from North Africa, whilst along the East Coast they came into contact with Muslim townsmen, living in stone-houses, skilled in trade and agriculture, and scarcely inferior to White men in the art of living. Another factor in the field of race relations was the fact that the Christians brought few women of their own colour to their colonies, for their country's population was small, and the carrying capacity of the Portuguese *naos*, tiny ships little larger than modern fishing-smacks, being extremely limited. The immigrants perforce established alliances with local girls, these unions sometimes receiving the blessing of the Church, whilst the authorities actually encouraged marriages between transported white convicts and local women, so as to stabilize the population, and get more work out of their 'felons'. The Portuguese moreover soon extensively employed local Africans as agents for their dealings inland, Bantu intermediaries rightly being considered more reliable than Muslims. The major dividing line between White and Black thus became religion rather than race, and this ancient tradition has never been quite extinguished since. Nevertheless, the Portuguese were by no means devoid of feelings of ethnic superiority, and these sentiments were perhaps heightened when they came into contact with the more primitive communities inland. Monomotapa's court of course was an impressive sight to Portuguese administrators and soldiers. But priests like Father Monclaro, representative of age-old civilization and the Christian religion, were prone to denounce the degraded state of the natives in terms no different from those subsequently used by more race-conscious observers in the nineteenth century.

The great majority of the Portuguese, however, came to trade rather than to argue and convert. From their base in Sofala the Portuguese imported cloth and beads into the interior, purchased gold and ivory which were sold in India for spices, the Portuguese trading posts in East Africa being little more than commercial appendages to the splendid dominion over the Indies. But in East Africa the Portuguese had come at the wrong time; Monomotapa's empire was already tottering under the blows of powerful vassals with the result that the flow of gold was diminishing. The captain of Sofala therefore decided to send out one of his own men to explore the source of the gold; Antonio Fernandes, a carpenter and a good linguist, though apparently a man with an unsavoury past, was sent to command the venture, the first expedition into the interior probably leaving about the year 1511. Fernandes brought back valuable reports about gold production in Karanga territory and about Monomotapa's Zimbabwe near the Utete River north of Sipolilo, not to be confused with Great Zimbabwe, the Rozwi headquarters in the south. Fernandes, the first European to visit

[1] Silva Rego, A. da. *Portuguese colonization in the sixteenth century: a study of the royal ordinances.* Johannesburg, Witwatersrand University Press, 1959

Mashonaland, undertook several other journeys, but the gold trade could not be revived to its former greatness, and the Portuguese settlements were reduced to a parlous state. For although the Portuguese were able to deprive the Arabs of their trading monopoly, they still could not control the interior effectively and had to continue employing African pedlars, 'feiras' being established where there had previously been *sembasas* or *baʒaars*. They also discovered that European trade goods were not accepted in barter and thus reverted to the practice of importing cloth and coloured clay beads from India.[1]

Much more serious was the fact that the overheads involved in maintaining their 'factories' and forts were heavy; there was much peculation; gold was produced but it was erratic in arrival, and the revenue of Sofala did not balance its expenditure. Many of the Arabs were antagonized by harsh treatment; much of their trade was destroyed, and the Portuguese failed to follow the advice of one of their wisest councillors who suggested that they should content themselves with a percentage of the profits, whilst leaving the coastal trade to the Muslims. This suggestion was probably sound, but quite out of tune with the 'bullionist' doctrines of economics then in vogue; as it was, the monopolistic policies of the Portuguese encouraged illegitimate trade and thus fraternization with the enemy, which in turn affected the efficiency of the administration as a whole.[2]

The Portuguese mainly wanted gold, and their interest in Central Africa declined with reports of new discoveries of the precious metal in the Moluccas in the fifteen-hundred and twenties; later on the colonization of Brazil diverted most of their energies away from Africa. A further weakness was the administrative subordination of the African East Coast to the Portuguese possessions in India, where conditions were very different; the general quality of many of the Portuguese officials also left much to be desired. But perhaps most serious of all was the medical problem. The Portuguese built their settlements in coastal plains, on low-lying sites where rain water accumulated, affording ideal breeding grounds for mosquitoes, they were consequently always plagued by malaria; the surprising thing about their settlers being not that their resistance and stamina were weakened, but that they displayed as much resilience as they did when assailed by unknown diseases, and faced with the ever present difficulty of getting a balanced diet in a country where it was difficult to grow vegetables or rear cattle.

Medical and climatic factors also affected military tactics and strategy in a manner unfavourable against the Portuguese. The Castilian *conquistadores* in South America possessed a tremendous advantage over the natives in being able to employ cavalry against armies devoid of horsemen. In South East Africa, however, the prevalence of animal disease made the employment of horsemen impossible to any large extent, and the Portuguese in the main remained

[1] Schofield, J. F. 'Beads: southern African beads and their relation to the beads at Inyanga' (in Summers, R. *Inyanga: prehistoric settlements in Southern Rhodesia*. Cambridge University Press, 1958, p. 183)
[2] Axelson, E. *South-East Africa 1488–1530*. Longmans, Green and Co., 1940

dependent on slow-moving infantry, weighed down by heavy armour, and not well adapted to bush fighting. The prevalence of 'fly', then as later, also interfered with the employment of wagons; this forced them to rely either on river transport or on carriers, the latter being a very unsatisfactory means of supply in a theatre of operations where lines of communications were long and insecure.

Nevertheless the Portuguese persisted and in 1560 Dom Gonçalo da Silveira, a Jesuit priest, set out for Monomopata's kingdom to preach Christianity. But Silveira was killed at the behest of local Muslim traders, the first well-documented Christian martyr in South East Africa. His death gave the Portuguese an excuse for military intervention and in 1569 a powerful expedition, consisting of five vessels, left Lisbon under the command of Francisco Barreto. The Captain-General's force, which included horses and camels, landed at Quelimane and marched into the interior. The enterprise, however, proved a complete failure. Barreto perished, and command of the expedition was taken over by Vasco Fernandes Homem who withdrew from the pestilential Zambezi to refit at Sofala. In 1575 Homem marched through Utete, but no lasting success was achieved. As far as Christianity was concerned, the Portuguese could make little headway amongst the Bantu, 'for their sorceries are many and of many kinds by which the devil deceives them, and if they have any form of worship it is rendered to the devil by all these spells . . . and even those who are brought up amongst us and made Christians leave us every day and return to their own people, for they value their own customs highly'. Portuguese influence was more of an indirect nature, the major contribution being in the field of agriculture where the Portuguese brought in a variety of new products from their possessions in the New World, India and the Far East, pepper, wheat, tobacco, sweet potatoes, manioc, haricot beans, lentils, onions, guavas, paw-paws and small bananas all being said to be Portuguese imports.[1] Maize, oranges, lemons, and onions, on the other hand were cultivated at Kilwa as early as 1505, the year in which the Portuguese first captured the port,[2] though the Portuguese also played a major part in bringing maize and Mediterranean fruit to Africa.

The white invaders subsequently pushed into the Zambezi valley, and in the course of the seventeenth century a Goanese by the name of Pereira established a settlement at Zumbo by the confluence of the Luangwa and the Zambezi, where a Portuguese garrison, church and trading colony were subsequently established. Zumbo developed into a centre for the gold and ivory trade, and from here Portuguese traders and travellers made their way to the north, and in the nineteenth century a Portuguese, born in Mozambique, known as Nicholas Almeida, thus recorded that he once travelled for twelve days from Zumbo where he found that the natives spoke Portuguese quite well. 'This they owed to the generosity and singular kindness of Emmanual Pereira, the representative

[1] Johnston, H. H. *A History of the colonization of Africa by alien races.* 2nd ed. Cambridge University Press, 1930, p. 92

[2] Baião, A., ed., *O manuscrito de Valentim Fernandes.* Lisbon, Academia Portuguesa da Historia, 1940

there of the king of Portugal, who finding them of quick parts, taught them also to dress in the Portuguese fashion and other things worth knowing.'

It seems likely that in the meantime the Maravi migrations continued, and emigrants made their way southwards by a route which led them past Lake Nyasa. Tradition has it that they were led by a number of different chiefs, amongst whom Karonga, Undi, Nkanda and Mwase were the most prominent, the Nsenga chief Kaluani being given the credit for having invented the rafts which transported their hordes across Lake Nyasa. The Maravi then occupied the vast region, roughly enclosed by the Zambezi on the south, Lake Nyasa on the north and the Luangwa River on the west.[1] They were mentioned by Gaspar Bocarro, a Portuguese who in 1616 made a daring overland journey from Tete to Kilwa during the course of which he discovered Lake Nyasa, 'a lake which looks like the sea from which issues the river Nhanha which flows into the Zambezi below Sena, and there it is called the river Chiry'.[2]

During the sixteenth century there also occurred a terrible invasion of ferocious hordes, variously known as the 'Zimbas', 'Ambeas', 'Cabires' or 'Mumbos', who swept down on the tribes along the Zambezi possibly from the Lake country. The cannibalism of the Zimbas proved even more horrifying to the Bantu than it was to the Europeans or Moslems, for the Africans believed that the Zimbas' horrible practice would destroy not merely their victims' bodies but also their souls, so that their descendants would be deprived of their supernatural help. The Zimbas are known to have arrived in the region of Tete on the Zambezi about 1570; in 1585 they once more attacked the Portuguese settlements, but subsequently withdrew to the north, marched to the coast and sacked Kilwa, where they are said to have eaten 3,000 of their prisoners. They were ultimately wiped out by a combined force of Malindi Arabs, Africans and Portuguese who all combined in self-protection against these warlike savages.[3]

Tribal migrations also continued beyond the Zambezi and about 1600 the Lamba-Ambo-Luano group of people may perhaps have migrated down from the Congo area, skirting the Katanga region and making their way down the Luangwa valley. Later on during the century the Luyi, later known as the Lozi or Barotse, moved in to the Zambezi valley from the north and gradually extended their authority right down the river, the primitive Subiya, Mashi and Shanjo people being driven to the outer confines of the plain. The Luyi then pushed outwards both towards the east and west, and established a complex kind of state which showed some affinity to the political organization characteristic of the Southern Congo.

Another movement during this period was connected with the great Lunda

[1] Lane Poole, E. H. *Native tribes of the eastern province of Northern Rhodesia.* 3rd ed. Lusaka, Government printer, 1949, p. 37–38

[2] Bocarro, A. 'Extracts from the decade ... of the performances of the Portuguese in the East'. (in Theal, G. M., ed., *Records of south-eastern Africa*. ... Cape Town, The Government of the Cape Colony, 1896–1905, v. 3, p. 416–417)

[3] Summers, R. *Inyanga: prehistoric settlements in Southern Rhodesia.* Cambridge University Press, 1958, p. 255

kingdom of Mwato Yamvo which perhaps came into existence some time during the sixteenth century. The Lunda subsequently expanded to the west where they were supplied with guns from Ovimbundu middlemen in exchange for slaves. The possession of firearms and the expanding commerce with the coast probably strengthened the Lunda rulers who built up a powerful state machinery, complete with an elaborate hierarchy of officials. Not all the princes of royal blood, however, could find suitable offices, and many of these dignitaries then set out to found new dependencies for themselves.[1]

It is possible that some time in the seventeenth century a number of Lunda leaders marched down south. These included Kazembe Mutanda (not identical with the Kazembe who later became chief on the Luapula, for Kazembe was a name denoting 'chief') who carved out a principality for himself; a second war-leader was Musokantanda who found a home for himself and his followers in what is now Katanga; a third was Ishinde who built up a chiefdom which was later divided between Angola and Northern Rhodesia. For many years these minor Lunda states remained tributary to Mwato Yamvo, but gradually the conquerors intermarried with the local population, adopted their way of life, and their links with the Congo weakened.

The great series of migrations also had its repercussions in North-Eastern Rhodesia, and it is possible that in the seventeenth century the Bisa and the Senga began to move southwards, travelling along the same course which the Chewa had taken before them, though other authorities place the coming of the Bisa and the Senga about the year 1700. In the eighteenth century there was further immigration into the region, where the population was probably not growing much; and it was perhaps during this period that the Aushi and Mukulu people found new homes for themselves in the Lake Bangweulu region. In addition Kazembe, a Lunda chief, broke away from the kingdom of Mwato Yamvo in the Congo and migrated into the fertile Luapula valley, which was rich in fish and cassava, and where he established a powerful kingdom.

Another group of invaders from the north were the Bemba, a warlike people of Luba origin, who perhaps settled in North-Eastern Rhodesia some time about 1740. Bemba tradition has it that the tribe became separated from the kindred Lunda and Bisa peoples, Chitimukulu (Kitimukulu), the Bemba captain, being killed by the Bisa with a poisoned arrow. The Bemba then revenged their chief's death on his slayers, and it seems certain that they extended their territory at the expense of the Bisa in the south-west and south-east, whilst the Lungu and Mambwe were pushed back to the north. The area as a whole was by now relatively densely populated in relation to the slender agricultural resources of its Bantu peoples, and competition for land stimulated inter-tribal warfare. The position was made more serious by the importation of fire-arms from the east and west coasts. The Bemba for instance acquired guns from Arab traders and became a military kingdom of formidable power. In addition more immigrants

[1] Turner, V. W. *Schism and continuity in an African society: a study of Ndembu village life.* Manchester University Press, 1957, p. 2

from the Congo moved into what later became North-Western Rhodesia; and some experts think that some time in the beginning of the eighteenth century Luchazi, Lwena and Chokwe tribesmen moved to their present place of residence, following the invasion route previously used by the Luyi. Much more research work, however, remains to be done on these population movements, which still raise formidable problems of a historical, ethnographic and ecological nature.

While these migrations were going on north of the Zambezi the Portuguese continued their attempts to assert their influence south of the river, where Monomotapa's power proved incapable of checking the powerful provincial magnates and where the 'Emperor' accordingly tried to play off the Portuguese against his rebellious feudatories. In 1607 a desperate Karanga Paramount presented all the gold mines in his kingdom to the Portuguese on condition that they should render him military assistance, and Portuguese influence inland for a time became sufficiently great to depose one of the Monomotapas whose successor became nominally a Christian.

The Portuguese were not, however, able to make much of these political successes. Portugal lost her own independence when in 1580 Philip of Spain managed to secure the Portuguese Crown and used the resources of his new possession to further the objects of Hapsburg 'grand policy' in Europe. It was only in 1640 that the Portuguese once again became masters in their own house, and by this time the Dutch had made heavy inroads into Portuguese commercial and maritime strength, whilst Portugal's resources were heavily strained by the vast commitments of an Empire that stretched from Brazil to the East Indies. The Portuguese moreover were meeting with bitter competition from French, English and other rivals, including Arabs from the Persian Gulf, who from the middle of the seventeenth century embarked on a vigorous counter-attack in the Indian Ocean and deprived the Portuguese of nearly all their possessions on the African East Coast north of Moçambique.

To make matters worse little could be made of the gold resources of the African interior.[1] Transport was always a difficult problem and in addition mining costs appear to have been so heavy that the Portuguese were forced to content themselves with trade rather than engaging in mining on their own account. African methods of production moreover left much to be desired for the native miners possessed no pumps; so their workers depended on gangs equipped only with pots to clear out the ground-water, which meant that they could not mine to any depth, and the resources of the 'ancient workings' remained only half-used. It also seems likely that the Portuguese had to contend with native sabotage, since some Monomotapas discouraged the working of valuable mines, lest their wealth might lead to further Portuguese penetration. Perhaps most important of all, the Portuguese never managed to solve the vital problem of labour incentives which also weighed so heavily on subsequent

[1] Axelson, E. 'Gold mining in Mashonaland in the 16th and 17th centuries' (in *Optima*, v. 9, no. 3, Sep 1959, p. 164–170)

European conquerors. The African tribal economies were largely self-sufficient; they required only relatively few trade goods from outside and it was difficult to increase production, as long as the indigenous people needed little in the way of foreign merchandise. For, as a seventeenth-century Portuguese chronicler complained in terms reminiscent of Victorian pioneers, the natives 'are so lazy and given to an easy life that they will not exert themselves to seek gold unless they are constrained by necessity for want of clothes or provisions, which are not wanting in the land . . . and the Kaffirs are inclined to agricultural and pastoral pursuits in which their riches consist'.[1]

The position of the Portuguese was shaken further when, at the end of the seventeenth century an aggrieved Monomotapa invited the current Rozwi ruler, Changamire, to get rid of the Portuguese. An *impi* made a surprise attack on Dambarare, a trading centre, the residents and Portuguese traders were all killed; Changamire disinterred the bodies of the dead and ground them to powder which he believed would guard his warriors against the Portuguese bullets. The dead Europeans were flayed, and with their skins Changamire struck terror into the hearts of the Portuguese native levies. The victorious Rozwi people absorbed a large portion of Monomotapa's empire and became the dominant power south of the Zambezi. The subordinate tribes now had to pay tribute to the Mambo and the appointment of their chiefs had to be confirmed by him; otherwise Rozwi's rule was a very loose one; the different Shona tribes continued to run their internal affairs, whilst internecine warfare between them continued.

Unable to exploit the gold resources of the interior effectively the Portuguese turned to the export of 'black ivory' and in 1645 the first slaves were exported from Moçambique to the great plantations of Brazil, which now required more and more unskilled labourers. The Moçambique and the Zambezi area replaced West Africa as a slave market. The exportation of labour was, however, a disastrous expedient, for local authorities were deprived of their workers, whilst the cruel commerce in human beings always proved speculative and uncertain in character.

In the political sphere the Portuguese attempted to consolidate their position inland by introducing white settlers, but these projects never succeeded. Instead a small group of magnates came into being, settled on huge estates, known as *prazos da corôa* who ruled the country as semi-independent chiefs. Neither was the position improved by the practice of sending hardened convicts to Moçambique, or by the expulsion of the Jesuits from the Colony, an ill-considered measure put into effect between 1759 and 1760.

In the latter half of the eighteenth century Portuguese enterprise in Moçambique revived with the appointment of the brilliant Dr Francisco José Maria de Lacerda e Almeida, a Brazilian scholar of note, to be Governor of Rios de Sena. Lacerda was a very far-sighted man and believed that the British seizure of

---

[1] Bocarro, A. 'Extracts from the decade . . . of the performances of the Portuguese in the East' (in Theal, G. M., ed., *Records of south-eastern Africa*. . . . Cape Town, The Government of the Cape Colony, 1896–1905, v. 3, p. 355)

c

Cape Town in 1795 was fraught with profound consequences for the future of southern Africa. 'The new possessors of Table Bay', he wrote, 'require very careful watching, or our want of energy will enable them to extend themselves northwards. Who will prevent the new colonists from selling the slaves of our southern interior thus palpably injuring our trade which has already lost one third of its value'? The English had to be excluded for they now could supply cloth more cheaply than the Portuguese. In addition the country inland possessed vast potential reserves of iron, sulphur and copper; both strategy and trade thus demanded that a permanent line of communication should be set up between the East and the West Coasts of Africa, which the Portuguese would control, and which one day might cut out the Cape route.[1]

Lacerda thus assembled an impressive expedition which left Tete in 1798. He got as far as Kazembe's town in North-Eastern Rhodesia, establishing for the first time direct contact between Europeans and a Lunda kingdom. Lacerda was impressed by Kazembe: 'clearly this king, though in the heart of Africa, is not the barbarian whom our closest geographers describe', and Kazembe was only too anxious to trade. His kingdom was already in commercial relations with the Portuguese in Angola through the good offices of Mwato Yamvo, whilst Yao traders kept him in contact with the Arabs in Zanzibar. Kazembe thus showed himself friendly to the Portuguese, but nevertheless Lacerda's great project came to naught; he was poorly served by most of his subordinates; his military escort proved practically useless, and worn out by fever and fatigue Lacerda died in the interior. His expedition was brought back to Tete by its chaplain, and nothing further was achieved.

The first known journey across Africa from coast to coast owed its successful completion, not to a European, but to two Portuguese-speaking Africans. In 1802 two *pombeiros*, bondsmen in the service of a Portuguese official left Muropoe in Angola; nine years later, the two men, known by the Portuguese as Pedro João Baptista and Amaro José, arrived at Tete after an incredible journey. Unfortunately neither of the two had any instruments, nor were they capable of making any scientific observations, so that their adventures did not add much to the geographical knowledge of the day.

The Portuguese made another attempt to secure their influence inland by setting up in 1827 a small garrison in what is now the Lundazi District of North-Eastern Rhodesia.[2] The site was chosen so as to control the route to Kazembe; had the Portuguese maintained it as a future base of operations in the interior, the course of Northern Rhodesian history might well have been different. As it was, the Portuguese withdrew after an occupation lasting only two years; and a further expedition, sent inland from Tete in 1831 under the command of Major José Maria Corrêa Monteiro and Captain Antonio Candido Pedroso Gamitto was no more successful.

[1] Lacerda, F. J. M. de. The Lands of Cazembe: Lacerda's journey to Cazembe in 1798, translated and annotated by R. F. Burton. John Murray, 1873, p. 14–21
[2] Lane Poole, E. H. 'An early Portuguese settlement in Northern Rhodesia' (in Journal of the African Society, v. 30, no. 119, Apr 1931, p. 164–168)

II

Nineteenth century invasions

For many centuries Bantu tribes moved southward from the Great Lakes and the Congo basin, but in the first quarter of the nineteenth century this tide was suddenly reversed, resulting in a trail of pillage and slaughter from Natal to Tanganyika. The change began amongst the Nguni, a peaceful group of pastoral tribes settled in the region between the Umgeni river in Natal and the Pungwe in Portuguese East Africa. One of their component groups, the Zulu, were welded into a great military power by the genius of Chaka, the Attila of Africa; Chaka taught the tribesmen how to charge in disciplined cresent-shaped formations, wielding stabbing spears and protected by great ox-hide shields, a tactical reserve being kept for the decisive thrust. Chaka was a ferocious tyrant but a brilliant soldier and his new military methods proved too much for the surrounding tribes who were decimated in a series of bloody campaigns. The Zulu people then began to increase; captive women and boys were incorporated into the tribe, the increase in manpower further adding to its war-making capacity. In addition, the Zulu raided for grain and cattle, their livestock providing them with much of their food and also with a kind of four-legged 'commissariat', able to accompany the Zulu horde over vast distances and providing it with great strategic mobility.

Chaka's military despotism was, however, subject to serious internal dissensions. Some time in the twenties the Matabele (Ndebele) broke away, and followed Mzilikazi, an outstanding leader, who had incurred Chaka's wrath. The refugees did not move south as their ancestors had done; such a course would now ultimately have brought them up against European settlers who were also pushing inland. Instead the Matabele host marched west, to the region of the Vaal, and then north-east of Kuruman. By employing Chaka's methods the Matabele soon put a broad belt of scorched earth between themselves and their erstwhile overlords, but they met their first great reverse when in 1836 they encountered Boer *trekkers* from the south. The Boers, anxious to escape British control at the Cape, and out to secure new land and grazing ground for their ever expanding pastoral economy, were also moving inland; the two competing groups of cattle farmers clashed, and the Afrikaners soon got the better of the struggle. The Afrikaners were mounted sharp-shooters, knowledgeable in fieldcraft, and extremely mobile. In addition they employed ox waggons, both for supply and for tactical purposes on the battlefield where they were drawn up in a hollow square, providing an almost impregnable base for their forces. The Matabele were not equipped to meet these tactics which more than four centuries ago had proved too much for the heavily armoured German knights battling against the Czech Hussites; the Matabele suffered a further defeat at the hands of the Boers, the situation being made even worse by further Zulu raids on Mzilikazi's people. The Matabele therefore withdrew to the north and in or about 1840 established a kingdom in what is now Matabeleland. Their state was organized on rigidly hierarchical lines. The *Zansi*, the original immigrants from the south, constituted the ruling class; the *Nhla*, mainly Sotho people incorporated on the march, came next, whilst the *Holi*, the despised indigenous people, constituted the plebs. Matabele hordes raided as far north as the Tonga country beyond the Zambezi, and deep into Mashonaland where the indigenous people were too disunited to resist them, having already been crushed by a second group of intruders from the south.

This new host was led by Zwangendaba, another Zulu chief who had opposed Chaka and had succeeded in making his way to the north. Zwangendaba advanced into Swaziland where he incorporated many of the Swazi into his horde, and then moved into the Makalanga country, where his hordes occasioned terrible devastation. In 1835 Zwangendaba's host crossed the Zambezi together with all their women and children, their captives and their cattle, the day of the crossing having been identified by an eclipse of the sun. The great horde, now known as the Ngoni, marched further north still, reaching the vicinity of Lake Tanganyika about 1845. After Zwangendaba's death the Ngoni host, weakened by two previous secessions but still vast and unmanageable, split up into various sections. One of these settled west of Lake Tanganyika where they became known as the Watuta. Others settled in various parts of Nyasaland. A further group, led by Mpeseni, marched to the west. Mpeseni's decision was an unfortunate one for about 1856 the Ngoni warriors encountered the Bemba, who were known raiders on their own account, and who were well supplied with muskets received from the Arab traders in exchange for ivory and slaves. The Ngoni suffered defeat, Mpeseni then retreated to the south where he finally settled in the Fort Jameson region of North-Eastern Rhodesia which became the home of another raider state.

A third branch of the Zulu under their chief Shoshangane established the so-called Gaza state which became a perpetual source of trouble to the Portuguese in East Africa; for long the Portuguese remained unable to expel these savage warriors who in 1833 managed to massacre a whole Portuguese garrison on the Spirito Santo.

A fourth group of invaders comprised the Kololo, another horde of cattle-keeping people who were led by Sebituane, a chief of the Patsa branch of the Bafokeng. Their migration, which may well rank with one of the most famous marches in history, say the wanderings of the Israelites through the desert, or the march of the Ten Thousand recounted by Xenophon, began about 1823 when the Bafokeng, later known as the Makololo, decided to seek a new and safer home for themselves in the Far North. Their route took them across the Vaal River and later through Bechuanaland; they subdued the Bakwena, but were forced to yield to the Bangwaketse, who were aided by the white men. Later on they invaded the Bangwato country and went to Lake Ngami where they overcame the Batawana. Thereafter in or about 1840 they crossed the Zambezi and for a time settled in the Tonga country.[1]

The Matabele, however, continued to press upon them and Livingstone relates a picturesque stratagem by which one of the terrible impis was wiped out. The raiders from the south came to the Zambezi in a large body. Sebituane then placed some goats on one of the large islands on the river as a bait to the warriors, canoes being left behind to co-operate in the manoeuvre. When all the Matabele were ferried over the canoes were removed, and the Matabele were trapped and easily massacred.[2] The Matabele threat, however, proved too great; and Sebituane's host moved into the upper Zambezi valley where Sebituane made himself ruler and consolidated the Barotse (Lozi) kingdom once again; Sikololo, the conqueror's language, becoming the *lingua franca* of the plain. Sebituane, however, died in 1851, and his people soon fell on evil days. The tall, light-skinned highlanders came from a country where malaria was almost unknown, and thus possessed little resistance against the fever prevailing in the Zambezi valley. There were moreover serious dissensions amongst them, and finally Sepopa, one of the remaining Barotse chiefs, fled to the north where the Makololo had been unable to penetrate; Sepopa then raised a new army; the Makololo were annihilated in 1864, and Barotse hegemony was re-established once more.

Under Sepopa's successors the Barotse continued to expand, their powers finally extending as far north as the Lovale country, deep into what is now Eastern Angola, and as far as the Kafue river. The Zambezi was dominated by Barotse war canoes, and the 'drifts' across the river strictly controlled. The fertile Barotse valley maintained a relatively complex economy based on cattle keeping, farming, fishing and agriculture; Barotse wealth was further increased by tribute from their subject tribes, who in exchange received gifts, loans of cattle and protection from their enemies. The Barotse of course need not be idealized; they too carried out bloody raids for cattle and manpower, and in times of trouble political liquidations were the order of the day. But the Barotse were not just conquerors pure and simple; their state was a highly complex one with elaborate checks and balances, so that a Portuguese observer was able to say that 'the political organization of the Kingdom ... is very different to that of the other peoples I have visited in Africa'.[3] The Barotse moreover were political realists, with a clear grasp of the complex balance of power which then existed in Central Africa and the flexibility of Barotse policy and its ability to adjust itself to changing circumstances profoundly affected the subsequent course of history in Central Africa.

The main problem that soon came to face all Bantu rulers in Central Africa occurred in what might be called 'the gun-powder revolution'. The interior of Africa had little to offer to foreign traders, except three kinds of merchandize:

[1] Smith, E. W. 'Sebetwane and the Makololo' (in *African studies*, v. 15, no. 2, 1956, p. 49–74)

[2] Livingstone, D. *Missionary travels and researches in South Africa.* John Murray, 1857, p. 86–88

[3] Pinto, A. da S. *How I crossed Africa. . . .* Sampson Low, Marston, Searle and Rivington, 1881

wild rubber, ivory and men. Rubber was not of much importance south of the Congo and does not greatly affect this story. Elephant tusks, however, became a major source of wealth, especially when the European luxury industries began to expand in the course of the nineteenth century; ivory was needed for knife-handles and combs, billiard balls and piano-keys, ornaments and all kinds of Victorian knick-knacks; the average annual import of ivory into London more than doubled between the eighteen-forties and the eighteen-seventies, and by the time of the Franco-Prussian War, Africa was supplying some 85 per cent of the world's total consumption of ivory.[1]

As far as manpower was concerned, the main demand came from non-Europeans. The nineteenth century saw the abolition of the 'Christian' slave trade, as well as profound changes in the great transatlantic plantation econo-mies on which this immoral traffic had rested. But as the White trade came to an end, the Muslim countries appear to have increased their purchases, making ever greater inroads into the remaining preserves of Central Africa. Slaves worked in the clove plantations of Zanzibar and Pemba; they were taken to the markets of Turkey, Persia and Arabia as domestic servants and concubines. In addition the great *prazo* holders in the Zambezi valley and the cocoa plantations owners of São Thomé in the west employed numerous slaves, whose high mortality required a constant replenishment of supplies.

Ivory and slaves were paid for mainly by cloth, gunpowder and firearms, the exportation of guns from Europe being stimulated by the technological revolu-tion that was coming over the European armament industries. During the first half of the nineteenth century, the old smooth-bore flintlocks gave way to the percussion musket, a new and improved model being introduced into the British army in 1842. The percussion musket in turn was replaced by the rifle, the En-field being adopted by the British forces in 1855, with the result that more obsolescent weapons became available for sale overseas. Bemba and Lovale warriors in time became keen customers for the old muskets that had served Wellington's veterans; in addition a large number of specially manufactured trade-guns of very inferior quality—as likely to blow up in their owners' faces as to hit their target—found their way inland to swell the local supply of fire-arms.

This barter in guns, ivory and slaves depended on four main streams of in-vaders who came from the coasts and converged in the heart of Central Africa. The first group consisted of Arabs from the East Coast, whose caravans reached the Great Lakes and the Congo basin during the sixties, two adventurous 'Moors' from Zanzibar having crossed the Continent to Benguella as early as 1852. The Arabs then pushed up the Tanganyika-Nyasa plateau and established their influence over much of what is now North-Eastern Rhodesia. The routes through southern Nyasaland were dominated by the Yao, a Bantu people who were drifting into the country in search of land and slaves and subjugated the local Nyanja. In addition Portuguese half-castes from the Zambezi made their

[1] Information kindly supplied to the author by Dr J. R. Gray from an unpublished paper.

way up the Luangwa valley, pillaging and laying waste wherever they went. Other raiders came from the west, the most important of these being the Ovimbundu, who reached the mouth of the Kafue about 1878, the traders from Angola dealing in slaves, ivory, and later on in rubber, and relying far more on local agents than the Arabs, whilst at the same time completely lacking the Muslim's political ambitions.

The effects of these multiple invasions were far-reaching, and some of them proved of benefit to the indigenous people; Africans acquired new goods like guns and gunpowder which made the hunter's task easier, whilst cloth and beads changed indigenous fashions. The trading caravans themselves needed food in their lengthy journeys, and this may have given the tribesmen an incentive to grow more crops, whilst acquainting them with the vagaries of market prices.[1] At the same time the introduction of firearms strengthened all those indigenous leaders who managed to acquire the new weapons. Better armed than before, they were now able to attack their neighbours with greater ferocity; more warriors would join the successful warlord's ranks, additional slaves were captured and more guns bought in turn, so that the new raider-state soon expanded. This explains the emergence of a 'gunpowder' kingdom such as the one founded in the Congo, by Msidi, a Munyamwezi freebooter, whose influence extended down into Northern Rhodesia. The gun trade also led to sharp reversals of the local balance of power. The Chokwe and the Lovale for instance, better placed geographically for the importation of firearms from Angola, began to turn upon the once-victorious Lunda whose empire under Mwata Yamvo disintegrated in the latter half of the nineteenth century, and the Western Lunda themselves became the victims of the trade.

Admittedly, not all areas were affected equally. The Barotse did not engage in the slave trade to any large extent, for they wanted their manpower at home to sustain a relatively complex exchange economy. Neither did the Matabele participate in the traffic; they preferred to raid on their own account to strengthen their tribe. But this was small consolation to the weaker tribes, for wherever the slave-caravans appeared pillage and slaughter followed in their wake. 'We passed a woman tied by the neck to a tree and dead', Livingstone noted in his diary in 1866, 'The people of the country explained that she had been unable to keep up with the other slaves in a gang. . . . We saw others tied up in a similar manner, one lying on the path shot or stabbed, for she was in a pool of blood'.[2] Burton, another explorer, who observed the trade elsewhere estimated that in order to capture fifty-five women, at least ten villages had been destroyed, each with a population of between one and two hundred souls. Recovery from these raids was difficult, for the Bantu could not draw on accumulated reserves and their margin of survival was a narrow one at the best of times. The advance of

---

[1] White, C. M. N. 'A Preliminary survey of Luvale Rural Economy' (*Rhodes-Livingstone paper*, no. 29, 1959, p. 37–40)

[2] Livingstone, D. *The last journals . . .* edited by H. Waller. New York, Harper and Brothers, 1875, p. 59

the 'gunpowder frontier' from the opposite coasts into the heart of Africa thus proved a disaster of the first magnitude, whose consequences can hardly be exaggerated.[1]

III

European exploration in the mid-nineteenth century

The traffic in ivory and slaves, for all its devastating effects had its positive side, and the expansion of trade into the interior also facilitated the work of white explorers, who were now becoming fascinated by the challenge of one of the last undiscovered regions of the world. The news of Africa also was of burning interest to missionaries, anxious to redeem these vast benighted heathen lands, where the Gospel had never before been preached. In addition there was a growing awareness of Africa's commercial possibilities, the economic motive being foremost in the mind of Silva Pôrto, one of Northern Rhodesia's greatest pioneers. Antonio Francisco Ferreira da Silva Pôrto was born in 1817, the son of a Portuguese private soldier who had fought with distinction in the Peninsular War. His father was unable to give him more than a primary education and Pôrto accordingly emigrated to Brazil, the land of promise to many poor and ambitious Portuguese emigrants. The New World did not, however, fulfil his expectations and in 1838 he permanently settled in Angola; here he set himself up as a trader, but subsequently made his way inland where he became one of Portugal's greatest frontiersmen. By 1845 he was permanently established at Bihé and from there he undertook a series of remarkable journeys about which unfortunately little is known.

One of Pôrto's most important expeditions was put under way in 1847, when he made his way inland, crossed the Kwanza, and reached the Upper Zambezi in 1848. On 22 January of that year, he was able to write into his diary a vital piece of news. 'The Chief of the Grand Libata received us surrounded by his dignitaries and a great crowd. We presented our compliments to him and expressed our hope that relations between natives and foreigners would be maintained and strengthened. Then we delivered our present which consisted of cloth, powder, arms and beads. The Chief distributed them to the bigwigs without keeping any for himself. He told us that we should consider the land as our own, that no distinction would be made between foreigners and natives and that to him they were all his children. In return for our own present he gave us four large elephants' tusks, venison and other supplies. . . . The land of Lui properly thus called' Silva Pôrto added, 'is at present inhabited by the Genje or audacious people, the name which the natives give to the Macarrollos [Makololo]. . . .'[2]

Pôrto thus played a major share in opening Barotseland to the trade from

[1] See Gann, L. H. 'The end of the slave trade in British Central Africa 1889–1912' (in *Rhodes-Livingstone journal*, no. 16, 1954, p. 26–51)

[2] Pôrto, A. F. da S. *Viagens e apontamentos de um Portuense em Africa*. Lisbon, Agência Geral das Colónias, 1942, p. 76

Benguela, but his greatest journey was undertaken four years later when he crossed Africa from coast to coast, the first European to do so. Pôrto set out from Benguella in 1852 in company with some Muslim traders from Zanzibar; he again crossed the Kwanza river, proceeded to the junction of the Quando river with the Gaimbo, reaching 'Nariere' (Naliele), the 'capital of Lui', in 1853; Silva Pôrto recorded a fairly detailed description of the Barotse, their habits, customs and economic resources, which remains of considerable historical interest. Silva Pôrto fell sick, but his *pombeiros* continued the journey beyond the Loenge (Kafue), reaching the Indian Ocean at Ibo in August 1854.[1]

Another traveller from the west was Ladislaus Amerigo Magyar (also known as Magyar Laszlo); Magyar, an able and well-educated man, was originally trained as a naval officer, but emigrated to Africa in 1847. He subsequently undertook extensive journeys in southern Africa and finally settled in Angola where he became an ivory trader and married the daughter of an African chief. 'You may be surprised', he wrote to his father in 1853, 'that not only did I settle amongst the savage nations of Africa, but that I also got married there. But failing such a step I should never have been able to reach my objective. Now that I have succeeded I can tell you that there is no power or reward in Europe which would have been sufficient to enable even the most audacious traveller to pass through these wild wastes. My wife's armed slaves have been my companions for five years, obedient tools in the execution of my orders'. The majority of his bondsmen, Magyar added, died as the result of exertions, whilst he himself was completely ruined in health. Magyar's work was of considerable value to the Portuguese who gave him an official title. In a series of journeys between 1848 and 1855, he penetrated deeply into what is now the Congo Republic, visiting Mwato Yamvo's kingdom, bringing back a good deal of information about the geography, ethnography and commercial possibilities of the interior, particularly with regard to the trade in slaves and ivory. His importance for Northern Rhodesia is only marginal, but his work at least deserves being mentioned since, on a return journey from the Lunda country to the north, he passed through Musokantande and north of Kanongesha, thus establishing contact for the first time with the Ndembu branch of the Lunda people.[2]

Travellers from Portuguese territory were the pioneers of Northern Rhodesia. But the most important journeys beyond the Zambesi were undertaken by David Livingstone, the greatest traveller perhaps ever to set foot in Central Africa. Livingstone was born in 1813 at Blantyre, Co. Lanark, the son of a small farmer who had been forced to leave his holding and become a cotton-worker at Glasgow. At the age of ten young David too was sent to the mill to add to the family income, but worked his way up by sheer determination, saving enough from his wages as a cotton-spinner to take a course of medicine at Glasgow. He

[1] Agência Geral das Colónias. *Silva Pôrto e a travessia do continente Africano*, preface by de Sousa Dias, G. Lisbon, Agência Geral das Colónias, 1938

[2] Petermann, A. 'Die Reisen von Ladislaus Magyar in Süd Afrika' (*in Petermann's Geographische Mittheilungen*, 1857, p. 182–183). See also 'Ladislaus Magyar's Enforschungen von Inner-Afrika' (in *Petermann's Geographische Mittheilungen*, 1860, p. 227–237), including map on table 10

qualified as a physician in 1840, by which time he was firmly resolved to devote his life to preaching the Gospel amongst the heathen. Under the influence of Dr Robert Moffat, he decided to choose Southern Africa as the field of his labours, and having been ordained as a missionary, embarked for the Cape of Good Hope to work for the London Missionary Society.

The L.M.S., as it was popularly known, had by this time built up a great tradition of service. It was founded in 1795, at a time when the Evangelical Revival was gaining vast support, part of that major religious and humanitarian revolution that was helping Britain to solve the problems of industrialization. The Society's work was closely associated with social work amongst the poor at home whom reformers were hoping to convert to a life of Christian thrift, sobriety and self-help, enabling them to find their feet in the new industrial towns of England, and providing a practical alternative to revolutionary conspiracies. The L.M.S. thus maintained close links with a domestic 'Village Itinerancy Society' and the 'British and Foreign Bible and Tract Society'. The Nonconformist conscience was, however, as keenly interested in saving the heathen in the kraal as in the slum tenement. The Society thus began to send out missionaries to the remoter parts of the world, that were now becoming more and more accessible through the expansion of trade and the work of British explorers.

In 1796 work was first begun in South Africa, where the Cape had recently been occupied by British troops. From here missionaries pushed inland, a great step forward being the creation of a new station at Kuruman by Dr Robert Moffat. Kuruman developed into a major missionary centre and it was this settlement which was Livingstone's first destination. He arrived there in 1841 and subsequently undertook a number of extensive journeys into the 'Far Interior'. These expeditions took him as far as Lake Ngami, which he discovered in 1849, in company with William Cotton Oswell and Mungo Murray. During the course of these travels Livingstone acquired a wide knowledge of native languages and customs and also heard reports of the great Makololo state on the Zambezi. He made up his mind to follow the trail inland and in June 1851 he reached the river Chobe, meeting with a friendly reception from Sebituane, the Makololo king. The Black Paramount expressed himself anxious to receive European missionaries, though it seems that he regarded the whites as much as a potential source of firearms against the Matabele, as the bringers of Glad Tidings. Sebituane died shortly afterwards, but his successor permitted Livingstone to continue his explorations and in the same year he first reached the Zambezi, the mightiest river he had ever seen.

Livingstone subsequently embarked on another expedition to the north and arrived at Linyanti in 1853. By this time Sekeletu had become chief of the Makololo but proved as friendly as his predecessors. Sekeletu's sentiments were not entirely altruistic, for the Africans argued according to Livingstone, 'Jesus had not loved their forefathers, hence their present degradation. He had loved the white men and given them all the wonderful things they now possess. And as I had come to teach them to pray to Jesus and to pray for them, their wants would soon all be supplied.'[1]

The Makololo moreover gave support to Livingstone as an ambassador to negotiate 'non-agression pacts' with the chiefs to the north and west of the kingdom, including the Barotse whom the Makololo had driven out of their homeland. Livingstone also enjoyed great personal prestige as the son-in-law of Robert Moffat, and the Makololo hoped that he would prevent the dreaded Matabele from raiding.[2]

As far as the young doctor's purely religious message was concerned, Sekeletu was less interested; as he admitted to Livingstone, he needed at least five wives and had no intention of being content with just one. But the king was impressed by Livingstone's medical knowledge, tactfully exercized in consultation with the Barotse's own doctors; Sekeletu was also struck by his visitor's wide knowledge of the world and by his geographical interest, which coincided with the Makololo's own desire for more trade.

Livingstone, having decided that Barotseland was ripe for the Gospel, decided to open a pathway to the west coast. Sekeletu, keen on additional commerce between Barotseland and Angola, was only too glad to subsidise the venture by providing men and canoes, and on 11 November 1853 Livingstone set out from Linyanti for the long trek to the Atlantic coast. His journey took him to Shinde, past the Kasai and Kwango rivers, and he finally arrived at the port of Loanda on 31 May 1854. Rather than leave his Barotse followers in the lurch, he refused an offer of being taken home on board a British frigate and instead decided to make his way back to the Zambezi. The journey back, like the one to Loanda, was fraught with grave hardships, but Livingstone overcame all the obstacles and got back to Barotseland, where he received a hero's welcome. Many Makololo volunteers were now ready to join him in his next project, a journey to Quelimane on the east coast of Africa. With Sekeletu's blessing and support, Livingstone's expedition left Linyanti in November; he reached the Victoria Falls on 16 November, giving us our first description of this mighty spectacle.

Livingstone then continued his journey past the confluence of the Luangwa and Zambezi, arriving at Quelimane on 20 May 1856. From there he returned to England where honours were showered upon him. He then published his work, *Missionary Travels*, which became a land-mark in the history of African discovery and also provided its author with additional funds for the work of exploration, now his major interest in life; Livingstone accordingly severed his connexion with the London Missionary Society and in February of 1858 accepted an appointment as H.M. Consul at Quelimane and as officer in command of an expedition to explore Eastern and Central Africa.

Livingstone was now determined to open up a river-route into the African

[1] Quoted from Seaver, G. *David Livingstone: his life and letters*. Lutherworth Press, 1957, p. 177

[2] See Gluckman, M. 'As men are everywhere else' (in *Rhodes-Livingstone journal*, no. 20, 1956, p. 68–73)

interior whereby 'Commerce and Christianity' might alike be brought to the Dark Continent. A steam launch, the *Ma-Robert* was placed at his disposal and in May 1858 he arrived at the mouth of the Zambezi. He made three successive attempts to push inland beyond Tete, but in the end even Livingstone had to admit that the Kebrabasa Rapids constituted an insuperable obstacle to navigation inland. Livingstone then turned to explore the Shire river and to find the great reputed lake at its source. His progress inland was stopped by impassable cataracts which he named after his friend, Sir Roderick Murchison, President of the Royal Geographical Society, and he was forced to return to Tete. But he moved forward once again and in September 1859 arrived with his companions on Lake Nyasa, Central Africa's magnificent inland sea.

Livingstone subsequently undertook another journey to the Makololo country, and also took an ill-fated party of Anglican missionaries belonging to the Universities Mission to Central Africa (U.M.C.A.) up the Shire Highlands. But his further work was dogged with misfortune; his wife died; sickness and dissension stalked his party; native labour and supplies became unobtainable because of the devastation brought about by slave traders. After another trip which took him as far as Kota Kota on the west coast of Lake Nyasa, Livingstone returned to the coast. He reached the mouth of the Zambezi in February 1864, and the expedition came to an end. Livingstone himself arrived in London in July 1864, where he received once more a great ovation and was able to devote himself to the work of recording his experiences.

A year later he left for his last tragic journey. Livingstone was still convinced that the source of the Nile would be found somewhere in Central Africa, and was eager to solve the question of its origins. In addition he had not abandoned his hope that Africa might be opened up to peaceful economic penetration from Europe and was determined to find out more about the slave trade which was beginning to devastate the interior. On 19 March 1866 he departed from Zanzibar for the mouth of the Rovuma River and subsequently made his way once more to strife-torn Nyasaland. From there he struck inland where he got as far as the river Luangwa. He then made his way to the north, reaching Lake Tanganyika on 2 April 1867. Receiving a great deal of help from the Arabs, he explored the Muslim trade route to Lake Mweru and Lake Bangweulu, but neither of these proved to be the real source of the Nile. He then travelled to the Manyema country, getting as far as the Lualaba River which was reached in March 1871. Livingstone's position by now had become desperate; he was sick and exhausted, supplies were lacking and he was fortunate to be relieved by Henry Morton Stanley who brought new provisions and medicine. Between them the two explorers carried out further investigations, but Stanley was unable to persuade Livingstone to come home with him to England. Livingstone was obsessed with the idea that he must at all costs discover the source of the Nile and was certain that the Lualaba must be identical with its upper reaches; Stanley returned to England and Livingstone continued on his trek, making his way once more to the swampy shores of Lake Mweru. But by now the end was near. Tormented by swarms of mosquitoes and poisonous insects, half-starved and exhausted by almost super-human exertions, his wrecked body could no longer withstand the ravages of disease. He died on 1 May 1873 at Chitambo south of Lake Bangweulu in the lonely wilds of North-Eastern Rhodesia.

Livingstone's body was brought back to England by his faithful followers, and the news of his death made a tremendous impression overseas. Science and Christianity, both equally dear to the hearts of Victorian Englishmen, had found a martyr of impressive stature. Livingstone's career, itself one of the 'great success stories' of his time, became an inspiration to Protestant Christianity, deeply influencing the future of both evangelization and exploration in Inner Africa.

Admittedly, in evaluating Livingstone's work, a number of reservations should be made. Livingstone was not, as he is sometimes thought to be, the prince of missionaries. He certainly preached the Gospel with force and conviction, but he never stayed long enough in any one region for his work to become effective, the whole purpose of his work being to extend the missionary frontier at breakneck speed, rather than progressing slowly and consolidating the Gospel's gains. Neither was he interested in, or indeed qualified by temperament, for that essential task of missionary administration, which occupied so much of the time available to the other great statesmen of evangelism who followed him on the African trail.

As a geographer Livingstone displayed some remarkable flashes of insight; he formulated an interesting theory about the direction of the Trade Winds in relation to the earth's rotation; he understood the difficult hydrological problems of the Upper Zambezi; and he saw that the central plateau of Africa was in some ways like a huge saucer, with slight rises inside, and a rim of higher hills outside, the rivers breaking through the rim in cascades and waterfalls.[1] But on the other hand Livingstone also made a good many mistakes. Sometimes these were caused by false information from others; sometimes clouds would impede star readings; his instruments would get damaged or lost altogether so that fate might perpetuate his errors. Lastly Livingstone had an obsessional streak in his mind which made him sometimes misconstrue his own evidence, such as in the case of the Lower Zambezi, which he firmly believed must be navigable, or the firmly held conviction that he would find the source of the Nile in the Lake Bangweulu region. Apart from that, Livingstone's admirers sometimes overlooked the fact that Africa from the geographical point of view was not simply a *tabula rasa*. The priority of various Portuguese discoveries cannot be disputed. Victorians moreover often wrongly imagined that the white pioneers were slashing their way through untrodden jungle. In reality, Livingstone like all other European travellers during this period, built on existing knowledge and had to rely on local help and advice. The European explorers did not always

[1] See Debenham, F. *The way to Ilala: David Livingstone's pilgrimage.* Longmans, Green & Co. 1955

make their way through completely virgin country; more often they used an existing though albeit extremely rudimentary system of communications, consisting of village paths, ill-defined caravan roads and canoe routes. The greatness of men like Livingstone consisted in their methodical and scientific spirit as well as in their trained intelligence, rather than purely in their ability as pathfinders, in which they were often surpassed by indigenous people. As an administrator and leader of men, Livingstone again had grave weaknesses. He was magnificent when it came to handling Africans, but his dealings with Europeans were sometimes open to grave censure, and often displayed bitter prejudices against Portuguese and Afrikaners.

But when all is said and done, Livingstone still stands out as one of the greatest figures in the history of African exploration. Previous travellers to Central Africa, with the exception of Lacerda, had lacked a proper scientific training. Livingstone now brought a methodical mind to the task, and his books supplied his contemporaries with an incredible wealth of geographical, ethnographic, medical, botanical, geological and other information, in most minute detail. Livingstone, after all, was a doctor, trained to observe with accuracy, and his insistence on precision added much to the value of his work even on non-medical subjects. This can be seen, for instance, in his anthropological observations, which are still of value to the scholars of to-day. In the days of Livingstone, medicine itself had only just abandoned the metaphysical and even mystical cast of old, preferring empirical observation to *a priori* reasoning. Most contemporary ethnographic observations, on the other hand, were still cast in an ethical form. The average missionary work on African customs thus tended to be an essay on the depravity of native ways rather than a clinical exposition. Livingstone, on the other hand, was more concerned with recording and analyzing the facts, rather than passing judgements, and in this connexion it is instructive to compare his comments with those of, say, Coillard, his brilliant missionary successor on the Zambezi who became the the self-confessed 'Micah' and moral critic of the Barotse and their ways.

Even more important were Livingstone's purely medical achievements. These are all the more outstanding when it is remembered that hardly anything was known of tropical diseases at the time that Livingstone first set out for Africa. No one was aware of the part played by insects in the transmission of sicknesses; black-water fever was not understood, and effective penetration inland was all but impossible to Europeans not possessing the African's semi-immunity to malaria. Many were the pioneers who attempted the dangerous journey into the interior, but the cost of life incurred by ventures such as the U.M.C.A.'s mission to the Shire Highlands was quite prohibitive.[1] Livingstone, however, was convinced that Africa would not remain the White Man's Grave. A firm believer in the cause of British expansion and of African economic development, he was convinced that it should be one of the 'chief objects of his work' 'to investigate the character of that disease which is the main obstacle to

[1] Gelfand M. *Livingstone the doctor* ... Oxford Basil Blackwell ,1957

Africa being opened to beneficial intercourse with the rest of the world'. In this object Livingstone obtained considerable success. Symptoms of malaria were immediately dealt with by quinine; he also discovered the value of this medicine for prophylactic purposes and the results of Dr Livingstone's treatment quickly became apparent in the surprisingly low death rate of his expeditions. The doctor's new knowledge fortunately coincided with a considerable expansion in the production of this essential drug. Throughout the first half of the nineteenth century English manufacturers were dependent on South America for their raw material, the cinchona bark, which was then still derived from wild trees; methods of collection were irregular and wasteful and the product accordingly expensive. The cinchona plant, however, was subsequently introduced to the Dutch East Indies and from 1861 to British India, with the result that production expanded tremendously, with far-reaching consequences for the future of the Dark Continent.

As a doctor, Livingstone also had various other claims to prominence. He was one of the first to make use extensively of the clinical thermometer, the first to use arsenic on animals with sleeping sickness, and the first to link relapsing fever with ticks. He also added a good deal to our knowledge of tropical medicine in other ways, for instance by accurately describing and diagnosing many diseases met with in the interior of Africa.

But the medical aspect was only one of many facets in Livingstone's work. Equally important was his role as a theorist of African colonization. Europe, he argued in a curiously modern strain, must bring the Gospel to Africa, but sermons alone would not suffice. The new religion would not strike roots unless accompanied by a major social and economic revolution. Trade must follow the Gospel; 'legitimate' commerce in tropical raw materials should replace the iniquitous traffic in human beings that was depopulating the Continent and keeping Africans in misery. Steam-power, Livingstone hoped, would one day throw the way open into the African interior, thus doing away with the need for native porters and making possible the cultivation of cash crops like cotton, of which Britain was growing desperately short during the 'cotton-famine' occasioned by the American Civil War. In return for its primary products Africa would import manufactured goods from Europe, not just gun-powder and 'Tower Muskets', so that White and Black alike would benefit from a new economic partnership. Development, however, needed pioneers, and Livingstone keenly favoured the cause of European settlement in Central Africa, hoping that white colonists would teach new techniques of production to the indigenous peoples.

These doctrines were more complex than the rather straightforward views expressed by Silva Pôrto that 'the Cross and the Sword, the former converting, the latter chastising, shall be the only engines of future redemption for the [native] people'.[1] Livingstone of course did not exclude military actions; gun-boats had a

[1] Pôrto, A. F. da S. *Viagens e apontomentos de um Portuense em África*. Lisbon, Agência geral das Colónias, 194, p. 20

part to play in Africa as much as the Gospel; and the great explorer was, in his own way, as forceful an advocate of Empire as Cecil John Rhodes after him. But Livingstone did not just think in terms of sermons and salvoes. For all his many miscalculations, he understood the complex interaction between economic, religious, political and military factors, all of which would play their part in effecting that decisive revolution in Africa, which alone could save the tribal African from his weakness and open a Continent to 'Commerce and Christianity'.

Livingstone's doctrines were just the kind to appeal to Victorian Britain, with its boundless self-confidence and firm belief in religious and economic expansion. Livingstone's appeal moreover transcended social class. To the industrial workers, he was one of themselves, an ex-cotton spinner who had made good and was now honoured by bishops and lords. To factory owners his teachings signified a constructive kind of Christianity, not merely for Africa, but also for Scotland, where Livingstone appealed to the Blantyre factory hands to work for increased trust between employers and employed. His religious message, expressed with brilliant powers of conviction, was enormous. Livingstone's dramatic death and moving burial further focused attention on Africa, while his books whetted the public's appetite for more information about the Dark Continent, the supposed land of mystery and pagan gloom, of lowest depravity and highest Christian endeavour. His life-work thus gave a great stimulus to exploration and missionary endeavour, and many others decided to follow his trail.

Chapter Two

The old order changes

I

Early missionary penetration into Nyasaland and North-Eastern Rhodesia

The first fruit of Livingstone's endeavour was an attempt by his own society, the L.M.S., to open work among the Makololo. The Reverend Holloway Helmore was appointed in charge of the mission and sailed from Southampton with his wife and four children in 1858. From Cape Town, the missionaries made their way to Kuruman from where, in July 1859, they left for the interior, together with the Reverend Roger Price and the latter's wife Isabella. In 1860, after many difficulties, the party arrived at Linyanti, Sekeletu's capital. Then disaster struck. 'We reached the Makololo on 14 February. On the third day Sekeletu gave us an ox and some beer, he came too and shared it with us. . . . We all got ill one after the other . . . and . . . after we had left the Makololo our men told us that they had heard from some of the Makololo poison has been put into the ox and the beer.'[1] The drug having been administered, the Makololo were said to have left the party and taken an emetic which made them vomit the poisoned food again, but most of the European guests died. The victims included Helmore, his wife and two children. Price himself was robbed of most of his equipment, and it was a miracle that he and the survivors managed to retrace their steps to the south, Price's own wife and child dying *en route*. Price was convinced that treachery was at the bottom of the tragedy, his view being supported by the testimony of his servants and the fact that ordinary medicines proved quite ineffectual against the dread sickness.

Medical evidence has, however, since rendered the poisoning theory unlikely, Livingstone himself being convinced that the deaths occurred as the result of fever; the illnesses as described in contemporary correspondence were too protracted to result from any kind of administered toxin; little mention was made of purging which would have resulted from poisoning, though delirium was stressed. If Africans had tampered with the missionaries' food, the whites would all have become sick at the same time, and not within a few days of each other, whilst the description of Helmore's coma points to cerebral malaria. The victims moreover all perished during the fever season in a country already previously mentioned by Livingstone to be terribly unhealthy, and where Makololo children died in such numbers that the future of their race itself seemed

<hr/>

[1] E. E. Helmore to O. Helmore: 1 Dec 1861 (HE 3/1/1, f. 99–104, Nat Arch MS)

D

in danger.[1] Price, who unlike Helmore was personally unpopular with the natives, adduced African testimony to support his poisoning charge, but black people were wont to attribute any otherwise inexplicable death to human intervention, and could hardly be expected accurately to diagnose the white strangers' disease. As far as Barotse rapacity was concerned, Livingstone expressed considerable surprise, for his own waggon remained in Sekeletu's care for several years without ever being touched.

Sekeletu himself was in the meantime walking on a political tight-rope. From the inter-tribal point of view of course his position actually improved, when the Matabele for a time gave up all ideas of raiding beyond the Zambezi, two of their impis having been wiped out by the Makololo, and Mzilikazi himself gave an assurance to Moffat that he no longer wished to make war against his northern neighbours.[2] But Sekeletu was unable to take advantage of this situation, and proved quite incapable of controlling the contending factions in his kingdom, who no longer felt Sebituane's tight reins; rebellion followed on rebellion, and even the Makololo lost faith in their king and he died shortly before the exiled Sepopa sent an army into the Valley in 1864, thirsting for vengeance and rooting out the Makololo ruling race with fire and sword.

The second missionary venture, made under the inspiration of Livingstone's work, proved just as disastrous. After a stirring appeal made in 1857 at Senate House, Cambridge, to the British Universities, the 'Oxford and Cambridge Mission to Central Africa' was formed in 1858, later becoming known as the 'Universities' Mission to Central Africa' (U.M.C.A.). The mission received support from High Churchmen and tended to rely on the most highly placed social groups within the Church of England, extensive powers being placed in the hands of the Missionary Bishop on the spot. At the same time the U.M.C.A. tried to put into practice Livingstone's principles, and its first settlement in Central Africa was intended to be a balanced economic unit, capable of promoting both commerce and agriculture, as well as the Gospel. In 1860 the U.M.C.A.'s first party left England under the leadership of Bishop Charles Frederick Mackenzie, who was accompanied by an agriculturist and a carpenter as well as several ordained ministers. They reached the mouth of the Zambezi early in 1861, but by this time Livingstone's journey had disproved his former theory of an open highway into the interior. After great difficulties the mission made its way up the Shire, and from there to Magomero where a station was set up. The missionaries, however, soon found themselves in a disastrous position; they were suffering from lack of supplies and from fever; the country was by now being devastated by bitter warfare between the indigenous Nyanja people and immigrant Yao who sold their prisoners into slavery. Mackenzie attempted to resist the Yao by force, and to gather together liberated slaves as the nucleus of his mission, but his work ended in disaster. Mackenzie himself died, so did three of his companions, whilst several others had to be invalided home. The remain-

---

[1] Gelfand, M. *Livingstone the doctor: his life and travels.* Basil Blackwell, 1957, p. 160–161
[2] R. Moffat to H. Helmore: 22 Feb 1860 (HE 3/1/1, f. 71–76, Nat Arch MS)

der moved to another site, known as Chibisa, and in 1863 re-inforcements arrived, led by William George Tozer. So desperate was the situation now that Tozer decided to remove the mission, first of all to Mount Morambala, and then out of the country altogether. The U.M.C.A. settlement was accordingly transferred to Zanzibar which was regarded as the most suitable centre for subsequent expansion, by reason of its geographical position, its character as a major trading depot for the interior, and on account of the extensive political influence wielded over the island by the local British Consul.[1] Work in Nyasaland itself was not resumed by the U.M.C.A. until 1881.

This disaster seriously impaired Livingstone's reputation as a missionary theorist for a time, but his death in 1873 gave a new impetus to the evangelization of Central Africa, especially in Livingstone's native Scotland, where a group of substantial Glasgow merchants banded together to provide the necessary funds. In 1875 the Free Church of Scotland, a dissident Calvinist body, sent out a party on which the Established Church of Scotland, however, also had a representative.

The Free Church mission was fortunate to count amongst its members a brilliant young doctor of medicine, Robert Laws, as well as a number of Scottish artisans. It was led by E. D. Young, a capable seaman, and the venture was much more successful than the U.M.C.A's ill-starred attempt. A site was chosen by a natural harbour on the shore of Lake Nyasa, where the settlement could receive supplies by water. A little log-fort was thrown up to give protection and 'Livingstonia' mission became the main centre of British influence in northern Nyasaland.

The site for the Established Church's station was chosen in the south, in the Shire Highlands, where the danger from fever was not as great as in the lowlying valley, and Blantyre was founded in 1876. The mission went through an initial period of grave mismanagement, the position being made worse by the internecine tribal warfare which was raging all around the station, and by the absence of any strong indigenous authority to which the Scots could turn. The missionaries accordingly were forced to take the law into their own hands, whilst their policy of giving shelter to escaped slaves once again presented them with the problem of theocratic government. The resultant judicial and administrative problems were, however, mishandled so gravely, that it was not until the arrival of David Clement Scott and Alexander Hetherwick some five years later, that the mission was reorganized and became a great centre for the Gospel in Central Africa.

In the meantime Livingstone's own former society had also taken up the challenge. It was enabled to do so by Robert Arthington, a Leeds business man who offered a most generous donation if the Society would found a station on Lake Tanganyika. The offer was accepted and Roger Price, the survivor from the disastrous Makololo mission, left for East Africa to report; Price approved

[1] 'Memorandum on the present state and prospect of the Central African mission: June 1864' (UN 2/1/1, f. 276–285, Nat Arch MS)

of the project and in 1877 an expedition assembled at Saadani on the mainland of East Africa, opposite Zanzibar. From there the missionaries made their way to Ujiji, the main Arab trading-centre on the Lake. The L.M.S. men hoped to master the supply problem, their main bugbear, by the use of ox-carts; but the prevalence of 'fly' made the use of draught animals impossible; the beasts died; and soon the missionaries, like the Arab traders to the interior, had to rely on human porterage till at last they arrived at Ujiji, having suffered the most extreme hardships. Their policy was to evangelize among the Africans around the lake shores, relying on water-borne transport, and a station was set up at Uguha on the west of the lake and another at Urambo. But all the usual difficulties made their appearance; there was disease, supplies were difficult to obtain, and in addition there was considerable opposition from the local Arabs who controlled the route to the East Coast.

The situation began to change when in 1878 the Livingstonia Central Africa Company, later known as the African Lakes Company, was founded by a group of Christian businessmen in Scotland. The Company aimed at supplying the Nyasaland missions via the Shire-Nyasa route and at developing that 'legitimate trade' which missionary labours were expected to stimulate. A year later Joseph Thomson, the well-known explorer, investigated the Nyasa-Tanganyika Plateau and the Directors of the L.M.S. realized the advantage of supplying the mission from the south rather than the east.[1] The generosity of James Stevenson, a Glasgow merchant, then made it possible for a track to be built from Karonga, on the north end of Lake Nyasa, some of the way up to Lake Tanganyika, and the L.M.S. gradually abandoned the East Coast route, becoming part of the Central African rather than the East African group of missions.

The change in supply position was linked to a shift in missionary policy. The L.M.S. men originally worked round the Lake shore, making use first of all of sailing boats, and subsequently of a steamer, the *Good News*. This method, however, proved very unsatisfactory, since it involved much dispersion of effort and prevented effective work at any single spot. In addition the L.M.S. was anxious to get away from Arab influence and in 1885 the Society therefore decided to concentrate its efforts on the southern shore of Lake Tanganyika. In the same year the Rev. John Harris, assisted by Arthur Brooks, an artisan, and Alfred James Swann, a sailor, went to Niamkolo on the south end of the Lake. The whole area, however, was in a desperate state. There was no strong, indigenous authority anywhere in the region which was being devastated by raiders; the indigenous people were thus only too glad to flock round the station to find protection there. Soon afterwards, Tippoo Tib, one of Central Africa's greatest slave-traders, decided to devote his attention to the region, and the arrival of his hordes caused so much panic and despair amongst the natives, that the work of the mission suffered a serious blow.

The L.M.S. remained undeterred and at the end of 1886 the Rev. David

---

[1] Hanna, A. J. *The beginnings of Nyasaland and North Eastern Rhodesia 1859–95*. Oxford, at the Clarendon Press, 1956, p. 45–50

Picton Jones and the Rev. Robert Stewart Wright established a station at Fwambo.[1] The pioneers once more were in a difficult position, for again there was no strong chief to whom to turn, whilst the local Mambwe people, a scattered tribe of cattle-keepers, were under constant pressure from the warlike Bemba. The situation of the missionaries was, however, eased a little when work was resumed once more at Niamkolo which, in 1889, became the headquarters of the Society's 'Marine Department'.

The Society's second major problem lay in the realm of what might be called 'local foreign policy' which was overshadowed by the question of Arab-White relations. The Muslims by now were under serious pressure. In 1884 the Germans gained a foothold in Tanganyika and then gradually began to push their influence inland. In Nyasaland, European settlement also led to conflict, for the African Lakes Company soon found that supplying missionaries was not a profitable business; the Company's expenses were too high in relation to its turnover and it found, like so many others, that almost the only commodity which would stand the cost of transport to the coast was ivory. In order to obtain more of this merchandise, the Company extended its operations to the north end of Lake Nyasa; but here it soon clashed with Mlozi, a Muslim East Coast freebooter who had made himself 'Sultan' and resented interference with his local monopoly. Between 1887 and 1889 there was a good deal of fighting between the Company and the Arabs in the north, but despite support received from most Nyasaland missionaries, and also from fighting men like Frederick Dealtry Lugard, the Company was unable to expel the Arabs from their well fortified stockades.

Fortunately for the L.M.S., the Arabs and Coastmen themselves possessed no co-ordinated policy. They were nothing but scattered groups of adventurers whose petty principalities, founded only for the sake of trade and self-protection, showed little cohesion; therefore whilst the 'North End War' was in progress, the local Muslims made no attempt to expel the Europeans from Lake Tanganyika. The L.M.S. was able to continue upon its policy of neutrality when the Germans came into collision with the Tanganyika Arabs. It appears that at this time Muslims considered an attack on the L.M.S. settlements, but in the end Mohammed-bin-Alfan, Tippoo Tib's local representative, decided against war; the missionaries were left undisturbed, but abandoned their centre on Kavala Island as a precautionary measure.[2]

In addition to the problem of foreign affairs, there was the equally pressing one of internal management. The L.M.S. missionaries, like their Scottish brethren in the south, were settled in that extensive belt of territory, stretching from

---

[1] London Missionary Society. *Ninety-fourth report . . . for the year ending April 30th, 1888, p. 207,* Gelfand, M. *Northern Rhodesia in the days of the charter . . .* Oxford, Blackwell, 1961, p. 59. Since the completion of this work, the author has also been shown the manuscript of a valuable work by Rotberg, R. *Western man in African society: Christian missionaries and the history of Northern Rhodesia 1882–1924,* a detailed, though highly critical study of the period.

[2] London Missionary Society. *Ninety-sixth report . . . from May 1st, 1889, to March 31st 1890* p. 150

Lake Tanganyika to Nyasaland and thence to the Zambezi, where there were no strong indigenous chiefdoms. The Lungu and Mambwe people who lived near the L.M.S. stations regarded the white man's villages as centres of refuge from Bemba and Muslim raiders; native settlements grew up round the stations, and whether they liked it or not, the emissaries of the Gospel were forced to become chiefs. Heads of stations became responsible for judging disputes and specifying building sites, whilst offenders were punished by fines, hard labour or the rhino-whip. Discipline was severe, though the L.M.S. was never guilty of such grave abuses as occurred at Blantyre in its unreformed days, when a native was executed and another brutally flogged to death. The whole system of missionary government of course gave rise to serious differences of opinion and the Society's Home Committee always disliked the system. But under existing circumstances there was nothing else the missionaries could have done. Theirs was not a theoretical problem; they were face to face with the harsh realities of running little stations full of broken refugees, devoid of natural leaders; responsibility had to be accepted and it was thus a matter of governing or getting out. As it was, their tiny theocracies ensured peace and order, whilst their stations were never attacked by the formidable Bemba, who were well aware of what European discipline and firearms could do.

The policy of direct rule, however, also led the missionary into a serious moral predicament. The white preacher came to Africa as a bringer of Glad Tidings to teach the word of God to the benighted heathen. Now suddenly he became a ruler, able to impose godliness by word of command. From the purely administrative angle this was well enough, for churches and schools were always full, there was never any shortage of labour, whilst drunkards and adulterers were punished by the secular arm.[1] But what was to happen if differences occurred between the missionary's and the African's view of right and wrong: should Christians make any concessions to immoral pagan customs? Most late nineteenth century missionaries would have answered this in the negative. The majority of Protestant missionaries in early Northern Rhodesia were fundamentalist by conviction; inner-directed men who got their education the hard way, many dissenting clergymen having come from lower middle class or working class stock, the U.M.C.A. forming something of an exception in this respect. In the bush they lived as pioneers, often doing the roughest kind of manual labour to keep their mission going, and having not so much time for intellectual pursuits. They were prepared to accept enormous hardships; sometimes their families would die before their eyes from disease; but these terrible sacrifices only seemed worth while to people who were convinced that they alone possessed the truth. The emissaries of the Gospel thought of themselves as a tiny army of God, alone in the wilds of Africa, battling against Satan, and felt convinced that Western Christian standards alone must prevail. They were rarely analy-

[1] W. P. Jones to L.M.S.: 1 Nov 1898; J. H. E. Hemans to L.M.S.: 2 Nov 1898; I. May to L.M.S.: 27 Oct 1898, enclosing minutes of Tanganyika district committee from 12 to 22 Oct 1898 (L.M.S. Arch)

zers; they were men of action intent on changing the world; and to people of such a stamp aboriginal cultures merely represented a lower stage of human evolution, and 'lying, stealing, gluttony, polygamy, licentious debauchery and cannibalism' were thought to be deeply ingrained in the Bantu mind. African ways tended to be judged from the point of view of Victorian morality, and were mostly condemned as evil. Tribal collectivism was bad, for it suppressed individual effort and all individual sense of sin. African family systems grounded in polygamy were morally wrong and must give way to a proper Christian family life. Africans were 'a nation of unemployed', they were in danger of hell-fire everlasting, and only a complete moral and spiritual revolution would save their souls.

In theory these views were straightforward enough. But for those who lived in daily contact with African tribesmen, they led to many practical difficulties. Some missionaries even began to challenge certain of their own basic assumptions. Was there not, for instance, an obvious similarity between the customs of African tribesmen and those of the ancient Jews? This was the conclusion arrived at by the Rev. David Picton Jones who rejected the belief in the Old Testament's Divine Inspiration on the ground that the Hebrews resembled the people around the Fwambo station, and that their stories were just about as reliable. Another Doubting Thomas was Alexander Carson, a University trained engineer, who resigned from the Mission on the grounds that he could no longer believe in the Resurrection.

Jones and Carson were very far from being typical, but even those missionaries whose beliefs remained completely unshaken had to ask themselves how much they should interfere with cases of native immorality in actual practice. This problem led to frequent differences of opinion which came to a head when the Society appointed a married West Indian schoolmaster, James Henry Emmanuel Hemans, who came to Fwambo in 1888. Hemans, a Negro, was an able, forceful and even violent man, very conscious of any colour prejudice which his white colleagues might feel against him. But a much profounder source of tension was the Jamaican's different approach towards the African; Hemans, though quick with the sjambok, was tolerant of native customs and was accused of being too lenient towards their immoral habits.[1] There was an enquiry; Hemans, though personally popular with the Africans, was suspended, but the deeper problem raised by his conduct was not thereby solved.

The extrordinarily difficult questions that faced the L.M.S. were made no easier by the fact that there was little unanimity between the missionaries themselves. Their stations were almost semi-independent principalities apt to engage in bitter quarrels with each other, a state of affairs linked to some extent with the whole organization of the Society. The L.M.S. was in theory a non-denominational body, but drew its support mainly from Congregationalists, whose doctrinal individualism placed effective power into the hands of individual

[1] H. Johnson to L.M.S., enclosing Tanganyika district committee resolution no. 1539. See also H. C. Nutter to L.M.S.: 25 Apr 1904 and 4 June 1904 (L.M.S. Arch)

congregations. Missionary government in Central Africa reflected these principles; wide powers were left to each station which could communicate directly
with the Home Authorities, the local District Committee exercising few important functions. This system of government sharply differentiated the L.M.S.
from the Scottish Churches in Nyasaland whose Kirk Sessions provided a more
tightly organized system of government. Wide scope was left to able individuals,
but this also encouraged internal dissensions; men of strong character and strong
opinions, willing to brave the deadly clime of Africa, were liable to quarrel at the
best of times. On the Tanganyika plateau, however, administrative decentraliza-
tion made matters worse, and there was unfortunately no great missionary
statesman, such as Laws, to pull the contending parties together again. The
ravages of disease, moreover, caused rapid changes in personnel which again
made co-operation more difficult.[1] But despite these difficulties the Mission was
now there to stay. Gradually its members gained more experience of the country
and as they left the unhealthy lake region for the more salubrious plateau there
was a sharp fall in the missionaries' death rate, which in time profoundly affected
the general atmosphere and character of the mission, whose foot-hold in
Northern Rhodesia was never shaken again.

II

The Missionary occupation of North-Western Rhodesia

In North-Western Rhodesia missionary history developed along different
lines. The key to expansion lay in the internal politics of Barotseland, a powerful
indigenous kingdom now making contact for the first time with white hunters
and traders from the south. For many decades past, daring frontiersmen, mostly
Afrikaners from the Transvaal, had been making their way north of the Limpopo in search of game. One of the earliest traders to reach the Zambezi region
was George Fleming, a coloured man from the Cape and a protegé of Livingstone,[2] who got to Linyanti in 1852 but failed to make a success of this venture.
In the meantime more hunters penetrated into what is now Southern Rhodesia,
but as time went on shooting elephants became less and less profitable further
south as the great beasts began to diminish in numbers, a serious matter for
big-game hunters who had to keep costs down; the ivory business after all was
a very speculative trade, depending on a small range of luxury industries subject
to severe fluctuations in price. Every European crisis was liable to affect a
hunter's prospects, so much so that even the Russo-Turkish War in the distant
Balkans made its repercussions felt in the wilds of Central Africa.[3]

The lands north of the Zambezi soon became the last remaining great reser-

[1] During the period 1880 to 1890, 8 missionaries died and 9 were invalided home. During the
following decade 2 missionaries and 2 wives died whilst 4 had to be invalided home.
[2] Seaver, G. *David Livingstone: his life and letters.* Lutherworth Press, 1957, p. 178
[3] F. C. Selous to F. L. Selous: 15 Oct 1877 (SE 1/1/1, f. 97–103 Nat Arch MS)

voir of ivory in the region, and its commercial possibilities were quickly realised by George Westbeech, a well-known trader. Westbeech first entered Matabeleland in 1863, where he and his partner, George Arthur Phillips, 'rationalized' methods of production by the extensive employment of native 'shooting boys' who killed big game on an enormous scale. By the 'seventies the finest tuskers were rapidly disappearing from the country south of the Zambezi, and about 1871 Westbeech began to trade with Barotseland, which had been neglected by traders from the south. In the early 'fifties a few white hunters followed in Livingstone's footsteps to the north. But Sekeletu soon raised the price of ivory, and in addition seems to have preferred Mambari traders from the west, who were in the habit of giving him all the goods in their possession, even their own clothes, in exchange for whatever the king chose to give them. Only Livingstone found favour in the eyes of Sekeletu, who was mainly interested in opening up commerce with the west, and neglected the southern route. Barotseland moreover was full of disease; and the dreaded 'fly' kept out English and South African hunters who preferred to shoot elephants from horseback rather than wearily trudge through the bush with their heavy muzzle-loaders. By the beginning of the 'seventies, however, the best hunting grounds south of the Zambezi were cleared of elephants which retreated into the remoter fly-belts where hunters could no longer follow them on horses, and where they could no longer use ox-wagons to take out ivory. Most of the Nimrods of an older generation could not adjust themselves to the change. Hunting on foot was much less profitable, physically more fatiguing, and also much more dangerous than going after big game on horseback. For, if a mounted hunter did not kill his elephant, but only wounded it, he could still swiftly ride to safety. But if he had to face the enraged beast on foot, he might easily be trampled to death.[1] Westbeech, however, met the challenge. He successfully employed African hunters who apparently became quite competent shots with the new breech-loading rifles that gradually drove out the more old-fashioned guns, and that required less skill than muzzle-loading smooth bores with percussion caps, whose terrific recoil might knock even a strong man off his horse. Westbeech opened up a profitable business, his arrival breaking the commercial stronghold of Ovimbundu traders from the west, whose flintlocks and gunpowder were inferior in quality to percussion muskets imported from the south. The southern merchants moreover did not normally deal in slaves; there was no market for the human merchandise in South Africa as there was in Angola, and British and Dutch traders used waggons which made the employment of porters unnecessary.[2] Westbeech and his partners accordingly became welcome guests in Barotseland and established their permanent headquarters at Panda-ma-Tenka, some seventy miles

[1] See Tabler, E. C. *The far interior* . . . , Cape Town, Balkema, 1955, which is the standard work on the subject of white hunters in Central Africa. The author calculates that until 1877, when trade declined for political reasons, Westbeech exported about ten to fifteen tons of ivory every year. He continued to work in Barotseland until his death in the Transvaal in 1888.

[2] Gann, L. H. 'The end of the slave trade in British Central Africa' 1889–1912' (in *Rhodes-Livingstone journal* no. 16 1954, p. 27–51)

south of Kazungula on the road from Tati. The little settlement became well known to scores of travellers from the south. Westbeech himself, with his courage and complete personal honesty, acquired great political influence in Barotseland where the indigenous aristocracy came to look upon him as their official adviser on European affairs.

The route to the north was becoming better known and its use was no longer confined entirely to traders. Emil Holub, an adventurous Czech doctor who had previously set himself up in practice at the Kimberley diamond fields, travelled to Barotseland via Panda-ma-Tenka, recording his impressions in considerable detail, and bringing back an extensive and valuable natural history collection to show for his efforts.

Then the pace of exploration quickened. Another expedition was launched by Dr Aurel Schulz, a medical man of independent means, and August Hammar, who set off in 1884 from Dundee, Natal, at their own expense to explore the Chobe River. The two of them crossed the Drakensberg, journeyed through the Transvaal and Matabeleland, visited the Victoria Falls, which by now was well known as a kind of 'tourist-attraction' for the traveller in the interior, a splendid sight none would miss, and then followed the Zambezi river to its confluence with the Chobe (Linyanti). They showed the connexion of that river with the Okovango and also brought back a good deal of valuable information with regard to the ethnography and the fauna of the country.[1] In the same year, H. Capello and R. Ivens, tough, bearded Portuguese naval officers both of them, started from Angola on the old project of crossing Africa à contra-costa for the purpose of opening trade between the West Coast and Moçambique and of making geographical and hydrographical observations inland. The two made their way to Barotseland, then up into the Katanga, finally travelling down the Zambezi till they reached the Indian Ocean at Quelimane.[2] Their labours, like those of their predecessors, added to the now considerable store of geographical knowledge with regard to the interior of Africa, as well as making a further contribution to that rapidly growing body of solid and well illustrated tomes with which our ancestors whiled away the long hours of the Victorian Sabbath.

The work of these savants and of traders in turn gave a new inspiration to the European churches that were now embarking on a great spiritual 'Scramble for Africa'; and the story now swings from the endless veld of Southern Africa to the mountains of Central France. The great nineteenth-century Protestant revival spread from Scotland to Switzerland, and from there to France, where the movement left a deep mark. Evangelical faith made a profound impression in a country where the Revolution and the subsequent wars had done much to discredit atheism, and where there was yet an intense longing for a creed that was socially constructive, and not just negative in nature. In 1828 the Paris Evan-

---

[1] Schulz, A., and Hammar, A. *The new Africa: a journey up the Chobe and down the Okovango rivers...* William Heinemann, 1897.

[2] Capello, H., and Ivens, R. *De Angola à contra-costa*... Lisbon, Emprensa nacional, 1886. 2 v.

gelical Missionary Society was founded, together with other charitable institutions, and French Protestants began to look outside the bounds of the kingdom for a suitable field of missionary labours. The Bourbon Government, however, was not prepared to let the new association work in the French Colonies, preferring Catholic priests to heretical parsons, and the Society turned to South Africa. Friendly relations were established with the London Missionary Society, and in 1835 the French built their first station in Basutoland.

It was thus in Basutoland that the Gospel was first preached by François Coillard, who was later to become Northern Rhodesia's greatest missionary statesman. Coillard came from old Huguenot stock and Protestantism was in his bones. His father was a substantial farmer from Berry in Central France, but only two years after young François's birth in 1834, he died leaving the family destitute; Coillard's mother bravely struggled on to bring up seven children on her meagre earnings as a housekeeper, whilst imbuing her family with her own deep piety. Through tremendous sacrifices Coillard acquired a good education, and it was then that he experienced his 'conversion', that intensely moving, sudden, personal experience that lit up the lives of so many early Protestant missionaries and deeply struck into the innermost core of their personalities: 'Never shall I forget the day, nay, the moment' Coillard wrote later on, 'when this ray of light flashed into the night of my anguish ... Oh my God, I cried in the depth of my heart, I believe ... a peace, a joy unknown before, flooded my heart'.[1]

Driven forward by intense faith, Coillard decided to devote his life to preaching the Gospel, and having attended a Protestant Training Institution at Paris as well as a course at Strasbourg University, he embarked for South Africa as a missionary. In 1858 he arrived in Basutoland, an earnest young clergyman barely twenty-four years old. Three years later he wedded Christina Mackintosh, the daughter of a Scottish minister, who was to share all his dangerous travels with a faith and steadfastness fully equal to his own.

Coillard's first missionary journey was undertaken in 1877 when an expedition was launched with the help of the Basutoland Native Churches to carry the Gospel to Mashonaland. The project aroused great enthusiasm among Christian Basuto who bore the cost of sending out Coillard's native evangelists, and welcomed the prospect of spiritual expansion at Matabele expense. The scheme, however, ended in complete failure. There was local opposition, and the Matabele were not prepared to let foreigners settle within their sphere of influence, especially when they were associated with the hated Basuto. The Coillards and their helpers were taken before Lobengula and then summarily expelled from Matabeleland. They found refuge among the Bamangwato in Bechuanaland and then decided to make a new attempt in Barotseland where Sesuto was understood and the task of preaching would accordingly be much easier. Khama, the Christian chief of the Bamangwato, gave his full support to the scheme, for he looked to Barotseland as a counterpoise to the dangerous Matabele, and in any

[1] Quoted from Mackintosh, C. W. *Coillard of the Zambesi* ... T. Fisher Unwin, 1907, p. 20

case welcomed the spread of the Gospel which he himself had accepted at the hands of L.M.S. missionaries.

After a long and weary journey the missionaries arrived at Leshoma on the Zambezi in July 1878, but the time chosen was unfortunately not a propitious one. Barotseland was now in the throes of a civil war which broke out a year earlier; Sepopa, the previous king, had chosen Sesheke for his capital, a decision influenced by his interest in elephant hunting, and strongly backed by West-beech; Sesheke, however, was not part of Barotseland proper and Sepopa, the man who had exterminated the Makololo, was himself murdered.[1] A struggle then ensued between two different candidates, Lobosi (later known as Lewanika), and Mwanawina, the latter being supported by the tributary hunters and the Portuguese traders from the west.[2] The tide of war flowed to and fro, but Lewanika secured power for a time and built his capital at Lealui in the centre of the Barotse valley. After considerable delays, Lewanika gave permission to the missionaries to open a station, and on the strength of his promise Coillard withdrew from the valley in 1879 for the purpose of making the necessary arrangements.

Coillard's party by now was reduced to desperate circumstances. True enough, no one actually harmed them whilst civil strife was in process, and their knowledge of Sesuto moreover gave them considerable prestige amongst the Barotse who still respected the Basuto though they had exterminated their Makololo conquerors. But the missionaries suffered terribly from fever, as did their native companions, three Basuto evangelists perishing in the deadly climate of the Zambezi valley, to which they were as little accustomed as the Europeans. In addition the Coillards had to take care of Major Alexandre de Serpa Pinto, a courageous Portuguese soldier and explorer, who tried to travel from Benguella to the East Coast, but had been robbed on the way and fallen desperately ill. The Coillards succeeded in making their way back, and in 1880 returned to Europe to gain support for their venture.

Financing the mission, however, was not an easy task. The French Protestant community was only small and the Paris Evangelical Missionary Society had to rely on support from well-wishers in Italy, Switzerland and Great Britain, as well as at home. The Coillards thus largely had to raise their own funds, a task of immense difficulty. Coillard, however, succeeded where lesser men would have failed, and enough money was raised to make a new expedition possible, many contributions being received from well-wishers in the United Kingdom, especially in Scotland, a country for which Coillard acquired a great admiration.

It was fortunate for Coillard that whilst he was away, another Protestant missionary, Frederick Stanley Arnot, also succeeded in making his way to Barotseland. Arnot, a member of the Plymouth Brethren, arrived in the country in 1882 and secured Lewanika's confidence through Westbeech's help. In the religious field nothing was accomplished. All the more important, however, was

[1] Arnot, F. S. *Missionary travels in Central Africa*. Bath, Office of 'Echoes of service', 1914, p. 21
[2] F. Coillard to [——]: 23 Aug 1878 (CO 5/1/1/, f. 400–406. Nat Arch MS)

Arnot's political role. 'During this period' Arnot relates, 'Lobengula, the chief of the Matabele sent a powerful embassy to Liwanika, bringing presents of shields and spears, and inviting Liwanika to become his 'blood brother', and to join with the Matabele in resisting the invading white man. I was able to persuade Liwanika that, apart from promises and the power of the respective chiefs, Kama was a better man to make friends with than Lobengula. Lobengula's men were treated with great hospitality and sent away with many presents, but Liwanika immediately decided to write to Kama asking for his friendship, his daughter to be Liwanika's queen, and a black hunting dog'. Lewanika added a postscript to the effect that Khama was to do all in his power to help M. and Madame Coillard.[1]

There is little further information about Lobengula's scheme for an alliance, for black kings in those days did not preserve any archives. But it does not seem unreasonable to link the project to the general state of Matabele politics. In 1878 Sir Bartle Frere, the Governor of the Cape, sent an embassy to Lobengula, which was headed by Captain R. Patterson. Patterson, a big-game hunter, primarily interested in shooting elephants up north, accepted the commission, hoping to combine business with pleasure. Frere's choice, however, was an unfortunate one. Patterson possessed little understanding of Matabele psychology and it seems that when discussing the grievances of white hunters in Matabeleland, he made the mistake of reminding the king of the rival claims of Kuruman, a pretender to the Matabele throne who had fled to Natal to escape Lobengula's assegais. The effect of Patterson's remarks appears to have been startling. Lobengula suddenly became profusely civil, and allowed the envoys to travel on to the Victoria Falls. The unsuspecting white men then left for the north but were all brutally slaughtered *en route*, merely as it seems, to relieve the king of his unwelcome guests,[2] at a time when Frere was beginning to press upon Lobengula's Zulu kinsmen in the south, but Zulu powers had not yet been crushed at Ulundi.[3]

As far as the Barotse were concerned, however, a Matabele alliance had little to recommend itself as a long-term policy, for as long as war continued to remain the national industry of Lobengula's 'Black Sparta', the surrounding chiefs were bound to regard his kingdom with the greatest suspicion. This was particularly true of the Barotse who feared for the safety of their dependencies north of the Zambezi. All the same, Lobengula's project might have been tried at least for a time, and if it had, Coillard's mission would have become impossible. As it was, Arnot helped to prevent a pro-Matabele course, and when he left

[1] Arnot, F. S. *Missionary travels in Central Africa*. Bath, Office of 'Echoes of service', 1914, p. 22

[2] Haggard, H. R. 'The Patterson embassy to Lobengula' (in Wills, W. A., and Collingridge, L. T. *The downfall of Lobengula* . . . 'The African review', 1894, p. 227–233)

See also F. C. Selous 'Notes regarding the death of Captain Patterson and his companions': n.d. (SE 1/1/1, f. 141–143, Nat Arch MS)

[3] In January 1879 the British suffered a serious reverse against the Zulu at the battle of Isandhlwana, where 800 European troops perished. In July 1879 the Zulu, however, were crushed at Ulundi, a battle which made a profound impression on Lobengula.

Barotseland for health reasons in 1884, the way was open for Coillard's return

The door to the lands of the Upper Zambezi was ajar, but the position in Barotseland was still critical; political turmoil continued and in addition there was a grave economic crisis caused by the continuous destruction of elephants. 'What are the riches of a kingdom' Lewanika asked in the course of a conversation with Coillard. 'The wealth of mine is ivory, and soon there will be none left. What shall we do then?'[1] The Barotse were moreover still suspicious of Europeans, with the exception of a few trusted traders like Westbeech, and the missionary's path was as yet strewn with many thorns.

Such was the tragic experience of a Jesuit mission which also attempted to preach the Gospel in the Far Interior during this period. In 1877 the Sacred College of Propaganda entrusted the Zambezi area, with its many historical memories, to the Society of Jesus and in 1879 an expedition set out from Grahamstown to conquer Zambezia for the Gospel. Panda-ma-Tenka was reached in 1880, and from there a party consisting of Fathers Henri Depelchin, Antoine Tereorde[2] and A. Vervenne, accompanied by George Blockley, one of Westbeech's partners, set out into the Tonga country beyond the Zambezi. Mwemba (Moemba), a local chief agreed that the Jesuits might establish a mission in his country, to be known as the House of St Cross, but disease took so heavy a toll of the Fathers that the mission had to be abandoned. The Jesuits then tried to establish contact directly with the Barotse. In 1881 another party, headed by Father Depelchin, made its way into the Valley. Lewanika made a number of very sweeping promises, and on the strength of these the Jesuits brought up reinforcements from the south. Further action was delayed for a time by internal troubles in the valley; in 1883 Jesuit emissaries once again went to Barotseland, but Lewanika changed his mind, and the missionaries had to depart without having accomplished anything.

On the face of it, their failure is not easy to explain. The Jesuits' resources were far greater than those of the Paris Evangelical Missionary Society; they possessed moreover, all the self-sacrifice, the discipline and the fine organization for which their Order has justly become famous; but they did not speak any Sikololo, and Lewanika moreover appears to have been bitterly offended by their attempts to settle in the Tonga country,[3] which the Barotse considered part of their sphere of influence. What was even worse from the Jesuits' point of view, though they do not appear to have realized it, was their failure to secure Westbeech's support. The well known trader's backing was essential to any European intending to work in the Valley, but Westbeech used his influence to keep the Jesuits out, and assist Coillard.[4] Emil Holub, an extremely friendly critic, also considered that Depelchin, for all his courage, lacked the right feel for missionary strategy. Barotseland was the key to the whole region; it was here that the Jesuits should have concentrated their efforts, but they dispersed

[1] Mackintosh, C. W. *Coillard of the Zambezi* ... T. Fisher Unwin, 1907, p. 328
[2] The spelling of his name differs, the versions of Terorde and Terörde also having been used.
[3] *Zambesi mission record*, v. 2, no. 19, Jan 1903, p. 196
[4] G. Westbeech: diary (WE 1/1/1, f. 14–26, Nat Arch MS)

their strength. Holub was also inclined to blame administrative over-centraliza-tion, and the fact that their Superiors in Rome were inadequately informed with regard to the physical and ethnographic conditions in the Zambezi basin. The Jesuits, moreover, had no doctor to give them expert medical attention. As it was, fever took a terrible toll, and further projects of expansion had to be aban-doned. Neither did they achieve any success at Panda-ma-Tenka itself, where a migrant population of white and half-caste traders and hunters proved almost impermeable to religion.[1] In 1885 Panda-ma-Tenka was finally abandoned and a tragic chapter in the history of the Order came to a close.

In the meantime Coillard completed his preparations for yet another thrust into the Barotse valley, and in January 1884 he left Leribe in Basutoland, to-gether with his wife, his niece Élise, the Rev. Dorwald Jeanmairet, a young Swiss pastor, and two British artisans, George William Middleton and William Waddell. They were accompanied by two Basuto evangelists with their families, and travelled by ox-waggon, voortrekkers of the Gospel, ready once more to brave the dangers of the interior. They reached Leshoma, one of Westbeech's trading sites, on 26 July 1884 and this settlement became Coillard's starting point in preference to Panda-ma-Tenka.

Once more, however, the political situation in Barotseland nearly wrecked the venture. Rebellion broke out again, unrest having been fomented by the powerful clan of the Banosha, who had also been the prime movers in the risings against Sepopa and Mwanawina. In September 1884 Lewanika was driven out of the valley, together with his son Letia; Mataa, the cruel and ambitious head of the Banosha, then installed a puppet king and massacred all Lewanika's adherents whom he could catch. In 1885, however, Lewanika's forces again managed to re-enter the capital, Mataa being defeated outside Lealui; Lewanika then carried out a mass purge of his own. 'All those,' wrote Westbeech, 'who were caught or came to surrender themselves, trusting to his [Lewanika's] former clemency, were immediately killed; even the women, wives of rebels, were ripped open by the assegai and thus left to die. Others were taken to the plain to what is called the 'Wizard's Antheap', their arms and legs broken and left for the wolves to finish or die of hunger thirst or pain. Boys and girls of tender age were carried off to the nearest lagoon and thrown in to the crocodiles'.[2] At Sesheke, things were not quite so bad; Westbeech with his hunters, armed with deadly breech-loaders, threw his support on Lewanika's side and nothing hap-pened to the missionaries. Soon the tide of war flowed the other way again and Akufuna (Tatira), the Barotse roi fainéant, then received Coillard at Lealui, where the Barotse expressed the hope that the intervention of the strangers would end civil war. The position, however, was still undecided. Internecine strife continued and anarchy reigned at Sesheke, where the missionaries never-theless established a station on 24 September 1885, the missionaries' abode being

[1] Holub, E. Von der Capstadt ins Land der Maschukulumbwe . . . Vienna, Alfred Hölder, 1890, v. 1, p. 354–362
[2] G. Westbeech: diary (WE 1/1/1, f. 25, Nat Arch MS)

respected by both parties as neutral ground. At the end of 1885 Lewanika finally re-established his power—this time with the help of Portuguese traders from the west who received certain trading privileges in return for their help; Mataa was slain; there were new proscriptions and blood flowed profusely. The main sufferers, however, were the Barotse aristocracy, the slaves simply rejoicing in another change of master,[1] whilst most of the older chiefs perished in the struggle, with the result that there appears to have occurred a considerable drop in the average age of the ruling group, and younger men now moved into the key positions.

Lewanika, however, was prepared to continue a pro-missionary policy, and on 23 March 1886 Coillard was formally presented to the king and his khotla (Lekhotla, National Council). There was still an element of opposition against the Europeans, but the Barotse were impressed by the benefits Khama had received from the missionaries and from the British connexion in general. British prestige at this time stood high, for in 1885 a British expedition under the command of General Warren broke up the Boer Republics of Stellaland and Goshen, Bechuanaland itself being formally taken under British protection on 30 September 1885 to the great satisfaction of Khama, who feared both the Boers and the Matabele. The missionaries having been finally accepted in the Valley, a station was founded on 11 October 1886 at Sefula near Lealui. The Frenchman had succeeded at last. The prestige of Khama, himself a keen Protestant, the renown of British arms, Coillard's outstanding personal ability and his knowledge of Sesuto, as well as the support from Westbeech, all played their part in this achievement, and the Protestants held fast to the Gospel's first bridgehead on the Upper Zambezi.

In the meantime the Plymouth Brethren were organizing yet another assault on pagan Africa, using the West Coast for the base. The Brethren were a puritan sect, more democratic in their church organization than most, holding that any kind of official ministry was a denial of the spiritual priesthood of all believers. The history of the Plymouth Brethren's Mission (known as the Christian Mission in Many Lands) was intimately linked with the life of Arnot, one of those remarkable Victorian Christians who did so much to impress their personalities upon the face of Africa. Arnot was born in Glasgow in 1858, his father being in the shipping trade. The Arnots and the Livingstones were close friends, and the youngster was profoundly impressed by Livingstone's example; Arnot was brought up in an intensely religious household and at the age of eight, his biographer relates, he found that he needed a saviour. 'He began then to seek the Lord; and when he was ten years of age, after lying awake one night wondering whether the Lord would save him, at two o'clock in the morning he was helped to commit his life and his eternal future into God's keeping by repeating the words of John iii: "God so loved the world, that He gave His only begotten Son, that whosoever believeth in Him should not perish but have

[1] Coillard, F. *On the threshold of Central Africa* ... translated and edited by C. W. Mackintosh. Hodder and Stoughton, 1897, p. 207

everlasting life" '.[1] Arnot subsequently entered a merchant's warehouse, but his missionary ideal remained with him, and at the age of 23 he set out for Africa to evangelize the heathen, entirely on his own, without any missionary or ecclesiastical organization to support him, save the help given by a few devoted 'Brethren'.

Arnot first attempted to carry the Gospel to Barotseland, but became ill and in 1884 he left for the West Coast in the Company of Silva Pôrto, the famous Portuguese trader. In Anglola he heard that Msidi, the powerful East Coast freebooter who was ruling in the Katanga, wanted white traders in his country. Once traders were welcome, Arnot thought, missionaries would also be able to establish themselves inland, and in 1886 he finally arrived at Msidi's capital where he succeeded in gaining the chief's confidence. Further reinforcements then came out from England and gradually a chain of stations was set up which linked Katanga to the West Coast, the Mission retaining its hold after Msidi's country was taken over by the Belgians, and the chief slain. From the Congo, the Brethren then pushed into Northern Rhodesia, a station being built near the northern shore of Lake Mweru in 1894 by Dan Crawford. Shortly afterwards the mission moved to the Luanza river, and in 1896 a new station was set up at Johnston Falls near the old Fort Rosebery, from which further expansion took place subsequently. A major advance was made in the present century when in 1906 Dr Walter Fisher, a devoted medical man, established a Sanatorium at Kalene Hill at the source of the Zambezi in the Lunda country. Fisher built up Kalene Hill as an important medical and evangelical centre, the earliest conversions amongst the local Lunda people taking place in 1911;[2] the first Christians characteristically coming from the ranks of the doctor's ex-patients. Mission and medical work remained closely linked throughout the religious history of Africa, during the course of which pastoral pioneers, treading in the footsteps of medieval churchmen in Europe, laid the foundations of modern social services on the Continent.

III

Background to Empire

Missionaries and hunters, traders and gun-runners formed the advance guard of white influence in Central Africa. But it was only in the last century that the European powers began to stake out effective political claims to the interior, and soon Britain followed suit to create a vast African Empire. In the preceding decades of the nineteenth century the British were not very interested in direct territorial expansion; British shippers, merchants and bankers possessed an unrivalled experience of affairs in the 'under-developed' parts of the world and

[1] Baker, E. *Arnot: a knight of Africa.* Seeley Service & co. limited, 1925, p. 19–20
[2] Fisher, W. S. and Hoyle, J. *Africa looks ahead.* . . . Pickering and Inglis, ltd, 1948

E

made full use of their opportunities. Throughout the last century extensive loans were made by British banking houses to *entrepreneurs* overseas, on the European Continent, in the U.S.A., Canada, South America and elsewhere, without leading to active political intervention on the British side. Even as far as the most backward regions were concerned, the British generally preferred not to get involved in the arduous and expensive task of administration and government. There was no point in 'painting the map red' as long as other countries did not discriminate against British merchants and investors; it seemed cheaper to work through existing governments. In the Near East a determined attempt was therefore made to shore up the tottering Ottoman Empire, even at the expense of going to war with Russia. In South Africa the British Government in 1852 concluded the Sand River Convention which at last guaranteed to the emigrant farmers beyond the Vaal freedom to run their own affairs; both parties agreed to facilitate trade; the Transvaalers promised to prohibit slavery, whilst the British engaged not to supply gunpowder to the tribesmen nor to make any alliances with the Bantu peoples north of the Vaal river. Two years later a similar Convention was concluded with the Orange River Boers. As far as West African affairs were concerned, British policy was summed up in the resolution of a representative of the House of Commons Committee which agreed that it would be inexpedient to conclude any further treaties of protection to native tribes. British influence on the east coast of Africa was exercised through the Sultan of Zanzibar, who was persuaded in 1873 to abolish the sea-borne slave trade. This policy of course did not exclude the occasional use of force. The British were willing occasionally to send out regiments to enforce respect for the British flag or to succour British merchants or to prevent slave-trading; the strength of British arms was thus shown in ventures such as the Abyssinian campaigns of 1867 to 1868, the Ashanti war of 1873 and British naval activity in the Indian Ocean, but these ventures were not supposed to lead to new annexations.

The 'client-state' approach, whereby Britain exerted her influence through local chiefs and princes, possessed however serious weaknesses. The local ruler might himself be incapable of maintaining effective control over his outlying dependencies. This was true of Zanzibar, which exercised only little power on the African mainland; it also applied—on a much larger scale—to Turkey, which failed to keep an effective grip on possessions such as Egypt and Tunis, and which was threatened, in its European provinces, by Balkan nationalist movements based on peasant-bred intelligentsias. As far as the 'tribal frontiers' of the world were concerned, the client-state principle was even more difficult to enforce, for indigenous authorities could not easily provide effective guarantees for European trade and investment on a large scale. In these backward regions there were several possible alternatives. Some theorists believed that missionary enterprise should be encouraged so that indigenous tribal communities might at the same time be civilized and converted to the Gospel, but the Missions themselves were not usually strong enough to succeed in such a policy. Another possible expedient was to encourage European settlement so that stable white states might come into existence which would themselves pay for the cost of maintaining law and order, whilst providing effective security for British merchants and investors. A third alternative, which came to be employed more and more in the last quarter of the century, was by means of setting up chartered companies, financed by private investors, but furnished with defined political and administrative powers, which would shoulder the risks and expense of colonization, without asking the general tax-payer to furnish the necessary funds.[1]

By this time moreover, a general shift in the balance of power was getting under way. America consolidated its unity through a bloody civil war which prevented the Union from breaking into two separate states; Italy became a unified country, and in 1871 a united Germany entered the ranks of the Great Powers. These changes were linked to a transformation in the economic field and Great Britain, step by step, lost some of her former industrial supremacy. The region grouped round the great coal fields of Western Germany, Northern France and Belgium, Western Europe's 'carbon core', also became the centre of great industrial combines, whilst foreign competitors who had started later in the race for industrialization, were able to begin production with more modern equipment. Other countries deliberately began to protect their own industries behind the shelter of tariffs; from 1879 Germany embarked on a policy of high tariffs; in the eighties Russia, Austro-Hungary and Italy all increased their duties, whilst in the nineties the U.S.A. became one of the world's most highly protected nations. In the cotton industry British exporters were thus driven to rely more and more on the markets of India, China, the Middle East and Africa, only goods of the highest quality now finding customers on the European Continent itself. Great Britain of course was still paying her way and in fact doing very well. But this was achieved by selling more machinery, ships and coal rather than goods for immediate consumption, and some British economists began to fear that by doing so, Great Britain was only enabling her foreign rivals to compete more effectively, whilst coal exports were diminishing an irreplaceable national asset. At the same time the financier became more and more important; England became the world's main banker, transport and com-mission agent rather than its main manufacturer, but even the former function was beginning to be disputed to some extent by her competitors. Continental countries like Germany and France no longer required so much British capital, having built up industries of their own and having themselves begun to lend to underdeveloped countries, especially in Eastern and South-Eastern Europe and the Middle East. Investments in the Eastern Mediterranean became unattractive when Turkey went bankrupt in 1876, a serious blow to economic theorists who had hitherto thought in terms of shoring up the Ottoman Empire. Russian securities fell in value as diplomatic relations between London and St Petersburg

[1] See Gallagher, J., and Robinson, R. 'The imperialism of free trade' (in *Economic history review* v. 6, no. 1, Jan 1953, p 1–15)

began to worsen, and France became Russia's main banker; this meant that some British investors began to look more and more to countries overseas, where they believed that better returns might be obtained for their cash than at home.

The gradual weakening of the British position relative to those of other Great Powers was also reflected in the field of naval policy; Britain was completely dependent for her defence upon her battle-fleets, her armies counting for little on the European Continent itself. British maritime supremacy went completely unchallenged as long as naval warfare depended on wooden ships which took a long time to build, and which, when once constructed, were serviceable for more than half a century. As long as the battle-line was composed of sailing vessels, Great Britain with her accumulated fleets could hardly be outstripped by any rival. The mechanization of naval warfare changed all this. Each year new guns, new kinds of vessels, new types of armour were designed, which made all existing ships obsolete: 'Supposing for instance', wrote R. C. K. Ensor, a distinguished English historian, 'that H.M.S. Rodney, launched in 1884 and completed in 1888, had been sent to fight a fleet comprising every ironclad launched in Great Britain down to 1881, she could, if properly handled, have sunk them all'.[1] Ship-building capacity now became at least as important as effective fighting strength and Britain had to engage in a constant race for technical improvements if she was to retain her former naval supremacy.

Admittedly, the immediate effect of these changes should not be over estimated. Britain for the time being did remain easily the world's first sea power, as well as one of the most important industrial states in existence. Her confidence in her own strength remained unbroken, but many theorists now began to argue that Great Britain could only keep up in the race if she relied more upon her Imperial connexions or even extended her possessions, for otherwise the small island kingdom would never be able to hold her own against great continental states such as the U.S.A., Russia or Germany.

The turning point in African Imperial policy occurred in the later seventies. In 1869 the Suez Canal was opened, completely revolutionizing naval strategy in the Mediterranean, shortening the sea-route to India, and making the East African coast more easily accessible to British shipping. At the same period there came a transformation in the political situation in the Mediterranean. The Egyptian Khedive owned about seven-sixteenths of the shares of a French Company that had constructed the Canal; his holding was important, but the Egyptians overstrained their financial resources by too rapid a programme of Westernization, by unwise territorial expansion in Africa, financial extravagance and administrative incompetence, their spending depending largely on their cotton crop, which constituted too narrow an economic basis for vast projects. The Khedive's financial position became disastrous and in 1875 he was forced to sell his shares in the Canal to the British Government. A year later he suspended payment on his obligations and an Anglo-French financial condominium was established in his country. Turkey's position was no happier than

[1] Ensor, R. C. K. *England 1870–1914.* Oxford University Press, 1936, p. 287

Egypt's; in 1876 she also defaulted on her debts, whilst the grievances of her European subjects landed her in war against Russia. Russian troops advanced down the Balkan Peninsula, reaching Adrianople, but the Ottoman Empire in Europe was saved, largely by British intervention. Russia received an increase in territory in Europe, as well as on the south-east corner of the Black Sea, whilst Serbia, Rumania and Montenegro were all recognized as independent states with an increase of territory. The Russians were, however, prevented from setting up Bulgaria as a powerful satellite state in the Balkans, whilst to balance Russian gains in Asia, Cyprus was assigned to Britain. The British thus acquired, for the first time, a base in the eastern Mediterranean and promised to defend Turkey in Asia.

France was appeased by a British promise not to interfere in the impending French occupation of Tunis, and in 1881 French troops marched into the country. In the meantime further unrest had broken out in Egypt. In 1881 Colonel Arabi Pasha led a rising directed against European and Turkish influence. The British, however, intervened and in 1882 the Egyptian nationalist forces were crushingly defeated at Tel-el-Kebir. The French would not participate in the expedition, and British influence in the country was then consolidated by Sir Evelyn Baring who went out to Egypt as British Agent and Consul-General in 1883. The Sudan for a time passed under the control of indigenous rebels led by the Mahdi. But the British held on to Egypt, and by the end of the eighties British strategists looked to Cairo and Alexandria rather than to Constantinople as the pivot of Mediterranean policy, the focus of British attention in that area shifting from South Eastern Europe and the Levant to the northern coast of Africa.

During the same period the Europeans began to intervene in West Africa. The race was started, not by the Great Powers, but by the King of the Belgians who in 1876 summoned a Conference at Brussels containing delegates from various countries. The gathering led to the formation of the 'International African Association' which soon became a Belgian-controlled body. When in 1875 Henry Morton Stanley returned from a great voyage of discovery down the Congo, the Association's ruling spirit, King Leopold III, turned his attention towards the Congo area, but soon both the French and the Portuguese began to put forward claims to the area. The British backed the Portuguese and in 1884 the two powers concluded a treaty whereby the British recognized the very extensive Portuguese claims in the area, whilst navigation on the Congo was to be controlled by an Anglo-Portuguese Commission. In addition the Germans, partly for diplomatic and partly for internal reasons, themselves entered the colonial field. In 1884 considerable tracts of territory were annexed in South West Africa, West Africa, as well as in East Africa.

As a result of a temporary Franco-German entente in Europe, a Conference was called at Berlin in November 1884 to discuss the future of the Continent. All the major European powers were represented as well as the U.S.A. and Turkey and as the result of their discussions the General Act of the Berlin Conference was signed on 26 February 1885. The Act represented a peaceful compromise between the different European powers. The interests of the various Imperial states in Africa were of course opposed to each other, but the deeper sources of friction between them lay in Europe, not on the Dark Continent, where they had enough in common to make some limited agreement possible. The signatories agreed that there should be complete freedom of trade 'in all the regions forming the basin of the Congo and its outlets'. The powers also pledged themselves to 'watch over the preservation of the native tribes and to care for the improvement of their moral and material well-being, and to help in suppressing slavery and especially the Slave Trade'. Freedom of religion was to be assured, whilst the navigation of the Congo and the Niger were to be open to all nations. In addition the colonial powers undertook to inform each other whenever taking possession of any new African territories, but occupation had to be effective. In 1885 Belgium authorized its king to become sovereign of the *Etat Indépendant du Congo*, Leopold explaining that the new state would—like Belgium itself—pursue a neutral foreign policy, that it would be policed and defended by black soldiers serving under European volunteers, and that it would remain linked to Belgium only through the personal bond of a common sovereign. The Belgian Legislature gave its assent without much enthusiasm, though all the great commercial and industrial enterprises as well as the municipal councils heartily congratulated Leopold on his *coup*, whilst the Lord Mayor of London personally called on the founder of the state to express his appreciation. Congo colonization thus began as it ended, as part of an international venture, though the *Etat Indépendant* itself proved short-lived, Belgium taking over the administration of the Congo in 1908.[1]

The settlement of the Congo question however constituted a heavy blow to Portuguese ambitions and greatly contributed towards subsequent Anglo-Portuguese friction. The treaty signed between Britain and Portugal on 16 February 1884 recognized Portuguese claims to the Congo, but also provided for free navigation on both the Congo and the Zambezi, whilst stating that Portuguese territorial claims on the Shire should not extend above the Ruo. But the treaty was never ratified and was finally killed by Bismarck's pro-French policy, with the result that the question of Portuguese claims to the lands discovered by Bocarro and Lacerda was opened once more. The Portuguese continued to uphold their claims to a belt of territory stretching from coast to coast, and in 1886 Britain came very near to accepting the Portuguese contention, so much so that for a time the Imperial authorities were still prepared to let the lands north of the Zambezi go to Portugal.

But British policy stiffened. The Portuguese published maps showing the whole Zambezi basin south of the Rovuma river, and including Nyasaland and Matabeleland as Portuguese territory. The Portuguese believed themselves in a strong diplomatic position for making such a claim, as a recent treaty with France and Germany had recognized Portuguese sovereignty in the territory

[1] Goffin, L. 'Histoire du Congo' (in *Encyclopédie du Congo Belge*. Brussels, Editions Bierleveld, n.d., v. 1, p. 1–44)

between Angola and Moçambique, provided the rights of 'other powers' were not prejudiced. But by now the general diplomatic position was worsened from Portugal's point of view. Bismarck was by no means an Anglophobe, neither was he specially interested in African expansion as such, but only in Germany's continental position. This was now endangered by the fact that Austro-Hungary, Germany's ally, had come into conflict with Russian policy in the Balkans, and Bismarck required British support in South-Eastern Europe, so that relations between the two powers quickly improved. Britain and Germany concluded agreements with Italy, assuring her of the *status quo* in the Mediterranean against France, and in March of the same year an exchange of notes between Britain and the Hapsburg Empire spoke of maintaining the *status quo* particularly in the Aegean and the Black Sea. Great Britain at the same time secured the support of Italy and Austria, Germany's partners, in Egypt, where France was still attempting to resist British influence and Britain needed diplomatic support from other powers. In December of 1887 British bonds with Italy and Austro-Hungary were tightened further still, the British aiming at keeping Russia out of Bulgaria and Asia Minor against Russia.

In these circumstances Portugal's diplomatic position was weak, and the Portuguese overplayed their hand. In 1888 they refused to permit the passage of artillery to the African Lakes Company for use against Mlozi's Arabs, but had to yield to British pressure in the matter. A year later Harry Johnston was sent to Lisbon to negotiate an agreement with the Portuguese. Johnston was ready to abandon the Shire Highlands to the Portuguese, provided the way was left open for British influence to be expanded north from the Zambezi and the Portuguese relinquished their claim for a continuous belt of territory from coast to coast. In the face of Scottish missionary opposition this compromise proved, however, unacceptable and the Portuguese sent a military expedition, commanded by Major Serpa Pinto, to occupy the Shire Highlands and the regions north of it. The British in 1889 replied by declaring that 'the Makololo country and the Shire Hills commencing at the Ruo River have been placed under Her Majesty's Protection', and political intervention in Central Africa became an accomplished fact.

By now, however, the dispute with Portugal over Nyasaland was no longer an isolated affair and the whole question merged with the wider South African one. British expansion in East Africa was linked to the enterprise of missionaries, traders, and later of coffee planters, from the United Kingdom. But in addition, a new power centre, situated on the Continent of Africa itself, was now in existence with an expansionist drive of its own. This was the South African 'miner's frontier' which was born in 1867 when diamonds were discovered at Kimberley, and Southern Africa suddenly moved into the forefront of the world's economic stage. So great indeed did the profits from the diamond industry become, that producers could largely pay for the initial expansion of the industry from their own earnings, and also accumulate sufficient funds for investment in other enterprises, and new territorial acquisitions.

The whole story is summed up in the name of one man—Cecil John Rhodes. Rhodes, greatest of Victorian empire-builders, was born in 1853, the son of an Anglican vicar; at the age of sixteen his health broke down and he was sent to Natal where he joined his elder brother Herbert in order to grow cotton. In 1871 the two young planters joined the rush for diamonds and the parson's son soon became a financial power in the land. The precious stones at Kimberley were at first secured by small *entrepreneurs* practising open quarrying; but mining operations became more complex and expensive, and direction over the industry was wrested from the diggers by a few powerful companies. Rhodes and his partners managed to secure a major share in the control of the industry and in 1880 the De Beers Mining Company was formed.

Rhodes's ambitions, however, were not merely of a financial kind. In 1881 he was elected to the Cape Legislature and soon assumed a prominent part in Cape politics. He was a keen believer in colonial autonomy, though he looked to the Imperial factor to smooth the way for Cape expansion into the Far Interior that would make his own Cape Colony the gateway to a great new African Empire. Rhodes's policy, however, met with serious opposition from the Transvaal which in 1881 recovered its independence after a short-lived period of British occupation. The Transvaalers were bent on expansion in order to obtain more land for their cattle farmers and cast ambitious eyes to the lands north and west of their territory. Their interest in Bechuanaland was particularly serious from the British point of view by reason of the German occupation of Angra Pequeña on the south-west coast in 1883; for if the Boers and the Germans joined hands in the interior, the British would be cut off from further expansion into the Far North. Imperial intervention however, was secured, and at the end of 1884 a British force under Sir Charles Warren was sent to Bechuanaland. In 1885, in the year that saw the fall of Khartoum before the Mahdi's hordes, the Berlin Conference, and the recognition of the Independent Congo State, the British acted in Bechuanaland. The country south of the Malopo River, known as British Bechuanaland, became a Crown Colony, whilst the lands to the north of it, including Khama's country, were proclaimed to be a British protectorate; the 'Suez Canal into the Interior' was secure at last.

In the meantime Rhodes also strengthened his economic position in South Africa. In 1886 gold was discovered at the Witwatersrand which turned out to be possessed of almost astronomical wealth, though its deep level of mines afforded opportunities for big companies only, not for the small diggers who first opened up Kimberley. Rhodes quickly stepped in, and in 1887 the Gold Fields of South Africa was founded in which Rhodes held a major interest. The new Company, later renamed the Consolidated Gold Fields of South Africa, soon became a huge trust company with shares in many deep level Rand mines and greatly added to Rhodes's standing. In the diamond industry Rhodes had even greater success, and in 1888 acquired complete control over the Kimberley mining industry. Concentration assured efficiency and permitted of prices being maintained at an economic level; the private digger, on the other hand, was squeezed out, as was the small diamond trader outside the ring patronized by the new monopoly, whilst shopkeepers lost much custom by the companies' practice of selling directly to native workmen, so that a good many European settlers in Kimberley and elsewhere became willing to look to the north to make a living in easier circumstances. Kimberley for all practical purposes became a company town, as well as the financial dynamo for Rhodes's plans of future expansion.

By now the 'great amalgamator' was looking beyond the Limpopo and even the Zambezi. Travellers such as Carl Mauch, an adventurous German school master, and Thomas Baines, an English explorer and artist, had brought back glowing reports of the golden riches supposedly buried under the northern veld; the popular fancy was stirred by imaginative works such as Sir Henry Rider Haggard's novel *King Solomon's Mines*, whilst scholars proved to their own satisfaction that Zimbabwe had been built by Semitic settlers who exploited Zambezia's boundless riches in the past. Rhodes took all these reports very seriously indeed and became convinced that a second Rand must lie somewhere north of the Limpopo. Here he meant to assume undisputed financial control, something which he did not enjoy at the Witwatersrand. Rhodes's scheme was all the more grandiose in view of the special position which gold then possessed in the economy of the world, but fundamentally Rhodes did not think in purely economic terms. He wished to extend British power inland so as to create a magnificent African Empire which one day would stretch from Cape to Cairo, whilst at the same time pushing forward the frontier of white settlement inland, uniting Boer and Briton in a common task.

Northward expansion, however, again involved opposition to the Transvaal which in 1887 sent a Consul to Matabeleland to arrange terms with Lobengula in what the Transvaalers regarded as their own hinterland. The Reverend John Smith Moffat, then Assistant Commissioner for Bechuanaland, rushed to Matabeleland, and on 18 February 1888 Lobengula was persuaded to sign a treaty whereby he engaged not to conclude any treaties with foreign powers without the previous sanction of the British High Commissioner for South Africa. On 30 October 1888 Lobengula put his name to another document, known as the Rudd Concession, whereby Rhodes and his associates received all the mineral rights in Lobengula's kingdom in exchange for one thousand Martini-Henry Rifles and the promise of a gun-boat on the Zambezi.

Having amalgamated with other rival financial interests, Rhodes then asked for a Charter for his British South Africa Company, and after lengthy negotiations this request was granted. Lord Salisbury aimed at forestalling foreign advances to the Nile valley and the highlands of East and Central Africa; for the Conservatives were now resolved on a prolonged occupation of Egypt, and argued that the security of this vital spot depended on reserving Uganda and the Nile valley to Imperial control. In 1888 the British Government granted a charter to the Imperial British East Africa Company; and a similar policy now seemed advisable in Southern Africa, where the previous policy of indirect expansion through the Cape government had broken down. Rhodes offered to the Conservatives what the Cape seemed unable to achieve; his company would relieve the Colonial Office of extensive commitments in the Bechuanaland Protectorate; his financial associates would construct a much-needed railway through Bechuanaland; he would contain the Transvaal to the north, and also relieve the Imperial authorities of the task of keeping order on this troublesome African frontier. Rhodes would likewise promote white settlement in the interior, a desirable object at a time when even anti-expansionist Radicals like James Bryce regarded 'colonies of settlement' as imperial assets, unlike native dependencies which required large public funds for their pacification and development. Ultimately the Company would develop a Second Rand which would balance the Transvaal's newfound wealth, and create a strong British community which would secure a future South African confederation to the Imperial connexion. North of Zambezi, the Company would keep vast native territories open to British influence at a time when Parliament would not vote the necessary funds.[1] A Chartered Company moreover would be more directly subject to Imperial control than a body of private capitalists who decided to incorporate themselves under the Joint Stock Companies Act, as they were entitled to do. In addition he believed that the example of the Imperial British East Africa Company proved that such a group of people might to some considerable extent relieve Her Majesty's Government from diplomatic difficulties and heavy expenditure. The Royal Charter was signed on 29 October 1889, just after the assumption of the Imperial Protectorate over Nyasaland. The definition of the charter's field of operations was left deliberately vague, comprising 'the region of South Africa lying immediately to the north of British Bechuanaland, and to the north and west of the South African Republic, and to the west of the Portuguese Dominions'. The Company was put under an obligation to preserve peace and good order and was accordingly permitted to maintain a police force, native civil law was to be respected and freedom of religion was to be maintained; the Company was to uphold freedom of trade, but its concessions were recognized. The Imperial Government retained the right to supervise the Company's affairs, but no local machinery of control was set up for the time being, so that the Company's local officials in fact had little to worry about from outside interference. A year later in 1890 Rhodes sent out a small, privately paid and equipped force known as the Pioneer Column, which successfully occupied Mashonaland, Boer trekkers from the south being effectively warned off from the region by a show of superior force.

At the same time, however, Rhodes looked further north, and financial policy now became entwined with tribal affairs north of the Zambezi. Lewanika was well aware of the treaty with the Matabele, and on 8 January 1889 Coillard wrote a letter to Sir Sidney Shippard, the Administrator of British Bechuanaland, informing him that Lewanika wished to be placed under British protection. 'Many a Zambezian' Coillard argued, 'has found his way to the Diamond

---

[1] Robinson, R. E. 'Imperial problems in British politics; 1880–1895' (in *The Cambridge history of the British Empire.* Cambridge University Press, 1959, v. 3, p. 166–167 and 173–174)

Fields and come back deeply impressed with the prestige of the British Government. The tale of what they have seen and heard, and of its dealings with the Native races, naturally leads their Chiefs and their countrymen to yearn after the protection of Her Majesty the Queen's Government'. The Barotse moreover were stated to be seriously upset about the possibility of a renewed Matabele invasion in 1889 and wished to be informed whether such at attack could be carried out with the British Government's sanction.[1] In addition Lewanika was apprehensive of Portuguese encroachments from the west and of the possible infiltration of white prospectors from the south, whilst he also believed that the British alliance would strengthen his still shaky throne.

Coillard's own motives in advocating the treaty were of a different kind. Whilst Lewanika hoped to shore up existing tribal institutions by means of a British alliance, Coillard expected to achieve exactly the opposite. As far as Coillard was concerned, the market-economy of Western Europe with its free flow of capital and labour was the only rational mode of conducting the affairs of a civilized state; the Barotse kingdom with its monopolies, its tributes and raids, its 'distributor-king' endowed with priestly powers, its caste distinctions and slavery, its bloody internal disturbances, was simply a savage empire held down 'by chains of abject and disgraceful servitude'. Coillard moreover was impressed by the foreign dangers threatening Barotseland. He was staggered by the German annexation of South West Africa, and he dreaded the approach of white gold-seekers and adventurers, having been made aware of the South African investing public's interest in Zambezia as early as 1888.[2] The Barotse— Coillard felt—required protection both against themselves and their own form of depraved feudalism, as well as from the impending depredations of Europeans; the best possible trustees for them were his wife's people, the British: for 'in spite of all her hesitations and all her blunders, England has always shown herself the protectress of the aboriginal races.'[3] In addition of course Coillard had strong personal reasons for wishing to see a European protectorate in Barotseland. He was plagued with constant transport troubles which were made worse by the royal monopoly of canoe transport; he was also in constant difficulties over the question of postal communications, and he believed that all these things would change for the better once British administrators had assumed the reins of government.

The High Commissioner for South Africa, Sir Henry Brougham Loch, urged that the Barotse country should be included in the British sphere of influence and that a continuous connexion should be secured at the same time between Lake Nyasa and Lake Tanganyika.[4] The Foreign Office, which was still

[1] F. Coillard to Sir F. Shippard: 8 Jan 1889 (enclosure in H. A. Smyth to Lord Knutsford: 26 July 1889), C. 5918 (1890)
[2] J. Smith to F. Coillard: 22 Nov 1889 (CO 5/1/1/1, f. 886–889, Nat Arch MS)
[3] Coillard, F. *On the threshold of Central Africa* . . . translated and edited by C. W. Mackintosh. Hodder and Stoughton, 1897, p. 184
[4] Sir H. B. Loch to Lord Knutsford: 7 Apr 1890, and Colonial Office to Foreign Office: 12 Apr 1890 (in *Further correspondence respecting the affairs of Bechuanaland and adjacent territories*. African (South) no. 392)

engaged in negotiations with the Portuguese, hummed and hawed, stating that the time had not yet arrived for the inclusion of the Barotse country within the British sphere, though Her Majesty's Government would be prepared to uphold treaties made therein, once they were in full possession of the required information.[1] This was the time for Rhodes to step in and Frank Elliott Lochner, a former member of the Bechuanaland Border Police, went to negotiate with Lewanika. Lochner's progress was impeded by unexpected heavy rains and after a long journey of great hardships Lochner arrived at Lealui, weakened by fever and without provisions. The missionaries fortunately took care of him and Coillard also assisted in the negotiations, vitally contributing to the success of the venture which Lochner, with his barrack-square manner and ignorance of the country, would hardly have been able to carry out on his own. The position was made even more difficult for the Europeans by the fact that there was considerable local hostility to the project of an alliance. The resident European traders, led by George William Middleton, formerly one of Coillard's missionary artisans, feared the prospect of Chartered Company rule which they thought would interfere with their own trade. In addition there was powerful native opposition which appears to have been led by the chiefs from Sesheke.

The pro-Treaty party, however, won the day and on 27 June 1890, the day on which the Pioneer Column set out for Mashonaland, the treaty was signed. The document gave to the Company a monopoly of mining rights over the Barotse territory, whilst the Company undertook to defend Lewanika from all outside attacks though there was to be no interference with the King's internal authority. The Company moreover made sweeping promises with regard to assisting in the propagation of Christianity, the establishment of schools, churches and trading stations, the equipment of telegraphs and the institution of regular postal services, whilst promising also that a British resident would reside with the king. The Company agreed to pay to the king an annuity of £2,000, a sum sufficiently large to get the king over the problem of diminishing revenue from ivory. The king at the same time retained his monopoly of elephant hunting, subject to minor modifications, whilst the Company agreed that the existing iron mines that were being worked by natives would remain their property. The Company also bound itself 'to respect the feelings of the people by not commencing mining operations in the country between the waggon road and the river from Sesheke and Lealui without the consent of the King', so that the core of the kingdom was to remain untouched by European influence. In addition the king agreed to suppress slavery and witchcraft in his kingdom, the latter being an ideal with which the king's subjects would have heartily concurred, though not in the sense meant by the white men, who disapproved of exterminating suspected witches. As far as European immigration was concerned, the Company agreed that the country should not be thrown open to whites without the consent of the king and his people, whilst the Company engaged itself not to

[1] Foreign Office to Colonial Office: 5 May 1890 (in *Further correspondence* ... African (South) no. 392)

enter the king's territory except by the Kazungula drift, unless special permission had been obtained, so that the king would retain control over the vital route of entry.[1]

Rhodes, in the meantime, had also turned his attention to the north-east. In March 1889 he arrived in England to get his Charter settled and when in England he met Captain Frederick Dealtry Lugard who gave him a first-hand account of events in Nyasa, and the best way of combating the Arab peril there. Rhodes was impressed, for Nyasaland to him was both the stepping stone to the north and possibly a future source of wealth. He made a financial offer to Lugard to suppress the slave trade in Nyasaland, but the scheme broke down, and Rhodes was unable for the moment to secure that controlling interest in the African Lakes Company which he coveted. Later on, about May, Rhodes met Johnston at a party and gave the young Consul for Moçambique a cheque for £2,000 to cover the expense of treaty-making in the interior so as to give the British a better claim to the country between the Zambezi and Lakes Nyasa and Tanganyika. Johnston subsequently called on Lord Salisbury who in the meantime had received Rhodes's application for a Charter; Salisbury decided that the Foreign Office should pay for Johnston's travelling and treaty-making expenses in Nyasaland itself, so that the Government would not be committed to handing the territory over to the future Chartered Company. Outside the limits of Nyasaland, however, there was no objection to Rhodes defraying Johnston's expenses.[2] Salisbury's decision is not difficult to explain. He was now aware of the financial power wielded by Rhodes, and the possible help of the great South African capitalist might come at a time when Parliament was reluctant to finance further Imperial expansion. In addition the existence of the Chinde mouth of the Zambezi was now known to seamen, who gained relatively unhampered access to the Nyasa area by means of a water route.

In May 1889 Johnston left for Central Africa to take up his duties as Consul for Moçambique. He travelled inland and managed to conclude an armistice between the African Lakes Company and the Arabs, as well as various other treaties with native chiefs in Nyasaland and on the Nyasa-Tanganyika plateau. On these journeys which got him near to Lake Mweru, he met with a friendly reception from the Tanganyika Arabs, Johnston himself being convinced at the time that the real danger to peace was the more warlike indigenous tribes, not the Muslim settlers.

In addition two further British agents were sent out to conclude treaties in North-Eastern Rhodesia. One of these was Alfred Sharpe (later Sir Alfred), a solicitor who had originally come to Africa for the purpose of big-game hunting and subsequently joined the British Central Africa administration. In 1890 Sharpe travelled west of Lake Nyasa but did not get very far; in March 1890 he was sent on a second expedition by Johnston. Sharpe travelled to Mpeseni, chief

[1] Enclosure in Sir H. B. Loch to Lord Knutsford: 20 Sep 1890 (in *Further correspondence respecting the affairs of Bechuanaland and adjacent territories.* African (South) no. 392)

[2] See Oliver, R. *Sir Harry Johnston and the scramble for Africa.* Chatto and Windus, 1957

òf the North-Eastern Rhodesian Ngoni, but Mpeseni was unwilling to sign any document. He then went up the Luangwa which was by this time largely depopulated by Portuguese half-caste raiders from the Zambezi valley, and before turning back to Nyasaland he declared the whole country west of the Luangwa and north of the Zambezi 'to be under British protection'. Subsequently he travelled to the north-west where he concluded a treaty with Kazembe, the only important indigenous chief in the area willing to sign an agreement with the British. Sharpe then continued to the country of Msidi (Msiri, Mushidi) the great freebooting chief in the Congo, but Msidi refused to enter into any engagement and Sharpe had to leave without having accomplished anything.[1]

To make quite certain of their interests, the Directors of the British South Africa Company despatched another envoy, Joseph Thomson, a well-known African explorer, to make treaties on their behalf. Thomson, accompanied by A. J. Grant, travelled independently, going as far as the Luapula and the Upper Kafue. He was, however, unable to reach Msidi's country, his real destination, and had to return to Kota Kota by way of Mpeseni's country.[2]

By signing these documents the chiefs bound themselves to accept the British flag and to grant a monopoly of their mineral rights to the British South Africa Company. In terms of local tribal politics these treaties of course meant very little. Neither the Ngoni nor Chitimukulu, the Paramount chief of the Bemba, affixed their signature to any one of them. The only powerful indigenous chief to do so was Kazembe, who was aware of his predecessor's previous dealings with the Europeans and may have looked upon the treaty as a means of strengthening himself against Msidi, his traditional enemy in the Congo. As far as the minor chiefs were concerned, the treaties to them were nothing but a vague promise of support against Ngoni or Bemba raiders. As Professor J. A. Barnes put it, men who only knew how to fight with spears were asked to sign little pieces of paper which would then be negotiable in a property system of which they knew nothing, by manipulators who knew little about them.[3] The treaty makers on their part imagined in fact that there was a patchwork of stationary kingdoms spread about the region, each with a chief powerful enough to conclude binding agreements over his country, whereas in fact there was only an unstable group of shifting cultivators, each liable to attack from the Ngoni or other more powerful neighbours. Contemporary observers came to rather similar conclusions. These petty princelings, wrote Captain Lugard during this period, had no conception that a bond in black and white constituted a sacred obligation; all they understood was blood-brotherhood. This of course did not

[1] H. H. Johnston to Foreign Office: 30 Sep 1890 and enclosed report by A. Sharpe: 26 Mar 1890 F.O. 84/2052)

For a map of the journeys, see Hole, H. M. *The making of Rhodesia*. Macmillan and co. ltd, 1926, facing p. 240

[2] Thomson, J. 'To Lake Bangweolo and the unexplored region of British Central Africa' (in *Geographical journal*, v. 1, no. 2, Feb 1893, p. 97–121)

For copies of the treaties, see Appendix to Foreign Office print 6337 (1892); for the Johnston treaties previously concluded, see H. H. Johnston to Foreign Office: 1 Feb 1890 (F.O. 84/2051)

[3] Barnes, J. A. *Politics in a changing society*. . . . Cape Town, Oxford University Press, 1954

apply to a comparatively developed kingdom like Uganda[1] or, one might add, Barotseland, where a relatively civilized aristocracy was running the state. The local Arab settlers of course also knew what they were doing when they put their signatures to these documents or persuaded their native protegés to do so. Potentates such as Simbesi, 'Sultan' of Western Iramba, or Salim bin Nasser, 'protector' of Chief Kambwiri, had everything to gain from being on good terms with the British, for their main enemies at this period were the Germans in East Africa, not the Chartered Company which was still quite incapable of interfering with the slave trade; some of the Arab adventurers inland even imagined that they might become salaried officials under the British, with a free hand in their dealings with the local population.[2]

The British promise of protection meant nothing at the time, a fact of which a chief like Kazembe must have been well aware, for there were no military forces on the spot available for use in North-Eastern Rhodesia. The real significance of the documents lay in the field of financial and international, not of tribal politics. The agreements, subsequently recognized by the British Government, provided the basis of the British South Africa Company's claim to the mineral rights of North-Eastern Rhodesia. The treaties also asserted British rights against foreign claimants and strengthened the hands of British negotiators at the Conference table.

The only region where nothing was achieved was the Katanga and the rich copper deposits of the Congo remained within the Belgian sphere. Even if Sharpe had been able to get Msidi to sign a treaty, Msidi's country would not have become British territory. The Katanga lay within the boundaries of the Congo Free State, as defined by a Belgian declaration in 1885 and the Chartered Company never succeeded in getting a grip on the country. In 1890 talks took place between Leopold and the Chartered Company. The King at first suggested that the 14th parallel latitude should become the boundary; later the negotiators provisionally agreed that the border should extend 'from the source of the river Kuango up to the point where the exit of the River Luapula from Lake Bang-weolo takes place, the line being the centre of the water parting between the tributaries of the Congo and the tributaries of the Zambezi.'[3] The Chartered Board at first would even allow the Congo Free State access to Lake Nyasa, but Rhodes vetoed this project. Much to the Belgians' disgust, the Chartered Company in turn tried to stake out new claims. In 1890 Alfred Sharpe visited Msidi's kingdom in the Katanga, hoping to secure a treaty. The black potentate, however, had no intention of making a deal. He was previously warned by Arnot, the missionary, not to put his hand to any pieces of paper which would assuredly rob him of his country, and when Sharpe suggested a concession, the chief burst out into a wild fit of anger. In any case the Foreign Office assured the Company that the country certainly fell under Congolese jurisdiction, whilst the

[1] Lugard, F. D. 'Treaty-making in Africa' (in *Geographical journal*, v. 1, no. 1, Jan 1893, p. 53–55)
[2] See Hanna, A. J. *The beginnings of Nyasaland and North-Eastern Rhodesia 1859–95*. Oxford, at the Clarendon press, 1956
[3] Memorandum of a meeting at Burlington Hotel: 16 May 1890 (CT 1/11/3/9 Nat Arch SR). See this file also for the remaining negotiations.

Belgians—for their part—took speedy action to make their influence felt inland. In 1891 the *Compagnie du Katanga* was founded with a capital of 3,000,000 francs for the purpose of exploiting the resources of the regions, the Chartered Company finding itself too weak financially to participate in this enterprise. The new concern organized several ventures into the interior, and Jules Cornet, a Belgian geologist serving with the so-called 'Bia-Francqui mission', acquainted his employers with the wealth of the area. A further expedition, led by Captain William Grant Stairs, a British officer in Belgian employment, hoisted the flag in Msidi's country; the old *condottiere* was killed in a scuffle, and his gunpowder kingdom quickly disintegrated.[1] A few years later in 1894, a treaty was signed between King Leopold and the British Government which further delimited Congolese frontiers;[2] the Belgians remained firmly established in Katanga whose 'pedicle' nearly cut Northern Rhodesia in half, Anglo-Belgian agreement being made easier by good diplomatic relations between the two countries, and by the existence of close Anglo-Belgian financial ties in Africa.

As far as Portugal was concerned, however, Lord Salisbury was willing to adopt a more peremptory tone, for Portugal was now unable to obtain any real diplomatic backing in Europe. In January 1890 an ultimatum was despatched and in February Portuguese forces received orders to withdraw from below the Ruo. On 20 August plenipotentiaries signed a convention between the two countries with regard to their respective spheres of influence in East Africa, which was relatively favourable to the Portuguese. The British did not wish to press Portugal too hard, as they did not intend to endanger its monarchical institutions, but Rhodes himself, an out and out expansionist, little interested in the European repercussions of his policies, was infuriated by the agreement for which he partly blamed Johnston.[3] Rhodes was very angry at losing Manica, a supposedly rich gold-bearing country; he was also indignant about the settlement of Barotseland which was neatly bisected by the treaty, which specified that the boundary should follow the Upper Zambezi to the junction of the Kabompo and then up that river.

The treaty nevertheless also met with passionate opposition in Portugal where the Republicans were especially keen to take up the issue as a stick with which to belabour, not only the British, but also the royalist regime. The Cortes assembled under great popular excitement, troops and police had to stand in readiness, and the Portuguese representatives finally refused to ratify the agreement. The British negotiators could thus take up the whole issue once again. By this time official notification from the High Commissioner had reached the Colonial Office about the Lewanika Treaty,[4] and the Portuguese on the whole did less well than in the previous convention. First of all a temporary

[1] Moloney, J. A. *With Captain Stairs to Katanga.* Sampson Low, Marston and company, 1893

[2] Published as C. 7358 (1894). See also Cornet, R. J. *Katanga: Le Katanga avant les Belges et l'expédition Bia-Francqui—Cornet.* Brussels, Edition L. Cuypers, 1946, p. 69–71

[3] C. J. Rhodes to H. H. Johnston: 22 Sep 1890 (JO 1/1/1, f. 130–133 Nat Arch MS)

[4] Sir H. B. Loch to Lord Knutsford: 5 Sep 1890 (in *Further correspondence respecting the affairs of Bechuanaland and adjacent territories.* African (South) no. 392)

agreement recording a *modus vivendi* was signed on 14 November 1890.[1] In the following year another Anglo-Portuguese Convention was concluded at Lisbon (on 11 June 1891), which again re-defined the frontiers between the Portuguese and the British territory.[2] This specified that the Barotse Kingdom 'shall remain within the British sphere; its limits to the westward, which will constitute the boundary between the British and Portuguese spheres of influence, being decided by a joint Anglo-Portuguese Commission, which shall have power, in any case of difference, to appoint an umpire'. The treaty thus left the westward extension of Barotseland undefined; at the same time the British agreed not to oppose the 'extention of Portuguese administration outside the limits of the Barotse country', which of course begged the whole question of its extent. The boundary between the British and Portuguese possessions thus continued to remain a source of dispute between the two countries, particularly as the Portuguese gradually began to drive a chain of forts westward from Angola. The whole issue was not settled until 1905 when the matter was put to arbitration and the frontier was finally settled in a manner very unfavourable to Lewanika,[3] who lost almost half the area claimed by the Barotse to be under their influence.

In the south the British obtained a large share of Manica, though Beira, which Rhodes would have liked to acquire as an outlet for Rhodesia to the Indian Ocean, remained firmly in Portuguese hands; the Portuguese also secured a larger tract of territory north of the Zambezi and west of the Shire. Freedom of navigation on the Zambezi and the Shire continued to be recognized as before, and Britain obtained a lease of a piece of territory on the Shire mouth for the purpose of setting up a customs house. The Portuguese agreed to construct a railway from the Pungwe to the British sphere. In addition, each of the two contracting partners bound itself to give preferential rights to the other should either of them ever decide to part with any of its territories south of the Zambezi, a provision which secured Southern Rhodesia against any possible German acquisition of the vital port of Beira.

The most important settlement, however, was the one arrived at with Germany, and this had implications much wider than those concerned with Africa, directly linking affairs on the Zambezi with those of the European Continent. In Germany a bitter conflict broke out between Bismarck and William II, the young Emperor. Bismarck was by then out for an armed showdown with the Social Democrats, but William II, with much greater realism, decided to embark on a more pacific policy. In March 1890 Count Georg Leo von Caprivi, a distinguished German general, took over the Chancellorship and decided on a 'New Course' of restrained liberalism at home and friendship with Great Britain abroad. Caprivi had no patience with the Russophile Prussian estate owners who despised him for not being a great landed proprietor himself; whilst in the field of foreign policy he was unwilling to

[1] The treaties of 1890 and attached correspondence were published in C. 6212 (1890)
[2] Published in C. 6370 (1891)
[3] The treaty was published as Cd. 2584 (1905)

F

continue Bismarck's delicate balancing of Russia and Austro-Hungary. The Reinsurance Treaty with Russia, concluded in 1887, and binding Germany amongst other things to give diplomatic support to Russia over the questions of Bulgaria and the Straits, was dropped. In August 1890 Caprivi agreed with the Austrians that no Russian solution of the Straits question could be admitted, and that no changes could be allowed in the Near East without Austrian and German consent.[1] The same period saw the high-water mark of Anglo-German friendship, a relationship not as yet disturbed by German naval ambitions, and cemented by a common distrust of Russian plans in Eastern Europe and the Middle East.

The British were just as anxious to make a deal. Their relations with France, then their chief opponent in Africa, and Russia, their principal adversary in the Near East and Central Asia, were far from cordial; they were anxious to secure their position in Egypt and to prevent any foreign power from gaining access to the Sudan, which Great Britain was not then in a position to reconquer from the Mahdi. A treaty was signed on 1 July 1890[2] which constituted a general settlement and was widely interpreted by foreign statesmen as an *entente* between the two powers. Britain ceded to Germany the island of Heligoland, whose importance was not at that time appreciated by either party in terms of its strategic value in a possible Anglo-German War. Zanzibar was recognized as a British protectorate. The British sphere of influence in East Africa, substantially corresponding to what are now Kenya Colony and the Uganda Protectorate, was mapped out in such a way as to bar German ambitions to the Upper Nile. South West Africa was enlarged by the addition of the Caprivi Zipfel which gave Germany access to the Zambezi. Agreement was also arrived at as to the frontiers in West Africa. The frontier between German East Africa, and what later became known as North-Eastern Rhodesia was fixed in such a way as to leave the Stevenson Road in British hands, though the northern end of Lake Nyasa was recognized as falling within the German sphere. The north end of Lake Tanganyika was declared to lie within German territory, and the British plan for a corridor running from north to south between German East Africa and the Congo Free State, for which a number of local treaties had already been concluded, was given up to meet German wishes. For a time Anglo-German relations continued to be friendly; and in 1893 Rhodes—finding that his company was running into grave financial difficulties—even went as far as to suggest an Anglo-German partnership. He thus put forward to a member of the German consular staff in South Africa the truly astounding idea that the territories of the two countries in East and West Africa should be placed under joint rule, the Union Jack and the Imperial Eagle flying side by side. Rhodes explained to the astonished German that the existing share-out of territory would not prove satisfactory to either of the two nations concerned, and that the suggested

[1] Taylor, A. J. P. *The Struggle for mastery in Europe 1848–1918.* Oxford, at the Clarendon pres[s] 1954, p. 328–330
[2] Published as C. 6046 (1890)

condominium would help to educate public opinion in Britain towards accepting the idea of an Anglo-German alliance. But nothing came of Rhodes's scheme, which seemed all the more utopian later on, when relations between Britain and German sharply deteriorated over the Jameson Raid, and Rhodes's own prestige received a smashing blow.[1]

Nevertheless, despite their numerous disagreements in Africa, the colonial powers had enough in common to formulate jointly the rules of the Imperial game on the Dark Continent. In the liberal tradition of the nineteenth century, they conceived their objects of government to be of a negative rather than a positive kind; the colonial administrator was to see that bloodshed and violence stopped, and that life and property were secure; his functions were to be more like those of a policeman on his beat than of a development officer. As far as economic progress was concerned, his main task was to create a network of communications, whilst the main burden of development should be carried by the private *entrepreneur*. This approach found expression in the General Act of the Brussels Conference, signed on 2 July 1890 by all the European colonial powers as well as the U.S.A., Turkey and Persia.[2] The signatories agreed to fight the slave trade, whether by sea or by land, and settled such technical matters as the exchange of information with regard to the traffic, the stopping and examination of suspected vessels, the use of their flags, the position with regard to liberated slaves and so forth. They also pledged themselves to establish roads, railways and telegraph lines in the interior, to set up administrative stations and to ensure internal security by means of the necessary police action. Commercial undertakings and missions were to be protected, whilst steps were to be taken 'to diminish inland wars between the tribes by means of arbitration; to initiate them into agricultural works and in the industrial arts so as to increase their welfare; to raise them to civilization and to bring about the extinction of barbarous customs, such as cannibalism and human sacrifice'.

This incipient doctrine of trusteeship rested on the military superiority of the European powers and to prevent this from being lost, the powers agreed 'that the importation of firearms, and especially of rifles and improved weapons, as well as of powder, balls and cartridges, is ... prohibited in the territories comprised within the 20th parallel of north latitude and 22 parallel of south latitude', subject to certain conditions. Only 'flint-lock guns with unrifled barrels and common gun-powder' might be sold freely, but even these weapons were to be excluded from regions infected with the slave trade. Restrictive practices of a comparable kind also came into being with regard to the importation of liquor into the area mentioned above, so as to prevent that disastrous traffic in spirits, which ruined the health of tribal communities as far afield as North America, Siberia and the South Sea Islands.

[1] See despatch by Consul von Nordenflycht to Reichs-Chancellor von Caprivi: 18 Mar 1893, printed in an interesting article by Holzhausen, R. 'Deutschland und die Gebiete nördlich des Limpopo in den Gründungsjahren Südrhodesiens' (in *Afrikanischer Heimatkalender*, Windhoek, Kirchenbundesrat des Deutschen Kirchenbundes für Süd-und-Südwestafrika, 1955, p. 58–70)

[2] Published as C. 6048 (1890)

IV

The beginnings of European control

The treaties signed in London, Lisbon and Brussels at first meant very little in the interior. In 1890 British influence inland was limited to a precarious foothold in Mashonaland and another in the country around Lake Nyasa and near the south of Lake Tanganyika. Missionaries, traders and administrators were holding on to a few stations; the Europeans wielded some powers locally, but they were not noticeably stronger than many of the chiefs amongst whom they dwelt, and their dealings with the indigenous powers resembled for the most part those between equals rather than those between conqueror and subjects. Nor did there seem any likelihood of sudden change. Money was short, for the Imperial Parliament was still unwilling to finance extensive colonization; the Treasury, then the core of the British administrative machinery at home, was wedded to Gladstonian doctrines of low taxation and limited state expenditure, and was even more unsympathetic to the idea of spending money on the colonies. Even the Foreign Office itself, which helped to map out these vast spheres of influence, liked its African responsibilities so little that Johnston could write, with pardonable exaggeration, that his friend Sir Percy Anderson was the only one in the Foreign Service who possessed any faith in Africa.

This accusation of course could not be levelled against the British South Africa Company. But the Company's energies were absorbed in Mashonaland where the pioneers disbanded to look for gold without finding the promised Ophir. Hardships and disease were rife in the new settlement; prices rocketed sky-high, and there was bitter discontent amongst many colonists. The Company was also under an obligation to extend the Cape railway and telegraph systems from Kimberley to the north, both in order to carry out its part of the bargain for the Charter and to break the isolation of its newly acquired territory in Mashonaland, so that there was little money available for anything else. It is in fact difficult to realize nowadays just how speculative the Chartered venture appeared to the initiated at the time. 'Only a few years ago' wrote the German Consul at Pretoria, a sensible and well-informed man, 'no one could have imagined a more fantastic piece of nonsense than the idea that a great empire might be brought into being in this dark, unexplored and inaccessible part of the Continent'. The Matabele military monarchy still remained a formidable power and in addition there were other warlike tribes who still remained to be subdued. More serious still, the German argued, was the problem of transport. A ton of coal was worth £20. 0. 0. at Cape Town, but could not be brought to the diggings for less than an additional £8. 0. 0. or £9. 0. 0. But what was to happen in Mashonaland, some seven hundred miles from Kimberley, a distance as far as Berlin to Birmingham? The problem of logistics would alone prevent the effective exploitation of the new Chartered Empire. Nevertheless, the German argued, South Africa was the land of the unpredictable; and Rhodes, who was always chasing the bird in the bush instead of holding on to the one in hand, might yet bring it off.[1]

Rhodes himself was untroubled by any such doubts. He was now at the height of his career, he enjoyed support from Dutch farmers at the Cape, who liked his policy of agricultural protection and his preoccupation with their economic interests, and from the English-speaking townsmen. On 17 July 1890 he became Prime Minister of the Cape, and no one could now be unaware of his power. During the same period Rhodes proceeded to make good his claims to the lands north of the Zambezi. The key to the situation lay in Nyasaland where the African Lakes Company was now financially crippled by the long war against the North End Arabs. The Chartered Company therefore agreed to subsidize the Lakes Company by £20,000, the Lakes Company being subsequently absorbed in the Chartered interest. The British South Africa Company also pledged itself to spend money for the purpose of maintaining law and order north of the Zambezi and for the protection of the mission stations.[2] In addition negotiations were begun with the Imperial Government with regard to the question of administrative control. The African Lakes Company lacked both the men and the means to assume any administrative powers itself, whilst Johnston himself had not the slightest intention of governing Nyasaland under the supervision of that 'miserable grocery business'. The Scottish missionaries, on the other hand, were unwilling to be placed under the rule of the British South Africa Company, whilst Johnston himself argued that Chartered Company rule without Imperial supervision was out of the question in the North, as the Company's officials would be too far away from their base at Kimberley, and as high-handed action on their part might possibly lead to complications with Germany, Belgium and Portugal.[3] Nyasaland moreover seemed of little immediate value without the Katanga, now in Belgian hands; and lengthy discussions between Rhodes and Johnston finally resulted in a preliminary agreement in which Rhodes agreed to meet the objections of the Scottish missions; Nyasaland being placed under Imperial Administration, whilst the balance of the Northern Zambezi country came under the Charter. The area south of Lake Tanganyika was originally also intended to form part of Nyasaland, but was subsequently excluded from the imperial sphere for purely technical reasons arising from the Berlin Act.

The matter was formally settled in an agreement between the British South Africa Company and the Imperial Government, signed in February1891.[4] The Company agreed to pay the sum of £10,000 per annum for the upkeep of a police force which was to be controlled by Her Majesty's Commissioner and Consul

[1] Von Treskow, H. 'The future empire of Zambesia and its founder': 6 Mar 1891 (GE 1/1/1, f. 1–9 Nat Arch MS)

[2] British South Africa Company. *Directors' report and accounts, 21st March 1891*, p. 16

[3] H. Johnston to Sir P. Anderson: 9 Feb 1891 (in F.O. 84/2140)

[4] Published as C. 7637 (1895)

General for British Central Africa and which could be employed either in Nyasaland itself or in Chartered territory at his discretion. In return for this payment, the
Chartered Company's sphere of operations was extended beyond the Zambezi,
though Nyasaland was excluded from its field. Administrative control over the
Chartered sphere was placed in the hands of Her Majesty's Commissioner who
was to exercise his control on the Company's behalf, and also had to be consulted as to the appointment of the Company's officers in its sphere. Justice was
to be administered in accordance with the Africa Order in Council, 1889, by
which judicial powers could be granted to consular officers in specified parts of
Africa, with powers to try cases concerning British subjects, aliens who submitted themselves to the jurisdiction of the courts set up under the order, as well
as foreigners 'with respect to whom any State, King, Chief or Government,
whose ... subjects they are, has ... consented to the executive power or
authority by Her Majesty', a very flexible phrase which subsequently enabled
the consular courts to extend their sphere of jurisdiction. The negotiations with
the Company having been concluded, Johnston became 'Her Majesty's Commissioner and Consul General for the Territories under British influence to the
North of the Zambezi', and on 14 May the 'Nyasaland Districts' were formally
announced to constitute a British Protectorate. The country was administered
under the supervision of the Foreign Office, and on 31 July 1891 the British
sphere beyond the Zambezi was constituted 'a local jurisdiction under the
Africa Order in Council, 1889, for which the Supreme Court of Cape Colony
became the highest Court of Appeal.

To the man on the spot of course all this meant little. Johnston's energies
were still fully absorbed in fighting the Yao slave dealers in the south, whilst the
area of European influence in the north was limited to the narrow strip of territory between Lake Tanganyika and Lake Nyasa where the African Lakes Company established a few depots. The Arabs were left strictly alone and nothing
was done even when the followers of an Arab named Abdallah-bin-Suleiman
murdered Nsama, one of the chiefs with whom Sharpe had concluded a treaty.
In 1890 Richard Crawshay was sent to Lake Mweru to build a station where the
Chiengi stream enters the lake, for the purpose of opening up trade to the
Katanga and preventing encroachments from the Belgians; this was known by
its native name of Mputa and was abandoned in 1891. In 1892 Alfred Sharpe sent
Kydd and Bainbridge to build another station and they built a fort at the point
where the old road to Kazembe crossed the Kalungwishi. They called this
Rhodesia but the name was later changed to Kalungwishi.[1] In 1893 Hugh
Charlie Marshall, another Protectorate official, was despatched to the Tanganyika plateau, and instructed by Johnston to make his headquarters at Zombe,
which was to be renamed Abercorn, the name originally given to the proposed
administrative station at the south end of Lake Tanganyika, the existing post of
that name being near Zombe and belonging to the African Lakes Company.
Marshall's sole resources consisted of a small detachment of Indian soldiers,

[1] H. Johnston to Foreign Office: 14 Dec 1891 (in F.O. 84/2114)

'together with a supply of postal and revenue stamps,' accompanied by an Imperial exhortation from Johnston who warned his subordinates that there would be many white people only too ready to find fault with his administration, but cheerfully explained that the new post was perhaps the most interesting in Africa 'from its geographical position, from the beautiful scenery that surrounds the south end of Lake Tanganyika, the remarkable native tribes inhabiting the District, and the fact that it will before long become one of the stepping stones of a continuous British Empire from Cape Town to Cairo.'[1] Another station was Ikawa, known from 1898 as Fife, the original Fife lying somewhat further to the north and first having been set up as a station for the African Lakes Company.

As far as Barotseland was concerned the Company did not even attempt to assert any influence as long as its hands were tied in Southern Rhodesia. Coillard thus found himself in the unhappy position of becoming the King's scapegoat for the Company's sins of omission; Lewanika's distrust of both missionaries and the Chartered Company was heightened by the trader Middleton, under whose influence Lewanika tried to repudiate the Lochner Concession on the grounds that it had been obtained by fraudulent means and that Lochner had misrepresented the Company's constitutional position.[2] For once, however, the Imperial Government reacted swiftly and Loch sent an assurance to the Barotse Paramount that he was indeed under the Queen's protection.[3] Coillard's position gradually became easier and in October 1892 he was permitted to shift his headquarters to Lealui, the royal capital. The prestige of the Europeans was not, however, fully secured until 1893 when the British South Africa Company's forces smashed the Matabele warrior state to the delight of the Barotse and their subjects. Jameson himself wanted to avoid war, hoping to assimilate the Matabele peacefully through the process of labour-migration.[4] Lobengula and most of the older chiefs, who had already gained high office and prestige would also have preferred to avoid hostilities. But the younger chiefs wanted war to make their names, and in any case, peaceful co-existence between a Western wage economy and a tribal raiding state, geared to perpetual war, was impossible as a long-term policy; the Matabele could not give up raiding women and cattle from weaker tribes along the periphery of their state; and their attacks interfered with the settlers' property and labour supply. The colonists on Mashonaland's western border wanted war to end the Matabele threat and on 2 October 1893 the Company's forces, consisting of mounted burghers, supported by eight machine-guns and two light field guns, moved westwards to engage the enemy. Lobengula's regiments, though possessed of a good many firearms, failed to adjust their tactics to the new military conditions; they continued to fight in close formation, the Matabele officers being convinced, like many of their

---

[1] Instructions to H. C. Marshall from H. Johnston: 26 July 1893, copy enclosed in L. A. Wallace to B.S.A. Company: 2 Nov 1912, annex. 9 to minutes of 19 Dec 1912 (in LO 1/2/75, Nat Arch SR)

[2] G. W. Middleton to Lord Knutsford: 27 Oct 1890 (in *Further correspondence respecting the affairs of Bechuanaland and adjacent territories*. African (South) no. 414)

[3] Sir H. B. Loch to Lewanika: 18 Sep 1891 (in *Further correspondence. . . .* African (South) no. 426)

[4] L. S. Jameson to S. Jameson: 4 Oct 1893 (in JA 1/1/1, f. 109–111, Nat Arch MS)

counterparts in European Guards regiments, that cold steel was the answer to accurate rifle and machine-gun fire. The Matabele had numbers on their side, but the mounted burgher force opposing them had superior fire power and greater mobility; the Matabele were crushed, and Bulawayo fell to the white invaders, whilst Lobengula perished in his flight.

European prestige in Barotseland now went unchallenged and the years that followed saw the hey-day of missionary influence in Barotseland, a kind of golden age, when the missionary was regarded as the King's supreme adviser, without having to reckon with interference from government officials or any other Europeans. Coillard used his position in an entirely disinterested manner. No attempt was made to acquire estates for the missions, as was done by the L.M.S. in North-Eastern Rhodesia; Coillard was content to have his stations delimited by the chiefs so that the Barotse would not imagine the missionaries had come to deprive them of their precious land.[1] Coillard's main objective, apart from preaching the Gospel to all and sundry, was to strengthen royal authority, whilst at the same time adjusting Barotse judicial procedure to European ideals; Coillard thus welcomed the introduction of a royal police; from 1891 the poison ordeal was no longer administered to witches, and though accusations of witchcraft did not thereby disappear, at least the poison ordeal was gradually stamped out. In 1892 the Mbundu medicine men, who were amongst the leaders of the conservative and anti-European party, were deprived of all political influence. Torture, hitherto employed against criminals by ex-posing them on the rack to the burning sun or by having them devoured alive by fierce ants, was abolished; so was the burning of witches, who instead of being executed were interned in separate villages; deportation as a punishment was apparently not opposed even by the missionaries, for as Coillard remarked, the subjects of witchcraft accusations were generally cantankerous persons who did not get on with their neighbours, so that Coillard believed the idea of in-terning such people might be capable of some extension.[2] At the end of the century Coillard's influence became so great that he had practically acquired the rank of a 'Natamoyo' a minister empowered to grant sanctuary. Coillard also fought to have the Christian view of morality enforced with the King's help. At the turn of the century the *Seferu*, an orgiastic dance, swept the country, but this was stamped out with the help of the King's bodyguard. Lewanika even outdid the teachers by attempting to prohibit the manufacture and sale of strong beer, an idea adopted from Khama; but the Frenchmen did not hold the prohibitionist views of many of their British nonconformist colleagues and thought that the king would only bring his own authority into disrepute by promoting legisla-tion which he would be unable to enforce.

Coillard also used his influence to help other Protestant missionaries in the area. The occasion arose when the Primitive Methodists, a British breakaway group from the Wesleyans, despatched an expedition, consisting of the Rev.

[1] F. Coillard to K. Mackintosh: 8 Jan 1903 (in CO 5/1/1/1, f. 2279–2284, Nat Arch MS)
[2] Mackintosh, C. W. *Coillard of the Zambesi.* . . . T. Fisher Unwin, 1907, p. 361

Henry Buckenham, his wife, and the Rev. A. Baldwin, to Barotseland where they arrived in August 1890. The Methodists had made the mistake of sending out a fully equipped Mission instead of taking Coillard's advice to investigate first with a small party.[1] The position was made worse by internal politics. The dispute over the recently concluded Lochner treaty was at its height and the Barotse were bitterly suspicious of the British missionaries. To make matters worse, Baldwin especially was ignorant of local conditions and was nearly executed for entering a Barotse town at night and going into the Queen's yard,[2] an offence which the Barotse probably associated with witchcraft. Perhaps the gravest objection from the Barotse point of view was the Methodists' intention of starting missionary work among the Ila (Mashukulumbwe) in the Kafue region. The Ila, cattle-keeping warriors, were noted for the fierce spirit of independence possessed by each of their petty tribal groupings. Though warlike, they were incapable of co-operating with each other against outside enemies, and the Barotse thus regarded their country as one of their traditional raiding areas, a major campaign being waged against them in 1888. The Ila thus hated anyone who came from Barotseland, and in 1886 they attacked Holub who was then trying to make his way from the Cape to Egypt by way of the Upper Zambezi. Holub and Rosa, his indomitable wife, were lucky to make their way back alive, though one of Holub's men, a European, was murdered. Two years later Selous was attacked by the Ila at Magoye and again was fortunate to escape with his life. But things might not always go so well, and as far as the Barotse were concerned, a European mission to the Ila country might lead to grave complications; in any case it was undesirable to have an uncontrolled foreign mission working within the Barotse sphere of influence.

The Methodists thus had a hard time in Barotseland, but Coillard's say was sufficiently great to prevent the missionaries being expelled, and he was able to smooth the way for his British colleagues. At the end of 1892 Barotse policy towards the Methodists changed for the better, the new course being linked to a radical transformation in Lewanika's approach to the Ila problem. Lewanika now decided that peaceful penetration was to be preferred to raiding, and arrangements were accordingly made to found a Barotse village in the Ila country; at the same time the Primitive Methodists were allowed to set up a station.[3] Coillard was overjoyed with this decision which he believed would help the spread of the Gospel beyond the Zambezi, and create a link with the Plymouth Brethren's mission further north in Garenganze. In December 1893 the Primitive Methodists finally arrived in the Ila country where they were introduced to the local chiefs by a Barotse sub-chief. The Barotse made it clear that any attacks on the missionaries would be followed by Barotse reprisals; he also added that there was no need to fear the Europeans, who had already brought considerable spiritual and material benefits to Barotseland, and who would neither raid for

[1] F. Coillard to J. Smith: 30 June 1891 (in CO 5/1/1/1, f. 1014–1021, Nat Arch MS)
[2] Undated letter from A. Baldwin (in *Record: journal of the Primitive Methodist Missionary Society*, Oct 1891)
[3] Letter from A. Baldwin: 30 Nov 1892 (in *Record . . .* , June 1893)

slaves nor molest the Ila in any other way, but pay for all their purchases with cotton bales.[1] The Ila were satisfied with this explanation and the Primitive Methodists constructed their first station at Nkala, just south of the Kafue river, in December 1893, a further station being put up at Nanzela in 1895. The missionaries suffered terribly from disease, but at least there was no hostility from the Ila who feared the Barotse, and who were probably also impressed by the defeat of the Matabele, their traditional enemies from the south, at the hands of the British.

Coillard's interregnum in Barotseland itself was much more prolonged than the Company intended. Barotseland was more than 800 miles away from Zomba, as far as London is from Corsica, and Johnston could not possibly exercise any authority there, even had he wanted to do so. The task of keeping control in Nyasaland alone taxed his resources to the utmost, for the Yao, into the bargain, were difficult to subdue; Sikhs and Imperial gunboats had to be brought into the Protectorate, and neither men nor money were available for the Company's sphere proper. To make matters worse, there was soon friction between Johnston and Rhodes, both forceful and strong-minded men who did not easily work in harmony. In 1893 Johnston went to Cape Town to discuss a new agreement with Rhodes, but subsequent negotiations broke down, Rhodes fulminating against the idea of setting up 'an independent King Johnston over the Zambezi' with the help of Chartered funds. At the end of 1893 the Treasury decided that it was preferable to make a fixed annual grant to the Protectorate, rather than to be badgered year after year with repeated requests for specific payments designed to supplement the Chartered Company's inadequate subsidy.[2]

On 24 November 1894 a new agreement was finally signed between the Company and the Foreign Office.[3] Control of the Chartered sphere north of the Zambezi was withdrawn from Johnston's control, whilst the British Central Africa Protectorate (Nyasaland) became responsible to the Home Government for all its expenditure as well as for its general policy, bringing to an end a highly unsatisfactory system of dual control. Direct administration in the Chartered sphere was to be transferred to the Company not later than 30 June 1895; the treaties made in the Chartered sphere were sanctioned by the Imperial Government in so far as they contained nothing contrary to the Charter of the Berlin Act. There were also provisions to sort out the tangled financial situation, and the question of mining and land rights acquired by the Chartered Company from the African Lakes Company in Nyasaland.

The new constitutional arrangement, however, made little difference at first. The Company was still incapable of devoting much money to its northern dependency which remained an administrative Cinderella. The Company's first Deputy Administrator was Major Patrick William Forbes, who arrived at Zomba on 23 June 1895. As far as Forbes was concerned, the new appointment

[1] Letter from A. Baldwin: 23 Dec 1893 (in *Record* . . . , Mar 1894)
[2] Hanna, A. J. *The beginnings of Nyasaland and North-Eastern Rhodesia.* Oxford, at the Clarendon press, 1956, p. 247–263
[3] C. 7637 (1895), p. 3–4

in the Trans-Zambezian wilds was little more than a slight, for a man in Forbes's position might have expected something very much better. A regular officer, educated at Rugby and Sandhurst, he had been sent to South Africa in 1882 where he saw a good deal of soldiering; in 1889 he received an appointment in the British South Africa Company's Police under Lieutenant Colonel Edward Graham Pennefather, an officer in Forbes's own regiment, the 6th (Inniskilling) Dragoons; later on Forbes was appointed a Magistrate in Mashonaland and when the Matabele War broke out in 1893, he was placed in command of the Salisbury Column, soon reinforced by the Victoria Column. Forbes commanded his troops with considerable success, and victory over the Matabele might in other circumstances have laid the foundations of a distinguished military career. But when a patrol commanded by Major Allan Wilson was wiped out on the Shangani, Forbes fell from favour. The blame for the massacre must in the main be borne by Wilson himself; but Wilson died a soldier's death, and Forbes, as Wilson's commanding officer, was made to take the blame, his position being made no easier by Rhodes's dislike of professional soldiers. Forbes was rusticated to the Far North and subsequently took up residence at Blantyre. The main object of Forbes's mission was to look after the construction of the African Transcontinental Telegraph line, which was then being built for the purpose of linking up Nyasaland with the south, the line to be subsequently continued across the Nyasa-Tanganyika Plateau, through German East Africa, Uganda, and then to Egypt. In 1895 the telegraph was taken up from the Zambezi to Blantyre, and in the following year to Zomba. Apart from thus acting as a glorified building supervisor, there was little Forbes could do with the means at his disposal, apart from inspecting his Chartered domain, in which he travelled as far as Kalungwishi. In December 1895 Forbes went to Cape Town for an operation which effected a cure, but made it impossible for him to ride, a fatal handicap for a soldier of proven ability.[1]

During Forbes's stay at Cape Town, Jameson committed his tragic folly of raiding the Transvaal. The fault was not his alone, for the Chartered Company and allied financial interests had for some time been fomenting revolutionary activity in Johannesburg for the purpose of overthrowing President Kruger's government, which they considered unsympathetic to their interests and hostile to the British element in the Transvaal. In order to back the rising, the Company concentrated the bulk of its Police in the Transvaal, leaving the country beyond the Limpopo almost unprotected. But the whole affair was bungled. No rising took place in Johannesburg; and unsupported by the revolutionary party, Jameson was forced to surrender near Doornkop on 2 January 1896.

The consequences of Jameson's action were far-reaching indeed. Relations between Boer and Briton were poisoned, and the Transvaal began to prepare for a war of defence. On 5 January 1896 Rhodes resigned from his position as Prime Minister of the Cape where the Afrikander Bond would no longer support him. Worse still, in March 1896 the Matabele rose in revolt against their conquerors

[1] Altham, E. A. *Some notes on the life of Major Patrick William Forbes.* For private circulation, 1928

The Matabele thought that the strategic opportunity had now come to rid themselves of the invaders whom they suspected of having brought the dreaded rinderpest into the country, who had crushed Matabele military supremacy, seized much of their cattle, conscripted labour, and imposed taxes. Many Mashona communities also took to arms, and it was not till September 1897 that the country south of the Zambezi was completely pacified. Six hundred and eighty three Europeans died during the rebellion, including some 327 settlers or nearly ten per cent of the white population of the country, and for a time most enterprise in the country came to an end. The Company, which was losing almost all its revenue, was at the same time forced to engage in crushing financial expenditure to suppress the rising, and it was only with difficulty that it survived the storm.

Its position became equally serious from the political point of view. The Colonial Office lost much of its former confidence in the Company and more stringent control began to be exercised over its affairs. As far as affairs north of the Zambezi were concerned, there was a further delay in the setting up of an effective administration. At the end of 1895 the Company proposed to send Hubert John Antony Hervey as Resident to Barotseland,[1] but he was killed in the Rising, and for the time being no replacement could be found.

The position became more acute when in 1895 a group of tough prospectors made their way to the Hook of the Kafue to explore the area on behalf of the Northern Rhodesia (B.S.A.) Exploration Company (later known as the Northern Copper Company), one of Edmund Davis's many financial interests. The expedition was led by Frederick Russell Burnham, one of the small band of American Frontiersmen who made their way to Africa when the open frontier closed in the West. Burnham's father, a stern, unyielding Congregationalist, used to live on the border of Indian country in Minnesota, and when his child was only two years old, the Redskins struck, massacring the white population in the nearby township of New Ulm; Mrs Burnham at the time was alone in her log-cabin, and realizing that she would never escape with a small infant in her arms, hid the toddler in a stack of green corn, enjoining him not to make a sound or move till she was back. She managed to get out just before a band of warriors surrounded and burnt the log-hut, and on the next day Burnham's mother returned with armed neighbours to pick up the child, who was still quietly waiting in the corn. Later on the family moved to California, and after an adventurous career in the West, Burnham fell for the spell of Rhodes and decided to give up gold mining in Arizona to offer his services to the great Empire Builder, believing that his own knowledge of scouting and fighting Indians would be of value in Africa.[2] Burnham saw much in Southern Rhodesia where he made a name for himself, one of the small but important group of Americans who introduced special skills to Central Africa, first of all as frontier fighters and missionaries, and later

[1] Foreign Office to Colonial Office: 25 Nov 1895 (in *Further correspondence relative to affairs in Mashonaland, Matabeleland and the Bechuanaland protectorate*. African (South) no. 498)

[2] See Burnham, F. R. *Scouting on two continents*. Los Angeles, Ivan Deach, 1934, and Burnham, F. R. *Taking chances*, arranged by Everett, M. N. Los Angeles, Haynes Corporation, 1944, for Burnham's career.

on as growers of Virginia tobacco, and as mine managers and engineers. In 1895 Burnham, together with another prospector by the name of Pearl Ingram, made his way through famine-ridden Tonga and Ila country to the Kafue. Their reports were so favourable that two years later a further expedition, led by Frank R. Lewis, made its way into the Kafue region, where extensive claims were pegged, and where the Northern Copper Company was subsequently given a concession of about 500 square miles of copper-bearing land.[1]

Lewanika was now thoroughly worried, and Coillard again wrote to the High Commissioner, bitterly complaining that no Resident had been sent to him, and charging the British South Africa Company with letting loose in the country 'parties of prospectors and diggers who without any control can go where they like, do what they please, bully the natives and threaten to burn their villages'.[2] In addition Lewanika was faced with the problem of continuous Portuguese penetration into what he claimed were his western dominions, two new Portuguese stations being founded in the west in 1895.

The Chartered Company's reaction to this was to try and get the Matabeleland Order in Council, 1894, extended beyond the Zambezi.[3] This instrument, issued after the conquest of Lobengula's kingdom, was designed to define the Company's administrative rights both in Matabeleland and in Mashonaland; it provided for the appointment of an Administrator and Council by the Company, subject to the Secretary of State's approval, very extensive powers being placed into the Company's hands. Had the Order been made applicable beyond the Zambezi, the history of Northern Rhodesia might well have taken a very different course; a unified administration would probably have come into existence right from the start, and the Zambezi might not have become that political dividing line which subsequently split two territories.

Events, however, took a different course. The Jameson Raid intervened and there was a public outcry. Joseph Chamberlain, the British Colonial Secretary, was deeply implicated, but the responsibility of the Colonial Office was hushed up, a few scapegoats being selected to bear the brunt of public disapproval; Francis James Newton, the Resident Commissioner for Bechuanaland and later one of the architects of Southern Rhodesian self-government, was sent as Colonial Secretary to British Honduras, 'an infernal hole' where his only child died; Sir Graham Bower, the Imperial Secretary in South Africa, a very loyal public servant, was posted to a minor appointment in Mauritius and his career was ruined. In addition action was taken against the Company. There were suggestions that its Charter should be rescinded, but this the Imperial Government was unwilling to do, for it had no intention of assuming any additional responsibilities. All the same there was to be no repetition of the Raid. The Company therefore had to be prevented from carrying out an independent military policy of its own, and was accordingly deprived of control over its

[1] In 1899 the Silver King and Sable Antelope mines were discovered in the area.
[2] F. Coillard to Sir H. B. Loch: 4 July 1895 (in *Further correspondence. . . .* African (South) no. 498)
[3] Foreign Office to Colonial Office: 24 Dec 1895 (in *Further correspondence. . . .* African (South) no. 517)

police force which was placed under Imperial supervision. The Company was also obliged to communicate all its minutes, orders and resolutions relating to the administration of its territories to the Colonial Office, the Secretary of State being permitted access to the Company's records. This provision went some way toward facilitating control over the Company's affairs, though it was not entirely effective in its purpose, since much confidential matter now found its way into private correspondence between the Board and its Administrators. In Southern Rhodesia the Southern Rhodesia Order in Council, 1898, also provided for the appointment of a Resident Commissioner as an Imperial 'watchdog' over the Company's affairs, available on the spot, though without any administrative machinery of his own. In addition a Legislative Council came into being, fashioned according to the normal British Colonial pattern, containing for the first time settler representatives who now secured a foothold on the legislature, and were able to balance the Company's powers to some extent.

As far as the Northern territories were concerned, the Colonial Office at first temporized: for the time being no further Order in Council should be issued giving increased powers to the Company beyond the Zambezi, whilst the Charter was still under a cloud.[1]

With this view the Foreign Office heartily concurred, and for the time being no new legislation was issued, despite the Chartered Company's efforts to get the position settled.

The attitude of the Colonial Office became even more hesitant as it began to have some doubts about the Lochner Concession itself. This document, the argument went, did not convey any administrative powers and was never sanctioned by the Foreign Office; its provisions giving to the Company a monopoly of trading rights were in conflict with the provisions of the Charter; the £2,000 a year promised to Lewanika had never been paid. The Lochner Concession in fact had not been carried out by the Company, its main values having consisted in keeping out the Portuguese. The best thing would be for the region to be administered under the Company by an Imperial police officer. An Imperial appointment would cause less public criticism than one which would further add to the Company's power before the Report of the Select Committee on the Jameson Raid had been received. An Imperial police officer would also be more capable of keeping order amongst the white immigrants who were now drifting into the country; it was also better for British interests to be represented by an Imperial man. Barotseland in any case should be treated as a separate entity on the grounds that, according to Johnston, the Kafue River formed a natural dividing line, that the Barotse were of South African origin, that the country was most readily accessible from the south, and that it should therefore form part of the 'South African system', its affairs to be controlled under the High Commissioner for South Africa.[2]

[1] Colonial Office to Foreign Office: 4 Apr 1896 (in *Further correspondence. . . .* African (South) no. 517)

[2] Colonial Office to Foreign Office: 16 Jan 1897 (in *Further correspondence. . . .* African (South) no. 517)

These views formed the basis for the future settlement of the Barotse question, except for the appointment of an Imperial police officer.[1] Robert Thorne Coryndon, the first Resident to be appointed for Barotseland was in every sense of the word a 'Company' man. A South African, born at Queenstown in the Cape Colony, he was educated at St Andrew's College, Grahamstown and then at Cheltenham, an English Public School. In 1889 he signed up with the British Bechuanaland Border Police, a *corps d'élite*, distinguished by its high standard of training and morale, which was attracting many youths of good family and high ambition, and which during this period developed into a kind of 'nursery' for military and administrative officers for the whole of Central Africa. In 1890 Coryndon joined the Pioneer Column, one of Rhodes's 'Twelve Apostles', young men dedicated to Rhodes's views, and subsequently saw service in the Matabele War and the Native Rising. In 1896 he was appointed Rhodes's Private Secretary at a critical period when passions were running high after the Jameson Raid, and again justified Rhodes's confidence in him. Apart from a short spell in the Surveyor General's Office at Salisbury, Coryndon had little administrative experience proper, but nevertheless, the Company could hardly have made a better appointment for its purpose. For what was needed at the time was not a bureaucrat but a diplomat and Coryndon possessed all the attributes of a sound negotiator—skill, patience and tact. A big-game hunter of many years' experience, he knew the veld inside out, and in addition he was possessed of phenomenal physical strength, one of those men who could bend a half-crown piece with one hand. His whole training and outlook moreover thoroughly identified him with the spirit and outlook of the European colonists in the country, and with the whole object of the Company's rule.

When Coryndon received his appointment he was only 27 years old, not much older than a Cadet would have been in the Northern Rhodesian service of later years. But he was able, keen, enthusiastic and self-confident, all qualities in great demand at a time when the Company was still quite unable to spend even the barest minimum on its Northern possessions. He arrived in Barotseland in October 1897, accompanied by his Secretary, Frank Vigers Worthington, and an escort of only five European policemen, a force which the Barotse found much too small to be impressive. Coryndon nevertheless was given a ceremonial welcome and the Resident set up a station near Coillard's establishment, from where he subsequently moved to a house at Mongu.

Coryndon during this period was still responsible to the Foreign Office and the Company had only limited control over what he was doing. The Company then suggested that 'Northern Zambezia' should be split into two sections, each under a Deputy Administrator, one of whom was to be answerable to the Administrator of Matabeleland, the other to his colleague in Mashonaland. Roman-Dutch law was to be introduced, just as it was south of the Zambezi, for the immigrants would mostly come from Southern Rhodesia and South Africa.

[1] Coryndon was formally given the rank of Major in the British South Africa Police as Staff Officer of its 'Northern Division' but was given 'full freedom of action in Barotseland'.

The Foreign Office did not object to the principle of splitting up the lands beyond the Zambezi for administrative purposes, a course of action well justified by the differences in geographical access. But the Imperial Government strongly opposed the Company's view that Northern Rhodesia would become the furthermost extension of the South African frontier. Instead, the Foreign Office argued that the region was much too unhealthy to absorb many white settlers, and that it should come under British law, like British Central Africa with which it had far more in common than Southern Rhodesia.[1]

After further lengthy negotiations the matter was finally settled in 1899. The country north of the Zambezi was divided into two sections, and the Kafue River became the dividing line between the two regions, 'with so much of any territory belonging to the Bashukolumbwe tribe as may lie east of the Kafukwe'. The Government was placed in the hands of an Administrator appointed by the High Commissioner for South Africa on the nomination of the Company, judges and magistrates receiving office in a similar manner. The High Commissioner was also empowered to make Proclamations for the administration of justice, the raising of revenue and the imposition of taxes and customs dues, though it was made clear that 'the High Commissioner should, before issuing any such Proclamations have regard to any suggestions or requests made to him in respect thereof by the Company', whilst no Proclamation concerning the raising of revenue was to be made without the Company's previous approval. English law was put into force, whilst the customs duties to be levied were not to exceed those of the South African Customs Union.[2] Under the new Order, Coryndon was promoted to be a full Administrator, his appointment dating from 15 September 1900.[3]

In addition to the settlement of the constitutional question, a new agreement had to be negotiated with Lewanika to take the place of the old Lochner Treaty. On 25 June 1898 a document, known as the Lawley Treaty, was signed between the Barotse and the Company.[4] For various technical reasons, including the fact that the original document lacked Lewanika's signature, the Imperial Government refused to sanction this agreement, and a third treaty, almost identical in its terms was signed on 17 October 1900 at the Victoria Falls. This

[1] Foreign Office to Colonial Office: 14 May 1898 and Foreign Office to Colonial Office: 22 Dec 1898 (in *Further correspondence. . . .* African (South) no. 559)

[2] The nomenclature of Northern Rhodesia is somewhat confused. The rather hazy definition of 'the British Sphere north of the Zambesi' was subsequently replaced by 'Northern Zambesia', and an Administrator's Proclamation, dated 1 May 1895, issued at Salisbury, stated that the Company's territories should collectively be known as 'Rhodesia', to be divided into three provinces, Matabeleland, Mashonaland and 'Northern Zambezia.' This Proclamation was subsequently disallowed, though at the end of 1895 the use of the term Rhodesia was sanctioned for postal purposes. Two years later a Government Notice informed the public that the Secretary of State had sanctioned the use of the term 'Rhodesia' to denote the Chartered territories (Government notice no. 82 of 1897, in *B.S.A. Company government gazette*, no. 140, 2 June 1897, p. 1). On 19 July 1897 the Foreign Office concurred in a suggestion made by the company that the regions beyond the Zambezi should collectively be known as 'Northern Rhodesia', and it is from then that the official use of the term can be dated.

[3] Barotseland—North-Western Rhodesia order in council, 1899

[4] Enclosure in B.S.A. Company to Colonial Office: 9 Apr 1900 (in *Further correspondence. . . .* African (South) no. 656)

was rather more unfavourable to the Barotse than the original Lochner treaty. The king's annual subsidy was reduced to £850. In addition the Company received 'the right to make grants of land for farming purposes in any portion of the Batoko or Mashukulumbwe country to white men approved by the king', on condition that existing native gardens and cattle posts should not be interfered with. Within Barotseland itself, however, the Paramount's existing 'constitutional power or authority' was to continue unchanged, whilst the Barotse reserve was specifically exempted from prospecting. Elsewhere the Company retained the mineral rights, though a number of iron mines worked by Africans were specifically excluded from this provision. At the time this reservation seemed an important consideration to the Barotse who were still receiving iron hoes, assegais and axes as tribute from Totela craftsmen. European-made goods of this type were as yet expensive, for traders had to bring their wares by ox wagon through the fringe of the Kalahari desert at rates of up to £7. 10. 0. per lb, and merchants could not therefore afford to import heavy goods at reasonable prices. As communications improved, costs dropped, and during the first decade of the present century the importance of the Barotse iron mines and of many indigenous crafts rapidly declined.

Under the circumstances the treaty was almost certainly the best Lewanika could obtain. The king was still seriously worried by the encroachments of the Portuguese who were pushing a chain of forts from the west into the interior. At home, moreover, Lewanika was still afraid of the danger of domestic upheavals and the claims from possible rivals. In addition there were a number of minor boundary questions, including a dispute with Segkhomi, a chief living to the south-west. Compared with these questions, the grant of the mineral rights meant little, for the Barotse were not interested in the copper deposits outside their Reserves, copper hoes being too soft to work the land, and the red metal being used only for ornamental and not for utilitarian purposes. The Barotse also promised to assist in the suppression of slavery, but the aristocratic structure of their kingdom remained unchanged, and their king stood out as the only chief in the whole of Rhodesia whose power was guaranteed by a treaty, and who was in receipt of a substantial annual income. As far as the permission for Europeans to enter Ila and Tonga country was concerned, there was nothing the Barotse could do anyway; they realized that their influence was coming to an end in the periphery of their territory, but managed to keep the core of the kingdom inviolate from permanent European settlement.

Coillard, on the other hand, was very dissatisfied with the treaty, which formed a landmark in the decline of the missionaries' local influence; he would have nothing to do with the document which he refused to sign on the grounds that its terms were extremely unfavourable to the Barotse.[1] He was also disappointed in the Company's failure to carry out its promised civilizing mission; he bitterly criticized the personal morals of some of the white men, and saw himself deprived of influence. Coillard, moreover, was faced with a problem of

[1] F. Coillard to K. Mackintosh: 20 Oct 1900 (in CO 5/1/1/1, f. 1814–1819, Nat Arch MS)

G

even greater potential consequence. The Barotse now had a number of literate people at their command, who had been taught by the missionaries, and who could conduct their own correspondence. This meant that the Barotse aristocracy was no longer dependent on the missionaries' secretarial help; the kingdom developed a rudimentary Chancellery of its own, where standards of correspondence quickly rose, and the missionary's local political importance accordingly decreased. At the same time, a new cleavage opened up—no longer that between Christians and pagans, but one of an entirely new kind, the rift between government officers and 'educated natives'. Coillard himself saw this quite clearly and became convinced that Coryndon, though personally a likeable man, was full of the most bitter aversion for Litia, the king's Christian son, because 'Litia is a Christian',[1] that is to say a man of education. After Coillard's death in 1904 the rift between the Mission and Company widened further, for the Administration owed no debt of gratitude to Coillard's successors, whilst at the same time the Company's older pro-Barotse policy was gradually modified.

In North-Eastern Rhodesia the process of establishing European control proceeded somewhat more quickly. The Yao slave traders in adjacent Nyasaland were gradually mopped up in a series of small campaigns and the slave-routes across Central Nyasaland were closed. In 1894 the Protectorate Administration peacefully took over Jumbe's country on the west coast of Lake Nyasa, the local chiefs not being opposed to the British like the Zanzibari party. A year later Johnston was able to turn his attention to the 'North End' Arabs, having by now convinced himself that his former pro-Muslim policy was mistaken, that the East Coasters were the backbone of the slave trade and could not be turned into peaceful agricultural producers, only Jumbe being a genuine colonist.[2] A sea-borne expedition was launched against Mlozi's stronghold, and after heavy fighting, his fortifications were stormed, and Mlozi was captured, tried and hanged.

Johnston's victory profoundly affected events in Northern Rhodesia. The North Nyasaland route was now blocked, and the tribes inland were deprived of their supplies of guns and gunpowder, their isolation becoming even more complete as the result of German operations in Tanganyika and of the Belgian advance into the Congo. The Bemba were impressed by the British victory, but could not agree on a concerted course of policy,[3] their kingdom perhaps not having been as rigidly centralized in the first place as subsequent observers have assumed.

In April 1896 J. M. Bell, one of the Chartered Company's 'Collectors', was informed that an Arab caravan was on its way to Chitimukulu, the Paramount chief of the Bemba; Bell hurried after it, and having overtaken it on the Chozi River, attacked and dispersed the Muslims, two of their principal leaders being killed.[4] In June John A. Drysdale, another Company official, was able to report

[1] F. Coillard to K. Mackintosh: 3 Oct 1899 (in CO 5/1/1/1, f. 1656–1663, Nat Arch MS)
[2] H. Johnston to Foreign Office: 20 Feb 1892 (in F.O. 84/2197)
[3] Report by J. M. Bell: 16 Jan 1896 (in A 6/2/2, Nat Arch NER)
[4] Report by J. M. Bell: 24 Apr 1896 (in A 6/2/2, Nat Arch NER)

from Ikawa the breaking up of a caravan bound for the Bemba country[1] and in July he pursued another beyond the Songwe River, liberating 35 slaves and seizing 1,000 lb of ivory.[2] The Arabs reacted by forming a temporary alliance between three prominent Muslim leaders, Kapandasaru, Mana Matondo and Chalooma, who combined with a group of Bemba against Chiwala, a Nsenga chief who enjoyed British support. Robert ('Bobo') Young, another of the Company's 'Collectors', quickly marched to Chiwala's help with fifteen native policemen. The Bemba failed to take the village and Young constructed a 'crow's nest' in a tree, doing heavy execution amongst the Arabs stockaded in their 'town,' which was then captured and burnt; Young was soon reinforced by Drysdale and their combined forces marched to Chalooma and Dakara, two further Arab strongholds which they destroyed.[3] The Nsenga, who had been compelled to grow grain and collect ivory for the Arabs, were released from their bondage, the last caravan in their country being dispersed in March 1898.[4] Arab influence in North-Eastern Rhodesia came to an end, never to revive again. The Muslims (very few of whom were pure-bred Arabs) had not been in the country long enough either to make any real impact on the culture of the indigenous people or to promote the spread of Islam, as in parts of Nyasaland. A few East Coasters remained as settlers, but the majority made their way back to the coast, their real home, and Arab political power became a thing of the past.

The destruction of the trade in ivory, slaves, powder and guns, in turn struck a fatal blow to the position of the more powerful indigenous kingdoms which had to some extent become economically integrated with the Muslim regime. The Arabs' most important trading partners in the country were the Bemba and their Lunda kinsmen on the Luapula, both of whom soon found that their political fate was also sealed. The Bemba, though highly organized politically, were economically weak. Theirs was a poor country, dry and harsh; they had almost no cattle; and unlike their neighbours, the cattle-keeping Mambwe, the Tabwa salt-makers and the Fipa iron-producers, they were dependent on raiding if they wanted a surplus for trade.[5] War became a major industry, so much so that a man's rank came to depend on the number of heads cut off from the bodies of his enemies.[6] The Bemba, however, failed to back up the Arabs when they still might have done so with some success, and what was worse from their point of view, they failed to maintain any sort of political cohesion in the face of the advancing Europeans. This was in the first place

[1] Report by A. Drysdale: 25 June 1896 (in A 6/2/2, Nat Arch NER)

[2] Report by A. Drysdale: 26 July 1896, enclosure in A. Sharpe to Foreign Office 4 Nov 1897 (in F.O. 2/129)

[3] Report by C. McKinnon: 10 Oct 1897, enclosure in A. Sharpe to Foreign Office: 21 Dec 1897 (F.O. 2/129)

[4] H. C. McKinnon to Capt. Daly: 14 Mar 1898 (in A 6/2/2, Nat Arch NER)

[5] Wallace, L. A. 'The Nyasa-Tanganyika plateau' II (in *Geographical journal*, v. 13, no. 6, June 1899, p. 595–621)

[6] Von Wissmann, H. *Meine zweite Durchquerung Äquatorial-Afrikas.* Berlin Globus Verlag 1907 p. 254

perhaps due to the fact that they learnt a hard lesson when in 1893 they attacked Hermann von Wissmann, the German Commissioner for East Africa, who inflicted a crushing defeat on one of Chitimukulu's raiding parties,[1] a feat of arms which so worried Johnston that he despatched Hugh Charlie Marshall to the Tanganyika Plateau to keep an eye on affairs.[2]

The Bemba, however, came to be faced with more than just German magazine rifles. As the result of missionary endeavour, they also found themselves confronted by a great Christian organization, endowed with discipline, drive and enthusiasm of formidable proportions. This was the Society of the White Fathers, founded in 1873 by Archbishop (later Cardinal) Charles Martial Allemand Lavigerie. Lavigerie, later the leader of the *ralliés*, those Catholics who were willing to abandon the cause of the Bourbons and 'rally' behind the middle-class Republic, was a keen supporter of French colonial expansion which he believed would spread the Gospel. He was also in favour of Leopold's schemes to open the Congo and strove to co-ordinate his mission work with Belgian efforts.[3] From the Congo his interests were drawn to Central Africa and the White Fathers then made an attempt to set themselves up in Nyasaland. This was unsuccessful and in 1891 their mission, largely for political reasons, was ordered to move over towards Lake Tanganyika. The White Fathers then established themselves amongst the Mambwe who welcomed them, but their site on the caravan route, with a floating population of Africans, possessed many disadvantages, and the Fathers decided to move further inland. In 1895 Makasa, a provincial governor of Chitimukulu's, gave them permission to build a station in country conquered from the Mambwe, and the Fathers set up a mission at Kayambi. Makasa was one of Chitimukulu's sons, and under the Bemba matrilineal system he was therefore not entitled to advance in the traditional Bemba hierarchy.[4] In the face of the European advance he tried to make himself independent of his overlord, and resisted all pressure from Chitimukulu to get rid of the whites. All the same, the White Fathers' position was an extremely dangerous one, and they were very lucky in having a very remarkable man for their leader. Bishop Joseph Dupont, a peasant's son like his compatriot Coillard, was outstanding for his moral and physical courage; he also had an inborne gift for dealing with African tribesmen, and when he established his station at Kayambi, Bemba warriors flocked to his 'court' as if he were a great chief. Dupont quickly acquired an astonishing reputation as a great hunter and wielder of magic, and his fame grew apace. In 1897 he made an expedition to Mwamba, a powerful chief in the Bemba hierarchy, but his mission failed, partly as the result of Arab intrigue against him. In 1898, however, Dupont received another invitation from Mwamba who by now had fallen very ill and wished to be cured by the strange and powerful medicine man from beyond the seas. Dupont was

[1] H. von Wissmann to H. Johnston: 14 July 1893, enclosure in H. Johnston to Foreign Office: 31 Aug 1893 (in F.O. 2/54)

[2] H. Johnston to Foreign Office: 14 Sep 1893 and enclosure (in F.O. 2/55)

[3] Clarke, R. F. *Cardinal Lavigerie and the African slave trade*. Longmans, Green and Co., 1889

[4] See Brelsford, W. V. *The succession of Bemba chiefs*. Government printer, Lusaka, 1944

unable to save his patient's life, but was able to gather Mwamba's followers around him, who acknowledged Dupont as their chief. The precise circumstances under which this happened are not quite clear, but according to the White Fathers' own account, the followers of the defunct chief feared the Royal Clan of the Bena Ngandu, who were in the habit of slaughtering a deceased lord's retainers. Dupont, however, took over the government, judged cases, warned the surrounding Bemba chiefs from invading 'his' territory, and restarted farming operations; it seems unlikely, however, that he also assumed the ritual functions of a chief, for at the end of the following year Mwamba's body still remained unburied and was finally handed over to the Bemba Paramount. Dupont also got Mwamba to make over to him the whole of his country and the rights in the soil.[1] This meant that at a critical moment in Bemba history, when only concerted resistance on the part of the whole tribe could have held up the advancing Europeans, the most powerful vassal of the Bemba state passed under European influence without a shot being fired. From then onwards, the remaining areas were taken over with negligible bloodshed. The only serious trouble arose when in March 1899, Ponde, a rival chief, advanced into Mwamba's country to claim the headship; Ponde built himself a fortified stockade, but was quickly driven out by McKinnon and a small force of 60 native policemen. Mporokoso, another Bemba chief, was also subsequently forced to submit. The administration then appointed a new chief, who was installed on condition that all blood sacrifices would end and mutilations cease. The White Fathers were forced to relinquish their political and territorial claims, but received five square miles of land for mission purposes.[2] In 1899 the White Fathers transferred their work to Luombe to which they gave the name of Kilubula, the name of their previous station at Mwamba's kraal. Dupont, who became involved in friction with the Administration over the question of land rights, was, much to his chagrin, transferred from the Bemba country, where he had wielded so much moral and political influence.[3]

The destruction of Arab and Bemba power left Kazembe's state isolated, and the Lunda community on the Luapula now constituted the last remnant of an older political and commercial system which depended on a partnership between indigenous rulers and Muslim slave traders. The river kingdom was still a relatively formidable one. Kazembe's town, with a population of some 20,000 people,[4] constituted the largest settlement in British Central Africa, and its economic resources were considerable; the fertile Luapula valley provided fine crops of manioc, millet, maize and beans and there was plenty of fish, so that Kazembe's people had provisions all the year round. The Paramount himself traditionally owned various salt deposits, and ever since the eighteenth century

[1] A. Sharpe to Foreign Office: 10 Mar 1899 and enclosures (in F.O. 2/208)

[2] Report by E. Codrington: 4 Sep 1899, annex. 13 to minutes of 13 Dec 1899 (in LO 1/2/1, Nat Arch MS)

[3] He subsequently became the first Vicar Apostolic of Nyasa and died in 1930. For details of his career, see Pineau, H. Évêque roi des brigands. . . . Quebec, Les Pères Blancs, 1949.

[4] A. Sharpe to Foreign Office: 29 Dec 1899 (in F.O. 2/210)

had been conducting an extensive trade in slaves, ivory and malachites in exchange for cloth and guns.[1] The commerce was conducted through Muslim intermediaries, the proceeds from trade and tributes being passed on to his vassals, so that the Lunda chief, like the Barotse Paramount and indeed like all Central African potentates, appears to have acted as a 'distributor-king' whose power depended on a complex system of internal exchange that ran without money.

Kazembe's community was also militarily strong. Victor Giraud, a French naval lieutenant who visited the country in 1883, was impressed by the fortifications of the settlement which consisted of a high stockade a thousand yards long, strengthened by a nine-foot deep trench. The stockade was entered by three defended gates, one of which opened onto the river, so that there was never any shortage of water, even in the event of a siege.[2] Kazembe, described by Giraud as a cruel and despotic ruler, was sufficiently confident of his power to refuse to have anything to do with the Europeans; at the same time he gave passive support to the Bemba and Arabs by giving shelter to refugees from Mlozi's fortress, to Bemba raiders and to Arab and half-caste traders on the run from the Company's forces; he also continued to raid the surrounding areas, and even attacked villages in the vicinity of Kalungwishi station. But his foreign policy was inconsistent; opposition against the Europeans made no sense unless the Lunda were willing to ally themselves with the Bemba and Arabs whilst these were still holding out against the Europeans. Kazembe, however, preferred a policy of armed neutrality with the inevitable result that, once the Bemba and Arab menace were removed, the Administration turned against the Lunda state itself.

For this task the Chartered Company's local forces were inadequate, and the Company then called on the Nyasaland administration for help. A striking force consisting of 13 Sikhs, 70 native troops and 100 Chartered Company native civil police, strengthened by a field gun and a machine gun, was then despatched to the north under the command of Captain E. C. Margesson, the expedition reaching Kalungwishi in October 1899.[3] Kazembe appears to have been surprised by the strength of the expedition sent out against him and evacuated his stockade without fighting, taking refuge across the Luapula River in Belgian territory. Negotiations were then started through the British Plymouth Brethren's Mission in the Congo, and Kazembe was assured that if he voluntarily returned, no harm would befall him. The Chief, who was now rapidly being deserted by his followers, was only too glad to make peace on these terms, and the Company's authority henceforth went unchallenged in his country.

In the meantime action was also taken against Mpeseni's warrior kingdom in the vicinity of present day Fort Jameson. This branch of the Ngoni, a patri-

[1] Lacerda, F. J. M. de. *The lands of Cazembe* . . . , translated and annotated by R. F. Burton. John Murray, 1873, p. 125–126, 232

[2] Giraud, V. *Les lacs de l'Afrique equatoriale.* . . . Paris, Librairie Hachette et cie, 1890, p. 369–372

[3] A. Sharpe to Foreign Office: 29 Dec 1899 (in F.O. 2/210)

lineal, cattle-keeping people, maintained few contacts with the Arabs and did not form part of the Bemba-Lunda-East Coast trading system. They rarely sold slaves and only had a few guns, but all the same, their *impis* were a terrible menace to their neighbours. 'The Ngoni used to come when the grass was long', related an elderly Lala from the Luano Valley, 'sometimes we were warned by the drums in the next village and then we fled and hid ourselves in caves in the hills. At other times we knew nothing until we saw the heads of their spears in the long grass. They killed all the old people and the children and took our young men and women'. The raiders, having struck with the leopard's silent swiftness, would retreat along hidden roads previously prepared through uninhabited country, and disappeared with their victims into the forest, where pursuit was impossible.[1] The captives were absorbed into the tribe so that the old Ngoni blood soon became greatly diluted with Chewa, Senga and other stock. In addition the Ngoni accumulated great herds of cattle, the only 'interest-bearing' investment available to a tribal community, and they were thus able to maintain a standard of living appreciably higher than that of the surrounding communities.

For a while the Ngoni were saved by their isolation. They refused to make treaties with either Thomson or Sharpe, and for a time negotiated with the Portuguese, the conversations being conducted through Carl Wiese, a daring German-Jewish adventurer, who married a black Portuguese wife from the Zambezi valley and, like Westbeech in Barotseland, built up considerable local influence through armed native retainers; Wiese was more than a filibuster, he understood something of finance and wrote on Ngoni ethnography. The Anglo-Portuguese agreement of 1891, however, placed Mpeseni's kingdom into the British sphere. Wiese, who had obtained a vast concession from Mpeseni, now left for Europe where he tried to turn his claims into cash. The search for financial support ended in February 1893 when the Mozambique Gold Land and Concessions Company Limited was incorporated in London to make use of Wiese's concessions, for which the German was paid £1,500. The British South Africa Company, however also advanced claims to the region and in support produced treaties concluded by its emissaries with other chiefs. After lengthy negotiations, agreement was reached between the Mozambique Company and the Chartered Company. On 8 May 1895 the Mozambique Company was granted mineral and land rights in a block of ten thousand square miles within Chartered territory, a huge area which included the Ngoni kingdom, and a new Company was formed known as the North Charterland Exploration Company in which the Chartered Company was to hold shares to the value of £300,000 out of a total capital of £1,000,000.[2]

The North Charterland Company was founded on the misconception that there was plenty of gold in Mpeseni's country, and the Directors expected quick results. In the same year the Company thus sent out an expedition under Lieu-

---

[1] Bradley, K. 'The turn of the tide' (in *The African observer*, v. 5, no. 2, June 1936, p. 31–32)
[2] A. Sharpe to Sir P. Anderson: 9 July 1895, and enclosure (in F.O. 2/89)

tenant-Colonel Wharton, formerly the secretary of a cricket club, whom Johnston considered to be neither a 'very capable nor a very prudent man'. Johnston,
not always a friendly judge of his fellow men, may not have fully appreciated
Wharton's difficulties, but in any case Wharton could not make much headway.
Mpeseni did not object to gold mining as such, but soon friction arose between
some of the prospectors and the Ngoni, whilst Wharton made things worse by
quarrelling with Mpeseni, who would neither abstain from raiding, permit taxes
to be raised, nor accept a British flag.[1]

The Protectorate Administration, however, was now ready to take a strong
line with the chief. In 1897 Johnston explained to the Foreign Office that
Mpeseni was nothing but an immigrant robber, that his country was both
healthy and auriferous, and that it was situated on a strategic route from British
Africa to Tanganyika. What was worse, Mpeseni was under the influence of
Wiese, a 'conscienceless and intriguing German'; sooner or later Mpeseni had to
be dealt with for he was now the only powerful and avowedly recalcitrant chief
left in British Central Africa.[2]

On the Ngoni side, Mpeseni appears to have opposed war, being well aware
of British military superiority. The war-party was led by Nsingu, the Paramount's son, who spoke for all those who considered that fighting was the only
occupation fit for a Ngoni, and who became commander-in-chief when the
Ngoni took to arms. In December 1897 word arrived in Nyasaland that Wiese,
now an employee of the North Charterland Company, and F. C. Worringham,
one of the Chartered Administration's local Collectors, were in imminent
danger from the Ngoni; Alfred Sharpe, Her Majesty's Commissioner for the
Protectorate, then offered help to Captain Henry Lawrence Daly, who in 1897
had succeeded Forbes as Acting Administrator for the Chartered Company's
territory north of the Zambezi. Daly accepted the offer with alacrity and on 29
December a detachment consisting of 15 Sikhs and 80 Africans was ordered to
proceed to the small settlement of Fort Jameson (not identical with the present
township) to draw off Mpeseni's forces.[3] In addition further troops were collected for the main thrust. On 4 January Lieutenant-Colonel William Henry
Manning, the Acting Commissioner, heard that Wiese was safe and stopped the
further advance, but was unable to contact the Fort Jameson party which was
now out of reach. On 10 January word arrived from Cummings that Mpeseni
was massing his troops, that an attack on Fort Jameson was likely, and Manning
therefore ordered the campaign to be resumed, arguing that the time had now
come to crush the Ngoni once and for all.[4] The operations were commanded by
Captain H. E. J. Brake who had 50 Sikhs, 4 African companies, 2 seven-pounders
and 2 maxims at his disposal. The Ngoni were able to mobilize about 10,000
warriors and should have been able to do some execution in the unmapped,
roadless and wooded country through which the British forces were advancing,

[1] Memorandum by H. Johnston: 14 June 1896 (in F.O. 2/107)
[2] H. Johnston to Foreign Office: 6 Feb 1897 (in F.O. 2/127)
[3] A. Sharpe to Foreign Office: 30 Dec 1897 (in F. O. 2/129)
[4] W. Manning to Foreign Office: 13 Jan 1898 (in F.O. 2/147)

especially at a time when the rains were falling and the ground swampy.[1] Brake's straggling column, consisting of some 350 soldiers and 200 porters provided plenty of opportunity for flank attacks and there were moreover a good many suitable defensive positions which they might have used. Ngoni leadership was, however, quite inadequate both from the strategic and the tactical point of view; the Ngoni, used only to sudden forays against weaker tribes, had failed to study the problems of a defensive campaign against a well-armed enemy, despite the fact that the military lessons of the Matabele War and the Matabele Rising should have been familiar to them. Their best chance would probably have been to try and massacre the Protectorate forces through a swift and silent night attack, in which case the Ngoni weight of numbers would have been overwhelming, Ngoni veld-craft and knowledge of the local terrain would have counted, and the British would not have been able to use their artillery and deadly smokeless automatic fire to their best advantage. As it was, the Ngoni fell victim to the cult of cold steel, and preferred to charge in close formations during broad daylight, relying on the thrust of the stabbing spear. The result was a foregone conclusion, for the smokeless rifle and particularly the Maxim gun had by now become supreme in the battlefield, lances and bayonets largely having lost their usefulness.[2]

The story of the military operations is quickly told. Captain Brake arrived at Loangweni on 19 January 1898. He was then met by a strong force of Ngoni who collected in a village near the Fort. The Protectorate troops attacked in four companies, opening fire at 100 yards and, in the face of their silent and disciplined advance, the Ngoni fled. Subsequently the Ngoni delivered another attack in their traditional semi-circular formation but they were bombarded by the British seven-pounders at a range of 1,200 yards, the artillery preparation being followed up by automatic fire from the maxims and a counter-attack. The Ngoni, who had never encountered weapons of such a kind before, showed considerable courage but could neither face volleys nor charges at close range. There was some subsequent fighting, more Ngoni concentrations being broken up and further villages burnt. On 25 January the British forces reached Mpeseni's town, where Brake was reinforced three days later by a further three companies of British Central African Rifles and the remaining Sikhs.[3] There were a few additional clashes but Ngoni moral was now cracking; Nsingu was captured on 4 February, sentenced by Court Martial for raiding into British territory, and shot on the following day, his death representing the first and last political execution in Northern Rhodesia under British rule. Mpeseni subsequently surrendered and was later permitted to settle in his old district. The Protectorate forces also captured a considerable amount of cattle. Much of this was later returned to Mpeseni, the question of the loot becoming the subject of an acrimonious dispute which found its way into the columns of *Truth*, a Radical journal

[1] Report by Capt. Brake: 20 Jan 1898, enclosure in W. Manning to Foreign Office: 17 Feb 1898 (in F.O. 2/147)

[2] The maximum throwing range of an assegai was about 70 yards.

[3] W. Manning to Foreign Office: 17 Feb 1898, and enclosures (in F.O. 2/147)

edited by Henry Labouchere, the well-known English Radical and humanitarian, who bitterly criticized the Chartered Company, without however going
into the question of the Ngoni's own title-deeds to the land and cattle in their
possession!

It is possible that the Ngoni war might have been avoided, just as there was no
Bemba war. The Ngoni settled in Northern Nyasaland were after all peacefully
absorbed into the European system, but in Northern Nyasaland there were no
prospectors; there were no reputedly auriferous regions; and there were
European missionaries willing and able to act as a buffer between the Administration and the tribesmen. In North-Eastern Rhodesia, on the other hand, the
Administration was willing for a 'show-down' and the *Central African Times*, the
organ of the colonists in Nyasaland, itself expressed some sympathy for the
Ngoni, arguing that no Europeans had actually been massacred, that nothing
specific had been said about Nsingu's crimes of raiding and that a great deal of
public sympathy had therefore been alienated from the expedition.[1] But war or
no war, the Ngoni state had to go; a military community in which each generation of leaders needed to glorify themselves in battle, had become an anachron-
ism under the changed conditions of life, and the prohibition of raiding would in
any case have struck at the roots of the State, both socially and economically.
War, followed by the confiscation of cattle and the destruction of the large and
densely populated villages, made the transition more painful. Yet even had there
been no European intervention, Ngoni military society was too unstable to
survive. According to Professor John A. Barnes, Ngoniland at the time of
conquest had become far too densely populated for the carrying capacity of the
land, the large Ngoni villages being appropriate only to a victorious warrior
society relying for at least part of its subsistence on raided crops and beasts
produced outside its borders. 'It is certain that in pre-conquest times the Ngoni
were settled at a density even more in excess of the critical value than it is now,
despite alienation . . . and the state was exhausting the wealth of its neighbours',
so that Ngoni society could not for long have continued to exist without either
making new conquests or breaking up.[2]

This campaigning had a profound over-all effect on the country. From the
soldier's point of view, the skirmishing that took place on the Nyasa-Tanganyika
plateau during the late 'nineties is of but little interest. But as far as the local
tribesmen were concerned the whole pattern of their lives was altered. Raiding
ended; the slave caravans disappeared and the blood-curdling Ngoni war song
'Chenjera! Adza Kaluangwe! Moto! Moto!—Beware, the hawk comes, Fire!
Fire!'—no longer rang through the northern veld. The stronger tribes were
reduced to political impotence, to the level of their erstwhile victims, and
European supremacy was assured.

Particularly hard hit were the Ngoni. Defeat did away with the traditional

---

[1] *Central African Times*, 12 Mar 1898, p. 4
[2] Barnes, J. A. *Politics in a changing society*. . . . Cape Town, Oxford University Press, 1954, p.
104–105

manner of recruiting the tribe and with the accustomed military hierarchy wherein a man could only make his name by means of taking prisoners in battle. The Ngoni moreover lost much of their cattle, a great many more beasts being sold to European traders after the campaign was over, and the tribesmen were in despair. This interfered not only with the traditional livelihood but also with the ancient institution of giving cattle as 'bride wealth', a major feature in Ngoni culture.

The warlike Bemba were not affected to the same extent, for the bridegroom in Bemba society did not pay beasts, but used to work for his parents-in-law for a number of years, sometimes residing permanently in the village where his wife was born. But Bemba society too was changed by conquest which did away with much of the chiefs' former punitive powers. 'The cruelty hitherto practised by the Awemba, not only towards captive slaves, but towards free-born men of their own tribe, is incredible. The number of mutilated people is enormous. In nearly every village are to be seen men and women whose eyes have been gouged out; the removal of one eye and one hand is hardly worthy of remark. Men and women are seen whose ears, nose and lips have been sliced off and both hands amputated. The cutting off of the breasts of women has been extensively practised as a punishment for adultery but . . . some of the victims of these atrocities are mere children . . . indeed these mutilations were inflicted with the utmost callousness; every chief for instance has a retinue of good singers and drummers who invariably have their eyes gouged out to prevent them from running away'.[1]

At the same time, the chiefs' military functions disappeared and so did the trade in guns. Strict control over firearms was gradually established by the Administration[2] and European military supremacy made secure. This of course did not mean that guns disappeared from the native village; on the contrary considerable numbers remained in African hands, but powder became more expensive and better weapons hard to acquire, whilst the guns that remained in the African hut were inefficient, and no match for magazine rifles. They ceased to have major military significance, becoming a kind of investment for people without cattle, something that could be used as dowry or pledges, for hunting or as a symbol of prestige to its owner.

The suppression of raiding and of the slave and gun-trade also proved decisive in the economic field. The weaker races found safety, and the terrible drain on their man-power disappeared; the period of vast tribal migrations came to an end so that the geographical position of the tribes became more stabilized. Within a village community, however, there was greater mobility. The tribesmen were no longer forced to live together in comparatively large stockaded villages, constructed with an eye to defence as much as for farming, so that cultivators were enabled to spread out further afield in search of better land and pastures. The government officials disliked this process, arguing that the natives became

[1] Codrington, R. 'Report by the Administrator of North-eastern Rhodesia for two years ending March 31st, 1900' (in British South Africa Company. *Reports on the administration of Rhodesia, 1898–1900*, p. 68)

[2] Government notice no. 4 of 1901 (in *British Central Africa gazette*, v. 8, no. 1, 31 Jan 1901, p. 6)

more difficult to control as a result of this dispersion, but the villagers probably gained, for safety from the raiders meant perhaps that they could look further afield for land and springs, and utilize their country's resources more effectively.

As far as the Europeans were concerned, economic penetration became possible for the first time on a large scale. The only white men who fitted easily into a tribal community were men like Carl Wiese or J. Harrison Clark ('Changa Changa') an adventurer from Port Elizabeth, who made himself chief in the Feira district, traded in ivory, married the daughter of a local Chikunda chief, raised a little army of native retainers and levied tolls and taxes in his domain. But the days of these colourful adventurers, European, Arab or half-caste, were now ending. Wiese became an employee of a land company and Harrison Clark, characteristically, ended up as the first beerhall manager at Broken Hill mine.[1] Mining, farming, and trade on a larger scale required very different conditions, which could only be brought about by conquest so that 'prospectors no longer had to be called in whenever Mpeseni had a bilious attack'.

Pacification was of even greater importance in the field of labour relations and racial contacts in general. The disappearance of the Arab slaver and his native auxiliary put an end to the slave trade, Africa's primary form of labour-migration, with all its attendant savagery and blood-shed. The interests of European employers, anxious to secure hired hands for their railways, mines and farms, prevailed over those of Arab clove-planters, and of half-caste lords in the Zambezi valley. The slave trade in Harry Johnston's words, represented 'a different type of civilization'. The Arab and Mulatto slave owner, however cruel and depraved he might be, did not stand apart from the black man to the same extent as the European. For slavery itself was an institution that allowed of an infinite number of gradations between slave and free. 'That gaily-dressed man with riches of cloth for exchange is a slave', wrote E. C. Hore, a Protestant mariner, describing the settlement of Ujiji on Lake Tanganyika, 'and the poor woman who has brought her basket of meal into market to sell looks up to him in awe and envy as she walks past with her companion who carries her wares and is *her* slave . . . you may see a gang of poor creatures (newly captive) chained together in their misery; at another, a party of poorly-clad native porters carrying loads, and led by an amply-dressed and armed superior, who is, however, a slave, while they are free hired labourers'.[2] Assimilation was made easier still by the Mohammedan religion which allowed polygamy, a form of marriage which the African practised himself, and the Arabs, though by no means devoid of colour feeling against the Africans, thus tended to merge imperceptibly into the indigenous population, especially as they had no women of their own in the interior. The European conqueror's outlook however was different. He paid wages, and relied on voluntary recruitment. But at the same time he segregated his labourers,

[1] Brelsford, W. V. 'Harrison Clark: king of Northern Rhodesia' (in *Northern Rhodesia journal*, v.2, no. 4, 1954, p. 13–31)
[2] Hore, E. C. *Tanganyika: eleven years in Central Africa*. Edward Stanford, 1892, p. 73–74

with whom he had nothing whatever in common. Two different systems of society were in conflict, neither of which could peacefully co-exist with the other for any appreciable length of time; conflict was inevitable, and the more efficient and, for all its aloofness, the more humane of the two carried the day.

In the political sphere, pacification permitted of a more effective administration which in turn required a firmer legal framework than the one established under the African Order in Council, 1889. North-Eastern Rhodesia, militarily and economically dependent on the British Central Africa Protectorate was treated in a different manner from the north-western portion which was only accessible through Southern Rhodesia. The Colonial Office argued that the same system of dealing with the natives and the same legal system prevailing in Nyasaland should also be introduced across the border in Company territory, whilst the indigenous chiefs should be permitted to dispense justice 'as far as possible in accordance with their own laws'; English common law was to prevail, rather than Cape law as demanded by the Chartered Company.[1] Negotiations on these lines continued all through 1899, and in the following year the North-Eastern Rhodesia Order in Council, 1899, passed onto the Statute Book.[2]

The new Order was modelled on the Southern Rhodesia Order in Council, 1898. It gave considerably greater powers to the Company than it possessed in North-Western Rhodesia, where the Imperial Government was more anxious to have a greater say by reason of the unresolved Portuguese boundary dispute and the existence of a relatively strong native kingdom with recognized treaty rights. The linch-pin of Government was the Administrator, the 'Lord-High-Everything', as he sometimes became known to local residents, the Administrator being appointed by the Company subject to the Secretary of State's approval; provision was also made for the appointment of an Administrator's Council, when the Company's Board so desired, though no use was ever made of this clause in practice. The Administrator was empowered to make Regulations for 'the administration of justice, the raising of revenue and generally for . . . peace order and good Government', but not for any subject connected with the raising of a military police force. All his Regulations had to be approved by Her Majesty's Commissioner for British Central Africa and were subject to disallowance on the part of the Secretary of State. The Commissioner himself could moreover initiate legislation by means of instruments known as 'Queen's Regulations', which the Queen could disallow, and the Commissioner remained in control of any military police force. In addition a High Court of North-Eastern Rhodesia was set up which was to administer English common law, except in so far as it was modified by local legislation, the Judge or Judges being appointed by the Company subject to the Secretary of State's approval. Minor matters were dealt with by Magistrates' courts, the Magistrate being appointed

---

[1] Colonial Office to Foreign Office: 4 Mar 1899 (in *Further correspondence. . . .* African (South) no. 574)
[2] North-Eastern Rhodesia order in council, 1899 (in *British Central Africa gazette*, v. 7, no. 5, 31 May 1900, p. 1)

by the Administrator with the Commissioner's consent. Native Commissioners and Assistant Commissioners also owed their appointment to the Administrator, subject to the Commissioner's sanction.

The Company was enjoined to assign sufficient land to the natives for their use 'suitable for their agricultural and pastoral requirements, including in all cases a fair and equitable proportion of springs or permanent water'. At the same time Africans were allowed to acquire and sell land on the same conditions as Europeans, though land sales were not to be recognized unless sanctioned by a Magistrate, who had to satisfy himself that the native understood the trans-action and got a fair price for his land. The Order also made it clear that 'no conditions, restrictions, shall without the previous consent of the Secretary of State be imposed upon natives by Regulations which do not equally apply to persons other than natives, save in respect of firearms, ammunition, liquor, or any other matter in respect of which a Secretary of State, upon the recommenda-tion of the Administrator thinks fit to authorize any Regulation'. As far as native jurisdiction was concerned, the Order stated that in civil cases between Africans the High Court and the Magistrates' Court were to be guided by native law in as far as this was not 'repugnant to natural justice or morality' or to any recognized legislation; polygamous marriages according to native law were to be regarded as valid. All legislation was similarly to respect native law and custom, provided it was not 'incompatible with the due exercise of Her Majesty's power and jurisdiction'. The jurisdiction of indigenous chiefs, which was still continu-ing did not, however, receive any official sanction; native law could not be codified, so that the last word on what did or did not constitute indigenous law remained with the European Magistrate, or with the Native Commissioner, who himself was given magisterial powers by the Administrator. The purely econo-mic clauses of the Order were very simple. Customs duties might be levied but were not to exceed the tariff in force in the South African Customs Union, whilst the Company's mineral rights were specifically recognized.

v

The establishment of administration north of the Zambezi

The Orders in Council, passed at the end of the century, provided a general framework for a new administrative system. But much hard work on the spot still remained to be done, the changeover from the old order being symbolized in the career of Robert Edward Codrington. Codrington was born in 1869 into an old Gloucestershire family which had long been imbued with a strong naval tradition. He was educated at Marlborough College, but instead of entering the Royal Navy, he went to Virginia for a time; later on he made his way to Africa where he joined the Bechuanaland Border Police, that great 'prep school' for Central African administrators where his colleague Coryndon also saw service.

Codrington's promotion was quick and by 1893 he was already a Sergeant-Major; during the Matabele War the twenty-four year old soldier participated in the advance from Tati into Matabeleland, where he was wounded in an ambush. Codrington subsequently left the police and in 1895 he became Collector of Revenue in Johnston's pioneer administration in Nyasaland. His new superior had very strong views about the type of people whom he wanted to serve under him; in the early days Johnston was forced to employ a motley crew, big-game hunters, former employees of the African Lakes Company, and a few ex-Indian army officers; but he showed a strong preference for men with Indian experience rather than what he called 'local adventurers', and in 1895 he asked the Foreign Office to take over the selection of candidates, suggesting that they should select the sons of Consular and Diplomatic officials,[1] not applicants from self-governing colonies 'without a proper governing class'. He was particularly anxious not to have South Africans whom he regarded as 'without any conception of justice where natives are concerned.'[2] Johnston got his young upper middle class Englishmen, but he soon found, that though he could get youngsters to come out for very little money, just to see the country, he could not keep them without decent salaries and pensions, especially at a time when the mortality in British Central Africa was still frighteningly high. Therefore from 1897 a regular Civil Service was set up with a system of recognized grades and a settled system of promotion, all candidates having to start as Assistant Collectors, an arrangement which gave permanency to the service but prevented the rapid rise of keen young people to top posts as in the early days.

Codrington did well under Johnston; in 1896 he helped to defeat Gomani's group of Ngoni and received their formal surrender, symbolized by the handing over of twenty-nine stabbing spears. In 1897 he went home on leave. Here he appears to have met Rhodes who was favourably impressed by Codrington. In May 1898 he left for Africa to take up his new appointment as Deputy Administrator of North-Eastern Rhodesia, his predecessor Forbes having been forced to resign on grounds of ill health. The young Deputy Administrator was at first still hamstrung at every turn. For a time he continued to reside in Blantyre, and as long as he was dependent on military help from the Protectorate, he had of necessity to play second fiddle to the British Central Africa administration. Effective pacification, however, changed the picture, and in October 1898 a site was selected at Kapatamoyo's kraal, which became known as Fort Jameson, the name being taken from another station previously established twenty miles to the north.[3] Building operations started in April 1899; the new post became the capital of the territory, where Codrington took up permanent residence; in

---

[1] H. Johnston to Sir C. Hill: 8 Oct 1895 (in F.O. 2/89)

[2] Sir H. Johnston to Lord Salisbury, enclosure in Sir H. Johnston to Foreign Office: 31 May 1897 (in F.O. 2/128)

[3] See Barnes, J. A. *Politics in a changing society*. . . . Cape Town, Oxford University Press, 1954, p. 84. The name was applied in 1896 to a camp at Chinunda's and possibly from October 1897 to another at Mafuta's; from December 1897 to March 1898 again to Chinunda's, and from October 1898 to Kapatamoyo's. In 1902 Fort Jameson was declared a township.

August 1900 he was promoted to full Administrator under the North-Eastern Rhodesia Order in Council.

Codrington's first job was to put Fort Jameson into some sort of order. Brick and iron dwelling houses were put up, and within a few years Fort Jameson developed into a trim little township, with attractive houses and trees, and possessed of a pleasant little hospital as well as a communal centre, known as the Queen Victoria Institute, which served as a library and meeting place for the small population of officials and planters. There were no white workers about; Codrington with his tiny budget preferred to employ African mission-trained artisans and clerks from Nyasaland, so that the whole atmosphere of settlement resembled that of the Protectorate, with its white middle-class society of civil servants and planters, who looked to England as their home, where they would retire when their careers had come to an end.

Codrington's next job was the organization of a local civil service which was taken in hand on Johnstonian lines. Codrington shared his former chief's dislike of local men and asked for young recruits from England, with a middle class background, good physique and education, giving special preference to University men with teaching experience, locally known as 'bum-switchers'. Codrington himself, tall and commanding of presence, with a neatly clipped moustache and military bearing, gruff of speech but with a strong sense of fair play, was just the sort of man who would have made a stern but respected headmaster in a British public school, and it was the schoolmaster's rather than the soldier's outlook which he brought to Northern Rhodesia. Company rule, he argued, was based on prestige, for the amount of military force available was very small; the natives moreover were but children, an interpretation well in tune with the views of social and biological evolution current in late Victorian England. Codrington therefore thought that officers who could produce testimonials as disciplinarians over British boys, would do equally well as district officers in remote outstations.

The new Administrator also understood the importance of bureaucratic method and of treating his staff well, and in 1901 he set up a graded Civil Service,[1] designed to provide an administrative career for recruits who normally had no other source of income. The Company was by no means satisfied with these arrangements which involved fixity of tenure and the payment of pensions, but Codrington had a way of getting what he wanted from his Directors—more so than Coryndon—and his scheme was adopted, the Company benefiting in the end by obtaining a good type of man. At the same time Codrington, with his almost fanatical belief in efficiency, purged the service of all people who did not live up to his own ideas of what a good official should be like, and no matter how well a man had done in the past, he was axed when his work suffered. Perhaps the most tragic case was that of Dr A. Blair Watson, a medical man who,

---

[1] R. Codrington to B.S.A. Company: 23 Nov 1900, annex. 9 to minutes of B.S.A. Company: 30 Jan 1901 (in LO 1/2/10, Nat Arch SR) and Government notice of no. 1 of 1901 (in *British Central Africa gazette*, v. 8, no. 1, 31 Jan 1901, p. 1)

like Codrington himself, had first joined the Nyasaland administration. Watson rose to be Magistrate and District Commissioner for the Mweru and Luapula Districts, but in the loneliness of his little kingdom he fell victim to the morphia habit. He was removed from the North-Eastern Rhodesian administration in 1904 and 'given another chance', but unable to get rid of the habit, he shot himself.

North-Eastern Rhodesia from the administrative point of view thus began to develop on lines very different from those of North-Western Rhodesia. A greater proportion of the officials in North-Western Rhodesia possessed previous experience of South Africa or Southern Rhodesia, where a regular civil service on Cape lines was set up in 1898. Some of these men started as labour agents, others had been policemen in the British South Africa Police or clerks in the Southern Rhodesian service. There was at first no established civil service in the North-West, for the Company preferred to engage its officials on contracts like commercial employees, being unwilling to pay for an established civil service until it had wrested full control of the Administration from the High Commissioner. The results were unsatisfactory, for there were frequent resignations and much discontent amongst its officials.

In the military sphere there was a similar contrast between the two territories. North-Western Rhodesia, the northward extension of Southern Rhodesia, originally employed European police from the south, and Coryndon's small escort consisted of troopers from the British South Africa Police. This tiny force was largely 'for show', but the position became more urgent when reports began to reach the Company that white ruffians were making their way across the Zambezi to steal cattle from the natives under the guise of trading; in 1898 a British South Africa Police detachment was therefore sent to Monze's kraal in the Tonga country.[1] A year later building work was begun at Kalomo, but European policemen soon proved too expensive; they were always liable to become ill, whilst their skill as horsemen was of little value in an area badly infected by the tsetse fly. In 1901 the European police force was replaced by a black one, known as the Barotse Native Police, of which Colin Harding became the first Commandant and which began its career with five Europeans and 71 native policemen, later being increased to a strength of a few hundred men but with a good stiffening of European non-commissioned officers. In North-Eastern Rhodesia public safety depended on the North-Eastern Rhodesia Constabulary, a force consisting entirely of native N.C.O.s with just a European Commandant and Quartermaster. By 1904 the force comprised some 500 men, recruited almost entirely from Ngoni, Bemba and Lunda people, the erstwhile 'military races', who possessed a warlike tradition. For whatever the law said, the Company's police was in effect a military rather than a civil force, a characteristic which it shared with other early police forces in the colonial territories; the native constables were drilled, armed, and commanded by experienced soldiers, and could be considered as second-rate troops, suitable for bush-

[1] High Commissioner to J. Chamberlain: 18 Jan 1899 and enclosure (in *Further correspondence*. . . . African (South) no. 574)

H

fighting though not for a European campaign. Their function was to enforce the Native Commissioner's orders; they carried out extensive patrols, were available for guard and escort duties, but they received no training in how to get to know the criminals in their area, or its officials and residents; and being illiterate they could not be taught how to use an entry-book, that essential tool, which is to the policeman what the rifle is to the soldier. The policeman was thus necessarily far removed from anything like the London 'Bobby'; and all he could do was to maintain the district officers' authority and the Company's prestige. Real authority remained with the civil administration, and the Company's rule was thus profoundly unmilitary in character. The policeman could never become an instrument of tyranny, for the whole of Northern Rhodesia was held down by a force that never exceeded 800 men, supported only by unarmed messengers. Whether he liked it or not, a Native Commissioner thus had to use a great deal of circumspection and rely on the help of local chiefs, unlike say, his German colleague across the Tanganyika border who was able to rely on much stronger military backing.

The process of extending European rule through the territory was usually fairly simple. A caravan was collected, consisting of a hundred or more native porters who enlisted for a short spell to earn some calico and get regular meals of venison; some were detailed to carry bales of cloth and beads, the precious currency on which the traveller was dependent inland; others picked up the tents, kitchen utensils, camp furniture and medicine chests, all carefully packed into loads weighing 40 to 60 lbs, which the carriers skilfully balanced on their heads. In addition there was usually a small bodyguard of native police, armed with Snider rifles, a tough crew who needed constant watching to prevent them from looting or getting hold of the village girls. Then the expedition would slowly make its way to its destination, travelling perhaps between twelve and fifteen miles a day through the bush. On arriving at his destination, the Native Commissioner built a small station of wattle-and-daub huts; the Company flag, with its lion rampant grasping an ivory tusk—the 'dog and bone' as it was called—was hoisted from a tree above. Then the new Native Commissioner would receive a deputation of local chiefs. The scene has been graphically described by John Edward ('Chirupula') Stephenson, a former postal official who in 1900 was appointed an Assistant Collector in North-Eastern Rhodesia and sent to the Lala country together with Francis Emilius Fletcher Jones. The chiefs and their people assembled in a great half-circle; Jones stood up and addressed them through his capitao, an English-speaking African. 'Tell them, tell these great ones of the Lala nation', he said, 'that we come from the Great White Queen. We are fresh from conquering the Angoni. We have three things to say. First, in this country there shall be no more war. Secondly, in this country there shall be no more witchcraft. Thirdly, in this country there shall be no more slavery. In regard to all other things, men shall do as they have done, and as their fathers have done before them'.[1] There was no reference to any treaties past,

[1] Stephenson, J. E. *Chirupula's tale.* . . . Geoffrey Bles, 1937, p. 62–63

present or future, but the Lala were impressed by the white man's guns. From the Lala point of view, there was of course nothing whatever objectionable about Jones's speech. Wars had indeed ceased and the Ngoni were no longer roaming through the land; witchcraft, that evil consequence of wicked actions or a depraved heritage, would of course go on as long as there was a cause for bewitching people, that is to say, as long as human nature remained what it was; still—if the white strangers thought they could introduce a new moral order, they could but try. The prediction that there would be no more slavery was also a pious hope; for bondsmen usually were convicts or men captured in war, and the absence of slavery thus implied to the Lala that in future quarrels, disputations and litigation would all cease, an improbable contingency, but one which no sensible man could reasonably oppose.

Gradually a network of stations was extended right through North-Eastern and North-Western Rhodesia, the process reaching completion in the years that preceded the First World War, when the remote Lunda country in the north-west was opened up.

Chapter Three

The birth of a new economy

I

Labour and taxation

The prediction, so confidently made by Francis Emilius Jones that men would continue to do as their fathers had done and their fathers' fathers before them, was not borne out by the facts. For the Native Commissioner's remote little 'boma' became itself a centre of social change. The new official's first task was to assert his authority and drive out such undesirables as Mambari ivory and slave traders, who were still coming in from the west. Their caravans were gradually checked by the setting up of police posts and by patrols, work often carried out with the active support of the local population. In North-Western Rhodesia the task was made particularly easy by co-operation from the Barotse whose state was based on the interchange of goods between the fertile flood plain and the surrounding bushland; their economic system was comparatively complex and needed a large number of different tribes with different skills to keep it going. The Barotse valley moreover was not densely populated and it was preferable to import labour. More important still was the fact that when ivory became exhausted, the country found a new source of wealth in its cattle. The export of stock became profitable when the great Rinderpest epidemic of 1896 wiped out most of the herds of European farmers and African pastoralists in Southern Rhodesia; Barotseland was fortunately spared this disaster, and from 1897 traders from Bulawayo, many of them Eastern European Jews, made their way to Barotseland, where they found no difficulty in buying stock. The Barotse did not then possess the institution of 'bridewealth', based on the exchange of cattle for women, and stock thus had less emotional significance for them than it did say for the Zulu. The traders used to take their wares by ox-wagon to the Zambezi, the wagoner, a highly skilled man, usually being an Afrikaner. Then the trader went up the Zambezi by canoe, on an uncomfortable and often dangerous journey. He bought his cattle, paying due regard to the royal right of pre-emption, and the herds were driven down to Bulawayo, the whole journey taking seven months. The trade was very risky; there was blackwater fever; lions would prowl round the traders' encampment at night, and the stock might be attacked by crocodiles when they were driven across the Zambezi. But profits were high and some of the traders made their fortune. As far as the Barotse were concerned, they welcomed the strangers from the south, and the old commercial bonds with the west largely disappeared. The Angolan slave-trader, once a prominent figure in many parts of North-Western Rhodesia, was gradually driven out, the liquidation of the Mambari being simplified by a Portuguese expedition against the Bailundu state which took a major part in the traffic. In 1904 Portuguese engineers started constructing a railway line from the West Coast to the regions inland, and the steam engine in time did away with the need for slave porters; lastly more effective steps began to be taken against slavery by the Portuguese authorities themselves, when Portugal became a republic in 1910.

Once the Native Commissioner's word had become supreme in his district, taxation could be introduced, and soon the tax receipt became an even more potent instrument of social change than the gun. From the Company's point of view taxation was an administrative and fiscal necessity. The whole theory of Company government was based on the assumption that Chartered rule could be turned into a profit-making institution; the so-called commercial revenue of the Company was derived from land sales and from investment in shares, especially railways, as well as from mining royalties, the Company constituting a kind of sleeping partner in the work of other mining companies whose work it encouraged. In addition the Company maintained a separate administrative revenue derived from customs duties, native taxes, postal rights, timber revenue and other sources. The administration of an under-developed country, however, was a much more expensive job than the Company had anticipated; Rhodesia was starting from scratch; all the institutions possessed by older countries such as transport and educational services, hospitals, roads, railways, and telegraphs, had to be built from nothing; there was little capital and less skill; and with its huge area and small population, the country resembled a firm with enormous overheads and a tiny turnover, so that no possible source of revenue could be neglected.

This was true even of Southern Rhodesia, a comparatively well established territory, where it was only in 1906 that there was for the first time a small excess of administrative revenue over expenditure. In Northern Rhodesia the position was even worse from the Company's point of view. The resources of the territory were little developed, and as late as 1911, when most of the Africans were already being taxed, the two administrations north of the Zambezi were running up a deficit of some £54,000 on a combined income of £95,000. These shortfalls had to be made good from the Company's commercial revenue, which were derived largely from Southern Rhodesia, a policy that did not appeal to the Company's 40,000 shareholders for the sake of whom the whole venture existed, and who constituted quite a powerful pressure group overseas. There was moreover little likelihood of any other income being developed from the north, for the European settlers were far too few to make anything from land sales. Direct taxation of Europeans was not resorted to until after the Great War, for the Company wished to attract colonists, and taxation would merely have kept them out.

The question of taxation in turn was closely linked to the labour problem, for the need to earn money for tax was one of the most important incentives to induce Africans to take up paid employment. All the white immigrants needed African labourers to a greater or lesser extent. The Administration itself was always in need of carriers, and if the Africans were unwilling to work they had at times to be forced to do so. In a report to Captain Daly, a District Officer by the name of McKinnon stated that where local resistance was great, compulsory labour in the early days was sometimes enforced by the burning down of huts and similar measures which unsettled the districts. Once tax was introduced, however, people would know where they stood, and the white residents thus advocated a tax that would compel natives to work regularly for a few weeks in the year. In any case the Imperial Government detested any kind of obligatory labour, and taxation would avoid it.

The local settlers were also in favour of taxing the Africans for they would then be more ready to work. Taxation, moreover, affected the colonists south of the Zambezi. From about 1900 onwards there was a considerable increase in the output of gold there, and farming had received an impetus with the creation of markets in the mine townships and with the influx of settlers after the Boer War, when many ex-soldiers came from South Africa. All these new immigrants desperately needed labour. The small workers who played such an important part in gold mining could not afford much equipment, and in any case machinery was often uneconomic owing to the vast distances over which it had to be transported. Moreover, the farmers did not enter the country with the intention of becoming peasants working with their own hands. They acquired estates, but too often lacked capital to buy machinery. Many were ex-officers or ex-officials whose savings and farming experience were often very limited, while the poor Afrikaans immigrants were even less able to afford labour-saving devices. Many of these immigrants, who were always faced with the counter attractions of prospecting, transport riding or hunting, did not always handle their labour well. Indeed there was 'an immense wastage of labour . . . largely, if not entirely, due to inefficiency'. In any case the African workmen, used to a different kind of life, were themselves generally incompetent; their wants were few, their treatment often poor. They returned to the village after a few months usually without acquiring any great skill. Southern Rhodesia complained of an everlasting shortage of native labour and was prepared to employ any black man asking for a job. The opportunities for earning tax money were there, and money taxation was thus a feasible proposition. The Chartered Company was bound to regard the settler demands with sympathy; it relied for its income mainly on the sale of land and royalties in mining ventures, and its financial interests were thus involved in the fate of miners and farmers. Nevertheless it should be made clear that taxation in the north was not imposed mainly with a view towards helping the south; the southern need for labour provided the opportunities for earning the tax money, but it was not the main reason for its imposition. Whilst taxation was being considered for Northern Rhodesia, the Southern Rhodesia Chamber of Mines demanded, not migrant tribal labourers coming out of their villages for a few months to earn their tax money and buy a blanket before returning, but a 'non-spasmodic supply' of permanent wage-earners, who would not retain one foot in the tribal economy. Between 1900 and 1905 the Company therefore made great efforts to find such labour, scouring the world from Aden to India, from China to Abyssinia, in a recruiting campaign that would have made Rhodesia a sociologist's paradise and a politician's hell, had it succeeded. All these attempts, however, failed, though neither the *Bulawayo Chronicle* nor the *Rhodesia Herald* seriously raised the cry for Northern labour at that time.

Lastly the Imperial Government was interested in the matter. Having entrusted Northern Rhodesia to the Company in order to avoid taking over further commitments itself, it did not wish to embarrass the Company. In any case the principle of taxing the Africans was not in dispute; it was an accepted means of policy; the African should pay for the protection he received, and he should take part in the development of his country, and not 'idle' about in the villages. Every South African territory taxed its natives. The only question at issue was the amount to be paid. The Imperial Government acted as a constant restraint on the Company, preventing it from raising imposts to too high a level, determined that tax must only be paid if accepted by Africans without serious reluctance and that in North-Western Rhodesia tax should only be imposed with the consent of the Barotse king. Critics might even argue that the Imperial Government actually made the work of the Company easier by preventing the pressure from becoming too heavy, thus avoiding African unrest and saving the Company from increased expenditure on its police force.

Native taxation was introduced in North-Eastern Rhodesia in 1900. It was enforced almost at once over most of the Territory. In North-Western Rhodesia taxation was first authorized a year later, but delayed at Rhodes's request till the Administration was established. Tax was gathered from 1904, but its collection was enforced gradually, following the general economic development of the country, beginning in the Victoria Falls and Tonga country, spreading to the 'Hook of the Kafue', and finally to the mineralized regions of the north. By 1913 even the remote Lunda paid their dues.

The new tax was enforced most easily amongst people with a strong tribal organization as well as recent memories of British military power, such as the Bemba, the Ngoni, and Kazembe's people; these people were easier to rule once conquered, and this fact may be linked to the general British preference for 'martial races'. The Barotse too possessed an efficient internal organization. They were, however, in a somewhat privileged position compared with the others in view of their treaty rights. Their cause was further strengthened by a visit which Lewanika paid to England in 1902 in order to attend the coronation of Edward VII. Lewanika had long wished to go overseas, a project which the missionaries disliked as they feared that it would diminish their own influence over the king. In 1902 Lewanika was able to carry out his plan and the Barotse king, with his excellent manners, aristocratic bearing and shrewd realism, made a favourable impression on the Colonial Office. The Chief himself was by no means entirely satisfied with the conversations held on the subject of the hut tax and the Portuguese boundary dispute; but all the same he was deeply impressed by the enormous crowds, the massive buildings and the boundless size of London, the railways, the huge grey ships and the massed British regiments, so that he returned determined—come what may—to stand in well with the Imperial power, his awe-struck accounts seeming so improbable to some of his subjects, that they thought the whites must have dazzled their king with magic mirages. From the Barotse aristocracy's point of view, co-operation was of course the only policy that would bear dividends, and at the insistence of the Colonial Office the Barotse received ten per cent of the tax collected in the area which Lewanika claimed to be under his suzerainty. The Barotse Paramount thus became the only chief in Northern Rhodesia who held a considerable financial stake in the collection of the tax. He failed to put into effect his plan to collect the tax on behalf of the Company through his own *indunas* (officers) a project which would almost have made his chiefs a part of the Government bureaucracy. Nevertheless though he lost the old tribute in kind which he once received, he remained a wealthy man as compared with all other chiefs in Northern Rhodesia. It is thus not surprising that the Administration found no great difficulties in collecting the tax, especially since they attempted to use the Barotse system of administration, as they understood it, for the purpose. The more 'difficult' tribes were those which lacked a strong central organization. Amongst these were the Senga, the Bisa, the Lenje and the Aushi, the latter being particularly hard to deal with as they lived in swampy country, difficult of access. The Tonga tribe on the other hand were an exception. They paid readily, despite the fact that they had no tribal organization. However, they had been utterly crushed by a long series of raids against them and they were geographically near to the labour centres of the south where they had long been drifting in search of work. Resistance to the introduction of the tax was only encountered amongst two peoples, the Ila and the Western Lunda. Neither of the two tribes liked to work in Southern Rhodesia. Both had warlike traditions, engendered by long periods of internecine warfare and by their prowess as hunters, whilst the Lunda possessed the tradition of the Mwata Yamvo Empire to sustain their pride.

But resistance was nowhere successful, for there was not really much the Africans could do about the new imposition. The punishment for failing to pay the tax was to have one's hut burnt down, an action admittedly not as drastic as it would appear, for African huts are rapidly and cheaply built. All the same, tax-gathering expeditions were a distasteful business to Collectors and subjects alike. 'I remember at Mukonchi's village, one of the princesses proved obdurate', relates J. E. ('Chirupula') Stephenson. 'She said she saw no reason on earth why she should give me money: and I said I would burn her house down if she didn't. We were both obstinate: and so the firebrand was laid to the thatch, and sure enough the hut went up in flames—after a gentleman friend had removed most of her goods to safety'. The princess was even more surprised than she was indignant but paid up in future, a poorer but wiser woman.[1] Not all the Company's

[1] Stephenson, J. E. *Chirupula's tale.* . . . Geoffrey Bles, 1937, p. 227–228

officers were as philosophical about the matter as 'Chirupula' and in 1906
Colin Harding, the Commandant of the Police left the Company's service after
a sharp dispute about tax enforcement.[1]

Punitive measures of the severer kind were subsequently discontinued, but
taxation itself became a regular and accepted feature of village life. The tax was
levied as a money tax on each adult male and also on each wife except the first
one. In North-Eastern Rhodesia it stood at first at 3s. In North-Western Rhodesia it varied initially between 5s. and 10s. depending on the district, and was
finally unified at 10s. for the whole of Northern Rhodesia in 1914. Although
tax was by no means excessive by South African standards, it constituted a
revolutionary innovation. Before the coming of the Europeans many tribes had
indeed paid tribute—but tribute was rendered in articles in which the country
was rich, and could often be evaded. White administrators in fact envisaged
native tax as the equivalent on a month's tribute labour given to chiefs, and tried
to make the yearly tax equivalent to one month's pay. The new obligations,
however, could not usually be met from local resources. Payment in kind was
theoretically legal, but the tax-payer was responsible for transporting the goods
to a usually non-existent market. The Administration had no wish to be saddled
with a lot of unsaleable stock or grain and adopted the same policy as Southern
Rhodesia, where payment in kind was abolished in 1895. By 1905 the tax was in
practice collected everywhere in cash only; from the point of view of the Company the results were successful, for between 1910 and 1911 the income from
African tax amounted to over £57,000 out of a total income of £95,000 for the
two northern administrations.

Taxation had major effects on tribal life. There were too few Europeans to
employ all tax-payers locally, and when some officials attempted to provide
employment in lieu of taxation, the Imperial Government, fearing forced labour,
stepped in. In any case the Administration could not have given employment to
all, and migration to Southern Rhodesia became a permanent feature of tribal
life. In theory the tax could be earned by working only a fortnight in Southern,
or a month in Northern Rhodesia for wages. These calculations, however, took
no account of travelling time, of the dangers and risks of traversing lion-infested
country or seeking shelter amongst strange and sometimes hostile villagers, nor
of the fact that the migrant could not save all his pay. Besides, it was quite impossible for every man in the village to undertake an annual journey, for there
was much work which women could not do, and every tribesman was expected
to bring back enough money to pay the tax for some of his kinsmen. This meant
that the journeys away from the village became lengthier and lengthier, and
large numbers of young men were away from their homes throughout the
year.

In discussing labour migration, it should be stressed that taxation did not
constitute its original or indeed its only cause. Taxation only speeded up a
process that had already begun. In the 'eighties already 'Zambezi boys' were

[1] Harding, C. Far bugles, 2nd ed. Simpkin Marshall, ltd, 1933, p. 141

travelling to the distant diamond fields of Kimberley; the Tonga began to work in the south at about the turn of the century, and in Barotseland during this period a missionary could already remark that 'the aristocracy of clothes was replacing the nobility of blood'. But taxation gave an enormous impetus to migration; it created a regular instead of a seasonal demand for cash, and extended this demand over the whole of the territory.

As far as the actual recruitment was concerned, the Native Commissioner's hands were tied. He was not allowed to sign on Africans, and in 1901 the Colonial Office even threatened to deprive the Company of its administrative powers in Southern Rhodesia, if official pressure on Africans did not stop. Recruitment in Northern Rhodesia was thus left to private touts, but some of these were undesirable characters who lured away ignorant villagers with lying promises, and their work was to some extent taken over by a state-approved Native Labour Bureau, constituted in Southern Rhodesia in 1903. As the result of pressure from the Chartered Company, recruitment for the Transvaal stopped in North-Western Rhodesia and the Bureau for a time gained a local monopoly.

The effects of the Bureau's work were twofold. On the one hand it is probable that the monopoly of recruitment enabled the Bureau to keep down wage rates by keeping competitors away; this at any rate is what the Bureau's Northern Rhodesian Manager himself believed to be happening. The Bureau moreover imposed a uniform head-charge and laid down uniform rates of pay, almost no attempts being made at grading labour. This policy may well have discouraged employers from offering incentives in the form of higher wages to good men for outstanding individual performances. On the other hand the Bureau could afford to look after its recruits better than private touts were able to do; it established a country-wide network of recruiting centres and rest houses; it distributed blankets and food, and maintained a staff of responsible persons, so that Africans soon became used to going down to work without waiting for the recruiters.

Conditions in the early days were bad, and the newly mobilized labour force suffered heavy losses. On the way down to the mine the individual tribesman might be attacked by wild animals, get lost or be assaulted by men from other tribes. Even the introduction of railway transport did not at first improve things. 'During the cold season horse boxes are used and the natives are packed together without the slightest consideration of their comfort or welfare...', wrote a Northern Rhodesian Government official who accompanied one of the gangs down from Kasempa. 'The natives who have to sleep close to the open sides of the boxes must, during the night ... catch their death of cold, as they are packed so closely that they are unable to move, there being not sufficient room'.[1] Once the new recruit had arrived on the mine he found himself in a new kind of community where the compound manager was boss, where tribal distinctions counted for nothing, and life was hard. The sudden concentration of

[1] W. Frykberg to F. V. Worthington: 1 July 1910 (in A 3/18/20/2, Nat Arch SR)

workers, labouring much harder than they had previously done, under strange conditions, living in overcrowded quarters with poor ventilation, promoted the spread of dysentery and pneumonia. Some of the larger mines provided buildings of wood and iron, and also proper latrines, but many of the 'raw' workers preferred to live in huts and seek out the long grass rather than the latrine. This sort of thing was all right in a small native village, but when many people were crowded together water supplies were infected, flies contaminated the food and dysentery followed. At the same time the workers' resistance suffered. The usual diet at the time was 3lb of maize a day, supplemented by some canned meat and sometimes a ration of beans, groundnuts and pumpkins. The workers were unable to get fresh meat, or the customary herbs and green plants which they used at home for a relish, and were soon attacked by scurvy, which together with pneumonia became the scourge of the compound.[1] The result was a very high death-rate, which amounted to 42·68 per thousand between the years 1907 to 1908 for North-Western Rhodesian Africans on the Southern Rhodesian mines. In 1912 the total death-rate rose to 65·43 per thousand, but then a sharp decline set in, the death rate dropping to 20·93 eight years later. Many factors were responsible for this success. Pressure was exercized on individual mines, both by the Northern Administrations, and by the British South Africa Company which approached the London offices of some of the offending concerns. In addition the Southern Rhodesian Administration itself began to issue regulations for the care of mine workers, ensuring the appointment of qualified mine managers on large mines, medical supervision, regular inspection by government officials, better sanitation, housing and an improved diet. In 1913 this early social legislation was tightened up by empowering the Government to limit hours of continuous employment of miners, the number of labourers on one shift, and the number of blasting shifts. The railways improved the transport facilities with the result that mine work became more popular, so much so that now the farmers began to complain that they could no longer compete with the mines for African labour.

As far as the individual migrant was concerned, the journey to the south became an event in his life. His wages might be low, but they did enable him to buy consumer goods such as pots and pans, clothes, blankets and such like which his own people did not produce at home. In the opinion of many Government officials, the migrants also acquired greater initiative and new tastes, but also much more critical opinion of their tough-fisted European foremen and shift-bosses, with the result that they were often inclined to 'leave their country to seek employment as ignorant and tiresome children but return offensive and often rebellious men'.[2]

The social effects of labour migration were far-reaching. As early as 1908 the Rhodesia Native Labour Bureau recruited 6,831 workers from North-Western

[1] Gelfand, M. *Tropical victory.* . . . Cape Town, Juta & Co. Limited, 1953, p. 134
[2] Statement by Col. C. Harding to the Native Labour Commission, Johannesburg: 6 Aug 1903 (in *Further correspondence.* . . . African (South) no. 717)

and 2,404 from North-Eastern Rhodesia, these figures rising sharply during the following years; the Labour Bureau statistics moreover took no account of those men who went independently; their number must have been high for the number of Africans ferried across the Zambezi at Feira alone amounted to 7,921 in 1908. The development of the copper resources of the Katanga also led to a demand for Northern Rhodesian labour there, and many Africans from the Luapula and Bemba regions crossed the border. As conditions on the mines improved, and as Africans became more familiar with the wage system, the number of labour migrants rose sharply with the result that many native villages became denuded of their men. In 1913 a District Commissioner in the Mpika district complained about the effects of this process in terms reminiscent of those used by trained anthropologists in the 'thirties. Bembaland, the District Commissioner argued, was being turned into a hungry rural annexe to the mining townships, for the exodus of labour left insufficient manpower for local needs. The departure of so many able-bodied people to the south left their dependants inadequately provided for, with the result that those who stayed behind had to work harder.[1] Other officials complained that adultery was growing in the villages, that Government officials could no longer get the labour they required, and that some of the migrants preferred not to come back at all, becoming 'lost ones' to their own people.

The effect of this migratory movement was of course not quite the same in all districts. Bembaland was particularly hard hit for the Bemba method of agriculture depends on a type of slash-and-burn cultivation where branches are cut off trees to a considerable height and then dragged into the centre of a clearing, where they are burnt to make seed beds where millet can be grown. The soil of the country is poor and this means that a new patch of trees must be pollarded every year if fertility is to be maintained. The work of cutting down branches up to a height of 20 or 30 feet high is one that requires great skill and daring; it cannot be done by women, children, or old men, the people who stay behind in the village. When farming has to be done by these people without the help of the strongest and most agile men in the village, the results are disastrous, for existing plots have to be worked over and over again, so that the yield from the country's poor soil falls rapidly. There are other tribes where the effects of labour migration are not quite so severe. The Mambwe neighbours of the Bemba occupy grassland and also have cattle. In order to grow their main crops, they put grass into the centre of mounds where it rots to form a rich humus. This sort of work can be done without the help of tough youngsters, so that agriculture is not affected to the same extent by labour migration.[2] The position may have been similar amongst the cattle-keeping Lungu south of Lake Tanganyika who proved keen students of missionary methods of farming, many native converts adopting the use of manure and the European manner of laying out gardens in

[1] Report by District Commissioner, Mpika, for 1913 (in KSD 4/4/1, Nat Arch NR) Compare with Richards, A.I. *Land, labour and diet in Northern Rhodesia.* . . . Oxford University Press, 1939
[2] Watson, W. *Tribal cohesion in a money economy.* . . . Manchester University Press, 1958

beds, as well as the cultivation of wheat and vegetables taught by L.M.S. Missionaries.[1] The effects of labour migration could, to some extent, also be overcome by the introduction of labour-saving devices, such as the plough, introduced to the Ila by the Primitive Methodists, and to the Tonga by the Jesuit Fathers. The Jesuits showed their pupils how to break in their oxen and how to yoke them together, so that hoes became unnecessary for the purpose of turning the sods, and much more land could be cultivated by far fewer people.[2] The Barotse, with their much more diversified system of agriculture, also appear to have made various innovations, and in 1910 a missionary doctor was able to write from Sesheke that grain was now being cultivated on a considerable scale for export to Livingstone.[3] But all the same, these cases were exceptions. Methods improved little; the labour migrant never lost his rights to the land; he could always return to his village where the chief remained under an obligation to allot new gardens to him, with the result that the old ways continued, whilst the great majority of migrants had little incentive to make themselves more efficient at their work in the town which, like many other peasants overseas, they regarded at first as a supplementary and not a full-time occupation.

The effects of labour migration were also far-reaching in other ways. Taxation and wage employment soon struck a major blow at the Barotse aristocracy, who depended for their income on the labour of their serfs, and who in the past obtained man-power from their outlying provinces by means of human tribute and raids. The first inroad into the institution was made by the Barotse themselves when in 1894 Lewanika, partly acting under missionary influence, freed all slaves who could prove that they were of Barotse descent and whose relatives were prepared to pay the required ransom.[4] The arrival of Coryndon aroused great hopes amongst the slaves that British rule would bring about their liberation, but Coryndon at first did nothing, except to stop further raids. The next step was taken by the missionaries, who from 1900 attempted a new policy of preaching the gospel to slaves, a course of action entailing house-to-house evangelization which was thoroughly disliked by the king and chiefs alike.[5] The subsequent establishment of British control over the Tonga country did away with human tribute from this region, whilst the loss of Lewanika's western dominions to Portugal in 1905 further reduced the area of Barotse tributary serfdom. Serfdom, or domestic slavery as it was commonly known, finally came under direct fire from the Administration. Bondsmen would not work for wages

---

[1] London Missionary Society. *Second decennial report: 1890–1900*, and Wright, S. *Annual report: Niamkolo*, 28 Dec 1906 (L.M.S. Arch)

[2] Casset, A. 'The Chikuni Mission' (in *Zambesi mission record*, v. 4, no. 49, July 1910, p. 92–94). See also unpublished mss. by Fr. Moreau on his experiences in Northern Rhodesia, kept at Chikuni mission, Northern Rhodesia.

[3] Reutter, G. 'L'oeuvre religieuse, sociale, scolaire et médicale à Sesheke' (in *Journal des missions évangéliques*, 1911, p. 67)

[4] Jalla, A. *Pionniers parmi les Ma-Rotse*. Florence, Imprimerie Claudienne, 1903, p. 224

[5] F. Coillard to K. Mackintosh: 18 June 1900 and 22 Sept. 1900 (in CO 5/1/1, f. 1758–1761 and f. 1799–1804, Nat Arch MS)

enabling them to pay their taxes if their earnings were confiscated by their masters; it was obvious moreover that the serfs could not at the same time perform corvées and go down to Southern Rhodesia for work.[1] These arguments gradually began to make some appeal to Lewanika and the Ngambela, his Christian Prime Minister, who were both anxious that taxation should be started, and they themselves began to preach the Christians' new gospel of work.[2] The Barotse aristocracy moreover feared that, if they did not abolish the institution themselves, receiving some compensation for doing so, the slaves might just run away, and the chiefs get nothing at all.[3] As far as the slaves themselves were concerned, they welcomed the prospect of liberation; tribal 'feudalism' possessed no charms whatever for the under-dog, and according to missionary evidence at the time, it was the slaves who were least worried about the introduction of taxation, a measure otherwise feared by everyone in the land. After lengthy negotiations Lewanika in 1906 issued a proclamation abolishing the institution, subject to various safeguards for the nobility. Slaves were permitted to buy their freedom for £2. 0. 0. each; all children born of slaves after the Proclamation were declared free; compulsory labour for the Paramount continued, but was reduced to a maximum of 12 days a year, all additional labour having to be paid for at the current rate of 5/– a month.[4] The new Proclamation thus did not abolish slavery all at once; there were still certain restrictions on freed slaves, but all the same a major blow was struck at the Barotse structure, the political change involved owing much to the diplomacy of a Coloured journalist from South Africa named Peregrino, who helped Worthington to get Lewanika's reluctant consent to the Proclamation.[5] Once the new measure was passed, many people left their former residence and the Barotse chiefs were often forced to do their own work.[6] Some tried to get out of their difficulties by imposing services illegally, in addition to the tax, and their impositions led to more discontent, giving the Administration a further incentive for interference in Barotse affairs to prevent what they held to be injustice. The blow was particularly hard, as the Barotse chiefs could not compete with European wage rates,[7] and as they themselves considered that the loss of their tributary rights was not made up by the money payments received as their share from taxation. The Barotse of course may not have taken account of the fact that their own demands were rising, and that they were now getting accustomed to buying goods like clothes, furniture, sugar, tea and coffee; but

[1] F. V. Worthington to R. Coryndon: 5 Dec 1904 (in A 3/14, Nat Arch NWR)

[2] F. V. Worthington to R. Coryndon: 7 Apr 1905 (in *Further correspondence.* . . . African (South) no. 763)

[3] Memorandum by F. V. Worthington: 27 Nov 1906, annex. 13 to B.S.A. Company minutes: 3 Jan 1907 (in LO 1/2/55, Nat Arch SR)

[4] Proclamation of 13 July 1906 (in *Further correspondence.* . . . African (South) no. 802)

[5] F. V. Worthington to Acting Administrator: 13 July 1906, annex. 20 to B.S.A. Company minutes: 20 Sep 1906 (in LO 1/2/51, Nat Arch SR)

[6] Report by District Commissioner, Lealui: 1906–1907 (in KDE 1/5/2, Nat Arch NR)

[7] By about 1908 wages for miners ranged from between 6/- to 20/- in Northern Rhodesia itself, the minimum wage on the Congo being 10/- a month for underground work, going up to about £1. In Southern Rhodesia higher wages still could be earned, the 'aristocracy of labour' consisting of domestic servants, cooks and certain skilled categories.

all the same there was considerable unrest in the Valley which found expression
in a number of plots against the king, who was forced into yet greater dependence on the Administration.

II

The second wave of missionary enterprise

The consolidation of European influence in the administrative and economic
field was followed by a corresponding increase in missionary activity. Religious
work remained open to the free enterprise of all denominations, whilst the older
establish edcommunities extended their spheres of influence in a kind of ecclesiastical 'Scramble for Africa'. In North-Eastern Rhodesia the main religious,
like the political, impetus, came from Nyasaland. One of the pioneer societies in
the field was the Mission of the Free Church of Scotland (Livingstonia). The
Society was excellently led, relatively wealthy and well organized, its training
institute at Livingstonia becoming a centre of learning which soon attracted
pupils not only from Nyasaland but from North-Eastern Rhodesia. In 1895 a
station opened under the Reverend A. Dewar at Mwenzo on the Tanganyika
Plateau, for the purpose of linking the Mission with the London Missionary
Society's stations on Lake Tanganyika. Work was subsequently extended to the
west, a milestone in the Mission's Northern Rhodesia history being the foundation of Chitambo. The initiative for this enterprise came from the British South
Africa Company, which erected a monument to commemorate the spot where
Livingstone had died, and then marked off a square mile of land around it,
inviting the Livingstonia Mission to take charge of the site and send a medical
missionary to the country. This was agreed to, but the Scots soon found that
Chitambo was too unhealthy, being situated in a marshy and unhealthy spot
where the tsetse fly abounded. In 1908 a more suitable site was selected, situated
about 20 miles away, to which the name of Chitambo was given. Malcolm
Moffat, a nephew of Livingstone's was placed in charge at the Mission. Moffat at
first met with great difficulties, the local people not proving very responsive to
his efforts, the exploitation of minerals at Broken Hill having led to a general
exodus of labour and a sharp rise in local native wages. Moffat, however, proved
to be a good organizer as well as an able agriculturist, and the mission soon
extended its sphere of work.[1]

Further to the south, in Ngoni country, the earliest move was made by the
Dutch Reformed Church. In South Africa, where there was at first almost no
town-bred Afrikaans-speaking middle class of the type which had done so much
for missionary enterprise in Europe, the evangelistic impulse came from the
predikants of the Church who formed a Mission Union whose members agreed

[1] Laws, R. *Reminiscences of Livingstonia*. Edinburgh, Oliver and Boyd, 1934. See also *The Livingstonia mission report for 1911*, p. 45–48

to contribute a fixed sum to missionary work. Gradually the movement gained well-wishers amongst the laity and was able to broaden its financial basis by the formation of laymen's unions, gaining support on a very extensive scale after the tremendous spiritual and national upsurge that followed upon the South African War. In 1885 Dr Andrew Murray, an Afrikaner of Scottish origin, approached the Free Church of Scotland and the Scots agreed to allocate a sphere of work west of Lake Nyasa to the Dutch Reformed Church whose Presbyterian doctrines they shared.[1] In 1897 Andrew Murray wrote to Rhodes asking whether he could work amongst Mpeseni's Ngoni. Rhodes advised him to wait in view of the possible danger of war, and the Afrikaners held back for a time. Had they decided to go ahead, the history of the Ngoni tribe might well have taken a different turning, but as it was the project was only taken up again after Mpeseni had been defeated and imprisoned. Mpeseni then sent a message to the missionaries enquiring whether they would be willing to start work amongst his people. A. C. Murray and P. J. Smit visited the chief in person and having received his approval for a station, Murray gained the support of the Dutch Reformed Church of the Orange Free State to support a mission in Mpeseni's country. In June 1899 the Reverend J. M. Hofmeyr, later joined by the Reverend P. J. Smit, set out with two hundred carriers and founded Magwero station, 12 miles from Fort Jameson. Work was held up by the South African War, but in 1903 the missionaries received strong reinforcements, and the Afrikaners then gradually extended their work towards the west, to the Senga and the Chewa peoples.[2]

The missionary thrust into Central Africa from the east was supplemented by another from Southern Rhodesia. Some of the most outstanding pioneers were the Jesuits who had never abandoned their hope of carrying the Gospel beyond the Zambezi where their first efforts had ended in such grim disaster. By 1902 the Society of Jesus was well established in Southern Rhodesia; and the future looked promising, for the railway from Salisbury to Beira was finished, another line from Bulawayo to the Victoria Falls was being surveyed, whilst help was promised by Rhodes; the Jesuits then decided on an exploratory mission to the Tonga country. The leaders of the expedition were Father B. Prestage, and Father J. Moreau. The missionaries travelled by ox-wagon but when they reached the Zambezi they were forced to abandon their beasts so as not to carry any cattle disease across the river, and carriers were recruited. They received an encouraging welcome from Coryndon, getting much help from Stephen Martin Lanigan O'Keefe, the Secretary of the Administration, and a fellow Roman Catholic. The missionaries proceeded to Monze, who proved very friendly to the Fathers. Monze, a famous Tonga rain-maker, claimed to be Paramount Chief over the whole of the area, though he was quite unable to make good his claims over the scattered and broken Tonga communities. Monze was, however, in

[1] Hofmeyr, A. L. *Het land langs het Meer*. Stellenbosch, Christen studenten vereniging van Zuid Afrika, 1910, p. 119–125

[2] Cronje, J. M. *En daar was lig*. . . . Bloemfontein, Sinodale algemene sendingkommissie, 1948, p. 62–93

close touch with the Administration, and as anxious to change the customs of his people as he was for support from the Administration against European raiders. In 1904, a station was set up at Chikuni, a well populated region where the local African proved friendly; Kasisi mission was opened up in 1907 north of the Kafue River by Father J. Torrend, a famous Bantu scholar.[1]

During the same period another missionary venture was launched from the south into the Tonga country, this time by the Seventh Day Adventists, who had been established south of the Zambezi since 1894. The mission to Northern Rhodesia was led by W. H. Anderson who visited the Tonga country in 1899 but found the indigenous people terrified of Barotse raiders and apt to hide at the approach of strangers. Anderson paid another visit to the country in 1903 and returned in 1905 to occupy a mission station in Monze's country.[2] Both the Jesuits and the Seventh Day Adventists acquired a reputation as fine farmers. The Tonga, who had been broken by a long series of Barotse and Matabele raids, and who had long been used to working in European employment, proved apt pupils, and for long were the missionaries' 'model Africans'.

African labour migration also facilitated the work of the Wesleyan Methodist Missionary Society, which had been established in Southern Rhodesia since 1891. The missionaries there got in touch with the son of a chief from the Luano valley about a hundred miles south-east of Broken Hill, who was working on one of the Southern Rhodesian mines. The young man implored the Wesleyans to send a missionary to his people, and his country was subsequently visited by the Reverend John White. He selected a site and in 1912 the Reverend S. D. Gray went north with two Africans and founded Chipembi station. Work was subsequently extended to Broken Hill and outstations were extended down to the Zambezi, the Wesleyans subsequently linking up with the Primitive Methodists west of the railway line.[3] During the same period the Brethren in Christ Church, another group already established south of the Zambezi, sent up Miss Davidson, together with another lady, who began work at Macha on the Tonga plateau, a further station being subsequently started at Sikalongo.

Missionary penetration into the extreme north of the territory was spearheaded by two Protestant sects endowed with the simple, earnest and sometimes fundamentalist faith that had been so strong in mid-Victorian Britain, but which was by this time almost disintegrating in England. The first mission amongst the Lamba owed its origins to the Nyasa Industrial Mission which had been set up in the Shire Highlands at the turn of the century for the purpose of instructing the Africans in the better cultivation of their soil and in other industries. In 1905 W. A. Phillips and Henry Masters, two Baptist members of the mission, made their way to the Lamba country, accompanied by a number of native Christians from Nyasaland, starting their first station at Kafulafuta. The missionaries

---

[1] *Zambesi mission record*, v. 2, no. 18, Oct 1902, p. 133; v. 2, no. 20, Apr 1903, p. 218–222; v. 3, no. 31, Jan 1906, p. 18–20; v. 3, no. 32, Apr 1906, p. 53–63; v. 3, no. 43, Jan 1909, p. 509–513
[2] Anderson, W. H. *On the trail of Livingstone*. Mountain View, Pacific press publishing association, 1919, p. 200
[3] Smith, E. W. *The way of the white fields in Rhodesia*. . . . World dominion press, 1928, p. 90–91

I

established themselves amongst the scattered and broken Lamba people, their method of approach being of a kind that was already going out of fashion in most of the remainder of the mission field. 'There was a period of great drought' relates one of their missionaries in almost Biblical fashion, 'and the people were in want. They had made offerings to the spirits, and had for days been praying for rain. I was led to put God to the test. Going up to the people and addressing the spirit-medium, I said "We will ask for a sign to prove who is able to give rain, the spirits or God. We believe that God alone can send it, and that it is useless to pray to the spirits. The sign shall be, if rain is sent before the end of this week (this was on Monday) that the spirits have sent it, but if no rain falls until early next week, that shall be the proof that the spirits cannot help you, but that God can". The missionaries beseeched God morning, noon and night that rain might be withheld—and so it was. On Sunday the missionaries called on God once more; all the local chiefs assembled; there was a great prayer meeting, and then the rains came; Jehovah was vindicated, and the missionaries' reputation made.[1] People of a similar stamp were recruited by the South African General Mission which first established itself in Northern Rhodesia in 1910, on the Chisalala stream, where they worked under very difficult conditions.

The pioneering history of missionary enterprise in Northern Rhodesia concluded with the setting up of an Anglican diocese beyond the Zambezi. This was first decided upon in 1907, the new move no longer being motivated by the need for missionary expansion alone, but also by the exigencies of European work. Since about 1905 an Anglican chaplain, supported by the Society for the Propagation of the Gospel and responsible to the Bishop of Nyasaland, was working amongst the small settler community at Fort Jameson. In addition the South African Railway Mission occasionally sent an itinerant clergyman by train to North-Western Rhodesia. The white community apart, there was still an enormous field left amongst the African population, most of whom remained quite untouched by missionary work of any kind. In 1909 a synod of South African bishops thus agreed that the Zambezi was to be the northern limit of the South African Province; work south of the river was to remain primarily 'Colonial', that is to say European in character, whilst to the north the Church was to concentrate on the indigenous population.[2] A new diocese of Northern Rhodesia was founded in the same year under the auspices of the U.M.C.A., but great difficulties were experienced in finding suitable staff. The first bishop appointed was John Edward Hine, a former medical doctor who had taken Holy Orders, risen to be bishop of Likoma and then of Zanzibar, but subsequently resigned owing to health reasons, and returned for a spell of service in Europe. In 1910 Hine arrived in his new diocese, where he only had two ordained European priests, W. G. Webster and A. G. de la Pryme, to help him. The new bishop displayed considerable energy. He carried out an extensive survey of his domain and in June 1910 the foundation stone was laid for a

[1] Masters, H., and Masters, W. E. *In wild Rhodesia*. . . . Francis Griffiths, 1920, p. 198–199
[2] *Central Africa*, v. 27, no. 315, Mar 1909, p. 57

Church at Livingstone. In addition a site was selected at Mapanza in the Tonga country where Webster took over a disused government house. Despite his limited resources Hine also decided to start work elsewhere in his diocese, and on being told by the White Fathers that they would not for the time being expand into the inhospitable and little accessible area between Fort Rosebery and Lake Mweru, a further station was set up amongst the Ushi people 60 miles south east of Fort Rosebery at Ngomba, where the indigenous people proved much more anxious to be taught than the Tonga dwelling round Mapanza station.[1]

Some work was also done at Fort Jameson where the Anglican Church was responsible for a remarkable new departure by appointing an African, the Reverend Leonard Mattiya Kamungu, as its first fully ordained priest in Northern Rhodesia. Kamungu, a Nyasalander, was trained at Kiungani College and subsequently worked at Likoma as an evangelist. In 1902 he became a deacon at Chia where his relatives lived, and he was as it were, 'the product of the Lake-side work of the mission steamer'. He was subsequently sent to Kota Kota where Mohammedan opposition was strong and in 1909, when the Northern Rhodesian mission was formed, he volunteered for work in Nyasaland's 'Far West'. In 1909 he was ordained a priest and placed in charge of Msoro station. A man of stern, unyielding personality and a rigid disciplinarian who was willing to place the exigencies of his Church even beyond those of his clan, Kamungu gained the respect not only of the local Africans but also of European planters; his death in 1913 proved a serious loss to the young and understaffed diocese. In the following year Hine was forced to retire, his place being taken by Bishop Alston James Weller May. May received the remarkable distinction, probably unique in Anglican church history, of being translated to a bishopric after having occupied the lowly office of curate for nearly twenty years in England, his appointment alone providing sufficient indication of the difficulties then experienced by the Anglicans of getting suitable recruits for this remote diocese.

As more mission stations were established in Northern Rhodesia, the problem of the relationship between the different societies became more acute. In the olden days the question had hardly arisen. The different stations were often separated from each other by hundreds of miles of inhospitable country and were able to work in complete isolation. Gradually, however, stations multiplied, sub-stations were set up in charge of native 'evangelists' and teachers, for the missionaries believed in rapid expansion of their work. They cultivated their spiritual acres in as extensive a fashion as the farmers worked their secular ones; and so anxious were they to extend Christianity quickly, that they would rarely confine their efforts to a few selected areas, the tendency being for the man on the spot to demand expansion whilst the Home Committee urged caution. Attack on a broad front, however, necessitated the employment of native auxiliaries who were cheaper to maintain than Europeans and spoke the

[1] *Central Africa*, v. 29, no. 344, Aug 1911, p. 203–205

indigenous tongues fluently. The new policy greatly speeded up the work of evangelization but at the same time encouraged competition between the sects who accused each other of poaching on their chosen preserves. The Administration tried to solve the problem by mapping out 'spheres of influence', a colonial variation of the principle of *cuius regio eius religio* adopted in Germany after the Thirty Years' War. This policy, however, itself became an incentive to occupy the most territory before some other rival could get to work. However sound in theory, it could never be enforced in practice. Protestants might be able to co-operate with each other, as was the case between Scottish and Afrikaans speaking Presbyterians, but Catholics and Protestants could not, since the Catholic Church would not limit its field in the struggle against heathendom and heresy. From about 1905 constant disputes arose between the L.M.S. and the White Fathers and there was also friction between the Dutch Reformed Church and Catholic missionaries in the Fort Jameson region. The position became even more complicated as new societies kept making their appearance in the country. In any case, as Northern Rhodesia developed, some areas became more 'valuable' than others, and it was hardly practicable to give a monopoly of a single township or of an accessible area, served by roads or railway, to just one society. Even had the Company wished permanently to enforce the principle of religious segregation, it could not have done so, for the Charter laid down that 'all form of religious worship or religious ordinances may be exercized . . . and no hindrance shall be offered thereto . . .', and any violation of this provision would have plunged the Company into major political difficulties. The system of establishing 'spheres of influence' thus gradually fell into disuse, and by the time the Company abandoned its rule north of the Zambezi it had completely disappeared.

Despite the friction that arose from competition, there was nevertheless also a good deal of co-operation between the different societies, personal relations between the ministers of differing sects being sometimes much friendlier than those between servants of the same Church. Co-operation was first placed on an institutional basis when the first General Missionary Conference for Northern Rhodesia was held at Livingstone in 1914 under the Presidency of the Reverend Edwin W. Smith, a Methodist minister who subsequently became a distinguished Bantu scholar and the doyen of Central African anthropologists.[1] Practically all societies working in Northern Rhodesia came to be represented on the Conference, including the White Fathers and the Jesuits. The objects of the Conference were to promote co-operation between the different societies, to labour for the more effective evangelization of the Africans, to enlighten public opinion on the mission question, and to watch over the interests of the native races; the Conference thus for the first time provided machinery for the expression of an incipient Christian 'public opinion' in the territory.

[1] Other distinguished Bantu scholars who emerged from the Northern Rhodesian mission field were Father J. Torrend, a Jesuit and a famed Tonga linguist and Professor C. M. Doke, a well-known anthropologist and an expert on the Lamba people who started off as a Baptist missionary.

III

The development of the miner's frontier

The first white settlers to bring their families to the inhospitable wilds of Northern Rhodesia, and the first white child to be born beyond the Zambezi, saw the light of day in a missionary household.[1] Clerical colonization, however, meant subsidized settlement; the stations were supported by well-wishers from overseas and rarely expected to maintain themselves, much less to generate new capital. Immigration on a large scale was impossible unless the country found a permanent and easily exportable source of wealth which would justify the expense of bringing Europeans into the country and of creating the first essential services. In this respect Southern Rhodesia was much better off than her northern sister colony; Southern Rhodesia possessed considerable deposits of gold, of the kind that could be worked by 'small workers' without much capital. But Northern Rhodesia was not so lucky; little gold was found in the Fort Jameson country, and the Missale mine did not prove profitable; the enormous concession to the North Charterland Concession Company proved a 'white elephant', which bitterly disappointed the hopes of its founders, whilst locking up much valuable land.

Northern Rhodesia's real wealth lay in its base mineral resources which could not be worked by petty *entrepreneurs*. Right from the start the lands beyond the Zambezi thus largely became 'Company country'. The majority of the early development work was done by two financial groups, both of which were closely associated with the Chartered Company, which also controlled the railways. The first of these combines was controlled by Edmund Davis. Davis was born in Australia in 1862 of Jewish parentage, and at the age of seventeen made his way to Cape Town where he obtained employment with a firm of merchants; within four years the firm ceased business, and Davis took over some of its assets, including a number of leases of small guano and sealing islands near Table Bay. Spending six miserable months of the year on the islands, he exploited their resources to the utmost, and although the life was a hard one, he did very well financially by the time the leases elapsed. Going up country he became interested in the Barberton Gold Fields and subsequently embarked on other enterprises. One of these was the Bechuanaland Exploration Company founded in 1888. In 1895 he formed the Northern Territories (B.S.A.) Exploring Company which in 1899 became the Northern Copper (B.S.A.) Company. This concern was closely associated with Rhodes and in time acquired various other concessions. Davis's copper interests were reorganized in 1909 when the

[1] The baby's name was Marguerite Jeanmairet, daughter of the Reverend Dorwald Jeanmairet and his wife Elise née Coillard. Little Marguerite was born at Sesheke in 1886 but died shortly afterwards. Marguerite had a sister called Eugénie who was born in 1888 but left the country in 1890 together with her parents.

Rhodesia Copper Company was formed, with extensive mineral interests all over the world.[1] Davis was a man of considerable perspicacity as well as personal courage (he held the Bronze Medal of the Royal Humane Society), and was extremely anxious to 'push' Northern Rhodesian copper. Davis's group was responsible in the 'nineties for sending out expeditions under Burnham and Lewis to which reference has already been made. In 1899 Lewis led a second expedition from Bulawayo, together with Orlando Baragwanath, an experienced prospector from South Africa, and news of further discoveries reached home. A number of copper mines were located in what was known as the 'Hook of the Kafue', with names as romantic as Silver King, Sable Antelope, Hippo, Sugar Loaf and North Star. Sable Antelope, the most important of these, re-mained in production off and on until the 'twenties, but management was faced with numerous technical problems, and transport proved a major obstacle. At first the miners tried to get the copper out by means of ox-wagon to the nearest railhead, but the dreaded 'fly' soon put an end to that. The answer lay in traction engines, ungainly steam monsters which pulled wagons through the bush in a straight line, and once they had steam up, there was little that could stop them. The trouble was to keep them going, for the appetite of the engines for wood and water was insatiable, and gangs of Africans had to remain at work constantly for cutting wood and feeding it into the furnaces, so that this strange marriage between the ox-wagon and the steam-engine did not prove satisfactory from the economic point of view.

Much more important was the discovery of Broken Hill by T. G. Davey, the Consulting Engineer to Davis's group. Davey in 1902 was actually looking for copper, but having got 'bushed' in the wild northern country, he stumbled across a curiously shaped *kopje* which so struck Davey by its appearance that he decided to investigate it more closely. On ascending the hill Davey kept 'knapping' the stone and it was not long before he broke off a heavy piece of rock which was perfectly white and which he immediately recognized as carbonate of lead. Delighted, Davey stumbled on to the summit, finding car-bonates and sulphates of lead as well as carbonate of zinc all the way up.[2] Davey was acquainted with Broken Hill in Australia and recognizing a resem-blance in the formation, named the prospect after it. The Rhodesia Copper

[1] The Rhodesia Copper Company later changed its name to Rhodesia Copper and General Exploration and Finance Company. It controlled substantial share interests in West African and Chinese mining concerns. By 1925 Davis was also Chairman of the Bechuanaland Exploration Company, the Bwana Mkubwa Copper Mining Company, the Kasempa Concessions and Serenje Concessions (two Northern Rhodesian prospecting concerns), Rhodesia Asbestos and Chrome Syndicate, Rhodesian and General Asbestos Corporation, the Charterland and General Exploration and Finance Company, Rhodesia Broken Hill Development Company and Wankie Colliery Company. Davis also became a Director of Rhodesia Railways and in 1925 acquired a seat on the Board of the British South Africa Company. He represented the major figure in the field of zinc, coal and asbestos in Rhodesia. He was one of the country's leading copper magnates and held an interest in its transport system. He was knighted in 1927 and made his name in England where he became High Sheriff of Kent and a patron of the arts. He died in 1939.

[2] For Davey's account see Bradley, K. *Copper venture....* Mufulira and Roan Antelope copper mines limited, 1952, p. 58, which also tells the story of Collier's discoveries.

Company then formed the Broken Hill Company to work the new deposit, which became an important link in Davis's financial empire.

In the same year the Davis Group sent out yet another expedition to the north. The venture was organized by Howard Unwin Moffat, then Manager of the Bechuanaland Exploration Company, one of Davis's trusted associates, later to become Prime Minister of Southern Rhodesia. The party was led by William C. Collier, one of those many hardy adventurers who were then coming into Rhodesia. Collier was born in 1870 near Dorchester, England, and being the youngest of a large family, he decided to emigrate to South Africa where at the age of eighteen he arrived at Cape Town; here he drifted from job to job, trying his hand at being a prison warder, a farmer, a prospector and a soldier. Like most other prospectors during this period, he possessed no formal geological training, but in time picked up a wide knowledge of the veld and of native ways which stood him in good stead at a time when prospecting was still largely concerned with looking for 'ancient workings', getting information from Africans and checking their reports by field-work.

Collier slowly made his way to the north, using donkeys as transport. Once he was across the Kafue, he entered tsetse fly country and the donkeys had to be killed, to be replaced by Ila carriers. They made their way to the Silver King where they were instructed to prospect in the vicinity of modern Ndola. Collier and his associate, J. Donohoe, 'struck lucky' and discovered enormous deposits at Roan Antelope, Rietbok and Bwana M'Kubwa. Collier thus deserves to be remembered as one of the great pioneers of the modern 'Copper Belt', but not much use was at first made of his discoveries. On both sides of the border, in Northern Rhodesia as well as in the Belgian Congo, the early finds were of oxidized ores. But whereas in the Congo much of the ore averaged 15 per cent copper and some was as high as 25 per cent, in Northern Rhodesia the oxidized ores only averaged between 3 to 5 per cent of the red metal, and ores as rich as these were thrown on dumps as waste matter on the Belgian side of the border. Only the later discoveries of sulphide ore bodies in Northern Rhodesia made the Copper Belt what it is today, but in Collier's time ores of this type were not as yet worked, and the Northern Rhodesian fields remained the Cinderella of high finance.

Real development was concentrated north of the border, the story of the Katanga being intimately linked with the career of Robert Williams (created a baronet in 1928). Williams, a dour Aberdonian, was born in 1860 and trained later as a mining engineer. In 1881 he went to Kimberley where he became one of Rhodes's many associates; Williams too was convinced that great mineral resources would be found along the great divide between the Congo and Zambezi river systems, just as vast wealth had been located along the Rand, along the watershed of the Orange and the Limpopo. Rhodes for his part was still anxious to find minerals that would assist his ambitious railway projects by supplying trucks with enough traffic to make railway building a payable proposition. Williams first made his mark by helping to found the Zambezia Exploring

Company of which he became Managing Director, and which absorbed several of the speculative, under-capitalized prospecting and land companies which were mushrooming in Southern Rhodesia at the period.[1] Williams also floated Tanganyika Concessions Ltd., which was formed in 1899 with an authorized capital of originally only £100,000, at a time when Rhodes was still hoping to take a railway from Bulawayo to Lake Tanganyika as part of his grandiose Cape to Cairo scheme, the Company being founded on the understanding that it would be given an area of 2,000 acres with all surface rights, which the concessionaires would be entitled to locate on the terminus of the railway at the south end of the Lake, where a township would be established. In addition the Company was allotted an area of 2,000 square miles within the B.S.A. Company's territory north of the Zambezi and the exclusive right of prospecting for two years, as well as the right to peg 1,000 claims on any open ground north of the Zambezi. The British South Africa Company was to retain a 35 per cent interest in the new concern, a condition considerably more favourable than those prevailing south of the Zambezi where the Chartered Company at that time generally insisted on a fifty per cent share.

Rhodes's ambitious railway project was never carried out, but prospecting continued, donkey wagons forming a popular means of transport, the patient grey four-footers being imune from various kinds of diseases that struck down horned cattle. What a prospector's journey was like may best be described in the words of an old-time miner who kept what he called a rhyming diary, which recorded his experiences in artless but down-to-earth verses:

> On the 28th day of June
> In '98 you see
> We started from Bulawayo Town
> Bound for the Zambesi
> . . . . .
> Our outfit was a heavy one
> And the best that trekked that road
> With waggons 7 and a Scotch Cart
> And each one had its load.
> Our white men numbered up to 5
> And donkeys six score eleven
> While Kaffir Boys were thirty five
> And Dogs amount to seven
> A Kaffir vrow we had on board
> To cook for the transport rider
> But none of the other four of us
> Could get near or beside her . . .

The Company shot game for the pot, but lions proved an ever-present menace.

[1] The companies which were absorbed included the Bembesi Syndicate, Zambezia Rand Investment Company and Central Monomotapa Ltd.

Worse still, the 'king of beasts' might even attack Africans asleep in their roughly-made huts and the company, white and black alike, was only too glad to get back to Bulawayo, the prospectors' main base for the north.[1]

The most important part of this prospecting work was done at the initiative of Robert Williams. In 1899 at a time when copper prices were rapidly rising,[2] he sent up a party led by George Grey and Fred Crewe, and assisted by John Grootboom, a famed scout, and a geologist. Grey missed the main Copper Belt deposits but in 1899 he discovered and pegged Kansanshi mine to which his attention had been drawn by an African.[3] Grey's main discoveries, however, were made in the Katanga where he obtained a vast concession and where a new company, the Union Minière, was floated, in which Tanganyika Concessions held a major interest, and which soon developed into a major copper producer; Tanganyika Concessions Ltd intended to follow up Grey's work by another expedition, but the Boer War created so many transport difficulties that the next venture could only be launched in 1901. The enterprise once again was directed by Grey, who formed an advanced camp at Kalomo where 120 head of cattle, brought from Barotseland for draught purposes, were trained. In April 1901 the two sections of Grey's expedition left Bulawayo and Abercorn respectively, and in October a permanent settlement was affected at Kansanshi, the Abercorn party being led by Michael J. Holland, and destined to form the nucleus of the Katanga party. The going was hard; the twelve ox-wagons were heavily laden, and the miners walked along with them through the bush, a major problem being presented by the Zambezi which took about two weeks to cross. On the north bank six trained spans of Barotse oxen were waiting, but the miners still had to take about 200 donkeys and the vehicles across the crocodile-infested river where there were no bridges. The men drove their animals to Sekuti's drift, a few miles above the Victoria Falls; and once the beasts were in the water, their heads were tied to African dugout canoes, and they were paddled across. The wagons were likewise pushed into the water; African boatmen would tie a long dugout canoe on each side; and twenty black paddlers then managed to take the vehicles to the other side of the river; then the expedition slowly moved northwards, reaching Nkala and making its way up the west bank of the Kafue through remote country where the local tribesmen had never seen a wheel before, and followed the miners for days to gaze in wonderment at the way these strange wooden circles kept turning over. The miners were fortunate in getting African help, for many of their oxen died, and eventually the expedition had to employ nearly 1,000 carriers, without whom the work could not have been completed. Eventually Kansanshi was turned into a base for future operations, George Grey proving a forceful and tireless leader, the best type of those

---

[1] Extracts from a rhyming diary by Barnes, J. B. (BA 3/1, Nat Arch MS). Barnes was employed by the Mashonaland Agency, which in 1898 despatched an expedition to investigate coal deposits in the Wankie area.

[2] Copper rose from £52 per long ton in 1897 to £55·4 in 1898 and £76·7 in 1899.

[3] Wills, W. H. and Hall, J., ed. *Bulawayo up-to-date*. . . . Simpkin, Marshall, Hamilton, Kent & co. ltd, 1899, p. 235–236

younger sons of aristocratic British families, who at that time were seeking employment and adventure overseas; Grey was a brother of Sir Edward, later Viscount Grey of Fallodon, but did not in the least correspond to the conventional but most inaccurate picture of the bluff, hale and hearty empire builder of late Victorian mythology. Meeting him for the first time, no one would have suspected that the middle-aged man of medium height, who suffered from a terrible stammer which got worse whenever anyone looked at him, was a born leader with a distinguished fighting record, who was admired by white and black alike. Grey managed to do his work without any show of armed force, a policy which gave astonishingly good results in an African country where there were a mere score of prospectors scattered over an enormous area and seldom more than one or two white men were together.[1] The most important of his new discoveries were then inspected by J. R. Farrell, the chief engineer in Williams' employment, who was most impressed by the Katanga finds. 'When it is recalled', wrote Farrell a year later, 'that since the days of Dr Livingstone and Commander Cameron, many expeditions have attempted to reach the mines of Katanga and failed, it is almost marvellous to find that Tanganyika Concessions' employees have gone there quietly and unostentatiously, explored a large portion of the area and mapped it well, located over fifty properties, built substantial camps, laid in supplies of serviceable foods and implements, and are carrying on a regular mining enterprise.'[2] Grey's achievement was all the more impressive in view of the enormous difficulties he met; his transport animals were continuously struck down by tsetse fly; he had to build his own roads, organize food for his white and black workers and even hunt down slavers who were making the Kasempa area unsafe and disorganizing labour supplies. What is more, he managed to carry out this operation without losing any of his employees from disease, a success largely due to the way in which his men regularly took prophylactic medicines and benefited from the services of a doctor.[3] As far as expenditure was concerned, Grey wrote laconically that the total outlay incurred up to 1902 'including purchase of stores in England and payments of salaries and travelling expenses of the members of the expedition' amounted to £36,659, a ridiculously small sum in relation to the astronomical riches discovered. In 1910 James Moffat Thomson, the local Native Commissioner, making his way through an area known to be mineralized, stumbled across a lonely green outcrop which later turned out to be Nkana, one of the greatest deposits in the Territory.

But for the time being Northern Rhodesia benefited relatively little from these discoveries. Northern Rhodesian copper production was neglected in favour of

---

[1] See reminiscences by White, W. R., in Scannel, T. 'A pioneer of 1901 comes to the Copper Belt' (in *Horizon*, Mar 1961, p. 10–14). See also Sharp, R. R. *Early days in Katanga*. Rhodesian Printers, Bulawayo, 1956, p. 2 and 36–37. Grey was killed in 1911 by a wounded lion.

[2] J. R. Farrell to R. Williams: 6 Jan 1903 (in Tanganyika Concessions ltd. *Reports on the discoveries made by Mr George Grey's expedition in Northern Rhodesia and Congo Free State*. The company, 1903, p. 97)

[3] Gelfand, M. *Tropical victory.* . . . Cape Town, Juta & co., limited, 1953

the much more profitable developments in the Congo, though a little work was done at Kansanshi, and also at Bwana M'Kubwa where a small concentrator was erected in 1912 to treat high grade ore. Some development also took place in the Hook of the Kafue, but though some mines were rich in their copper content, they suffered from water and foul air seeping through the limestone formation. At Kafue, moreover, too much work was taken in hand all at once, and when the price of copper dropped in 1907 the mines closed, except Sable Antelope which carried on for a time. Difficulties were also met with at Broken Hill, where it was found impossible to separate zinc and lead economically and work could only be done where there was a clear cleavage between the two metals. All the mines were faced with major transport difficulties; much time had to be wasted in cutting wood for fuel; work in general being characterized by lack of capital, scant use of machinery, frequent stoppages, and the speculative nature of the enterprise.

The miners employed in these isolated little communities led tough lives, and whenever a mine ceased production, they would have to start looking for new jobs, a difficult task in a country where there were few opportunities for employment. There were no amenities of any kind, and at the end of the month, after pay-day, the miners in the Hook of the Kafue would send for their supplies to Mumbwa. Most of these were in liquid form, and the men would go on a drunken spree which often necessitated the virtual closing of the mine for a few days. Then the hard round in the bush began once more, but the Hook of the Kafue did not prove an economic success; and today Sable Antelope is a ghost mine where only charred walls of Kimberley brick and heaps of rubble reveal what once were offices and billets, whilst an old stamp battery decays close to the main shaft, and a few abandoned traction engines still gather rust in the bush.[1]

Existence was harder still for the African labourers employed on the early mines. At Kansanshi for instance the local district officer reported that conditions were poor, the food indifferent and there was no regular day of rest.[2] Abuses were sometimes made worse by the employment of inferior types of Europeans or of African *capitaos* as labour agents who scoured the villages for men, and sometimes secured labour by false promises or threats. Contracts of course were short, which meant that the labour force was constantly changing, and white foremen were faced with the unenviable task of having to handle men whom they hardly knew, whose language and beliefs they did not understand, and whose incompetence irritated them. Understandably enough they considered severe discipline, backed sometimes by corporal punishment, to be the only suitable remedy, much reliance being placed on 'boss boys' who were often chosen from the same tribes though not necessarily from chiefly families. As far as the rank and file of African miners were concerned, they only worked for a few months, enough to earn their tax money and make a little extra to buy some clothes or pots and pans, the idea of bargaining for higher wages never entering

[1] 'The Ghost mines of Mumbwa' (in *Horizon*, v. 3, no. 3, Mar 1961, p. 18–19)
[2] For conditions on early mines see Quarterly report for Solwezi: 30 Sep 1913. (LO 1/1/154 Nat Arch SR)

their heads. Nevertheless there is one recorded case of an anti-European movement before the First World War which, characteristically, was organized by a
head *capitao*. A former district officer, Edward Arden Copeman, thus recalls
that at Kansanshi the management complained of constant desertions. Copeman
hurried to the mine and finally learned that the *capitao* kept a gruesome collection of skulls and human bones in his hut and practised the black art. As soon as
the foreman was arrested, the African mine hands, who previously would not
talk, became only too eager to tell all they knew; and their evidence showed that
the *capitao* by claiming supernatural powers, tried to force his workmates into a
brotherhood of which he was the leader. He used his position to ill treat those
who wanted nothing to do with his movement; but many others joined,
impressed by the *capitao*'s threats that he would live for ever, that the Europeans
would soon die, and that he and his friends would then seize their property.
The candidates for the *capitao*'s society were promised a share in the loot, but
before qualifying had to undergo a training of the most revolting kind. Together
with the *capitao* they had to go to the burial place and dig up the latest buried
corpses and possess themselves of certain portions; they also had to break the
arm and leg bones, suck out the marrow, as well as indulge in various other
loathsome practises. Copeman had the culprit beaten and sentenced for two
years, the *capitao*'s implements of magic being ceremonially burnt before the
assembled workers, with the result that mass desertions ceased from that date.[1]
But Government by and large took relatively little notice of the mines, the problem being primarily regarded as disciplinary in nature. The Masters and Servants
legislation, passed in 1908 in some ways resembled the code of an army, making
desertion and other kinds of misdemeanour a criminal offence, as they already
were south of the Zambezi.[2] The measure did not specifically apply to Africans
only, but to unskilled workers in general; but since there were in fact no unskilled whites in the territory, the regulations formed an important legislative
barrier between the two races. At the same time, however, Africans received
some protection against dishonest employers so that the law also contained a
paternal element. Social welfare legislation of a more positive kind had to wait
until the Administration first began to regulate conditions of work in greater
detail. The Mines, Health and Sanitary Regulations of 1917 made provision for
various improvements as well as for proper inspection, with the result that
mining became far more attractive to Africans, and farmers began to complain of
local competition for labour. Nevertheless mining in Northern Rhodesia
remained on an extremely small scale and employed very few workers,[3] so that the
territory as a whole remained almost unknown to the world of international finance.

[1] Copeman, E. A. Reminiscences: n.d. (CO 3/4/2, Nat Arch MS)
[2] See High Commissioner's proclamations no. 37 of 1908 and no. 18 of 1912, based on the Masters
and servants ordinance, 1901, of Southern Rhodesia.
[3] In 1913 Kansanshi employed 85 local workers and 778 imported labourers. Broken Hill at this
period employed about 2,000 workers, mostly non-local, and conditions at Broken Hill appear to have
been consistently better than at the smaller mines. See for instance interview with G. T. Davey in
Bulawayo chronicle, 4 Oct 1904.

IV

The railway

Mining could never emerge from the experimental stage until railway transport became available to carry machinery, fuel and ore. There was no other alternative, for porters could not carry more than 40 lbs to 50 lbs per man, and in addition, they had to carry their own food; they were always liable to fall ill, or desert, and were difficult to manage. Transport by ox-wagon was impeded by the prevalence of the tsetse fly and the history of mining in Rhodesia is thus linked to the development of the railroad. In 1897 Bulawayo was connected with the South African railway system, and during the first decade of the present century the bulk of the Southern Rhodesian lines were completed, their construction forming one of the major achievements of the Chartered Company which was able to raise capital at relatively low rates of interest, and which was able to build the lines through private, rather than state enterprise as was done in most of Southern Africa.

As far as Rhodes was concerned, railway building was, however, not merely an economic but also an Imperial necessity; in 1898 he induced the share-holders of the British South Africa Company to authorize the extension of a line beyond the Zambezi.[1] Rhodes intended that the new railway should go on to Lake Tanganyika tapping more African labour, opening up good ranching country, and leading to the creation of a port on Lake Tanganyika. Whilst Rhodes was putting forward this scheme, the Imperial Government had already agreed to build a railway to Uganda to put down the slave trade, open a strategic backdoor to the Nile Valley, and to secure the newly acquired Uganda Protectorate. Rhodes then arranged with Kitchener that the Egyptian and Sudanese system should be brought down to the borders of Uganda, the trans Zambezi railway thus forming part of a gigantic design that would ultimately join the Cape to Cairo. The Imperial Government, however, refused financial support to the projected line through North-Eastern Rhodesia,[2] and the discovery of new coal deposits soon altered the situation. In 1894 Albert Giese, a German-born prospector, found coal in the Wankie area. A year later Giese pegged a concession of 400 square miles which was secured by the Mashonaland Agency, one of Edmund Davis's concerns; enormous coal resources were located and production started in 1903, the 'combustible stone' completely changing the country's economic outlook. Both the mines and railways were supplied with cheap fuel which did away with some of the ruthless deforestation which was then being

[1] For details of the railways' financial history see [D'Erlanger, E. B.] *The history of the construction and finance of the Rhodesian transport system.* Printed by Burrup, Mathieson & co., ltd, 1939

[2] Colonial Office to C. J. Rhodes: 1 May 1899 (in *Further correspondence....* African (South) no. 574)

practised in order to keep the boilers going.[1] The existence of these coal resources persuaded the planners that the new northern extension should go via
Wankie, a decision made even more palatable by the fact that the original route
to Lake Tanganyika would have involved difficult and extensive engineering
problems. The extension of the railway from Bulawayo to Wankie was completed in 1903, and in 1904 the Victoria Falls were reached, the construction
being entrusted to George Pauling, an outstanding railway contractor who was
financially aided by the banking firm of Erlanger. Then followed the building of
the Zambezi bridge to span the vast gorge below the Victoria Falls. The bridge
stands out as a magnificent piece of engineering, the rail level being about the
same height from the river bed as the dome of St Paul's Cathedral from the
ground. The line was then pushed forward through the Tonga plateau, its
direction being determined not by agricultural but by engineering needs, the
exact course being planned in such a way as to incur the minimum expenditure
on bridges, cuttings and viaducts; it then continued beyond the Kafue river to
where Lusaka now stands. 'The night that the rails reached Lusaka' relates an
old-timer, '. . . the siding was laid. As usual, some ten ox-wagons were in waiting, the backs of the wagons close to the siding, and the spans of oxen lying
down tied to their trek-tous [ropes], stretching away into the darkness beyond,
all ready for loading and moving off at daybreak. Lusaka was the worst place
on the section for lions, and they had caused a certain amount of trouble with
ox transport already. There were no lights in the new siding, except for the head-
lights of the engine the world was in darkness. Heedless of the noise of the engine and the shunting, the lions actually came in that night and killed some of the
leading oxen. . . .'[2] In 1906 the line reached Broken Hill where the available
mineral deposits were thought to be capable of more immediate exploitation
than the copper resources of the more distant Hook of the Kafue. Up to now the
building of the railway had been financed through the Mashonaland Railway
Company which was linked to Chartered interests. The completion of the last
lap to the Congo, however, was due to the initiative from Katanga, for in 1908
Robert Williams sponsored the linking of the Congo with Northern Rhodesia,
principally with the object of obtaining cheap coke from Wankie for the Congo
copper mines. The Rhodesia-Katanga Junction Railway was formed with
Williams's support, and in 1909 the Rhodesian system finally linked up with the
Congo railway,[3] the completion of the line proving a great boon to farmers who

---

[1] Trees were cut down, but the roots and lower section of the stem remained in the soil, being too
troublesome to shift. New growth then sprouted forth in profusion, which tended to compete successfully with the grass cover, leading to soil erosion.

[2] Varian, H. F. *Some African milestones*. Oxford, George Ronald, 1953, p. 125

[3] The financing of the trans-Zambezi system was part of a major railway-building scheme propoun-
ded by Rhodes to the shareholders of the Chartered Company in 1899. £4,250,000 Bechuanaland
Railway Company debentures were to be issued, their interest being guaranteed by the Chartered
Company and convertible into Chartered shares, all debentures bearing 4% interest. With the proceeds of the loan the line was then carried from Bulawayo to Gwelo, the link with Salisbury being
completed in 1902. In addition several branch lines were constructed in Southern Rhodesia, as well as
the line to Kalomo in Northern Rhodesia. The stretch from Kalomo to Broken Hill was constructed

could for the first time rail their maize and beef up to the Katanga mines. Six years later the Germans finished a railway from Dar-es-Salaam on the East Coast to Lake Tanganyika, with the result that Rhodesians living on the Tanganyika Plateau could now reach the Indian Ocean within five days; and goods no longer had to travel by the more expensive Chinde route.[1]

V

The farmer's frontier in Northern Rhodesia

While the railway was being extended north of the Zambezi, a substantial white farming community had already settled in Southern Rhodesia. Farming there was at first amateurish and speculative in character, since the available markets were so small. The farmer was dependent on the miner for his sales, but as long as mining south of the Zambezi largely consisted of the reckless buying of gold claims and the flotation of companies, settlers had little incentive to do more than scratch the soil. The men who went north usually had little capital; being able to acquire 3,000 acre farms for small payments they only cultivated a small portion of their estates, moving on to work another patch as soon as the land had been exhausted. This type of farming, characteristic of any 'frontier', did not yield much of a living and the settlers' lot was made worse by droughts, by unfamiliar cattle and plant diseases, and by the lack of transport facilities. Most of the early farmers therefore had to eke out their living by prospecting, transport riding, the sale of firewood and trade in native cattle.

After the Boer War conditions in Southern Rhodesia slowly began to improve. The building of the railway and the exploitation of the new coal resources gave a stimulus to mining which at last was carried on in a more businesslike fashion, and less in the spirit of a Rhodesian lottery. In the years that elapsed between the turn of the century and the Great War, gold production in Southern Rhodesia rose from 58,981 to 3,580,209 ounces; gold became the country's chief export and the mainspring of her economy. As the mining townships and market towns grew in size, their people—white and black—required more food; the demand for maize and 'boys' meat' went up by leaps and bounds. Farmers for the first time acquired an internal market, even though most of the goods required were still of low quality. Farmers were thus able to devote less time to subsidiary occupations, specialization of labour being aided also by other factors. A considerable amount of 'kaffir-trade' for instance, was taken over by people who devoted the whole of their working time to commerce; the gradual disappearance of game from many parts of the Colony led to the decline

by the Mashonaland Railway Company. The line from Broken Hill to the Congo was financed by the Rhodesia-Katanga Junction Railway and Mineral Company, and Erlanger in 1909 offered for sale £800,000 first mortgage debentures of the Company at 5½% interest being guaranteed by the Tanganyika Concessions Ltd. Northern Rhodesia thus got its railway relatively cheaply.

[1] Gelfand, M. *Northern Rhodesia in the days of the Charter.* Basil Blackwell, Oxford, 1961, p. 115

of hunting, whilst the arrival of the railway diminished the need for transport riding, except for the purpose of 'feeding' the lines. Some farmers improved their methods; fertilizers were introduced; breeding stock was imported from England; dips, dams, fences and roads slowly began to make their appearance in the Southern Rhodesian countryside. At the same time there was a medical revolution in the country, and in the decade that preceded the Great War the Company's medical officers as well as doctors in private practice won that great 'Tropical Victory' which at last made Southern Rhodesia a fit country for white people.[1] More families settled down south of the Zambezi, the country's European rural labour force becoming more stabilized than hitherto.

At the same time land prices began to rise and the explanation for this was simple. The alienated land, generally speaking, comprised the highest and the most accessible, though not necessarily the most valuable portions of the territory;[2] and under conditions where the average density of the white population on the land was less than one person per four thousand acres, there was soon no longer enough unalienated land available near the railway lines. Land companies and farmers willing to sub-divide their estates were able to get somewhat better prices for their land, and the palmy days of 'a tickey (3d) an acre' became a thing of the past. The Chartered Company itself woke up to the fact that settlement was beginning to push up land values. 'The Company', wrote its London Manager sadly, 'has been willing to sell unlimited areas of land in a limited market at prices considerably below its true economic value. In Stock Exchange language the Company has been a persistent bear of its own land! It has created an artificial depression in prices and having done so, it has forced sales.'[3] The Company, in other words, was subsidizing land sales at a time when capital was extremely short and applicants few. Initially this policy mainly profited mining companies and land-holding companies, whom the Chartered Company wished to attract in order to divert more investments to Southern Rhodesia; but the long-term effect of this policy was probably to give further encouragement to the extensive farming methods customary in Rhodesia, as on any other frontier. In the first decade of the present century the Company changed its general economic policy so as to benefit the smaller *entrepreneur* both in the field of gold mining and of farming. From 1907 a more vigorous settlement policy was put into force; there was a marked improvement in the agricultural, medical and veterinary services provided, while at the same time land sales began to be carefully scrutinized.

[1] See Gelfand, M. *Tropical victory*. . . . Cape Town, Juta & co. limited, 1953
[2] In Southern Rhodesia in 1912, 8,030,549 acres were held by companies, 14,092,486 by individuals, 24,877,150 acres were comprised in native reserves, 156,209 were comprised in B.S.A. Company Estates and 47,931,561 in unalienated land. Of the unalienated land 25,646,700 acres were situated below the 3,500 ft level of altitude and, being low-lying and hot, were regarded as generally unsuitable for European settlement in the ordinary sense. The total number of whites on the land in Southern Rhodesia was estimated not to exceed 5,000 persons.
[3] Between 1908 and 1912 the average value of land in Southern Rhodesia rose from 1/8 an acre to 3/6 an acre. In 1912 the minimum price at which land was sold by the Company was raised to 4/-.
  Wilson Fox, H. *The British South Africa Company: memorandum . . . containing notes and information concerning land policy*. . . . British South Africa Company, 1912, p. 12

The efforts of this development became noticeable north of the Zambezi, for the poor frontier farmers, with little money to spend, now began to look beyond the river where land prices were still low. Immigration first began about 1898 when small groups of immigrants had trekked to the Zambezi. More settlers came after 1904 when the railway was extended to Northern Rhodesia, settlement along the 'Railway Belt' speeding up when Congo markets became accessible.[1] In addition a few colonists found homes for themselves near Fort Jameson and Abercorn.

As far as the Company was concerned, the Directors did at one time consider the possibility of 'locking up' Northern Rhodesia to prospective immigrants, keeping the country as a kind of *terra clausa* which could be held in reserve when the Company sold out its possessions in Southern Rhodesia as part of a general settlement. This possibility, however, was never considered very seriously, and the Company's Administrators on the spot were keen advocates of the cause of European settlement. Coryndon thus argued that conditions should be made easier for prospective settlers, and that the Company should look to financial returns from indirect sources such as increased customs duties and railway revenue and the benefits to be derived from cheap agricultural produce, rather than to profits from land prices.[2] Land sales in the early days were in any case carried out in rather a lackadaisical fashion, as the local staff tended to look on large tracts of unalienated land as a drug on the market, whilst the Company itself, when making grants from London was frequently unaware of local conditions, so that little care was exercised in the selection of immigrants.

The Imperial Government was at first very sceptical of the wisdom of thus encouraging white settlement. In 1899 Lord Milner, then High Commissioner for South Africa and at the zenith of his prestige, advised the Colonial Office that the Zambezi was the natural boundary of what would one day be a self-governing British Africa. Beyond the river there was tropical country which would never hold a sufficiently numerous white population to be a self-governing state. The North, he argued, must ultimately become a Black Imperial dependency, like Uganda or Nigeria.[3] Milner's outlook, not an unreasonable one at a time when whites were dying in scores from malaria in the disease-ridden veld of the North, dominated the outlook of the Colonial Office at the time when Northern Rhodesia's constitutional framework was being created at the turn of the century. The Chartered Company did not, however, share Milner's view, and neither did it agree with that of Lord Selborne, a later British High Commissioner. Selborne was a pessimist. Settlement in Northern Rhodesia, he

[1] In North-Western Rhodesia extensive land concessions were at first given to the various railway companies next to the railway lines; in addition land was sold to private individuals. Pricing was done on a system of zoning depending on proximity to the railway. Within 20 miles of the railway the maximum of acreage sold was 3,000 at a price of 2/6 an acre; outside this zone land was sold at 1/- an acre or less (the prices refer to the period 1911 to 1912). Previously land had been sold for values ranging between 3d and 1/6 an acre.

[2] R. Coryndon to B.S.A. Company: 13 Dec 1904 (in A 2/2/3, Nat Arch NWR)

[3] Lord Milner to Colonial Office: 5 Apr 1899 (in *Further correspondence. . . .* African (South) no. 574)

argued in 1907, should be confined to getting big planters to buy estates in the country and carry out experiments in tropical products like cotton and rubber; existing farmers should be confirmed in their holdings, but no further white immigration should be encouraged. Northern Rhodesia, the High Commissioner believed, was not suitable for white farmers; the land was too poor and the low-lying *vleis* would turn out to be hot-beds of fever. European settlement more-over would involve many political risks. The settlers were not likely to succeed; economic failure would turn them against the Company; they would expect to be 'feather-bedded' and come to look at politics as a means of alleviating their distress, whilst at the same time living on the natives.[1]

The Company, however, was not convinced. It argued that the expense of administering Northern Rhodesia and building the railways fell on itself, not the Imperial Government, and that it should therefore be entitled to do what it thought fit. Settler discontent was nothing like as great in Chartered territories as in Nyasaland. Even the suggestion that the settlement should in advance be limited to certain regions was unacceptable. For 'until experience has been gained', argued Lawrence Aubrey Wallace (later Sir Lawrence), the Company's Administrator in North-Western Rhodesia at the time, 'it seems to me better that those who risk their capital should not be limited to areas which may not contain the conditions they require'. The Company promised that it would not artifi-cially promote large scale land settlement; in fact few applications from eligible settlers were being received, but the Company would regularize the position of existing colonists and continue to make grants on vacant land, where native rights were not being interfered with. Permission to purchase land would be given only after a specified period of *bona fide* occupation.[2] Selborne declared himself satisfied with this policy and so did the Directors, who, after a visit by one of their number, Henry Birchenough, in 1912, became convinced that Northern Rhodesia was, from the farming point of view 'a singularly promising portion of the Company's territory . . . with . . . possibilities for cattle, mealies, cotton and citrus', that land sales should be concentrated along the line of rail, that land prices could now be raised, and that the point had been reached where land settlement had to be actively promoted. At the same time Birchenough thought an attempt should be made to exclude 'speculators, wastrels, amateurs and low Dutch', all of whom were to be found amongst the ranks of present Permit of Occupation holders in the North.[3] The Company's policy of promot-ing land-settlement, even if only on a limited scale, entailed the extension of the rather vague treaty rights hitherto granted by Lewanika. The Barotse king was gradually put under more and more pressure, till the Company acquired full land rights in the territory nominally under Barotse control. In 1904 Lewanika

[1] Lord Selborne to Colonial Office: 11 Nov 1907 (in *Further correspondence. . . .* African (South) no. 872)

[2] Lord Selborne to Colonial Office: 3 May 1909 and enclosure L. A. Wallace to Lord Selborne: 23 Apr 1909 (in *Further correspondence. . . .* African (South) no. 932)

[3] Birchenough, H. 'Report . . . on Land policy and land settlement in Northern Rhodesia' (in Wilson, Fox, H. *The British South Africa Company: Memorandum . . . containing notes and informa-tion concerning land policy. . . .* British South Africa Company, 1912, p. 99–103)

agreed to give authority to the Administrator to issue land from the territory outside the Barotse reserve; though no farms were to be issued 'where many people are, or many gardens which are for my [Lewanika's] people'. A year later the boundary of North-Western Rhodesia was extended to the west, until it spread across the narrow part of North-Western Rhodesia between the Congo and Portuguese East Africa, bringing under the terms of the Barotse treaty a vast stretch of territory never previously controlled by the Barotse kings. Lewanika's tax percentage was then extended over the whole of the area, and the Company's administrator on the spot was informed that he should not raise the question of delimiting Lewanika's sphere for the purpose of allotting the additional revenue.[1] In the same year Lewanika granted away a piece of territory situated within a radius of fifteen miles of the north bank of the Zambezi at the Victoria Falls, and in 1906 he formalized the land grant over the territory over which he was chief, 'within the territories of Barotzi-land, North Western Rhodesia', excluding Barotseland proper, this being followed up in 1909 by an even more comprehensive concession.[2]

The first Europeans to take up land under these conditions were mostly adventurous amateurs. They comprised amongst their ranks former members of the British South Africa Police, the armed forces, especially men who had seen service in the Boer War, retired members of the Administration, the railways, the Post Office, or even traders who had built up a little capital dealing in cattle. To such immigrants Northern Rhodesia offered the attractions of cheap land, cheap labour and cheap cattle, so that men with little capital had a chance of setting themselves up on their own, having to call no man master. Land was also acquired by a number of great noblemen resident in England, such as the Duke of Westminster, Lord Wolverton and Lord Winterton, as well as by a number of big companies whose directors bought real estate as a future investment against the time when the land should appreciate in value, under conditions where the capital invested was unlikely to be made subject to confiscatory taxation.[3] Some of these concerns did a little development work under hired managers on the spot, whilst the Chartered Company itself also opened up an estate as well as two small experimental stations.

The most numerous group of early farmers, however, was made up of Afrikaans-speaking immigrants who pioneered settlement in various parts of the country, especially in the Lusaka area, where land was bought cheaply from the Northern Copper Company, which had found no minerals in the area and became only too anxious to sell. Most of the newcomers appear to have come from the Transvaal and the Orange Free State where distress was rife after the devastation caused by the Boer War. The Afrikaners, like most of their English-speaking fellow pioneers, raised cattle and a little maize. They were on the look-out

[1] B.S.A. Company to R. Codrington: 14 Oct 1905 (in A 3/16 Nat Arch NWR)
[2] These have been printed in Appendix II of Gann, L. H. *The birth of a plural society*. . . . Manchester University Press, 1958
[3] By 1912 over 7,000,000 acres were held by land, mining and railway companies, and only 1/10 of this amount by farmers.

for open rolling savannah or thorn-tree country which could easily be 'stumped', and accordingly kept away from the denser forest land of the Congo type further to the north which defeated the efforts of most white farmers, except of a very few possessed of ample capital. The Afrikaners—like Sarie Marais, the poet's sweetheart in South Africa's most popular folk-song—usually made their homes 'down yonder by the mealies, by the green thorn tree'; and early white settlement largely remained confined to a strictly defined fly-free area by the side of the railway line, south of Broken Hill, the exception being a few patches of settlement in the Fort Jameson area and in the extreme north-eastern corner of the territory.

The Afrikaners' agricultural methods were little distinguished from those of English-speaking settlers, but socially the Afrikaners differed from these in that they employed white 'bywoners', poor men, often indigent relatives of the farmers, who were unable and sometimes unwilling to acquire farms of their own. They worked for the landowner either as foremen or as share-croppers, and on some farms no Africans were employed at all. The 'bywoners' in some cases had to give one third of their crops and trading profits to the 'baas'. They lived in mud huts whilst their masters lived in brick huts with a superior standard of living, though on terms of social equality with their wealthier countrymen. The Administration was hostile to these poor Europeans and argued that 'their appearance, condition and manner of living are having the worst effect on local natives. They now see that the largest portion of whites in the district consist of people whose habits of life and morals are as degraded as their own.'[1] The poorer immigrants who often suffered from malaria and other diseases, did not readily conform with game laws and other regulations, and this, as well as their poverty, explains something of the Administration's antagonism towards them. The *Livingstone Mail*, the country's European newspaper, on the other hand, was much less hostile, and there were others who thought that the poor Dutchmen in fact constituted an asset since they would tackle land of a quality which British people would not usually touch. The 'bywoner', like the poor Colonial-born Britisher, was never a 'poor white' in the sense of being unemployed and unemployable. As long as there was an open frontier, he could exist. Rough of manner and ridden by endemic malaria as he often was, he was yet adjusted to life in the wilderness; he knew how to handle a span of oxen in rough country, how to 'prospect' for the best soils in the bush, and to eke out a living with hunting, transport-riding and odd jobs such as making rhino whips for sale, his usefulness only coming to an end when the old frontier conditions ceased to exist.[2]

[1] B.S.A. Company to Northern Copper Company: 2 Oct 1913, annex. 9 to B.S.A. Company minutes: 9 Oct 1913 (in LO 1/2/78, Nat Arch SR)

[2] Henri Rolin, a contemporary observer from Belgium, found that by 1912 in Southern Rhodesia about 95 per cent of the farmers came from South Africa, of whom about 70 to 80 per cent were English-speaking. The Company's emigration offices in Britain had great difficulties in giving efficient guidance to prospective emigrants as these offices were themselves inadequately informed of local conditions, the main effort to recruit settlers being made in South Africa. South African farmers were said to succeed better in the country than those from the United Kingdom. The Northern

But no matter where or who the farmers were, their methods of farming were always of a very extensive kind. The old story of lack of markets and transport facilities was repeated over and over again, for the Belgian Congo mines at first proved the farmers' only regular customers, though a certain number of cattle were also sold in Southern Rhodesia. Equally difficult was the problem of getting the crops to the market away from the line of rail, the motor lorry only coming into use from about 1913. Little machinery was employed, partly because native labour was so cheap, and partly because of the high cost of transport. Yields accordingly were low; production remained limited largely to cattle and maize, whilst methods were so backward that Harry Rangeley, a Government official, could lightheartedly write that all the farmers did was 'to watch a very small herd of native-bred cattle increase until such time as the increase had become noticeable in Salisbury'. Another local observer wrote at the time that the 'probationary years of farm life in North-Eastern Rhodesia fulfil all the requirements of the "simple life" '. The two-roomed house or hut on the side of a hill overlooking some lovely valley enclosed with lonely hills, with the cattle kraal below and the herds close by resting during the heat of the day under the shady trees, the herd boys beside them playing some game with pebbles, like English boys do with marbles, [constitutes] as peaceful a scene as one could well imagine. Food is plentiful enough. Guinea fowls and partridges are always near at hand, and larger game is never far to seek . . . while milk, butter, eggs and vegetables can be obtained from the farm. Constant watch, however, has to be kept against the attacks of wild animals, for lions and leopards constantly fall upon stray cattle and even endeavour to enter the kraals. Wild pigs also do much damage to gardens. In the wet season it is difficult to get about owing to swollen rivers and swamps, for as yet there are but few waggon roads. Indeed all the year round farmers are dependent to a large extent upon their bicycles. . . .'[1]

The man who made good under these conditions was the good all-rounder, who could do his own building, carpentering and nursing, as well as being able to gain the trust of his native 'boys'. The specialist farmer did not put in an appearance until very much later in the day, and this is how a local resident described the way a colonist started off his career in the Fort Jameson area in the days that preceded the First World War. 'In selecting a farm, water supply is the first consideration; then, if he is going in for cattle he must consider the quality of the grass, whether it is in sour veldt or sweet. . . . When he has chosen his land, and obtained his Permit of Occupation, the next thing for the settler to do is to build a wattle and daub house. Perhaps a circular native hut will content him at

Rhodesian administration, on the other hand, made no special effort to recruit farmers from South Africa and tended to rely more on emigrants from Britain, about half the farmers coming from South Africa and the remainder from Britain and other parts of the Empire. In Northern Rhodesia Rolin was told that the best colonists were those who came from Britain since the effort involved in emigrating so far was weeding out the unenthusiastic. The Southern Rhodesian emigrant was expected to have a capital of between £500 and £1,000, the Northern Rhodesian could manage with less. (H. Rolin. *Les lois et l'administration de la Rhodésie.* Brussels, Établissements Emile Bruylant, 1913, p. 396–397 and 413–415)

[1] *Northern Rhodesia journal* (published locally at Fort Jameson), v. 1, no. 6, July 1909, p. 6

first. He will find it quite comfortable and watertight, and only costs six shillings to build. Next he should turn his attention to providing a house for his cattle. Twenty boys at the rate of 3/– a month will bring him in a sufficient number of long poles to build a 'kraal'. . . . The cattle he can either buy for himself or hire on a three years' system from the Administration. At the end of three years half the original herd has to be returned to the Administration, the remainder being made up out of the increase, whilst the other half of the original herd and the rest of the increase becomes the property of the settler. After being three years in possession the settler is also expected to pay up what is outstanding of his purchase money, when his Permit of Occupation will be exchanged for the title-deed of his newly acquired estate.'

The early settler could start with very little, but all the same, his was a hard and lonely life. The farmer and his family were usually far away from the nearest school or hospital; teaching had to be done in the home, and if anyone fell ill, it took a long time for a doctor to be called. There were few roads, markets were precarious and a single drought or an outbreak of one of the many little understood cattle diseases might ruin a man.

Nevertheless, despite their lack of capital and simplicity of methods, the early colonists made a valuable contribution to the country's economy. They were the first to produce farming products for export on any appreciable scale, and this became even truer when the Barotse herds were decimated by an outbreak of pleuro-pneumonia during the Great War. By and large, the indigenous tribal economies were geared to produce for subsistence, not for a market. This was true at first even along the railway lines, where the native population was sparse and the standards of farming attained by broken and scattered people like the Lamba and the Tonga were extremely low, much more so than those of the Barotse away from the line. Some tribesmen near the mines did well out of selling grain and meat to the mines, but once the demand began to increase, local native resources proved quite inadequate, and the mining companies had to purchase food on a bigger scale from elsewhere.

The settlers' farming standards gradually began to improve, though the process was extremely slow.[1] A number of farmers began to import breeding stock. Others started to use machinery and by 1913 a Livingstone merchant was able to advertise 'a large assortment of agricultural implements amongst which are: Deere Disc Plows, 2, 3 and 4 furrow; Groote Trekker Mouldboard Plows; Disc Harrows; Zig Zag Harrows; Cultivators; Mealie Mills; Wire Trek Tows and Trek Chains and Stinkwood Yokes'. In addition there was a good deal of experimentation. In the Fort Jameson area attempts were made to grow cotton, but the most important step forward proved to be the introduction of tobacco. The new crop was first grown in North-Eastern Rhodesia in 1903, where the experiment was backed, from 1913, by the United Tobacco Company, which established

[1] In 1911 there were 159 holdings in Northern Rhodesia with 713,663 acres under cultivation of which only 9,736 were under crops and 7,214 classed as fallow. Of the land held by farmers in 1911 only 770 acres were classed as orchards or gardens, whilst the average yield of maize per acre amounted only to little over 2 bags.

storage facilities, gave free advice to farmers and was able to pay cash for the farmer's products, the incipient industry receiving some encouragement from the existence of a protected market in South Africa.

The immigration of European farmers raised a new problem in the field of race relations; for the first time a group of white immigrants came into competition with the Africans for the latters' source of livelihood, the land. Along the 'Railway Belt' the position was not a very serious one for the local African population along the highveld was relatively sparse, whilst the cultivation of maize and the breeding of cattle did not require a very numerous settled labour force. Compensation was paid to the Africans living on land alienated to Europeans, payment being made at the rate of £1. o. o. to £2. o. o. per hut and 8/– to 10/– per cultivated acre, payment being calculated on the basis of the poll tax and of existing wages which then amounted to between 8/– and 15/– per month. Only very few Africans elected to stay on as tenants as there was plenty of land available elsewhere.

In the Fort Jameson region the position was different, for the country was already well populated before the Europeans arrived, and some of the land granted away by the North Charterland Company possessed a native population of 140 people per square mile, the average being perhaps about 20 per square mile. As long as the whites mainly confined their efforts to keeping cattle—as they did in the earlier stages of development—they needed only a few African herdboys, and the demand for native labour was small. When the Europeans began to improve their stock, they became even more anxious to see the last of the Africans on their estates. Like the 'enclosing landlords' of eighteenth century England, they did not like to see expensive pedigree cows mingle on the same pastures with the villagers' small and diseased beasts. Some Europeans therefore began to demand territorial segregation. In 1904 a Reserves Commission was set up which considered that 490 square miles of land should be constituted a native reserve, and that natives were to stay on European land only in the capacity of tenants, though compensation at the rate of 3/– per hut should be paid for those who elected to move out.[1] This policy, however, did not work. The overwhelming majority of Africans preferred to stay on the European farms, no African being ejected without his consent.[2] In addition there was also a change in the labour position. When Europeans started to experiment with cotton and tobacco, they required more labour and they were also able to employ African women and even children, so that the introduction of a reserve policy made little difference at first.

New difficulties, however, arose wherever European cultivation of land became more intensive, for the farmers' interests then began to clash with their tenants' whose time-honoured methods of 'shifting cultivation' involved the

[1] East Luangwa commission. *Report*: 29 Feb 1904 (in *North-Eastern Rhodesia government gazette*, 15 Mar 1904)

[2] In 1905 the Administrator reported that of 137 villages on European land 112 elected to stay. Those who remained had to work two months every year at the current wage rate. They also obtained defined water, timber and land rights from their employers.

burning down of extensive areas of timber which caused many veld fires. Complaints moreover came from the North Charterland Company, which found itself in grave financial difficulties. In 1911 the Company's local manager complained that the British South Africa Company refused to grant farms in regions where many Africans had settled, but which constituted the most valuable of the North Charterland Company's lands. Neither was his company permitted to charge rent to Africans living on its land, despite the fact that the local Africans themselves were now able to sell maize and other products at Fort Jameson. It was therefore essential to define his Company's rights, otherwise more effective European settlement would be impossible. Negotiations for new reserves began in 1913 when the local Nkunda, Chewa and Ngoni chiefs were called to Fort Jameson to discuss the matter. The chiefs themselves approved of the principle of separating white and blacks, provided they got land of good quality, and several scattered reserves were suggested by the Administration rather than one big consolidated bloc. A policy of splitting reserves was expected to facilitate administrative control, speed up the recruitment of labour, and also make the allocation of water supplies an easier matter. The soil selected varied in quality, ranging from very barren country to good, cultivable land, the allocation being made on a basis of 11·75 to 34 acres per head of native population, depending on the kind of country selected.[1] Then the Great War intervened and the reserves question was left in abeyance, though Africans were encouraged to move into those areas chosen.

In the meantime the demand for reserves also grew on the Railway Belt, where the subsequent War boom led to more intensive European production. Farmers complained of thefts of grain, whilst many objected to Africans living on the boundaries of their property because of numerous arguments over the right of way to water-holes. There was, moreover, some incipient competition from Africans who began to sell mealies and cattle, a type of enterprise which some farmers considered all the more objectionable because they thought it 'spoilt' their local labour supplies. From 1914 provisional reserves began to be laid out in the area, on the basis of about 25 acres per head, but again nothing was done till after the end of the war. The Chartered Company itself was at first far from jubilant about the whole question of laying out reserves. Some economists have since argued with a considerable degree of justification that the true function of the native reserves has been to subsidize urban enterprise at the expense of the tribe: reserves made it possible for old and unfit workers to be repatriated without getting sickness benefits and old age pensions, in much the same way as European employees thrown out of work had to go back home when Northern Rhodesia could no longer afford them a living. But at the time when the system first came into use, the Company looked upon the matter in a very different light. Henry Wilson Fox, the Company's London Manager, who possessed previous administrative experience of Rhodesia, thus argued that territorial segregation

[1] A peasant in Eastern Europe would have regarded a holding of about 6 acres as adequate, whilst 12 acres would have made him a substantial owner within the village community.

was wrong in principle. Reserves prevented development and stood in the way of native advancement. The country's African labour resources should rather be made available by encouraging education, by taxation and by the progressive destruction of tribal land ownership, which Fox imagined lay at the root of all evil. Fox at the same time was very critical of the Native Department; he said that the Native Commissioner was 'an expert in natives; he speaks of them as "my natives". His whole idea is segregation, if for no other reason than that he consciously or subconsciously realizes that when there is no native district, there will be no Native Commissioner. When Europeans enter his reserves . . .' Fox continued, 'there is often trouble. He only asks to be left alone . . . and it is not surprising that the more progressive citizens have begun to call for his elimination'.[1] As far as Northern Rhodesia was concerned, all efforts on the Imperial Government's behalf to delimit reserves should therefore be resisted, especially since the absence of a large European population north of the Zambezi made such measures unnecessary. The country's real need was education, to be accompanied by 'the gradual concentration of population in the most fertile and accessible districts'.

Whatever value Fox's ideas may have had for the future, at the time of writing they were visionary. An extensive development programme was quite impossible with the limited resources which the Chartered Company could command; skill and capital were scarce, and for the time being there was no possibility of revolutionizing native systems of land ownership. European pressure on land however hardly it may have borne on some individual Ngoni or Chewa tribesmen, was localized as far as Northern Rhodesia as a whole was concerned. North of the Zambezi there was still an area larger than France, Holland, Belgium and Switzerland between them available for the use of a population no larger than that of a big provincial town.[2] This meant that chiefs were still able to allocate land to their followers in the traditional manner; the returning labour migrant could still insist on being given a plot to work; his contacts with Europeans mostly remained of short duration, and tribalism continued to operate, as long as its economic basis remained little shaken.

The only conceivable solution from Wilson Fox's point of view would have been the individualization of African tenure. The Administration on the spot, however, made no attempt to put such a policy into practice, for they considered that the African's place in the new economy was that of a wage-labourer rather than that of a producer.[3] This view of course was not in accordance with the

---

[1] Wilson Fox, H. *The British South Africa Company: Memorandum . . . on problems of development and policy.* . . . British South Africa Company, 1910, p. 26.

[2] In 1911 the African population of the territory was estimated to number only 820,000. This figure probably constituted an under-estimate, but the total is unlikely to have much exceeded 1,000,000.

[3] Even in Southern Rhodesia, where more markets were available and where the Mashona were able to pay their taxes by selling grain and cattle, there was practically no individual tenure. A small Fingo colony at Bembesi had been attracted from the Cape by the offer of plots tenable on quit-rent title. A few farms were also bought in the Victoria District by Basuto or Shangaan people and two Matabele bought plots near Bulawayo where they carried on market gardening. The overwhelming majority of Africans, however, continued to hold their land on tribal tenure.

declared policy of the Imperial Government which by several Orders in Council had specifically guaranteed the right of Africans to buy land on the same conditions as Europeans. But as long as the necessary conditions for such a policy were lacking, it could not be enforced. Lewanika, for one thing, was bitterly opposed to the individualization of African tenure, for sound practical sociologist that he was he understood perfectly well that such a move would do away with the traditional functions of Barotse chieftainship. African tribesmen moreover lacked both the capital, and the knowledge of European ways and administrative procedure to enter the land market. Even had they done so, they still would have had to cope with all the problems that worried European farmers, who were much more used to such a system than they were; individualization of tenure implied exchanging the relative security of tribalism, with its time honoured co-operation between a wide circle of kinsmen and neighbours, for the stark insecurity of a man working his plot on his own, assisted only by his immediate family, and depending on the vagaries of a small and inadequate market. No wonder that at the time no tribesmen elected to lead such a life, and tribal tenure continued throughout Northern Rhodesia.

VI

The beginnings of urban life in Northern Rhodesia

The first towns in Northern Rhodesia all began as European settlements which were started up for the purposes of trade, mining or administration. All these centres had one thing in common: they were intended to serve specific functions, and most of their European inhabitants were at first labour migrants just like their African employees, intending to make some money and then return 'home'—wherever home might be. The earliest of these little posts was at the 'Old Drift' which was situated at the narrowest and deepest portion of the Zambezi river between the Victoria Falls and the first Rapids which extend as far as Kazungula. The 'Old Drift' owed its importance to the fact that all stores for Tanganyika Concessions Ltd, the Northern Copper Company, the Administration, and the traders bound for the Barotse valley had to be unloaded there. F. J. ('Mopani') Clark, a trader and hotel-keeper, settled there in 1898, and managed to pick up some business as a forwarding agent.[1] Another of these old-timers was Leopold Frank Moore, a Londoner who struggled for his education in night classes until he finally qualified as a chemist; in 1892, at the age of twenty-four, Moore joined the Cape Town Branch of Lennon Ltd, but a year later went to Mafeking where he set up a chemist's shop. In 1898 he went into business with his brother-in-law at Bulawayo and took a prominent part in the campaign against the introduction of Chinese labour, earning bitter hostility from the Chartered Company. Six years later he moved over to the 'Old Drift', a hot,

[1] A list of surviving 'Old Drifters' was published in the *Livingstone mail*, 28 Jan 1939, p. 5

steamy and miserable little place where malaria and blackwater fever were a constant menace to health and life. The few dozen Europeans had little to enter-ain themselves with but drink, and the bar was kept open all night if there was enough custom; an American gambler used to keep a roulette table drawling monotonously 'Round and round the little ball goes, and where she'll stop there's nobody knows; now gentlemen make your stakes, if you don't speculate, you can't accumulate'.[1] The 'Old Drift', like all Rhodesian settlements, was however, a very quiet place. The Rhodesian frontier was never crime-ridden like the American West or even Kimberley; the early Rhodesian owned a hunting rifle but never carried a revolver; he might start a drunken brawl, but murders were almost unknown in small communities where everyone knew everyone else, and where there was a relatively efficient administration and police almost right from the word go. Besides the mere fact of belonging to a small white community surrounded by a huge black majority gave white men a feeling of fellowship for each other which was much stronger than that which existed in Australia or the American West, and no Ned Kelly or Billy the Kid ever arose to become a folk-hero of the Rhodesian frontier.

In 1905 the 'Old Drift' lost its significance as an *entrepot* when the Victoria Falls bridge was completed, the bridge being sited, at Rhodes's characteristic request, in such a fashion that the spray from the Falls would hit the carriages. With the railway creeping towards the north the British South Africa Company decided to move the township and in spite of protests from the pioneers, the township of Livingstone was established on its present site, the first sale of stands being held on 23 February 1905. Two years later, the township obtained a new source of income when the capital of North-Western Rhodesia was moved from Kalomo to Livingstone. In 1903 Kalomo was a tiny outpost with an administrative staff of only fifteen officials who lived in little brick houses or African-style huts. In the same year a hospital was completed at Kalomo, but the place was administered very badly; poor sanitation and inadequate drainage made the post a paradise for the anopheles mosquito so that between 1905 and 1906 fourteen Europeans out of seventy died in the area. Matters came to a head when the Standard Bank of South Africa, which opened a branch at Kalomo in 1906, refused to carry on in the fever-stricken settlement, unless more satis-factory arrangements could be made. In 1907, therefore, the administrative centre was shifted to Livingstone and the riverside settlement became the head-quarters of Robert Codrington, who had been transferred as Administrator of North-Western Rhodesia in June of that year. Codrington, a stern believer in efficiency and sanitation, managed the place very well; the water supply was taken over from the railways, and Livingstone was spared the dreadful typhoid outbreaks which struck Salisbury and Bulawayo in the early days; the Adminis-tration also bought a cold storage plant which facilitated the supply of fresh meat, improved the sanitary services and supplied the little community with

---

[1] 'Discovery and historical associations' by Baxter, T. W. (in Clark, J. D., ed., *The Victoria Falls*. Lusaka, Commission for the Preservation of Natural and Historical Monuments, 1952, p. 21–48)

electricity. By 1910 the white population had grown to 277 (191 men, 49 women and 37 children). Livingstone was the only settlement in Northern Rhodesia which could boast of a permanent newspaper,[1] and was the centre of whatever European political activity was going on. As in all other Rhodesian townships a large variety of different voluntary societies sprang up to cater for sporting and social purposes amongst the mixed population of railwaymen, traders, and civil servants, club membership cutting to some extent across national and professional ties. As far as entertainment was concerned, Livingstonians were thrown on their own resources; there was of course plenty of sport, the Zambezi affording an opportunity for the running of regattas, there was drink and politics, and there were home-made variety shows. 'Messrs Nunn, Drew and Probyn' reported the *Livingstone Mail* on one of the local 'Cafes Chantants', 'sang a pretty glee "The Little Farm", and with the assistance of Mr McKiever gave "Sweet and Low" as an encore. Mr C. H. Drew sang "This is my Heart" but declined an encore which was a pity. The Reverend Moffat just returned from England came on with a new song "My Word" or "Jones of the Lancers". He sang it capitally with absolute and appropriate gestures and action and had to be coerced into an encore "I've got a mother", an old favourite. Mr T. F. Nunn sang "Bid me Love" and Mr T. B. Probyn rendered a new number "Onaway Awake". . . . Another quartette "Oh who will o'er the down so free" terminated the programme' which the audience undoubtedly appreciated!

During the same period another little settlement came into being. This was Lusaakas, later known as Lusaka, situated some 250 miles up the railway line from Livingstone. Like several other small villages along the line, Lusaka took its origin as an agricultural marketing centre, serving a community of farmers, most of whom were Afrikaans speaking. When the railway first came up, a few stores were opened by Jewish traders from the south, willing to face the bleak loneliness of a bare, wind-swept siding on the open veld. The tiny dorp grew a little bigger when traffic increased, 'the railway put up a 12 × 12 wood and iron room, called it the station [and] put in a Station master who also acted as Postmaster. Trains began to run more frequently, a few more farms were taken up, a European policeman was allocated to the village as well as a veterinary officer who . . . "was allowed to charge for visits to farms . . ." '.[2] The only link with the outside world was the train which arrived once a week and brought up supplies; the only local excitement was derived from lions who used to prowl around in the neighbourhood and attack the cattle. Life was made even more uncomfortable because the place was so low-lying. In the haphazard fashion customary

---

[1] Northern Rhodesia's first newspaper was *The Pioneer*, a cyclostyled sheet which appeared irregularly, published by W. Tranter. This was succeeded in 1906 by the *Livingstone pioneer and advertiser*, published by Tranter at his office in Empire Street. This did not survive the year, probably being 'killed' by the *Livingstone mail* which Leopold Moore started soon after Tranter commenced his venture, and which is now the oldest newspaper in the territory. The *Northern Rhodesia journal* began publication at Fort Jameson in 1909, edited first by the Reverend W. J. Bell and then by A. C. Hayter. Only a few issues were printed.

[2] Sampson, R. *So this was Lusaakas.* . . . Lusaka publicity association, 1959, p. 20

in the selection of most early Rhodesian town sites the planners chose the line of least resistance, the sole reason for the construction of a halt at the place being that the area was flat. Twenty years later a Government doctor could still write that 'there are pools of stagnant water in every street and almost every stand. Several houses are entirely surrounded by water. Between the township and the hospital is a square mile of swamp. The school is surrounded by water. There is a large lake of stagnant water knee deep on the north side of the school, and swamp on the other sides. The children are unable to reach the school with dry feet. . . .'[1] To make matters worse, Lusaka was characterized by that 'spread' which characterized most other Rhodesian settlements; land was cheap; time was no object; people liked privacy and built their houses far away from each other, a practice encouraged by the poor facilities for sanitation, the Administration itself usually making a point of building their offices in a separate area. This 'spread' gave Rhodesians plenty of elbow room, but made the subsequent provision of municipal services more difficult than it might have been. All the same, more immigrants came in; maize-mills and stores were built; an Italian started up a lime kiln which provided the settlement with its first industrial enterprise; by 1913 the village was sufficiently large to justify the setting up of a Village Management Board.

Broken Hill, further north from Lusaka, took its origin from a mining camp, the settlement starting with a collection of pole and daga huts and a few stores which were constructed close to the workings where the railway line was scheduled to pass. In the early days of Broken Hill the place was controlled through the Manager of the Rhodesian Broken Hill Development Company who kept law and order amongst his employees, whilst a Magistrate stationed nearby dealt with criminal matters. The railway line was then hurriedly pushed northwards, Pauling and Co. working under a heavy penalty clause and completing the work with such speed that when the line reached Broken Hill in 1906 the whole place was empty, as the inhabitants had not expected the gangers to arrive so quickly. As soon as proper communications had been established, calcined zinc began to be exported to Wales, and a cosmopolitan population of white labour migrants began to collect in the little settlement, including a number of destitute Europeans in search of jobs. Anglican clergymen used to hold religious services in the place, which appear to have been something of a social occasion for 'there were present at these services, Jews, Germans, American Methodists, Scotch Presbyterians, Romanists and others, while at the open-air service held for the boys, there were natives from twenty-four different tribes'.[2] Broken Hill, however, had a hard struggle. Lead and zinc were found in large quantities, but the different metals could not at first be economically separated and the mines had to close down with the result that Broken Hill became a miserable little place, at the edge of beyond. 'The spot represents desertion', wrote an Anglican missionary in 1910, 'for the numerous buildings and works around are

[1] Sampson, *op. cit*, p. 63
[2] De La Pryne, A. G. 'Broken Hill' (in *Central Africa*, v. 28, 1910, p. 230–232)

all falling into decay from disuse and dreariness prevails'. The show-place was the hotel, 'an iron room built on piles and divided into two, one half of which was the dining room, and the other place the billiard saloon . . . the rest consisted of squarely built native huts one of which was allotted to each guest as a bedroom'. A railway journey to Broken Hill was no luxury trip, and it was nothing out of the ordinary to see a couple of lady missionaries jammed into an ordinary luggage van with all their baggage and crates of live fowls, no light, seats, food or even water for the whole journey! All the same, things began to improve, and from the medical point of view Broken Hill was not the worst spot to live in. The mines administration drained the surrounding swamps by cutting dykes, and in addition a government hospital was set up, and life gradually became a little more comfortable.

Ndola, on the extreme northern edge of the territory, typified a third kind of settlement along the 'Railway Belt'. 'Old Ndola', situated some five miles from Bwana Mkubwa, was first selected by 'Chirupula' Stephenson, a well-known Native Commissioner in the Company's service, who in 1904 picked the site as his administrative headquarters. Later the railway line came up on its way to the Congo; a halt was constructed, the Railway erecting a number of wood and iron houses next to the line for their staff, and Pauling and Company built a local office; a few traders then moved in to profit from whatever local custom there was, and buildings were erected on both sides of the Luembwe River which ran in a valley parallel to the line, the main township being laid out on the sloping ground between river and railway. The white population of Ndola sub-district in 1910, including Bwana Mkubwa, was tiny, and included sixteen railway employees, thirteen traders, seventeen mine employees, seven farmers, five officials and a labour agent. Ndola nevertheless became a marketing centre of some local significance, supplying Bwana Mkubwa mine whenever it was in operation; in 1911 the local District Commissioner moved his headquarters to the little settlement.[1]

The most stationary section of the floating population in these little settlements tended to be the store-keepers. Missionaries and officials were always liable to be posted away, but the trader who successfully built up a business often remained where he was known, and where he had invested his savings, his little tin shed gradually being replaced by a decent brick house, topped by a corrugated iron roof, and surrounded by a huge veranda, where friends would gather at sundown to enjoy their drinks. The miners and artisans, on the other hand, belonged to a labour force that was far more unstable, both from the 'job' point of view, and as far as residence was concerned. An interesting 'case history' for the latter category was that of Charles Theodore Eriksson, known as 'Dynamite Jack', a Finn of Swedish extraction who was one of Robert Williams's early employees. Eriksson started off in life as a sailor in the Russian merchant navy, but in 1895 the nineteen year old seaman deserted his ship at Cape Town and

---

[1] Based on Gelfand, M. *Northern Rhodesia in the days of the Charter*. Blackwell, Oxford, 1961, p. 240–241

two years later made his way from Johannesburg to Bulawayo on a bicycle. He then tried to earn a living mending bicycles, but was lucky to find a job with the Bulawayo power station. When the Boer War broke out, he fought on the British side and took part in the relief of Mafeking, together with other Rhodesian troops. On being demobilized he went back to the power station, but in 1901 volunteered for Grey's expedition to the Katanga where he pegged several copper mines and remained with the Company until 1906, working just across the Northern Rhodesia border, exploring, pegging and digging shafts, generally 'bossing up' native workers, and building an almost wholly 'home-made' plant to turn out the first bars of tin and copper to be smelted in the Congo. When the job came to an end he became a 'white hunter', shooting game for the University of Helsinki, his native city, and later he returned to Russia to prospect in Siberia. Eriksson could not, however, resist the spell of Africa and came back to Bulawayo where he finally became a successful businessman, receiving a commission in the Great War in East Africa, becoming a City Councillor after the end of hostilities, and finally retiring to spend his old days on a Rhodesian farm.[1]

Eriksson's career sounds adventurous and romantic in retrospect—and so in many ways it was. But the golden glow that always gilds the past should not disguise the fact that the European labour migrant's lot was hard and insecure— like the African's. Unemployment was always round the corner—and so was death. The white death rate in North-Western Rhodesia between 1904 and 1905 stood at 64 per thousand, comparable to the losses an army might sustain in wartime. Nearly all the deaths were due to malaria and blackwater fever. The people who were forced to live outside the settlements in rough country, transport riders, traders, prospectors, and railwaymen suffering even more severely than the remainder.[2] With better housing and better medical care conditions gradually improved, but malaria and blackwater fever remained a serious problem until well after the First World War.

The European workers' condition was in fact comparable in some ways to that of his African fellow worker. The native who drifted into the poverty-stricken townships by the railway line also regarded these settlements, not as places to live in, but designed just to make money. Like his white shift-boss the black navvy or miner drifted from job to job and from compound to compound, remaining inefficient at everything he tried. Unlike his European workmate, however, he remained tied to a tribal economy, the average mine contract at first not exceeding two or three months at a time. This meant that the mine-worker had neither the chance nor the inclination to rise beyond the ranks of unskilled labour, and the process of stabilizing black labour was infinitely slower than the equivalent process at work amongst the Europeans. Nevertheless, as soon as the black worker entered the town, he immediately had to fit into a new society. There were two kinds of communities: the mining compound, rigidly

[1] See the Eriksson papers (ER 1, Nat Arch MS)

[2] According to M. Gelfand's figures, there was a sharp improvement in 1908, when the death rate dropped to 25·71 per thousand, but the white man's life expectancy was still only 34½ years, which is considerably lower than the Southern Rhodesian African's today.

controlled by the mine administration and composed only of mine workers, and the ordinary urban location, housing a variegated lot of hawkers, general labourers, domestic servants and its contingent of chancers and prostitutes. The mining settlement in some ways resembled a military camp where the foremen and sub-managers were the officers and the General Manager took the place of the Commanding-Officer. The Europeans were separated from their African hands by a rigid colour bar, culture, skill and living standards, even though the European in the early days was also very poor. The white foremen, faced with the unenviable task of having to handle crowds of men whose languages and beliefs they did not understand and whose incompetence irritated them, considered that tough treatment of Africans was the only thing possible, becoming convinced that there must be no 'weakness' in dealing with them. In this respect there was not the slightest difference between a man like Eriksson, born in a country where the colour issue was unknown, and the South African workers, who had come from a Colony where white superiority had become part of the country's historical tradition.

Discipline was re-enforced by the Masters and Servants legislation, passed in 1908,[1] which resembled the code of an army, making desertion and various other kinds of misdemeanour a criminal offence, as they already were south of the Zambezi. The measure was not specifically applicable to Africans but to unskilled labourers in general. But as there were no white unskilled workers in employment, the measure constituted an important new legislative barrier between the two races. At the same time, however, the Africans received protection against dishonest employers so that the law also contained a paternal element. Discipline on the spot lay in the hands of the mine administration itself, the local Magistrate only entering upon the scene in very rare cases. In the early days the European miners hit their 'boys' as they thought fit, but on the mines at the Hook of the Kafue the power to punish Africans was soon confined to the manager, and fines or forcible seclusion took the place of beatings, a reform which led to the disappearance of desertion.[2] Similar reforms were introduced at Kansanshi where the condition of the compounds was gradually improved and the power of inflicting lashes was taken from the compound manager.[3] Broken Hill pursued a similar policy; no man-handling of natives was permitted, and Broken Hill was unusual in that Africans were allowed to bring their wives with them, with the result that the workers became more contented with their lot.[4] Order on the lowest level depended on African 'boss-boys' and 'police boys' who tended to be drawn from the same tribes as their charges, though not necessarily from chiefs' sons, so that in the mine it did not matter whether a man came from the highly aristocratic Bena Ngandu or Crocodile clan from Bembaland or

[1] High Commissioner's proclamations no. 37 of 1908 and 18 of 1912, based on the Masters and servants ordinance, 1901, of Southern Rhodesia
[2] 'The minerals of North-Eastern Rhodesia: interesting interview with Mr. T. G. Davey', (in *Central African times*, 21 Feb 1903, p. 7)
[3] Report for Kasempa district 1909–1910 (in A 4/2/2, Nat Arch NWR)
[4] *Livingstone mail*, 9 May 1919, p. 3

from the ranks of commoners, mine-work tending to produce a rough egalitarianism, comparable perhaps in some ways to that which developed amongst the European workers. An even more important means of control, however, was to be found in the economic power which the mines were able to wield over their 'boys'. Only the mines could supply the labourers with food. The few neighbouring African villages could not produce enough provisions, for the mining sites, unlike indigenous African settlements, were not chosen for the fertility of the surrounding countryside. The system by which labourers received their pay in truck goods which they bartered to local villagers soon broke down, and the mine began to trade itself, developing a commissariat service that became responsible for feeding the whole of its labour force. Trading operations soon had to be extended over a large area, a strong incentive to this being the fear of 'spoiling' local labour supplies by giving other opportunities for earning cash.[1]

The first piece of social welfare legislation of any importance was not passed until 1917,[2] the law again being modelled on a code already in force south of the Zambezi. The administration laid down that every mine employing more than 300 Africans must have a compound manager, that compounds must be kept clean, whilst medical and compound inspectors obtained the right of inspection. The mines were forced to provide adequate accommodation for their workers, whilst provision was made for a compulsory day of rest. In addition there were clauses dealing with obligatory medical treatment for Africans; every mine employing more than 300 workers had to maintain a doctor, and a hospital had to be provided by the mine authorities. A minimum scale of rations was also laid down: African workers became entitled to $1\frac{1}{2}$ pounds of grain per day, as well as 2 pounds of beans, 2 pounds of meat, 2 pounds of vegetables, a pound of peanuts and $3\frac{1}{2}$ ounces of salt a week. The mines might feed their workers according to alternate ration scales, but these had to be equivalent in food value to the first mentioned, with the result that the average mine worker became much better fed than he was in his village, where famine still remained an ever present threat. These measures resulted in a better cared for and therefore more efficient labour force; they also meant that mine work, once the most unpopular type of employment, came to be preferred to farm work, where food and pay was often worse, with the result that a new kind of cleavage opened up between the white farmers and miners of Rhodesia, who were both competing for the same labour supply.[3]

At the same time a variegated crowd of African labour migrants began to collect at Livingstone, the only urban centre of any size in Northern Rhodesia.

[1] The labour force in question was of course small at first. Kansanshi in 1913 employed 85 local and 778 non-local Africans. In 1920 Broken Hill employed an average of 1,845 Africans, Bwana Mkubwa 212, and Sable Antelope only 196.

[2] Mines health and sanitation regulations (Government notice no. 17 of 1917, *Northern Rhodesia government gazette*, v. 7, no. 3, 13 Feb 1917, p. 38)

[3] Wages at Kansanshi before World War I ranged from 6/- a month above ground up to £1. o. o. underground.

L

The earliest native 'townsman' of whom we possess any record in Northern Rhodesia was a Basuto called Richard, a former pupil of the Paris Evangelical Mission in Basutoland who settled in the vicinity of the Victoria Falls where he worked as a transport rider and gardener.[1] In 1907 a new type of African made his appearance for the first time on the railway line when Codrington brought over a number of mission trained African craftsmen from Fort Jameson to build a government camp at Broken Hill. The local Europeans protested, but Codrington went ahead all the same, arguing that in a country like Northern Rhodesia where the climate was against the settler, skilled Europeans should only act as supervisors, a sentiment which the *Livingstone Mail* shared at the time.[2] Codrington of course was used to North-Eastern Rhodesia where skilled African labour had first been introduced from Nyasaland, and where there were no European artisans. His only concern was to be able to get the job done on the tiny budget available, and he saw no reason why he should employ skilled Europeans at 35/– a day, if he could get the work done for less. A year later the *Livingstone Mail* angrily wrote that 'in defiance of the prejudices of the British race the world over, the Administration is trying to create a class of skilled native artisans who are intended to perform the work elsewhere entrusted solely to white men'.[3] To some extent the *Livingstone Mail*'s point of view was, however, accepted, and in 1910 Wallace, the new Administrator, assured a European deputation that whilst Africans would continue to be employed as telegraphists, typists and compositors, no use would be made of them locally as carpenters or bricklayers.[4]

A similar case of colour tension being heightened by economic competition arose in the case of the Indians. Here the quarrel was not one between two different groups of artisans, but between two conflicting sections within the trading community. The Indian question first made its appearance in Fort Jameson, a cultural extension of Nyasaland, where Sir Harry Johnston had encouraged Indian immigration for the sake of getting clerks, telegraphists and traders to come into the country. In Nyasaland there were no poor white traders comparable to those in North-Western Rhodesia, and Indians soon made some headway. 'No profit is too small or inconsiderable; no time too long to devote to the successful driving of a bargain', wrote a former British Consul of the Asian of the time. 'His manner of life, domestic in the extreme is nevertheless so thrifty, so frugal and his wants, bounded by a little curry and rice, are so inexpensive, that few there are who cannot remit a few rupees to India at the end of the year, to add to the store which . . . shall support them in an honoured old age in Goa or Bombay.' Indians were inured to a tropical climate, they mixed easily with the Africans and possessed considerable aptitude for learning native languages. The immigrant from Asia usually came as a young man to engage himself as a salesman in the stores of those of their countrymen who were already established

---

[1] A. Coisson: 28 Feb 1905 (in *Journal des missions évangéliques*, 1905, p. 312–314)
[2] *Livingstone mail*, 13 July 1907, p. 4   [3] *Livingstone mail*, 12 Sep 1908, p. 3
[4] *Livingstone mail*, 10 Sep 1910, p. 5

in the country. 'At the end of such an engagement, they endeavour as a rule to start business on their own account, and as there is rarely an opportunity of doing so in the towns, the enterprising young "Banyan" invests a portion of his savings in the purchase of a small stock of native barter goods, and with these, borne on the heads of a few native carriers, fares forth . . . into some outlying district where the opposition is slight and native villages many. Here he builds a good-sized hut, and arranging his calico, beads, matches, brass wire, and other tempting wares on roughly constructed shelves, publishes to the small surrounding community that the new establishment is now open for the transaction of business and commends his future to Allah'. The small profits from selling his goods were invested in buying up a stock of maize, millet, oil-seeds or groundnuts, beeswax or rubber, which were then sold to European wholesale traders. Gradually the Indian became more prosperous and sent for some of his relatives from India who would open up branch establishments, whilst the merchant had a proper shop built for himself in the nearest important trading centre. At this stage he opened a bank account, learned the European language and acquired a working knowledge of local law and custom, becoming a man of considerable importance in the local community.[1]

Much of the trade at Chinde, Tete and in the Zambezi valley came to be monopolized by Indian and Goanese merchants and North-Eastern Rhodesia became the eastward extension of this new 'trader's frontier', most of these immigrants apparently coming to the country via Beira. They first made their appearance at Fort Jameson in 1905 when a direct route was opened up to the Zambezi. There were bitter protests from local white traders, including the African Lakes Company, but Codrington, then in charge of the territory, would not listen to any of these complaints; Indians, he argued, catered almost exclusively for the native trade, in hides, wax, grain and oil-seeds, which was too troublesome for Europeans to undertake.[2] The Indian village trader would help to develop the country by helping Africans to get rid of surplus produce, without having to trek hundreds of miles to the nearest store, and Indian enterprise in the end would improve the European wholesale merchant's business The Chartered Company itself was in agreement with these sentiments; Wilson Fox at one time even thought in terms of settling Indian peasants in the Zambezi valley; and all European efforts to exclude Indians from the territory proved in vain.[3]

The Administration did, however, insist on residential segregation. When Fort Jameson was laid out the Administration planned an Asian quarter, just as had already been done in the Nyasaland townships. This type of separation was not at first looked upon as a hardship, for the Indians naturally preferred to be

---

[1] Maugham, R. C. F. Zambezia. . . . John Murray, 1910, p. 27

[2] R. Codrington to B.S.A. Company: 11 July 1905, annex. 12 to B.S.A. Company minutes: 20 July 1905 (in LO 1/2/44, Nat Arch SR)

[3] Immigration of course was still very small. In 1911 there were only 39 Indians in Northern Rhodesia, among whom were 13 Moslems and 22 Hindus. 20 were engaged in trade, 11 in agriculture, mostly as market-gardeners, 6 as domestic workers and 2 as tailors. 23 out of 39 could read and write.

within reach of their friends. More important still was the fact that land values did not matter at first in an under-developed little community, where land was cheap and where there was at first not much difference between one stand and another; in Blantyre the Europeans even argued that when the township was first laid out Asians were given all the best positions near the trunk roads.[1]

Whatever the merits or de-merits of these local controversies, Indians were, however, accepted as townsmen right from the start. Africans, on the other hand, were not; and all early laws were based on the assumption, universally accepted in Southern Africa at the time, that the township would never form the African's permanent home. Legislation was passed to enforce residential separation, which was considered to be essential both from the point of view of sanitation and that of discipline. Segregation enabled the Europeans to control the labour migrants from the village, who were as yet without any permanent stake in the towns and who lacked any kind of indigenous authority in the new settlement. The Africans could now be kept under a new kind of restraint, either on his master's premises, or in 'compounds'. The first legal instrument to enforce this policy was provided by the Natives in Townships Regulations of 1909[2] which applied to North-Eastern Rhodesia and was first put into force at Fort Jameson. No African who was not permanently employed by a European or an Asian, was permitted to reside in the township. Africans who wished to be outside their location between the hours of nine and five had to have a pass. In 1914 similar regulations were published with regard to Livingstone where since about 1907 Africans were housed either at Maramba or what was known as the 'employers' compound'.[3] In addition the manufacture of native beer was prohibited in urban settlements, only Village Management Boards being allowed to sell beer under specified conditions, which constituted a further unintentional blow against tribal customs, as many ritual purposes demanded the use of home-brewed beer. The compound came under the supervision of the Local Village Management Board and a compound inspector was appointed to look after the mixed crowd of Africans who gathered in the place; violence and drunkenness made their appearance there from an early period and in 1913 the *Livingstone Mail* reported that a gang of intoxicated Africans from North-Eastern Rhodesia had stoned the compound inspector.[4] The compound also brought different tribal groups into contact with the result that there was a certain amount of inter-marriage. In 1917 the *Livingstone Mail* reported a murder case involving a Yao bricklayer married to a Lamba woman,[5] a type of union that would not easily have been contracted in other parts of the territory.

[1] Nyasaland times, 11 Sep 1913, p. 4
[2] Government notice no. 9 of 1909 (in *North-Eastern Rhodesia government gazette*, 4 June 1909)
[3] Government notice no. 20 of 1914 (in *Northern Rhodesia government gazette*, 18 April 1914, p. 1)
[4] *Livingstone mail*, 24 Oct 1913, p. 7
[5] *Livingstone mail*, 30 Mar 1917, p. 6

Chapter Four

Politics, war and aftermath

I

Administration and politics

Economic development gradually imposed new tasks on the Administration, and despite the Company's constant clamour for economy, there was a slow but steady expansion of its civil service north of the Zambezi. Small technical departments were built up, including rudimentary medical, veterinary and agricultural services; the formalization of justice necessitated the appointment of a trained Legal Adviser, whilst the growth of legislation necessitated the setting up of a Printing and Stationery Department. The need for closer administration and taxation in the districts also promoted the expansion of the civil service, and this resulted in the familiar phenomenon of growth in one direction resulting in additional expansion in other departments, as the newly appointed staff in turn needed more staff to look after their pay, their transport, their health and other needs.

The complexity of the administrative machine must of course not be exaggerated. The civil service was still limited in its functions, designed primarily for the maintenance of law and order. The bulk of social work continued to be shouldered by the missions, though the Administration did set up a small and at first rather inefficient Government school for Barotseland, as well as giving some support to European education. Under these conditions the administrative machine remained sufficiently small to be effectively supervised by the Administrator, who remained the king-pin of government. The Administrator, a carefully selected and relatively highly paid man, supervised the work of all departments and attended to all political problems, centralized government not yet having been slowed down by the existence of a complex Secretariat. The Administrator was able to rule his domain with little interference from outside, his power only being limited by financial stringency and by any such 'remote control' as the London Board and the Colonial Office chose to exercise, the latter acting through the High Commissioner and, from 1911, through a Resident Commissioner stationed at Salisbury.

The mainstay of the Administration and its 'maid of all work' was, however, the District Officer. Northern Rhodesia was as yet regarded as a native country, a reservoir of labour, a speculative investment for the future, but not as a major area of white settlement. This attitude was reflected in the country's administrative structure. South of the Zambezi the Company maintained two different hierarchies, the Civil Commissioners and Magistrates, concerned primarily with European matters, and Native Commissioners, who looked after African affairs. North of the river, on the other hand, there was but a single pyramid. A young man would join the Administration as a clerk and probationer, then he rose to be an Assistant Native Commissioner until such time as he was given a district of his own. The next step was to become a Magistrate, Magistrates and Native Commissioners alike exercising judicial functions, so that at the lower level the administrator was also a judge. In addition to trying cases, collecting taxes and collecting census material, the Native Commissioner was expected to carry out an enormous range of additional duties which ranged from repairing roads to shooting man-eating lions. In many ways a Native Commissioner's lot in the early days was more enviable than it is now. As long as communications were poor he was largely his own master and enjoyed a considerable degree of independence. The invasion of Government by the expert had not yet begun; the Native Commissioner was not as yet expected to correspond about soil erosion, tsetse control, or veterinary problems; half the year might still be spent on 'ulendo' trekking through his district on foot with native carriers, and much of his work was still done under the village tree, surrounded by a semi-circle of half naked tribesmen who had come to hear him adjudicate on their local disputes.

The spirit of this Administration was one of paternalistic despotism, and nothing can better illustrate the early district officer's benevolent, sometimes amused attitude towards his charges, as well as his own image of himself, than this facetious doggerel, reminiscent of school prefects' poetry, written by Codrington himself in praise of a subordinate:

> On Luapula's banks by rock and pool
> Bwana Kijana exercises rule.
> Around his boma turmoil ceases not,
> Belgians intrigue and missionaries plot,
> Witchdoctors brew decoctions to destroy him,
> But all these things are powerless to annoy him:
> Unmoved, undaunted, undismayed he still
> Will bend or break them to his iron will.
>
> On Luapula is much zeal administrative,
> I should like to be a native
> On the Luapula where Harrington is ruler,
> Where the revenue is full and always growing fuller,
> Where the rubber and the vine tree grow.
> Oh I wish I was a negro
> For the revenue is big and always growing bigger.
> Oh what luck to be a nigger
> On the Luapula where Harrington is ruler.[1]

[1] Quoted from 'The Taming of North-Eastern Rhodesia' by Harrington, H. T. *Northern Rhodesia journal*, v. 2, no. 3, 1954, p. 3–20

Boma meant a stockade and came to be used for an administrative station of Government in general. *Bwana*, 'Lord' was the title used for the Europeans, all of whom were given native nicknames by the Africans.

Under these pioneer conditions the white officials, like the traders, lived in close contact with the African population, and one of the inevitable results of their isolation from their own kind was the prevalence of temporary unions between white men and black women. Exact figures are of course impossible to obtain and estimates differ, but what information there is available indicates that the practice was widespread, despite many attempts to stamp it out. As long as there were no European women in the country the practice even found its defenders. In 1910 Judge P. L. Beaufort, then acting Administrator of North-Eastern Rhodesia, could even suggest that Native Commissioners entangled in liaisons of such a kind should not be punished, provided their unions remained 'decently veiled', confined to one woman, and not flowering forth into 'libertinage'. The writer, whose previous colonial experience had been in Borneo, not South Africa, went on to say that such practices were being defended on the grounds that they were beneficial to health, that they were of material comfort to many a lonely official in the outposts, that they prevented the influx of South African prostitutes, and that they protected the official from contempt and suspicion on the part of Africans, who might otherwise suspect the whites of being prone to much more degrading and unnatural practices. In addition the Judge thought that such unions facilitated the learning of native languages and native ways of thought, and served to keep the Administration informed of what was going on in the villages.[1] Judge Beaufort's views proved most unpalatable to his superiors and were never accepted, but many of the men on the spot shared them, and miscegenation only began to diminish when more white women came into the country and succeeded in imposing a new tone on back-veld society.

The impact of European immigration created many new problems and these in turn necessitated more formalized administration. More letters had to be written and answered, and in order to deal with the increase in clerical work typewriters came into use. The typewriter however in turn added to office work; carbon copies could be reeled off and documents could be produced much more quickly than before; these were circularized to other offices, read and acknowledged, so that the art of filing became more important. Offices now acquired a kind of artificial memory with the result that administration achieved greater permanence and impersonality than in the past, when the Native Commissioner relied on a few notes hastily scribbled down in a pocket diary. At the same time a greater premium was put on 'chair borne' work; more time had to be spent in the office and less on trek, so that by 1910 an intelligent Magistrate in the Bemba country complained that Native Commissioners were becoming nothing but 'transport and postal clerks'. Office work, he protested, 'showed up' more for promotion, with the result that the chiefs were recovering something of their older powers as popular leaders, whilst the Native Commissioner was regarded as a man who collected taxes, inspected census papers and put people into gaol.[2]

[1] L. P. Beaufort to High Commissioner: 4 Oct 1910 (A 2/1/2, Nat Arch NER)
[2] Melland, F. *Report on Mpika district for 1908–1909* (KDS 4/6/2, Nat Arch NER)

The increase in paper work also influenced the selection of the officials. More emphasis was now placed on education, and from 1914 onwards the Administration attempted to engage University trained people only. The average Native Commissioner was no longer an ex-labour recruiter or a former police sergeant; he was the son of a barrister or a merchant who had learnt how to play games at a public school, taken a 'Second' or a 'Third' at Oxford, or just failed to get through the 'Indian Civil', the plum of the administrative profession overseas. The new kind of civil servant was considerably removed in background and outlook from the ordinary settler, over whom he had an additional advantage in possessing a regular source of income, independent on the vagaries of mining or farming. It is thus not surprising that the *Livingstone Mail* began to rail at what Moore mistakenly believed to be the 'younger sons of British aristocracy', with their 'assumption of arrogant superiority.'[1]

The formalization of administrative work also gave employment to a new kind of African, the mission trained clerk, for whom there was no outlet in the traditional village economy. Typists, compositors, junior telegraphists, clerks and court interpreters were all Africans, most of them being recruited at first from Nyasaland with its old established system of mission schools.[2] Native clerks and interpreters were cheaper than whites, an important consideration to an Administration with a perpetual deficit; they also knew the indigenous languages better than Europeans. For in Northern Rhodesia a South African tongue was of little use, except Sesuto, and the needs of the Administration could not be filled by bilingual white South Africans. In this respect Northern Rhodesia was very different from the southern sister colony where Sindebele was widely understood and many Zulu speaking whites from Natal found employment. The 'new men' became a privileged group receiving better rations and quarters than the ordinary Africans,[3] and some of them became semi-Europeanized and did not return to their homes. The majority of these people came from Nyasaland and they were drafted all over the country, with the result that knowledge of Chinyanja spread to many parts of North-Eastern Rhodesia. Even ordinary native chiefs found it useful to cultivate people of that stamp and to encourage them to settle in their villages; a man who could salute the Europeans with becoming dignity and correctness was after all well worth cultivating, with the result that 'Nyasaland boys' could be found on terms of intimacy with the local headmen in many parts of the country.[4]

In Barotseland, with its comparatively complex state apparatus, the position

---

[1] In 1905 the Administrator of North-Eastern Rhodesia was paid £1,200. The minimum salary in the service amounted to £200, which was the annual income of the Comptroller of Posts and Telegraphs. A foreman in the Public Works Department got a maximum of £300, a doctor up to £400 and a magistrate up to £600. The purchasing power of money was of course many times what it is now.

[2] The best-paid African Clerk in North-Eastern Rhodesia received £48 p.a.

[3] In 1906 the so-called 'class B' clerks in North-Western Rhodesia were entitled to a daily ration of a pound of meat, 2 ounces of sugar, a pound of meal and an ounce of coffee.

[4] Webster, W. G. 'The Goths and Northern Rhodesia' (in *Central Africa*, v. 29, Sep 1911, p. 236–239)

of the mission educated man, usually a local aristocrat, was even more important. From 1899, when Letia, Lewanika's son, received baptism, Christians gradually came to dominate the state. Mission trained men were responsible for putting forward repeated requests to be put under direct Imperial protection, demands to this effect being made through missionary channels as early as 1907.[1] The Barotse were not successful in this policy; for the Imperial Government at the time was unwilling to be saddled with any additional administrative responsibilities, especially since these would have entailed leaving the Company in possession of the most promising part of North-Western Rhodesia, and the Imperial Government with a poor and isolated section. The demands of educated Africans, however, increased, and four years later in 1911, Lewanika for the first time put forward a request that 'those who understood the notion of progress' should be allowed to advance, and that there should be no discrimination on grounds of colour.[2]

The chiefs in the remaining parts of Northern Rhodesia were, however, not yet worried about issues of this kind. Their problems were much more pressing ones and were concerned largely with finance. The theory of Administration at the time was that of Direct Rule. The Native Commissioner was supposed to be responsible for everything that went on in his district. Chiefs, who formally owed their appointment to the Administrator, were nothing but 'constables', minor executive officials receiving no fixed salary in reward for their services. They were responsible for the apprehension of criminals, for assisting in the collection of taxes, and a great variety of other duties, including, ironically enough, the suppression of witchcraft and divination, even though the chiefs' powers themselves were partly of a magical kind. The chiefs' judicial powers were not recognized in law, but in practice their informal courts continued to operate, for the Native Commissioner had now little time to concern himself with the marital affairs of his charges or with their disputes about water and fishing rights. The retention of power by the chiefs meant cheap administration, and long before 'Indirect Rule' became an officially accepted doctrine of Government, chiefs were encouraged to adjudicate in minor cases with the blessings of the Administration, whilst attempts were made to appoint chiefs even in 'stateless' societies. In return for their services some chiefs received small salaries, 7/6 a month being a fair average. This was, however, no more than a 'raw boy' might get down a mine, so that chiefs might find themselves worse off than their subjects—a basic weakness in the Company's administrative scheme, but one for which no remedy could be found as long as Government continued to be run on a shoe-string.

Immigration and economic change also presented the Company with a European political problem. In the early days this did not exist, for the last thing the poor frontiersman wanted to do was to engage in politics. The trader, often an

---

[1] A. Jalla to High Commissioner: 30 Sep 1907 (*South Africa: further correspondence....* African (South) no. 872)

[2] Lewanika to High Commissioner: 17 Sep 1911 (A 2/2/1, Nat Arch NR)

alien, could not afford to alienate the Administration on which he was dependent for the issue of his annual licence; the staff of the big trading companies, the mines or the railways knew that they were only labour migrants and did not meddle in local affairs, unless their most immediate interests were concerned, whilst their employers preferred to approach the London Board of the Company directly, if they wanted anything. As far as the farmers were concerned, they lived in isolation from one another; few could afford the time to attend regular political meetings or to quarrel with the Administration which sold them land at cheap rates and helped them to get stock.

The first stirrings of political interest were at Livingstone, the only settlement with any pretensions to being a township. Livingstone was moreover the centre of administration of North-Western Rhodesia; in 1911 its position was further strengthened when North-Eastern and North-Western Rhodesia were amalgamated and Livingstone became the 'capital' for Northern Rhodesia as a whole. The new move was itself a recognition of the fact that the centre of gravity had shifted to the Railway Belt, communications now being sufficiently good to admit of the whole country being run from a single headquarters. It might be added that the Directors had the mistaken view that amalgamation would lead to a reduction of staff and expenditure, an expectation not fulfilled in practice.[1] At Livingstone, budding politicians could easily get into contact with senior officials and hear the latest news. Livingstone was also able to boast of the country's only newspaper, the *Livingstone Mail*; political meetings and scurrilous speeches moreover formed one of the few forms of entertainment available in this isolated little settlement on the Zambezi, and Livingstonians were not slow to take advantage of a change from the monotony of daily life. The first man to build up an interest in local politics was Leopold Frank Moore. Moore, honest, but narrow-minded, sometimes 'woolly' in thought and full of prejudice, hated the Chartered Company with all his might. The Company to him represented Cobbett's 'Thing', that unholy combination of financial monopoly, social privilege and political absolutism, which he believed was holding up the country's development. Moore also held the most ill-conceived notions about the ability of a handful of European settlers to run a vast territory with nearly a million African people, and possessed little understanding of the financial and administrative realities of the situation. The *Livingstone Mail* moreover gave expression to that lunatic fringe which is found in every frontier society, and entertained its readers with Moore's musings regarding the evolution of humanity, the future of the soul, as well as other topics nearer to the interest of Livingstonians such as the current price of mealies and grain! But for all his idiosyncrasies, Moore was a man of great drive and force of character; he was genuinely and deeply attached to his adopted country and was willing to spend a

---

[1] By 1914 the European staff of central and technical departments had shot up and numbered 125 persons, the Northern Rhodesia Police numbered 33 and the District Administration 103. The Secretariat now comprised 9 persons, and the Treasury 10, the most remarkable increase being in the Medical Department which now comprised 16 doctors, 3 entomologists and 9 dispensers and nurses.

great deal of his time and money to fight for the policies in which he believed. The *Livingstone Mail*, printed by Moore himself under enormous difficulties, was originally subsidized from the profits of his chemist's shop, and without Moore's energy this paper could never have been produced. At first his paper dealt mainly with local grievances, such as the supposedly high price of land and the restrictions imposed on the export of breeding cattle. But he soon tackled more general issues such as the mining policy which he believed to be responsible for locking up the country's wealth; then he questioned the Company's land-rights and finally demanded self-government for the territory, his paper becoming a catalyst for the colonists' incipient political ambitions.

Moore's efforts by themselves would have availed little, but the strength of the Europeans gradually increased, as more economic opportunities came into existence. Farmers banded themselves together in Farmers' Associations, and this new political lobby was reinforced from home when Lord Winterton, in association with the Duke of Westminster and Lord Wolverton, all wealthy absentee landowners, formed an association of Northern Rhodesian farmers resident in England.[1] Helped by three Peers of the Realm, white Northern Rhodesians became one of the best represented communities in the British Empire.

Admittedly, care must be taken not to exaggerate the importance of these developments. The settlers were still extremely weak, and Rhodesia as a whole entirely lacked any properly constituted political parties with a mass backing, and a bureaucratic backbone to give continuity to their work; politics were still run by local 'notables', and a sundowner party might matter more than a meeting. Most of the issues that interested the colonists were local ones and concerned with immediate grievances, rather than the theoretical issues of Company versus elective Government, which loomed so large in Moore's mind. There were complaints with regard to land prices, the steadily rising cost of living, veterinary matters and the expense involved in trading licences. 'What are these exorbitant licences?' asked Sir Starr Jameson, the Company's President at an interview with a deputation at Lusaka. '£60 for a bottle store' the farmers' spokesman firmly replied, 'it makes our sundowner too dear. We have to pay customs duties, £10 for trading licence, £60 for liquor licence, and it makes our food too dear— whisky, I consider is food in this country.'[2]

All the same, increasing note was being taken of the opinion of the colonists whose ranks were now being reinforced by men of more substantial means, including a number of retired army officers who took to farming with the help of their pensions. The new trend was symbolized by Lawrence Aubrey Wallace (later knighted), who became Administrator of North-Western Rhodesia in 1909. Wallace, a civil engineer by profession, was a very different kind of man from Codrington with his Public School, military and Nyasaland background. Before coming to Northern Rhodesia Wallace had 'knocked about' widely, having built railways in South Africa and South America, and travelled and

---

[1] *Livingstone mail*, 5 Sep 1913, p. 6
[2] Sampson, R. *So this was Lusaakas.* . . . Lusaka, Lusaka publicity association, 1959, p. 45

hunted extensively in Central Africa. In 1902 Wallace accepted an appointment as Chief Surveyor of North-Eastern Rhodesia where he achieved rapid promotion, rising to be Administrator five years later, before being sent to North-Western Rhodesia to take over after Codrington's sudden death, at the end of 1908. Wallace was the man of much more conciliatory disposition than his predecessor and proved friendly towards the settlers' demands for representation in local government.[1] In 1912 he agreed to discuss all matters of interest to the Farmers' Association with their delegates. Two years later he reported to his Directors after the break up of an ephemeral 'Political League' that much of the old animosity towards the Company had gone and that he was now personally in favour of an Administrator's Council with some local representation.[2]

The Company, had Moore but known, was itself far from hostile to the settlers' political aspirations. Its main object by now was to secure a favourable deal by which it would be enabled to get rid of its expensive administrative commitments, and in the pursuit of this policy it was willing to make political concessions. Its policy in Southern Rhodesia, where the bulk of European strength was concentrated and where a Legislative Council with elected representation had been conceded since 1898, is best summarized in the words of Fox, the Company Manager, himself. '. . . On the one hand it was necessary in the shareholders' interest to carry the political power of the settlers to such a point as to constitute them an effective bulwark against encroachment by either the Union [of South Africa] or the Imperial Government, it is on the other hand inadvisable and dangerous to further or acquiesce in the extension of their political power up to a point when it can be used effectively against the commercial interests of the shareholders.'[3] In Northern Rhodesia this critical point was as yet far from being reached, and the outlook for further political concessions to the settlers was bright, when World War I burst upon the Western World.

II

Northern Rhodesia and the Great War

(a) *Military operations*

The outbreak of hostilities was wholly unexpected and the Company's administration was quite unprepared for the shape of things to come. The only military force available was the Northern Rhodesian Police which was formed in 1912 by amalgamating the North-Eastern Rhodesia Constabulary and the

[1] Livingstone was provided with a Village Management Board in 1911, Lusaka in 1913 and Broken Hill in 1915.
[2] L. A. Wallace to B.S.A. Company: 5 Sep 1914, annex. 1 to B.S.A. Company minutes: 29 Oct 1914 (in LO 1/2/80, Nat Arch SR)
[3] Fox, H. W. *Memorandum . . . containing notes and information concerning land policy. . . .* (British South Africa Company, 1912), p. 27

Barotse Native Police.[1] In 1912 the entire force only numbered 27 British officers and N.C.O.'s and some 750 Africans, armed with rifles and bayonets. There were a few machine guns, but artillery, technical equipment and properly organized motor transport were all lacking. The askaris' training was indifferent in quality, which was not their officers' fault, but that of a military system by which a small and scattered body of men was made responsible for the military defence, security and the policing of a territory a good deal larger than France. The force was split into a small section of European police, known as the 'Town and District Police' which kept order along the line of rail, and the military branch, which was regarded as available for active service. There were practically no reserves, as the Administration could not as yet draw on any trained cadres of ex-askari who might serve in wartime. The only other source of recruitment available was the small white population in the Territory. Northern Rhodesia contained a relatively large number of young people with military experience and an aptitude for soldiering; in 1909 in the North-Western Rhodesian Rifle Association numbered 360 members, a large number for such a small population and the Association even put forward a suggestion to turn itself into a Volunteer Reserve.[2] Financial stringency, however, made further action impossible, especially since the Administration always reckoned to be able to call on Southern Rhodesia in times of trouble. The only bright spot in the picture was the internal security position. Throughout the whole of Rhodesia the tribes never thought of making any attempt at shaking off British rule at a time when they might well have done so, whilst African communities on the exposed Tanganyika border, such as the Lungu people, actually tried to assist the Administration.

When war started, the Company's troops adopted a purely defensive strategy. Alfred Hamilton Mackenzie Edwards, the Imperial Commandant General of the Rhodesian forces north and south of the Zambezi, rightly argued that the Company could do nothing else, that there were in any case no strategic points to strike at nearby, and that the allied Belgian forces in the north were themselves barely adequate to defend their own far-flung frontiers. Neither were the Germans ready to embark on a major offensive, and the Company's main object was merely to hold on to the Northern Border, the distant 'N.B.', which the Administration considered important not so much for military reasons but to protect the area available for taxation.[3]

Operations in 1914 were accordingly on a very small scale. A detachment of Northern and Southern Rhodesian Police, previously concentrated on the

[1] Some Northern Rhodesian Africans also joined British military units in Nyasaland. One of these was Sergeant Kashema, who became the country's oldest veteran. Kashema joined the King's African Rifles in 1890, fought in the later Ashanti campaign, the 'Mad Mullah' campaign, the Nandi and Kisii expedition in Kenya and the Great War. He died in 1958. See *East Africa and Rhodesia*, 16 Jan 1958, p. 647

[2] L. A. Wallace to B.S.A. Company: 19 Nov 1909, annex. 16 to B.S.A. Company minutes: 5 May 1910 (in LO 1/2/66, Nat Arch SR)

[3] L.A. Wallace to B.S.A. Company: 24 Nov 1914, annex. 1 to B.S.A. Company minutes: 7 Jan 1915 (in LO 1/2/81, Nat Arch SR)

strategically vital Victoria Falls Bridge, occupied the German post of Schuck-
mannsburg without fighting and thereby cleared the Caprivi Zipfel, thus covering the British rear. In addition a mobile column of Northern Rhodesia Police
was rushed to the Tanganyika border, which was threatened from Bismarckburg,
where the Germans maintained a strong military post only thirty-eight miles
from Abercorn, Lake Tanganyika being controlled by armed German steamers.
Abercorn was attacked in September, but the assault was repulsed by local
police and volunteers, the position finally becoming stabilized by the arrival of
the Northern Rhodesia Police Mobile Column, which succeeded in driving the
enemy across the border, after another unsuccessful German attack. In November German troops from Bismarckburg landed at Kituta Bay, fourteen miles
west of Abercorn but were subsequently forced to re-embark by Northern
Rhodesian Police and Belgian troops, after having secured a large amount of
telegraph material of which they were very short. In December two German
attacks were made, this time on Fife, but again the invading force, numbering
between 200 and 300 African troops, was obliged to withdraw.

In February 1915 the Company's men received welcome reinforcements in
the shape of the Northern Rhodesia Rifles (known as the Northern Rhodesia
Volunteer Force, Mobile Column), the country's first purely European military
force. The creation of this unit was due to the private initiative of Major Boyd
Alexander Cuninghame, a Scotsman who saw service in the Boer War, subsequently worked for Tanganyika Concessions Ltd, and then took up land to the
west of Lusaka where he bred cattle for the Katanga market. Cuninghame, with
the help of Major Robert Gordon, organized a defence force of about 300 volunteers under his command. He intended that the new defence force should eventually provide the nucleus of a permanent Territorial Corps, and with this object
in view officers and men were carefully selected from people holding permanent
positions and interests in Northern Rhodesia.[1] Cuninghame proved himself a
man of ability, and his column contained some first class fighting men; discipline
admittedly was poor, and so at first was training, but standards quickly improved
and the Northern Rhodesia Rifles gave an excellent account of themselves. The
first operation these still raw and untried troops were asked to perform was a
gruelling march through the bush, in the midst of the rainy season over a distance of more than 550 miles, as far as from London to the Pyrenees. The only
transport available was some ox-wagons, but most of the beasts perished on the
way. 'We marched along' recorded one of the survivors, 'carrying our rifles
and equipment with Haseriis [the bugler] playing marching tunes on his bugle.
Everyone tried to march in front, we existed on bread made with baking powder,
and in the heat and the rain I wonder still how we survived on the last stretch'.
On arrival at the 'N.B.', the Northern Rhodesia Rifles took part in a number of
border clashes, the most serious of which was a series of attacks on the post of
Saisi between June and August 1915. This was held by 10 British and 8 Belgian
whites and 160 Northern Rhodesia Police and 280 Belgian native soldiers, the

[1] B. A. Cuninghame to L. A. Wallace: 3 Mar 1915 (CU 1/1/2, Nat Arch MS)

entire garrison being under the command of Major J. J. O'Sullevan. The Germans had superiority of something like four to one, but, lacking heavy artillery, they were unable to break into the allied fortifications. The Northern Rhodesia Rifles[1] also took part in numerous border raids, where fighting was mostly at close quarters in forest or savannah country where the grass might be anything up to twelve feet high, and patrols suddenly stumbled upon one another. Much of the Northern Rhodesia Rifles' work was, however, taken up with pure garrison duties and Cuninghame himself was bitterly disappointed that his column was being used merely as a border guard. There was constant friction with the Northern Rhodesia Police and Cuninghame complained that his men were neglected in every department of commissariat and transport; the Northern Rhodesia Rifles, he felt, should be given an opportunity of seeing some real action rather than being rusticated along the 'N.B.' where the native troops' state of morale made it inadvisable for white troops to be brigaded together with them. The men were just getting bored, especially since quite a number of them were actually being offered commissions in other units after their enlistment in the Northern Rhodesia Column.[2] Cuninghame was not exaggerating, and certainly was right about the opportunities available in other fighting formations, about 200 Europeans, or ten per cent of the European population in the country having by that time left Northern Rhodesia to join military units outside the territory. In 1916 the Mobile Unit was finally disbanded. This was a sensible decision, for the Column contained so many potential officers and N.C.O.s that its personnel was wasted on garrison duties. The Northern Rhodesia Rifles Mobile Unit was paid off, but many went to fight overseas, whilst others joined Southern Rhodesian formations. The organization remained in being for the purpose of providing local defence and training, but by 1918 attendance had become so low that the utility of the corps could no longer be relied upon. By this time operations had so far moved away from Northern Rhodesia that interest had completely died down; most of the best fighting men had left for other regiments; conscription remained politically impossible, even had there been enough men left to conscript; and to make matters worse, the settlers did not produce an outstanding leader after Cuninghame's death from typhoid fever in 1917.[3]

As far as Northern Rhodesia was concerned, the war effort thus came to be shouldered entirely by the Northern Rhodesia Police and by those Northern Rhodesian Europeans who joined the British South Africa Police and other colonial units. Fortunately, from the end of 1915 onwards the general strategic position began to improve. The surrender of the German forces in South West

[1] In March 1915 the Mobile Column of the Northern Rhodesia Rifles amounted to 135 officers and men. The Northern Rhodesia Police then numbered 26 European officers and Warrant Officers, 6 British N.C.O.s, 23 European volunteers and constables, 813 native N.C.O.s and men and 93 special native police.
[2] B. A. Cuninghame to R. Gordon: 10 May 1915 (CU 1/1/2, Nat Arch MS)
[3] A. H. M. Edwards to Administrator: 19 Sep 1918, annex. 1 to B.S.A. Company minutes: 12 Dec 1918(in LO 1/2/88, Nat Arch SR)

Africa enabled the British to concentrate on the Northern Border, and in 1915 two European companies of 125 men each were sent north, known as the Special Service Companies of the British South Africa Police, and consisting of serving policemen, Southern Rhodesia Volunteers, and some ex-members of the 1st Rhodesia Regiment who had fought in South West Africa. These two companies proved a welcome reinforcement on the Northern Border, especially since a Belgian unit which had garrisoned Abercorn was about to be withdrawn. Sporadic fighting continued but assaults from either side failed, as these could not be carried against heavy machine gun and rifle fire without artillery support.

The British did, however, score an important strategic success in a brilliant little naval 'side-show'. The Germans were still controlling Lake Tanganyika with a small squadron and thus remained in a position to conduct constant raids on the British-held coast, and threaten any coastwise advance by landing troops in the rear of the attacking forces. In July 1915 a tiny expeditionary force, led by Commander G. Spicer Simson, R.N., assembled at the Cape, together with two $4\frac{1}{2}$ ton motor-launches, bearing the Gallic names of *Mimi* and *Toutou*, both as fast as their names suggested, armed with a 3-pdr gun each, and able to outclass the three or four German vessels on Lake Tanganyika. The boats were taken to the Belgian Congo by rail, and then through forest tracks over a distance of over 150 miles, mounted on specially made wagons drawn by traction engines. The expedition had to cross the most difficult country imaginable, including a range of mountains 6,000 feet above sea-level; then the vessels were taken down the Lualaba to Kabalo, and finally by rail to Lake Tanganyika where the two boats were launched. *Mimi* and *Toutou* captured a 53 ton German gun-boat, the *Kingani*, which was converted into a British warship under the name of *Fifi*. Then the *Hedwig von Wissmann*, three times as big as the *Kingani*, was sunk, while the biggest of the German boats, an 850 ton vessel known as the *Graf von Götzen*, was scuttled by the Germans after a successful bombing attack by a Belgian sea-plane. The Belgians apparently also accounted for a fourth German vessel, and German command of Lake Tanganyika came to an end.[1]

Equally important was the establishment of a joint command for the forces in Rhodesia and Nyasaland which had hitherto operated in wasteful isolation from one another; Brigadier-General Edward Northey, an infantry officer with previous experience in South Africa and Flanders, was appointed to take command of the two fronts, and in 1916 preparations were begun for an advance into German East Africa in connexion with a major drive from British East Africa under General Jan Christian Smuts. In May 1916 two columns left Northern Rhodesia. The first of these marched northwards from Abercorn under the command of Lieutenant Colonel R. E. Murray, and consisted of 250 men of the British South Africa Police Special Service Companies and 450 Northern Rhodesia Police, whilst the second column, containing 300 Northern Rhodesia Police, one section of South African Mounted Rifles and 200 South African Rifles,

---

[1] Lucas, Sir C. 'The Lake Tanganyika expedition' (in Lucas, Sir C., ed. *The Empire at war*, v. 4. Oxford university press, 1925, p. 243–247)

concentrated at Fife. Their advance into German East Africa proceeded extremely quickly, and within a fortnight Northey managed to occupy the whole of the Langenburg and Bismarckburg districts. Murray's Column was then ordered to Neu Langenburg, his column becoming known as 'Murray's Rhodesians' and consisting of two and a half companies of Northern Rhodesia Police and two companies of British South Africa Police; Murray advanced, Northey himself taking considerable pride in these operations which were carried out in the face of enormous obstacles, since it was difficult to feed the troops over the vast distances involved, despite the excellent work done by South African engineers. Northey was only commanding 2,500 men, who were being opposed by 1,500 Germans recently reinforced by another 500 men, and he was therefore forced to take far more risks than General Smuts with the main force of 70,000 men, or the Belgians with 10,000 men and the Portuguese with 14,000.[1]

After the capture of Iringa the first of General Smuts's troops arrived from the north and the plan of campaign now was to push the enemy across the Ruhuje on to the Mahenge Plateau towards the main German forces under Paul Emil von Lettow-Vorbeck. The advance began in August 1916, and to meet a possible threat to his lines of communication, Northey brought over two Northern Rhodesia Police companies from Lake Tanganyika. Murray's column was then called to go to the relief of the Rhodesia Native Regiment. The Germans were driven off and Murray followed up his success, but the opposing forces under General Wahle succeeded in getting away and linking up with the main force under Lettow-Vorbeck.

Murray was more successful in another engagement near Ilembule Mission where he succeeded in forcing Wahle's rearguard, consisting of 260 askari and 54 Europeans with one gun, to surrender unconditionally. This little operation was a brilliant exception to the almost invariable failure of the British troops to close the net on the retreating Germans in the endless bush, where visibility was poor and the terrain difficult.

The Rhodesian troops then engaged in a number of further actions, designed to keep the enemy on the move, the campaign in German East Africa itself being finally brought to an end with the surrender to Deventer of a German force numbering 148 Germans, 1,400 askaris and 3,000 porters, all under the command of Major Tafel. Von Lettow-Vorbeck, however, escaped with a picked force and marched southwards through Portuguese territory where he was able to pick up supplies from local depots. Von Lettow had no mechanized transport to worry about; there were no problems of getting fuel or spare parts, and neither was his column encumbered with an administrative 'tail', so that he could live off the country, and from what he might capture on the way. Von Lettow, for all his archaic political ideas, was a first-class commander, and in the absence of proper air reconnaissance, his force could never be permanently pin-pointed in the bush. The difficulties of the allied forces in the East African campaign as a whole were increased by inadequate transport and supply arrange-

[1] E. Northey to F. D. P. Chaplin: 24 Aug 1916 (CH 8/2/1, Nat Arch MS)

M

ments, neither Smuts, nor Major-General Louis Jacob Deventer, by now commander of the military forces in East Africa, showing particular ability as administrators. Though excellent work was done by British army doctors, including the members of the Northern Rhodesia Medical Corps (formally instituted in 1917), there was an unnecessarily high rate of casualties from disease and exhaustion; the lack of adequate staff work on the East African front having to be made up by the sheer grit and marching powers of the troops. As a Cockney Private of Deventer's army grimly said to a man from France next to him in a Cape Town hospital, '*You*'ad food in France—*we* didn't; *you*'ad boots, we didn't 'ave boots; you didn't 'ave to march for six blinkin' months on end or fight niggers on mountains . . . and if you was 'it or sick, within twenty-four hours yer was back in Hengland . . . nex' time there's a war, they can ask someone besides yours truly ter fight it. I've 'ad enough, I 'ave. They messed us abaht till we didn't know which was Thursday and which was our helbows'.[1] Many similar remarks must have been made in Chinyanja and other African tongues, for white and black alike suffered badly in this foot-slogging. Worse still, inadequate planning, as well as the natural conditions of the terrain prevented the numerical superiority of the allies from being brought to bear on the retreating Germans, so that Lettow, alone of all German commanders in Africa, managed to fight on right to the end of the war, immobilizing a disproportionately large number of allied troops.

The story of this pursuit is quickly told. The British first of all imagined that the Germans might try to double back into German territory, and during December 1917 the Rhodesians were kept on patrol along the Rovuma. The Northern Rhodesian Police, on the other hand, were now for the first time concentrated in one place and reorganized. The Northern Rhodesia Rifles, by this time a fine, war-hardened force of veterans, consisting of Bemba, Ila, Ngoni and other African troops numbering over 1,000 men and commanded by some 60 British officers and N.C.O.s, mostly Rhodesians, was constituted into a self-contained battalion of four companies with its own machine gun and Lewis gun companies, signallers, medical units, scouts and transport units. In February 1918, after the retirement of Colonel Murray, the Northern Rhodesia Police were moved down to Lake Nyasa for a rest, but in June the force had to be rushed down to Limbe to try and intercept the Germans in Portuguese territory. At this point Brigadier G. M. Hawthorn took over the command of the 'Rhodesia and Nyasaland Field Force'. The pursuit of Lettow-Vorbeck, however, proved unsuccessful and the German force, consisting of some 1,500 men and an equal number of carriers finally managed to move into Northern Rhodesian territory. Lettow was unable to capture Fife, but then moved inland to seize the supply depot at Kasama which he reached on 9 October, but found completely deserted. News of the armistice in Europe reached von Lettow on 13

---

[1] Quoted from Letcher, O., by Bradley, K. 'The 1914–18 campaign' (in Brelsford, W. V., ed. *The story of the Northern Rhodesia regiment.* Lusaka, Government printer, 1954, p. 48) on which the narrative of the military operations has been largely based.

November, two days after the war had come to an end. Lettow, unaware up to then of the fall of the Imperial Government accepted the armistice. A last telegram was sent to the German Emperor who in the meantime had fled to Holland, 'Majesty. Berlin. General Deventer officially informs me that the Armistice terms subscribed to by Germany stipulate the unconditional surrender of the Colonial Troops. This I shall carry out. Lettow. 14.11.18'.[1]—Africa was at peace once more.

The burden of war on the Territory had been a heavy one. 88 Northern Rhodesian civil servants had fought on various fronts, nearly all of whom obtained commissions, and 19 of them lost their lives. 355 settlers had gone to war, apart from those who had joined local defence units, so that 40 per cent of the adult white population of the territory had been on active service, a very high proportion, especially in view of the fact that many district officials were precluded from volunteering, whilst many of the colonists could not be spared for economic reasons. In addition 1,839 Africans served in the Northern Rhodesia Police which, after four years of fighting, developed into an excellent force, expert in bush-fighting. Equally severe was the strain on the African civilian population. The war in East Africa was a war of movement, but a war in which the fighting troops still largely depended on carriers. Carriers for their part needed more carriers to carry their food, so that even small operations were immensely wasteful in manpower. Matters were made worse by sharp fluctuations in demand, which threw a heavy load both on the recruiting organization and on the native population; the number of troops engaged changed constantly, so did the front line and the lines of communications; which meant that demands had to be met as they arose. In addition, the ordinary requirements of the Territory had to be provided for, with the result that the manpower resources of Northern Rhodesia became desperately strained. In normal times carrier-work was far from unpopular, for carriers were simply given their loads and a definite time in which to complete their task, so that they could determine their own rests, a state of things always popular with workers. In war-time all this was different. Carriers had to be ready to work at all times, they were exposed to wind and rain, to heat and cold over long periods; sometimes high mountains had to be traversed, and sometimes low-lying, fever-ridden swamps. The carriers, who lacked the military pride and discipline of regular troops, yet had to share the same dangers and hardships, hurled as they were into the white man's incomprehensible war; where men did not just seize women and cattle and go home again, but where they would slog on endlessly, without knowing where the enemy gathered, or what was the purpose of the operation. No wonder carrier-work was unpopular and men had to be impressed.[2] Recruitment was done through

[1] Telegram in German by P. E. von Lettow-Vorbeck: 14 Nov 1918. (The original is in the Rhodes-Livingstone Museum)
[2] The aristocracy amongst porters were the machine-gun porters, as well as the 'blue boys' or hospital porters, the latter receiving 12/6 a month. First line porters received 10/- a month and lines of communication porters 7/6. Rations were supplied, and after the war small gratuities were paid in the shape of hoes and axes.

chiefs who had to supply a specified quota, a task which made their position with the tribesmen no easier, and goes some way towards explaining the bitter propaganda that was subsequently made in North-Eastern Rhodesia by African sectaries against the institution of chieftainship. The numbers mobilized were considerable. In 1917, 37,000 Northern Rhodesian Africans were on war-work, of whom 31,000 came from North-Eastern Rhodesia; the taxable males of North-Eastern Rhodesia however only numbered 120,000, so that 40 per cent of all available African men in North-Eastern Rhodesia were at times employed— 30 per cent being in fairly constant service.[1] In order to keep up this supply, all recruitment for Southern Rhodesia and the Katanga mines had to be suspended for a time, and since the current wages were double those paid for war-work, the African population suffered bitter hardships in a period of sharply rising prices. Worse still were the physical losses. Rather more than 2,300 carriers never returned to their villages, the number of carriers killed being much heavier than those of the Northern Rhodesia Police of whom about 100 men lost their lives. When the fighting ended, the remnant of these stout mercenaries were largely demobilized, spent their pay and returned to the villages, where the wounded drew their disgracefully inadequate pensions,[2] and the fit went back to the customary ways of farming, without apparently causing much upset in the village communities.

(b) *War and the African home front*

The severity of the impact of war on the African population differed in the various parts of Northern Rhodesia. The Barotse remained relatively little affected and co-operated in providing men, though they were seriously hit when pleuro-pneumonia wiped out a large percentage of their herds, striking a major blow at their export trade to the south. Nevertheless there was a certain amount of friction between the Barotse ruling class and the British administration, the major point at issue being the jurisdiction of the Khotla as against the Magistrates' Courts. The Lewanika Concession of 1900 clearly specified that the Administration would only deal with cases between Europeans and Africans, cases affecting black men only remaining reserved to the king. The Company's civil servants were, however, inclined to regard the Barotse brand of tribal feudalism as oppressive in nature, and the needs of war and closer administration forced them to take a more active part in the country's judicial structure. Step by step, Barotse powers were further restricted and in 1905 the jurisdiction of the Khotla was limited to civil proceedings amongst Africans, and criminal matters amongst Africans where the punishment did not exceed six months, a dozen lashes or a

---

[1] Figures from Wallace, Sir L. 'Northern Rhodesia and the last phase of the war in Africa' (in Lucas, Sir C., ed. *The Empire at war*, v. 4. Oxford university press, 1925, p. 296 and 308–309)

[2] In the Legislative Council almost a quarter of a century later Lt Col Sir Stewart Gore-Browne drew attention to the case of a tenant of his. This ex-askari was shot through the head during the War and became half-witted as the result of this injury. The Imperial Power paid him a pension of 7/6 *per annum*. See Northern Rhodesia Legislative Council debates: 11 Dec 1942, col. 330

fine of £100.[1] Even this provision, however, proved inadequate as far as the Administration was concerned. Africans took a growing share in the white economy which in turn affected judicial problems, and by 1914 the Company's Legal Adviser argued that Lewanika and his Khotla were never intended to have the power of punishing offences against English law or against the statute-law of the Territory, unless these also happened to be offences against customary law. This was a vital point for administration could not be separated from justice; statute-made offences were now forming a major part of the court cases and it was essential for the Company to try them. Prosecutions for tax evasion breaches of the fire-arm regulations or of labour contracts were all unknown to tribal life; they owed their existence to contact between tribal Africans and the dominant European group, the whole problem becoming further intensified by the stress of the war.

The question of Barotse-British relationship was made no easier when Lewanika died in 1916. The shrewd old king who ruled for more than a generation always possessed a profound respect for an Empire whose might had impressed him so greatly on his visit in 1902, and whose backing strengthened his hold on a somewhat shaky throne. Letia, his son who succeeded him as Yeta III, was the child of a different age; his succession symbolized the advance of the newly literate and Christian element in Barotseland, who by then had also captured the key office of Ngambela or Prime Minister in the person of Mukamba, Letia's Christian half brother-in-law and close personal friend. The position of the new king was admittedly still a delicate one for, as a French missionary put it 'it is very difficult for a Christian chief to break with the religious past of his dynasty without shocking his *entourage* through innovations', especially since royalty was so closely linked with pagan notions. Letia, however, possessed some diplomatic ability and managed to steer through these dangerous waters. He held firmly to Christianity and for a time even to monogamy without offending the pagan section of his kingdom, a policy made easier by the fact that Barotseland was far away from the fighting, and relatively little affected by hostilities.

Along the Railway Belt the effects of war were felt in a different way. For once agricultural prices went up; farmers found more customers for meat and mealies, and production was increased, the average yield of maize per acre rising from 2·2 bags between 1915 to 1916, to 5·28 between 1919 to 1920.[2] Africans benefited from the rise in prices in the same way as Europeans, and the *Livingstone Mail* began to publish complaints from farmers that labour was more difficult to get because of native competition. The War and the few years of prosperity that followed upon it also seems to have given rise to Northern Rhodesia's earliest African *kulaks*. Perhaps the first African pioneers in this new type of farming were two brothers, both Christians, named Theodore Kachesa

[1] High Commissioner's proclamation no. 6 of 25 Feb 1905
[2] *Northern Rhodesia—Statistical statement of crops* (Supplement to Northern Rhodesia government gazette, 25 May 1921)

and Henry Jariso, who set themselves up as partners just at the edge of Chikuni Mission farm, the Jesuit establishment in the Tonga country. By 1924 the two owned a prosperous homestead, complete with five rooms and covered by a corrugated iron roof, with properly made doors and window frames and well-designed fireplaces; the farm had its own carpenter's shed and a shed for black-smith's work; there was a lime kiln, as well as an artificial water reservoir over 200 yards in length and 110 yards in breadth. The two Africans ploughed up 80 acres of land, farming operations being made easier by a mealie-planter, two cultivators and three ploughs. The partners employed 21 'boys' and, the Jesuits reported proudly, 'every Sunday without fail the two families come to Mass—the two men, their wives and their twelve children, besides a big girl, a relative who acts as a nurse to the double household'.[1] Men like Kachesa and Jariso were of course exceptions. Nevertheless African enterprise was for the first time beginning to be of some importance, and the intensification of agriculture sharpened competition for land between white and black, so that the Europeans demanded that native reserves be mapped out along the railway.

In North-Eastern Rhodesia the effects of war were felt most severely of all; the drain of labour was heavier than anywhere else in the territory, and the proximity of German troops in the early and the final parts of the war induced a greater loss of confidence in British power. At the same time, the general rise in prices, occasioned all over Southern Africa by wartime shortages, was not made up by increased opportunities for earning money—rather the reverse, for compulsory carrier work meant that wages were artificially deflated. North-Eastern Rhodesia was moreover in close proximity to Nyasaland which supplied the country with many of its mission-trained teachers and clerks. Some North-Eastern Rhodesian Africans were probably aware of the John Chilembwe rising of 1915, a small revolt set off by the grievances of labour-tenants on European estates and the political ambitions of mission trained Africans who were inspired by an incipient African nationalism, cast in ecclesiastical form. Chilembwe's attempt to set up a black state on theocratic lines admittedly proved a complete failure; few Nyasalanders would join, and the outbreak was quickly suppressed, even though practically the whole of the available British forces were engaged against the Germans. Nevertheless, the movement left its mark, and North-Eastern Rhodesia, which was geographically closest to Nyasaland, witnessed the first manifestation of a new spirit of independence, which again found expression in Biblical terms.

Religious opposition to European rule was of course nothing new in Nor-thern Rhodesia. As early as 1900 Willie Mokalapa, a Basuto evangelist of the Paris Evangelical Mission, an ex-student of Lovedale and one of the ablest teachers of the French Protestant Mission, set up an independent 'black' Church in opposition to the European dominated mother-church. The move-ment began with a teachers' strike for higher salaries; this was led by Moka-lapa, who got in touch with the Basutoland 'Ethiopian Church' which had been

[1] *Zambesi mission record*, v. 7, Oct 1924, p. 425–429

condemned by a French Protestant Synod in the previous year for its immorality, and for its pastors' poor education and character.[1] Mokalapa gained Lewanika's support by making extensive promises to build schools 'on the cheap'. The Ethiopians, however, were not able to carry out their programme, and to make matters worse, Mokalapa lost a sum of money entrusted to him by the king for making purchases at Cape Town, the fault apparently resting with his unsavoury business associates in South Africa.[2] The movement lost Lewanika's support, and quickly disintegrated, for the Ethiopians had nothing tangible to offer. Their position was rendered even more precarious by intervention on the part of the Administration which passed a law controlling the influx of alien Africans.[3] In 1905 the Church collapsed. One of the Ethiopian leaders, a half-caste born in Morocco, subsequently taken to South Africa and educated at Lovedale, went back to the missionaries, asking for a job and complaining of his existing small salary and of friction with his Ethiopian colleagues,[4] whilst the last representative of the movement in Barotseland put his education to better financial use by taking a job with a trader at Nalolo.[5]

The leaders of the 'Ethiopian' Churches usually consisted of discontented schoolmasters and evangelists, who appealed to ordinary tribesmen and took a more lenient attitude towards polygamy than European clergymen, and who frequently promised to supply education more cheaply and readily than the whites. But in addition there was prophesying of a different kind which was addressed to the illiterate and which promised—not an African society cast in a European mould but the disappearance of white society altogether. In 1909 a seer thus arose in the Monze sub-district, one of those areas where life was being most seriously affected by the European impact. The prophet enjoined the villagers to go to sleep and promised that after five days he would wake them all up with a pistol shot when—lo and behold—the District Officers would all miraculously die, Kafue Bridge would collapse, and the property of the whites be seized. In 1913 an educated African in Lambaland gave himself out as Jesus Christ and proclaimed that he would issue a new law, based on the Ten Commandments, whilst instructing his followers to erect standards smeared in fowls' blood. None of these movements, however, genuinely challenged the Government. The Barotseland Ethiopians, for all their belief in the equality of white and black, attempted to work within the existing framework of government and set up a European type of organization. The 'prophets' relied on a miracle which at one blow would do away with the whiteman's taxes and technology. In addition Northern Rhodesia was influenced from Nyasaland which supplied the country with numerous clerks, interpreters and evangelists who spread their

[1] Jacottet, E. 'Le Synode de Thaba-Bossiou' (in *Journal des missions évangéliques*, 1900, p. 33–37)
[2] High Commissioner to Colonial Office: 3 July 1905 and enclosures (in *Further correspondence. . . .* African (South) no. 763)
[3] High Commissioner's proclamation no. 19 of 6 Aug 1904
[4] Jalla, A. 'A Lealuye' (in *Journal des missions évangéliques*, 2ième semestre, 1905, p. 186)
[5] Boiteux, E. 'Rapport sur la mission du Zambèze pendant l'année 1905' (in *Journal des missions évangéliques*, 2ième semestre, 1906, p. 254)

own tongue and often became the intellectual leaders of the backvelders across the border; Nyasaland influence helped to put the country in touch with new notions, including ideas spread by American Negro missionaries, who played some part in Nyasaland's ecclesiastical and social history, and supplied a special flavour to evangelical work, which blended revivalist Protestantism with a drive towards social reform and an assertion of black colour pride. About the turn of the century an American Negro was said to have come to Northern Rhodesia, together with two Nyasaland interpreters, preaching the gospel of 'Africa for the Africans' before being thrown out by the Police, the American probably being attached to John Chilembwe's separatist Providence Industrial Mission in Nyasaland, which maintained native helpers in Northern Rhodesia.[1] Chilembwe never seems to have made an appreciable number of converts in Northern Rhodesia; and his rising in 1915 found no echo in the backwoods beyond the border where tensions between white landlords and black tenants were nothing like as severe. All the same, travel between Northern Rhodesia and Nyasaland became a regular feature which must have left some mark on the indigenous people; whilst American Negro thought probably exerted some influence, however tenuous, on the small educated minority, at any rate to the extent of Lewanika becoming a member of the Negro Society for Historical Reasearch, an American organization founded in 1911 to promote Negro interests in the academic field.[2]

Trouble of sorts also arose in the East Luangwa district where the Dutch Reformed Church was exercising very inadequate control over its vast network of village schools, which were rapidly being set up in competition with the White Fathers. There were no cases of actual subversion, but the Administration received numerous complaints that African teachers were trying to over-ride the authority of local Ngoni chiefs. Conservatively-minded Africans also attacked the *Chipe* dance, which originated with pupils and teachers from the Mission, and which involved the mixing of the sexes, the theme being that 'God will come, Dear, and no one can say what we are doing here. There are no witnesses'. This entertainment was called the 'dance of God'; only Mission Africans were said to take part in it, most of the girls present being the wives of men away at work; whilst the chiefs sighed that the adulteries of the teachers were becoming too many! The local Native Commissioner took a serious view of the position and thought that the Mission's rule of monogamy was partly responsible for the trouble, since Mission teachers often remained unmarried or divorced their wives, in order to keep a few mistresses—usually the spouses of labour migrants away in Southern Rhodesia—the local administrative officer becoming all the more incensed by the fact that poorly supervised native teachers often

---

[1] See Shepperson, G. 'The literature of British Central Africa' (in *Rhodes-Livingstone journal* no. 23, June 1958, p. 42–43). On the Chilembwe movement as a whole see the monumental work by Shepperson, G., and Price, T. *Independent African: John Chilembwe and the origins, setting and significance of the Nyasaland native rising of 1915.* (Edinburgh, University Press, 1958)

[2] Shepperson, G. 'Notes on the Negro American influences on the emergence of African nationalism' (in *Journal of African history*, v. 1, no. 2, 1960, p. 309)

opposed the recruitment of labour. After lengthy discussions the Administration in 1918 decided, against strong clerical opposition, to impose some control over mission schools, the difficulties with the Dutch Reformed Church constituting a major factor in initiating this policy, which however, was not seriously implemented until after the end of Chartered rule.

Pre-war and war-time agitation was never very important in Northern Rhodesia, but post-war troubles became rather different in quality. For the first time there was something more like mass action, linked to open defiance of authority. The new resistance movement was connected with the Watch Tower sect, a chiliastic movement, partly inspired by American teaching, which foresaw the coming end of the world, the Day of Judgement being followed by the destruction of the Evil Trinity of Government, Church and Business, whilst the true believers would inherit Life Eternal. In 1917 a number of African preachers, most of them connected with the Scottish Mission at Mwenzo, and members of the Wiwa tribe, were expelled from Southern Rhodesia where they had come under the influence of Watch Tower teachings. Back home, they foretold to village audiences that the world was coming to an end, that Native Commissioners and African chiefs alike would lose their power to the King of Heaven, that true believers should no longer work for the Europeans, or even cultivate their own gardens. Rather should the faithful prepare themselves for the Day of Judgement by prayer, baptism and shouting to the Lord by night, and by discarding their wives, unless their spouses also took the true faith. The Administration attempted to suppress this novel movement of religious anarchism, and in 1919 there was a mass trial at Kasama. One Daniel Kawensa and eight other Watch Tower men were accused of forcibly liberating a number of their co-religionists imprisoned at Chinsali. The most serious offenders got two and a half years' hard labour and ten lashes, the lesser fry getting off with lighter sentences; Shadrash Shankila, the leader of the sect in the Fife and Chinsali division who had also led rioting, received three years and twenty-four lashes. Others were sentenced to lesser terms of imprisonment for passing the word round that Kafwimbi, the Paramount Chief of the Wiwa, had become a woman and was now expecting a baby of unspecified paternity! Five men were charged with committing a public nuisance, one of the tenets of the sect being that at each village someone must keep shouting to the Lord at night to show that they were watching for His Coming, a practice objected to by their less enthusiastic fellow villagers who preferred a good night's rest. In addition 119 other Watch Tower adherents were tried for various offences, including rioting and assault.[1]

The Kasama trial dealt with the first mass action of a non-tribal kind to take place in the Territory. The Watch Tower people appealed to a rural proletariat in an isolated part of Northern Rhodesia where there were few opportunities for economic advancement and much distress; Watch Tower teaching moreover for the first time opposed chieftainship as an institution, an unheard of doctrine in

[1] *Livingstone mail*, 16 May 1919

the past. The tribesmen had of course always been used to rebels out to instal a new chief whenever the existing holder of power was no longer giving satisfaction, but no African ever previously argued in Northern Rhodesia that men should accept no earthly authority whatever, and that chiefs should be disobeyed for religious reasons. The Administration dealt with the problem by arresting trouble-makers and controlling native schools, the Administrator being given powers to close subversive institutions,[1] which prevented the organization of propaganda cells amongst the young, the Administration's counter-measures proving very successful. The Watch Tower people were unable to build up a proper administrative framework, a course of action which was in any case not encouraged by their doctrines, and one very difficult to carry out amongst widely scattered and backward rural communities. Neither were the preachers able to formulate precise or realistic demands, or attempt to infiltrate their men into local key positions. They left their Party Programme to the Almighty, and when Jehovah failed to intervene much of their enthusiasm evaporated, though the movement continued to smoulder on in a few areas, especially Fife and Abercorn.[2]

(c) *The whites in war-time*

Whilst African political and religious activity remained of peripheral importance, the European managed to move nearer to the centre of the political stage. War resulted in higher prices for mealies and cattle; farmers for the first time managed to make some money; more settlers entered the Railway Belt and the Europeans became a more numerous, a somewhat wealthier and also a politically more self-confident community than in the past.[3] Economic development was speeded up by the introduction of the motor car which was now beginning to make its appearance in the country. The arrival of the first car at Lusaka, for instance, was a major social occasion. 'It was a very imposing vehicle with I think a wooden body and the whole village and District turned out to see it doing its stuff. Cairo Road was then a deeply rutted track covered with grass and many holes . . . so Percy [Morton, the owner] did his motoring between his house and the town on the Railway reserve between Cairo Road and the Railway line which had many tracks . . . and the speed would be 10–15 miles. . . . The firm who supplied the car sent a mechanic to Lusaka with it to show the new owners where to put the petrol and the water, what the steering wheel was for and so forth. He had not long gone when the car refused to start. . . . All the experts in wagon driving and also anyone who knew anything about a steam engine, including the village blacksmith were consulted, but without result. Eventually a wire was sent for the mechanic to come back which he did,

---

[1] Northern Rhodesia proclamation no. 3 of 5 April 1918. This was subsequently altered after discussion with the missions who were anxious to avoid possible abuses.

[2] Annual report by Secretary of Native Affairs for 1920, annex. 92 to B.S.A. Company minutes: 23 Dec 1920 (in LO 1/2/92, Nat Arch SR)

[3] Between 1911 and 1921 the white population rose from 1,497 to 3,634.

turned on the switch, cranked up and away she went . . . Percy had forgotten to turn [it] on'.[1]

The internal combustion engine was destined to bring a major social revolution to Rhodesia. Towards the end of the war and during its aftermath, lorries came to be more widely used; the back-veld farmer ceased to be as isolated as he was before and merchandise and ideas alike flowed more easily through the countryside. The lorry was of particular importance to the Fort Jameson tobbacco growers who were far away from the railway line, but in North-Western Rhodesia too the motor car proved of inestimable benefit to traders, farmers and their families. It also had some indirect economic effects; for buying cars was a new way of spending money, whilst their presence in the country provided an incentive for road making. As far as the problem of race relations as a whole was concerned, the coming of the motor car tended to pull white and black further apart. Africans could not afford to buy cars, but some Europeans could, and step by step the white man became the car-borne man. Yet, in other ways, the internal combustion engine did more for the downtrodden African carrier than a whole regiment of reformers. 'Natives are often grossly over-loaded' wrote a Native Commissioner in 1914, 'and there is no method at present of proceeding against the culprit. It should be illegal, I think, to give a load weighing more than 50 lb. It may be roughly estimated that no native can carry a greater weight for long. . . . It must be remembered that natives nowadays want to carry at least a blanket in addition to their loads. Some years ago they would sleep by the fires in the coldest weather, naked—and many probably died indirectly of exposure to wet and cold. Now most natives possess at least one blanket. The people *en route* too are not so obliging as they were in the matter of pots and food and a carrier with 65 to 70 lb to carry cannot bear anything more. Natives loaded with no more than 50 lb arrive here [at Kafue] from Broken Hill over 200 miles away showing considerable distress. Carriers are not in a position as a rule to refuse to carry a load because it is too heavy for them.'[2] The writer, a conscientious district official, suggested that handcarts might be used, but the real answer was provided by the internal combustion engine, which at long last relieved the sweating *tenga tenga* from his back-breaking labours.

As far as skilled workers, that is to say the white artisans, were concerned, War and its aftermath greatly strengthened their position. War occasioned a great shortage of skilled operatives, as so many fit men left for the front, and those who stayed behind found themselves much better placed for the purpose of collective bargaining. On the mines their strength admittedly remained limited, for the Rhodesian mines were mostly small and widely scattered, so that the white workers were unable to build up that powerful hold which they occu-pied on the Witwatersrand. But their status did improve and the people who

[1] Reminiscences of R. B. Dean quoted in Sampson, R. *So this was Lusaakas.* . . . Lusaka publicity association, 1959, p. 58–59

[2] Heath, L. C. *Annual report for the Mwengwa sub-district of the Kafue district for the year ended 31st March 1914* (Enclosure in High Commissioner to Colonial Office: 25 May 1915. African (South) no. 1034)

gained most were the railwaymen. Before the war their position was precarious, and the so-called 'aristocracy of labour' was itself a depressed class. Jobs were scarce, the work hard, and wages low;[1] men were discharged on the spot for refusing to obey unreasonable orders; there was no redress, and if there was any trouble, Management would simply enforce discipline by stopping people's pay. 'You say you have a grievance' a railway worker was told, 'then you can go off and get yourself another job, because we don't want people with grievances on the railway.' There were few other posts to go to and there were always many people only too anxious to get signed on at the railways. Much of the semi-skilled work was done by Afrikaners of the *bywoner* class, hardworking and conscientious men, whilst many of the gangers were Italian labour migrants glad to work at £12. 0. 0. a month, save their wages and return to their home-land with what they put by. The only consolation which the European workers had was that no Africans were employed, but this did not mean much at the time, for there were in any case very few skilled native workers, and African competition was not at first a major issue.[2] The white workers' position did not improve till the War came. Then the artisans got their chance for there was no direction of labour. In 1916 the Bulawayo firemen went on strike; their demands were met, and the drivers and guards then joined them in forming the Rhodesia Railway Workers' Union.[3] The Union rapidly spread to all important centres, including the Northern Rhodesia depots, and the railwaymen at last became a political pressure group of some importance in the Territory.

(d) *War-time politics*

Northern Rhodesia remained the most insignificant of the Chartered Company's domains, and local politics amounted to little more than the backwash of events in the south. Southern Rhodesia in turn was strongly affected by what was happening in the Union of South Africa, where the Chartered Company possessed important financial links with the mining industry; and a short digression is therefore essential to make events north of the Zambezi more intelligible. Whilst the railway was being pushed into Northern Rhodesia, the extreme northward limit of the South African 'miner's frontier', the political interests of the British mining magnates in the Transvaal, as well as those of English-speaking shopkeepers on the Rand, were represented by the Progressive Party. One of the Progressives' most outstanding Parliamentary representatives in the Transvaal was Francis Percy Drummond Chaplin, Joint Manager for the Consolidated Gold Fields of South Africa Limited, and later Administrator of

---

[1] Before the railway strike of 1916 guards got 11/- per day, but were expected to work up to twelve hours a day; firemen got £14. 0. 0. a month. By 1921 wages had risen to 18/6 for guards to start with; shunters got £1. 6. 0.; firemen received £22. 0. 0. per month. An engine driver's maximum was £42. 0. 0. Gangers obtained between £23. 18. 0. and £27. 0. 0. Coloured gangers were expected to do the same work for between 13/- and 15/- a day.

[2] Personal information given to the author by F. Squair, a former railway worker.

[3] Hall, J. H. 'Reminiscences of a Rhodesian railwayman' (in *Rhodesian railway review*, May 1923, p. 4–5)

Southern Rhodesia;[1] Chaplin's views can be accepted as being representative of those of his principals. He was bitterly afraid of the influence of the Afrikaans speaking countryside, especially the poor farmers, and was convinced that once the Transvaal received self-government, power would pass to the rural areas, to the detriment both of the Imperial connexion and of the urban interests. Chaplin's fears turned out to be only too well founded; in 1906 a British Liberal Government granted full autonomy to the Transvaal, on terms that enfranchised the white *bywoners*, a group of people who were excluded from the electoral roll in Southern Rhodesia where a property qualification kept poor Afrikaners off the voters' roll, the Boer from the backveld being regarded by the Chartered Company as a much greater potential danger than the emergent African, who as yet professed no nationalism of his own, and never thought of criticizing big business.[2] In the Transvaal, on the other hand, power passed out of British control and many of the key positions in the civil service fell into Afrikaner hands, quite a number of 'purged' British officers and administrators making their way north of the Limpopo where their presence contributed to anti-Afrikaner sentiments. In the Transvaal, on the other hand, British supremacy came to an end and in 1907 General Louis Botha became Premier of the Transvaal and an Afrikaner-dominated Administration also took over in the Orange River Colony. In February 1908 the Progressives in the Cape, led by Jameson, and representative mainly of British mercantile interest in the towns, fell from office, and were replaced by a Bond-Moderate coalition, headed by Merriman. This meant that only six years after the signing of the Treaty of Vereeniging the British had lost that supremacy for which they had shed so much blood, and Natal remained the only Colony where the Afrikaners played no political part. Under those conditions the Progressives and their sympathizers would not hear of the inclusion of Rhodesia into the Union, a point of view shared by the majority of Rhodesians themselves: better let the country remain a separate political entity, which could be slowly built up as a bastion of British Imperial power in Southern Africa; if the country joined the Union now, British Rhodesians would soon find themselves hopelessly outnumbered by Boer immigrants from the back-veld with their large families.[3] and the mine-owners' interests would be jeopardized.

The formation of the Union of South Africa in 1910 did not in the least improve matters from the 'Rand Lords' ' point of view. The Progressives in the

[1] The Consolidated Gold Fields owned extensive claim holdings on the central and other sections of the Witwatersrand, mostly deep-level, as well as mines in other parts of the Transvaal. It also acted as Secretaries and Consulting Engineers for many of Edmund Davis's mining interests in West Africa. It was linked to the Chartered Company through Rochfort Maguire, Rhodes's old associate, who sat on the board of Consolidated Gold Fields and was the Vice President of the Chartered Company. Maguire was also a director of the Rhodesia Railways.

[2] The Southern Rhodesian property qualification limited the vote to literate British subjects, permanently resident in the country and receiving a wage of not less than £50 per annum, or owning a mining location, or occupying premises worth at least £75. This was a 'colour-blind' franchise in the Cape tradition, but determined both by national and by property considerations.

[3] Sir P. Fitzpatrick to P. D. Chaplin: 7 Oct 1908 (CH 8/2/1, f. 639–667, Nat Arch MS)

Transvaal joined with the sister party in the Cape, led by Jameson, and also representative mainly of British urban interests, but the new united 'Unionist' Party still could not make any headway against the Boers, especially when Labour was beginning to attract many British working class votes on the Rand. Under these conditions the British South Africa Company was not anxious to further the cause of Southern Rhodesia's joining the Union, arguing that it was better to wait till its assets north of the Limpopo had appreciated in value and till the general political position had become more favourable. In order to pursue such a policy successfully, it was, however, necessary to strengthen Rhodesia, which a banking expert privately described in very forceful terms as a business with a tiny turnover and staggering overheads. The most obvious way of improving the situation from the political point of view was by linking together the two Rhodesias. This was first suggested in 1915 when the question also became urgent for financial reasons, for the Imperial Government was expecting the Company to meet local extra War expenditure arising from hostilities with Germany and economy became the order of the day. Chaplin himself, the Company's Administrator in Southern Rhodesia, did not think that a great deal of money would be saved by amalgamating the two territories, but loudly stressed the political advantages of such a move which would put Rhodesia into a stronger position *vis à vis* the Union and also strengthen the Company's hands in dealing with the Imperial Government. Amalgamation, he argued, would also place the settlers in a better position with regard to the Africans, since the Legislative Council was elected almost entirely on a European vote. Chaplin did not regard this prospective access to European strength as an unmixed blessing, but nevertheless favoured complete amalgamation, arguing that a purely administrative fusion of the two Rhodesias, as suggested by Henry Birchenough, was not feasible. The Southern Rhodesian Legislative Council could not possibly be excluded from legislating for Northern Rhodesia; but would have to contain Northern members and be responsible for the Territory as a whole. As far as the prospects of amalgamation were concerned, Chaplin was optimistic; the measure would probably be welcomed by many of the farmers north of the Zambezi, and would add to the English element in Southern Rhodesia. Amalgamation might not save much money, but would lead to greater administrative efficiency, and once union was brought about, a number of the older type of Southern Rhodesian officials might be replaced by their more capable and better educated colleagues from the north, most of whom were British-born.[1] This latter point was one of some importance; the 'frontier' official admittedly had many good qualities; he was a fine linguist and able to do excellent work in the more backward districts; but now the progress of white settlement necessitated the employment of more highly educated people, for the most difficult administrative problems were now those which arose from contacts between Europeans and Africans.[2]

[1] P. D. Chaplin to Sir H. Birchenough: 10 Aug 1915 (CH 8/2/2/2, f. 12–17, Nat Arch MS)
[2] P. D. Chaplin to Sir H. Birchenough: 21 Sep 1915 (CH 8/2/2/2, f. 24–32, Nat Arch MS)

The scheme, as finally suggested, was workmanlike. The two territories would be administered as a single unit, and Roman-Dutch law would be made applicable over Rhodesia as a whole, so that there would be a uniform code from the Cape to the Congo. The administrator would continue to conduct affairs from Salisbury, but a senior official would remain at Livingstone to give special attention to northern affairs. The Administrator would remain his own Secretary for Native Affairs, as he was south of the Zambezi, and be assisted by two Chief Native Commissioners, one for Northern and one for Southern Rhodesia. There would be a single Legislative Council empowered to pass ordinances for the whole of the Territory, except Barotseland which would remain under the High Commissioner's authority. Northern Rhodesia would get three elected members in a united Legislative Council which would also contain two nominated members to represent the natives, so that the Legislative Council would number 8 nominated and 15 elected members, with the Administrator as Chairman.[1]

The project had much to commend it, but its reception in Northern Rhodesia was mixed. Some farmers favoured amalgamation on the grounds that unification would facilitate cattle exports to the south, whilst others were attracted by the idea of 'Greater Rhodesia'. There was however, a great deal of opposition, especially from Livingstone where amalgamation became a kind of 'dirty' word soon after the idea was first mooted. Moore himself might originally have been won round to the idea, for the *Livingstone Mail* at first seemed far from unfriendly, and might have been satisfied with certain economic guarantees. But the Company failed to canvass the idea properly, and Moore as well as A. A. Willis, an attorney, and F. J. Clarke, a substantial farmer and shopkeeper, the two leading lights in local politics, soon denounced the whole idea. Livingstone would be reduced to the status of a village, a very serious matter for those who had invested their money in property there; what was more, Northern Rhodesia would be left to the mercy of a bunch of junior officials. The only people who would gain from the scheme were the Directors and shareholders of the Company who would thus spend less money for administrative purposes, but who would find themselves saddled with an unprofitable territory north of the Zambezi, once Southern Rhodesia joined the Union of South Africa.[2] A public meeting at Livingstone took a similar line. Amalgamation would, it was said, entail the loss of the Congo markets; the Northern Rhodesian representatives in the common Legislature would be swamped; Company rule would be perpetuated, whilst the Territory would suffer from a continuous drain of native labour to the south.[3] Jameson, the Company's President, doubted just how representative this opposition was, and was convinced that amalgamation would receive a good deal of support from Northern Rhodesian farmers. He was

[1] B.S.A. Company to F. P. D. Chaplin: 18 March 1916, in Annex. 1 to B.S.A. Company minutes: 23 March 1916; *Draft scheme of administration*, in Annex. 3 to B.S.A. Company minutes: 13 April 1916 (in LO 1/2/83 Nat Arch SR). The scheme was published as *Draft scheme of administration. . . .* (Salisbury, Government Printer, 1916)

[2] *Livingstone mail*, 3 Dec 1915   [3] *Livingstone mail*, 10 Dec 1915

probably right in this surmise, but Livingstone was more vocal; Livingstonians were the only people in the country with a newspaper to voice their views, and were nearer to the seat of the administration than isolated farmers who could never put forward their views to the same effect.

But the decisive battle was fought south of the Zambezi, and here the Company failed to carry the day. The arguments used on both sides possess a curious modernity; many of them turned up in a new dress forty years later and may therefore be worth summarizing. The best case for the Company was put by Francis James Newton, the Company's able Treasurer, who subsequently went over to the settlers. The Zambezi was not a natural boundary; rather should Rhodesians look upon it as a natural asset where water-power would be used one day and great sugar plantations and vast cottonfields might develop. Equally valuable were the grasslands of the Kafue which might give rise to cattle breeding on a big scale. Amalgamation would mean cheaper administration, avoid duplication of services and entail a common native policy, though Barotseland would remain a special native reserve, a kind of Rhodesian Basutoland. Amalgamation would be a step towards constitutional advancement by adding more elected members to the Council and including in it spokesmen of additional economic interest groups from the North. Lionel Cripps, a pioneer farmer from the Eastern Districts, backed the Administration's proposals. Northern Rhodesia possessed vast untapped resources and nothing would be more foolish than to neglect its possibilities. The argument that, by taking in a vast black population, the whites would be swamped, was unsound. Amalgamation would not give the northern natives any rights which they did not at present hold in Southern Rhodesia. In any case, mining, Southern Rhodesia's chief industry, was employing 40,000 blacks and less than 2,000 whites. Rhodesians therefore would have to live for all time alongside the native races, and would have to suit their policies to the Africans' wants and needs. Amalgamation would improve Rhodesia's position, if the country was ever to join South Africa. In any case, if the two Rhodesias did not amalgamate, there was a distinct possibility that Northern Rhodesia would do so with the territories to the north of it. 'In that case' he argued prophetically, 'Southern Rhodesia would be wedged in between a Northern federation and a Southern unification. One would be under English law, the other under Roman-Dutch law. Towards which would they gravitate? ... There could be no doubt. ... They would inevitably drift, not in their own good time, but by force of circumstances into union with the South which they might not, at the time, desire to do'. In any case, why should the natives always be regarded as a source of weakness? Northern Rhodesia posessed a great reservoir of manpower, and, with a loyal native population behind them, Rhodesians would go far. It was easy to underestimate this factor, but if the Germans had not been able to count on the support of their Africans in East Africa, the Hun would have been crushed more quickly! The Company also received some support from Raleigh Grey who represented Salisbury Electoral District and was himself a director of several mining companies, as well as General Manager of the United Gold Fields Rhodesia Company, a subsidiary of

Consolidated Gold Fields of South Africa. Grey generally used to take the 'Chartered' side in politics, and now once again backed the Company's line, stressing the economic benefits to be expected from amalgamation. In any case the Europeans in the north were people of their own blood, 'they were white people trying to colonize the hinterland, the interior of Africa, in a country which they believed to be their own. . . . Were they to leave those people alone to stew in their own juice?' No, a thousand times no, for such a thing would be iniquitous, reprehensible and entirely unworthy of Rhodesians!

The opposition was led by Sir Charles Coghlan, a prominent lawyer from Bulawayo, and the most influential of the settler leaders. Amalgamation, Coghlan argued, would indefinitely delay the achievement of Responsible Government, and though the project would benefit the Company financially, it would not improve the position of the public. He was not impressed by the argument that a unified civil service would attract more and better recruits, whilst the advantages of a common Roman-Dutch law on both sides of the Zambezi might be achieved by simply passing an Order-in-Council. Northern Rhodesia would throw a heavy additional burden upon the South; neither was a united Rhodesia more likely to get a worthwhile increase of territory at the end of the War. The worst of it was that white Rhodesians would find themselves swamped by a vast black majority, but they would have none of it. They had slaved and struggled for twenty-five years, and they were not going to put the fruits of their labour at the mercy of educated African agitators. He did not like colour bars, Coghlan added, but Rhodesians were stuck in a country, side by side with a huge black population, and under those conditions there was much to be said for excluding even educated Africans from the franchise. Taking in Northern Rhodesia would only make things worse. 'If one went to Fort Jameson or to Broken Hill what would they see? They would see the place full of black clerks, black typists and black mechanics. And how many white men were there in Fort Jameson? He did not think there were thirty. They found black men who could read and write and use a typewriter, who could satisfy the educational tests and the electors there would largely consist of black men. . . . One wondered whether . . . the British South Africa Company . . . had taken into consideration . . . the mixing of oil and water in the shape of white and black?'[1]

Despite Coghlan's eloquence, the Chartered Company managed to steamroller the proposals through the Legislative Council with the support of their six nominated members, joined by three elected members. The remaining six elected members, however, voted against the proposal and now the Imperial Government intervened. The Chartered Company had, as one of the Rhodesian speakers pointed out, waited with its proposals until Sir Lewis Harcourt, a Liberal and a critic of the Company, had left the Colonial Office. There was indeed a time when the Colonial Secretary used to be so unpopular with the

[1] For the principal debates see Southern Rhodesia. *Debates in the Legislative Council*, 4th Session of the 6th Council, April–May 1917, p. 309–386

N

Board that *'Gott strafe Harcourt'* became a customary morning greeting at London Wall, the Company's head-office! No one was better pleased than the Directors when Andrew Bonar Law, an ex-iron merchant and a sound Unionist, took over the Colonial Office in 1915. Law, however, relinquished his portfolio only a year later to become Leader of the House of Commons, and his successor, Colonel Walter Hume Long, was much less sympathetic to the Company. Long admittedly was a good Conservative, as well as a personal well wisher of Chaplin's. But, Wilson Fox wrote, Long was 'absolutely under the thumb of [Sir George] Fiddes [Permanent Under Secretary for the Colonies],'[1] Wilson Fox, now himself a member of Parliament and a back-bencher of some influence, probably being sufficiently well informed of such matters to be quoted as a trustworthy source. Fiddes himself was not a particular admirer of the Company, and his attitude appears to have been fairly typical of the permanent staff of the Colonial Office as a whole, which was now much less friendly towards the Chartered Company than in the early days. Dougal Orme Malcolm, an ex-Colonial Office man, and now an influential member of the Company's Board, certainly thought that this was the case, though Malcolm did not analyze the reasons which led to this ideological shift. But one can venture upon a certain amount of generalization to account for this transformation. The Company had all too often 'blotted its copy book' from the civil servants' point of view, the Jameson Raid only being the worst instance of all. Then there was the Boer War, and in the minds of some officials the Company was associated with those Capitalist interests which were accused of having engineered the conflict. But what was perhaps more to the point, the Company was active, it was pushful; it was a great deal more enterprising than the conventional type of Colonial Office administration, and there existed a good deal of professional jealousy against this body of rich 'money-bags' who were always asking for things, and always ready to over-tax the natives, thereby provoking inconvenient questions in Parliament! In actual fact Company Government came out well in comparison with contemporary Colonial Office rule. The Company's administration was efficient; letters were answered quickly, and in a businesslike fashion, instead of being held over for weeks and even months on end. Board meetings, and meetings of the Board's Executive Committee, an inner ring formed in 1913, took place at regular intervals; the Directors were well informed and a good deal more aware of economic issues than the civil servants at Downing Street. In addition some of the Directors repeatedly visited Rhodesia; and though the old personal touch with the settlers was lost with the death of Rhodes in 1902, there was infinitely more contact between the Board and its colonial domain than there was between the senior Colonial Office men at headquarters and their admittedly much more extensive charges.

But to return to the amalgamation issue, the Colonial Office would not budge, and the project was vetoed on the grounds that such a scheme should not be forced through against the declared opposition of the majority of elected

[1] H. Wilson Fox to P. D. Chaplin: 3 Jan 1918 (CH 8/2/1, f. 2027-2031, Nat Arch MS)

members. 'Once you allow a country to elect representatives', Long wrote rather apologetically, 'it is impossible . . . for H.M.G. to ignore the opinions of elected members or to go into direct opposition to the majority of them.'[1] The Company then tried to get round the opposition by making the very reasonable suggestion that the two Rhodesias should be put under a single Administrator for the purpose of ensuring economy and a greater measure of political uniformity.[2] The scheme was perfectly sound and would have facilitated the extension of various Southern Rhodesian services to the north. There were moreover precedents for such a step, and so unobjectionable was the measure, that in 1921 a joint Administratorship was in fact brought into being under Chaplin. But at the time even this modest measure could not be enforced, for Long was afraid of questions in the House and, so Wilson Fox believed, tended to give an exaggerated importance to the speechifying of Rhodesian politicians who could always become vocal through Radical Members of Parliament,[3] who at that time often spoke up for the local settlers just as they later spoke in defence of African nationalists.

Had amalgamation gone through, the question of representation for the white Northern Rhodesians would have solved itself, for their delegates would have taken their seats in the Legislative Council at Salisbury. But when the scheme fell through, the problem of local representation in a purely Northern Rhodesian Advisory Council became more urgent. A Northern Rhodesian delegation visited London to confer with the Colonial Office and in 1917 Long agreed that, if the Southern Rhodesian Legislature were to reject amalgamation, Northern Rhodesia would get a local Advisory Council.[4] The only question now at issue was how the Council was to be constituted. The Chartered Company, for reasons of administrative convenience, would have preferred members to be nominated by the Northern Rhodesian Farmers' Association, which represented agriculturists as well as cattle traders. This suggestion, however, was opposed by artisans and railway workers, and the final scheme provided for the election of delegates, every literate male British subject of European descent over the age of 21 and in receipt of a salary of £150 p.a., or occupying premises worth £150 being eligible to be a voter.[5] Africans had no part whatever in the agitation, remaining completely uninterested in the issue; but though they were formally excluded their loss was not great. The Council had neither legislative nor executive functions; it was devoid of any statutory basis, and remained in fact a talking-shop, empowered to discuss matters affecting European settlement.[6] All the same, the Council was of some use for the purpose of political publicity, as well as a kind of barometer indicating the relative strength of the various sectional

[1] W. H. Long to P. D. Chaplin: 28 Dec 1917 (CH 2/2/8, f. 8/187–195, Nat Arch MS)

[2] P. D. Chaplin to High Commissioner: 28 May 1917, to B.S.A. Company minutes: 2 Aug 1917 (in LO 1/2/86, Nat Arch SR)

[3] H. Wilson Fox to P. D. Chaplin: 3 Jan 1918 (CH 8/2/1, f. 2027–2031, Nat Arch MS)

[4] *Livingstone mail*, 29 June 1917. This contains copies of correspondence between the Colonial Office and W. Burkitt and J. W. Little, the two Northern Rhodesian delegates.

[5] *Livingstone mail*, 1 Mar 1918   [6] See *Livingstone mail* 22 Mar 1918

interests in Northern Rhodesia. The greatest political surprise in the first Council election was the failure of the Northern Rhodesia Farmers' Association to get any of its candidates in; the Association represented most of the country's local wealth, and was the most vocal of all local groups, but was heavily outvoted, so that the first council thus represented companies and small traders rather than the farming community.[1]

III

Post-war politics and the end of Chartered rule

At the end of hostilities the West found itself starved of food and the whole world cried out for raw materials—for grain and copper, for maize and lead, and for all manner of merchandize to make good the wastage of war. Prices rose sharply, and the result was a short-lived boom, the effects of which were felt as far afield as Rhodesia. The Company was now anxious to promote further white settlement in the two Rhodesias, not only for economic reasons but as part of a last outburst of Imperial enthusiasm. The Empire had won through at last, and the men who had fought for it should be rewarded. Ex-servicemen, mostly ex-officers, were encouraged to come to Rhodesia; a very large area of land, amounting to 5,000,000 acres, half of which was situated in Northern Rhodesia, was set aside, and an attempt was made to pick the new settlers for their suitability. Land grants were free, but prospective colonists were expected to possess a minimum of £1,000 capital and undergo a specified training period. But the boom did not last, and when agricultural prices began to slump in 1921 most newcomers found themselves in desperate straits; equipment had been bought at exaggerated prices at a time when quick returns were confidently expected; but now farmers could no longer get enough money for their cattle and maize; the position being made worse by high freight charges and high prices for agricultural implements, fertilizers and other imported goods. The people who suffered most were the beginners who had not yet had time to get themselves properly established, whilst prospective settlers at home found difficulty in liquidating their assets before coming to Rhodesia. Some of the soldier settlers stayed on; some left the Territory; others again drifted into townships and made a precarious living from trading, contracting and transport. The experience of Major Hugh Kennedy McKee, later a Member of the Northern Rhodesian Legislative Council, was typical of many. McKee was born in 1896 in Lanarkshire. He was only eighteen years old when the Great War broke out, but at once enlisted in the Royal Scots; he was subsequently commissioned, wounded and decorated

[1] The voters roll numbered 582 whilst the Farmers' Association with its exclusive membership only numbered 56. The first to be elected was Moore, a chemist and journalist; the manager of the North Charterland Company; the manager of the Rhodesia Katanga Railway and Mining Company; an ex-civil servant who had become a trader; the fifth member appears to have been an auctioneer. Later on the railway men also got one of their members on the council.

with the M.C. and Bar. When the War was over he decided to settle in Northern Rhodesia where his Commanding Officer was already established; he came to Choma in 1920 and worked for six months on a farm as a learner, but did not make a success of agriculture, and opened a store and hotel at Choma where he stayed for twelve years before moving to Lusaka to start a business.[1] McKee, however, was one of the more lucky ones. The slump hit every form of trade and industry with equal severity; mineral sales dropped; railway trucks ran empty, and it was in the shadow of deepening financial gloom that the final negotiations began for bringing Chartered rule to an end.

The Company's principal assets lay in Southern Rhodesia; the story of the final takeover is therefore largely concerned with Southern Rhodesia. The Southern Rhodesian settlers had previously challenged the Company's claim to the commercial ownership of the land in their country. The question was taken before the Judicial Committee of the Privy Council which in 1918 gave its long expected answer to the question of who owned the unalienated land in Southern Rhodesia. The Council argued that the land did not belong to the Company in its commercial role. The Company might only sell the land in its administrative capacity to make good its deficits incurred in the work of administration as an agent of the Crown. The Company then retaliated by refusing to make any further capital expenditure on the settlers' behalf, and thus cut the ground from underneath its feet. A change of government became essential, for Rhodesians were after all still desperately dependent on the outside world for financial support. But now the Elected Members found themselves in a position where the Company would no longer provide funds for development purposes, whilst no money could be raised by means of public loans until a new form of Government was set up.

The British South Africa Company was itself only too anxious to get rid of its administrative responsibilities. Government had turned out to be a far more costly business than was anticipated in the past, when magnates and humble prospectors alike had dreamt of a 'Second Rand', and when no one had really understood the immense amount of expenditure that would be required to create even the most sketchy system of transport, administration and other essential services. As a commercial speculation Chartered Government proved a flop. Individual directors admittedly may have benefited from their position on the Board through their financial connexions with associated concerns, by inside information, legitimately acquired in the work of governance, and by reason of the social position which their status entailed. But the ordinary investors, some 40,000 of them, more numerous than all the settlers in the two

[1] Rhodesia as a whole seems to have been less kind than Kenya to ex-officers without an agricultural background who turned to colonial farming, partly for economic reasons, but partly also to acquire the social status of a country gentleman. The soil fertility of the White Highlands was in many cases higher than that which was found along the Rhodesian railway lines. This meant that the amateur in Kenya could perhaps often afford to make more mistakes, and still get a crop of sorts, which tided him over the critical period needed to acquire a thorough agricultural training by dint of hard experience.

Rhodesias, had not as yet received a single dividend. Aid for an underdeveloped country was being supplied from the pockets of private lenders, and the lenders did not like it. Provided the Company received an adequate offer for its railway and mining interests as well as adequate compensation for its administrative deficits, the Directors were only too anxious to get rid of their unpopular and expensive commitments, and the only question at issue was, how this was to be achieved.

There were three possibilities. Southern Rhodesia and Northern Rhodesia might become a Crown Colony under Imperial Rule. Southern Rhodesia, with or without its northern sister colony, might join the Union of South Africa, or alternately Responsible Government might be instituted. Crown Colony Government was advocated for a time by some Southern Rhodesian politicians who expressed their views through the so-called 'Rhodesia League', but the scheme did not prove popular in Southern Rhodesia. The country was now paying its way, even if only because of the Company's policy of stringent economy, and the Imperial Government was in any case not anxious to add further to its administrative responsibilities. Great Britain had taken on several new mandates; there was fighting in Ireland and trouble in Egypt; after a short outburst of Imperial and patriotic fervour, imperial sentiments were ebbing and no British statesman wanted new commitments. The only people who were looking towards the Colonial Office for their salvation were the Northern Rhodesian settlers. Their descendants might find their attitude incomprehensible, but in 1919 an Imperial solution seemed good sense; Northern Rhodesia could not possibly finance its own expenditure—only the Imperial Government was in a position to do so. Britain was giving grants to other colonies, and in neighbouring Nyasaland Imperial administrators seemed well disposed towards the colonists. The Nyasaland planters and traders had a fully fledged Legislative Council of their own where they could air their views, despite the fact that Nyasaland's white population was now much smaller than Northern Rhodesia's. Northern Rhodesians also liked the system of taxation in Nyasaland which benefited local labour users rather than their competitors south of the Zambezi. The Protectorate Administration which, unlike the Chartered Company, had no financial stake in Southern Rhodesia, was satisfied to waive half the tax of those Nyasaland Africans who worked for a European for one month in the year. This provision did not please Southern Rhodesian employers who wanted labour for much longer periods, but greatly helped Nyasaland estate owners who could make do with local manpower for a shorter space of time. In addition the Nyasaland Government discouraged the exodus of migrants from the Protectorate, believing that the local planters could not be expected to pay Southern Rhodesian wages. Imperial civil servants also thought that labour migration was disrupting tribal life, an argument also put forward with the same relish by local planters who argued that Africans should not come into contact with 'low whites', with 'cads and bounders' from the south, who did menial work on the mines and whose example would undermine the prestige of better-class Europeans in the

Protectorate. Nyasaland policies made a considerable appeal to Northern Rhodesians. They were just like white Nyasalanders; they could no more compete with Southern Rhodesian wages than their compatriots beyond the Eastern border; they found difficulty in getting farmhands, and as one enraged farmer put it at a public meeting, 'all they got in the way of native labour was the smell of the railway coaches on the way to Bulawayo'! The Northern Rhodesian settlers moreover wanted more representation and soon got tired of playing at politics in the Advisory Council. Even greater anxiety was occasioned by the question of land titles, the colonists feeling that they must get their titles confirmed. Imperial rule seemed the best solution, at a time when few settlers as yet seriously envisaged a British Labour Government, and in 1919 the Advisory Council and all branch chairmen of the recently founded Political Association demanded that the Territory should become an Imperial responsibility.

The settlers' view was shared, though for very different reasons, by the Barotse aristocracy, the only politically conscious African community with an organized administrative apparatus to be found in the Territory. The Barotse argued that they had made a worthwhile contribution to the British war effort by recruiting 6,000 war carriers and by offering armed levies to the British, even though this latter offer had never been accepted. They had been completely loyal to the Crown but received nothing in return. The Caprivi Zipfel should have gone to Barotseland at the end of the War, but the region formed part of the South-West African mandate, a bitter blow to the Barotse who had already lost a large portion of their territory as the result of the Anglo-Portuguese boundary settlement of 1905.[1] Like the settlers, the Barotse questioned the right of the Company's land and mineral concessions which, they said, were obtained under false pretences. These concessions should be cancelled and replaced by new agreements, to be based on the fact that the Company was a commercial body. The Barotse Reserve, at the same time, should be extended in area so as to include the lands from the headwaters of the Dongwe River to the junction of the Anglo-Portuguese boundary with the Zambezi.

The Barotse, like the European colonists, were also faced with the problem of creeping inflation, which was becoming ever more serious, especially since tea, sugar and other imported goods were coming into wider and wider use, whilst the Barotses' ability to pay for these imports was sharply diminished by the destruction of their herds through anthrax and pleuro-pneumonia before and during the Great War. The Barotse contended therefore that the ten per cent of the tax money to which they were entitled should all be paid to them, without deductions for money spent on the Barotse for educational purposes, and that the Company should itself finance the Barotse National School. The Company, the Barotse complained, had not met its promises to maintain schools and industrial establishments or to promote transport services. In addition the Barotse objected to the Company's contention that the Chief of Barotseland had no

[1] *Award of His Majesty the King of Italy respecting the western boundary of the Barotse Kingdom* (Cd. 2584: 1905)

authority over the people outside the Barotse concession. More serious still was the general economic situation. For a time, the Barotse said, 'we went on fairly well, depending on our cattle, and also the cost of living had not increased as it is now; but now many misfortunes have fallen on us, such as the loss of our cattle [through pleuro-pneumonia], the abolition of Free Labour System [by which chiefs were able to enforce corvees] and the going out of the young men from the country for work, it is very difficult to keep the same standard of Chieftainship as before'. There was only one solution. 'The territories defined as Barotziland, North-Western Rhodesia, in the Order in Council of 1899 ...' should be put under the direct rule of His Majesty the King and His Imperial Government, as a Protectorate Native State with a British Resident Commissioner to reside permanently with the Paramount Chief. In asking for direct Imperial rule, the Barotse neither objected to British governance nor to white immigration as such. Constitutional change was to be a means of re-asserting the chiefly powers of old, relieving the economic position of the Barotse ruling group and enabling them to exact great financial benefit from mining and land settlement. But the Imperial Government was not in a position to meet these major economic and social demands. The High Commissioner, for one thing, would not accept the Barotse argument that the various concessions granted by Lewanika and his Councillors were made in ignorance of their true content. The Barotse knew very well what they were doing at the time, and they should not go back on their pledged word now. In any case, cancelling the concessions would hardly have been feasible from a purely administrative point of view; repudiation would have led to legal chaos, for if the Chartered Company had no right to make any of the existing land or mineral grants, who had? The only real promise the Imperial Government could make was in the constitutional sphere, and here the High Commissioner agreed that, if any change were made in the form of government in Northern Rhodesia, Barotse wishes with regard to Imperial rule would be borne in mind.

The Imperial Government, however, was as yet far from anxious to assume a new Protectorate in the North, for there was still a third alternative; Rhodesia might join the Union of South Africa. Rhodes always dreamt of a united Southern African community where the British would hold the balance of power; and the makers of the Union's constitution envisaged that Rhodesia might join at some time in the future. Events down south now seemed to make such a course of action feasible. In 1919 Dougal Orme Malcolm wrote that a great political transformation was going on in South Africa; if General Smuts managed to fuse the Unionists and the moderate South African Party, and beat the Nationalists and Labourites, that is to say rural and urban radicals, Rhodesian opinion might as yet come round to see the advantages of a Southern solution. Milner, the new Colonial Secretary, an Imperialist of the old school and a staunch friend of the Chartered Company, also spoke in favour of Union. Southern, and possibly North-Western Rhodesia should become part of South Africa, whilst North-Eastern Rhodesia would be best off by being linked to Nyasaland, German East

Africa, Kenya and Uganda, which should be joined into a British Central African Protectorate to be administered from Britain. Responsible Government was impracticable for financial reasons, and Milner himself was not prepared to set up a Crown Colony administration.[1]

Malcolm's and Milner's views were shared by Chaplin, the man on the spot, and Chaplin became even more of a 'Unionist' when Smuts won the South African election in 1921 with a crushing majority. The inclusion of Rhodesia into South Africa, Chaplin argued, would strengthen the British and the loyalist cause in South Africa. The Union could easily purchase the Company's mineral and railway rights, and set up an efficient administration; Responsible Government, on the other hand, was not feasible for financial reasons, and all those who had anything to lose in Rhodesia were against it. A Responsible Government Administration would have no funds; it would have to take over the Company's public works, stores and other financial liabilities and would therefore require another £1,500,000 to £1,750,000;[2] the new administration would have no money; it would own neither the land rights nor the railways; all it could do would be to tax the wealthier people in the country and the local companies for the doubtful privilege of putting local men into top jobs. The Company's property itself might not be safe from confiscatory legislation; capital would take fright and Rhodesia would go to rack and ruin. Smuts on the other hand was a sound man; there was no mollycoddling of white workers in the Union, and much could be said for the Union's policy of lowering costs of production on the mines by employing more blacks and taking a firm line against white radicals.

Chaplin, himself a former manager of Consolidated Gold Fields, knew what he was talking about from the Company's point of view, but the poorer Europeans in Southern Rhodesia of course took just the opposite line. The Union issue in fact became the first major class cleavage in white Rhodesian politics, faintly reproducing the savage clash between white skilled workers and foremen on the one hand, and mine-owners on the other that shook the Rand to its foundations in 1922. The position was obscured a little by the fact that the poorer Afrikaners in Rhodesia generally favoured the cause of Union, where their own language was officially recognised in 1925 as the country's second official language, unlike Rhodesia, where English remained the sole official tongue. But the remaining white workers and salary-earners tended to fight a South African solution. The railwaymen were warned by their leaders to oppose Union, for wages on the South African Railways were low and strikers could be punished.[3] The mine workers were appalled by the Rand Lords' policy of substituting white skilled labour by means of lower paid African labour, and their opposition to Union became even more bitter when Smuts in 1922 smashed the

[1] D. Malcolm to P. D. Chaplin: 16 Apr 1919 (CH 8/2/2/11, f. 387–395, Nat Arch MS) amalgamation between the two parties took place in South Africa in 1921.

[2] P. D. Chaplin to Sir T. Smartt: 28 Feb 1921 (CH 8/2/1, f. 2433–2445, Nat Arch MS)

[3] Keller, J. W. 'Responsible Government or Union' (in Rhodesia railway review, Oct 1921, p. 1–5)

Rand Rising by sending in the Union Defence Force.[1] From the purely political point of view Labour was in any case far more likely to play an influential part within a small Southern Rhodesian state than within the Union as a whole. The European clerks and junior civil servants thought much the same; they did not want centralized Pretoria rule either, and they were not going to have their promotion prospects interfered with by their inability to speak Dutch. The poorer Europeans (the very people who a generation later opposed the cause of Central African Federation) then were mostly determined not to have Union. Their cause was strongly reinforced by fervent appeals to British patriotism and Imperial loyalty: sooner or later the Nationalists would come into power south of the Limpopo anyway; Rhodesians would all be made to become citizens of a hated Republic where men of British blood would have no say. The Indians and Coloureds also appear to have opposed Union, and so did the Negrophiles and most missionaries who criticized the Union's native policies.[2] Many of the farmers also disliked Union which they thought would lead to an influx of Boer whites from South Africa in search of cheap land, whilst some of them anticipated that Union would speed up the exodus of black labour to the south. In addition there was also the wider issue of general economic policy. South Africa was beginning to develop secondary industries of her own which could only be fostered by means of protective tariffs. Protectionism might not hit so badly the mining companies which bought much of their specialized machinery from South Africa. But as far as the remaining Rhodesian producers were concerned a policy of low tariffs was essential; Rhodesia was still dependent on the export of a few primary products; her interests were thus best served by a policy of low taxes to attract capital, and low tariffs to keep down the cost of living and to promote Rhodesia's export trade. These sentiments were widely shared in Northern Rhodesia, a poor back-veld community whose economic interests were very similar to those of the poorer Europeans in Southern Rhodesia. The Union, the *Livingstone Mail* argued, had no capital to spare for developments in the North.[3] If Northern Rhodesia joined South Africa the settlers would have to pay higher taxes as well as having to perform universal military service; the Union's native policy was open to criticism in many respects, whilst no civil servant would possibly want to become a South African. Neither was there any point in joining a great East African Protectorate as was suggested by some, for none of them were self-supporting; none of them could support a modern government, and none of them had enough funds at their disposal for future development.

The British South Africa Company, however, firmly continued to push the cause of Union, and as far as the Trans-Zambezian territories were concerned,

---

[1] The Rhodesian Mine and General Workers' Association, though a very moderate body, was linked to the South African Mine Workers' Union in 1921 and shared the South African workers' insistence on the need to protect civilized standards against black competition.

[2] For an analysis of Rhodesian political attitudes see P. D. Chaplin to J. C. Smuts: 30 Oct 1922 (CH 8/2/1, f. 2861–2865, Nat Arch MS)

[3] *Livingstone mail*, 24 Jan 1919, p. 6

Union meant partition. 'Northern Rhodesia', argued the Company in a forceful memorandum to the Imperial Government 'is ill adapted to be a separate single unit of Government. The eastern part of it, which prior to 1911 was separately administered . . . is wholly distinct ethnologically, economically and geographically from the western part. The only centre of white population in the east, and that a very small one, is at Fort Jameson, whence the natural outlet for trade and every other purpose is through Nyasaland. . . . Communications between Fort Jameson and Livingstone otherwise than by telegraph, having to cross the deep trough of the Luangwa valley and the high wall of the Muchinga Mountains takes at least a month. . . . The western parts of Northern Rhodesia consists of the Barotse Reserve and of the Kasempa District and the Western portion of the Kafue District which . . . are purely native areas . . . the Central part . . . is the area in which the railway runs through to the Congo. All its trade runs north to the Congo and south to Southern Rhodesia and the Union of South Africa. All its affinities are with the south whence, except for some direct immigration from Great Britain, its colonization . . . has proceeded.'

The company went on to say that the best course of action would therefore be to partition Northern Rhodesia, get rid of its expensive headquarters administration, placing the eastern portion under direct Imperial rule on lines similar to those of Nyasaland and Tanganyika. Barotseland and the native areas adjoining would be linked to the Bechuanaland Protectorate, whilst the central part should be united to Southern Rhodesia. The Imperial Government ought not to pay too much attention to the clamour of a handful of 4,000 Northern Rhodesian settlers. Their importance should not be overestimated, even though 'in proportion as the white population of Northern Rhodesia is politically more ignorant and inexperienced than that of the south, so the expression of its views by those whom it allows to act as its spokesmen is more vehement and less courteous'. In addition the British Government should find out whether it would be possible to raise native taxation in the central portion of Northern Rhodesia to the Southern Rhodesian level, so that the region might not form a burden on any other territory to which it was joined. Besides a Native Reserves Commission should be set up to get the African areas delimited once and for all.

There was of course a fourth alternative. Northern Rhodesia might be linked to the 'black' countries to the north of it. The first suggestion of this kind appears to have been put forward in 1917 by Alexander Hetherwick, a Nyasaland missionary, who argued that Nyasaland should be joined to Northern Rhodesia. 'Nyasaland is a black man's country. There is no scope within it for the settlement of a white population such as the South African Colonies or Southern Rhodesia afford. The place of the European in the Protectorate is that of administrator of its Government or director of its commercial and agricultural enterprises. . . . The natural future of Nyasaland will be in association with its neighbour on the west—Northern Rhodesia. In both the conditions of life—European and native—are very much alike'. A new united Protectorate would have the advantages of double lines of communications, one on the west by means of the railway to Cape Town and on the east through the Shire-Zambezi-Beira route to the Indian Ocean. Union between the two territories would make possible a common native policy as well as a joint customs tariff, and might lead to a wider association of all British Protectorates in East and Central Africa.[1] Hetherwick's idea was taken up, though in a modified form, by Frank Melland, a senior civil servant in Northern Rhodesia. Melland advocated a Central African Confederation, which was to include Northern Rhodesia, Nyasaland, German East Africa, Kenya and Uganda, forming a great British bastion stretching from Ethiopia to the Zambezi. 'Great Britain', Melland wrote in the mood of contemporary trusteeship principles, 'should keep this and hold it in the interests of Africa and the world at large. No other country has shown more disinterested rule, and no other nation need fear anything from our guardianship. Our commercial policy is extraordinarily unselfish, and we would raise no objections to any safeguards in the interests of other nations and of the natives being enforced internationally'.[2] Melland's ideas, characteristic of those of many of his colleagues in the Native Department, and foreshadowing in some ways the theories so brilliantly expressed a few years later by Sir Frederick Dealtry Lugard,[3] did not, however, appear feasible at the time, There were both geographical and international obstacles in the way of such a project; even the more limited scheme of joining Northern Rhodesia and Nyasaland would have entailed great administrative and logistic difficulties. Joining North-Eastern Rhodesia to Nyasaland as the Company suggested was a much more feasible project, but then Southern Rhodesia would have had to take over the Northern Rhodesia Railway Belt, and even Herbert James Stanley, the Imperial Secretary for South Africa, a good friend to the settlers and the cause of a Responsible Government, was convinced that Southern Rhodesia, poverty stricken as she was, could not take on the extra burden of the Railway Belt. A similar point of view was held by most of the North-Western Rhodesian settlers who objected to partition because it might add unnecessary difficulties to their labour problems, whilst the farmers in Fort Jameson were scared that they might lose their market for tobacco, assured to them under existing customs agreements with the Union of South Africa.

The whole matter was investigated by a Committee headed by Viscount Buxton, a former High Commissioner. Buxton was far from unsympathetic to the colonists and the Chartered Company thoroughly disliked his report. The Committee suggested that Northern Rhodesians might be represented on the Legislative Council, though the Company should retain an 'Official' majority.

[1] Hetherwick, A. 'Nyasaland to-day and to-morrow' (in *Journal of the African Society*, v. 17, no. 65, 1917, p. 11–19)

[2] 'Africanus' (pseudonym for F. H. Melland) 'A Central African Confederation' (in *Journal of the African society*, v. 17, no. 68, 1918, p. 276–306)

[3] Lugard, F. D. *The dual mandate in British tropical Africa*. Blackwood, 1922. This book, which was awarded the Gold Medal of the Royal Colonial Institute, exercized a major influence on the formulation of British colonial policy, forming its major apologia at the time.

In addition the Commissioners went into the vexed question of the Company's land and mineral claims in Northern Rhodesia which the Northern Rhodesian Advisory Council challenged in 1920. The Committee argued that the matter should be referred to the Judicial Committee of the Privy Council; a legal decision on the highest level was essential because of the complexity of the issues involved, and because the Privy Council's judgement on Southern Rhodesia did not deal with the lands north of the Zambezi. In Northern Rhodesia the position was somewhat different. There was no conquest, the Commissioners stated (by no means correctly as far as North-Eastern Rhodesia was concerned); there was only a series of treaties concluded in circumstances very different from those obtained in Southern Rhodesia, and it might even be held that the unalienated land belonged to the natives. The Committee also referred to the possibility of partitioning the Territory on lines very similar to those suggested by the Company, though no final opinion was expressed on this point.[1]

The Buxton Enquiry, like most of its kind, was a waste of time and money. Not one of its recommendations was accepted; the Company refused to instal a Legislative Council which it considered to be an unnecessary expense, whilst the matter of the land and mineral rights was kept out of the Courts. The Colonial Office at first tried to take a strong line, the suggestion being made that His Majesty's Government should take over Northern Rhodesia on condition that the Company surrendered all land and mineral rights there, as well as making various other important concessions. But Philip Lyttleton Gell, the Company's President, was not going to knuckle under to what he called the 'perfide Albion' spirit prevailing at Downing Street. The Company was in a strong position on both sides of the Zambezi. If the Colonial Office were to persist, the Company would be willing to refer Northern Rhodesia to the Privy Council. But in the meantime the Company would only pay for the native administration, the one obligation incumbent upon it under the Charter, whilst the settlers would only get such services as they themselves were willing to pay for. As far as Southern Rhodesia was concerned, the Company was well entrenched and able to exert pressure, forming the main supplier of capital, and there was always the possibility that it might call in Land Bank loans.[2] Even more important was the Company's control of the railways, for the Company could refuse to send down native labour or interfere with railway transit through Southern Rhodesia.[3]

Matters, however, never came to such a pass. Instead a final decision was brought nearer when a plebiscite was held in Southern Rhodesia in 1922 on the future of the country. The electors decisively rejected Smuts's offer of Union, and Responsible Government was accepted as the only possible future form of administration for the territory. Responsible Government for Southern Rho-

[1] ... *Second report of the Committee appointed by the Secretary of State for the Colonies to consider certain questions relating to Rhodesia* (Cmd 1471: 1921)
[2] Gell was referring to the Rhodesia Land Bank ltd, a Chartered-controlled concern. This was distinct from the Land and Agricultural Bank of Southern Rhodesia subsequently established by the Coghlan Government in 1924.
[3] P. L. Gell to P. D. Chaplin: 7 June 1922 (CH 8/2/2/6, f. 377–382, Nat Arch MS)

desia in turn implied an Imperial solution for Northern Rhodesia, for Coghlan was still unwilling to have anything to do with the Black North; the Union could not now even consider extending its influence northwards, whilst the Company had no intention of holding on any longer to an isolated territory that was running up an annual deficit of over £157,000 per annum, despite an income tax that had been imposed on the settlers in the face of fierce opposition in 1921. The final settlement involved lengthy bargaining between Imperial Government and Company, the Board's hands being strengthened to some extent by the appointment in 1922 of William George Arthur Ormsby-Gore as Parliamentary Under Secretary for the Colonies. Ormsby-Gore was a personal friend, as well as a connexion by marriage of Malcolm's;[1] he was convinced that the treatment received by the Company in the past had not been very generous, and that the Colonial Office should now deal frankly with 'London Wall', especially since the Company had influential friends in Parliament. Southern Rhodesia's future, he argued, was with the Union of South Africa. Northern Rhodesia, on the other hand, should become a Protectorate of its own, under a separate Governor; its laws and policies should be assimilated to those of the East African Colonies, and there was no point in putting the territory under the High Commissioner for South Africa. The country, moreover should be treated as a single unit, though the idea of linking the 'railway-strip' to Southern Rhodesia should as yet not be ruled out. In the course of subsequent negotiations, the Colonial Office for a time attempted to make the Company give up its land claims under the Lewanika Concessions, but the Board put up a stout resistance. After all, the Directors argued, the Colonial Office had itself sanctioned the various concessions in the past, and whereas the Company's receipts from land only amounted to £120,000 in Northern Rhodesia, private investors had poured out £1,500,000 on the administration of the territory, not counting the liabilities incurred in guaranteeing railway debentures. In the end reference to the Privy Council was avoided, for the Imperial Government itself felt that litigation would be a lengthy and expensive affair, and that the British Government might find itself landed with the Company's accumulated Northern Rhodesian administrative deficits. The mineral rights would in any case be hard to contest. It was best to strike some sort of a bargain, for the Company could hardly be compelled against its will to continue its administration in Northern Rhodesia, once Southern Rhodesia became a self-governing colony, at a time when the Northern settlers themselves were demanding the end of its administration.

After lengthy delays, arising partly out of Irish and Near Eastern complications, an all-round settlement was finally concluded in 1923.[2] Southern Rhodesia became a self-governing colony and was formally annexed to the Crown, but the Company retained the mineral rights, and also received specific guarantees against confiscatory legislation with regard to its railway interests, an important

---

[1] D. Malcolm to P. D. Chaplin: 1 Nov 1922 (CH 8/2/2/11, f. 1629–1633, Nat Arch MS)

[2] *Rhodesia: agreement between the Secretary of State for the Colonies and the British South Africa Company ... : 29 September 1923* (Cmd 1984: 1923)

consideration from the Board's point of view, for most of the Directors, except Sir Edmund Davis, had at first little confidence in what they regarded as government by back-veld farmers and bush-lawyers. The new Government of white Rhodesians was in fact looked upon in some ways rather like a 'native' administration, incapable of giving satisfaction to investors, and likely to land the country into national bankruptcy, though Gell himself thought that the Colonial Office was just as liable to mulct the Company as the Rhodesians.[1] As far as the Company's accumulated administrative deficits were concerned, the Crown agreed to pay £3,750,000 in quittance of the amount due to the Company under the so-called Cave Award.[2] The unalienated lands of Southern Rhodesia and the public works passed to the self-governing Colony of Southern Rhodesia for the sum of £2,300,000, Southern Rhodesia thus becoming the only community in the British Empire which had to pay for the privilege of acquiring self-government. The Crown moreover relinquished its claim to the £2,000,000 of war expenditure against the Company.

As far as Northern Rhodesia was concerned, the Imperial Government promised to relieve the Company of the Administration of the Territory as from 1 April 1924. The Crown agreed to pay to the Company half of the actual realized administrative deficit for the year 1923 to 1924 subject to certain deductions. The Company handed over all public works and buildings to the Crown, as well as all its land rights, the Crown becoming completely free to administer the lands 'in such a manner as the Crown may in its discretion deem best in the interests of the Native population and in the public interest generally'. The Imperial Government, however, agreed to pay one half of the sums received from land sales up to 1965 to the Company, after making provision for the expense of land management. The Company retained three big freehold areas held by it in virtue of 'Certificates of Claim' issued by Harry Johnston, whilst the Crown reserved for itself the right to lay out native reserves in the concession granted to the North Charterland Exploration Company. All existing land alienations in Northern Rhodesia were recognized, and the Company remained the owner of the country's mineral rights. This latter concession meant little as long as no one had any idea of the Copper Belt's true wealth, and the Company was at first bitterly disappointed at the settlement obtained. But unknown to themselves, the Directors in fact pulled off a brilliant bargain. Their investors' economic rights were fully safeguarded, and as the Company passed out of the ranks of the world's rulers, the last representative of its kind in British Africa, it was able to pay its first modest dividend of 6d in the £. Even more important was the fact that 'London Wall' at last found itself in command of a relatively large amount of liquid funds, and with this money at its disposal, added to its vast local knowledge, the Company was able to play a major role as a supplier of

[1] P. L. Gell to P. D. Chaplin: 7 June 1922 (CH 8/2/2/6, f. 377–382, Nat Arch MS)
[2] The Cave Award in 1921 fixed the amount due to the Company under the Privy Council Judgement which had stated that, whilst the unalienated lands belonged to the Crown, the Company could look to the Crown for the reimbursement of its accumulated administrative deficits.

capital for Rhodesia. But the most decisive change in the Company's economic fortunes was to derive from the little regarded northern mineral rights which soon rocketed up to heights which even the most daring speculators would never have dared to foresee.

As for political control, government south of the Zambezi passed into the hands of the white colonists. The new Administration in Salisbury of course remained hedged around with many restrictions; it was unable to expropriate the Company's railway or mineral rights; neither could it conduct an independent foreign policy, and there were extensive safeguards against the passing of discriminatory legislation against Africans without Imperial sanction. But for all practical purposes, Southern Rhodesia now enjoyed full internal autonomy, its affairs being conducted by a Cabinet, formally appointed by a Governor, though responsible to a Legislative Assembly, which in turn was elected on a non-racial franchise, based on a 'colour blind' property qualification which in practice only gave the vote to white men, the better-off Indian traders and a handful of well-to-do Africans. In Northern Rhodesia, power was assumed by the Imperial Government through the Colonial Office, which took over the Company's civil service and set up an administration of the conventional British colonial pattern, complete with Governor, an 'Official' Executive Council, and a partly elected Legislative Council to which more detailed reference will be made in later chapters. Sir Herbert James Stanley, a brilliant administrator of partly German-Jewish descent, was made the country's first Governor. Stanley's appointment was a popular one, for the Governor was identified with the 'South African' rather than the 'East African' school of thought, having previously held the position of Imperial Secretary for South Africa, and having earlier championed the settlers' cause against the Company when serving as Resident Commissioner in Salisbury during the Great War. After much ceremony the new Governor was solemnly sworn in at Livingstone, and as he took his oath of office a new and momentous chapter opened in the history of the colony.

IV

Northern Rhodesian society in 1924

When Stanley first drove into Government House as the King's representative a whole generation had gone by since the treaty-making days of old, and the world was changed beyond recognition. The Royal Navy no longer ruled supreme over the seven seas, whilst the Hohenzollern, Hapsburg and Romanov dynasties were a matter of history, as much as the royal house of Mzilikazi. The Communist Party held undisputed sway over the Soviet Union, whilst in the West the balance of economic power was shifting beyond the Atlantic to the United States. In layout and type, *The Times* for 1 April 1924, the day when

Stanley assumed office, still looked the same as in the days of Rhodes—but what a difference in content! Victorians would have been familiar with its leader pages, the discussions of industrial unrest in Britain and of taxation problems, more important from the long-range point of view were the less conspicuous items. On the first page there was an 'On Active Service' column where bereaved wives and parents mourned the victims of the Great War. The last page was filled with offers of magnificent country estates and mansion houses, all up for sale, as the landed aristocracy was crumbling. A British 'plane on a world flight reported engine trouble at Corfu, but such items were now becoming common-place as aircraft ceased to be news and became a commercial proposition; a small column described the opening of the new Baghdad University on the Anni-versary of Arab Independence, symbolic alike of the breakup of the Turkish Empire and the emergence of a new native-born intelligentsia in the East. Another item dealt with a Soviet disarmament scheme, whilst three short lines reported 'an imposing display of Fascist forces' before Signor Mussolini; from Canada there was news of a serious agricultural labour shortage, as the trans-atlantic industries were tuning up and young men left the prairie farms to work in factories. In the House of Commons the National Health Insurance (Cost of Medical Benefits) Bill was getting its Second Reading, part of a much wider trend towards social legislation and the creation of a Welfare State in the West-ern world. The Kenya Europeans were opposing a political union of the British East African territories, where immigrant races were coming into conflict with the indigenous Africans. The world was in the throes of change, and Northern Rhodesia little more than a stagnant backwater.

To all outward appearances village life in the Territory seemed little changed. The ordinary Lenje cultivator still prepared his bush gardens as his forefathers had done, by dragging the branches of felled trees into piles about the stumps; then the clearing was burnt and the land between the stumps hoed, kaffir corn forming the main crop. Still there were changes. The Lenje woman's hoe was now probably machine-made; the villagers would wear cloth rather than skins or bark cloth, whilst khaki drill jumpers and shorts were replacing the loin cloth, except with carriers and the roughest manual labourers. Among the Ila and Tonga ploughs were used on an increasing scale; more maize was cultivated and native farmers could boast of a vastly increased number of cattle.[1] In some communities where European influence was strong, Africans built square huts, provided sometimes with three or more rooms, a separate sleeping apartment, a veranda in front and a courtyard at the back whilst inside the visitor might find properly made chairs and bedsteads.[2] Buildings of this type were however still the exception. 'A stranger wandering through an African village might well believe that he had struck a human race of dwarfs . . . as the walls [of the houses]

[1] In 1921 the estimated number of cattle in African hands was 310,623 as compared with 3,520 in European ownership; 150,000 beasts were found in the Barotse District, 71,000 in Namwala, 61,310 in Magoye and 5,746 in Chilanga.

[2] 'After twenty-two years, 1902–24' (in London Missionary Society. *Report of . . . deputation to South and Central Africa, January–July 1924*. London Missionary Society, 1924, p. 77–82)

are low and the entrance available even smaller, making it impossible for ordinary human beings keeping in an erect position to enter or use the hut. Once inside, the caller would find himself in total darkness, and if the hut belonged to a woman, he would cough and search for his breath as the air was getting foul, the outside sanitary arrangements being so inadequate that flies would breed round the settlements with disastrous effects for the peasants' health'.[1] The overwhelming majority of the country's estimated population of some 970,000 Africans was still living under such conditions, though labour migration was now universal, and the tribesmen were becoming familiar with the world of the mine and the workshop; and also learning more about other black people in the territory.

Contact with the white man spread new ideas and knowledge, but perhaps the most revolutionary concept of all was a new way of measuring time and space. Bantu people of course could reckon the time quite accurately for their purposes; they divided the year into months and seasons; or they used the growth-cycle of a staple crop, the day being further sub-divided by the sun's position, or by what the people would be normally doing. But in the villages there were neither printed calendars nor mechanical clocks; time was an everlasting stream, and the villagers thought of it more like the Hebrews of the Old Testament who wrote that 'to everything there is a season and a time to every purpose under the heaven: A time to be born and a time to die; a time to plant, and a time to pluck up that which is planted'. The white man's beliefs were, however, very different. Time to the European was something that could be minutely sub-divided like a loaf, a commodity for sale; 'time was money', and this was the labour migrant's first lesson when he was working his 'ticket', or labour certificate indicating the monthly period worked. New terms for hours, minutes, months of the year and times of the day began to enter into Bantu languages, characteristically in their English dress. Linked to these novel concepts was a new sense of space, one that very slowly began to percolate down to the Africans in the town and by the railway line. To the tribesman in the village land was a continuum; land was in unlimited supply and went on forever, like time. The Europeans, however, had a different idea; they conceived of land in terms of individual tenure; space was apportioned with an imaginary grid, and each of the little bits became marketable pieces of merchandise.

The whites moreover brought another revolutionary invention; they taught the villagers the art of storing ideas. In the past tradition depended on memory and word of mouth; the old knew most, and the young knew least, but missionaries and others showed how words might be committed to paper and permanently preserved, with revolutionary effects for the future. Not only were labour migrants enabled to communicate with their village homes by means of inky marks on paper; they were also enabled to enter the white man's world by reading his books and newspapers. Of equal significance was the creation of a vernacular literature which began, as in Europe, with missionary trans-

[1] Boer, H. D. de. 'Native health' (in *Livingstone mail*, 17 Jan 1934)

lation of the Scriptures and the compilation of hymn books in indigenous languages.[1]

The effects of missionary work were of course still limited. By 1924 well over 100,000 Africans were reported to be followers of the missions, but it is difficult to say just what these figures meant. The missions certainly succeeded in training a group of people, evangelists, clerks and artisans, who were emancipated to some extent from tribal life and tribal conventions; people who sometimes were said to turn to a ruthless individualism and accepted no obligations whatever. The village folk moreover were becoming increasingly familiar with Bible stories which became part of their own folklore, and many Africans began to adopt Biblical names. But the missions did not succeed in drastically altering the structure of African family life; most rural Africans held on to polygamy as their ideal, in many cases even when they were nominally Christians; and the missionaries continued to report constant cases of backsliding in sexual matters even amongst their most trusted followers, and many Church members would lapse and take a second wife. The missionaries usually thought that this was the result of lechery, but this interpretation was not always right. Housewives in an African village could neither buy labour saving devices nor hire servant girls, whilst their husbands' prestige, like an ancient Teutonic chief's, depended to a considerable extent on lavish hospitality, on cooking and beer brewing, which was women's work, and which one wife alone could not easily manage. Children moreover brought prestige as well as influence, whilst the Africans' desire for regular sexual intercourse could not always be satisfied by one wife in a society which imposed all kinds of conventions and taboos on this side of marital relationship. As far as African morals were concerned, the missionaries of course did not regard all African systems to be of equal standing. Patrilineal people like the Ngoni, who—in theory at least—insisted on strict standards for their girls before marriage, got a much 'better press' than matrilineal ones like the Chewa, whose marriage bonds were much weaker, and who were constantly accused of immorality. Ngoni ideals were nearer to European ideals; they were also much closer to those of the ancient Hebrews, another cattle-keeping patrilineal people, the only primitive race with whose manners and customs the missionaries thoroughly familiarized themselves in their Theological Training Colleges before coming out to Africa. As far as the ordinary villagers' religious concepts were concerned, one may doubt whether mission teachings had as yet taken very much effect. By and large there was enough land left to support old ways; chiefs and headmen were still able in most areas to allocate ground to all those who asked for it, and this meant that traditional ways of life and traditional beliefs also continued. Africans were far from being an uninventive people but the village economy and the old religion, now sometimes strangely blended

[1] By 1923 the speech of the Bemba, Mambwe, Lungu, Mwanga, Ngoni, Nsenga, Lala, Lamba and Wisa, Lenje, Tonga, Ila, Barotse, Lovale and Mbunda, Lunda and Kaonde had all been reduced to writing in some form or another. Some work was done by Native Commissioners interested in linguistics, but most of it by missionaries, and by 1928 there were five missionary presses at work in Northern Rhodesia.

with Christian doctrines, made comparatively few allowances for change; village children still learned that the ancestral spirits disliked innovations, that men should try to live as their parents and grandparents had done before them, that individual striving brought unhappiness, and that none should aim beyond his proper station in life; the old gods continued to wage a tenacious underground warfare, and all too often Jesus, the Virgin Mary and the Saints merely became additional spirits in a tribal pantheon.

Numerically the most important of the missionaries were the Catholics, the White Fathers alone accounting for something like half the Christians in the territory. Critics argued that Catholicism was a mass-movement simply because the Church of Rome was satisfied with extremely low standards of religious knowledge and education amongst those who were accepted for baptism. This was certainly true when Catholic practices were compared with those of the Paris Evangelical Mission, which tried to train an elite, but there were also other factors. Catholic priests did not marry; they did not have to bring up families and worry about their children's education; they did not require much leave; and their social links with the remainder of the European settlers were weaker than those of their married colleagues. The priests were sworn to poverty, poverty in turn made for a cheap ecclesiastical labour force; for the same outlay the Catholics could put more men into the field than the Protestants whose spiritual army was encumbered with families, with young children and a bigger administrative 'tail'. In the Catholic Church there was also much less delegation of authority to African catechists and evangelists, for the Church of Rome was based upon a rigid hierarchical structure; the priests' sacramental office possessing a very different significance when compared with the Protestant clergyman's, whilst much less attention was given to Bible readings, a spiritual labour that any literate Protestant evangelist could perform for his flock. The Catholics moreover were generally more willing to bend native customs and beliefs to their own purposes, rather than fight them outright (a policy which they shared with High Anglicans). They did not try to stop singing and dancing—they only preached against excesses; they took away pagan charms—but they gave their converts amulets instead; they appealed to the tribesman's love of colour and ceremonial by providing a magnificent ritual for his edification.

But the Protestants too made progress, especially in view of the importance which they attached to education, a commodity now much in demand amongst Africans. The average attendance at all the mission schools in the Territory amounted to some 40,000, of whom about 10,000 attended Catholic schools, all the remaining children in these 'bush schools' being in the charge of Protestant clergymen and African teachers. As far as the number of followers was concerned, the London Missionary Society, the oldest established group, ranked first with some 17,000 converts. Then came the Dutch Reformed Church with a following of nearly 13,000, led by Afrikaans-speaking clergymen endowed with an almost Judaic conviction that Afrikaners were elected particularly by God to bring salvation to the native races of Africa. The Paris Evangelical Mission ranked far behind most other sects with regard to their numbers, but the Society insisted on relatively high standards of Biblical knowledge before admitting Africans to Church membership, and its converts were strategically placed in influential posts all over Barotseland.

Despite all these advances missionary work was still an uphill struggle, and nowhere more than in the new urban centres where Africans came into contact with whites who were only nominally Christians, and whose way of life was often in marked contrast to missionary precepts. The story went that an African chief asked his District Commissioner for advice on what religion he should adopt. 'Tell me, Bwana,' he said, 'should I become a Moslem like the Yao?' 'Well,' said the District Commissioner, 'the Moslems can't drink but they are allowed several wives'. 'Not a very good religion—what about the Dutch Reformed Church'? continued the chief. 'They are pretty strict, you know; they don't let you dance; they don't let you drink and you can only have one wife'. 'No use to me' said the chief, 'What about the Catholics?' 'The Romans allow you to dance and drink, but you can still only have one wife'. 'None of these religions suit me' replied the chief, 'But could I not adopt the creed of the white Bwanas in the Secretariat?' The District Commissioner's answer is not recorded, but whatever it was, it could not explain away the discrepancies in the Europeans' own standards; neither could it possibly satisfy the chief because of the confusing nature of the different competing creeds. What was even more significant from the labour migrant's point of view was that when he did come to Broken Hill or Livingstone, the missions were not much in evidence, as their main efforts were made on the rural front. The total of African urban congregations in the Territory does not appear to have exceeded some 1,300 people in 1923, the bulk of the initial work being done by Protestants.[1]

As to the social structure of the African population in general, it is difficult to come to any hard and fast conclusions. There were as yet no proper sociological or statistical surveys of the rural areas, and the statistical material left much to be desired, with regard to quality and quantity. The position was not much better for the towns where the problem was complicated by the existence of a floating African population, not in 'gainful employment', who either lived on their wits, or who supplied much needed services to other Africans as pedlars or shoe makers. The number of these people was unknown, but it is significant at any rate that even before the First World War there were complaints in the Livingstone Mail that native 'shop keepers' were doing better than white ones. Most Africans were, however, still working on European farms, the number of farm labourers in the Territory being stated in 1921 to have been 13,843. The next important means of making money was in domestic service, the 1921 figure amounting to 3,815, which meant that there was a 'houseboy' for every European. This was an important factor in shaping racial attitudes, for the ordinary

---

[1] At Broken Hill the Dutch Reformed Mission had 558 members and the Jesuits 260. In addition some work was done by Wesleyans. At Livingstone most of the work was done by the Paris Evangelical Mission whose congregation at Coillard Chapel amounted to 2

white men picked up their ideas of the African from the man who polished his shoes and kept the house after a fashion. Mining came third on the list with only 2,534 of a total black labour force of 34,693 employed within the territory. As far as the number of 'advanced' Africans is concerned, the enquirer is again largely reduced to guesswork. In 1921 there were 1,222 teachers and 2,108 persons in Government service, the latter figure being an interesting indication of how far the Administration was already depending on the services of African messengers, clerks and interpreters. 513 made their living in shops and stores and offices, another 1,149 worked in building and allied trades and 178 in factories and workshops, but most of these were probably still unskilled.

A good deal more is known about the European population, and the census figures for 1921 may be accepted with a greater degree of confidence. The European population was still very small, numbering no more than 3,634 people for the whole Territory; this was in other words still a country where everyone knew everyone else, a gigantic village community spread over a vast territory. Northern Rhodesia was still a man's world, whilst the age structure of the population showed that characteristic 'bulge' in the group of people at the height of their working capacity which is characteristic of all settler countries in the early stages of their development.[1] There were few old people in the Territory, no grandmothers to help with the young children, no grandparents to pass on tales of the past, with the natural result that the young Rhodesian was, then as now, not tradition minded. Many of the older children were away at school in Southern Rhodesia or in England when the parents could afford it, but a high birthrate resulted in a relatively large number of young children, the general youthfulness of the population probably contributing to that mood of confidence and optimism that is characteristic of most pioneering communities. All the same the population was becoming a more stable one and since 1911 there was a striking increase in the percentage of married men in the Territory. The natural result of this development was a much more settled family life though a considerable proportion of wives still remained in the immigrant's country of origin.[2]

As far as occupations were concerned, the most important kind of work was agriculture which accounted for 19·65 per cent of the labour force. Mining, quarrying and industrial occupations between them only amounted to 6·72 per cent. Professional posts with 6·27 per cent constituted a relatively high proportion, giving a good indication of the importance of the clerical element in the territory where many of the outlying areas remained 'missionary country' pure and simple. The only other important form of employment was

[1] The following was the age distribution of the European population in 1921:

0–4	11·66	5–9	7·92
10–14	5·48	15–19	4·95
20–24	6·47	25–34	24·41
35–44	21·58	45–54	12·74
65–74	1·16	75 and up	0·17

[2] Between 1911 and 1921 the proportion of women per thousand men increased from 335 to 605.

provided by the railways and other forms of transport which absorbed 8·39 per cent, whilst administration and defence were in themselves major 'industries' with 7·05 per cent.

Northern Rhodesian white society as a whole was still fairly egalitarian in character but there was an improvement in general living conditions, and an old-time missionary who re-visited Northern Rhodesia in 1924 after an absence of more than two decades, was impressed by the appearance of the houses, now sometimes double-storeyed and mosquito-proofed and the rise in farming standards, cotton, corn, lucern, oranges and lemons now being grown by some enterprising settlers in addition to the inevitable 'mealies' (maize). Medical aid was still hard to get, but all the same Europeans were now much healthier and the traveller noted with satisfaction that there had been no deaths in the L.M.S. Mission for 22 years. There were as yet no great fortunes to be made in the country, and the only kind of aristocracy to be found was in the higher ranks of the civil service. The Governor, with an annual income of £3,000 and an entertainment allowance of £1,000 was not only the most powerful, but also the wealthiest man in the country and the only one able to entertain on something like an extensive scale, so that Government House remained the apex of the social pyramid, where anyone of any pretensions hoped to be invited to some suitable function. The civil service itself was also sharply stratified socially, or, as the poorer settlers grumbled over their whiskies, riddled with class distinction and snobbery, a state of things not surprising in an organization where differences of pay were high,[1] and the sense of rank and precedence highly developed accordingly.

In a society such as this, the relationship between white and black became almost wholly identified with that of employer and employed. Some 'bosses' might be extremely considerate; many farmers took an almost patriarchical interest in their labourers, whilst the farmer's wife was expected to be a nurse and midwife for Africans as much as a domestic manager. Bad employers, known as 'skellums', soon found great difficulties in securing labour; for once word went round that Bwana So-and-so treated his men unfairly, there might be a sort of unofficial boycott against him. But whether a farmer was a good employer or a bad one, his outlook towards the African was moulded inevitably by his everyday experiences with a poorly paid and grossly inefficient labour force; 'he knew his African'; and was not impressed by what he saw. Missionaries might criticize the farmers' outlook. But, the farmer would reply, it was easy for a clergyman to talk; a mission station was not expected to yield a profit, neither was a school; the missionary's salary was paid by well-wishers from overseas and the missionary's and his family's livelihood were not dependent on his ability to get the 'boys' to work. The farmer was in a very different position, and his point of view became generally accepted. The white mineworkers' outlook was similar. African competition was as yet not a major factor, but

[1] In 1924 the Chief Secretary received £1,200 p.a. and a stores clerk £300. In 1953 the Chief Secretary received £2,200 and a Grade I Clerk in the Accountant General's Department received £815 p.a.

African labour management was. The African miner or navvy only worked for
a maximum of something like three months a year, and when he returned to
European employment after a prolonged stay in his native village, all he had
learnt was usually forgotten. The white foreman's task under those conditions
was most unenviable; keeping control of vast numbers of backward people from
different tribal backgrounds, speaking different languages, was hard; and when
the Africans did not understand the foreman's 'kitchen kaffir', the new *lingua
franca* imported to the Railway Belt from the southern mines, the foreman's
patience might give way. Tempers ran even higher in situations where everybody's life might depend on the taking of a few elementary safety precautions,
especially when the tribesmen could not be made to understand how essential
these were. In any case, the white supervisor's own job rested on his ability to
make his gang work; if he could not, he was sacked, and unemployment was a
terrible scourge in a poor and backward territory where there were no social
security payments, and few alternative jobs. By force of circumstances alone the
farmer's and the miner's image of the African became stereotyped into that of
the idle and unreliable 'boy', a perpetual minor who would always have to be
'bossed up', and usually let the boss down! In this respect there was no difference
at all between men with a South African background and those who came from
overseas without ever having been in contact with Africans before, men who
had never heard tales of 'kaffir warfare' in their youth. The diaries of Eriksson,
the Finnish miner previously mentioned in this work, contain just as many
uncomplimentary references to 'niggers' as those of South African-born people.

The economic motive was of course not the only determinant in forming
white-black relationships; European women were incensed at the idea of liaisons
between white men and black women which they considered to be degrading to
both, whilst white men, especially those living on lonely farms, sometimes
worried what might happen to their womenfolk if they were left alone amidst
backward tribesmen. In the early days there was also often an undercurrent of
fear, for even though Northern Rhodesia never saw much serious fighting
between white and black, apart from the Ngoni campaign, many early Northern
Rhodesians served during the Mashona and Matabele Risings, Gifford's Horse, a
Bulawayo unit, containing many miners and prospectors like Collier, Baragwanath and Lewis who made a name for themselves beyond the Zambezi. The
impression made by the fighting was never erased from the participants' minds,
and stayed with them for as long as they lived, not as the dry abstractions of
historians and sociologists seeking to disentangle impersonal causes, but as
memories of horror. More than sixty years later an octogenarian pioneer of
Northern Rhodesia could still vividly tell of those bloodstained days when, in
1896, he found himself cut off on a gold mine outside Bulawayo; on hearing
that the Matabele were coming, the little white community all went into laager,
and kept out of sight as they saw the huge host of thousands of black warriors,
arrayed in warpaint, with their shields and assegais. 'We went into a quick huddle
and decided that when they attacked, we would shoot our womenfolk and

children—I know how people feel when they are condemned to death; we all felt we were condemned that particular day.'[1] Fortunately the danger passed for the people in question, but about one tenth of Southern Rhodesia's white population was slain in battle, swiftly murdered, or tortured to death, with the result that even those who never took part in the fighting still listened to these tales, which were still vivid enough a generation after it was all over. For all we know, deeper psychological motives may also have played their part, but as far as can be judged from the written evidence, the economic relationship and—very secondarily—the military position remained the most important factors in moulding the colonist's attitude towards the Africans around him.

From this point of view, the professional man's position was somewhat different from that of the ordinary farmer or miner. The Native Commissioner was expected to rule his charges, but in doing so he was not under any immediate economic pressure; the ex-University man, or the ex-officer, lucky enough to have got a job with the Chartered Company after the Great War, was assured of his regular salary and his pension, and therefore more inclined to be critical of Europeans whose dealings with the Africans were determined by harsh economic necessity. At the same time life was no longer as hard as it used to be, and there was a general 'softening' in the official's attitude towards what were now 'his' natives. The Victorian servant of Empire, the ex-trooper from the Bechuanaland Border Police, used to be somewhat different in his outlook; a man like Codrington, faced with the difficult task of policing a huge slice of Africa on a budget fit only for an English parish, did not idealize the old Africa; he was convinced that toughness alone would pay when it came to dealing with Arab cut-throats or hard-bitten African adventurers. As far as he was concerned Africans only had one duty—and that was to obey. But by 1924 the official's problems were no longer quite the same; he was beginning to appreciate the value of native chieftainship as an instrument of government, and was now more anxious to protect his charges, not against the threats of slave traders and foreign raiders, but the exaction of Europeans. All the same, the African was still regarded as a child, the white man's ward, a sort of black-skinned Peter Pan who would take a long time to grow up, if he ever managed to do so at all.

Furthest removed from ordinary European society were the missionaries, and it was probably amongst them that the greatest changes in outlook were taking place. The old-time preacher had to be a man of a heroic stamp. As long as malaria and blackwater fever could not be prevented, the missionary's life was in infinitely greater danger than that of a convict in Siberia; missionary death rates were often higher than those of Commandos and paratroopers in modern warfare, and only the hardiest would face such perils for the purpose of saving souls.[2]

---

[1] Quoted from the reminiscences of White, W. R., as written up by Scannell, T. 'A pioneer of 1901 comes to the Copperbelt' (in *Horizon*, Mar 1961, p. 14)

[2] The connexion between malaria and the *anopheles* mosquito was established only at the turn of the last century and not universally accepted throughout the Empire till about some ten years afterwards. In Northern Rhodesia the key date is the year 1902 when Dr George Reutter, a Swiss mission doctor with the Paris Evangelical Mission, caused the first fly-proof house to be introduced into the Mission.

People of that type were not inclined to be analyzers; they had to be men with a burning faith to accept suffering and deaths for themselves and their families whom they brought out to Africa. They found consolation in the conviction that they were fighting Satan and all his works; the heathen around them were sunk in unspeakable depravity, and unless they were converted, eternal torments would await them. These convictions were well in tune with an uncompromising Victorian Protestantism which often survived longer in the mission field than at home, for the missionary in the wilds had not much time to read literature concerned with the 'Higher Criticism', and books were in any case hard to come by. There was thus a considerable 'time lag' before the newer theological and sociological theories made themselves felt in the African mission field. But now life was changing. Northern Rhodesia was a perfectly healthy place to live in for those who took proper care, a fact not always understood by missionary supporters at home who were still inclined to invest the clergyman overseas with a martyr's crown. Bearded prophets like Coillard, rigid in their faith, were now less frequent, and the missionary was becoming more of an administrator, supervising the work of mission educated Africans. The newer kind of missionary in some ways was becoming more like the members of the Administration, and also inclined to place a less uncompromisingly harsh interpretation on tribal life, especially since the country had long since been pacified and the cruelties of tribalism were falling into oblivion.

All the same, the European's dominant role in Rhodesia was as yet accepted without question. The overseas public was not yet Africa-conscious; Parliamentary debates rarely dealt with Central Africa, and journalists hardly ever came out to this sleepy backveld colony where nothing seemed to happen. If they wanted excitement, there was Ireland, there was Mesopotamia or Eastern Europe; there was labour unrest at home, which provided their readers with all the stirring headlines which they could possibly desire. Central Africa was a backwater from the 'news' point of view, a fact not without influence on colonial administration. Neither was there as yet a great professional body of secular scholars ready to embark on critical analyses of social institutions in distant Rhodesia. Methods of anthropological work were still being perfected, and what research there was in Central Africa was carried out by missionaries and civil servants.[1] The first professional academic man ever to have conducted a theoretical enquiry in Rhodesia was Henri Rolin, a brilliant lawyer; Rolin was a Belgian, a member of a nation whom the British had severely censured for their colonial practices in the Congo, and Rolin was quite ready to pay Belgium's critics back in kind; but his massive work was published in French only;[2] and few Rhodesians read it. As far as criticism from England was concerned, its impact on Central Africa was small; the wrath of Negrophiles and Left Wingers raged against the

---

[1] The first major anthropological work on Northern Rhodesia was Smith, E. W., and Dale, A. M. *The Ila-speaking peoples of Northern Rhodesia.* Macmillan, 1920. An early book is Gouldsbury, C., and Sheane, H. *The great plateau of Northern Rhodesia.* E. Arnold, 1911

[2] Rolin, H. *Les lois et l'administration de la Rhodésie.* Brussels, Établissements Emile Bruylant, 1913

Chartered Company rather than the settlers, whom English Radicals supported in what they regarded as a struggle against a ruthless financial monopoly.[1] Nevertheless Britain during this period saw the beginning of a major change of outlook in colonial affairs. Imperial pride, as exemplified in the Great Empire Exhibition, was still strong; but the terrifying losses of the Great War and the weariness of its aftermath all destroyed the invincible self-confidence of old; whilst the gradual erosion of the older middle class by war and taxation, the intellectual swing towards socialism, the victory of Communism in Russia, and the emergence of a large number of newly independent countries, including the Irish Free State just across the water, all contributed towards the shaping of a new climate of opinion, which was further influenced by the general reaction against Victorian middle class ideals and their economic, religious and sexual standards. There was, however, a time-lag before these new trends of thought made themselves felt in Central Africa, and Northern Rhodesia for the time being remained a backwater, little affected by the changing ideas of the Western World.

[1] See Harris, Sir J. H. *The chartered millions; Rhodesia and the challenge to the British Commonwealth.* Swarthmore Press, 1920

Chapter Five

Economic development in the 'twenties

I

King Copper: 1923–1930

When the new Governor took over at Livingstone, Northern Rhodesia was a poverty stricken backveld Protectorate which only few people could have identified on the map. But at this time a group of financiers came together in London whose deliberations were to usher in the most far reaching economic changes ever to have come over Central Africa. In 1923 world demand for copper revived; prices rose as the scrap supplies dating from the Great War were gradually used up. In addition there was a new industrial revolution for electrical, automobile and light industries were coming into their own overseas, with the result that more orders went out for wire, pipes and a host of other products made of copper, a metal both malleable and possessing excellent conductive properties.[1] The second change occurred in the realm of technology. Investors for long would rarely look at the Northern Rhodesian deposits where oxide ores only contained an average of 3 to 5 per cent as compared with the rich reserves of 15 per cent ores available on the Belgian side of the border, where even 6 to 7 per cent oxides were thrown away with contempt, being too poor for profitable treatment. In the Katanga, however, ore bodies did not alter to workable secondary sulphides at depth, but suddenly changed into lean primary ores of no value. Mining engineers at first assumed that the same thing would happen in Northern Rhodesia, where shaft sinking down to water level gave poor results; their reasoning, however, overlooked the different geological structure of the Copper Belt, where drills ultimately struck enormous deposits of valuable sulphide ores, once work was continued to a sufficient depth. In earlier times miners did not know how to work these low grade ores profitably, but then experts discovered the so-called 'flotation method' of concentration which allowed them to exploit sulphides successfully.

The first phase in Northern Rhodesia's copper revolution began in 1922 with the reconstruction of the Bwana Mkubwa mining company which had carried on a little intermittent mining during the war. Bwana Mkubwa, formerly a small

[1] For general historical surveys see Gann, L. H. 'The Northern Rhodesian copper industry and the world of copper: 1923–1952' (in *Rhodes-Livingstone journal*, no. 18, 1955, p. 1–18). See also Rhodesian Anglo-American ltd *Mining developments in Northern Rhodesia*. Johannesburg, 1929; Bradley, K. *Copper venture. . . .* Selection Trust ltd, 1953; and Prain, Sir R. L. 'The Copperbelt of Northern Rhodesia' (in *Journal of the Royal Society of Arts*, 18 Feb 1955, p. 196–216)

concern, was now launched with an impressive authorized capital of £1,500,000, its new board containing some of the most powerful mining magnates to be found in Southern Africa. Edmund Davis with his extensive Rhodesian base mineral and coal connexions was chairman, whilst Dougal O. Malcolm provided the link with the British South Africa Company. Equally important was Alfred Chester Beatty, an American-born financier who had started off in life as a consulting engineer in the U.S.A. where he made his name in the search for low grade copper deposits. Beatty, unlike most other experts, possessed enormous financial and administrative ability as well as technical knowledge, and gradually worked his way on to the directorates of several important American copper companies. In 1913 he settled in London where a year later he founded the Selection Trust Ltd, an investment corporation which later also bought its way into Bwana Mkubwa. The South African mining industry was represented on the Board by Sir Ernest Oppenheimer, one of South Africa's most influential mining men. Oppenheimer's career provides a vital link between the pioneering period of Southern Africa's mining history and its subsequent consolidation and is therefore worth mentioning at some length; Oppenheimer was born in 1880 in Friedberg near Frankfurt-on-Main in Western Germany. The Oppenheimers, by a strange twist of fortune, came from the same region as the Hochschilds, American metal magnates who later also heavily invested in Northern Rhodesian copper, with the difference that the Hochschilds were already well established in the German metal trade before they took their upper class Frankfurt Jewish liberal tradition across the Atlantic, whilst Oppenheimer, the eighth son of a small-town merchant, started off with little. At the age of sixteen Oppenheimer went to London in order to learn English and modern methods of commerce at the hub of world trade. The young apprentice began his business career on a salary of £1 a week in a dingy room in Camden Town, but London proved a stepping stone to South Africa; and when Oppenheimer was only twenty-one, his employer, a diamond merchant, sent him as representative to Kimberley, Oppenheimer's career thus affording a parallel to that of Alfred Beit, Rhodes's great financial ally. Things went well with the young immigrant who soon became a successful and highly respected diamond dealer, and became Mayor of Kimberley.[1] During the First World War, however, anti-German feelings ran high; his house was stoned and he had to be given protection, with the result that the Oppenheimers had to leave town. Misfortune, however, turned out to be the high road to success; Oppenheimer subsequently settled in Johannesburg, became greatly interested in gold mining, and got to know an American mining engineer by the name of W. L. Honnold who was convinced that the Rand's mineral content had not yet been fully gauged. Oppenheimer, in one of his famous 'hunches' believed that the American must be right, and between them the two in 1917 formed the Anglo-American Corporation which managed to secure big American credits and soon became a great power in the South African gold industry. Later on, Oppenheimer bought out extensive German diamond

[1] For his obituary see *South Africa*, 30 Nov 1957, p. 418–419

interests in South-West Africa as a prelude to an attack on De Beers, Rhodes's old firm, where he captured a directorship in 1927 and the chairmanship two years later, his position being further strengthened by a seat on the Board of Barclays Bank, one of the 'Big Five' of British banking.

The next step in the development of Rhodesian copper was taken in 1923 when the British South Africa Company decided on a new policy of giving out vast concessions to strongly capitalized concerns. This decision was made easier for the Chartered Board by the fact that in Northern Rhodesia the Directors did not have to contend with organized opposition from small European prospectors who formed a powerful pressure group south of the Zambezi and bitterly opposed large monopolistic grants. In addition Britain was now conscious of her war-time dependence on American copper and became anxious to remedy this state of affairs at a time when she was still trying to maintain parity with the U.S.A. as the world's leading naval power. In February 1923 Beatty and Oppenheimer, assisted by some other financiers, floated the Rhodesian Congo Border Concession Ltd which received an exclusive grant of 50,000 square miles; the Chartered Company then made a number of further concessions and within a few years the whole of the Protectorate outside Barotseland and the north-eastern region was parcelled out into six vast areas, each bigger than a European principality.[1]

Prospecting proceeded and in 1926 Beatty reconstituted the Selection Trust with American backing and holdings in the Balkans as well as Northern Rhodesia. During the same year, at a time when Northern Rhodesian copper was still regarded as a speculative kind of investment to be avoided by the cautious, Oppenheimer laid his plans for the setting up of a Rhodesian Branch of Anglo American with headquarters at Broken Hill, the influence of his company having already been vastly expanded by the fact that it served as consulting engineers to several prospecting concerns. Two years later, in 1928, Rhodesian Anglo American was incorporated with a capital of £3,500,000 much of which was provided by co-operation between Davis and Oppenheimer, whose financial power still exceeded that of the rival Selection Trust. Work then proceeded on such a scale that the supply of British capital became inadequate, the London market being less receptive to copper shares than the American markets because of earlier disappointments in Rhodesia. In 1927 Dr Otto Sussman, a German-Jewish mining engineer and at that time Vice President of the American Metal Company, visited Southern Africa, and immediately recognized the potentialities of the Rhodesian deposits. He quickly cabled to New York that Roan promised to become a major producer and advised American Metal to acquire an interest. The first share acquisitions took place in 1927, and two years later arrangements were made to advance £1,500,000 to the Rhodesian Selection

[1] Between 1925 and 1926 Kasempa Concessions ltd, Loangwa Concessions (Northern Rhodesia) ltd, and Serenje Concessions ltd, were founded on similar terms. These were subsequently amalgamated under the Loangwa Company in 1928 which in 1938 was absorbed by Rhodesian Anglo American ltd.

Trust, the American Metal Company committing itself to by far the largest portion of this amount. In 1930 the American Metal Company vastly extended its holdings by acquiring 800,000 shares of Roan and 1,000,000 shares of R.S.T. against which it issued 350,000 new shares of its own common stock and paid $1,000,000 in cash to an affiliated company of Selection Trust Limited in London.[1] Apart from its financial advantages, the transatlantic connexion helped the Rhodesian copper industry to secure the services of American metallurgists, the best known experts in the field at a time when the U.S.A. was dominating the world's copper production. There followed further financial consolidations for the purpose of facilitating marketing, cutting down over-production, assuring a more efficient utilization of technical services, and more effective representations to the Northern Rhodesia Government. The details of these negotiations would be tedious to relate, but in the end two powerful, partially inter-connected combines controlled the entire Copper Belt.[2] The first centred on the Rhodesian Anglo American Corporation, linked in turn to the Broken Hill Mine, the South African gold and diamond industries and the British South Africa Company. This group owned Nkana, Bwana Mkubwa and Nchanga. Sir Ernest Oppenheimer himself would have liked a financial union between the two copper-producing groups, paralleling comparable arrangements in the diamond industry, but could not achieve this aim. He did, however, help in keeping the Copper Belt primarily an 'Imperial' interest. In 1928 he prevented Bwana Mkubwa from largely falling into the hands of the American Metal Company. A year later a powerful British financial alliance, comprising Rhodesian Anglo American, the Rio Tinto Company, the Rothschilds and other interests, stopped Nchanga from being bought by transatlantic investors, Nchanga becoming definitely part of the Anglo American empire, whilst Americans only held a minority share in the Northern Rhodesian copper industry.[3]

The Selection Trust for its part controlled Roan Antelope and Mufulira mines, Beatty himself receiving a seat on the American Metal Company's Board, his transatlantic connexions rendering his policies much more independent of local South African considerations than those of his rival Oppenheimer.[4]

Financial combinations on this scale raised vast problems and left the Governor practically powerless with regard to the mining policies which decided the country's future. But without these imposing concentrations of capital the Copper Belt could never have come into its own. Individual prospectors and white 'small workers' who took the lead in creating Southern Rhodesia's gold industry, and exerted such a strong influence on the country's social policies,

---

[1] The author is indebted to personal information from Walter Hochschild of the American Metal Climax Inc. for this section. By the end of 1930 the American Metal Company owned 1,777,198 shares in Roan at a cost of $8,756,000 and 1,641,361 shares in R.S.T. at a cost of $7,766,000.

[2] For a detailed chart see *Economist*, 12 May 1934

[3] See for details the authoritative work by Gregory, Sir T. *Ernest Oppenheimer and the economic development of Southern Africa*. Oxford University Press, 1962

[4] By 1941 the American Metal Company had issued 1,224,585 shares. Of these Harold, Walter and Gertrude Hochschild owned 144,117 and the Selection Trust 289,000.

were excluded from vast areas, which were thus 'locked up' and probably still present great opportunities for future prospectors. But from the copper industry's point of view, this restrictive policy was sound, for base mineral prospectors looking for copper found themselves gravely handicapped in a country where intense leaching made surface indications of the red metal rather scanty. 'When I was working on the Roan Antelope', related a well known German geologist who now occupies a Chair at Göttingen University, 'I remember that out of twenty rock samples as big as my fist, I noticed just one tiny speck of copper . . . this one being only as big as the point of a pin'.[1] Distances moreover were great; labour not easy to get, difficult to feed, and harder to keep healthy; transport alone posed a major problem, and drilling below the water level, often at a depth of several hundred feet below the ground, exceeded the resources of small investors. Work on a really big scale began with an aerial survey over the 52,000 square miles alloted to the Rhodesian Congo Border Concession, and landing grounds were established at 20 mile intervals. Surveying by 'plane, however, met with difficulties; in the rainy season heavy layers of clouds obscured the view, whilst in the dry months photographers could not see through the heavy palls of smoke from veld fires, which still show up on early photographic maps as grey blotches; clearing the landing fields taxed the tempers of the most patient, for meadows would flood during the rains, whilst the huge termite hills characteristic of the northern bush could not be blasted by dynamite. Worse still, aerial surveying failed to show up those 'blind dambo' clearings in the vlei characteristic of the Katanga fields where acid solutions from surface copper ores interfered with growth. The main burden of work thus fell on teams of first-class young geologists, who were only too glad to find a job during the years of depression and came from many different countries, including Britain, Germany, South Africa, Canada and the U.S.A. These teams systematically slogged through the bush, covering some 20 miles a day, armed with a couple of yards of graph paper, a compass, and the front wheel of a bicycle which counted the number of miles traversed.[2] Their reports were then collected at headquarters, where Dr J. Austen Bancroft, a Canadian professor of fiercely autocratic temperament but most outstanding ability, was in charge of affairs in his new capacity as Chief Consultant Engineer to Rhodesian Anglo American Ltd. Bancroft, who previously had made a name for himself by his bauxite discoveries in British Guiana drew on extensive knowledge previously accumulated under the direction of Raymond Brooks who first located many of the major deposits. The Professor also received much assistance from Dr T. D. Guernsey, a scholarly and able man, who also hailed from Canada, and between them they managed to publish a great deal of most valuable geological work, and saw to it that the areas in their charge were worked in uniform fashion, a

[1] Quoted from an account by Professor Ernst Ackermann, supplied to the author and now deposited with the National Archives (MISC/AC 2, Nat Arch MS)
[2] I am indebted for some of these reminiscences to W. H. Reeve, formerly Director of Geological Surveys for Northern Rhodesia.

unique achievement in those days. In addition, the companies undertook drilling on an extensive scale, drilling teams, complete with foreman, workers and equipment arriving from North America by plane, the prospecting companies sparing no expense since they were in any case contractually bound to spend large, specified sums of money.

After many expensive disappointments which, according to a German expert, would have discouraged any Continental prospecting company, copper deposits were proved on a vast scale. By 1929 work was sufficiently advanced for the opening of a branch railway from Ndola to Roan Antelope, the first of several others, and the Copper Belt experienced its first construction boom. Shafts went down; houses went up; the native labour force rose from a monthly average of some 10,000 workers in 1927 to nearly three times that number in 1930, the initial reluctance of local Africans to work underground being overcome by the use of black workers specially imported for the purpose from Southern Rhodesia. European artisans, foremen and miners were recruited on an extensive scale in the Transvaal, a small percentage of the more highly qualified men being imported from Britain.[1] By 1930 Bwana Mkubwa, Roan, Nkana, Mufulira, Nchanga, Chambishi and Kansanshi were all producing or under development, and even the cautious *Economist* foresaw a magnificent future for the distant North.

The new white communities in the bush were composed of all sorts and conditions of men—Texan drillers, hardbitten Afrikaners, Yugoslav timbermen, fitters and turners from South Africa, smeltermen from Wales, American construction experts with experience in the copper mines of Arizona or Latin America, Cornishmen, and others. But all faced similar problems, the most important being that of health. The early pioneers lived in huts made of Kimberley brick, or rondavels of corrugated iron; when the sun was hot they were scorched; when tropical storms burst down they waded through the mud; worse still was the ever-present peril from mosquitoes. When Sir Malcolm Watson, Director of Tropical Hygiene at the famous Ross Institute in London, arrived at Cape Town on his way to visit the Copper Belt, he got quite a shock. 'No need to get a return ticket' said the booking clerk at the station 'you won't come back—no one does!' Rumour fortunately exaggerated the position, but reality was grim enough. The rich mineralized area was riddled with disease; malaria, blackwater fever and other sicknesses formed a constant menace to the health of miners, white and black, and many Africans deserted rather than brave the terrors of the mysterious 'Snake' that was supposed to haunt the compounds. The tiny Government Medical Department was numerically quite inadequate to cope with the problem, and its solution was left to private enterprise. The mining companies fortunately took a most enlightened attitude, and in 1929 Beatty's group approached the Ross Institute for advice. Within two months an expedi-

---

[1] At the time suggestions were made that unemployment in the United Kingdom should be relieved by the employment of British miners. Davis actually considered their use at Bwana Mkubwa, but the project fell through, though the *Engineering and mining journal* considered the idea feasible.

P

tion was on its way. The party contained Sir William Simpson, then the most distinguished sanitarian in the British Commonwealth, Dr Charles Dalzell, an experienced research worker, and Christopher Robert Harrison, who started off in life as a young rubber planter in Malaya where he familiarized himself with problems of swamp drainage and mosquito control. Harrison proved an outstanding organizer and there is no better way to sum up his achievements than to quote Watson's dry-as-dust, and yet so dramatic report:

'When C. R. Harrison began the control of malaria on the Copper Belt Mines of Northern Rhodesia in 1929, he found A [nopheles] gambiae widespread. In addition to natural depressions on the ground, a construction programme to house 10,000 people and extract copper from 10,000 tons of ore a day provided a succession of artificial depressions entirely suitable for A. gambiae. It began to increase with the arrival of the rains in October. Harrison's organization was so excellent that the normal increase of the malaria wave caused by it was aborted by December, and when I visited the mines on April 4th 1930, no A. gambiae were found by me, except outside the controlled areas, where they were breeding freely.'[1]

This decisive victory over Anopheles gambiae was paralleled by the defeat of Anopheles funestus which lives in swamps rather than in small pools as does its equally deadly cousin. The mines thus embarked on an extensive programme of swamp drainage which eliminated disease as well as providing fertile gardens for Africans. In addition, feeding arrangements vastly improved and hospitals went up in all the mining townships with the result that death rates dropped dramatically and the Copper Belt became as healthy a place as any in Africa.[2]

Life in these new communities was rigidly controlled. Right from the start the Administration approved of the American system of 'company towns' which seemed to offer many advantages. Company local government was efficient, and it also kept out white 'riff raff', for no one might live in a mining township without the permission of the management; the system also avoided that hotchpotch of ownership which existed at Broken Hill where uncontrolled sprawling characterized the pioneer settlement. The Government avoided expenditure, saddling the companies with the expense of providing public services for settlements whose future as yet seemed uncertain; the companies, for their part, obtained full control of their townships, a valuable privilege; for if outsiders were allowed to come in and acquire property, they would demand local self-government, raise rates and wrest the companies' property out of the shareholders' hands.[3] The mines thus received land at favourable rates and developed their own electrical, sewerage and water supplies as well as houses,

[1] Watson, Sir M. *African Highway: the battle for health in Central Africa.* J. Murray, 1953, p. 23. This provides a detailed account of medical work on the Copper Belt.
[2] At Luanshya for instance, the death rate from all causes went down from 13·23 per 1,000 in 1930 to 9·9 in 1938 for European employees. The corresponding figures for African workers were 34·6 and 6·6
[3] Statement by Chief Secretary (in Northern Rhodesia. *Legislative Council debates*: 8 Mar 1932, p. 551–558)

roads, cinemas and sports grounds, a task undertaken with accustomed efficiency. The Administration, for its part, set up small 'public townships' next to the mines to house independent traders, hotel keepers and artisans.[1] Luanshya thus came into being to serve Roan Antelope, whilst Nkana was at first wholly developed by the Rhokana Corporation, before Kitwe Public Township was declared there in 1935. Ndola, the original railhead, became the main commercial and distributive centre for the Copper Belt, and in 1931 the Chartered Company launched a local building programme to facilitate the Governor's policy. Development of the public townships, however, proceeded slowly. The Administration, with a regrettable excess of caution, would only grant leases of up to 99 years which proved an inadequate incentive for small investors; mining developments moreover at first fell below expectations, whilst Ndola turned out to be inconveniently far away from some of the bigger mines.

The layout of the mine townships faithfully reflected their social composition. Mining enterprises are like armies, requiring a strict chain of command from management downwards, and the rough egalitarianism of malaria-ridden pioneer settlements soon gave way to the social cleavages of a well-run garden city. As early as 1930 an angry correspondent railed in his paper at the undemocratic structure of the new townships; an 'A' house for heads of departments, containing ten rooms, costs £10,000, whilst an 'F' house for the ordinary worker with just one bedroom is put up for a mere £800. Worse still, the writer added, houses of different types are grouped into separate areas with rigid divisions between them, with the result that even the native servants take their social status from their masters and 'A' house boys presume to give orders to 'F' house boys and refuse to mix with them socially.[2] Residential segregation between white and black was even stricter. The unskilled workers were at first housed in temporary little cabins of sun-dried brick with thatched roofs and imported wooden doors. Once the continued life of the mines was assured, these dwellings gave way to permanent, fireproof little houses of burnt brick and cement, much thought being given by their designers to the questions of ventilation and insulation. The labourers themselves were encouraged to bring their wives, though their working periods on the mines remained strictly limited, the main recruiting area being the more distant and poverty-stricken Northern Province, especially the Bemba country.[3] Recruiting was at first done by the mines individually, but in 1930 the companies joined to found the Native Labour Association, the repatriation of the workers being undertaken at the end of their contracts by the mines themselves.[4] The companies also provided elementary training and Nkana soon boasted of a complete dummy working place where Africans were taught

---

[1] The legal instrument for this was provided by the Mine townships ordinance, no. 11 of 1932

[2] Mussell, F. 'The outlook in Northern Rhodesia' (in *Livingstone mail*, 26 Feb 1930)

[3] The earliest contracts were for six 'tickets' (periods of 30 labour days). In 1930 these were raised to 12. In 1937 Nkana Mine employed 3,319 from the Northern Province out of a total of 6,495 Africans. The corresponding figures for Mufulira were 3,001 out of 4,526.

[4] See the valuable contribution by Robinson, E. A. G., in Davis, J. Merle, ed. *Modern industry and the African*. Macmillan, 1933

how to use drills, their instruction resulting in a sharp rise in output.[1] Skilled work at first remained entirely in European hands, for European workers were the only ones available at the time and had to be brought in from the Rand and elsewhere. Semi-skilled work, on the other hand, soon became a black preserve and by 1929 'machine boys', 'timber boys' and hoist drivers were listed on the companies' paysheets, receiving between two and three times the wages paid to ordinary labourers; four years later Africans held 73 out of the 265 blasting certificates issued on the Copper Belt, and black workers were driving lorries and underground trains, as well as sharpening drills, and occasionally working as carpenters.

II

White farms and black reserves

For the farmers the construction boom seemed to be the first stroke of good fortune they had ever experienced. Right through the early 'twenties, the growers on the Railway Belt grimly struggled on, but luck was against them; Katanga continued to import beef, but in 1922 Southern Rhodesia was declared free from East Coast fever, and stockmen from the south captured the Katanga markets. Maize for a time seemed a good investment, but a sharp slump in prices followed in 1923, with the result that a good many farmers abandoned their holdings to become traders or transport contractors. Hopes that cotton might provide a suitable alternative were shattered between 1924 and 1925, when plant disease and bad weather ruined the crop. Fort Jameson continued to rely on its tobacco, the only commodity able to stand the transport charges, but farmers complained that the United Tobacco Company of South Africa pushed down prices by reason of its virtual monopoly. The growers then tried to set up a co-operative society, but their attempt failed because some of them stayed outside, the Co-operative being unable to provide adequate supervision during the growth, curing and grading of the crop. Moreover farmers lacked capital, and in 1928 interest stood at 8½ per cent, so that diversification of production proved difficult. A few growers tried their luck with beans and groundnuts, but soon got discouraged; markets were inadequate; Government could provide but little in the way of technical advice; there was no adequate selling organization, the small amounts grown proving insufficient to attract big contractors; Northern Rhodesians indeed found that there were not enough petty village traders about, willing to deal in 'penny-packets' and thus able to play their part in diversifying the economy. Many settlers also lacked experience; and though

---

[1] Between 1926 and 1931 wages were reported to have risen by 50 per cent. Native artisans received up to £8. o. o. a month, native clerks a maximum of £5. o. o. Underground locomotive drivers earned up to £3. o. o. Unskilled men received about £1. o. o. In addition the men received housing, rations and medical attention.

some were beginning to improve their land by ploughing in green crops, general standards remained low in the 'twenties. The position was made worse by the haphazard way in which farms were strung out over huge areas, the Government never having made any attempt to plan properly grouped settlements. No wonder that farmers looked enviously to the south where in 1924 a Responsible Government Administration established a Land Bank independent of the Chartered Company and encouraged the development of creameries, cheese and bacon factories and refrigerator plants.—'I have sunk all my capital into my farm'—a despairing grower from Kafue wrote to the Chief Secretary during this period—'but now I am "sunk" myself, I can't get a loan, and even though my wife and I never had a holiday for the last eight years, we can't save a penny; when I started to farm I had to pay as much as 25/– a bag for native grown grain to traders to feed my "boys"; then I lost some of my cattle from obscure diseases and wild animals; to make matters worse, my wife had to go to hospital to have her appendix taken out; my child died from malaria. Afterwards I needed medical attention myself for diabetes, and my farm had to be left in charge of a white manager who made all sorts of mistakes. I came back, lost some more stock, and to cap it all, my labourers deserted in the middle of the rains "because it was too wet to work" [or possibly because the Africans' agricultural peak season coincided with his own]. Being single handed, I can't get away to supplement my income from trading or contracting, as some do, for if I left my holding in charge of a native foreman, the place would just go back to bush.'

The farmers then tried to put pressure on the Government in various ways. Demands for an increased public spending programme topped the list: there should be more research; the Government's Veterinary Department should become more than just a 'fire brigade' to stamp out outbreaks of disease, and should actively promote research. More ought to be done to investigate the country's arable potentialities; more should be spent on health, forestry services, roads and rural credits; Northern Rhodesia after all was still a young country, and it was not unreasonable that the United Kingdom, as well as future generations of local taxpayers should pay for the foundations of progress. Sir Herbert Stanley was personally sympathetic to the farmers, but there was little he could do, for he was after all expected to balance his budget; and the means at his disposal remained extremely limited. The British taxpayer, he argued in the Legislative Council, could not be expected to subsidize all the colonies, and there was no point in saddling the country with a heavy debt charge like Nyasaland.[1] There were also demands for reforms in the Survey Department. The inadequacy of the governmental machine was itself said to promote extensive farming, and one applicant found that he could not get 50 acres to start a dairy-poultry farm, the minimum size offered being 1,200 or 2,000 acres, the country only having been surveyed in blocks of this size.[2] In addition farmers asked for a

[1] Northern Rhodesia. *Legislative Council debates*, 28 May 1925 p. 230–236
[2] Letter by M. H. Fisher in *Livingstone mail*, 10 June 1926

revision of land values.[1] Interest on existing farms, coupled with heavy cost of dipping and fencing was leaving no profit; the only farmers doing well were said to be those who had bought their holdings in the halcyon days before and during the early days of the Great War, when land stood at between 3d and 1/– an acre. Again the Administration disagreed. The land now being sold at between 1/2d and 13/6d an acre was not over valued; interest rates of 6 per cent were not unreasonable. Remitting liabilities was equivalent to a subsidy; Government in any case was bound by its agreement with the Chartered Company to remit to the Company half the receipts from sales in North-Western Rhodesia, and could not simply write off debts.[2]

The copper boom suddenly altered the position; some optimists began to dream of a 'second Jo'burg' in the lonely northern veld, and even the more cautious found that local markets were expanding. In 1928 Northern Rhodesia for the first time became a net importer of food, and a year later Sir James Crawford Maxwell (Stanley's successor as from 1927) set up a Land Settlement Board to encourage immigration; loans were made available for dips, boreholes and fences, and in 1929 an agricultural research station opened its doors at Mazabuka. Maxwell also stressed the need for a comprehensive ecological survey, and pointed out that land should be alienated in economic units rather than in the haphazard fashion of old. Caution, he added, was admittedly still essential. Small farmers should not be brought in until a great deal more knowledge became available, and settlement should be regarded as something in the nature of an experiment. Maxwell, who had qualified as a doctor at Edinburgh and once served as a Medical Officer in Sierra Leone, was particularly worried that Europeans might not be able to retain their vigour in the tropics over several generations, his medical theories influencing his views on land settlement. But whilst Maxwell imagined that care should be exercized in promoting white settlement, and that maize growing might ultimately even become an African industry, he never doubted that European production should be encouraged, and even complained that farmers were not doing enough to meet the copper companies' insatiable demand for food. The Imperial Government was in broad agreement with these views, and in this respect there was little difference between the Conservatives and a Socialist like Lord Passfield (formerly Sidney James Webb) who became Secretary of State for the Colonies and the Dominions under the Second Labour Government in 1929. Passfield became something of a bogeyman to white Northern Rhodesians, who regarded him as a sort of arch fiend and a sworn enemy of white settlement, but in fact their fears were quite unfounded. The Africans, Passfield agreed, were quite unable in the near future to supply enough cattle and grain to feed the workers in the mine compounds, a perfectly reasonable assumption at a time when Lamba and Tonga cultivators were using extremely backward methods of production near the

---

[1] Improved farms, complete with homesteads and dips, were advertised during 1927 at prices ranging between £4,000 and £6,000, repayable over 20 years at £200–£300 per annum.

[2] Northern Rhodesia. *Legislative Council debates*, 22 Sep 1926, p. 157–177

railway line, and when agricultural surpluses from the villages remained small and irregular. An early increase in the number of European farmers was therefore desirable; agriculture should preferably be of the mixed kind, but settlers with too little land or capital should as yet not be encouraged in view of Northern Rhodesia's little known potentialities and tropical climate. Until the resources of the country were better known, settlement ought not to be actively promoted by publicity, so that all risks and responsibility remained with individual white colonists.

Settlement raised two major problems: on what basis the settlers were to hold their land, and their relationship with the Africans. As far as tenure was concerned, there were two possible choices—leasehold or freehold. Stanley, with his South African background, was a forceful advocate of freehold tenure. The Europeans, he argued, should be able 'to make in Rhodesia a permanent home for themselves and their children, and to become an integral part of the local population, socially superior to the natives, politically dominant no doubt, but conscious of a more than temporary association with the country and all its inhabitants and obliged therefore, in the long run, by the logic of facts to recognize the economic interdependence of the two races'. The recommendation of the East Africa Commission, that Northern Rhodesia should consider the Tanganyika system of leaseholds, was unsound. This concept, according to Stanley, regarded the European as nothing but an interloper, and would actually encourage him to exploit the soil as fast as he could before retiring for home. Settlers moreover would be able to borrow money on less advantageous terms than on the security of freehold titles. As far as Northern Rhodesia was concerned, there was no likelihood of native interests being disregarded, for Northern Rhodesia was thinly populated; plenty of land existed for all; the country's aridity might eventually be cured by water boring and soil conservation, whilst the eradication of cattle diseases would permit of more efficient stock farming. Permanent settlers moreover would take a much more enlightened view of Africans than birds of passage: indeed 'the general attitude of the settlers in Northern Rhodesia towards proposals for the education of the native and his moral and material betterment need not fear comparison with the attitude in other East African territories' and Stanley wisely added, 'if my impression is correct, I should be inclined to submit that the explanation is to be found in the psychological factor of security.'

Stanley's views were broadly shared at the time by Sir Edward Grigg, then Governor of Kenya, whilst Sir Donald Cameron, Governor of Tanganyika and a strong advocate of the system of 'Indirect Rule', preferred to encourage native peasant production. Maxwell, Stanley's successor, showed little interest in the theoretical issues involved, but was guided more by purely practical considerations. The new Governor, a dour Scotsman from Dundee, known to his opponents as 'Sir James Not-a-Penny' from his habits of rigid economy, had nothing against the settlers, despite his 'West Coast' background. But, he argued, the present system of freehold tenure was opposed to the needs of sound farming, and also encouraged over-building in towns; Europeans, moreover, were able to sell land in white areas to non-Europeans both in the towns and the country, which defeated the policy of creating white zones. Similar points were expressed in the Legislature. Freehold tenure, the Chief Secretary stressed, would only encourage land sharks to buy out property on easy terms for the purpose of getting an unearned increment from improvements that were being made on the farms next door. Alienation of large areas led to loss of governmental control which was particularly undesirable in a territory where European settlement was still in its infancy, and where speculation already was rampant to such an extent that in North-Western Rhodesia alone over 2,000,000 acres were alienated, much of it to big companies which were not using the land. There was the added danger that owners in fee simple might lease their land to Africans, an undesirable state of affairs, and one opposed to the Government's declared policy of providing land for natives in their own areas.[1] Maxwell's policy met with bitter opposition from 'Unofficials', but was successfully carried in the Legislative Council. In 1931 the former policy of only alienating land in freehold, subject to a quit-rent, was dropped; purchasers could still acquire farms within a distance of up to 25 miles from the railway in 'fee simple', after five years' occupancy during which certain conditions as regards cultivation had to be fulfilled. In the remainder of North-Western Rhodesia farm land was only granted on a 999 year leasehold, with a rent revisable after 30 years, whereas ranching land over 6,000 acres was made subject to 30 year leases. In North-Eastern Rhodesia, which the Colonial Office regarded more particularly as a native area, leaseholds were given out for 99 years only, with rents revisable after 33 years, as in Tanganyika. The long leases handed out in North-Western Rhodesia could hardly be regarded as onerous. Much more serious, however, was a provision which limited tenure in the mining areas from 30 to 99 years and to 99 years in all new townships, though freehold continued in Livingstone, Broken Hill, Ndola and Fort Jameson. These limited leases took no account of the possible needs of later industries, which were not even considered at the time; neither did they provide any incentive for settlers to put up substantial structures, with the result that urban development was probably retarded.[2]

The promotion of European settlement inevitably meant that land must be controlled. However backward the white farmer might be, there was generally a vast gap between his methods and those of the African *chitimene* cultivator. Northern Rhodesian Railway Belt farmers found that their labour needs were more limited than those of their colleagues in Kenya and Fort Jameson, and the majority thus favoured big consolidated reserves which would facilitate the construction of dips and veterinary supervision,[3] the European farmers in their own interest being more anxious than anyone else that stock diseases should be

[1] Northern Rhodesia. *Legislative Council debates*, 25 Nov 1930, p. 104–107
[2] For a summary of conditions see *Report of the Commission appointed to enquire into the financial and economic position of Northern Rhodesia* (Colonial no. 145, 1938), p. 16
[3] Northern Rhodesia. *Legislative Council debates*, 20 Sep 1926, p. 130

kept out of the native areas. As far as their own lands were concerned, the farmers wished to be rid of neighbours who would start uncontrolled bush fires, cut down timber, damage fences, occasionally 'lift' a cow, and who allowed their scrub-cattle to mingle with the settler's improved stock. Others complained that Africans would take money from a settler to leave his piece of veld; the tribesmen would then move on to adjacent land where they would again accept payment for getting out when a newcomer bought up property, a practice which may have indicated that in certain areas, such as in the neighbourhood of Broken Hill, land was beginning to be of specific value to Africans near a market.

On the whole, there was a good deal of similarity between the white farmer's attitude and that of 'enclosing landlords' in eighteenth century England; the native neighbour at the time was not normally feared as a competitor, but as a bar to agricultural progress; and at the time public opinion both at home and overseas was overwhelmingly on the settler's side in this respect. The 'twenties, admittedly, saw a certain amount of anti-imperial writing, but the attack against the white colonist started on the northern and southern end of the arc of British African settlement—in Kenya and South Africa—not in Rhodesia.[1] The British 'Right' blamed Afrikaner Nationalists for their anti-Imperial and Republican proclivities, whilst 'Right' and 'Left' wingers alike condemned the Union's colour bar, albeit for different reasons. The Kenyans were associated in the public mind with the British military and landowning class, which was coming under heavy fire at home. Anti-colonial critics also damned the Kenyans for using compulsory native labour in the intensive cultivation of tropical products, requiring a great deal of manpower to work them and thus putting a strain on tribal life. Rhodesians, on the other hand, were not tarred with the same brush. Journalists had no occasion to write exciting headlines about Central Africa, and if the ordinary Englishman's attention was ever drawn to this part of the world, it was only by a tobacco advertising poster showing a burly farmer in a broad-brimmed hat!

Rhodesia in fact still seemed a legitimate area of white colonization; in 1929 Lord Olivier, a prominent Labour theorist, could thus write that territorial segregation might as yet still be workable in a country where there was so much unoccupied land left, and where whites could not be legitimately excluded from farming.[2] A local correspondent for the *Anti-Slavery Reporter* deplored the effects of the migrant labour system, and accordingly welcomed European settlement at Abercorn in North-Eastern Rhodesia, on the ground that settlers would give employment to Africans near their own homes.[3] Missionary opinion acclaimed the principle of reserves, and in Rhodesia the Rev. Arthur Shearly Cripps, an anti-settler Socialist, whose laboured poems contrasted the unspoilt innocence of primitive tribal life with the white man's insolent materialism,

[1] Gann, L. H. 'The changing image of the white settler' (in *Race*, v. 2 no. 2, May 1961, p. 28–40)

[2] Lord Olivier. *White capital and coloured labour.* Hogarth Press, 1929, p. 122–124

[3] *The Anti-slavery reporter and aborigines' friend* (organ of the Anti-Slavery and Aborigines Protection Society),v. 19, no. 3, Oct 1929, p. 79

wrote a book which extolled the merits of territorial apartheid.[1] Anthropologists took a similar line and Dr C. M. Doke, an expert on the Lamba of Northern Rhodesia, equally stressed the need for separate reserves which ought to be tribal in character and avoid the dangers of the South African precedent where Africans had not been provided with enough land. Similar thoughts were current in Southern Rhodesia, where much more was being done to improve native agriculture than in the North, and where local Africans, the Colony's Missionary Conference and later the Aborigines Protection Society all approved of the principles of the Land Apportionment Act, 1930. Cabinet ministers in Salisbury remained similarly convinced of the merits of apartheid, though in Southern Rhodesia territorial segregation was linked with the creation of separate native purchase areas where Africans might buy land on an individual tenure. The Southern Rhodesian authorities, whilst wishing to meet the wishes of white farmers, imagined that their Land Apportionment Act of 1930 was the only way of safeguarding native society and protecting the country from subversion. They argued that in passing the Act, they would help to promote better agricultural methods in African areas, and set aside sufficient land for Africans whilst there was still time, thus avoiding the mistakes made in South Africa, and preventing the creation of a landless black proletariat by preventing too much of the available land being bought up by Europeans with more capital than Africans could command. Educated African opinion in Southern Rhodesia at the time shared the view that territorial segregation was desirable, and whilst demanding more land, thoroughly approved 'the principle of separate Purchase Areas for Europeans and Natives respectively'.[2]

Segregation in fact was 'in the air' during a period when even Stalinists were thinking in terms of separate black republics for South Africa and the American 'Deep South', in accordance with the Russian dictator's theories on the problem of nationalities. Territorial separation accordingly went unchallenged, and the only question at issue was how it should best be applied.

The Administration first tackled the problem of reserves in the East Luangwa District of North-Eastern Rhodesia where the problem of overcrowding was most serious.[3] Stanley was gravely worried about the general feeling of insecurity amongst the Africans whose existing reserves were proving inadequate. In addition there was pressure from the North Charterland Company which was anxious to alienate more land from its vast 10,000 square mile concession, and also wished to grow more tobacco on its own account. In 1924, therefore, the Governor appointed a Reserves Commission, headed by Philip James Mac-

[1] Cripps, A. S. *An Africa for Africans*. Longmans Green, 1927
[2] Southern Rhodesian Native Welfare Association: Meeting on 11 July 1927, resolutions forwarded by Native Commissioner, Gwelo, to Superintendent of Natives, Bulawayo: 30 July 1927 (S 138, file 18, Nat Arch SR). For the views of Southern Rhodesian statesman at the time see the private papers of Sir F. Newton and H. U. Moffat (NE 1/1 and MO 13/1, Nat Arch MS)
[3] In 1924 the population per square mile was given as 19·1 for Fort Jameson district as compared with 14·7 at Lealui, 7·6 for Magoye, 5.5 for Petauke, 4·3 for Chilanga and 2·3 each for Livingstone, Broken Hill and Kalomo.

donell, a Judge of the High Court, who was later knighted for his services and presided over another reserves commission two years later on the Railway Belt. Macdonell stood out as a man of pro-African views, and resolved that the Fort Jameson District should give a lead to the remainder of the country in the matter of native policy; the pro-African element also censured the Fort Jameson farmers for paying inadequate wages and using the iniquitous *posho* system whereby black workers were supplied with money or cloth in lieu of rations, and had to scour round the neighbouring villages to buy their own food. Defenders of Africans now began to argue that the African cultivator was by no means as ignorant as he was made out to be. Native agricultural systems were best under existing circumstances, in view of the tiny capital possessed by Africans, and the lack of scientific knowledge available. Even European planters were now using the indigenous method of cutting timber and abandoning old gardens. The Government's chief task, the Judge thought, should be to develop the reserves, enabling Africans to produce economic crops and prevent the exodus of native labour with its disastrous consequences to the stability of village life.

In settling down to their work, the Commissioners had to recognize certain limitations. They were anxious to retain existing reserves and only to make such proposals as would not involve the Africans in extensive movements. The Commissioners argued that one third of the concession was uncultivable, that each adult required $1\frac{1}{4}$ acres to produce enough food for himself, though this was in fact the area normally cultivated by a family of two or three persons. 17,000 head of cattle were assumed to be grazing in the region, and eight acres per head was taken as providing the necessary pasture. The Commission also attempted to take into account the natural growth of population, and added 50 per cent to the land requirements existing at the time, considering that the remaining increase could be achieved by improving methods of cultivation. The Commissioners finally proposed nine reserves with a total of 3,558 square miles and an average of 14·9 acres per head, which they considered ample for a total population of 151,000 of whom they though 32,000 would have to be moved in from outside. They also insisted that no land should be leased or sold to Europeans within the reserves, a suggestion that raised a storm of disapproval from missionaries. They also pointed out that government should undertake a programme of sinking wells, checking deforestation, and developing export crops by experiments with cotton and sun-dried tobacco.

The Commissioners' report received a very mixed reception. The local farmers thought that the Commissioners were just ignoring the facts of life. High transport costs made cotton and tobacco the only possible economic crops, the bulk of the land being suitable only for bright, flue-cured tobacco; this type, however, needed much skill and capital, neither of which the Africans possessed. Cotton, the settlers added, had been grown for a number of years, but yields remained low despite careful cultivation; the natives' haphazard methods were bound to make cotton a failure; and the African population was so scattered that ginneries would prove to be an uneconomic proposition. The cultivation of native cotton moreover would lead to insect pests, and injure existing European planters who were trying to fight boll-worm.[1] Judge Macdonell himself was also dissatisfied with his report, but for very different reasons. He felt that the senior official on the Commission made a number of concessions to J. H. Phipps the 'Unofficial' European member, and further complained that most of the white witnesses were only looking at the question from their own point of view, adding that an allocation of 14 acres per head would turn out to be inadequate. Stanley then went over the recommendations once more, but in the main agreed with the Commissioners' official findings. He insisted, however, on two modifications. The Msoro reserve was too small, the Commissioners having been influenced too much by Chief Msoro, who was simply concerned to see that he and his immediate followers were all right, and did not worry too much about the rest. Neither would Stanley agree to the suggestion that white people should be wholly kept out of the reserves; provided that the natives agreed that the Europeans' presence was in the Africans' interest, and that the land occupied by white residents remained rigidly limited in extent.

Macdonell's prediction that the suggested reserves would prove inadequate, turned out to be correct, for the suggested improvement programme was not effectively carried out. But the immediate difficulties did not arise from the local Africans, but from the North Charterland Company, which considered itself aggrieved, and embarked on a bitter and long-drawn out campaign against the Colonial Office. The North Charterland Company's case was simple. The Commissioners agreed that one third of the Company's territory was uncultivable. Now they wished to give 3,558 square miles to the Africans, which meant that the Company would lose half of its worthwhile land. In addition the Company disliked the idea that native needs should be determined by the requirements of economic crops, rather than of subsistence cultivation. This was a new principle, and the Company objected to it, partly perhaps because the Company was itself trying to make money by growing crops. The Imperial Government, the argument continued, had no right at all to make such an award, the North Charterland Company not having been a party to the agreement concluded in 1923 between the British South Africa Company and the Colonial Office, whereby the Crown reserved itself the right to set apart reserves in the North Charterland area. The North Charterland Directors also considered themselves to have been 'let down' by the Chartered Company which until 1925 had managed to dominate the Company's affairs through its appointees on the directorate.

The Colonial Office went to considerable trouble in investigating the question, and vast piles of correspondence accumulated on its files. Enquiries as to the North Charterland's affairs revealed the full history of the huge land concession which was made in 1895, at a time when the Chartered Company possessed no land rights whatever in the area, but followed its accepted Rhodesian policy at the time of attracting capital and immigrants by the formation of subsidiary companies; the North Charterland Company only raised £250,000

[1] *Livingstone mail*, 14 May 1925

since its inception, its affairs were going badly, no dividends ever having been paid on its ordinary shares, and only one tiny payment on its preference shares. The Colonial Office then despatched a somewhat curt letter to the North Charterland Company. The Chartered Company possessed no land rights in the area. This meant that grants could only be effected in the British South Africa Company's administrative capacity, and were of course subject to the legal obligation to set aside adequate reserves. By 1923, the Colonial Office argued, these reserves had not yet been fully determined, and the Colonial Office would never have recognized the North Charterland's huge concession without reserving to itself the right to set aside adequate reserves. The North Charterland Company stuck to its guns, and there followed a bitter legal conflict, which led first to a Petition of Right and finally to a full scale enquiry under Justice Maugham. Maugham decided against the Company, holding that its title was from the first subject to native rights.[1] The Company, however, still refused to give way, and H. B. Spiller, its belligerent Chairman, launched a propaganda campaign against the Colonial Office, getting some 100 Members of Parliament to support him in the cause of private property, buying up whole pages in the newspapers, and calling ex-ministers and senior civil servants all sorts of uncomplimentary names to which they were not accustomed. Spiller's publicity, however, reached such a pitch of violence that it defeated its own purpose, and in 1936 the Company's resources came to an end. Spiller lost his seat on the Board; the concern was reconstructed with South African money, the new company taking no further active interest in tobacco growing which in the meantime had been largely wiped out by the Slump.

The administration next turned to the problem of the Railway Belt. This area was much more thinly populated than the East Luangwa area, and more land therefore remained available for both races. But the Railway Belt, on the other hand, also saw the first instances of economic competition between white and black growers in Northern Rhodesia. For maize, the main crop, posessed many advantages which turned it into an ideal proposition for cultivators with little working capital, be they English-, Afrikaans- or Chitonga-speaking. 'Mealies' could be grown without a great deal of hired labour, and required neither superfine seed beds nor 'thinning out', whilst harvesting was a comparatively simple matter involving little loss from shedding and relatively little damage from rain during the long dry season ahead. Poor Afrikaners in the Chilanga area solved some of their manpower problems by getting 'bywoners', friends or indigent relatives, to help on their farms on a share-cropping basis, whilst Tonga cultivators also made use of traditional kinship obligations for the purpose of raising economic crops. The better-off farmers at the same time started to speed up production by the use of machinery, and tractors began to replace

---

[1] See *North Charterland Concession enquiry: report to the Governor of Northern Rhodesia by the Commissioner Mr Justice Maugham, July 1932* (Colonial no. 73, 1932) as well as the supplementary report of 30 May 1933 (Colonial no. 85, 1933). The first report with its annexures constitutes a veritable gold mine of source material on the history of the Fort Jameson area.

trek oxen. In addition motor cars and lorries were coming into use, and from 1926 a Livingstone firm began to advertise trucks and big Ford cars for a down payment of only £70. o. o., the remainder being paid off by monthly instalments, a credit arrangement which allowed even some of the less opulent farmers and traders to provide themselves with transport.

By 1926 the position was sufficiently acute for Stanley to ask for the setting up of a Reserves Commission on the Railway Belt, both in the interests of the Africans themselves and of the country's economic development. He explained to the Secretary of State that the region would attract most of the new settlers, and that it was furthermore being explored for mining purposes. There were only two other alternatives. The Africans might be exposed to the risk of gradual encroachment from the whites—or else the Administration would have to lock up all the unalienated land indefinitely against European settlement, whether needed for Africans or not. Stanley of course approved of neither the one nor the other, and again called on Justice Macdonell to head a Reserves Commission, assisted by a senior official and a local settler.

The Commissioners' terms of reference directed them to set aside adequate reserves able to provide for present needs and future economic production, and to consider at the same time the requirements of over 300 European farmers already settled in the region. In addition the Commissioners bore in mind that Government was also thinking in terms of additional white land settlement, though no one knew exactly just how many immigrants were going to come. Macdonell's task proved thus to be very difficult, and in order to arrive at some sort of solution, the Commissioners laid down certain fundamental principles. The reserves were to be situated away from the railway line, but, where possible, corridors were to be marked out giving access to the nearest siding. This admittedly conflicted with the idea of giving equal economic opportunities to white and black, and a number of Chilanga and Mazabuka chiefs (that is to say those most affected by the new economic changes) objected to the idea, adding that they did not wish to move away from their present land. Lima and Swaka witnesses before the Commission on the other hand agreed that the land by the railway should be reserved to white men, a statement which would seem to indicate that they had not as yet begun to sell grain or cattle in appreciable quantities. Apart from that, the Commissioners were faced by other arguments. The railway, after all, was built with European capital for the purpose of promoting European enterprise; white men were already settled by the side of the line, and buying them out would be too expensive. In any case, even the most advanced Africans were not mainly producing for the market; when their grain bins were full, they would sell the surplus to the nearest trader, but the amounts available for sale would vary greatly from year to year. The European farmers, on the other hand, were much more fully integrated into the market economy, and compelled by force of economic circumstances to produce that steady and continuous supply of local food which alone would satisfy the mining companies. Next, the Commissioners decided, the reserves ought to be homogeneous in character and should not intermingle with the white areas, so that the Africans might develop on their own lines. On this principle there were again some sharp differences of opinion. A minority of farmers, that is to say those who got their labourers from nearby, preferred to have African villages next door. The majority, as represented for instance by the Northern Rhodesia Farmers' Association took the opposing point of view and insisted on rigid segregation, stressing that native villages were apt to become 'beer halls' and a place of refuge for loafers and deserters, the kind of people whom eighteenth century English landlords would have described as 'the idle poor'. Thirdly, the Commissioners ruled that the reserves should be tribal in character; in doing so, they made an important contribution to the theory of 'Indirect Rule' which shortly afterwards was adopted as the official principle of native policy throughout Northern Rhodesia. Tribal reserves, they argued, would avoid administrative difficulties and enable Government to build on existing foundations, since chiefs were still being respected—a statement not wholly in accordance with all the evidence presented. Many official witnesses also stressed the value of tribal reserves which would encourage Africans to take more interest in their own affairs, build better houses and adopt more efficient means of cultivation. A minority party opposed this policy on the grounds that Africans would only stagnate in their reserves, but their argument failed to make much impression. The Commissioners also recommended that the reserves should be permanent and perpetual in character. Not all European witnesses agreed on this point, holding that the final delimitation should be delayed until more was known about the quality of the land in question. The Commissioners, however, would not hear of such a course, arguing that some of the Mazabuka chiefs had already been moved once before, whilst past promises to Chiwala and his Swahili had not been kept. The reserves ought to be fixed here and now—before Europeans took up all usable land, and the native areas should be of adequate size. On this point all witnesses were agreed; none of the white farmers who gave evidence wanted the reserves skimped, one European indeed insisting that Africans should get as much as 120 acres per head. The reserves finally were expected to form part of a general scheme for improving African conditions, involving the systematic provision of water, economic instruction, the teaching of hygiene and the gradual promotion of local self-government. The Commissioners accordingly looked towards a future where the Africans and Europeans would live side by side, separated socially and politically, but with equal economic opportunities. The white and black economies were expected to be complementary, in that African labour migrants would go to the towns where they would acquire the necessary capital for agricultural improvements at home by working a while for European employers. Government itself, the Commissioners added, should provide education, whilst the missionaries ought to concentrate on the task of evangelization alone.

After lengthy deliberations the Commissioners decided on the formation of 16 reserves with an estimated total of 38,866 square miles and a population of some 268,000 giving an average of 92·8 acres[1] per head, and an average density of 6·89 per square mile. They estimated that about 26,000 natives would have to be moved into the reserves either from European farms or from other areas, but that these moves would only involve 'squeeze ins' rather than extensive migrations. Few or no chiefs would have to seek new homes, though a contraction of a tribal area would be involved in the case of Nkambo, a Lamba chief in Ndola Sub-District; Chikupiri, a Swaka chieftainess, would have to shift a few miles, and so would a small number of Tonga chiefs. The only bigger movement concerned Chirimina, a chief in the Ndola area who was required to find new land some 30 miles away. The Colonial Office calculated that 24,874,000 acres would be reserved from nine districts containing 48,556,000. This would leave 23,682,800 acres of Crown land of which 2,980,636 had been alienated to the Europeans, and a senior official accordingly expressed his satisfaction that Macdonell had managed to secure unanimity in getting more than half the area in question reserved.

Another Commission was finally appointed in 1927 for the area south of Lake Tanganyika. Here the first settlers originally came to raise stock, but after the War a few enterprising farmers experimented with coffee, a difficult and delicate crop which required much skill. The position was further complicated by a huge estate acquired by the British South Africa Company, which owned 4,310 square miles, a concession recognized in the old days by means of Certificates of Claim issued by the Imperial Government's representative. The Company was anxious that reserves should be laid out, so that land might become available to European coffee planters, a suggestion quite acceptable to some local Africans who appreciated the benefits of local employment. The Chartered Company, however, adopted a much more co-operative attitude than the North Charterland Company; 'London Wall' first suggested that some 31·7 per cent of its holdings should be turned into native reserves, but when the Commissioners recommended that the Company should relinquish 41 per cent of its land, the Directors accepted the position with a good grace, retaining 1,600,000 acres for their own use in an area which, they assumed, would appreciate in value by the opening of a port and a steamer service. The Commissioners' final recommendation allowed for a total of nearly 8,000,000 acres giving a density of 8·5 per square mile.[2] In addition they again insisted that the reserves should be tribal in character, that they should involve the minimum of population movement, preserve rights of access to Lake Tanganyika, that no plateau people ought to be moved to the valley or vice versa, and that ancestral graves should remain in the reserves.

The three Commissions did their work conscientiously, with what they thought was due regard for both African interests and the needs of general

[1] The acreages per head differed very widely from reserve to reserve, ranging from 228 per head of the population in the Nkoya reserve to 124 in the Toka, 92 for the Tonga (Choma), 48 for the Tonga (Magoye) down to 23 for the Sala.

[2] Population densities again differed sharply, ranging from 21·38 acres per head in the Mambwe (Fwambo) reserve to 213 in one of the Tabwa reserves.

development. Many of their assumptions moreover were perfectly sound. They were correct in believing that European farmers would provide more stable and intensive agricultural production, and so was their view that white and black cultivators would not merely prove competitors, but would supplement each other's efforts. A good deal of evidence, for instance, points to the theory that settlement cleared empty land of the tsetse fly; white farms certainly provided work and wages, and what is more, European farmers themselves became customers of native-grown food, especially when they concentrated on more specialized kinds of crops, like flue-cured tobacco which required skill and capital not available to African peasants. Nevertheless, the Administration's reserve policy soon showed serious weaknesses. In demarcating African lands, the Commissioners were labouring under the same disadvantages which were preventing the Administration from making adequate plans for European land settlement. Not a single trained agriculturist or ecologist served any of these bodies, which simply relied on evidence from white farmers and black chiefs. The very composition of say, the Railway Belt Commission, symbolized its function; the African side was represented by a Native Department man, the European side by a settler, and a learned and sympathetic Judge held the balance between them. Naturally enough, there was little scientific basis for the resultant apportionment, for Macdonell possessed no soil maps, no vegetational or water surveys to help him, there being no money available to pay for such services. Worse still, the colonial administration as a whole was not very scientifically minded. Admittedly, there were exceptions in high places; Maxwell, the shrewd Scottish doctor, possessed a very good idea of the potentialities of scientific work. But the best educated, the ablest and most efficient Native Commissioners were normally Arts graduates; and it was they who rose to top administrative jobs, whilst the scientific services remained the Cinderella of the Administration, the last to be expanded in times of prosperity, the first to be cut in a slump. The very knowledge of what science might do was often lacking; to mention just one example, no Government Geological Survey was started until 1951, for the mining companies seemed to be doing excellent work already, an assumption which was based on the idea that geologists were people who looked for metals, and which ignored the immense contribution geology could make to the study of soil and water resources. The output of officially sponsored scientific work at first remained inadequate, and the results of this weakness made themselves felt in every sphere of policy. The Commissioners also made other errors of judgement. They failed to allow adequately for population movements within the territory, for the influx of Africans from the Zambezi valley to the Tonga plateau, and from Portuguese East Africa to the Fort Jameson region. Neither did they fully envisage the extent of subsequent overstocking and the erosion which ploughs would occasion in congested areas. But in any case, the Commissioners' own recommendations were never fully heeded and the Administration failed to develop the Reserves. Whereas Southern Rhodesia embarked on a comparatively big programme of well sinking and dam building in the reserves,

Q

and also opened up a small but highly efficient Department of Native Development for the purpose of undertaking technical training, Northern Rhodesia at first did little, and much of the work done was wasted by failure to secure adequate maintenance. The policy of concentrating Africans into reserves was carried out to a varying extent along the Railway Belt, the work being made more difficult by the general unreliability of population estimates. Many Africans, however, remained in the European areas, and subsequent estimates of population in the reserves sharply differed from those made by the Commissioners. Besides, white settlement at the time never developed to anything like the extent anticipated, partly because certain regions were later found to be unsuitable for European methods, partly because the bottom fell out of the market only a few years afterwards; large tracts from which Africans were evacuated thus remained practically empty, difficulties caused by the scarcity of water and the presence of fly remaining important contributory causes, so that thousands of acres turned into manless 'silent lands'.

Chapter Six

Administration and Politics in the 'twenties

I

Black judges and village Messiahs

When the Colonial Office took over from the British South Africa Company, it inherited the Company's administrative machine as well as its personnel. The Chartered administrators were trained in South African methods of 'direct rule' according to which chiefs in theory were nothing more than 'constables', minor executive officials who possessed no recognized powers of jurisdiction outside Barotseland. In the late 'twenties, however, a different point of view began to prevail, which was influenced, amongst other things, by practice in Nigeria and later in the Tanganyika Mandate, whereby attempts were being made to build up Native Authorities as governing bodies. Conservative thinkers hoped thereby to preserve all that was best in native institutions, which were now looked upon with much greater approbation than in the early days of Imperial conquest. They also believed that tribesmen should develop on their own lines, and feared the rise of an uprooted native intelligentsia who would drift to the towns where there would be no jobs for them. In Northern Rhodesia in the 'twenties this reasoning seemed sensible enough, for the country was after all still very backward; the extent of its mineral wealth was not fully appreciated by Government; and village agriculture was the only opening available to the overwhelming majority of the African people. Liberals also generally supported 'Indirect Rule', hoping to apply contemporary theories of national self-determination on a tribal level and to promote the emergence of local authorities in contact with the people.

The new theory never envisaged that district officers should abdicate all local responsibility. There was no question of trying to build up small African client states, but rather to build up a system of dual administration which would use the power of chiefs to strengthen the machinery of local justice and government. This system seemed to offer many advantages: throughout Northern Rhodesia, native headmen, councillors and elders were still hearing cases, though the kind of authority they wielded differed widely from tribe to tribe, the difference between a Barotse or a Bemba chief and a minor Lenje dignitary consisting not only in the number of people in his charge, but also the type of power which he could legitimately exercize. Chiefs were cheaper than bureaucrats, and some advocates of indirect rule stressed its value as an economy measure; chiefs were moreover in touch with local needs, and their rule was expected to prove more popular than government by civil servants. Another argument in favour of indirect rule, though not one of immediate application in Northern Rhodesia, stressed the supposed general political advantages of the system. As long as the Africans were governed by chiefs and councils they would regard themselves as members of tribes rather than as members of the coloured race as such; and the time when the Bantu would be pitted against the whites as a whole would be indefinitely postponed.

The opposing arguments went along different lines. Chiefs might be turned into agents of government pure and simple which would cause them to lose power; chiefs were doomed to disappear anyway, so there was little object in relying on their support; there was no point in endowing them with a criminal jurisdiction which was entirely different in character from the sort of civil jurisdiction which they were exercizing at the moment. Some officials expressed strong criticism of the Barotse national *Khotla*, the only experiment of its kind, and argued that the Barotse were simply using their powers to exert an oppressive rule on their manifold subject tribes, one of the examples quoted being the local 'prohibition' rules which were supposedly being used as an instrument of extortion, whilst not in fact affecting the consumption of alcoholic liquors one whit. Indirect rule, however, won the day as the adherents of the older school of thought gradually left the Service. In 1927 Stanley, the ablest of the 'South Africans', departed from Northern Rhodesia to take up a Governorship in Ceylon; in the same year 'Dicky' (Richard Allmond Jeffrey) Goode, the Chief Secretary, took up a seat on the newly established Railway Commission for the two Rhodesias; and in 1928 Edward Samuel Bourn Tagart, the Secretary for Native Affairs, a protagonist of the 'Chartered' ways, went on leave, pending retirement. Maxwell, Stanley's successor, was a 'West Coast Man', having previously served with some distinction as Colonial Secretary on the Gold Coast, and he cautiously sympathized with Indirect Rule. In November 1927 he assembled an important conference of administrative officers which recommended that chiefs should be endowed with recognized judicial powers, and that the legislation passed in Tanganyika during the year 1926 should be adopted as a suitable model.

In drawing up his legislation, Maxwell aimed at a pattern which would not prove too elaborate, and which could be applied to tribes of widely differing organization. At the same time he insisted that the Native Courts should not be hampered by too rigid a code of procedure, and strongly objected to placing them under the direction of the High Court, which he thought would introduce too complex a system. The legal machinery for Indirect Rule was first established between 1929 and 1930. The Governor became empowered to appoint chiefs and obliged to notify such appointments in the *Gazette*. In addition he was able to create Superior and Subordinate Native Authorities; where there was no chief of sufficient standing he might set up a council of Chiefs, or alternatively abstain from establishing a Superior Native Authority altogether. The Native Authorities retained all their real or supposed customary powers, and also became entitled to issue minor administrative 'orders', subject to the District Officer's control. They likewise received the right to make 'rules,' the theory being that 'orders' would enable them to cope with the day-to-day work of administration, whilst 'rules' would provide the machinery by which they could adapt their administration to new needs.[1]

The Native Courts Ordinance was drawn up according to a similar pattern.[2] Native Courts were officially established, and the Governor became entitled to make regulations concerning their jurisdiction and other administrative details. Subsequent Government Notices provided for two grades of Native Courts, those of the first and of the second class; these administered native law and custom, provided these were not repugnant to 'natural justice' and morality, though what exactly did constitute native law was not clearly defined. The native courts obtained jurisdiction in minor criminal and civil matters where Africans alone were involved, though black Government servants remained exempt from the jurisdiction of the Courts, unless the District Commissioner's previous authority was obtained. Native Courts of the first class would award jail sentences up to three months, ten strokes of the cane, or fines up to ten pounds, the corresponding punishment in the second class being one month, five pounds and six strokes. Barotseland, which had its own system of courts, at first remained exempted from this legislation, separate arrangements being made later on.

The next task consisted in actually setting up these various bodies, a determined attempt being made to find out who constituted the 'legitimate' chiefs, and to follow tribal custom, a policy that stimulated anthropological enquiries. Unfortunately from the *boma*'s point of view, administrative needs and ethnographic reality did not always coincide. 'Theoretically one would like the paramount chief of a tribe nominated as president of a native authority and native court, superior to all other authorities and courts in his tribal area', explained the Secretary for Native Affairs. But in practice such an arrangement might not always prove practicable, owing to the existing divisions of the territory into districts and provinces. A hierarchical structure moreover did not necessarily correspond to tribal ideas of government. Administrative pyramids were convenient from the governmental point of view, and also much more intelligible to white civil servants who themselves formed part of such a structure. But in Northern Rhodesia tribal kingdoms like those of the Barotse or the Bemba, with clearly defined ladders of authority, formed the exception rather than the rule. This fact has been obscured to some extent by the belief, reiterated over and over again in scores of official reports, summaries of evidence and reminiscences, that 'the power of the chief is decaying'. But many of the Northern Rhodesian tribesmen never knew powerful chiefs at all; some followed local leaders; others resembled the Tonga who possessed no formal courts, but relied on the support of their matrilineal kinsmen who alone would back an injured relative in

[1] Native authority ordinance, no. 32 of 1929   [2] Native courts ordinance no. 33 of 1929

recovering stolen stock or exacting compensation for an arm broken during a beer-drink. Even where more powerful chiefs existed, their judicial functions did not necessarily correspond to authority of a European type, often containing a sacral element which was not concerned with 'the suppression of prostitution . . . , the making and maintenance of inter-village roads . . . , assisting in the compilation of the census and the collection of taxes' and a host of other administrative duties for which chiefs became responsible. Neither did the new laws make any provision for councillors and headmen who in fact were doing the bulk of the work, but got no pay for helping the chief.

The new policy soon met with difficulties. Chief Kopa, for instance, was appointed Superior Native Authority for the Bisa in North-Eastern Rhodesia, but the remaining chiefs complained that they were all of equal standing. The Secretary for Native Affairs then had to explain to them that tribes should be governed by a Paramount, because a united tribe would be much stronger. Similar trouble arose among the Tonga, where no local dignitary would recognize the authority of any other, the position being made no better by the low calibre of some of the Native Authorities appointed. 'Chief Mwemba is obviously despised by his people', wrote a District Commissioner, 'he has no personality, little intelligence and very little control. . . . He is an ex-slave.' What administrative action was taken often failed to coincide with either the District Commissioner's ideas or the legal code. In 1930 the Secretary for Native Affairs thus censured chiefs who instituted wrongful prosecutions to enforce labour services. He also blamed Kazembe of Kawambwa for putting minor offenders into 'stocks', whereas Tafuna, the Paramount of the Lungu, was said to have prohibited the entrance of other natives into his reserves, and prevented the Tabwa from traversing his country on the way to Abercorn, so as to keep the local market for dried fish and other goods reserved for his own people. Another chief, an ex-mission teacher, failed to conform to tribal custom and granted a divorce to a woman whose husband had married a second wife; this was stopped on the grounds that the tribe permitted polygamy.

Indirect Rule also had other drawbacks. Economy was one of its supposed advantages, but where Native Authorities were so weak that they had to be newly created or improved, European officials were needed all the same, and administrative savings were unlikely to result for many years. This meant that when retrenchment became necessary, the expansion of Indirect Rule was retarded. From the purely administrative point of view, Indirect Rule thus at first proved a failure. Most chiefs possessed neither the training, the inclination nor the machinery to become efficient auxillaries of government, and most early reports remained full of complaints as regards the chiefs' supposed apathy or incompetence. The same accusation, however, did not recur with the same frequency as regards the chiefs' judicial work, which from the early days onwards gained a much greater measure of success in its limited sphere.

Indirect Rule created a new group of recognized chiefs, but was not designed to solve the Africans' economic and social problems. Earnings remained low and taxation high,[1] with the result that there was a good deal of discontent, some of which found expression in religious or magical forms. In 1923 a native detective thus reported a prophet by the name of Hanok who preached that God sent the whites to bring free gifts to Africans and teach them about God. But the Europeans—he said—appropriated the divine gifts, keeping their superior knowledge to themselves, and therefore all ought to go back to England. Hanok himself was familiar with Watch Tower literature, supplied from the Society's headquarters in Brooklyn, U.S.A., which circulated in Northern Rhodesia from the 'twenties onwards. But Hanok was only one of many preachers, a common story being that the British were only in Northern Rhodesia by permission of the Americans, or that the British were not clever enough to make aeroplanes which were all manufactured in the U.S.A.[2]

Another version of this primitive anti-colonial doctrine was the so-called Banyama myth. The Banyama were imagined to be Africans who haunted the bush at night to commit murders under European direction, using their victims' blood and brains for magical purposes. This rumour first apparently began in Tanganyika where chiefs were supposedly implicated in these murders, receiving payment from the whites for their help. The Tanganyika Game Department was accused of organizing these killings, possibly because its wardens wandered through the bush—away from the paths—like outlaws. Migrant workers from the Tanganyika sisal plantations carried these tales to Northern Rhodesia, where they were current in the Kasama region from about 1929 onwards. Chief Chitimukulu was said to be implicated, an accusation which might seem to indicate the unpopularity of his rule. The myth was also current in Abercorn, Mporokoso, Chinsali, Mpika and Luwingu, whilst Africans at work in Ndola and Broken Hill believed that the Banyama were making their way into the Railway Belt, a myth possibly linked to the unexplained disappearances of labour migrants who either died, or decided not to return to unpleasant domestic responsibilities in their villages.

These stories seemed all the more credible, since murders for magical purposes certainly were being committed, though evidence is difficult to obtain, as District Commissioners themselves did not always know what was going on. There appear to have been killings, for instance, in high places in Barotseland, though these were never linked to Banyama stories. Some scholars have since suggested that such murders were themselves symptoms of decay: under the colonial dispensation, the argument went, chiefs found themselves in a difficult plight, unhappily sandwiched as they were between Government and their own

---

[1] From 1914 to 1920 the tax stood at 5/- in North-Eastern Rhodesia and 10/- in North-Western Rhodesia. In 1920 the North-Eastern tax was raised to 10/-, despite strong protests from Native Commissioners, but reduced to 7/6 in 1923, a further reduction being made in the Balovale District in 1925, the tax going down to 5/- there. In 1929 the taxation of plural wives was abolished, but at the same time the tax went up again by 2/6 throughout the Territory.

[2] See for instance letter by 'Nimrod' *Livingstone mail*, 7 July 1927. The writer blamed the Seventh Day Adventists for introducing these doctrines, a charge which the Adventists then indignantly repudiated.

people, whilst their traditional position in the tribe was becoming steadily undermined by the impact of a money economy and modern administrative requirements. The Barotse aristocracy certainly were having a difficult time, and were complaining of many grievances, particularly when all traditional labour services were abolished in 1924 in return for a subsidy of only £2,500. But no historical evidence has been brought forward that ritual murders increased in numbers under white rule, as compared with the pre-colonial period, when some chiefs as individuals suffered from a much greater sense of personal insecurity during lengthy periods of civil strife, standing in constant danger of being liquidated by rival factions, a fate which they no longer had to fear under the *Pax Britannica*. But whatever the explanation, there were ritual murders, and corpses were used for magical purposes. In 1929 lengthy trials took place which involved some of the highest in the Barotse state. Ngambela Mataa, the Prime Minister, Kamilatu Mataa, his son, and Namuyama, a Divisional Chief and the Prime Minister's nephew, were all accused of murder, but acquitted for lack of evidence. The charge arose out of another unpleasant case where a small child was said to have been done to death by Kamilatu and a medicine man named Kaiwala; in 1927 the child's mother was still persisting in her accusation and was summoned to Lealui, where she disappeared without a trace. Kaiwala and Kamilatu were then charged with the baby's death, the infant's bones having been found in Kamilatu's hut. Murder, however, could not be proved and Kamilatu and Kaiwala each got away with three years' hard labour for offences against the witchcraft laws.[1]

Murders of this kind were committed by persons trying to practise black magic. But there were also killings which were committed for exactly the opposite reason, that is to say for the purpose of liquidating witches, supposed public malefactors, whose depredations were said to have become worse since the whites stopped their execution with ulterior motives of their own. This agitation as a whole was clothed in a religious garb, and assumed a millenarian, sometimes Messianic, and usually anti-white and social-revolutionary flavour. The worst outbreak occurred in 1925, during a period when the temporary cessation of recruitment for the Congo and Southern Rhodesia in the previous year had caused much distress. The leader of the programme was one Tomo Nyengwa or Nyirenda, a Nyasalander, educated at Livingstonia Mission, who drifted to Northern Rhodesia to look for a job. Tomo for a while worked as a cook in Broken Hill where he was sent to jail for an offence against a small girl. In 1925 he was received into a 'Watch Tower' group by one Gabriel Aphiri, and became a pastor in the faith. Tomo was now apparently once more unemployed and became a wandering preacher, later assuming the name of Mwana Leza, or Son of God. Tomo's doctrines combined indigenous witchcraft beliefs with dis-

[1] *Livingstone mail*, 8 Aug 1929. It should be added in this connexion that in 1929 a new Prime Minister, Ngambela Munalula, succeeded to the dignity. Munalula, a man of about 50 years of age, was a highly respected dignitary who had succeeded his father in the position of Muleta, that is to say Chief Councillor of the Libonda Kuta. He died in 1941.

torted Biblical teaching and a belief in social revolution by Divine Grace; he taught that baptism was necessary to see whether people were infected by witchcraft; that witches ought to be exterminated, but those who accepted baptism would never die. The Elect would get help from the Americans who were expected to carry out an extensive foreign aid programme, whilst the settlers' wealth would be parcelled out amongst Tomo's adherents. Taxation would then cease and food drop from heaven. Another version stated that at the day of reckoning calico would drop from 500/– a bale to 1/–, that the Elect would control the 'bomas' and the stores, and that the Churches represented the Scarlet Woman, and were robbing the poor by means of church collections, or that Tomo could kill by the touch of the wood. The prophet apparently also claimed freedom from the bonds of sexual morality, and was said to have told the Lala women that if they lay five on each side with him under a blanket at night, they would all have heavenly dreams!

These stories are difficult to check, but there is no doubt that Tomo was leading a militant group, and that the so-called 'Watch Tower' men (they had in fact little in common with the American Sect of that name) were envisaging a future of violence.

> *'Paul is back, let there be persecutions, warbeatings'*

sang the congregations at their prayer meetings:

> *'Simon of Jesus, let there be war*
> *Yonder there is war*
> *Amen, alleluja'*

Another hymn proclaimed:

> *'War with all people*
> *Christ is Lord, our Protector*
> *Soya is fierce, let Christians go*
> *Let us go to fight*
> *We shall go in the morning*
> *To the meeting place.'*[1]

The immediate objects of Tomo's wrath were not the well-armed Europeans, but African 'witches'. The prophet first of all received a request from Shaiwila, a Lala chief who supplied Tomo with a list of people to be killed, at least two of these being personal enemies of Shaiwila's. Tomo murdered these unfortunate persons with the help of locally recruited 'deacons', young men who supplied his bodyguard and assisted with baptismal ceremonies, acting under the belief that they would mysteriously die if they deserted their leader. Tomo's executions were apparently carried out by means of drowning, the official doctrine being that all those who did not immerse completely during baptism were

---

[1] Contributed by J. E. Stephenson to the *Livingstone mail*, 22 Oct 1925. Stephenson was a former Native Commissioner who settled down in the country, married several African wives, and made a living as a labour recruiter and farmer. In the *Livingstone mail* of 24 Sep 1925 he contributed his own version of the Mwana Leza affair. He stated that Tomo assumed the name of Mwana Leza on his return from the Congo and that witches were killed by being hit over the head with a knobkerry.

witches. Having killed some sixteen people at Shaiwila's, Tomo's gang departed for the Ndola Sub-District where four more 'witches' were slain, the purge apparently being welcomed by the local Lala villagers who kept their mouths well shut whenever a member of the Administration was within hearing. Tomo subsequently crossed over into the Congo where something like 176 lost their lives, the Congo having previously been subject to another prophetic outbreak which was originally initiated by a preacher named Simon Kibangu. But Tomo at last met his match. His band was attacked and dispersed by Belgian askari, and Tomo fled to Serenje where yet another murder took place. The Messiah was finally arrested by two courageous Native Messengers, assisted by a local headman and his villagers. Tomo received a fair trial, the defence pleaded extenuating circumstances on the grounds that Tomo was sincere, though deluded; that the natives at large were still in the 'pre-logical stage', and that white civilization had itself introduced numerous disturbances into native life; the defence particularly blamed the preaching of Christianity, arguing that 'the Bible itself is unfit reading for the unguided native', and drawing attention to the way in which Tomo quoted Mosaic injunctions about not permitting a witch to live, and Ezekiel's denunciations of sorcerers. This kind of nonsense was outdone by Watch Tower publications, which filled their readers' minds with stories about Anti-Christ and the Beast of Revelation, Government being partly responsible for allowing these doctrines to be preached at all. Stanley went over this evidence very carefully, and in the end decided to commute thirteen out of the sixteen death sentences. Tomo and two of his associates were hanged, and no further outbreaks occurred.

Tomo represented the militant and violent branch of a millenarian movement which preached purification and redemption from present ills. In addition, more pacific preachers were wandering through the countryside who also purported to 'cleanse' the people, but by peaceful means. Some were known as 'Watch Tower' men, though they possessed no recognized connexion with the official American organization, the Watch Tower Bible and Tract Society which until 1935 was not permitted to maintain an accredited representative in the country. Others called themselves 'Mchape' and maintained no links with Christianity at all. Nevertheless, there were marked similarities between the two movements which both served identical purposes. The Mchape cult appears to have originated in Nyasaland about 1930, and the movement subsequently spread to Northern Rhodesia. In 1933 the District Commissioner, Lundazi, thus arrested five Africans, four of whom came from the lakeside Protectorate. These Mchape accepted invitations from local headmen to cleanse villages in return for a fee. The tribesmen would squat round the strangers, who used to hold a mirror before their eyes, so as to make them confess the use of evil medicines. These concoctions were then produced for inspection and tested; 'bad' medicines had to be destroyed, and their owners were adjured to make no more. The villagers finally gulped down a cleansing drink, made of a reddish-brown powder which acted as a mild purgative, and was supposed to possess purifying qualities. The Mchape themselves were said not to know its composition, but only acted as agents of bigger medicine men in Nyasaland.

The Watch Tower people adopted similar practices, though they used the Christian device of baptism by water in order to effect the required cleansing. Before being immersed, converts had to produce their charms, philtres and horns, baptism being said to be otherwise ineffective. In addition, hymn singing was universal, and the secretaries also seem to have displayed a puritanical streak in that they disapproved of dancing. Their sexual morals, on the other hand, came under severe attacks from unbelievers who told hair raising tales of Watch Tower wives making free with their male Brethren, their husbands not being allowed to interfere in these affairs. These accusations, however, may merely have arisen from the fact that Watch Tower folk permitted a different status to women, allowing them to sit together with men at prayer meetings, and giving them other privileges.

Watch Tower doctrines also possessed other attractions, as against those of the established Churches; Life Eternal was envisaged as a material rather than a spiritual state; only the Elect were expected to inherit the Kingdom, and witchcraft and magic were accepted as active forces. The preachers moreover stressed the social nature of guilt, and attracted many African Christians who had become alienated from the Missions by the practice enforced at some stations of insisting on a public admission of sins.[1] Watch Tower men, moreover, stressed the part played by the congregations in the services, encouraging hymn-singing and responses, which made the faithful think that it was *their* service, and not just some foreign importation. Watch Tower teaching also satisfied some deep felt psychological needs. The doctrine that men were now living in times of unequalled woe seemed reasonable enough to poverty stricken villagers, shaken out of their old ways by new ideas and impositions; it was even more comforting to be told that these times of woe were themselves a sure sign of salvation at hand. The District Commissioner, Ndola, for instance, felt convinced that the Watch Tower faith had helped people through the misery of moving to the reserves, to the loss of valued village sites, and made them indifferent to the tax and the Slump. For what was the use of worrying too much about these things? The day of judgement was at hand, and then the Just would gain their reward whatever happened!

From the general economic point of view Watch Tower possessed enormous advantages over other Churches. True enough the movement could not supply educational or medical services, and thus tended to appeal to more simple people. But Watch Tower, on the other hand, was adapted to the needs of a backward rural economy in a way which the white Missions were not, the sectaries needed few Church collections and no foreign subsidies; their services

[1] Quick, G. 'Some aspects of the American Watch Tower movement in Northern Rhodesia' (in *International review of missions*, v. 29, no. 114, Apr 1940, p. 216–226). For later accounts see Cunnison, I. 'A Watch Tower assembly in Central Africa' (in *International review of missions*, v. 40, no. 160, Oct 1951, p. 456–469)

took place in the open, or in unpretentious wooden structures which could be built at little cost, whilst itinerant preachers could live almost at subsistence level, their needs being largely met by hospitality. The movement as a whole was self-supporting, self-propagating and free from outside control; possessing those very qualities which Protestant missionaries prized as long term objectives but could not easily achieve. Watch Tower thus continued to gain influence, remaining a powerful contender in the battle for the mind of Africa.

II

European politics: 1924 to the Slump

The end of Chartered rule in 1924 had little immediate effect on the lower ranks in the civil service; the day-to-day work of administration continued in the hands of the District Officers, who were assisted by a small number of technical and central departments, their work being co-ordinated through the Secretariat at Livingstone, where the Chief Secretary acted as the Governor's principal adviser and Head of the Civil Service.[1] Protectorate status, however, led to some expansion at the top, in accordance with the time-honoured tendency for major constitutional change in the colonial field to lead to a multiplication of dignitaries! Whereas Chaplin, the Company's last Administrator, used to run the two Rhodesias almost single handed, assisted only by a small Executive and Legislative Council south of the Zambezi, the two successor Governments were much better staffed; Southern Rhodesia acquired a full scale Legislature, Cabinet, and Governor, whereas Northern Rhodesia obtained a Governor, an Executive, and a Legislative Council of its own, so that Chaplin used to grumble privately that he must have been grossly underpaid for doing all their combined work!

The Governor formed the king-pin of Administration in Northern Rhodesia. He owed his appointment to the Crown and was not therefore dependent on local pressure. He presided over both the Executive and Legislative Councils, headed the executive branch of government, and represented the King for ceremonial purposes, the Governor constituting the head of the social as much as of the administrative hierarchy in the country. The Governor made appointments, suspended officials and gave pardons; he was titular Commander-in-Chief of the armed forces; he could grant land, subdivide the Territory into Provinces; his assent was necessary for all local legislation. The Governor was assisted by an Executive Council of senior civil servants, to whom all instructions from the Secretary of State had to be communicated, but whose advice he might disregard, provided he informed the Secretary of State of his reasons.

---

[1] In 1927 the machinery was strengthened by the creation of a full-scale Secretariat. Two years later the Provincial organization was revised. Districts were placed in charge of District Commissioners, known as 'D.C.s', and the Territory was sub-divided into nine Provinces, each under a Provisional Commissioner or 'P.C.'

In addition there was a Legislative Council, which was responsible both for voting supplies and for making local laws, known as Ordinances. The powers of this embryonic Legislature were of course restricted; the British Parliament remained the ultimate source of all law, major constitutional or policy changes being effected through the instrument of Orders in Council, promulgated by the Crown. All local Ordinances were bound to respect native law and custom, in as far as these were compatible with public safety, natural law and morality. No member of the Council might introduce money bills for the raising or disposing of public revenue, except with the Governor's sanction. Once a bill was passed, the Governor could either refuse his assent, or reserve the bill for the signification of the King's pleasure. Certain classes of bills had to be specifically reserved. These included laws discriminating against non-Europeans, except those dealing with arms, ammunition and liquor. Specific protection was given to powerful investors in the matter of bills affecting mining revenue or railways; whilst Imperial uniformity was assured in major fields like currency, banking, customs duties, treaties and foreign policy, as well as divorce. The executive moreover completely dominated the Legislature through a bloc of 'Officials', comprising five *ex officio* and four Nominated Members who at first were all senior civil servants. These men were all bound to vote as the Governor said, except when allowed a free discussion, and the Government could always sway the debate, both by its special knowledge and by force of numbers:

> '*Their's not to reason why*
> '*Their's but to answer 'aye*'

Moore defined the Officials' role, which for long remained much more important than the Elected Members'.[1]

The Unofficials initially only numbered five persons. They were chosen on a 'colour-blind' franchise, but despite Imperial trusteeship theories, black and brown people in Northern Rhodesia at first found greater difficulties in getting on the voters' roll than they did in Southern Rhodesia under settler self-government. Voters all had to be British subjects, and this provision at one stroke excluded Northern Rhodesian Africans, whose status was that of British Protected Persons, Northern Rhodesia only counting as a Protectorate, whereas Southern Rhodesia had since 1923 been annexed to the Crown. The same disqualification also affected the great majority of Coloureds on the technical ground that illegitimate children of British fathers, born outside His Majesty's Dominions, did not count as British subjects, though Africans and Coloureds could become British subjects on payment of a fee.

The Northern Rhodesian franchise qualifications moreover stood at a higher level than they did south of the Zambezi. Voters had to prove an annual

---

[1] The first Legislative Council thus contained the Chief Secretary, the Secretary for Native Affairs, the Attorney General, and the Principal Medical Officer as well as the Treasurer, and several other officials. The exact composition was varied from time to time, but the key departments always remained well represented.

income of at least £200, or the occupancy of a dwelling worth £250 or the ownership of a mining claim of equivalent value. (Illiteracy, the receipt of poor relief, undischarged bankruptcy or a recent criminal record also served as disqualifications). This property qualification not only excluded Africans from politics, but also indigent white back-veld farmers, white unemployeds, and down-at-heel white pedlars who were all regarded by Government with an equal measure of distrust. The more prosperous Indian traders, however, became eligible for the vote and entered their names on the Register.[1] The early Unofficial Members contained no European working men within their ranks; for miners and railwaymen were migrant labourers who did not at first show much interest in politics, being too much concerned with immediate matters of bread and butter. The Unofficials thus only spoke for the settled whites in the country, the shopkeepers and farmers. The former were represented by Leopold Frank Moore, the Livingstone chemist and editor of the Territory's only newspaper, an old-fashioned Radical, stubborn, honest, contemptuous of all privilege—social, financial or ecclesiastical—and always inclined to be 'agin the Government'. The farmers were more numerous and comprised men like Captain Thomas Henderson Murray, a gentleman of the old school, with an Eton and Sandhurst background, who became a rancher at Kalomo. The farmer members were normally the wealthier and more conservative, for poverty stricken backwoodsmen could not afford the time to sit in 'Legco' at Livingstone. The farmers, however, never formed an organized pressure group, being scattered on their widely dispersed holdings, whilst the better-off Members used to spend considerable periods travelling abroad.

The importance of 'Legco' can easily be overestimated during the early days. The Council was no Parliament, the Elected Members' job being merely to ventilate the views current in their localities.[2] The debates took part in uninspiring surroundings; and right up to 1955 there was no full-time Clerk of the House, knowledgeable about Parliamentary law, procedure and traditions, and able to advise Members on such problems. The Unofficials of course were an honest, conscientious and, on the whole, an ultra-respectable lot; 'Legco' contained none of those colourful rogues who filled some of the early Australian State Legislatures; the worst offence committed by any Northern Rhodesian Member consisted of filling in a false income tax declaration which at once led to his enforced resignation under pressure from both Government and his indignant colleagues. But debates were deadly dull. Officials used to regard it as a penance to have to listen to Moore's interminable speeches, delivered standing, staccato fashion, like a spluttering machine-gun, with highlights like: 'I know perfectly well that there are many lions in the path of this suggestion—there are always lions—ever since we have had any Government in the country those

---

[1] The main constitutional instruments were the *Northern Rhodesia Order in Council* of 20 Feb 1924, the *Northern Rhodesia (Legislative Council) Order in Council* of 20 Feb 1924 and the *Instructions . . . to the Governor and Commander-in-chief of Northern Rhodesia* of 26 Feb 1924.

[2] Northern Rhodesia. *Legislative Council debates*, 28 May 1924, p. 110

lions have been prominent'; whilst Murray would gloomily predict the country's early decay to a mess of 'monopolies, myrmidons, and a mangled mass of martyrs to megalomania'![1]

Much of early politics, moreover, hinged on personalities to an extent much greater than would have been customary in a more numerous community. Northern Rhodesia's white population was no greater than that of a small town in England; and almost everyone knew everyone else's business.[2] There was no party organization of any kind; and a 'sundowner' might be a much more important political event than a formal meeting. Much of course depended on the Governor. Stanley always knew how to make himself respected, and even Moore had a grudging sort of trust in the brilliant, strongly Judaic-looking, little man who presided over the first Legislative Council. Relations between the Senior Member, and the Administration sharply deteriorated when Maxwell took office in 1927; for Maxwell, the stubborn Scotsman, and Moore, the Livingstone Radical, used to quarrel fiercely, so much so that Maxwell asked the Mayor of Livingstone to abandon the civic reception scheduled for the Governor's final departure in 1932. But, however small the scale of politics, and however petty some of its tin-pot scandals, politics dealt with matters of real importance and soon a number of major issues came to stand out which have ever since dominated the country's public life.

The Rhodesian frontier communities, like so many of their kind, displayed a strong leaning towards radicalism and egalitarianism; the new immigrants were in some ways like African migrants in that they too lost respect for traditional authority when thrust into a new environment;[3] and this attitude of mind often found expression in a raw anti-clericalism. Moore of course went further in this respect than most. Inside the Legislature and outside, he used to rail at parsons, at the 'hymns-and-holy-water' brigade who to him represented the cause of social privilege as much as of religious superstition. He used to slate Christianity which he regarded as a cracked foundation for white and black education alike;[4] and with the same gusto he would attack the Northern Rhodesian bishop's recognized status in the official Order of Precedence.[5] When an Anglican dignitary presumed to attack the settlers' morals, Moore's fury knew no bounds; Rhodesians were no worse than anyone else, but in any case, what harm could come of sexual indulgence;[6] these pleasures should come as natural as eating and drinking; frustrations were harmful, and only the starry-eyed could speak of the wanton seduction of young females, who knew all about life anyway. Moore added that the use of contraceptives was becoming common, an interesting

[1] Northern Rhodesia. *Legislative council debates*, 10 May 1935, p. 293, and 9 May 1935, p. 243
[2] In 1931 the white population numbered 13, 846, as compared to 3,634 ten years earlier.
[3] 'Respect for a parson's office is unknown' wrote a pioneer clergyman in the early days 'and unless he personally commands respect . . . he will be intensely disliked. In England one *is* the Church. Here all sects are lumped into one and the best all-round man has the largest following.' Quoted from Rev. D. R. Pelly to Canon and Mrs Pelly, his parents: 7 Mar 1893 (in PE 3/1/1, Nat Arch MS)
[4] Northern Rhodesia. *Legislative Council debates*, 26 May 1939, p. 104–110
[5] Northern Rhodesia. *Legislative Council debates*, 21 Dec 1932, p. 310–313
[6] *Livingstone mail*, 18 Feb 1929

comment on the changing values of the time, which were now also spreading into the backveld. The remarkable thing was not the publication of such views, but that they seem to have met with little protest except from clergymen, neither 'Pro Bono Publico' nor 'Mother of Seven' rallying to the defence of Victorian standards in the correspondence columns.

The question of social and ecclesiastical privilege became linked to some extent with the much wider issue of 'Native Trusteeship'. Moore, and the great majority of white Rhodesians bitterly resented the idea that upper class civil servants with Oxford accents and 'Thirds' from Balliol, or expatriate parsons from Cuddesdon, should regard themselves as impartial arbiters between black and white, and the African's chosen champions. The settlers made Rhodesia, they paid the bulk of its revenue, and they should ultimately run their country, self-government in any case constituting an Englishman's birthright.

The officials sharply dissented. They tended to think of themselves as the country's 'guardians' in a way Plato might have approved, and they alone regarded themselves as competent to hold a balance between conflicting class interests: their independent source of income, untainted by 'trade' would assure their freedom from local pressure groups. Over and over again official speakers would thus stress the settlers' supposed political immaturity, their lack of numbers, and the danger of entrusting power to a tiny white oligarchy. Official spokesmen would enlarge on supposed parallels of history, on the oppression of English workers by their employers in the past, on clashes between French noblemen and their serfs, and the conflicts between patricians and plebeians in ancient Rome,[1] these social struggles being capable in their view of only being resolved by the intervention of an impartial governing class.

The civil servants' thought was in tune with the era which saw the emergence of the Trusteeship idea as an undisputed dogma of colonial government. Trusteeship ideas existed in many different forms before 1914, but during the Great War they became part of an officially accepted doctrine which the Germans were supposed to have violated; trusteeship principles were accordingly built into the post-war settlement which disposed of the German colonies as 'Mandates', rather than as legitimate objects of conquest. Colonial administrators now had to decide how native trusteeship was to be interpreted, and two sharply differing views of government came into conflict. The 'native paramountcy' school, broadly speaking, envisaged the African's role in East Africa as that of a peasant producer, who would grow crops for the British market at low overheads and would also be relatively 'crisis-resistant'. The opposition for its part put its trust into European-run plantations, which were considered more efficient, neither school of thought being as yet concerned with large scale mining or industry.

The battle was joined in 1923, when the Duke of Devonshire issued a White Paper on colonial policy in East Africa, which started a long and bitter controversy over the definition of 'paramountcy', comparable in intensity with the

[1] See for instance Northern Rhodesia. *Legislative Council debates*, 18 Apr 1928, p. 63–69

debates that used to rage over the details of obscure theological doctrines in ancient Byzantium. The 1923 Paper explained that Kenya should be regarded primarily as an African territory, and that native interests should therefore be 'paramount' over those of immigrant races.[1] The new Paper did not at first arouse much discussion amongst Europeans, being directed against Indian rather than white immigrants, the Kenya colonists—tropical Ulstermen at heart—being willing at the time to fight even the Imperial government itself in defence of their interests. The Europeans in East Africa successfully maintained their stand, and in 1927 a new statement agreed, in the tortuous language of contemporary discussion, that the settlers should be associated in the Imperial trust. A White Paper was published which emphasized the right of the immigrant communities to share in the political and economic development of East Africa, arguing that both immigrants and indigenous Africans should take an increasing part in the government of their country; the Paper also stressed the complementary nature of black and white development.[2]

Two years later another Commission was sent out, which gained special authority by its inclusion of Dr Joseph Houldsworth Oldham, Secretary of the International Missionary Council, a well-known authority on Africa and a keen missionary lobbyist with many political and academic contacts, in its ranks. The commissioners mainly considered East African problems, but also dealt with general issues, and the question of closer association of the Central African territories.[3] The new commission recommended what amounted to a scheme of modified *apartheid* under Imperial Control: 'It appears to us,' they argued, 'that the white and black races can for a long time to come—possibly for all time—develop in the main with the greatest advantage to each along different lines. Our idea is that while each pursues its own distinctive and natural line of development they may be able to settle down together in a single state without the fear of a struggle for domination provided there is available an impartial arbiter to decide issues on which there is a conflict of racial interests. It can be the destiny of the Imperial Government to fill this role.'[4] The Commissioners accordingly envisaged 'some degree of political segregation at least for dealing with all but what are essentially common interests', a point of view which justified both Indirect Rule and native reserves.

These controversies still did not make much of a stir in Rhodesia, but when the Second British Labour Government came into power, there was yet another twist to Imperial policy, and this time the fat was in the fire. In 1930 Lord

[1] *Memorandum relating to Indians in Kenya* (Cmd. 1922: 1923)

[2] *Future policy in regard to Eastern Africa* (Cmd. 2904: 1927)

[3] *Report of the commission on closer union of the dependencies in Eastern and Central Africa* (Cmd. 3234: 1929). The other members were Sir George Arthur Schuster, former company director with a distinguished career in colonial and Indian Government, and Sir Reginald Arthur Mant, an Indian civil servant. The Chairman of the Commission was Sir Edward Hilton Young, Director of the Hudson Bay Company, the Southern Railway and the English General Electric Company, who had previously served in many important financial capacities in Britain, at The Hague and in India.

[4] *Report of the commission on closer union of the dependencies in Eastern and Central Africa* (Cmd. 3234: 1929), p. 235

R

Passfield, (formerly Sidney James Webb, an ex-Professor of Public Administration at London University) issued his much discussed 'Statement of the Conclusions of His Majesty's Government in the United Kingdom as regards Closer Union in East Africa.'[1] In this memorandum, the new Colonial Secretary affirmed British trusteeship for the under-developed native races of East Africa, and declared the need for retaining final political control in Imperial hands, even if unofficial majorities were eventually established in the local Legislatures. He endorsed at the same time the statement made in reference to Kenya in 1923 that the interests of Africans should remain paramount over those of the immigrant races in East Africa, and that if the two conflicted, African interests should prevail.

The Passfield Memorandum caused a storm of protest from whites in the various East African colonies, including Northern Rhodesia. The Europeans argued that it was they who did the pioneering, and not the Imperial Government; European enterprise was responsible for white and black development alike, and white interests should come first. Moore drew an interesting parallel between British policy in East Africa and British policy in Palestine, where 'Another Passfield Memorandum'[2] at this time restricted Jewish colonization for the supposed benefit of a backward and illiterate Arab peasantry. Governor Maxwell himself regarded Passfield's statement as both academic and unnecessary, and did his best to explain it away. Passfield's policy was nothing new, and would in no wise either injure existing European interests or interfere with future white settlement; 'paramountcy of native interests' did not imply that colour would be the determining factor in the settlement of disputes between white and black.[3] The Chief Secretary formally told Unofficials that there was nothing in the Passfield Memorandum which would retard the country's normal development, or militate against the settlers' legitimate aspirations to a larger share in the management of their own affairs.[4] The Europeans, however, were not finally mollified until 1931, when a Joint Select Committee of Parliament issued yet another report, signed by a group of members drawn from both Houses, and representative of all three major parties.[5] The new report 'dropped' paramountcy. Native Paramountcy, the Parliamentarians agreed, meant no more than that the interests of the overwhelming majority of the natives should not be subordinated to immigrant minorities, a diplomatic evasion which left the question of East Africa's *ultimate* political future undecided, but for a time silenced further controversy.

The settlers in the meantime developed a trusteeship doctrine of their own,

---

[1] *Statement of the conclusions of His Majesty's government in the United Kingdom as regards closer union in East Africa* (Cmd. 3574: 1930)

[2] *Livingstone mail*, 22 Oct 1930

[3] Northern Rhodesia. *Legislative Council debates*, 13 Nov 1930, p. 1–3. See also *An address delivered by His Excellency the Governor at . . . Livingstone, 27th October 1930*, printed in Northern Rhodesia. *Legislative Council debates*, 1930, app., p. 217–234

[4] *Livingstone mail*, 20 Oct 1930

[5] *Report of the joint select committee on closer union in East Africa* (in House of Lords no. 184 and Cmd. 4141: 1932)

which in some ways paralleled Imperial thinking, and which constituted a remarkable departure from pre-war theories. In the early days of settlement, the colonist's thought was dominated by the imperious needs of a backward and undifferentiated wage economy, avid for unskilled labour. The European's main problem consisted in getting tribesmen to leave their kraal for wage-work; missionaries and farmers alike would describe beer drinking as the native's sole sport, and fornication his only entertainment! After the War, these crude theories became less popular. Africans were now coming out of their reserves without pressure, and as the white economy became more differentiated, white aims began to diverge. European farmers of course still wanted cheap labourers, but they also wanted African craftsmen to put up homesteads and cattle byres; white manual workers objected to black competition, but thoroughly approved of black farmers growing cheap food; European traders discovered the value of the African custom, and began to emphasize the need for putting money into the black man's pockets. In addition the colonists too were coming under the influence of those humanitarian and trusteeship ideas that were becoming more current after the great holocaust, and settler ideas accordingly began to change.

The new ways of thinking found their clearest expression in a memorandum submitted in 1921 by Dougal Elliot Charles Romaine Stirke, a Northern Rhodesian farmer, on behalf of the Territory's Advisory Council. There were four ways of 'solving' the native problem, Stirke argued. The first was extermination, but this was unacceptable to any civilized community. The second was exploitation of Africans for their labour; this policy, though commonly accepted by whites in Africa, 'could not be described otherwise than cynically immoral and extremely dangerous'. The third policy was trusteeship, 'a doctrine unctuously proclaimed by the British Government ... but ... only spasmodically and sporadically tried in South Africa'. The fourth alternative was co-operation, and this was the policy advocated by the Advisory Council; both white and black races must be assured of a place in the sun, and the right to develop on their own lines. The natives should be granted security of tenure as regards their land, the present state of uncertainty being a fertile source of discontent; Africans should only be taxed to produce revenue, and not in order to mobilize labour. All income derived from African sources should be devoted to the purpose of helping Africans, and a portion of the tax should be earmarked for agricultural improvements, on the grounds that the abstract blessings of peace, good government and British justice did not particularly appeal to Africans, who preferred their own kind of law. The Government should promote education, for the Missions were too poor to do much on their own; more schools ought to be built for the African desire for education could no longer be stemmed, and 'we might just as well try to dam the Victoria Falls'. The memorandum further explained the undesirability of forced labour and the need to train African artisans. Finally, Stirke argued, there should be some kind of representation for Africans; natives could not as yet make their views heard on their own, but it was essential for their opinions to be considered, and three or four Europeans should therefore be appointed to keep in touch with Africans and express their demands.

In putting forward these views, Stirke probably failed to realize that there were already a small number of English-speaking Africans in the country who might have held their own in a European Assembly. By 1921, for instance, Barotse official correspondence already displayed a fair degree of expertise; by about 1923 the King's scribes were sufficiently good at their jobs to introduce a proper filing system into their Secretariat; and these African civil servants would have been perfectly capable of taking part in a debate. All the same, Stirke's demands constituted a new departure, and the white colonists could now justifiably claim that they helped to pioneer the cause of African as well as European representation. But, as far as ultimate control was concerned, the settlers were adamant. The white colonists thought they were destined to run the country, and politics hinged on their demand for constitutional advancement.

But politics at first remained at a tepid temperature. Stanley's regime gave little occasion for controversy; hopes in the country's future were high, and though Moore demanded an increase in the number of Elected Members once the budget balanced,[1] there were no serious clashes; the *Livingstone Mail* indeed professed general satisfaction with things as they were, whilst expressing fears of Responsible Government which might put more power into the farmers' hands.[2] When Maxwell took over, this back-veld calm at first remained undisturbed. Moore reiterated former arguments that two more Unofficials should be elected to the Council, but Maxwell proved by no means unsympathetic and in 1929 the Elected Members got an extra two Unofficials.[3] A year later Maxwell agreed to appoint an Unofficial, Captain John Brown, a well-known farmer, to be Agricultural Surveys Commissioner at a good salary, a decision which infuriated Moore who distrusted the farmers and objected to Elected Members who received paid appointments. Maxwell also initiated a system of Select Committees to which Estimates and Loan Expenditure were referred at regular intervals.

On the subject of ultimate control, however, Maxwell remained a good Colonial Office man. He was annoyed at the controversy over the Passfield Memorandum, and most unfavourably impressed by the settlers' strident response, and their demand for what amounted to paramountcy of European interests, a reaction shared at the Colonial Office. But Maxwell's criticism of the colonists went further. The country's future was still uncertain for no one knew how long the mines would last, or how Europeans would stand up to a tropical climate over a lengthy period of time; Chartered policy used to assume that Northern Rhodesia would inevitably become a 'White Man's country', following the South African pattern. But this whole idea needed reassessment. Nor-

---

[1] Northern Rhodesia. *Legislative Council debates*, 16 Sep 1926. In 1926 Northern Rhodesia was receiving a small imperial subsidy of £23,000 *per annum* as against a local revenue of £371,000.

[2] *Livingstone mail*, 3 Feb 1927

[3] Legislative council (amendment) ordinance, no. 37 of 1929

thern Rhodesia's agricultural population was not equal in type to Kenya's, and its soil was much poorer. The Territory in fact might never attract a big white population at all, apart from the Copper Belt, where Europeans would only come as temporary residents, most white workers being liable to get 'the sack' at 24 hours' notice. More thought should be devoted rather to Africans who were undoubtedly capable of taking on better jobs, African progress being encouraged by the mining companies, and facilitated also by the relative absence of an Indian intermediary class. In any case, Elected Members were seriously over-estimating the settlers' interest in politics. Neither Ndola nor Broken Hill would as yet accept the offer of municipal status, and Elected Members possessed quite enough influence for the time being. The Unofficials, Maxwell might have added, were also seriously divided amongst themselves; the farmers tended to vote with Government on many issues, Moore's permanent support being dependent on a small faction composed of Kennedy Edward Harris, an Nkana businessman, and Charles Sidney Knight, a Livingstone contractor and a fellow Radical.

III

The 'Closer Union' issue: 1924–1931

Internal politics closely affected the Territory's 'external' relations which hinged on the question whether Northern Rhodesia should look to a 'black' North or a 'white' South. A Northern tie-up was first seriously discussed in 1925 when an East African Commission recommended periodic conferences between the East African Governors. The first of these took place in 1926, Northern Rhodesia being represented, but no major decisions emerged from these and subsequent discussions. The Governors agreed on the need for a 'dual' policy of black and white development, and there were useful exchanges of views on various technical matters. But as far as major issues like land tenure were concerned, the different territories had too little in common for effective co-ordination of policies; and no further links were established. The Governors' meetings were paralleled by a series of Conferences between Unofficial Members from the East African territories, including Northern Rhodesia. The first of these assembled in 1925 at Tukuyu (the former Neu Langenburg in Tanganyika), but the settlers found practical co-operation just as hard to achieve as the Governors. The colonists of course all believed in further white settlement, additional government expenditure on technical services, and the paramount importance of keeping the Germans out of East Africa. But otherwise their interests diverged, the suggestion of an East African Federation meeting with little support, whilst the Northern Rhodesians felt that their problems differed too sharply from those of the remaining territories. Communications, for one thing, were extremely poor, and even the car journey to Tukuyu was something of an adventure; Northern Rhodesians moreover largely made their living by mining, and even the farmers in the Protectorate relied for their income on the sale of food to local 'compounds', rather than on shipping tea, coffee and other tropical crops to Britain, like their colleagues in Nyasaland, Tanganyika and Kenya. Northern Rhodesians could hardly give up their southern links; South African firms were sending men, money and machines to the Copper Belt, and even the local tobacco farmers all depended for an assured market on the existing Customs Union with South Africa. In 1926 the Unofficial delegates from the various East African territories thus agreed at a Victoria Falls Conference that, for the time being, a Federation of their countries was quite impracticable; and the northern link was rejected.

The obvious alternative was union with Southern Rhodesia. This issue was at first little concerned with the native problem, but hinged almost entirely on the railway question. The Railways, controlled by Chartered capital, enjoyed a natural transport monopoly which was bitterly resented by Rhodesian farmers and mine owners, who all complained that they were being strangled by high transport rates. The railways should therefore be controlled in the public interest, but effective control, the argument went, required the amalgamation of the two Rhodesias. Howard Unwin Moffat, the Southern Rhodesia Minister of Mines and Works, thus pointed out in 1925 that only about half the railway lines were situated inside Southern Rhodesia, and that nothing much could be done until the two Rhodesias possessed a single government which could supervise the system as a whole.[1]

Moffat's argument made no appeal to the Northern Rhodesian Administration. Southern Rhodesian control, they argued, might enable farmers from beyond the Zambezi to undersell Northern Rhodesians in the Katanga markets. In any case Northern Rhodesia was far more interested in the Lobito Railway, the new outlet to the West Coast via Portuguese territory, which was then being constructed, against strong Chartered and South African opposition, by Sir Robert Williams, the great Congo copper magnate. Chartered control over the railways, moreover, seemed preferable to Southern Rhodesian supervision, for the British South Africa Company held an important stake in local industries, whilst Livingstone was more likely to make itself heard in London than Salisbury. Amalgamation therefore ought to be rejected. Even the less ambitious plan of linking the Railway Belt to Southern Rhodesia should not be countenanced, for such a solution implied partition of the territory which might be fraught with serious effects on the mining companies' labour supplies, whilst African backwoods would be cut off from their main source of wealth. Besides Southern Rhodesians might not exercize as tight a control over expenditure as at present, which might affect financial stability. Everything else apart, the proposal would incur much local opposition and was therefore unacceptable.

The Northern Rhodesian settlers themselves were divided. Shopkeepers like Moore strongly opposed amalgamation, on the grounds that Northern Rhodesia would ultimately become a great dominion of its own, and that Southern

[1] *Bulawayo chronicle*, 2 Dec 1925

Rhodesians were taking away trade from the north; Livingstonians feared the loss of their township's status as a capital, whilst the majority of civil servants preferred Imperial to local conditions of service. Local patriotism in fact proved so strong, that various speakers in the Legislature even suggested a change of name for the Protectorate, Zambezia, Transzambezia, Cecilia, Windsoria and Zambeziland all being mentioned as possible alternatives.[1]

The anti-amalgamation cause received support from the mining companies whose case was effectively put by Sir Francis Percy Drummond Chaplin, now a Director of the Chartered Company as well as of the Anglo American Corporation. Chaplin, a South African by adoption and a strong supporter of General Smuts and the Rand mining interests, still hoped that the British cause might yet prevail in South Africa over Afrikaner nationalism; he also stressed the close financial links between the Union and the Copper Belt, whilst pointing out Northern Rhodesia's dependence on Imperial aid. Amalgamation with Southern Rhodesia, on the other hand, might lead to financial troubles. Southern Rhodesia's administrative services admittedly were of a high standard, but Southern Rhodesia might run into difficulties if it took over vastly increased responsibilities.[2]

The Northern Rhodesian farmers failed to agree; the opponents of amalgamation pointed to the danger of Southern Rhodesian competition. Pro-amalgamationists, on the other hand, were impressed by the quality of agricultural and veterinary services south of the Zambezi, so that the amalgamationist party in Northern Rhodesia found its main support amongst farmers who wanted improved facilities, and also perhaps hoped for a rise in real estate values if Southern Rhodesia's forward land settlement policy was adopted. These advocates of Salisbury rule first entered the political arena in 1926, after Sir Charles Patrick Coghlan, the Southern Rhodesian Premier, had unsuccessfully approached the Imperial government over the amalgamation question. Northern Rhodesian Members of the Legislative Council kept in touch with Salisbury, and at their own request received an invitation to talk matters over with the Southern Rhodesian Cabinet. A three-man delegation then took the train for Salisbury, consisting of Stirke, Captain Thomas Henderson Murray—both prominent farmers—and Louis Gordon, another member of the Northern Rhodesian Legislative Council. The Rhodesians then agreed that the northern Protectorate should not be split up, a stipulation firmly insisted upon by the Northerners, which placed 'Railway Belt amalgamation' outside the realm of immediately practical politics. The delegates instead demanded a fully amalgamationist programme whereby the laws of the two territories should be unified and Northern Rhodesia adequately represented both in the Cabinet and the Legislature. The southern land settlement policy was to be applied in the north, though certain limitations on the recruitment of native labour would continue

---

[1] Northern Rhodesia. *Legislative Council debates*, 5 Mar 1926, p. 21–23

[2] Oral evidence given by F. P. D. Chaplin to the Hilton-Young commission: 17 April 1928 (CH 8/2/1, f. 3177–3191, Nat Arch MS)

in the north. The Southern Rhodesian mining law was to be universally applied, whilst the Chartered land rights north of the Zambezi should be bought up—if possible. The Northern Rhodesians also asked for the construction of the Sinoia-Kafue rail-link, a most expensive proposition, and one unpopular with the Railways which were anxious to keep the traffic on existing lines; the Sinoia-Kafue link would of course have greatly simplified the farmers' transport problems in the Lusaka and Mazabuka regions; but Southern Rhodesians would not agree to this demand, until traffic greatly expanded.

These conditions were extremely favourable to Northern Rhodesian amalgamationists, but no immediate results followed upon the discussions, the railway problem being solved for the time being in 1927 by the creation of an inter-territorial Railway Commission in 1927.[1] A year later, however, the amalgamation issue once more came to the forefront, the initiative this time being taken by the Imperial Government which was anxious to secure more information on the subject. Another Commission now left for Africa, headed by Sir Hilton Young, a noted lawyer and financial expert, who later became a Unionist Member of Parliament. But the Commissioners completely disagreed on the country's future. The Chairman's recommendations followed the Chartered Company's old 'Malcolm' plan, whereby the Railway Belt was to be linked to Southern Rhodesia, North-Eastern Rhodesia should go to Nyasaland, whilst Barotseland would become a separate native reserve. Major policy should be co-ordinated by a Central Authority for the two Rhodesias and Nyasaland, the new body to be headed by the Governor of Southern Rhodesia as High Commissioner; the High Commissioner should receive the supervisory powers at present exercized by the Secretary of State for the safeguarding of both Imperial and native interests, and he should also co-ordinate policies with regard to defence, communications, customs and other important matters. The majority, on the other hand, advocated the status quo, evading the whole issue of amalgamation on the somewhat unconvincing ground that the future of mining in Northern Rhodesia was still too uncertain. They also objected to a Central Authority, arguing that the Southern Rhodesian Government should first solve its own problems before taking on new ones, especially since it still remained to be proved that the lands north of the Zambezi could really become a White Man's Country in the same sense as Southern Rhodesia.[2]

The Southern Rhodesian Government strongly dissented from these findings, but the Imperial Government sided with the majority. Governor Maxwell, for one thing, sharply disagreed with Sir Hilton Young on the grounds that

[1] The question was investigated by a transport expert who then issued the *Report by Brigadier-General F. D. Hammond, C.B.E., D.S.O. on the Railway System of Southern Rhodesia.* Salisbury, Government Printer, 1926 (CSR 2—1926). Hammond was impressed by the cheapness and efficiency with which the system was built, but agreed that rates were high and profits had sharply increased in 1924. He advocated control by agreement between all parties concerned, rather than nationalization or forced purchase, and in 1927 a Railway Commission was set up, on which Northern Rhodesia, Southern Rhodesia and Bechuanaland were all represented.

[2] *Report of the commission on closer union of the dependencies in Eastern and Central Africa* (Cmd. 3234: 1929)

amalgamation would give Southern Rhodesia control over the mines; 'Railway strip amalgamation' moreover had the further disadvantage of placing the mines under one administration whereas the labour centres would be placed under another, thus depriving African areas of the advantage of association with the wealthy Copper Belt. In any case, it was better to wait till the economic effects of the Lobito Railway were known. Apart from that the Imperial Government was impressed by what it considered to be its obligations to Northern Rhodesian Africans, as well as by the economic and strategic advantages of keeping the copper mines under Imperial control, now that the Territory was likely to become one of the world's big producers. The agricultural regions north of the Kafue should similarly remain linked to the mining areas. The most that Southern Rhodesia might be offered was an area of some 30,000 square miles between the Kafue and the Zambezi, but even this suggestion was never made public.

The amalgamation cause north of the Zambezi gained strength with the publication of the Passfield Memorandum in 1930, and in October of that year another Unofficial Conference took place between Southern and Northern Rhodesian Parliamentarians.[1] This time Moore was present, as well as Dr Godfrey Martin Huggins, a prominent Salisbury surgeon who was just beginning to make his name in politics as a strong advocate of a Greater Rhodesia. The Conference condemned the Passfield Memorandum, criticized the working of the Railway Commission, and agreed to hold further Unofficial Conferences in the future. Amalgamationist tempers south of the Zambezi rose still further as the result of Maxwell's silly and tactless remark that Southern Rhodesia had only 'redoubled her wooing since Northern Rhodesia had become a rich young lady', words which infuriated Moffat who pointed out that amalgamationist approaches first started when the northern sister-colony was still carrying a deficit. Soon, however, the amalgamationist front collapsed once more. Southern Rhodesian artisans disliked the idea of taking in the 'Black North', whilst Moore was pacified by Imperial assurances given with regard to the Passfield Memorandum; Moore accordingly swung round once more, and agreed that amalgamation should be held over until those more distant days when Northern Rhodesia had economically caught up with the south.

In the meantime the Imperial authorities had further considered the question, the Labour Government then in power taking counsel with the Opposition over the amalgamation issue. Once again the question was diplomatically shelved. The Imperial Government refused a request from Southern and Northern Rhodesian elected members for a conference on the amalgamation question; and professed itself unable to consider the issue at present, on the grounds that Northern Rhodesia should develop to a much greater extent before a final decision could be made; in any case Northern Rhodesia had already made considerable constitutional advances since 1924, and nothing further should be done for the time being; great further developments were likely to result from mining, but for the moment the European population was still too small, and the

[1] *Livingstone mail*, 1 Oct 1930

Africans too undeveloped to permit of their being taken away from Imperial control. But the statement added, the Imperial authorities would not reject amalgamation in principle. A Greater Rhodesia might come into being one day, but if it did, its frontiers would not necessarily turn out to be the same as at present, a compromise which still left the way open for 'Railway Belt amalgamation', or at any rate some minor territorial concession to Southern Rhodesia beyond the Zambezi.

Chapter Seven

The Depression and its aftermath

I

Slump and recovery

The late 'twenties were a period of optimism, and Northern Rhodesians saw their country's future in the rosiest colours. But suddenly this short-lived prosperity collapsed, and the story now shifts to the United States, which at this time was dominating the world's copper markets.[1] In America two mammoth companies, Kennecott and Anaconda, were exercizing control over most of the country's copper industry, and their position was further strengthened in 1926 when a vast combine known as Copper Exporters Inc. came into being. The new organization attempted to eliminate speculation, and comprised something like 90 per cent of the world's producing capacity, including mines in the U.S.A., their Latin American subsidiaries, the Katanga, and various European and Canadian companies. Copper Exporters Inc. restricted supplies in order to eliminate the price-fixing power of the London Metal Exchange, and from June 1928 to April 1929 prices shot up from $12\frac{1}{2}$ cents to 24 cents per pound.[2]

The copper magnates, however, miscalculated. High prices stimulated mining in other countries like Northern Rhodesia where production costs were lower and demand soon failed to keep pace with supply. Worse still, some of the manufacturers found themselves unable to afford their copper bills, and began to experiment with substitutes like aluminium. Soon huge unsold stocks accumulated at the mines, and prices slumped, going down to a mere $6\frac{1}{4}$ cents per pound by November 1931. The copper producers then came to an international agreement, and from January 1932 world output was limited to $26\frac{1}{2}$ per cent of its capacity; the Northern Rhodesian companies participated in this project, and contented themselves with a limited quota. But even this drastic remedy proved inadequate. Copper prices tumbled down further, reaching $5\frac{3}{5}$ cents in February 1932. The Americans then imposed a duty of four cents per pound with the object of helping their high cost producers who complained that they were being ruined by sweated labour from abroad. Several important companies withdrew from Copper Exporters Inc. and the organization broke up, though the limitation of output continued until the end of 1932.

In Northern Rhodesia the first rumblings were heard in February 1931, when

---

[1] By 1929 the U.S.A. produced some 905,000 metric tons of copper out of a total of 1,937,000 or about 48 per cent. Chile came second with 16 per cent, Africa as a whole producing only 8 per cent.

[2] *Economist*, 9 July 1932

Bwana Mkubwa, a high cost producer, was forced to close its gates. At Nchanga, it was first decided to curtail production, but then the mine was accidentally flooded, and work was suspended, the development work at Chambishi and Kansanshi being likewise abandoned. Just before Christmas, Mufulira was ready to produce, but then orders were received to shut down, and by the end of 1931 only Roan and Nkana were being worked, the companies deciding to concentrate all their efforts on these two mines. Results for the Territory were catastrophic, for Northern Rhodesia had few other sources of wealth on which to fall back, and all these remaining industries were hit as badly. In 1931 Sir Edmund Davis, one of the most farsighted of Rhodesian producers, approached the Colonial Office for help which might enable him to maintain zinc production at Broken Hill and prevent him from throwing 100 Europeans and 600 Africans out of work. The Imperial Government, however, refused to assist, for the Labour Administration in power was as much a believer in orthodox finance as its Conservative predecessor; Davis offered to pay back the money when zinc reached the price of £20, but Passfield professed himself unwilling to 'gamble' in zinc, his refusal being based on a number of similar requests from other industries.

The Rhodesian farmers fared even worse. The settlers on the Railway Belt always had to reckon with competition from the South, since the Railway Companies' policy of granting flat rates to Southern Rhodesians largely neutralized the Northerners' advantage of being nearer to the market. But now even this small internal market went to pieces; the mines reduced their native labour force from 30,000 in 1930 to a little under 7,000 men in 1932, a policy which left them with fewer mouths to feed, and did away with the farmers' best customers; no money could be made from tobacco, for yields were low, transport charges high, and no purchasers would buy the mass of inferior leaf that had been accumulating in Rhodesian warehouses since 1928. The slump in primary products in turn affected the shopkeepers, the general position being aggravated by the absence of any other industries in the country which might still have given employment to the jobless. Economic life nearly came to a standstill, and in 1932 even the Railways had to ask their debtors' consent for a moratorium.

Government now faced a major crisis which it turned out to be ill-equipped to handle. The country's administrative machine was understaffed at the best of times, but revenues suddenly dropped, and the Administration embarked on a major economy campaign to balance its budgets. Civil servants all accepted a levy on salaries, and some of the more senior officers were retrenched. The district staff for instance was reduced from 110 officers in 1932 to 90 in 1935, the number of provinces being diminished from 9 to 5 in 1933; technical personnel were 'axed' to an even greater extent, a policy which led to serious loss of morale, and gave rise to angry or despairing comments that Secretariat men were looking after their own, whilst throwing specialists to the wolves. The tiny Education Department lost some of its best European teachers, whilst the salaries of African schoolmasters were cut to an extent which put the teachers' real income below that of District Messengers. The Medical Department was similarly retrenched, with the result that until 1937 the organization managed to do little more than just 'tick over'. The Agricultural Department suffered even worse, its already inadequate establishment being cut from 23 to 5 officers, the water boring staff being sacked altogether, whilst all experimental work came to an end at Maza-buka Research Station. So serious indeed seemed the position in 1933 that the Governor even discussed with senior mining men the possibility of a complete break-up of the educational, veterinary and agricultural services. The disintegra-tion of these departments, he thought, would put an end to permanent white settlement, turning Northern Rhodesia into a superior kind of Bechuanaland, a prospect which he disliked. The mining people agreed that the position was serious, but felt that their industry could not run in a purely native state, so that even if the vital services were scrapped, they would only have to be built up again.

Administrative catastrophe was fortunately avoided; but Government could do little to relieve distress, as serious deficits were accumulating over the years 1933 and 1934. 'The wealth of the country is in the minerals which it does not own' the Chief Secretary gloomily explained, 'and direct revenue from this source is at present negligible. This is attributable to the absence of taxable profits, a position which accentuates the disability under which this Govern-ment suffers in a time of business depression through the alienation of mining royalties. The fact, however, that the companies are not earning taxable profits does not diminish the services which Government is compelled to supply to the mining areas'.[1] This meant that a large proportion of European taxation fell on the resident whites who themselves were unable to accumulate any savings. The local Europeans in 1933 thus contributed something like £279,000 out of a total, revenue of £778,000, paying tax at an average rate of £28 per head of the popu-lation, notwithstanding the fact that ten per cent of their numbers were unem-ployed, whilst the remainder were getting much smaller wage packets and salary cheques than before and the smaller farmers were practically penniless. The Africans were even worse off; recruitment came to a standstill; many African workers were content to work for nothing more than their keep, with the result that receipts from African taxes dropped to a mere £104,000, the fall in income offering a further incentive to diminish services for Africans.

Under these circumstances the Administration felt only too pleased that, as they imagined, the African worker possessed a sort of 'national home' in the reserve, where he might go without costing the country a penny. African un-employment need cause no undue anxiety to Government, argued the Chief Secretary, for native requirements were small, and Africans could support themselves in their villages, except when the crops failed; Africans possessed plenty of land; forests supplied them with fuel, some meat and roots, the rivers with fish; unemployed Africans could always work for their friends, though. some of the jobless might need help to get back to their kraals.[2] These views

---

[1] Northern Rhodesia. *Legislative Council debates*, 10 Mar 1933, p. 82
[2] Northern Rhodesia. *Legislative Council debates*, 15 Feb 1932, p. 146–147

which rather idealized conditions in the countryside, did of course possess some sort of justification; unskilled navvies made their way back home where they were accepted by their neighbours without difficulty. But all the same the Administration took rather an optimistic view of things; the countryside itself was badly hit by the Depression; recruiting stopped; crop sales slumped; the money economy almost broke down, the demand for 'luxuries' like sewing machines, gramophones, bicycles and ploughs dried up, whilst European traders were reduced to bartering their merchandise for African goods in order to get rid of their wares.

In the towns the position was even worse. The extent of native unemployment of course remains difficult to assess, but in Ndola alone about 4,000 black people found themselves without jobs. About ten per cent of these were supposedly making ends meet from their savings, whilst the remainder were living on the charity of friends or on their wits.[1] The *Livingstone Mail* spoke of thousands of unemployed in the Maramba Compound of Livingstone, and demanded that soup kitchens be set up to feed these hungry people, and that unemployed workers should be settled in camps from where they should be recruited, stressing the inhumanity of punishing people for failing to find jobs. Many of the workless of course could no longer return to the villages, for a backward subsistence economy found no use for their services. 'I am a clerk and an interpreter' explained Henry Chibangwa in an interview with the Secretary for Native Affairs. 'I have been without a post for eighteen months. People like me can't go home. We have settled in the towns, adopted European ways and no longer know village life'.[2] Chibangwa got no satisfaction, the Secretary for Native Affairs simply insisting that Chibangwa should return to his home in Mporokoso. People in Chibangwa's position who could not make their way back or find another job faced great temptations, and under these circumstances spivs began to plague the compounds. Burglaries sharply increased, and there developed a kind of black underworld, composed of deportees from the Congo, Southern Rhodesia and South Africa, professional criminals most of them, and unemployed Africans who used to 'pump' houseboys about their masters' habits, and then break into unprotected houses.[3] Even in the countryside the position got worse, and farmers complained about a sharp increase in thefts of trek-gear, cattle and growing crops, the security problem being further affected by retrenchments in the police force.[4]

The position of the white unemployed in some ways resembled the Africans'. Men got the sack at 24 hours' notice, the mining industry being under no obligation to provide further benefits, though return fares were paid under certain conditions. A small number of Europeans, mostly Afrikaners, went back to the land, and a few hundred people, including miners and their dependents, drifted

[1] Northern Rhodesia. *Report of the Government unemployment committee.* Livingstone, Government printer, 1933
[2] The *Livingstone mail*, 6 Dec 1933, printed a letter on similar lines from one I. W. Lisulo.
[3] Letter from N. M. Nalumango in *Livingstone mail*, 12 Dec 1934
[4] Northern Rhodesia. *Legislative Council debates*, 18 Dec 1934, p. 298–299

to the Lusaka region where they eked out a miserable living in tumbledown shacks on other peoples' holdings. The vast majority emigrated, and between 1931 and 1933 the country's white population dropped from 13,846 to 11,278.[1] The Northern Rhodesian mining industry, in other words, largely managed to throw the burden of supporting the white unemployeds on to other countries, but even so, the problem was not solved, and by the end of 1932 about ten per cent of the country's European population found themselves on the street.[2]

Maxwell, though personally sympathetic to the unemployed, took the line of ruthless economy. He decided that only people who had lived in the territory for five years or more should receive help, and that people who had no claims on local charity should be compulsorily repatriated. Some unemployed people of course did not wish to leave, and used to spend the day in the bush, only coming into town at night in order to get food, so that they might not be sent out of the country; some sold their belongings for a song and were packed on lorries, together with their families, to try and find posts in the Tanganyika Gold Fields; others had their fares paid to Britain, but here the labour position turned out no better, and despairing miners, who had spent twenty or even thirty years in Africa, used to call on the Colonial Office to get help in a strange country, where they no longer had friends or relatives to help them through lean times.

The Colonial Office in 1932 then formed a Northern Rhodesian Unemployment Committee, with representation from the Dominion and Home Offices. The Commissioners shared Maxwell's fears that the Territory might become burdened with a class of poor whites who would become a charge on the country, and whose upkeep might use up funds that ought to be devoted to Africans. But the Committee also opposed compulsory repatriation, a precedent liable to lead to renewed demands from the Dominions regarding British unemployeds within their borders, and apt to result in Parliamentary criticism. Maxwell thus received instructions to supply rations to all unemployeds who asked for them, and compulsory repatriation was abandoned, though the amount of food issued to the jobless was hardly enough to keep body and soul together.[3] European unemployeds were also given some work, including the building of a camp for workless people at Ndola, an expedient which worried Maxwell who felt that Africans could have done the job more cheaply, and that semi-skilled and unskilled whites should be treated on the same economic level as black men, lest Government should encourage the creation of a colour bar. Government moreover appointed an Unemployment Commissioner, and Gerald Chad Norris, the

---

[1] At the same time the number of workers in employment at the mines dropped from 3,326 to 964, so that most of the emigrants were probably mineworkers. The decline in the European population continued until 1935 when numbers dropped to 9,913. They recovered as from 1936.

[2] The exact figure was 1,064 in December 1932 out of 10,553 persons. The figure was made up of 150 workers with 247 dependents who were unemployed and in receipt of rations, and 334 workers, with 333 dependents who received no rations.

[3] Only 10/6¾d was spent per person per week. By the end of 1932 rations were issued to 667 people Between April 1932 and September 1933, the worst period, 453 persons were repatriated.

Member for the Northern Electoral Area, was selected to fill this rather difficult and unpopular post. Norris's hands of course were tied, for he had little money at his disposal, and major public works were out of the question. But all the same, something was done; the authorities instituted a Register of unemployeds, helping to put people back into employment, and allotted various skilled and supervisory tasks to white unemployeds, including the repair of Government furniture, the painting of road signs, or watching over black gangs engaged in drainage work and tree planting. Immigration was further restricted, a policy which met with the strongest possible approval from local Europeans, who feared competition from white newcomers even more than from black men. Local charitable bodies also supplied a good deal of help, their work being co-ordinated by a joint 'Northern Rhodesian Relief Organization.'

In the meantime, however, the world copper position began to improve, the Northern Rhodesian copper magnates holding a number of strong cards. Mining costs remained low, for most of the companies possessed mines with sections of high metallic content, where only small quantities of ore had to be mined, crushed and concentrated to result in a profitable tonnage of copper. The Northern Rhodesian mines moreover then required little timbering, and work did not have to be extended underground to any great depths. The companies also managed to engage in some profitable share dealings, their financial stability never being called into question. In addition, managements showed remarkable efficiency in improving techniques, with the result that Rhokana alone managed to reduce costs in 1933 from £31. 5. 0. per ton to £26. 0. 0. The competitive power of British producers was further strengthened when Britain departed from the Gold Standard, thus facilitating the task of export merchants. The Ottawa Agreement moreover introduced a preferential duty of 2d per pound on all non-Empire copper producers, providing Rhodesians with an assured market in the United Kingdom. Under these circumstances the Northern Rhodesian magnates could afford to take a strong line with their competitors; their delegates took part in another Copper Conference in New York in December 1932, but agreement between high and low cost producers proved impossible, and international control broke down. This meant that the Rhodesian companies now found themselves free to sell their copper at only 3 cents a pound, whereas the cheapest American producers would insist on 7 cents; Mufulira re-opened in 1933, and the Northern Rhodesian producers received further assistance, when in the same year the Colonial Development Fund agreed to advance money to Rhokana for the construction of an electrolytic refinery.[1]

Development in Northern Rhodesia suffered a temporary set-back, when in 1934 a new 'Copper Code' in the U.S.A. sharply raised internal copper prices for American manufacturers, whilst foreign markets were swamped with masses

[1] Production was started in December 1934. Originally the refinery was intended to be built in Britain, but estimated costs in Northern Rhodesia only amounted to £380,000 as compared with costs in the United Kingdom of £650,000 where operating costs would also have been higher. The new refinery was regarded as important both for economic, political and strategic reasons, helping to make the sterling area more independent of American refineries.

of American copper.[1] The Rhodesian companies, in self-defence, then entered upon another restriction scheme in 1935, limiting production to 70 and later to 75 per cent of capacity. But the new agreement did not last long. The copper mines retained their assured market in Britain, where copper intake doubled between 1930 and 1938, since copper was essential to the kingdom's rapidly expanding electrical, automobile and aircraft industries. The process of recovery was further speeded up when rearmament got into its stride from about 1937;[2] prices thus continued to rise, and from January 1937 all restrictions on output disappeared, the industry going full steam ahead into the future.

II

Building a new capital

Ever since 1909 Northern Rhodesian affairs had been run from Livingstone. But copper development shifted the country's economic centre of gravity to the north, and Livingstone became more and more inconvenient as a headquarters. As early as 1926 Captain Murray complained in Council of the capital's disadvantages,[3] and civil servants shared his misgivings.[4] Three years later the question became more acute; Northern Rhodesia's place as a metal producer now seemed assured, and the problem arose whether the Administration should spend any more money on a township where even the highest in the land were living under appalling conditions. Government House then consisted of an old hotel, roofed with corrugated iron, which caught the rays of the sun and turned the place into an oven; inside His Excellency was conducting the country's affairs from the former billiard room, whilst his Private Secretary had his office in the old bar. The remaining government buildings were no better, and the cost of replacing them in Livingstone was estimated at something like £200,000. Admittedly, if Northern Rhodesia was ultimately to be governed from Salisbury, there was no point in leaving Livingstone. But amalgamation seemed out of the question for the time being; and the new investment—estimated at about £500,000—appeared well within the country's capacity at a period when shares were still booming. Then there was the future to be considered. Livingstone lay right on the edge of the Territory, far away from the agricultural districts north of the Kafue, or from the Copper Belt; the township would never become an important road junction, and no branch lines were ever likely to start from there, for

---

[1] *Economist*, 2 Nov 1935

[2] The Germans at the same time were also buying Northern Rhodesian copper, coming second on the list of purchasers. In 1936 the territory thus exported 64,330 tons of blister and 13,589 of electrolytic copper to the U.K., whilst Hitler's Germany bought 40,119 tons of blister copper, whereas Italy bought 7,992 tons of blister and 10,827 tons of electrolytic copper.

[3] Northern Rhodesia. *Legislative Council debates*, 20 Sep 1926, p. 112–120

[4] A 'free debate' was held in 1929, in which 7/9 of the Officials and most Unofficials advocated the moving of the capital. See Northern Rhodesia. *Legislative Council debates*, 22 Mar 1929, p. 378–411

future rail development was expected to hinge on the West Coast, whilst the ultimate completion of the Sinoia-Kafue rail-link would further reduce the settlement's importance. The mining companies thought along similar lines and in 1929 Anglo American, Rhodesian Selection Trust, as well as three Unofficial Members, addressed a memorandum to Government, in which they emphasized that economic development would centre beyond the Kafue, that the capital should be nearer to resident communities having permanent business with Government, and that local foodstuffs were inadequate at Livingstone, where the climate was bad.

Livingstone was of course Moore's home, which he had seen growing up from its earliest beginnings and which filled him with the kind of proprietary pride that only colonists can truly appreciate. Besides, material issues were involved, for if the civil servants left, the local shopkeepers would lose their most credit-worthy customers and the value of real estate would drop. Moore thus never tired of pointing out Livingstone's advantages, its fine situation by the river, the proximity of the awe-inspiring Victoria Falls, and he insisted—quite correctly —that the place was perfectly healthy, a view with which Maxwell agreed as a medical man. Moore even went to the trouble of personally calling in 1929 on Lord Passfield and on senior officials in the Colonial Office, but received no satisfaction, and the project went ahead.

Government was now faced with the problem of where to put the new capital, and this issue aroused a great deal of heat. The farmers mostly wanted the new site in the midst of the agricultural districts north of the Kafue, and Moore caustically pointed out how such a move would appreciate the value of estates owned by a small clique of absentee landowners.[1] Broken Hill formed another powerful contender, and the township's case was ably put by Sir Edmund Davis, the local mining magnate; Davis pointed to the waste of money involved in the construction of artificial capitals like New Delhi and Canberra, and explained that Broken Hill already possessed a population of some 1,400 Europeans, the settlement housing the headquarters of the Northern Rhodesian Railway Administration; Broken Hill moreover was a mining centre, electric power being supplied from the Rhodesia Broken Hill Development Company's hydro-electric plant at Mulungushi.[2] From the geographical point of view, Broken Hill would in fact have made an excellent choice, lying about halfway between the farming area and the Copper Belt. But there were strong arguments against its selection. The town was poorly planned, and replanning was expected to entail further delay; the settlement moreover lay near a fly-belt, and its choice would necessitate the purchase of about 10 square miles from land companies, a prospect disliked by Government which remembered unhappy experiences with such bodies in the past. Ndola might have provided a third alternative, but

[1] *Livingstone mail*, 1 Jan 1930. It was calculated at the time that in this region the largest non-resident farmers were Sir Randolph Baker, Earl Winterton, Major J. V. Hermon and the Duke of Westminster, who between them held 157,354 acres.

[2] A plant was first installed there in 1925.

though the copper companies were anxious to have the capital nearer to the mines, they did not want it right in the Copper Belt itself.

In 1930 Government commissioned Professor Stanley Davenport Adshead, a prominent town-planner from London University, to investigate the matter. Adshead travelled all round the country and finally selected the little village of Lusaka, where he was impressed by the beauty of its windswept ridge. 'If it were not important that the site be a great city, but only a Government centre, Lusaka offered all the facilities', he jotted in his diary, and he predicted that the settlement could for economic reasons never become an important town. The site chosen lay near the railway; there was ample room for further expansion, and the choice of an existing village possessed the further advantage that—in Adshead's view—a capital would grow out more easily from a nucleus already in being than from nothing. Government accepted these recommendations which possessed further economic merits in that the bulk of the land round Lusaka belonged to the Crown, and might be expected to appreciate in value to the benefit of the public purse. Internally the town embodied the idea of white and black separation, a concept accepted at the time not only by poverty stricken back-veld farmers, but also by distinguished academics from overseas like Adshead himself. The Professor in fact went rather further in his views on the backwardness of Africans than many Rhodesians might have done at the time: 'The solution seems to be', he wrote in his diary, 'to keep them as slaves, to give them every encouragement when they are lazy and stupid and to see that they are, according to their own desire, comfortably well off as far as one can satisfy bodily needs. It would be a mistake to treat them as if they were Europeans: it would be ridiculous to expect them to accept the responsibilities of the white man, and it would be foolish to offer them those bodily comforts which they have never known and which generations and generations of habit have made necessary to the white man.' The Administration, however, adopted a more enlightened point of view, and attempted to discriminate between different kinds of Africans; African clerks, artisans and *capitaos* (supervisors) were allocated a special village, where they could build their own houses, and received garden plots at low rentals, only buildings of a relatively good type being permitted, whilst the settlement as a whole was controlled by the District Commissioner with the aid of an African Committee.

The Government offices lay a long way from the older township with its shops, whilst Lusaka as a whole was situated far from any of the other centres of settlement, emphasizing in space the social and political separation between government officers and the resident community, a characteristic feature of British Central Africa, where Zomba, Nyasaland's capital, was placed at some distance from Blantyre, the commercial centre, whilst Salisbury for a long time remained a civil servants' town, Bulawayo constituting the country's commercial focus, Salisbury itself being divided in the early days into an official and a trading section, separated from each other by swampy ground and social snobbery. Up in Lusaka the fine Ridgeway formed the backbone of what was still a kind of half-empty, artificial back-veld Canberra, centring on a big but unat-tractive Secretariat. On the map, the township was neatly zoned into adminis-trative, commercial, residential, African, Indian, recreational and 'undetermined' areas, the whole scheme resting on the assumption that Lusaka would only be the country's governmental, social and cultural centre, where industrial develop-ment would remain strictly limited.

The next problem concerned finance. Maxwell was pushing ahead with the scheme at a time when Northern Rhodesia seemed likely to escape the effects of Depression. But then the Slump hit Rhodesia, and when Great Britain went off gold, Maxwell took alarm and in 1931 temporarily suspended preliminary work on the site. In 1932 work was resumed, but in 1933 the situation again seemed so bad for a time that Sir Ronald Storrs, Maxwell's successor, thought of tempora-rily abandoning the project, the situation being saved by a generous offer from the Beit Trustees. The economic blizzard thus caused work to proceed by fits and starts, but even more serious was the absence of proper supervision. Maxwell at first wished to entrust overall control to an internationally known firm of Consulting Engineers. This suggestion, however, had to be abandoned for economic reasons, and Maxwell had to rely instead on his Secretariat and on local talent in his under-staffed Public Works Department; P. J. Bowling, the local Town Planning Engineer, did all he could but the whole of his staff was retrenched, and existing town planning legislation proved far from adequate. Trouble also occurred with some of the local contractors, and inadequate supervision resulted in waste, with the result that the original estimate of £500,000 had risen to over £800,000 by 1933. All the same work went on, giving some relief to the unemployed, and in May 1935 the new government headquarters were formally opened, the ceremony being associated with the King's Silver Jubilee.

Chapter Eight

European politics in the 'thirties

I

The changing social scene

The decision to change the capital turned out to be administratively justifiable, but the exact location of the site pleased hardly anyone, not even the traders in Lusaka who felt that their shops were too far away from the government offices. Merchants in Livingstone, Ndola and Broken Hill all imagined that Government had presented them with a grievance, and Moore in particular turned strongly against the Administration, becoming a staunch advocate of amalgamation with Southern Rhodesia, now that his home town would never be the centre of government. This relatively minor issue apart, the 'thirties also saw other changes in the structure of Northern Rhodesian politics. The revival of industry led to renewed immigration of white artisans whom the Slump had made more conscious of their interests, and who were now more willing to defend their position than in the dark days of Depression, when the men felt too worried about getting a job to turn up at meetings, and when even the well organized Rhodesia Railway Workers' Union lost most of its members. As prosperity came back, the workers' political interest increased, and in 1935 Nkana elected Mrs Catherine Olds, the wife of a small Copper Belt farmer, to represent the constituency in 'Legco'. She, the first woman ever to sit in the Northern Rhodesian legislature, was returned for the specific object of speaking for the mineworkers, a choice which appeared reasonable at a time when many miners were hoping to invest their savings in a farm, once they had earned enough money underground.[1] Richard Olds, Catherine's husband, in the meantime busied himself with trade union affairs, and invited Charles Harris, General Secretary of the South African Mine Workers' Union, to visit the Copper Belt and organize the local workers.

The mining companies disliked the idea that a South African Union should extend its activities to the north, fearing that this might involve them in purely South African disputes, and also lead to the creation of a legalized colour bar in industry. The Administration itself did not object to unions, rightly regarding them as a natural stage in the country's development, but strongly sympathized with the companies on the dangers of South African unionism gaining a foothold in the Copper Belt. The Government's difficulties were, however, resolved,

[1] Evidence is inadequate on this point, but few Copper Belt farmers seem to have made good under these semi-tropical conditions.

by constitutional obstacles within the South African Mine Workers' Union itself, and in 1936 the Northern Rhodesian Mine Workers' Union came into being as an independent body with its headquarters at Luanshya. The Companies then agreed to recognize the organization whenever its membership reached 60 per cent of the labour force, subsequently contenting themselves with a mere 55. The new body was all-white; the Constitution specifically limiting membership to Europeans.[1] Elected General, Executive and Financial Councils looked after the Union's affairs, the important day-to-day work remaining in the hands of an Organizing Secretary, the first to occupy this office being the Rev. Harold Ignatius Webb, a Luanshya clergyman. The Union at first steered an extremely moderate course and a dispute in 1937 was solved by negotiation. Admittedly, Unionists were now in control of the industrial key positions in the Copper Belt, and the political influence of white supervisors and skilled men could no longer be ignored. But in the industrial field, the Union's power was reduced by frequent differences of opinion between the different geographical branches, by lack of interest on the part of members, by horizontal divisions between mineworkers proper and artisans, by divisions between English and Afrikaans-speaking workers, and by the migrant character of its membership, some of the trade union officials themselves only staying in the country for a time and returning to South Africa on the completion of their work. The most able of the new generation of trade unionists turned out to be an unknown railwayman, Roland (Roy) Welensky, whose outstanding future as yet none could foresee.[2] Michael, Welensky's father, a tough Jewish pioneer from near Vilna in Lithuania, was one of those adventurous souls who drifted from frontier to frontier, trading furs in the Middle West, and selling ostrich feathers in Kimberley, before pushing on by ox-wagon to Bulawayo, where he served as a *burgher* in the Afrikander Corps during the Matabele Rebellion. Michael Welensky wedded Leah, an Afrikaans girl, the kind of marriage not uncommon on the South African frontier where women were few, and Afrikaner girls always amongst the first on the edge of white settlement. The Welenskys, however, had a hard and grim life, and when Roy was born in Salisbury in 1907, the youngest of thirteen children, the future looked indeed gloomy. His father lacked business ability, and affairs got even worse when, at the age of eleven, young Roy lost his mother, and his family went to pieces. Michael Welensky had previously made a precarious living as a boarding-house keeper, but was now reduced to doing odd jobs, including work as a *wocher*, a Watcher for the Dead employed by the Jewish community, and his son had to help make up the family income. Roy's formal education never continued beyond the age of fourteen, though the youngster acquired an extraordinary familiarity with the Bible which his father made him read out aloud, the two of them going twice through the whole of the Scriptures—from Genesis to Revelation. In 1921 Roy Welensky became a storekeeper in the back-veld, and subse-

---

[1] *Constitution of the Northern Rhodesian Mine Workers Union.* Bulawayo, 1936
[2] See D. Taylor. *The Rhodesian: the life of Sir Roy Welensky.* Museum Press, 1955

quently a professional prizefighter, holding for a time the heavyweight boxing championship of Rhodesia. The ring, however, did not provide much of a living for the men who gave and got the blows, and Welensky reckoned himself fortunate when, in 1924, he found a job on the Railways, where he became an engine driver. In 1933 Welensky was transferred to Broken Hill, and was appointed Chairman of the local Railway Workers' Union branch, which he completely reorganized, a difficult task at a time when apathy was widespread, and anti-semitic and Fascist feeling rife amongst some of the men; he soon made his name as a skilled and forceful negotiator, and became an influential personage in local politics, his background and upbringing having given him an instinctive sympathy with the underdog, but also a strong consciousness of the meaning of national minority-status, as well as a firm belief that white working class standards should be protected from undercutting by poorly paid Africans. Welensky in fact started off as a segregationist, a point of view which subsequent experiences slowly modified.

The young railwayman did not, however, attempt to enter national politics all at once. Having for a short period opposed the election of another candidate, Lieutenant-Colonel Sir Stewart Gore-Browne, who stood for the Northern Electoral Area in 1935, he swung round in the Colonel's favour: and there began one of the strangest political partnerships in Rhodesian history. On the face of it, few could have had less in common than the unknown trade unionist from Broken Hill, broad shouldered and burly, without a drop of British blood in his veins, and the tall, distinguished and aristocratic looking landowner from overseas, English to the core, though sometimes emotional in his approach to political problems and apt to get tired of causes that ceased to hold his interest. Sir Stewart was an accepted member of the 'Establishment'; his father was a well-known King's Counsel and his grandfather a soldier of senior rank; and whereas Welensky never got beyond 'Standard VI' at school, Sir Stewart went through Harrow and then through the Royal Military Academy at Woolwich, subsequently making a name for himself during the Great War. After the end of hostilities, Sir Stewart, a wealthy man in his own right, decided to settle in Northern Rhodesia. 'My original idea, born in those days of boundless humanitarian optimism . . .' he related later on, 'was to found a soldiers' settlement at Shiwa Ngandu which was to work in happy co-operation with the surrounding Natives who, one supposed, would only be too delighted to take part in this Utopia-on-European lines'. But the scheme turned out a failure. The soil proved unsuitable; transport charges mounted up; the soldier settlers became disgruntled and the Africans apathetic; and after two years Gore-Browne found that he could not even produce mealies. Undaunted, the Colonel made a new start. His brother came out from England with sufficient knowledge concerning the production of vegetable oils to set the settlement on its feet; a retired Provincial Commissioner joined the staff, as well as a carpenter and a handyman from England. Gradually the estate began to take shape: roads were built and motor transport started; Gore-Browne installed steam-power and a saw mill; native carpenters, bricklayers and brickmakers were trained, buildings went up, and nursery gardens were laid out. Gore-Browne, however, wanted to be more than just a businessman. He also envisaged his role as that of a traditional British squire, responsible for his tenants' welfare, and continued to provide all kinds of facilities for Africans which were well beyond the financial abilities of ordinary farmers. A dispensary opened its doors, as well as an infants' welfare clinic and a farm school; decent houses were provided; but the local Africans—amongst the most backward in the Territory—took little interest in these schemes, and all Gore-Browne's efforts at 'uplift' were dogged with misfortune.[1] Finally the Colonel embarked on a policy of segregation; the Africans on the far side of the lake might do as they pleased; the ones on the near side did as they were told!—a simple formula which did much to influence the Colonel's immediate thinking on larger issues. But the new approach succeeded, and Shiwa Ngandu became the showpiece of Northern Rhodesia, where a courteous squire, possessed of a taste for diplomacy, ruled his estate with benevolence and a hand of iron.

The Welensky—Gore-Browne partnership symbolized a somewhat unstable white class-alliance which soon became effective on the issue of closer association with Southern Rhodesia, which in itself was deeply influenced by local economic policies. The misery produced by the Slump made a profound impression on the skilled white workers who were now living in permanent fear for their jobs. Southern Rhodesia seemed to provide the answer when, in 1934, the Legislature in Salisbury passed the Industrial Conciliation Act. This provided for the registration of recognized trade unions, giving specific recognition to the principle of collective bargaining, though African workers were excluded from its provision. The protection given to European artisans in towns was strengthened by an amending Act in 1937 which added safeguards against the undercutting of skilled wages; Southern Rhodesia also undertook far more relief work for its workless whites. Policies south of the Zambezi also made a strong appeal to Northern farmers. During the five years between 1928 and 1933 alone, the Southern Rhodesian Government spent about £1,000,000 in the way of loans, debt liquidations or reductions, export bounties, rebates and research; a tight machinery of control came into being in order to keep up prices of agricultural commodities, partly for the purpose of favouring the producer over the consumer, protecting the small farmer against the big and shielding the maize grower from African competition. This policy produced a whole new spate of legislation which—apart from its colour aspect—bore some resemblance to the equally unplanned 'New Deal', and to those remedial policies current in many Western countries at the time, which aimed at subsidizing the producer as against the consumer. In 1930 a Board was set up to regulate the sale and export of tobacco; a year later the Dairy Control Board came into being for the supervision of the dairy industry, whilst a Maize Control Act established compulsory control of

[1] Gore-Browne, S. 'The relations of black and white in tropical Africa: an address to the African circle on May 20th 1935' (reprinted from *Journal of the Royal African Society* by the *Livingstone mail*, 18 Dec 1935)

maize and maize-meal sales. In addition, steps were taken to improve the quality of the country's agricultural produce by measures like the Tobacco Pests Suppression Act which was strictly enforced by expert administrators. In 1934 maize control was further strengthened, and a Cattle Levy and Beef Export Bounty Act was passed giving further help to ranchers.

The Northern Rhodesian farmers would have liked a similar policy, but specialist services north of the Zambezi were much more poorly endowed than those in Salisbury, whilst the local authorities remained wedded to a greater extent to older policies of *laissez faire*, which entailed less administrative expenditure. The farmers did however succeed in getting a Maize Control Ordinance put on to the Statute Book in 1935, at a time when the maize position was already getting better again. The new Act was based on current legislation in Southern Rhodesia, and aimed at making the internal price independent of foreign fluctuations, whilst dividing the market between white and black producers, the Africans being allotted a fixed quota corresponding to their existing share in the market, which was then calculated to amount to one quarter. The Director of Agriculture defended this decision by pointing out that maize was being exported at a loss, and that the only alternative to present legislation was direct restriction of production, a measure which could not possibly be enforced all over the countryside. Unless some sort of control was established, farmers would intensify their struggle for the internal market, with the result that white maize-growers might be gradually eliminated. But this would be a disaster, for African peasants would not maintain regular production, whilst their soil would become eroded in the absence of adequate care, with the result that in the long run crops would diminish.[1] These arguments made special appeal to Europeans —especially the smaller and weaker producers amongst them—who considered that Africans enjoyed a natural advantage in not having to pay rent or interest on the purchase price of their land. On the face of it, the Europeans seemed to get what they wanted, but oddly enough, the Maize Control law had just the opposite effect from the one intended. Governor Maybin went into the question a few years later and found that the scheme in fact led to that very expansion of African production which it was designed to avoid, for Africans were now getting a relatively high price which was fixed at a higher level than they would have obtained under free competition. Maybin also came to the conclusion that the original allocation of a quarter to the Africans did not injure their interests, because there was in fact no appreciable carry-over of maize which they could put on the market. African evidence seems to support Maybin's views; and an abortive African nationalist organization, founded amongst Tonga farmers in 1937, gave praise to the Maize Control Board, which Africans considered to be a valuable instrument, and of great benefit to African traders and farmers by paying them cash for their product.

It might be added that in this respect the views of the more advanced Tonga ran parallel with those of educated Africans in Southern Rhodesia who, despite

[1] Northern Rhodesia. *Legislative Council debates*, 19 Nov 1935, p. 59–74

other grievances of a more general nature, gave their whole-hearted approval to a Maize and Maize Meal Bill, when this was being considered by the Southern Rhodesian Legislature earlier on in the decade.

To return to the Closer Union question, the white artisans' and farmers' amalgamationist sympathies were shared by European 'stiff-collar workers' who resented the large scale employment of 'expatriates' with University degrees in the Northern Rhodesian civil service, the clamour for official jobs becoming louder when unemployment became a serious problem. As the result of 'Unofficial' pressure, the Administration in 1934 appointed a committee to consider the matter, and the following year the Governor agreed that selected jobs within the Administration should be filled locally, the newly appointed officers no longer being granted the privilege of free passage overseas, or of qualifying for free pensions under the European Officers Pension Ordinance like their privileged colleagues from abroad. But local jealousies continued, the position being made worse by Downing Street's declared policy of employing more Africans in the Administration. In 1931 Passfield asked Maxwell to give more jobs to Africans, a policy which seemed desirable both from the point of view of economy, and from that of African advancement. The immediate results of this move were not impressive, for Maxwell correctly pointed to the extremely low level of education prevailing amongst African clerks at the time, which made promotions difficult; all the same, a detailed scheme was published in 1931, which divided African government employees into five different classes according to their skill, African wage rates all lying far below the European level.[1] The process of building up a native civil service was delayed by the Slump, when some 45 native clerks and artisans, as well as 112 policemen, lost their posts; but these reductions to some extent proved a blessing in disguise by weeding out poorly qualified men. In 1933 the Colonial Office renewed its pressure for African advancement, the Colonial Secretary insisting in Parliament that Northern Rhodesia could not be administered economically or efficiently by a predominantly European staff.[2] The new policy, described for the first time as one of 'Africanization', not only perturbed many officials, but also did much to convert sceptical Elected Members to amalgamation.

[1] See Northern Rhodesia government notice 84/1931 of 10 June 1931, and *Livingstone mail*, 22 Aug 1931. The top class was composed of compositors, printers, binders, telegraphists, telephonists, motor mechanics and clerks. Below them came tailors, storemen, linesmen, road and dip tank foremen. The third class was made up of post, telegraph and district messengers, prison warders, guards for agricultural and health departments, as well as forest and customs guards. The two bottom groups consisted of unskilled men. Specialists in the top grades could earn maximum salaries at between £7. 10. 0. to £12. 10. 0. a month, but the ordinary tradesman would only get about £3. 10. 0. a month until he had served for at least 6 years.
[2] *House of Commons debates*, v. 266, 3 May 1933, p. 1599

II

The amalgamation struggle continues: 1932–1939

The newly established solidarity between white artisans, farmers and 'stiff-collar workers' found expression on the Legislative Council, where in 1933 Moore swung round in favour of amalgamation,[1] all the Unofficials throwing their weight behind the cause of a united Rhodesia.[2] Opposition to a southern link now remained largely confined to the top strata of Northern Rhodesian society, top mining men, civil servants without permanent roots in the country, and lawyers with a stake in the existing system of laws. The missionaries were divided: in the early 'thirties there still remained a few parsons like the Rev. J. D. Schonken, who led an amalgamationist gathering at Livingstone in raucously singing 'We'll hang Jim Thomas on a sour apple tree',[3] but the majority of clergymen were now fully convinced that Salisbury rule should be resisted, and that Imperial Trusteeship should prevail. Their views found expression on the Official benches of 'Legco', which dominated proceedings at Livingstone. But at the same time cleavages were beginning to appear within the ranks of the monied men overseas which profoundly affected the future of the Closer Union issue. The Chartered Company used to oppose amalgamation in the past, on the grounds that a government of back-veld farmers and bush lawyers could not be trusted to respect the shareholders' money.[4] Southern Rhodesians did in fact consider questioning the Company's mineral rights at law, but after having taken advice, including counsel from Denis Nowell Pritt, an eminent legal authority and a convinced Socialist, the Cabinet at Salisbury decided not to take the matter to court; instead the Southern Rhodesians in 1933 bought up the Company's mineral rights in the Colony, paying the sum of £2,000,000 for what appeared a somewhat speculative asset which would drop in value once the gold was worked out. In actual fact the bargain proved sound, but at the time the Company's directorate expressed thorough satisfaction with a deal that provided them with badly needed cash which they could now invest in various subsidiary enterprises and mining stock.

Government in Salisbury moreover showed unexpected stability. The ruling Rhodesian Party temporarily lost power in 1933, when the Reform Party, led

[1] Northern Rhodesia. *Legislative Council debates*, 6 Apr 1935, p. 430–441
[2] Northern Rhodesia. *Legislative Council debates*, 27 Nov 1933, p. 577–578
[3] *Livingstone mail*, 15 July 1931. James Henry Thomas, formerly General Secretary of the National Union of Railwaymen, became Secretary of State for the Dominions in 1930 in the Labour government.
[4] As a matter of fact, there were divisions on the Board itself. The extreme conservative position was taken up by Philip Lyttleton Gell, President of the Chartered Company and a Director of the Guardian Assurance Company. The pro-Southern Rhodesian wing was led by Sir Edmund Davis who took up a positive attitude towards the new administration right from the beginning of Responsible Government.

by Dr Godfrey Martin Huggins, was swept into power on the votes of discontented white artisans and poverty stricken farmers.[1] The Reform Party,
however, proved incapable of retaining cohesion, assailed as it was by a European Labour Party on the one hand and the conservatively minded Rhodesian
Party on the other. In 1934 the bulk of the Rhodesian and of the Reform Parties
then joined under Huggins's leadership in a conservative coalition—consciously
based on the precedent of Britain's National Government. Huggins, able and
forceful to the point of indiscretion, proved as resolute and competent in the
council chamber as in the operating theatre, and soon removed all traces of
opposition to his personal supremacy; a General Election, held in 1934, resulted
in a sweeping victory for his middle-of-the-road leadership, which favoured
amalgamation, whilst the remnants of the Reform Party and the equally isola-
tionist Labour Party only made a poor showing at the polls. The Chartered
Company reversed its former attitude, and in 1934 Sir Henry Birchenough, the
Company's Chairman, called on the Colonial Office in order to point out the
value of a British block which should include the two Rhodesias, Nyasaland,
northern Bechuanaland and possibly even Tanganyika. Birchenough also
expressed confidence in Huggins's leadership, as well as satisfaction with the
prevalence of industrial peace in Southern Rhodesia. Birchenough's views
coincided with Sir Herbert Stanley's who in 1931 returned from Ceylon to become High Commissioner for South Africa, moving house to Salisbury four
years later in order to take up the Governorship of Southern Rhodesia; Stanley
also became impressed with the need for an all-British grouping in Central
Africa to balance South African power, and seems to have urged the value of
this scheme on Birchenough.

Support for the idea of closer union was now also coming from Nyasaland,
where the *Nyasaland Times* backed the scheme on the grounds that it would
lead to administrative economy, and reduce taxation. In 1933 the British Empire
Producers' Organization put forward a similar project, and a delegation called
on the Colonial Office, composed of H. T. Pooley, a Director of the Organization, Captain T. H. Murray from Northern Rhodesia, Major L. M. Hastings
from Southern Rhodesia and Lieutenant-Colonel C. E. Ponsonby, the London
Representative of the Nyasaland European Unofficial bodies. Research, customs,
communications, mining, non-native education and defence should all be unified
—argued the delegates—and in addition the authorities should set up a common
Court of Appeal. The visitors justified these demands by pointing to the greater
economy which would result from their adoption, and by the need to put a stop
to Afrikaner influence which was spreading beyond the Limpopo. Southern
Rhodesia was culturally influenced by South Africa and many Rhodesian students went to South African universities. In addition the delegates advanced

---

[1] Huggins, like Dr L. S. Jameson before him, was a very able medical man in his own right, an
F.R.C.S., and author of a work on the amputation and after-treatment of stumps, as well as an article
on the treatment of gunshot wounds which was inspired by his war-time experiences as an officer in
the R.A.M.C. Huggins also acquired a personal stake in the farming industry.

strong economic reasons; the Imperial Tobacco Company, now the chief dealer in Central Africa, was maintaining its main centres at Limbe and Salisbury, and tobacco merchants were regarding Central Africa as a single economic unit. Besides, 80 per cent of the native labourers on Southern Rhodesian farms came from Nyasaland, and this fact alone emphasized the need for a common economic policy. Apart from anything else, there remained the need for solidarity between the three Central African territories in the field of customs tariffs, especially when the two Rhodesias failed to put up a united front at previous customs talks at Pretoria in 1930.

Whilst these negotiations were going on overseas, local agitation continued for direct amalgamation of the two Rhodesias. In 1933 Moore and Charles Sidney Knight, the Junior Member from Livingstone, called on the Southern Rhodesian Government, arguing that amalgamation was an urgent matter so as to stop Northern Rhodesia from being forced into an East African Association, to prevent Africanization, and to resist those great capitalist enterprises at home, whose operations Moore now considered to be inimical to the country's interests. Moore and Knight, Livingstonians both of them, also hoped that amalgamation might yet be achieved before Lusaka was completed, and the country saddled with a great, big, white elephant. Local pressure was also brought to bear on the Colonial Office and Southern Rhodesia associated itself with the Northerners' demands. In 1934 Huggins called on the Department and outlined a scheme whereby East and Central Africa would be split into separate white and black areas, the two Rhodesias being amalgamated into a single state; educated Africans would be free to reach top positions in the black areas of the North, a project which would have provided Huggins with an outlet for advanced native people who were leaving the efficient Southern Rhodesian schools in greater numbers and with better qualifications than were being turned out by the missions north of the Zambezi. A year later, in 1935, the Southern Rhodesians for the first time became seriously concerned about Nyasaland when the Union Government changed its policy towards the employment of tropical Africans. Recruiting now began on an experimental basis in Nyasaland for the Rand mines, thus competing with Southern Rhodesia for the Protectorate's labour supplies, and the Southern Rhodesians acquired an additional incentive to safeguard their position in the North.

These arguments, of course, made little appeal to the small minority of Africans who then displayed any interest in these matters. Black views still counted for little, for the vast majority of rural natives knew little about amalgamation, and cared less. But in the towns the first elements of a knowledgeable black opposition were beginning to appear. From about 1930 onwards educated Africans in Northern Rhodesia were banding themselves into 'Welfare Societies', informal little groupings along the line of rail, where black clerks, hospital orderlies and elementary school teachers used to hold regular meetings in English, airing local grievances as well as discussing those more general issues about which they read in the *Livingstone Mail*, the *Bulawayo Chronicle* and the

Northern Rhodesian Hansard, of which copies were beginning to find their way into African hands. In 1933 an African speaker, Nelson Nalumango, thus explained his views to the Livingstone Welfare Society: amalgamation, he argued, might improve trade and even give more work to Africans on the Railways; but all the same, Africans would oppose union with Southern Rhodesia, where Africans were often moved away from their holdings on to poorer land, whilst black clerks could not find jobs in Government offices—the latter argument carrying particular weight with Nalumango's audience. The Northern Rhodesian Government, on the other hand, recognized Native Authorities, laid out reserves and did not legally lay down any colour bar, whilst neither grazing fees nor timber royalties were required of Africans north of the Zambezi.[1] These arguments of course were not very radical, the budding African politicians remaining 'loyalists' rather than critics of Government, like the settlers. All the same, thought a senior Colonial Office man, Downing Street policies were in fact creating a new class of politically conscious Africans whose demands would create new problems, which the minute writer imagined might be left 'for solution by the efflux of time', his views conforming to the best Downing Street tradition of letting awkward matters slide. The Colonial Office now found itself faced with a difficult task which has bedevilled policy right to the present day; the Office would not accept amalgamation, or relinquish control over native policies beyond the Zambezi to the whites who had made their homes there. But the economic and administrative advantages of closer association seemed obvious, whilst 'the men on the spot' tended to favour some kind of larger Central African grouping. Sir Harold Baxter Kittermaster thus advocated union between Northern Rhodesia and Nyasaland, adding that the Protectorate must now look to the south rather than to Tanganyika and Kenya. But this suggestion proved unacceptable to Downing Street. Malcolm Macdonald, the Secretary of State for the Colonies, explained to the Governor that, in the event of a merger, Nyasaland would lose its capital at Zomba, and might suffer administratively; that there was little trade between the two territories, whilst existing international engagements with regard to the Congo Basin prevented a Customs Union between the two countries; Nyasaland was also carrying a heavy burden of debt, relying for assistance on the Imperial treasury, so that a merger would necessitate a Northern Rhodesian subsidy to the country. The local settlers moreover would only support the scheme if it formed a step towards amalgamation with Southern Rhodesia, which the Secretary of State regarded as undesirable.

The new Governor of Northern Rhodesia also advocated some kind of Central African association. Major Sir Hubert Winthrop Young was, like Gore-Browne, a product of the Royal Military Academy at Woolwich, and people who did not know him might easily take him for just another Blimp; he would bristle, and bang the table when he thought banging the table would do any good; and the story has it that when he first stepped into the new Government House at

[1] *Livingstone mail*, 4 Oct 1933

Lusaka, he just gave a snort which sounded like 'Hm, Metro Goldwyn Meyer!' But behind his deceptively tigerish manner and a neatly clipped moustache, there lay an acute intelligence; Young did well as a Staff Officer, subsequently represented Great Britain at Baghdad, before being translated to Government House at Zomba, and then in 1934, to Northern Rhodesia. Young—one might add —was also a keen chess player, an accomplished linguist, a lover of music, and keenly alive to the value of anthropological enquiry into African problems, his intellectual bent considerably influencing the country's cultural development.

As far as Rhodesian politics were concerned, the Governor felt that the white settlers had come to stay, that they were doing a good job, and that they merited a gradually increasing share in political power. He also considered himself as something of a heretic on the current orthodoxy of African government through 'Indirect Rule' exercized through Native Authorities, arguing that this way of controlling the rural areas should only be regarded as a training ground where black men might learn to conduct their own affairs, rather than as acceptance in advance of the idea that they should ultimately rule the country.[1] Young more-over received a most favourable impression, both of Gore-Browne, an ex-soldier like himself, and of Huggins, whom he met in Salisbury, and who struck him as willing to subordinate local Southern Rhodesian interests to a policy of creating a United British Central Africa. Young moreover also thought in terms of encouraging secondary industries, a novel idea at Government House; Central Africa should be joined into a local customs union, which should keep out cheap Japanese products and encourage the local manufacture of low-grade textiles of the type which Lancashire could not produce, thus affording employ-ment not only to Africans, but also to unemployed supervisors and skilled men from home. Transport between the three territories should similarly be co-ordinated, so that the individual territories should not play a lone hand against the Rhodesian Railways, comparable arguments applying in the field of air transport. Northern Rhodesia's links with East Africa, Young continued, were quite artificial, only having come into existence since 1924, and they should not be further strengthened, so that Southern Rhodesia might not be pushed into the arms of South Africa. Instead a new kind of association should be created, to be known as British Central Africa, which was to be placed under a common High Commissioner.

Young visited Southern Rhodesia and in January 1935 held informal dis-cussions with Kittermaster and Stanley on the long and weary train journey from Salisbury to Bulawayo. The three Governors got on extremely well and in April 1935 a formal conference took place between Huggins, Kittermaster, Young and Stanley, who stressed the need for closer relations between the three territories with regard to research, customs, communications, education, defence, publicity and trade representation in London and common currency. The delegates also agreed on the need for a common Central African Court of

[1] Speech by Young to the East African Group of the Overseas League, *Livingstone mail*, 24 Mar 1937

Appeal, for consultation on mining law, and for the avoidance of dual taxation of Africans. The first Governors' Conference formed a considerable advance on the road to closer association. The Colonial Office warned Young that he must take no steps likely to lead towards either amalgamation or federation of the Rhodesias, but the principle of regular consultation now became established, and also the idea of co-ordinating 'non-controversial services', a major step forward being the creation in 1939 of a common Court of Appeal for the two Rhodesias under the presidency of the Chief Justice for Southern Rhodesia. But modest proposals for the unification of technical services alone made little appeal to most white Rhodesians who wanted something more tangible, and a further Unofficial Conference at the Victoria Falls in 1936 passed yet another motion in favour of amalgamation, the Southern Rhodesian Parliament following suit with another resolution later on in the year. Moore and Huggins continued to advocate outright unification. Gore-Browne, on the other hand took a more cautious line: the Imperial Government would never agree to outright fusion, and Central Africa should therefore join into a Federation, where Southern Rhodesia and the Railway Belt would become a 'white' constituent state in which European interests should be paramount, whilst North-Eastern Rhodesia should be linked to Nyasaland, the resultant territory as well as North-Western Rhodesia becoming 'black' states, whose native policies would remain under Imperial supervision.[1] Gore-Browne of course realized perfectly well that if his project was ever accepted, his estate at Shiwa Ngandu would fall within the 'black' zone, but continued to advocate his scheme with complete sincerity, bitterly denouncing in 'Legco' the whole concept of Imperial Trusteeship: trusteeship was humbug, and—for all their wordy pronouncements—the Trustees in Downing Street were in fact doing very little for their charges; periodic famines continued to stalk the tribal lands, and Africans were losing confidence in an Administration whose policies were rendered ineffective by constant staff changes and lack of money. Native trusteeship made no sense, unless the British were prepared to give the whole country back to the Africans, a course of action which no sensible man could advocate. Repression, on the other hand, was morally indefensible, whilst segregation, for all its theoretical advantages, would no longer prove practicable, now that native and white interests had become so closely interlocked. The only way out of the Imperial dilemma was partnership between the races, a policy which would allow the partners plenty of room to get away from each other, as long as cultural discrepancies between them continued to remain as striking as they were at the moment.[2] 'Partnership' as first defined in Northern Rhodesia by Gore-Browne between 1935 and 1936, thus meant a measure of limited territorial separation which would protect European standards through a policy of political autonomy, whilst at the same time speeding up the provision of social services and the building of local self-government in

[1] Speech by Gore-Browne at Broken Hill, *Livingstone mail*, 11 Nov 1936
[2] Northern Rhodesia. *Legislative Council debates*, 29 Oct 1936, p. 245–254 and 2 Dec 1935, p. 195–209

the African areas, the two 'partners' having nothing in common socially, whilst Africans would continue in their status of political minors.

The amalgamationist cause received reinforcements when, in the middle of the 'thirties, Sir Ernest Oppenheimer became a convert to the cause of closer union, whilst Stanley himself came round in favour of outright fusion. Southern Rhodesia's record in the provision of services for Africans was an excellent one, an argument which the Colonial Office could not deny; South African leaders no longer opposed the idea of a united Central Africa; both Smuts and Oswald Pirow, a Nationalist Cabinet Minister, having assured Stanley that they would not object to such a policy, Smuts himself admitting that his former idea of incorporating Southern Rhodesia into the Union was a mistake. Southern Rhodesia—Stanley believed—developed faster under Responsible Government than before, and Salisbury would make a better job of running the North than London where British taxpayers displayed little interest in the lands beyond the Zambezi. In Downing Street itself opinion was divided; many officials were now beginning to be much more critical of white settlement in Central Africa than in the optimistic days before the Slump, some senior civil servants feeling convinced that Southern Rhodesians were merely out to get hold of the Copper Belt, a vital Imperial asset which, they thought, was no more dependent on white settlement than the mines of Ashanti or Nigeria. The 'West African' trend was strengthened by the now effective separation between Colonial Office and Dominion Office which to some extent helped to make Colonial servants think of Central Africa more in terms of a black country than of a white Dominion like New Zealand or South Africa.[1] But all the same, opinion still remained malleable, and some very senior officials were greatly impressed by Stanley's arguments in favour of a strong British bloc north of the Limpopo, whilst Ormsby-Gore was ready to consider Young's suggestions for a federal rather than a unitary solution. A meeting between the two Secretaries of State, attended also by senior officials from the Colonial and Dominion Offices thus agreed to re-open the whole question by means of a formal enquiry. Ormsby-Gore argued that co-operation between the three territories might be achieved by some sort of loose central authority which would assure co-operation with regard to economic matters, defence, and the judiciary, whilst certain technical departments might well be amalgamated, though the Imperial Government should retain control over native policy, native lands and labour, as well as the staff of the Colonial Service. Top-level discussions took place in 1937, when Moore, Huggins and Gore-Browne all visited London for the Coronation, and at Stanley's suggestion, yet another commission of enquiry departed for Central Africa, the Imperial Government having decided that closer links should be forged between the three territories, though amalgamation still remained out of the question, the

[1] The Dominions Office split off from the Colonial Office in 1925 to deal with the Dominions, which included Southern Rhodesia and the High Commission Territories of Bechuanaland, Basutoland and Swaziland in South Africa. In 1930 a separate Principal Secretary of State was appointed for the Dominions Office. The links between the two Offices at first remained close as the result of frequent interchange of personnel, but gradually weakened in the later 'thirties.

T

Imperial Parliament not being agreeable to any surrender of Imperial responsibilities in the field of native policy.

The new Commission was headed by Viscount Bledisloe, an expert in agricultural matters and a former Governor General of New Zealand, a shrewd administrator who once told an old Rhodesian that if he wished to be thoroughly misinformed about the position in any conceivable part of the world, he would always ask a man who had lived there himself for more than ten years! The Commission also comprised Thomas Fitzgerald, an ex-Postmaster General for the amalgamated services for Kenya, Uganda and Tanganyika, and Patrick Ashley Cooper, a Director of the Bank of England. In addition to these economic and administrative experts there were three political men: Ian Leslie Orr Ewing, Member for Weston-super-Mare, stood for Conservatism, and Ernest Evans, Liberal M.P. for the University of Wales and a distinguished King's Counsel, for the centre of the Parliamentary spectrum. William Henry Mainwaring, Member for East Rhondda, represented Labour, which was now beginning to take some interest in Central Africa, to which its attention was drawn by the Copper Belt Riots of 1935 (discussed later on in this book) and by the activities of an able group of intellectuals who read and wrote widely on colonial problems, and contributed to various left-wing publications, including a newly founded journal, known as *Empire*, which belied its name by fiercely attacking Imperialism.[1] As far as most of these young Socialists were concerned, all forms of colonial rule were bad; but there were degrees of iniquity; whilst Downing Street was content with seduction, Huggins stooped to rape, though both were equally lecherous,[2] the Central African settlers' cause now ceasing to be respectable in the eyes of Socialists and Radicals, who used to back Coghlan in the early 'twenties against the Chartered Company.

The Bledisloe Commission itself assembled a vast body of evidence which largely recapitulated former arguments for and against amalgamation. But there was one significant difference. Far more Africans now gave evidence, displaying a far greater political interest than ever existed in the past; a number of witnesses spoke in favour of amalgamation, though hardly along lines which would have greatly interested local Europeans; a Mkushi storekeeper thus considered that amalgamation would lead to uniformity of tax law, that Northern Rhodesians would no longer be regarded as foreigners south of the Zambezi, and that amalgamation would thus lead to the emergence of one African nation; many witnesses agreed that Southern Rhodesian Africans got better schooling and more pay, whilst the Lovale, who lived far from the Railway line, professed themselves

---

[1] *Empire* later became known as *Venture*, and became the organ of the Fabian Colonial Bureau. In their analysis of Empire, the Left was divided. There was widespread agreement with Lenin's thesis that imperialism represented the last stage of capitalism. But opinions differed as to the profitability of Imperialism. Some held that capitalists were making vast profits from their Empire and thus able to corrupt the metropolitan working classes with a small share of the loot. *Empire* on the other hand argued that far from being a source of riches, Imperial possessions did not in fact profit the Mother Country economically, the kind of argument with which 'Little Englanders' of an earlier period would have agreed.

[2] 'Huggins takes a trip', *Empire*, Sep 1939, p. 134–135

willing to accept amalgamation, provided they were not grouped into the same Province as the hated Barotse. The bulk of the African evidence, however, opposed the scheme. Many of the arguments against amalgamation rested on factual misconceptions, such as the belief that Southern Rhodesians put taxes on marriages, on collecting firewood, or even on children; whilst other witnesses adopted the sort of outlook that the known devil was better than the unknown saint! But some speakers presented a more cogent case: the Barotse, represented by a variegated group, including the Paramount, a teacher, a chauffeur, a judge and a policeman, stressed that chiefs were powerless south of the Zambezi, and that white pioneers came to the country as conquerors and occupied vast tracts of native land—the land question being of overwhelming importance to a community where even clerks, civil servants and artisans still retained a customary stake in tribal holdings. Other speakers emphasized the question of personal dignity, contending that the white man despised the black, and that Southern Rhodesians offended particularly badly in this respect. The African Civil Servants' Association at Lusaka, the best educated and also the most radical group of all, considered that chiefly rule should be preserved in Northern Rhodesia, and not done away with as in the south, adding that Southern Rhodesian pass laws and reserves policies should be rejected; they admitted that Northern Rhodesian schools were worse than those in the south, but concluded from this that there ought to be major reforms in Northern Rhodesia, where black men should get better houses, more money—and also the franchise. Africans at Choma location foresaw pessimistically that 'Our Heavenly Father and our Merciful King George of England are going to drop us in a great agony'; Salisbury should not rule the North, for the white man's country down south offered fewer opportunities to black traders and clerks, whilst imposing all sorts of undesirable taxes and pass-laws.[1] The question of the industrial colour bar then played a much less important part in the native testimony than the afore-mentioned problems, the colour bar being stressed more often by white speakers connected with management in the mining industry. Africans concentrated on questions connected with land, passes, taxes, chiefly rule, and legislation, pre-ferring the *status quo* to the allurements of the South. 'At present laws are made by the Bwanas' argued a clerk from Mkushi, 'but they have to be agreed to by the High Commissioner, [in fact the Imperial Government]. If we unite, the Bwanas will make their own laws and nobody will stop them'. No Africans as yet demanded home rule; they rather regarded the Imperial Power as a kind of rampart which ought to be preserved, a tribute to the District Commissioners' ability to impose their philosophy upon their black wards.

In Southern Rhodesia Africans also opposed amalgamation—but for exactly opposite reasons. The Southern Rhodesia Bantu Congress and the Bantu Community Association at Bulawayo feared that in the event of amalgamation, Southern Rhodesian Africans might be relegated to the backward North, thus

[1] Pass legislation was reinforced during this period in Southern Rhodesia by the Natives registration act, 1936.

echoing Huggins's theories of parallel development. They also stressed that
wages were higher in Southern Rhodesia than beyond the Zambezi. A further
delegation, led by the Rev. M. Tshiminya stated that they would rather accept
amalgamation with South Africa, where conditions were much better, whereas
fusion with the North would mean a reversion to barbarism,[1] a statement which
met with no publicity amongst Trusteeship advocates in the United Kingdom!
In the end the Bledisloe Commission produced an immensely learned, knowledgeable and informative report[2] which yet, in Gore-Browne's words, 'funked
the issue' on all essentials. The Commission demonstrated the need for co-operation between the three territories, and outlined the advantages which amalgamation might bring by effecting greater efficiency and economy in government.
Amalgamation was accepted as a good thing in principle but, the Commissioners
argued, immediate fusion of the three territories was undesirable, partly because
of existing differences in native policy, and partly because of the paucity of the
white population in the Northern territories. The investigators agreed that
Southern Rhodesia was providing more social services for Africans than the
Northern territories, but stressed the restrictive aspects of Southern Rhodesian
labour policies, designed to assure the 'rate for the job' to white artisans in
towns, and limiting opportunities for the employment of natives in clerical and
other subordinate posts in the central government service. The Commissioners
concluded that there should be a 'testing period' during which the Northern
Governments should expand their welfare services for Africans, whilst Southern
Rhodesia might as yet modify its native policies in the light of subsequent experiences. The Commissioners, at the same time, advised against federating the
three territories on the grounds that the wide disparity in constitutional and
economic development between the three countries would cause such an experiment to fail. They did, however, recommend the setting up of an Inter-Territorial Council which would examine and co-ordinate administrative services in
the three territories, as well as surveying the economic needs of the whole area,
and framing plans for future development. As far as the two Northern territories
were concerned, they advocated fusion under a single Government, provided
that a solution might be found to Nyasaland's pressing problem of railway debts.

These recommendations, not very courageous in themselves, were further
modified by conflicting notes which the Commissioners appended to their
document. Bledisloe and Ashley Cooper stressed Southern Rhodesia's remarkable progress since 1923 and the importance of establishing a solid British bloc in
Central Africa; they also wisely emphasized the need for caution with
regard to dogmatic pronouncements in official or semi-official publications to
the effect that large areas of territory were unsuited to human habitation or
economic utilization, such statements having frequently been falsified elsewhere
in the light of new discoveries and scientific achievements. They also agreed
with the Commission's main political representation, but welcomed the appoint-

[1] *Rhodesia herald*, 9 June 1938
[2] *Rhodesia—Nyasaland Royal commission report* (Cmd. 5949: 1939)

ment, at no distant date, of a single Governor for the three territories, or, alternatively, the appointment of the Governor of Southern Rhodesia for the Northern territories—Orr Ewing on the other hand considered amalgamation desirable but not inevitable, whereas Fitzgerald, a Colonial Office man to the core, felt that His Majesty's Government should not as yet commit itself to the principle of amalgamation, in view of the alleged failings of Southern Rhodesian native policies. Mainwaring, the Labour M.P., strongly opposed the idea of handing over the Africans of the Northern territories to the control of a white settler population, explaining away 'Southern Rhodesia's greater economic success' by pointing to the Territory's supposedly 'greater resources', an assertion which utterly ignored Northern Rhodesia's vastly greater wealth in minerals, and the fertility of the Luapula and Zambezi valleys. Evans rightly emphasized the need for a more active social policy in the North, whilst praising what he thought to be the 'comparatively happy and independent spirit of the Nyasaland natives', which he considered a tribute to missionary enterprise and colonial policy—factors which did not, however, stop Nyasalanders from emigrating in droves to seek the higher wages paid to them by white men in Bulawayo and Johannesburg.

In Northern Rhodesia itself, Sir John Alexander Maybin, the new Governor, a former Chief Secretary from Nigeria, subjected the report to a searching analysis. The Europeans were disappointed by the report, but there was no doubt that the natives were opposed to amalgamation, the officials having made no attempt to influence them either way in giving evidence. Maybin considered that the economic effects of amalgamation would almost certainly be beneficial, though he doubted whether the administrative economies resulting from unification would balance the loss of revenue from customs, income tax and the Colonial Development Fund. The main obstacle, however, lay in the sphere of native policy, the differences between the three territories being of such a kind that Maybin could not agree to the acceptance in principle of amalgamation as a future policy. If His Majesty's Government wanted amalgamation, they should only authorize it if native policies were harmonized between the three territories on acceptable lines. A future *rapprochement* of policy with Southern Rhodesia was not impossible, but Maybin disliked the 'Two Pyramid' policy on the grounds that the mines were excluded from the native areas, that it entailed an industrial colour bar, that the European areas depended on African labour, that natives ought to be allowed to rise in the Government service, and that Northern Rhodesia's policy of Indirect Rule should not be altered. Maybin elaborated these arguments in a letter to a friend in the Colonial Office. In labour matters the interests of both European employers and native labourers diverged from those of white workers who wanted 'equal pay for equal work'; existing differences in native policy, moreover, might well increase in time, as more Africans would rise in the Government service; 'vocational segregation' must be rejected, and Southern Rhodesia's policy of 'parallel development' would not prove a permanent solution. Amalgamation with Nyasaland was equally undesirable;

there existed no real economic links between the two Protectorates, one of which had an agricultural and the other a mining economy; trade between the two colonies was insignificant, whilst Northern Rhodesia would have to finance the lakeside Protectorate; Nyasaland moreover would be difficult to govern from Lusaka, whilst fusion was unlikely to result in any great administrative savings. Maybin finally produced a scathing indictment of the project of an Inter-Territorial Council: the new body, with its boards would lead to further expense and administrative elaboration, whereas the Government should aim at simplification; the suggested Boards would encroach on the time of senior officials who could use their working hours to better effect; apart from that Maybin thought that the system would create a new vested interest making a future reversion to the present system impossible, that it would prove a step towards amalgamation, and that the Official element of the Northern territories would be placed in a minority, thus endangering their present native policies. In England itself the report gave rise to some sharp political controversy. On the pro-settler side Lord Bledisloe argued in the House of Lords that Southern Rhodesians were showing a real desire to develop the country and to improve the health and education of Africans, whilst stressing the inadequacy of Northern Rhodesia's development. Baron Lugard of Abinger, Britain's greatest exponent of 'Indirect Rule' and the foremost exponent of the 'West Coast' pattern of development admitted some of Bledisloe's contentions, but on the other hand stressed Southern Rhodesia's colour bar, and argued that the growth of education promoted in the South would itself lead to further discontent. Perhaps the strongest argument in favour of amalgamation was the prospect that it might commit Southern Rhodesia to a 'northern' rather than a 'southern' kind of economic development, but this object might be attained more easily by looser economic ties, without political union, all the more so since the southern mineral industry depended largely on northern labour.[1] Lugard's arguments found a wide echo in the academic sphere; and Miss Margery Perham, then a Fellow of St Hugh's College and already one of the country's ablest Africanists, thoroughly identified herself with the Baron's views; amalgamation, she wrote to *The Times*, ought to be rejected, for it would prevent genuine self government, and entrench a white minority; amalgamation moreover was incompatible with the Trusteeship principle which in her view constituted the only moral justification on which a large empire could depend,[2] a view as unacceptable to British settlers in Southern Rhodesia, as to earlier colonists faced with backward tribesmen in New Zealand and North America. Margery Perham's views were shared by many other academic luminaries like Professor Arthur Berriedale Keith, a great Sanscrit scholar and an expert in the constitution of the Empire, and Professor Eric Anderson Walker, an outstanding specialist on South African history,[3]

[1] *House of Lords debates*, 31 July 1939, p. 683–731
[2] Letter in *The Times*, 29 July 1939
[3] Keith wrote against amalgamation in a letter to the *Manchester guardian*: 9 Aug 1941, and Walker expressed similar views in *The Times*, 12 Aug 1941

academic opposition to the settler itself becoming a factor of considerable long-term significance in the shaping of public opinion overseas.

In 1939 Huggins again came to London to discuss the amalgamation issue. But he was now dealing with a new Colonial Secretary who stood a little more to the 'left' than his predecessor, Ormsby-Gore (now Baron Harlech) who once served as Parliamentary Private Secretary to Lord Milner, and sympathized with the older school of South African Imperialists. He was succeeded as Colonial Secretary in 1938 by Malcolm Macdonald, a former Labour M.P. who went over to the National Government in 1931. Macdonald took a somewhat stronger line with Huggins, arguing that the Copper Belt should not be regarded purely as a white area, that Africans should be allowed to rise to the highest positions in the European zones, that they might perhaps have to be employed as engine drivers, and that the Africans would not necessarily content themselves with being outvoted for all time by a European majority in the Legislature. Macdonald would not commit himself to amalgamation, but thought that there would be much value in sending an independent expert to Central Africa in order to carry out a comparative survey of native policies. This idea was taken up later on, when Lord Hailey, Britain's greatest Africanist, left for Rhodesia: but for the time being His Majesty's Government found itself faced with problems of infinitely greater magnitude. In September 1939 German Panzer divisions clattered across the Polish border; Britain and France declared war upon Hitler's Reich, and the little matter of Central African amalgamation was shelved for the future.

III

The battle for 'Legco' control

Amalgamation formed one major feature in the country's political struggle—control of the Legislature stood out as the other, the 'thirties witnessing a considerable hardening of political fronts. The economic crisis made a deep impression on the white settlers, some of whom became the first in the Territory to criticize both the ideology of Empire and of the prevailing economic system. The *Livingstone Mail* now ran long articles condemning Imperialism, and right through the later 'thirties Moore reprinted lengthy articles from the *New Statesman and Nation*[1] and other left-wing publications from overseas, which thus made their first local appearance through a settler newspaper, their views gradually percolating down to such literate Africans as managed to buy the *Livingstone Mail* and the local *Hansard*. Moore began to call himself a Socialist, and though his views hardly coincided with those of orthodox Labour men overseas, he did begin to echo most of the anti-Imperialist theories widely

[1] Moore reprinted *New Statesman* articles until 1941 when the *Statesman* embarked on a campaign of bitter criticism against white settlers over the amalgamation issue.

current at the time: Northern Rhodesia, he now argued, was nothing but a milch cow of Empire; the cost of copper at the point of exit from Northern Rhodesia only stood at £17. o. o. a ton which was all that the Protectorate got out of its resources. The vast additional profits made by the magnates were spent overseas,[1] and the Territory was being grossly exploited by the British upper classes, an utterly self-centred lot who looked at the rest of the world through lorgnettes whilst politely suppressing their inclination to sniff![2] So much did Moore despair of the Capitalist system that the struggling shopkeeper even defended Hitler in 1933, arguing that the German dictator's only fault lay in his strident nationalism and hatred of the Jews.[3] But Moore soon changed his tune and stoutly condemned what he called totalitarian gangsterism, becoming convinced that Fascism was nothing but finance capital on the war-path against the workers. Moore's loathing of Nazism and British conservatism derived further heat from German colonial claims, and from what Moore regarded as British weakness in resisting Nazi pretensions in Europe and Africa alike; his habitual anticlericalism also fitted in well with these ideas, the Member for Livingstone remaining convinced that Christianity was nothing but an outworn creed, now serving to shore up an equally degenerate Imperialism, which hypocritically masqueraded as Trusteeship—the kind of thought as yet quite alien to mission-trained Africans who derived all their education from white clergymen.

These ideas also affected the settlers' outlook on native policy. Moore, like many others, came round to the idea that a white skin did not denote biological superiority, arguing that tribal barbarism in Scotland was no better than the system prevailing amongst the Bantu today,[4] and criticizing Pirow for saying that whites must remain supreme for all time just because they were white.[5] The natives of Africa, he believed, were as much enslaved in principle as the natives of Europe a hundred years ago; Africa must assert her independence as against Europe—like Russia and Japan before—white Africans being the only ones with enough brains and energy to permit of a general scheme of economic emancipation being carried out.[6] The Bantu, as far as Moore was concerned, were still a 'patient, willing, good-tempered, obedient' lot, who were being kept down, and needed more opportunities.[7] The colonists thus saw nothing inconsistent in both demanding more political power for themselves and at the same time championing African claims, their assumption being that white and black alike were being exploited from overseas. The new outlook[8] of course did not prevent Europeans from defending their *immediate* economic interests when these came under fire; white artisans continued to demand protection against under-

---

[1] *Livingstone mail*, 4 Apr 1934   [2] *Livingstone mail*, 28 Feb 1934
[3] *Livingstone mail*, 17 May 1933   [4] *Livingstone mail*, 13 Jan 1937
[5] *Livingstone mail*, 26 May 1937   [6] *Livingstone mail*, 2 Nov 1932   [7] *Livingstone mail*, 7 July 1937
[8] 'One never hears the old time South African "wallop your own nigger" creed nowadays', wrote Mrs Ethel Tawse Jollie, Southern Rhodesia's first woman M.P., in 1931. Mrs Jollie was probably exaggerating somewhat, but Dr Jesse Jones, the American Liberal, drew unanimous applause at Livingstone, when he demanded not 'equality of race', but 'equality of opportunity' for white and black alike, likening the racial set-up to white and black piano keys which gave the best music when both were struck. See *Livingstone mail*, 26 May and 28 Oct 1931.

cutting from blacks and white immigrants alike, whereas farmers viewed an undue expansion of maize production with fear, no matter who caused it. But as far as broader issues of a kind not likely to harm their constituents were concerned, Elected Members demanded many reforms on the Africans' behalf. Moore and Knight thus called on the Government to encourage cotton growing in Barotseland,[1] the Unofficials reiterating the demand that native reserves ought to be improved by dips, dams and boreholes. Government fiscal policy came under severe criticism from Elected Members who now thought that Africans were being grossly over-taxed, Moore suggesting that native taxation ought to be abolished altogether.[2] Moore also thought that beer was being sold to Africans at too high a price, and strongly attacked the municipal beer halls' monopoly in the native compounds, bitterly disagreeing with the whole principle that native amenities should be financed from their profits.[3] There was also some concern with civil liberties, and when native rioters were fired on during a riot on the Copper Belt in 1935, the *Livingstone Mail* thundered forth against the Government's detestable 'might is right' philosophy, whereas the Mayor of Ndola demanded a full scale enquiry into native tax policies.[4]

Elected Members also sharply clashed with Government on the Eurafrican question. Thomas Spurgeon Page—a prominent Unofficial—thus strongly pressed for separate schools for Coloured children, who were growing up in native villages as unwanted 'Ishmaes'l', rejected by their fathers and neglected by their mothers' people.[5] Page was only echoing the former views expressed by the Advisory Board of Native Education at Livingstone in July 1927 which demanded the provision of separate education for coloured children, but met with strong official opposition. Maxwell argued that a separate school system for Coloureds would create an artificial class, which would be regarded as neither white nor black, and would look to Government for jobs, the Governor considering that the Coloureds' unwillingness to return to native life constituted no reason for their preferential treatment. Maxwell's view met with support from the Advisory Committee on Native Education at the Colonial Office, where Oldham expressed himself opposed to the provision of separate schools for half-caste children, whereas A. G. Fraser, Principal of Achimota, thought that the half-castes should identify themselves with the Africans and become their natural leaders. The settlers' view was more in accordance with reality. In the past, Page pointed out in 1939, Coloured children of white fathers were re-absorbed in the villages as natives; but now there were people of mixed blood who lived like Europeans, owned lands and stores, and paid the non-native taxes, one of them even having won the first prize in the Southern Rhodesian State Lottery; these people were trying to advance Coloured folk who were still

[1] Northern Rhodesia. *Legislative Council debates*, 10 May 1935, p. 290–298
[2] Northern Rhodesia. *Legislative Council debates*, 14 Oct 1936, p. 90–91, and 3 Dec 1934, p. 40–57
[3] Northern Rhodesia. *Legislative Council debates*, 1 Dec 1933, p. 662–667
[4] *Livingstone mail*, 5 and 12 June 1935
[5] Northern Rhodesia. *Legislative Council debates*, 27 May 1938, p. 141. There were then about 400 Coloureds in Northern Rhodesia.

living in the villages like Africans, their efforts helping to prevent the absorption of Coloureds into native life, which was further impeded by the natives' own dislike of half-caste children. Page believed that the presence of mulattoes in the village was incompatible with the idea of Indirect Rule, the Coloureds being liable to become a prey to agitators unless they received proper schooling. The Elected Members accordingly put forward a motion, demanding the appointment of a Committee on Coloured Education, which was accepted by Government,[1] Coloured Education having been included within the scope of the European Education Department in 1938.

Regarding themselves with all sincerity as spokesmen of all the people against Government, the Elected Members pressed on with their campaign for an increased say on the Legislature. Under Maxwell they met with no success, their efforts being further impeded by electoral apathy amongst their supporters. Maxwell's successor, Sir Ronald Storrs, a handsome and gifted intellectual, perhaps the best prose writer amongst Rhodesian Governors,[2] made himself very popular in the country, but Storrs did not stay long enough to affect policy, being invalided out of the Tropics in 1934. Storr's successor, Young, embarked on a new course which vastly added to the Unofficials' status. 'I regard Hon. Elected Members as the permanent element in such a Council as this', he explained to a delighted House soon after attaining office. 'Individually they may change, but as a corporate body they represent those who intend to spend the whole of their lives in the Territory. They represent permanent local interests in a way that no official can claim to do . . . I look to Hon. Elected Members'—he continued—'for advice upon all local matters, not only upon matters affecting their own community, but also on questions affecting that larger and less articulate community of native Africans upon whose co-operation . . . depends their own prosperity', a remarkable admission which for the first time recognized the Unofficials' claim to a share in determining native policy. The Elected Members, he added, should be consulted not just on the way policy was being applied, but also on its original formulation.[3] At the same time Young strongly criticized more recent trends in Colonial Office thought, and bitterly complained in a private letter to a senior civil servant in 1935 that Cadets were coming out to the country who had apparently never heard of white settlement there, who knew all about 'native paramountcy', but nothing of the subsequent modification of this doctrine, and got their inadequate notions from 'a Professor Copeland' [Reginald Coupland, Beit Professor of Colonial History at the University at Oxford] who lectured to them before coming out to Africa.

Moore of course, with accustomed surliness, would do nothing to make the Governor's task easier, and even Gore-Browne, an ex-Woolwich man like

[1] Northern Rhodesia. *Legislative Council debates*, 3 June 1939, p. 330, 396
[2] His book *Orientations*, Readers Union ltd, by arrangement with Ivor Nicholson and Watson, 1939, deals with his earlier career in Cyprus, Palestine and the Near East; it only mentions Northern Rhodesia in so far as to explain that he found the social protocol of a country intolerable where the only native whom a white man could shake by the hand was the Barotse Paramount.
[3] Northern Rhodesia. *Legislative Council debates*, 1 Dec 1934, p. 3

Young himself, thought that toughness would pay. Having received no satisfaction on the amalgamation issue, the Elected Members in 1936 threatened to resign collectively on the ground that they could see no hope of further constitutional advance, their minimum demand amounting to parity on the Legislative Council. Young persuaded the Unofficials to reconsider their decision, and strongly advised the Secretary of State to give in to the request for equality on the Legislative Council, a concession which he thought would not effectively increase their power, though it might allay the discontent over the amalgamation decision. In 1937 further constitutional discussions took place in London, the settlers' case being put by Moore and Gore-Browne. The Unofficials now asked for an Executive Council, consisting of the Governor, four Officials and four Unofficials, one of whom was to be chosen by the Governor from the Elected Members' ranks for the purpose of representing native interests. The Europeans also reiterated their demand for parity on the Legislative Council, asking that the Governor should only exercize his casting vote on certain reserved subjects, whilst Officials should be allowed to vote according to their conscience, except on specified matters of major importance. As far as native policy was concerned, the Elected Members favoured a scheme of 'parallel development' which would enable Africans to build up representative institutions, though whites and blacks should never meet in the same Council. The irrepressible Moore immediately published this highly confidential interview in the *Livingstone Mail*, but Young was not deterred, and for the first time the Legislative Council became something more than a high-level debating society. Bills were now circulated well before each session, so that Members might study them in advance; arrangements were made for informal discussions between the Governor, Elected Members and Senior Officials: these became known as 'Huberts' and provided a more fruitful means of exchanging views than the formalized debates in the Council. Elected Members were represented on the Finance Committee, and Young endeavoured that they should put forward as many motions as possible, so as to associate them more closely with the work of administering the country. In the Legislative Council itself, Young agreed to act as Speaker rather than as Governor, except in the Committee stage, and always tried to avoid confronting Unofficials with decisions on which they had not been previously consulted, even agreeing to withdraw a controversial bill which met with united Unofficial opposition.

As far as Parliamentary representation was concerned, Ormsby-Gore was persuaded to accede to the Unofficials' main demand. He stressed of course that no changes should be made without safeguarding Africans, and that the interests of the copper industry must be protected. But within these limits, he agreed to the demand for parity which was attained by eliminating one Official, and appointing an extra nominated Unofficial Member to represent native interests, as was suggested by the Unofficials. The new regime came into force in 1938 when further elections were held. The Unofficial Members now comprised seven Elected Representatives, including Welensky, who was returned for Broken

Hill; whilst Gore-Browne accepted appointment as Member for Native Interests, a congenial task for a man who, at heart, did not like the hustle and bustle of electioneering in a white mining constituency. The Colonel now found himself in a key position. He deservedly took much of the credit for the new constitutional changes, which he thought gave the settlers all they could reasonably ask for at present; the Elected Members respected him for his experience, his knowledge of the world, and his London connexions; and apart from that, they needed his vote to attain parity with the Officials. Young himself promised that he would never give his casting vote against a combined front of all Unofficials before first referring the matter to the Secretary of State; in fact, this issue did not arise, as the Major and the Colonel respected each other, and got on extremely well. In 1939 Gore-Browne's hand was further strengthened when Moore resigned in protest against the Bledisloe Report without even consulting his colleagues, and though Moore was re-elected, he lost his position as Senior Member, his fellow Members—now thoroughly tired of his erratic behaviour— deciding that Gore-Browne should become Senior Member and also Chairman of the Unofficial Members' Committee.[1] Welensky himself was converted for a short period to Gore-Browne's view on the need to partition Northern Rhodesia, and remained a loyal supporter of the Colonel's, whilst at the same time representing the cause of white labour with infinitely greater effect than a back-veld housewife like Mrs Olds managed in the past. As far as general strategy was concerned, Welensky continued to advocate a coalition of all Elected Members for the purpose of bringing about amalgamation, his determination not to 'split' the Unofficials making him oppose for the time being the formation of a separate Labour Party.

[1] This was an informal organization which in 1945 was replaced by a more formal body, known as the Unofficial Members' Organization.

Chapter Nine

African life in the 'thirties

I

The rural scene

Politicians might debate and Commissioners recommend, but the overwhelming majority of Africans remained as yet little aware of these issues, their life being bound up with the village and the land, where change took a long time to become effective. But some changes there were. In the late 'twenties already European witnesses explained to the Railway Belt Reserves Commission that tribesmen near the markets of Broken Hill were growing more maize and less sorghum than Africans further to the north, and that some cultivators were using a crop rotation of monkey-nuts, maize and *nyouti*: isolated groups, such as Swahili-speaking settlers under their headman Chiwala near Ndola, descendants of slave traders, were employing greatly improved methods to grow food for Bwana Mkubwa mine, the Swahili pioneers being imitated by some local Lamba people. Tonga cultivators by the line of rail were learning from white farmers, and buying sledges, ploughs and oxen, their surplus being traded to European merchants. This changeover to a partial cash economy began to affect Tonga social institutions, explained an observant District Officer: in the old days land was held by the clan-head who acted as trustee for his people as well as a kind of High Priest, each clan possessing a treasured rain shrine of its own. But now the traditional system was said to fall into disuse by the railway line; in Kateya's village for instance the community was run by a stranger from Mwanza, and, if a man wanted land, he went to Kateya without even bothering to consult the clan-head, youngsters often having no idea on whose soil they were planting their mealies, and remembering little of the traditional ways. In Muyereka's country, wrote another official, Africans were growing food exclusively on alluvial soils along the Luangwa and its tributaries where land was fertile and could be cultivated year after year, the local peasants alternating kaffir-corn, maize and beans, the stalks of kaffir-corn being burnt on the gardens, whilst the bean leaves were dug in after the harvest; under these conditions the communal system of tenure was stated to have disappeared; gardens were laid out in strips going right down to the river, each peasant working his land for life, being succeeded on his death by his eldest son, who was, however, still obliged to look after his brother and could not sell his plot to strangers. Even in the far north life was changing. Mambwe cultivators near Abercorn for instance were now using a fairly stable system of mound-cultivation, well adapted to the conditions of a treeless country, though other sections of the same people adhered to the traditional ways of tree-lopping and burning. On Chilubi Island on Lake Bangweulu the local cultivators worked out a reasonably permanent system of crop rotation; Bemba villages around bomas like Kasama were said to have remained practically stationary for the last fifteen years, individual rights of cultivation being handed down to the next generation, though village land could never be bought or sold, Northern Rhodesia as a whole as yet lacked any legal provisions for individual African tenure in the Reserves, such as existed in the 'Native Purchase Areas' of the more progressive sister colony south of the Zambezi.

In some areas fishing also became a more valuable subsidiary occupation. In 1930 the Secretary for Native Affairs investigated the position and found that the industry could still greatly expand, for fish were abundant in streams and rivers. Men and women alike took part in the industry which was carried on in a variety of ways, by stationary and floating nets, by rod and line, by poison, fish-weirs and traps. On Lakes Tanganyika and Mweru fishermen used to take out nets with floats and sinkers by canoe, sometimes even working late at night with the help of flares, the demand having gone up so much in recent years that fish was now regarded as a commodity for sale. The industry was even more important on Lake Bangweulu and along the Luapula, where work was done at the instigation of store-keepers and capitaos who bought fish from local villagers. A Belgian firm maintained several depots in the swamps, the catching and drying of fish being left to Africans who traded grass parcels of ten to twelve fish for a shilling, their merchandize then being taken by lorry to Kabunda and Sakania, and then by train to Elizabethville. On the Kafue, near the railway bridge, a whole fishing village grew up, composed of Barotse, Nyasalanders and Africans from North-Eastern Rhodesia, who supplied fish for local Europeans, and also for sale as far as Ndola. Black settlers from Nyasaland also managed to make a living in the Lukanga swamps, some sixty miles from Broken Hill, from where they sold their catches to people on the mines, whilst the Barotse carried on their traditional fishing industry, despite the fact that former exports to Wankie were disrupted by Southern Rhodesian import duties.[1]

Trade in grain, fish and a few other primary products like beeswax and tobacco depended on the work of merchants whose work was now slowly being supplemented by native store-keepers and hawkers, many of them pioneers from Nyasaland, 'black Scotsmen' from the East, who came to seek their fortunes in Northern Rhodesia. The emergence of a village bourgeoisie was of course an extremely slow affair, and hardly seems to have got under way before the middle of the 'thirties. African barter is of course of ancient origin; the village was probably never fully self-sufficient; and a people like the plateau Tonga are known to have traded goods as varied as salt, hoes, spears, iron brace-

---

[1] *Livingstone mail*, 5 Nov 1930. Moffat Thomson, Secretary for Native Affairs, thought that about 1500 tons at least were being traded to Katanga and for local consumption, prices varying between 1d and 3d per pound, which was being paid to Africans.

lets as well as slaves, and agricultural commodities like fish, goats, game meat, poultry, as well as other kinds of merchandize, to neighbouring tribes, receiving slaves, guns, beads, cloth, iron ore and other imports in exchange. Later on, however, European and Indian traders successfully competed with the indigenous barter trade, buying up indigenous products and supplying at reasonable terms all the items formerly traded, or providing a substitute—often at better quality, except a few commodities like red ochre, spear shafts and such like, whilst the Government crushed the traffic in slaves. The most enterprising Tonga often looked for employment abroad, or took to farming, indigenous trade remaining of little importance.[1] In the late 'thirties, however, the recovery of the copper industry created new opportunities for exchange; townsmen became willing to pay good prices for poultry and fish, whilst game was becoming scarce, so that black traders found some scope for their enterprise. The Lovale also proved keen businessmen, having been used to commerce since the olden days of incursions from Angola; and traders exported their local cassava to Barotseland in exchange for beef; Angola and later the Copper Belt also providing various opportunities for Lovale enterprise.[2] But by and large these pioneer merchants still worked under numerous disadvantages. Capital was hard to get; markets poor; whilst the Africans' poverty prevented them from getting goods at wholesale prices like their competitors, a further obstacle to their prosperity being the scarcity of coins of low denomination.

Apart from that, recognized dealers had to meet heavy charges in rents and taxes; rents for a plot in the reserves amounting to £3. 0. 0. per annum, whilst a plot in a rural area outside a reserve required twice as much. In addition harried traders required a general dealer's licence which, up to 1935, cost them £7. 10. 0., the charge being subsequently reduced to £2. 10. 0. for people opening a store in their own village, the same sum being required as an annual payment from hawkers.[3] When it is borne in mind that a trader's annual profits rarely exceed £27. 0. 0., these expenses obviously weighed heavily on small men, so that a large percentage of hawkers had to eke out their living by working for Indian firms. Nevertheless, some enterprising folk amassed a little money by working down the mines, and then invested their savings in bicycles, which could carry goods of relatively high value; others got credit from Europeans or Indians, and others again bought secondhand sewing machines and started making up garments for sale in their huts.[4] A success story of this kind was the career of

[1] Miracle, M. P. 'Plateau Tonga entrepreneurs in historical inter-regional trade' (in *Rhodes-Livingstone journal*, no. 26, Dec 1959, p. 34–50)

[2] White, C. M. N. 'A preliminary survey of Luvale rural economy' (in *Rhodes-Livingstone papers*, no. 23, 1959, p. 37–42)

[3] Northern Rhodesia. *Legislative Council debates*, 18 Nov 1935, p. 43–50. The charge was reduced by the Trades licensing (amendment) ordinance, 1935, which amended previous legislation by discriminating against Europeans who still had to pay the older rate, whereas African traders who traded in their own village now paid at the reduced rate.

[4] The history of African village trade still remains to be written and estimates of its exact development are difficult to make, as side by side with the licenced trader and hawkers, there were also unlicenced men. In 1934, 3313 hawkers' licences were issued, and there were 49 stores owned by Africans

Saulosi Dimba, an African economic pioneer from Mazabuka District, who used to work as a little boy on a European farm. After the First World War Dimba became a waiter, but soon went back to farming, where he rose from the lowly job of leading oxen to the more responsible task of driving a span. Having looked after his master's wagon for some time, Dimba was fired with the idea of becoming an employer, like his white boss, who agreed to help him with farm implements to make a start; he threw all his energy into his new enterprise, and having amassed some capital from the sale of maize, he decided to buy a wagon to trade in the Mazabuka area. He again discussed the idea with his former employer who sold him his old wagon, which soon set Dimba up on the road to a modest fortune. Africans and Europeans came along to have their wares carried, and—acting on his old employer's advice—Dimba got a hawker's licence. He then began to buy soft goods from the Mazabuka stores, loaded them on to his vehicle, and took them to villagers further afield, taking in return for his merchandize not money but maize, which he sold at a profit along the line of rail. By 1937 Dimba felt that he had enough capital to put up a store of his own, and in time added a second and a third shop to his original enterprise.[1]

Government at first paid little attention to this emergent African bourgeoisie, but from the late 'thirties began to take a more active interest. In 1937 the Markets Ordinance was put on the Statute Book for the purpose of encouraging trade by reducing overheads and thus lowering prices. The new legislation aimed both at controlling existing markets in municipalities, where itinerant traders were offering their wares to African workers, and also to get Native Authorities to set up producers' markets where buyers (not sellers) would set up stalls to acquire mealies and cattle from the local villagers, all purchases in native markets having to be paid for in cash.

These advances, however, remained isolated and the Northern Rhodesian countryside as a whole continued poverty-stricken, backward and riddled with disease. The uneven character of rural development was influenced by many different factors. Lacking the two 'C's' of communications and capital, African villagers found themselves beset by exactly the same difficulties as white pioneers in the past, African farmers along the railway line facing the additional problem of generally being further away from the railway sidings than their white neighbours. The villages as a whole remained rural reservoirs of poorly-paid, unskilled labour, serving both the Copper Belt and Southern Rhodesia, the

but these figures can only serve as a rough guide. The assumption that African trade began to increase from the middle of the 'thirties seems confirmed by a correspondent in the *Livingstone mail* of 13 Oct 1937, who complained that native hawkers and storekeepers had become prominent in the villages since 1935 and were doing harm to established traders, a complaint which echoes earlier complaints by white traders against 'low white' hawkers. A detailed analysis of 'native domestic exports' for the years 1932 to 1936 is provided in *Report of the commission appointed to enquire into the financial and economical position of Northern Rhodesia.* 1938 (Colonial no. 145), appx. 11B, p. 351

[1] Mbasela, A. 'He copied his employer' (Reprinted from *Nshila* in *Success in Northern Rhodesia.* Lusaka, Northern Rhodesia information department, 1960)

position being further complicated by the uneven impact of labour migration on the different tribes, leaving some areas with far fewer fit menfolk than others.[1]

Agricultural methods moreover remained backward. Only about one tenth of the African population kept cattle, the beasts being distributed in a very uneven fashion, the vast majority of tribesmen finding themselves unable to buy stock by reason of the dreaded 'fly', or the lack of good pastoral land, or of money to buy animals. Cattle being so scarce, the use of stock manure did not apparently enter into any of the country's traditional systems, except in Barotseland; and even where Agricultural Officers patiently taught African farmers in the Pemba-Monze areas how to clean out their kraals and put the manure on the land, they found that the quantity available proved inadequate for large areas. In some areas the position in fact was getting worse rather than better, and as the population increased, the soil was allowed too little time to recuperate, with serious consequences to the villagers' diet. More rapid degeneration, coupled with a frightening destruction of land, took place on the Railway line, where the inexpert use of the plough became a major threat to the land. An agricultural expert pessimistically describing the position a little later, in 1945, concluded that labour migration formed the chief cause of general decay, further reasons for dangerous congestions of people being found in historical factors, such as the great Angoni 'bulge' near Fort Jameson, the concentration of tribesmen into reserves; African immigration from outside the territory—as in Lundazi and other parts of the Eastern province, the natural increase of the population which caused the carrying capacity of traditional systems to be exceeded, and voluntary migrations of black people towards the mines and the railway line. Admittedly, the writer added, labour migration removed the fear of starvation from the minds of able-bodied villagers, and the average income of an African family in Northern Rhodesia and Nigeria remained much the same, despite the latter country's incomparably greater rural development. But in Northern Rhodesia by far the greater part of this income was both earned and spent in the towns.[2]

Government of course was only too anxious to help, but sound and practicable advice for long remained an extremely scarce commodity in a country whose natural resources were so little known. Maxwell fortunately showed some real understanding of these difficulties, and just before the Slump burst on the country, the Administration agreed to an ecological survey to investigate the country's potential for European and African agriculture, this imaginative project forming a major pioneering effort, and the first of its kind in Africa.

[1] In 1936 53,462 Africans were stated to be employed inside Northern Rhodesia and 51,212 outside. Of the emigrants 34,212 went to Southern Rhodesia, some 15,000 went to Tanganyika and about 1,000 each to the Rand and the Congo. The percentage of adult men leaving their villages was 40–70 per cent from Mporokoso in the Northern Province, 60 per cent from Sesheke, 50–60 per cent from the Fort Jameson District in the Eastern Province, and 45 per cent from the Mumbwa District then in the Southern Province. The areas least affected were Namwala and Livingstone Districts with 5 per cent each, Mwinilunga and Broken Hill with 10 per cent and Balovale with 17 per cent. See *Report of the commission . . .* 1938, (Colonial no. 145), *op. cit.*, p. 36

[2] Allan, W. 'African land usage' (in *Rhodes-Livingstone journal*, no. 3, June 1945, p. 13–20). For details of soil erosion in the 'thirties see *Report of the commission . . .* 1938, (Colonial no. 145), *op. cit.*

u

'N.R.G.' moreover showed sound sense in the men whom it chose to carry out this work: Colin Graham Trapnell, an ex 'Arts' man from Oxford with a wonderful bent towards botany, a man completely absorbed in his work, with great powers of observation and a vast verbal memory, turned out to be perhaps one of the ablest civil servants ever to have drawn a salary from the Protectorate Government. John Neil Clothier, an able agricultural expert with a natural gift for getting the best out of African farmers, collaborated in much of this work, the engagement of a soil scientist to complete the trio being prevented unfortunately by the disastrous impact of the Slump. The survey amassed much information on the country's ecology and indigenous African systems, which for the first time permitted planners to work on a sound basis.[1] In addition valuable, though still somewhat isolated work was done by Agricultural Officers, an important step forward being the opening in 1936 of a station at Pemba, just within the Railway Reserve, and at Lunzuwa in the Abercorn District, where trained men investigated indigenous systems of cultivation, and taught better methods.

II

Administration in the countryside

The Northern Rhodesia Government's somewhat ineffective attempts to build up the African economy found a parallel in the administrative sphere through efforts to extend the system of Indirect Rule through recognized Native Authorities. Whereas Southern Rhodesians continued to govern Africans directly, through Native Commissioners who generally regarded the Colony as 'home', Downing Street orthodoxy now favoured Indirect Rule as the most practicable way of running African dependencies under the supervision of expatriate European officers, who regularly took their leave in Britain. Overseas opinion indeed now went further, holding that Indirect Rule possessed great intrinsic merits of its own, that the system would preserve all that was best in traditional institutions, whilst enabling Africans gradually to learn the arts of civilization, blending the old with the new without compelling black men to discard inherited ways prematurely, the colonial administrators assuming that they had almost unlimited time at their disposal for the purpose of slowly changing the accustomed ways. The theory and practice of Indirect Rule produced a new literature and mystique, much importance being attached to the

[1] See Trapnell, C. G., and Clothier, J. N. *The soils, vegetation and agricultural systems of North Western Rhodesia: report of the ecological survey.* Lusaka, Government printer, 1937; also Trapnell, C. G. *Interim report on methods of extraction of Landolphia rubber.* Lusaka, Government printer, 1942; Trapnell, C. G. *The soils, vegetation and agriculture of North Eastern Rhodesia: report of the ecological survey.* Lusaka, Government printer, 1943; Allan, W. and others. *Land holding and land usage among the plateau Tonga of Mazabuka district: a reconnaissance survey, 1945.* Cape Town, Oxford university press for the Rhodes-Livingstone Institute, 1948

researches promoted by the International Institute of African Languages and Cultures, headed by Baron Lugard of Abinger who once fought Muslim slavers in Nyasaland, a staunch Conservative who was now recognized as one of Britain's greatest African pro-consuls as well as the most outstanding advocate of Indirect Rule.[1] Government through chiefs was of course familiar enough to old-timers from Chartered Company days, who also used to make extensive use of important local men, but often regarded their approach as a matter of convenience and interpreted native customs in a manner very different from those usual in the 'thirties.[2] But now problems of Government were changing; law and order was secure, and District Commissioners had to shoulder a variety of new tasks. If African chiefs were to become effective and permanent auxiliaries of government, they required more strictly defined powers as well as a greater say in monetary matters. In 1933 the majority of Provincial Commissioners agreed that chiefs should have more financial responsibilities; and the only question at issue was how much power they ought to get, the Colonial Office favouring extensive devolution of authority on the lines of Tanganyika Territory, which was being administered as a Mandate under the League of Nations. Downing Street argued that the Native Authorities ought themselves to be entrusted with the collection of the native tax which would enhance their importance in Africans' lives and also provide 'the most valuable part of their education in administration and financial responsibility', the Tanganyika system strangely being stated to be best fitted to deal with the problems arising from industrialization and the decay of tribal customs. The Provincial Commissioners displayed greater caution, arguing that Northern Rhodesia should rather follow along the lines of Nyasaland which allowed chiefs to collect money for local Native Treasuries alone, the only dissentient voice being the P.C. for Barotseland, who was familiar with a more elaborate system of indigenous government. In 1936 the new policy found expression in a series of important ordinances,[3] which permitted Native Treasuries to be set up, though Native Authorities were not as yet entrusted with the collection of the general tax, a sharp distinction being drawn between Government and Native Authorities' revenue. Native Authorities could raise a small income from Court fees and fines, bicycle, dog, arms and game licences; in addition Government agreed to pay to the various Treasuries ten per cent of the native tax collected either inside or outside the district, from Africans belonging to the tribe. At the same time legislation concerned with Native Courts was further elaborated by an Ordinance passed in 1936. Native Courts wielded a wide authority in civil and criminal juris-

[1] See Perham, M. *Lugard: the years of adventure 1858–1898*. Collins, 1956; and *Lugard: the years of authority 1898–1945*. Collins, 1960

[2] The author was thus told by a pioneer official who helped to establish administration amongst the Lovale that the Lovale matrilineal institutions arose from the tribesmen's immorality, extramarital intercourse being practised on such a scale that the women did not know their children's fathers, with the result that descent was traced through the mother's line! A complex state machinery like the Barotses' on the other hand was held in much higher regard.

[3] Native courts ordinance, 1936, and Native authorities ordinance, 1936

diction in African cases, the courts being graded according to their importance. In addition the Protectorate legislation provided for a whole chain of appeals from Native Courts to Native Appeal Courts, and then to District Commissioners and to the High Court, whilst district officers retained wide powers of review over the decisions of Native Courts. Native Courts were soon regarded as the most successful venture into Indirect Rule, giving Africans a chance to be tried in a manner which they understood, by people who knew the ways of the village.

In defending its policy in the Legislative Council, the Administration argued that Indirect Rule would save both money and work, that it would help Africans to build up their own institutions, the new legislation making specific provision for the recognition of Native Authorities in accordance with law and custom, though unsatisfactory Native Authorities could still be removed. As far as the chief's financial powers were concerned, the Government considered the fact that in the early days chiefs used to collect traditional dues in the shape of ivory, venison, or forced labour services to meet the charge of what limited 'services' tribal government could supply; this archaic kind of revenue, however, could not now be enforced, with the result that some chiefs became unable even to travel round their own districts because they could not feed their carriers, whilst native courts could no longer summon assessors, as of old, because there was no food to provide them with meals. Existing legislation, the Senior Provincial Commissioner added, largely ignored the existence of native councillors and court officials, and something must be done to remedy these deficiences.[1] The Elected Members, who were previously consulted on the subject, found little to criticize in the new legislation, except Moore who believed that native courts were corrupt, that Indirect Rule was leading to a reversion to superstition and witchcraft, and that Africans themselves preferred the system of 'Direct Rule' practiced under the Chartered Company. Moore added—perfectly correctly—that the new legislation did not tackle the problem of 'detribalized' Africans, but his arguments met with little support amongst his colleagues; Gore-Browne in fact took just the opposite line, namely that the settlers could not ask for self-government whilst at the same time denying this boon to Africans, that the powers of the native courts in fact were still too limited, and that chiefs—or at any rate their sons—needed further education to cope with the laws introduced by white men.[2]

African reactions to the extension of Indirect Rule are difficult to judge, but on the whole the policy appears to have met with approval, not only from backveld villagers, but also from the so-called 'progressives', clerks, capitaos and school teachers, who gave evidence before bodies like the Bledisloe Commission, whilst an African nationalist organization, formed by educated people in the Mazabuka area in 1937, likewise welcomed the new measures on the grounds that they constituted 'an honour towards our Chiefs and natives in general'.

[1] Northern Rhodesia. Legislative Council debates, 2 May 1936, p. 5
[2] Northern Rhodesia. Legislative Council debates, 5 May 1936, p. 70–98

The development of native treasuries and tribal administrative services took time, however, to get under way, and 'Indirect Rule', properly speaking, did not make much progress until the 'forties. Rural poverty remained the main obstacle to administrative expansion, for 'Indirect Rule' with its local treasuries threw some of the cost of local government on the backward rural regions which lost a large proportion of their tax-payers to the towns. The Chief Acting Treasurer thus explained that the bulk of African revenue was derived from people in employment, many of whom worked down the mines or along the Railway Belt; he added that efficient Native Authorities in the tribal areas, able to collect taxes effectively, were unlikely to emerge as long as Northern Rhodesia depended primarily on wage-earning.

The Government tried to meet some of these difficulties by adjusting its fiscal system to the realities of labour migration—but at the price of contradicting some of the underlying assumptions of Indirect Rule! Taxes bore no relation to the peoples' capacity to pay, the Governor explained in 1935; the highest rate of 12/6 presented no hardships to a relatively well paid miner, but proved a great burden to a poor farm labourer. The fairest solution of course would have been some kind of income tax, but this was administratively out of the question, requiring more staff than the collection would have been worth. The Administration then attempted to arrive at a rough kind of justice by further differentiating tax rates by regions, the wealthier areas paying more than the back-veld.[1] More important still was the revision in 1935 of the whole basis of assessment, *temporary residence* replacing *domicile* as the criterion of collection. This meant that a Lovale miner who worked on the Copper Belt for a month now paid his tax at the higher rate prevailing at Kitwe or Luanshya, instead of the lower rate back home, the Administration trying to even out some of the local inequalities by the creation of a Central Treasury Fund in 1938.[2]

Nevertheless, the revenue collected by the different Native Authorities

[1] An earlier attempt to introduce some kind of income tax consisted in the taxation of plural wives, the assumption being that wives constituted an economic investment and a sign of wealth, whilst missionaries considered this measure as a weapon against the institution of polygamy. In 1929 plural taxation of wives was abolished, the Administration realizing that the possession of wives formed an economic burden on the man who took his traditional kinship obligations seriously, the tax leading to an increase in divorce. At the same time the rate was increased by 2/6, so that the Balovale paid 7/6, the remainder of North Western Rhodesian Africans 12/6 and the North-Eastern Rhodesian Africans 7/6, up to 1929, and subsequently 10/– with the abolition of tax on plural wives. The rates proved too high once the Slump hit the country, and taxes had to be remitted on an extensive scale, some reductions for various outlying districts being introduced between 1930 and 1935. In 1935 a further important change was made when the general rate of tax for the Territory was reduced to 7/6d, the rate already prevailing in Balovale and Mwinilunga districts. At the same time a graduated system was introduced in centres of employment. The 7/6 rate applied to all districts away from the line of rail, except in Fort Jameson where the rate at first remained at 10/– for most agricultural areas, 12/6 at Broken Hill, Livingstone and Ndola, and 15/– at the copper mines.

[2] Outside Barotseland, the wealthiest Native Treasury was that of the Bemba whose revenue in 1938 amounted to £1,303. Next came the plateau Tonga, the very people who possessed no traditional chieftainships at all, who collected £1,234. The smallest income was drawn by the Shila in the Northern Province who only raised £51. 0. 0. The Barotse on the other hand collected a total revenue of £13,446.

continued to vary enormously from district to district; and roughly speaking the poorer areas, which depended most on the provision of new services, drew the smallest revenue. Local chiefs and councillors thus found themselves in a difficult position; if they wanted to succeed, they had to show concrete results in the shape of schools, court-houses, dams and dispensaries. But such schemes cost money, and as funds remained desperately inadequate, chiefs often became apathetic. Poverty also prevented the recruitment of competent black officials. Once rain-makers became road-makers, the so-called traditional Native Authorities could no longer function without 'new men', skilled in the white man's way, and able to keep court records, total up accounts, or write letters. Trained clerks, however, would willingly settle down to village jobs where some drew as little as £3. 0. 0. *per annum*, their average rate amounting to no more than £3. 10. 0. or £4. 0. 0.; even the most frugal scribes could hardly manage to live on such a salary; though some were ex-Government clerks receiving pensions. Many chiefs thus tried to get out of their predicament by giving posts to relatives with a modicum of mission education who did their job part-time, and continued to work the land when they were not wielding the pen. This kind of unspecialized clerical labour proved as inefficient in the office as migrant labour down the mine; and the further development of African local government thus depended largely on the emergence of more highly trained administrators. This process, and the resultant development of local 'chancelleries' remains difficult to document, for Native Authorities kept their records badly, much of their correspondence being eaten by rats and white ants, going up in flames, or disappearing as the result of plain carelessness. But some professional specialization did occur, and by 1938 a few native Treasury clerks in favoured areas appear to have drawn enough money to devote themselves to office work as a full-time occupation.[1]

Barotseland in the meantime continued in its rather special position, many Britons looking upon the country with particular benevolence as a living embodiment of its ideals of Indirect Rule; one adviser argued that the country should become a self-contained native state under British protection, criticizing what he considered to be the present tendency of welding the territory too closely to the Railway. He enquired of the Governor whether the region could not be turned into a separate administrative unit, managing its own finances, making its own laws and employing its own civil servants, subject of course to control from Livingstone, stressing at the same time that the Barotse in the past handed over greater concessionary rights than any other people in Central Africa, though receiving relatively little in return for their services. Storrs shared Downing Street's enthusiasm for the Barotse system of government but Maxwell approached the subject with somewhat greater reservation. He explained that the Barotse should be asked to set up properly constituted Native Authorities and Native Courts which would prevent what the Governor considered to be abuses. He also favoured a reduction in the powers of the Paramount, adding that the

---

[1] Some Ila Treasury clerks thus managed to draw between £24. 0. 0. to £36. 0. 0. *per annum*.

Barotse at present were not as yet fitted for extensive financial responsibilities and required further training in the subject. Maxwell's more cautious approach was shared to some extent by Charles Cecil Farquharson Dundas, who came to the country in 1934 in his capacity as Acting Governor, Dundas found that the Paramount was using his own revenue indiscriminately for public and private purposes, unbusinesslike handling of funds throwing him into serious debt. The Acting Governor got Yeta III to draw up a regular annual budget, and thus established some indirect control over the revenue. Dundas argued however that the local administration merited support, though he added that government was still being conducted with too much thought to the pecuniary benefit of the ruling family and higher nobility, little consideration being shown to the common people. Similar strictures on the Barotse judicial system recurred in official correspondence lower down the administrative scale, the *khotla* being described by one senior official as 'lazy and grasping and devoid of public spirit'. But complainants did not always substantiate these criticisms, sometimes apparently acting on the assumption that the relatively undifferentiated law administered by the Barotse, who lacked the more formalized procedure of European courts, would necessarily lead to injustice.[1] The Government, by agreement with the Barotse, finally regularized the position in 1936 when the Barotse Native Authority Ordinance and the Barotse Native Courts Ordinance passed on to the Statute Book. The *khotlas* now for the first time received official recognition, acquiring a recognized legal status under Northern Rhodesian law, doing away with the previous period of uncertainty which proved so intensely irritating to tidy-minded District Commissioners, who used to resent their inability to interfere in the proceedings of local courts. The Paramount's *khotla* continued to be the supreme legislative, judicial and executive body and Barotse courts now acquired the power to imprison offenders, a practice unknown in the past. Provision was now made for appeals from the Paramount's Court to the High Court, whilst in criminal cases appeals were allowed to the Provincial Commissioners' Courts. Magistrates Courts could revise the decision of Native Courts in criminal matters, but minor civil cases remained outside their jurisdiction.

At the same time changes occurred within the Barotse system of law and administration itself. In the early days the tribal lands were divided into territorial administrative units for the purpose of controlling land rights and the requisition of labour. But for political and judicial purposes the Barotse employed a system of non-territorial 'sectors' whose members were scattered over the whole of the country, so that even in the same homestead, people might find themselves members of different sectors.[2] The system as a whole thus resulted in a marked concentration of power at the capital, with the result that even in times

[1] For a detailed treatise on Barotse law and related problems of comparative jurisprudence, see the major work by Gluckman, M. *The Judicial process among the Barotse of Northern Rhodesia.* Manchester university press, 1955

[2] See Gluckman, M. *The economy of the central Barotse plain.* (Rhodes-Livingstone papers, no. 7, 1941), and Gluckman, M. 'The Lozi of Barotseland in North-Western Rhodesia' (in Colson, E. and Gluckman, M., ed. *Seven tribes of British Central Africa.* Oxford university press, 1951)

of rebellion provinces rarely made war against the Paramount as a whole, except in outlying areas where entire tribes were administered through an indigenous system of 'Indirect Rule', exercized by the existing chiefs, advised and controlled by Barotse Residents. But when the British came, administrative change became inevitable. The new overlords naturally thought in terms of government on a territorial basis, the kind of system they used themselves; and wrongly assumed that the existing territorial divisions in Barotseland (*lilalo*) also formed the basis of Barotse administration, the 'sectors' only relating to military and labour matters. The British then employed the territorial units as the basis for the collection of the tax, and the importance of the 'sectors' declined. At the same time the functions of administration as a whole began to alter. Formerly the Council rarely dealt with matters concerning the day-to-day lives of ordinary folk, and questions like war and foreign policy, the organization of royal hunts or of the periodic moves of the king's residence formed the main subjects of discussion; but as time went on, Barotse Councillors had to deal with more mundane affairs like schools, missions, cattle sales and veterinary regulations, becoming more like modern civil servants in the process, whilst some of the traditional posts declined in importance, their holders settling down in well-paid but useless sinecures. Government at the same time became more difficult to understand and the common people and minor councillors were no longer consulted over complicated matters like the framing of estimates or the details of the Barotse Native Courts Ordinance.

At the same time there was a shift in the whole economic basis of government, both in Barotseland itself and in the outlying provinces. The traditional system of agriculture in the valley itself centred on fertile mounds which remained dry when the annual floods covered the plain. This system of agriculture gave a major say to such local dignitaries as controlled these mounds. But gradually the Barotse pushed out to the edge of the plain where they began to cultivate 'margin gardens', which possessed the additional advantages of being more suitable for growing vegetables and fruit for sale to white men; the Europeans set up stores and mission stations on the edge of the plain where they lived more comfortably, and this meant that the economic value of land on the margin further increased. The mound-owners thus lost something of their former importance, the traditional system being further modified by the increasing importance of wage labour. The change to a money economy also affected Barotse relations with their subject tribes. In early times, the conquered peoples used to bring tribute in kind to the capital, carrying back presents from their overlord in exchange. The tribute system, however, disappeared and the tribes which used to obtain herds of cattle from Lealui now argued that they got inadequate returns for their taxes, especially as the Barotse valley proper got far more in the way of government services than in the outlying provinces.

Under these circumstances relations with the subject tribes were bound to become more difficult. The Barotse on the one hand and the Lunda and Lovale on the other had for long quarrelled with one another; the setting up of a

Barotse Court at Nawinfa at Balovale in 1932 made matters worse, and in addition economic factors may have played some part in the dispute. The Barotse were said to be cutting the Lunda out of the Mongu meal market, whilst the Lovale competed with their overlords on the labour market on the basis of lower wages.[1] Geography also entered into the question, for unlike many other tribes under Barotse rule, the Lovale and Lunda were situated a long way from the Barotse valley proper, where the Barotse and many of the immigrant peoples were now inter-marrying, Silozi becoming the accepted *lingua franca* for the country. Trouble began in 1932 when the Barotse decided to consolidate their rule by setting up a *khotla* for the Balovale country. Daniel Kufuna, Yeta's son assumed the presidency over the new body, but acted with much tactlessness, the local tribes complaining that they were being deprived of various hunting, fishing and land rights, and that their customs were being superseded. Shinde, a prominent Lunda chief, then agitated to have the Barotse expelled, making propaganda, not only amongst his local subjects but—significantly—also amongst such of his people as were working down the mines. The dispute led to a bitter personal quarrel in which Daniel was accused of having attacked Shinde with a knife; Shinde then refused to accept Barotse rule and was joined by all the Lovale chiefs on the west bank of the Zambezi, despite the fact that Government recognized the Barotse *khotla* at Nawinda. The Administration in 1937 persuaded Yeta to restore certain rights to his subjects, but Yeta refused to recall Daniel, with the result that the indigenous people boycotted Barotse government, which ground to a standstill. Dundas then attempted to negotiate an agreement, acting on the principle that Barotse paramountcy should be upheld, that Yeta should not be compelled to withdraw the Nawinda *khotla*, though a section of the Lovale, and the whole of the Luchazi tribe remained loyal to the Barotse. Dundas also suggested to Yeta that he too should adopt Indirect Rule, that the subject tribes should have their own courts of appeal composed of indigenous chiefs, that subject chiefs should issue their own orders subject to Yeta's approval, and that fees and fines raised locally should be spent where they were raised, Dundas himself feeling convinced that the Barotse were just using their subject tribes as milch-cows. The Colonial Office concurred with this policy and stressed that Government should prevent the subordinate Native Authorities from seceding, Downing Street as a whole displaying greater sympathy for the Barotse than the local officials. Trouble continued, however, and in 1938 a Commission of Enquiry was appointed to adjudicate in the matter. The Commission disagreed with the Barotse claims, and in 1940 the Colonial Office came round to the Commission's view, agreeing that the Lunda and Lovale should be removed from the Barotse rule, and that they should receive their own system of Indirect Rule after a short period of direct administration. In 1941 the disputed *khotla* was finally wound up; almost the whole of the Lovale District was removed from Barotse jurisdiction, and transferred to the Kaonde-

[1] Gluckman, M. *The economy of the central Barotse plain.* (Rhodes-Livingstone papers, no. 7, 1941), p. 122

Lunda (later the Western and now North-Western) Province, the Barotse receiving compensation for land, mineral, game and fishing rights, as well as an increase in their tax percentage.

III

Urban administration

Whilst the Government was attempting to build up traditional or supposedly traditional chieftainships, African tribesmen continued on their periodic treks to the towns, wage labour being said to have become so much part of the accepted way of village life that girls would no longer even look at a youngster who had never been away from home! Many Africans drifted into Municipal compounds, where housing was bad, and amenities almost non-existence, local governments lacking the finance needed to supply adequate accommodation. The real burden of administration fell on poorly paid Location Superintendents, who were expected to 'make bricks without straw', and possessed neither the District Officer's social standing nor his financial security, despite the weight of responsibility which they shouldered.[1] The mining companies on the other hand looked after their men very much better, providing adequate food and housing, beerhalls, playing fields and cinemas, as well as hospitals and baby-clinics for the miners' wives. The system of migrant labour continued, though the men could bring their wives or mistresses to the mine compounds and live normal lives in their little huts, unlike their comrades on the Rand who remained cooped up in bachelor barracks. The white farmers took migrant labour for granted, but as far as the mining companies were concerned, opinion was at first far from unanimous. Before the Slump H. S. Munro, Chairman of the Native Labour Association, strongly attacked the system on the grounds that it proved uneconomic, that it was cheaper to settle labour on the companies' own door-steps, and that the present system called for three times as many Africans as were employed at any given time. A few Northern Rhodesian officials also spoke in favour of such a policy, Dundas as Acting Governor feeling convinced that more provision should be made for permanently urbanized miners, and deploring the way their children were lounging about the towns without getting a proper education, their future constituting a grave potential problem. The weight of official opinion, however, as yet went against such views, Thomas Frederick Sandford, for long Secretary for Native Affairs, showing himself particularly opposed to their implementation. The Administration must prevent the wholesale industrialization of Africans, he explained to the Legislative Council at the beginning

---

[1] In 1934 the position of Assistant Location Superintendent at Livingstone was thus advertised for an annual salary of £240 p.a. Applicants were expected to speak a native language, to have some experience in the work of native superintendence and be familiar with the brewing and sale of kaffir beer under municipal regulations. Cadets in the District Administration at this period drew salaries of between £400 to £475.

of the Second World War; the tribal system should be encouraged, and Africans in towns ought not to lose their links with home. The growth of a native intelligentsia living side by side but out of touch with ordinary Africans was undesirable.[1] A stabilized urban population moreover would present serious problems in times of unemployment and besides 'we do not wish to create a question of old age pensions and the like'.[2] Others pointed to the fluctuations in the value of copper shares, and tried to demonstrate that stabilized labour depended on stabilized metal prices which could not be assured under existing circumstances; a further argument (and not a very sound one) being that the benefits of the copper industry should continue to be spread throughout the countryside by remittances from the mineworkers, rather than being confined to a small section of townsmen. Apart from that, the Native Authorities themselves did not wish to lose permanently an appreciable number of their menfolk, and also tried to prevent women and children from drifting into towns where they might learn the ways of whores and crooks. In the fiscal sphere, however, Government took exactly the opposite line. As has been previously explained, the authorities in 1935 altered the whole basis of tax assessment, and an African labour-migrant now had to pay his tax according to the rates prevailing at his place of work in town, instead of those customary in his own tribal area. Payments were reduced in the countryside, but at Luanshya, Nkana and Mufulira taxes went up to 15/– per year. Government of course was acting with the best of intentions, hoping that the new scheme might serve as a rough and ready kind of income tax which would 'temper the wind to the shorn lamb', but overlooking that a man might in fact be assessed on his neighbour's income in the compound. The authorities really assumed that every black man in the mining areas had a job. But unemployment was rife and the townships full of people looking for work, or living on their wits, or on their kinsmen's kindness, the labour position having been made worse by the closing down of many white farms at Fort Jameson. The Ndola Native Welfare Association thus complained that wages (amounting to between £1. 0. 0. and £2. 15. 0. per month) did not suffice for a married man with children, even though the men drew rations free of charge, and that many employers were not paying their workers' rent as they should. An African deputation also deplored the way Africans were being prosecuted for trespassing on mine property. 'Our friends and relatives among the unemployed come and stay with us. . . . Some of them have grown up amongst Europeans, and they are accustomed to European life; you may try to chase them away, but they will not go away . . .'. The burden of unemployment benefit in fact was to some extent being borne by the poorest class of workers themselves, though the Africans did not put it this way, and still thought in terms of traditional kinship obligations. In addition Africans complained that workmen's compensation proved inadequate for families of men who met with accidents; that Africans were being prosecuted for leaving their Native Registration Certificates at home; and that

[1] Northern Rhodesia. *Legislative Council debates*, 12 Dec 1940, p. 383
[2] Northern Rhodesia. *Legislative Council debates*, 9 Dec 1942, p. 250–255

whites were muscling into the native trade in tobacco and fish in the compounds. A further grievance was that 'Europeans are making children among the native women. We do not like to see this at all—they are spoiling our nation',[1] white competition for black women proving all the more galling, since white men got more pay. The final cause of trouble on the Copper Belt—though no one actually said so—was perhaps just plain boredom. In the village life was never regimented and when the crops were good, the villagers would brew beer and drink till they dropped. In the townships on the other hand, life was strictly regulated; compound policemen maintained an all-round watch, and cinema shows and football matches formed perhaps an inadequate compensation for the relative freedom at home, at a time when African workers could not as yet purchase daydreams for the price of a lottery ticket or a football pool coupon. Life got a little colour from Hollywood films, and African youngsters, calling themselves 'Jacks' tried to model their behaviour on that of pistol-packing badmen in broad-brimmed hats, to the disgust of their tribal elders who had no patience with exhibitionism of that sort.[2] Alternately the labour migrant might listen to horrific prophecies of Watch Tower adherents, white or black, whose blood-curdling fire-and-brimstone sermons sent a tingle down their listeners' spines, and which foretold in picturesque language Satan's final overthrow, while the so-called Mbeni (or Beni Beni) societies staged elaborate ceremonies in which members gave themselves magnificent European titles in ceremonial dances where black 'Sixpence' became a white King.[3] But this was hardly enough, the position as a whole being made worse from the security point of view by the poor state of the police force, the absence of a ready-made plan to deal with disturbances, and the fact that officials were completely out of touch with miners whether white or black.

Unrest thus seemed likely on the Copper Belt, and serious trouble was sparked off on 20 May 1935 when the tax was suddenly raised and unauthorized mine policemen ran all over the compound at Mufulira bawling out that the people

[1] *Evidence taken by commission appointed to enquire into the disturbances in the copperbelt, Northern Rhodesia.* [London, H.M. Stationary Office, 1935], v. 2, p. 892–894. The deputation itself only contained one ex-miner, the remainder consisting of a caretaker in a native recreation-hall and two store-capitaos.

[2] The author's attention has been drawn to this point by Dr J. R. Hooker of Michigan State University.

[3] For their history, see report by Chief Commissioner of Police, Nyasaland: 29 July 1921 (N 3/23/2, Nat Arch SR) and *Evidence taken by commission appointed to enquire into the disturbances in the copperbelt, Northern Rhodesia.* [London, H.M. Stationery office, 1935], v. 1, p. 77. For a valuable sociological enquiry see Mitchell, J. C. *The Kalela dance.* (Rhodes-Livingstone papers, no. 27, 1957). The Beni Societies seem to have started in Tanganyika under German rule. They were introduced into Nyasaland by askari who saw service in East Africa and from there spread to Southern Rhodesia and Northern Rhodesia. African participants gave themselves titles like Field Marshal, King or Kaiser, the German love of rank and ceremony having perhaps made a particular impression on Africans. In Tanganyika members paid monthly subscriptions to provide feasts and pay bandsmen, and some of the people painted themselves white. In Northern Rhodesia dances were held at Old Fife, Abercorn and Kasama. The societies were entirely non-political in character and were not in any way responsible for the Copper Belt troubles, though some Europeans regarded them with a considerable amount of suspicion, the authorities in Nyasaland quietly discouraging them.

must now pay more money. On the next day the Africans struck, and though some went back to work, the majority, containing a large number of Bemba, continued to strike and threatened black-legs with violence. The next morning shift turned up at full strength; again the strike leaders interfered, but all the men returned to work on 23 May. At Nkana events followed a similar pattern: on 25 May Bemba workers harangued the men and called for a strike, and on the next day Africans assembled at the compound, invaded the copper-concentrator and threw out the people at work. The 'D.C.' tried to pacify the crowd, and the police was strengthened, but when the morning shift assembled on 27 May stone-throwing began, and in the evening the Provincial Commissioner got so worried that he asked for troops to be sent. African soldiers then flew in from Lusaka, this early airborne operation being carried out with considerable efficiency, and the position was stabilized. At Luanshya and Roan, however, events took a more serious turn. On 26 May a native from Nkana was said to have distributed pamphlets, and on the following day Bemba workers attempted to incite Africans to strike, stating that wages had been raised at Mufulira and Nkana. Evidence on the organization of the strike is almost impossible to obtain, but the Bemba clearly constituted the leading element, a Bemba 'Tribal Elder' himself being one of the leading agitators. The system of 'Elders', chosen on a tribal basis by their fellow workers to put the workers' case to management, now broke down, the Elders proving of little assistance, and not even carrying out their limited function of bringing grievances to the notice of the authorities. No one explained why the Bemba people should have been the most discontented—a possible interpretation being that they were not only the most numerous individual group, but also contained the smallest number of men in good positions, resentment between the Bemba and the more literate Nyasas in better jobs being said to have been considerable. But whatever the cause, the Bemba went on strike, and on 29 May pickets were posted. The 'D.C.' with considerable personal courage tried to pacify the angry crowd, but later on a huge mob of excited Africans advanced on the compound office, hurling stones, with the result that the police opened fire, killing six men. Troops arrived after the shooting stopped, just coming in time to prevent further looting of grain stores, but disorder continued, and rioting only ceased on 31 May when a detachment of British South Africa Police came up from Bulawayo. Most of the men went back on 1 June, and the strike was over on the following morning.

The Government then appointed a Commission of Enquiry which concluded that the firing was justified, that rations and wages were adequate, arguing that no demands were being made on native wages except for clothing, tax and luxuries, and that the men themselves were at fault if they provided idlers with food out of their allocation. The Commissioners thought that Watch Tower propaganda, individual abuses and the presence of a large number of workless or work-shy people on the mines all contributed to make trouble, and that the drift of unwanted labour to the Copper Belt should be stopped. They agreed that contact between District Officers and urban Africans proved inadequate, but hedged on the vital question of labour stabilization, simply stating that the only alternatives were either frequent repatriation, or permanent urbanization. The Commissioners were impressed by the fact that black miners offered no violence however to their white fellow-workers or their families, a fact from which Governor Young concluded that the state of race relations remained good. The European settlers themselves took a much less optimistic view of the situation, and bitterly attacked the Government for its real or alleged failings, the *Livingstone Mail* thundering away at the Administration's detestable 'might is right' philosophy, and the inequitable burden of tax which was proving a crushing burden to whites and blacks alike. Moore also pointed out—quite rightly— that the collection of the tax was technically illegal at the time, money having been collected before the formal enactment of the law.[1] As far as overseas opinion was concerned, Colonial Office government in Northern Rhodesia for the first time received extremely unfavourable publicity overseas, papers like *Time and Tide* and the *New Statesman and Nation* launching into bitter attacks on the country's affairs whilst Dr Norman Leys, an anti-colonial veteran, tried to explain that only the big companies, Government and well paid white employees were benefiting from the copper industry, adding—perhaps not altogether accurately—that Africans did not really want to work down the mines and were no happier for doing so.[2]

The Administration—hamstrung by lack of funds—tried to meet the problem by further controlling the influx of Africans to the mines, and also by setting up African villages in the vicinity of townships, where clerks, capitaos and traders could lease plots at low rates and build their own houses. In addition a Native Labour Advisory Board came into existence, consisting of senior officials, an Elected Member of the Legislature and several mine managers, but comprising no workers within its ranks. In 1938 moreover the Government agreed to set up Native Advisory Committees on the Copper Belt which were to be composed of selected Africans from the government townships and mining compounds. The inaugural meeting of the Nkana Native Advisory Council comprised six Africans, a Senior Boma Assessor, a head-messenger, a house-servant, two clerks and a 'boss boy', the latter being the only mineworker proper and, apparently, the only one not related to some chief or other. The meeting was told that the floating nature of the Copper Belt population made the continuity of Elders in office a matter of great difficulty, largely eliminating the hereditary factor in their selection. The Committee was instructed to fight 'detribalization' (now a fashionable word in governmental and anthropological terminology), and act as the 'eyes, ears and mouth' of the District Commissioner. The Committee was not, however, to concern itself with wages, which remained a matter strictly outside its competence, so that members could only deal with minor matters like the regulation of traffic, the provision of

---

[1] *Livingstone mail*, 29 May 1935 and 5 June 1935. See also Northern Rhodesia. *Legislative Council debates*, 3 Dec 1935, p. 242–268

[2] *Time and tide*, 12 Dec 1935; and *New statesman and nation*, 4 Jan 1936

transport and recreational facilities, the repatriation of destitutes or unattached females, and the registration of marriages. In addition the Government appointed African assessors in order to start urban courts, help District Commissioners and relieve them of some of their judicial work.

IV

African politics in the 'thirties

The Copper Belt riots remained an isolated occurrence and the remainder of the Territory stayed completely quiescent, so that some pioneers now tend to look upon the pre-war days as a golden age of race-relations. But there was discontent, and in 1934 a District Commissioner who toured Kawambwa was struck by the sullenness of the younger generation who no longer cheerfully greeted white men as of old, but just grimly stared, or ignored them altogether. The changed manner, the official thought, did not just arise from Watch Tower propaganda, but from the economic Depression in general, and also from the way the Belgians were deporting people from the Congo. The new kind of behaviour was of course far from universal, though the story still circulates of a fire-eating 'D.C.' who met a gang of carriers who would not raise their hats, so he punished them by making them light a fire and throw all their headgear into the flames! The old martinet with a strong personality and plenty of idiosyn-cracies was not necessarily the most unpopular of whites amongst local Africans, but in the 'thirties many Europeans began to remark on the way 'D.C.s' were losing contact with the people altogether, administration becoming much more impersonal. Critics blamed the increase in chair-borne work which prevented District Officers from touring their areas and maintaining contact with their charges as in the olden days, when 'D.C.s' acted as the 'fathers' and 'mothers' of their people. Some of these complaints were justified, and the matter seemed so serious that in 1939 the Governor himself made an investigation. Maybin, a sound and competent Scotsman, a bachelor devoted to his work, an able adminis-trator, and an Edinburgh graduate like Maxwell, produced a report which stood out as a model of good sense. He agreed that some 'D.C.s' were not travelling enough, but thought that this was not necessarily caused by an increase in their office work. There were no arrears of correspondence on the Copper Belt and, Maybin calculated, the number of letters written at the different stations investi-gated amounted to no more than $2\frac{1}{2}$ per diem for 300 working days. Hours of work varied from $6\frac{1}{2}$ to 8 per day, but the amount accomplished during this period did not always justify the time spent. This state of affairs resulted to some extent from an inadequate training in administrative methods; Cadets required a far better knowledge of subjects like filing and records administration in order to become proficient at their work. As it was, routine work took too long; office systems varied greatly, sometimes being over-elaborate, whilst methods of time allocation left much to be desired, few officers knowing their clerks' rate of typing. There were also more general causes for the increased office work and the growing flood of circulars; the technical departments all expanded, and the specialists' activities now required much greater co-ordination, whilst their extra expenditure resulted in more time being spent on accountancy. Attempts from London to achieve greater uniformity of method in the various colonies led to an increase in correspondence; and as the Governor had to provide more information to satisfy critics at the Colonial Office, in Parliament, or in the League of Nations, his subordinates were required to furnish more written reports. Finally, Maybin complained, African clerks were inefficient; few of them could keep accounts, type at a reasonable speed or write good English, some District Officers even having to do their own filing. A few officials taught their clerks, but the Administration as a whole needed much better training facilities for whites and blacks alike. The position was further aggravated by the migrant character of the administrative labour force itself, for continuity of local policy remained difficult to achieve under conditions when five Provincial Commissioners headed the same Province within a period of only two years,[1] each new 'P.C.' tending to sweep with a fresh broom, and reverse his predecessors' decisions in a way that did not occur within the more stable administrative system south of the Zambezi. Maybin attempted to cope with the situation by improving the training of African clerks, and by instituting various reforms in the Secretariat, the hub of the whole system, but the growth of bureaucratic method could not thereby be prevented, so that 'D.C.s' became yet further removed from the lives of ordinary villagers.

African political reactions continued in a mainly religious form, millenarian preachers continuing to address enthusiastic congregations all over the Territory. The full history of these little groups will never be written, for few African secretaries kept records, and those who did failed to preserve their material, so that most remaining evidence is of an indirect nature.[2] But preaching clearly continued in town and countryside alike, the organization of these various groups sometimes following perhaps on the lines of internal African social cleavages. The Livingstone Criminal Investigation Department reported for instance in 1934 that the local Watch Tower sect split into two groups, one of which consisted of domestic servants, and the other of unemployeds who were controlled by one Salomon Banda, neither group being subversive in character. In addition Livingstone could boast of two 'separatist' Churches organized more on the European pattern, the New Apostolic, and the African Methodist Church, both of which were controlled by black men themselves. As far as Northern Rhodesia as a whole was concerned, Young estimated in 1935 that about half of the African population were said to be professed Watch Tower

---

[1] Sir S. Gore-Browne in Northern Rhodesia. *Legislative Council debates*, 12 Dec 1935, p. 204
[2] By far the most brilliant study of this kind is Shepperson, G., and Price, T. *Independent African.* . . . Edinburgh university press, 1958, which deals with the Chilembwe rising in Nyasaland and its general background.

adherents, whilst a 'D.C.' reported from Ndola that the movement was now part and parcel of indigenous African life in his area. Watch Tower was even making some headway amongst white miners on the Copper Belt, whilst many Europeans themselves were impressed by the self-discipline which the preachers were able to impose on its adherents, Mrs Olds going out of her way in the Legislative Council to denounce persecution of black Watch Tower men, and stressing that they made very satisfactory workers.[1] The Administration at first continued to regard the movement with some suspicion, but then the conviction gained ground that it was better to tolerate and control the preachers than drive them underground. In 1935 the Watch Tower Bible and Tract Society thus received permission to send a white representative to the country in order to set up proper supervision over its adherents;[2] at the same time the more objectionable types of publication were prohibited, the Administration taking exception to the way selected passages from Isaiah, Micah and other Hebrew rebels were being bandied about in a manner destructive of existing authority.[3] Watch Tower preachers appear to have made least headway among the Barotse or Barotse-ized tribes, though many of the Mawiko immigrants from Angola became converts to the new creed. The Barotse Paramount, angered by the sectaries' refusal to give the royal salute, at first wished to expel the unwelcome prophets, but the Provincial Commissioner objected to what he regarded as interference with freedom of religion. In the end a compromise was reached in 1939 by which all religious meetings required the approval of the local chiefs, and Watch Tower as a whole lost its potentially revolutionary character.

In strong contrast to these religious movements, a number of secular societies of a moderate kind sprang up along the Railway Belt from the early 'thirties onwards. Then new Native Welfare Associations conducted their meetings in English, and comprised school masters, clerks, hospital orderlies and others, many of them immigrants from outside the Territory, the leading positions usually being taken by civil servants.[4] The most influential members of these societies depended on Government for promotion, and advocated peaceful co-operation with the authorities in order to bring about African advances. The Welfare Societies thus put forward ultra-'respectable' demands like requests to control the sale of native beer, whilst the Chairman of the Lusaka Association bitterly denounced Watch Tower fanatics who said that the Government was pouring tax money down the drains, and that a terrible war would break out between whites and blacks which only the Elect would survive.[5] As far as long

---

[1] Northern Rhodesia. *Legislative Council debates*, 11 May 1936, p. 287

[2] Northern Rhodesia. *Legislative Council debates*, 8 May 1936, p. 158

[3] See for instance Micah 3. 11 and 7. 3, and Isaiah 66. 22 which were often used as texts by migrant preachers.

[4] By 1938 the Northern Rhodesian Administration was employing black clerks, interpreters, telegraphists, telephonists, postal clerks, agricultural assistants and forest rangers, teachers, medical assistants, compositors, book-binders, District messengers, sub-foremen and sub-draftsmen, assistant surveyors able to plot bearings, veterinary assistants able to inoculate cattle and veterinary laboratory assistants.

[5] *Livingstone mail*, 25 May 1932

term aims were concerned, African adherents of these societies appear to have thought along two separate and partially opposed lines. On the one hand they attempted to speak for all groups of Africans, not merely their own section, and thus demanded assistance to unemployed workers, the re-opening of the copper mines, security for black squatters on European land, and permission for natives to carry modern weapons, a request echoed by rural Africans who wanted rifles to exterminate elephants and other wild animals which trampled down their crops. But in addition, the 'new men' also believed in special privileges for themselves, like separate hospital facilities on the grounds that 'educated Africans are accustomed to soft beds and cannot do well with existing coarse blankets without sheets',[1] an observation which symbolized the widening gaps between the 'white collar workers' and the peasantry. At the same time sharp differences of opinion appeared in the field of ideas. On the one hand many 'progressives' looked askance at the tribal ways, stressing that they were like Europeans, and wanted to be treated more like white men. On the other hand, some Africans who began to look back to the half-forgotten days of old, now plunged into a sort of hazy golden mist, when Africans all had their hoes, axes and spears, and happily practised their own trades before the whites came and interfered with black men in the land God created for Africans.[2]

The welfare associations do not appear to have been very effective at first, for membership fluctuated as clerks and schoolmasters were posted about to different parts of the country. In 1937, however, a more ambitious organization came into being amongst Tonga farmers along the Railway Belt, perhaps the wealthiest and most stable section of the 'new men'. Discontent was now said to be spreading in the Railway Reserves, where Africans complained that white men owned too much land and that Europeans were impounding native cattle straying on unfenced grazing grounds. Many Tonga farmers moreover were exhausting their land by over-grazing and over-ploughing with the result that yields began to fall, a misfortune which seemed all the harder to bear when maize prices went up. Some white observers also argued that polygamy—far from dying out amongst the more advanced Tonga—was in fact increasing, as wealthy farmers could afford to wed more wives to help in the fields; these polygamous marriages—the argument continued—produced many more children, with the result that the Tonga further exploited the land with dangerous effects on its carrying capacity. Whatever the rights and wrongs of this reasoning, Africans in the well-developed Mazabuka area were the first to form a more general kind of movement which called itself the Northern Rhodesian African Congress. The association began in 1937 under the presidency of Ellison H. Milambo, the position of General Secretary being held by George W. Charles Kaluwa, the new group receiving support both from local chiefs like Mwanza and Monze and from African farmers and traders in the Mazabuka area. The Congress put forward an extremely moderate programme which approved of Indirect Rule,

[1] Letter by R. I. Nyirenda and G. A. Mbikusita in *Livingstone mail*, 30 Nov 1932
[2] Letter by P.P. Mfukwe and S. P. M. Sinkala in *Livingstone mail*, 17 May 1933

existing maize control legislation, and the development of native education, but also aimed at giving publicity to matters injurious to Africans, at securing better treatment for black men and keeping in touch with similar organizations in Southern Rhodesia, South Africa and Nyasaland, at the same time asking for Government recognition. The Administration, however, showed itself extremely guarded in its reactions to this and other organizations. As far as the Native Welfare Associations were concerned, the Government would only recognize them in so far as they looked after the non-political interests of 'detribalized' Africans in towns, insisting that civil servants must not join them once they assumed a political character, and refusing to sanction an amalgamation of these societies. The Congress was even less liked by Government which argued that the proposed organization would interfere with the official policy of controlling Africans through Native Authorities in tribal areas, and of getting Africans in towns to express their views through native councils. The authorities thus refused to give their approval to Congress, which petered out for the time being, though Kaluwa again entered politics after the end of the Second World War. Government on the other hand showed itself willing to differentiate between educated and backward Africans on an individual basis, and in 1939 an African Exemption Ordinance passed through the Council, which freed African priests and professional men from existing pass legislation, the Ordinance going through without any serious opposition from Elected Members, though some objected to the use of the word 'African', which was now coming into official usage.[1]

[1] Northern Rhodesia. *Legislative Council debates*, 7 Dec 1938

Chapter Ten

Teachers, missionaries and scholars in pre-war Northern Rhodesia

On 28 February 1920 a cumbrous-looking bi-plane, a Vickers Vimy bomber named the *Silver Queen*, landed at Abercorn, the earliest aircraft ever to arrive in Rhodesia. The bomber continued its flight to Ndola and thence to Livingstone where Pierre van Ryneveld and Quintin Brand, the two pilots, were feted like royalty, before taking off for Bulawayo and then to South Africa to complete the first flight from Britain to the Cape. Ryneveld and Brand were knighted, but despite their achievement *The Times* still gloomily concluded that the art of trans-African flight consisted in a good knowledge of how to crash, and Rhodesia for a time continued in its relative isolation, dependent on the endless and miserable train journey from the Cape to the Copper Belt which exceeded the distance between London and Leningrad. Within the Protectorate itself, motor cars were beginning to make life a little easier, but roads were still bad and during the rainy season, tropical downpours would turn the tracks into brown quagmires where even the best vehicles would get firmly stuck. In the 'thirties things began to improve a little, and in 1932 the first regular airmail service was inaugurated to Rhodesia from Britain, whilst a year later Rhodesia and Nyasaland Airways, affectionately known as 'RANA', (Latin for 'frog') came into being, and air travel gradually ceased to be a rare adventure for the bold, becoming a more normal way of getting about the country.[1] At the same time wireless sets ceased to be expensive toys and in 1930 Moore thought that some of his readers would be interested in a programme of Wagner, Beethoven and Weber broadcast from Königswusterhausen,[2] whilst a year later the B.B.C. opened a new Empire Service from Daventry which could be clearly heard in Rhodesia and conferred a great boon on local listeners. The cinema was by now a popular source of entertainment in Rhodesian townships, whilst a greater air of sophistication began to enter into some of the letters written to the newspapers, where trusty veterans like 'Disgusted' now had to compete with correspondents who would quote H. G. Wells and Bertrand Russell in support of their views. In Livingstone itself the Public Library was now a recognized social centre; Livingstonians would read a good deal, J. B. Priestley joining 'Sapper', Edgar Wallace, Ethel Mannin and Margaret Peterson as the most popular authors, whilst few would take out any more novels of the 'servant maid...sex type' or tales with a reputedly Rhodesian background, some readers

[1] For a summary see 'Aviation in Central Africa' (in *Horizon*, v. 2, no. 11, p. 18–22). RANA was itself the successor of the Rhodesian Aviation Company, formed in 1931, which had previously absorbed the Rhodesian Aviation Syndicate formed in 1927. Previously the so-called Aircraft Operating Company had done aerial photographic work and reconnaissance on the Copperbelt.

[2] *Livingstone mail*, 8 Oct 1930

contenting themselves entirely with instructional works, biographies or adventure stories to fill in their daily 'siesta' break.[1]

Nevertheless Northern Rhodesia remained half cut-off from the world, and the state of general education left much to be desired. The country of course had enormous leeway to make up for only a few schools were started in the 'Chartered' days, when the 1911 Census revealed that out of 93 children between the ages of 5 and 14 who lived in the country, only 45 could read and write after a fashion, whilst the country's over-all white population included 14 per cent illiterate people. From about 1914 onwards existing schools at Fort Jameson, Livingstone and Lusaka were supplemented by miserable little 'farm schools', but even here teachers faced a difficult problem in that potential scholars either lived too far away, or their parents would move round from job to job, so that the youngsters could not continue in one place for long. Teaching moreover often took place under appalling conditions, little different from those at African 'bush schools', requiring an enormous amount of toughness and idealism from educational pioneers.

'. . . There was a tiny children's school at Lusakas kept by several Colonial and Dutch girls for the surrounding farmers' children. I can't think how they faced the life. . . . A mud house, swarming with white ants, which ate walls, furniture, clothes and everything else; poor food at famine prices; intense heat coming on; practically no society, no pleasures, nothing! The pay given them (by the Education Department) was cruelly insufficient and they got but scant thanks or recognition from anyone for the heroism that had brought them there and kept them there. They could all have left, for they had homes in Southern Africa, and could have got posts there. But someone had to come here, and now they were here, and they were trying to live it out. . . .'[2]

Things began to improve somewhat after the Great War. A new boarding school opened its doors at Mazabuka to supplement the small boarding establishment set up at Lusaka in 1914, and in 1925 a separate European Education Department was formed. In 1927 a few secondary subjects were first introduced at top forms in schools at Livingstone, Mazabuka, Lusaka and Broken Hill, though Elected Members would still complain with much justification that the brightest children were leaving the country to get their education in Southern Rhodesia, South Africa or England, taking up jobs abroad, with the result that Northern Rhodesia lost its best brains. By 1928 moreover some 400 out of 1,000 youngsters were still not getting any formal education at all, and tuition by correspondence courses which started in 1932, proved quite inadequate to cope with the problem of educating children in outlying areas. Conditions again improved a little after the Slump; a European Education Advisory Board was formed in 1935, this reform being followed up by Technical Evening Classes which started on the Copper Belt in 1939. But schooling still remained one of the Government's

---

[1] 'Livingstone's public library: "twenty-one years of service" ' (in *Livingstone mail*, 23 Nov 1932)
[2] Quoted from Mrs Maturin by Sampson, R. *So this was Lusaakas*. Lusaka, Lusaka publicity association, 1959, p. 25

many Cinderellas, only £21,000 being spent in 1936 on European education, though this sum still caused much head shaking at Downing Street, where the Colonial Office complained that Northern Rhodesian expenditure on white education far exceeded that of other African dependencies, and requested the Governor to find out whether Europeans were contributing their fair share. Young wrote back with some heat that white tax payers were paying about £25 per head in taxes, whereas Africans were only handing over an average of about 2/6 per head, stressing that Northern Rhodesia contained more white children than the ordinary kind of dependency the Colonial Office was thinking of, whilst a total of £27,000 was spent on African education. This spirited defence, however, proved of small consolation to local white colonists, who to some extent remained educationally under-privileged[1] and envied Southern Rhodesia, where schooling was better and education compulsory.

African education meanwhile remained mainly in missionary hands, but after 1919 the Colonial Office became more school-minded, interest being stimulated partly by current Trusteeship ideas, and partly by missionary research work. Much of the pioneering in their field was done by Dr Joseph Houldsworth Oldham, who became Secretary of the International Missionary Council, and later on Administrative Secretary of the International Institute of African Languages and Cultures. Equally important was the work done by Dr Thomas Jesse Jones, a Welshman who, before the Great War, conducted sociological research amongst Jewish and Italian families in New York, then turned to problems of American Negro instruction, before embarking on a thorough study of educational problems in Africa from 1919 when he was appointed by the Phelps-Stokes Fund, an American charitable organization, to head a Commission to investigate educational problems in Africa. Jesse Jones, like other contemporary experts, believed that the old-time mission teacher often followed the wrong track, that missionaries should no longer try to impose textbooks and curricula remote from their students' life, that the 'three Rs' should only be regarded as tools to acquire the arts of community life, and that the proper use of man's environment, including related activities like agriculture, home life, hygiene and recreation should be regarded as the essential of education.[2] Jesse Jones possibly over-estimated the 'academic' bend of existing mission schools, where standards of book learning remained low, whilst most missionaries in fact favoured an 'industrial' education, progress being held up more by lack of trained instructors and equipment than by an unreasoning preference for literary accomplishments. Nevertheless the missionaries naturally regarded education as a means of

[1] By 1936 1,043 children were at school, and 54 children getting correspondence tuition. Along the Railway Belt there were 9 Government 'controlled schools' where boys and girls went to the same classes. Primary education was provided, with Latin, French, algebra and geometry being given up to St. VII. In addition there were a few private schools receiving Government help, whilst a good education was provided by the Convents at Broken Hill and Ndola which received no Government help whatever. Average attendance at school was now 90·4 per cent of the total.

[2] Dougall, J. W. C. 'Thomas Jesse Jones: crusader for Africa' (in *International review of missions*, v. 39, 1950, p. 311–317)

spreading the Gospel to the masses rather than an object worth pursuing for its own sake, whereas the new-style educationist stressed the secular aspect to a much greater extent. At the same time Jesse Jones and his friends assumed that the overwhelming majority of their pupils would spend their life in the villages; that education should uplift the masses rather than create an elite; that advanced Africans would return to the countryside to teach their skills to fellow tribes-men, and that the higher positions in the townships would remain in European hands, a concept of society conservative in character, as well as in tune with contemporary trusteeship doctrines and a growing interest in native customs. These views made a great impression on Ormsby-Gore, then Under Secretary of State at Downing Street; he later invited Oldham to submit suggestions for a *modus vivendi* between missions and Government in the educational sphere. At Oldham's suggestion an Advisory Committee upon Education in Tropical Africa (later renamed the Advisory Committee on Education in the Colonies) was set up at the Colonial Office in 1923, Oldham becoming a foundation mem-ber.[1] The new Committee gave an opportunity for distinguished colonial administrators, clerics and university men to express their views on an official level with regard to educational matters, and also on related aspects like the industrial colour bar and race relations in general: the Committee strongly upheld current doctrines of Imperial trusteeship and sometimes strongly criti-cized the cause of white settlers in Africa, who were of course not represented in the Committee's ranks.

The new ideas gradually made themselves felt in Northern Rhodesia where the authorities discussed their problems with Jesse Jones, modelling their policy as far as possible on suggestions put forward by the Welsh scholar and also previous resolutions of the General Missionary Conference in the Protectorate. In 1925 a Sub-Department for Native Education came into being within the Department for Native Affairs, the new office becoming separated from its parent-body five years later, and achieving an independent status of its own. At the same time Government began to pay modest subsidies to the various mission societies, rejecting alternate suggestions that it should run the system on its own, on the grounds that the missions were already maintaining a staff of some 200 workers in the country, that they were familiar with local problems and 'knew their Africans', that the Christian faith should be encouraged, and that the Administration would merely fritter away its scanty resources by trying to run more than a few technical schools. In 1929 Geoffrey Chitty Latham, the first Director of African Education, an ex-Magdalen man from Oxford and a former Native Commissioner with a fine war record, submitted a more exten-sive scheme. The missions were to continue with most of the existing elementary education with the aid of grants, but age limits were to be gradually raised, and English was to be taught in the higher elementary school classes, where pupils should get a chance of either continuing a general education or specializing as

[1] Bennett, G. 'Paramountcy to partnership: J. H. Oldham and Africa' (in *Africa*, v. 30, no. 4, Oct 1960, p. 356–360)

teachers, carpenters, builders, agricultural assistants and such like. At the same time Government was to train 'Jeanes' teachers,[1] to act as supervisors of village schools; girls' schools were to be set up at missions, and Government should establish a trades school, an elementary day school at the Copper Belt and a 'normal school' at Mazabuka. Latham's scheme met with much support at Downing Street, where the Sub-Committee on Native Education called on the Imperial authorities to develop education by a development loan, as in the Sudan; and Latham, a strong believer in education through trained rather than untrained teachers, made some progress. In 1929 the Rev. J. R. Fell, formerly head of the well-known Primitive Methodist Training Institution at Kafue, joined the department in order to take over the Jeanes and Agricultural schools now under construction at Kafue. In addition a Trades School was begun a Lusaka in 1932, and native elementary school work began on the Copper Belt. But then the Slump burst on the country, and education suffered a disastrous set-back. Several white teachers left the service and so did many Africans who found their salary reduced below that of native messengers. A Government Middle School, founded at Mazabuka, closed its doors with the result that the supply of clerks for Government service dwindled, much to the annoyance of the Colonial Office. The Education Department moreover was thrown into a serious administrative muddle when Latham retired in 1931, a procession of six Directors and Acting Directors passing through head-office until 1936, when a new man was appointed and the financial position improved.

By now the demand for trained junior civil servants, artisans and teachers was rising once more, and at the same time considerable pressure was exercized at Downing Street by the Education Advisory Committee which now constituted an influential pressure group. The Committee was headed by Sir James Currie, Chairman of the Empire Cotton Growing Corporation, a bitter opponent of the industrial colour bar, who believed that the Railways might cut operating costs by about 30 per cent, if they would only replace white workers by lower paid Africans, reduce transport charges and provide an added incentive to the cultivation of native crops. Currie's views were shared, though for different reasons, by his fellow members on the Committee, including intellectuals like Professor Sir Reginald Coupland, a distinguished Oxford historian, Bishop Edward Myers, a Roman Catholic theologian, and senior civil servants like Sir William Frederick Gowers, a former Governor of Uganda. All these men condemned on moral or intellectual grounds the 'narrow' outlook of Northern Rhodesian settlers, and regarded themselves as more 'enlightened' than white back-velders, who retorted that the matter had nothing to do with superior education or morality, that academics deliberating at Downing Street were simply not subject to the economic pressures operating at Broken Hill or Livingstone, and were just making moral capital out of their favoured position. The Committee for its part

---

[1] 'Jeanes teachers' derived their name from a fund set up by Miss Anna T. Jeanes, an American philanthropist, who founded a charity to train Negro inspectors to supervise other teachers in works of community development.

strongly criticized alleged restrictions on native artisans in Government service, the colour bar on the Railways, and alleged discrimination against African building workers at Lusaka, whilst stressing the importance of advancing Africans in the civil service. James Henry Thomas, now Secretary of State for the Colonies, fully associated himself with the Committee's views, and emphasized the need to educate Africans to meet Imperial trusteeship obligations, achieve economy in government, and also to develop Indirect Rule, Thomas being perfectly well aware that the so-called tribal systems of government now required an adequate supply of trained 'non-traditional' administrative labour to run them. Young, for his part, strongly defended the Administration's record, arguing that it was not the settlers who were holding up African advancement, but that the basic cause lay in lack of finance, the Elected Members never having taken up an unsympathetic attitude towards Africans and always having welcomed benefits for black men. Young also tried to explain technical details of the sort that the complicated kind of machinery now used in the telephone exchanges and telegraph department precluded the employment of Africans, as long as they were so poorly trained. He stressed that African advancement in Government service often gave poor results, since educational standards were low, whilst the best men would take better-paid jobs with commercial firms. Young likewise pointed out that the Railways were beyond the control of his Government, and strongly repudiated charges of official discrimination against native artisans. On the whole the Governor was perfectly justified in his defence; the major factor was the financial one, for it was only in 1937 that expenditure on native education again reached that of the years 1931 to 1932. In 1937 £28,305 was spent on native education, an advance on the past, but still a small sum when compared with the £84,620 voted by a 'settler-Parliament' down at Salisbury for native development during the same period. Nevertheless primary education north of the Zambezi made some progress, and in 1937 the first modest beginnings were also made in the neglected field of secondary education, five pupils receiving bursaries for schools outside the Territory, while a junior secondary school opened its gates at Munali in 1939.

The main weight of education, however, continued to be borne by the missions whose interest in schooling vastly grew during the 'twenties. Oldham taught in and out of season that the mission must seize their educational opportunities with both hands, at whatever risk, and at a great Protestant Missionary Conference at Le Zoute in 1926 he told the assembled delegates that they would lose Africa, unless they adapted themselves to the new forces changing the Continent. The Conference approved the policy of co-operation with the British Government's new educational policy, and accepted the recommendations of the Phelps-Stokes Commissions: the Catholics soon followed suit, and in 1928 the Apostolic Visitor urged a conference of bishops and leading missionaries at Dar-es-Salaam that they should, if necessary, even neglect their churches, in order to perfect their schools.[1] The new departure in time also made itself felt in

[1] Oliver, R. *The missionary factor in East Africa.* Longmans, Green and co., 1952, p. 271-275

Northern Rhodesia, though standards still differed widely from one area to the next, depending on the local mission's financial support overseas, and the kind of recruits who would volunteer, which meant that some tribes found themselves in an educationally much more favoured position than their neighbours. Government to some extent tried to counteract this uneven rate of development by helping inefficient missions as well as good ones, and in 1938 the Director of Education bitterly complained that money was being wasted on buttressing inferior establishments at the expense of more advanced bodies.

The best education of all was provided by the Church of Scotland, whose previously divided presbyteries at Blantyre and Livingstonia united in 1924 into the Church of Central Africa, Presbyterian. Work centred on the institutions in Nyasaland, with the result that 'Nyasa boys' and trainees from Scottish stations in North-Eastern Rhodesia continued to play a leading role as clerks, capitaos and schoolmasters. The mission believed in relatively high standards and led in experiments like the 'Central Village School', whilst devolving much more authority to Africans than their fellow Calvinists in the Dutch Reformed Church. Good work was also done by the London Missionary Society, despite the fact that bitter inter-station quarrels retarded progress. The 'L.M.S.' excelled in the field of industrial education, and Mbereshi station acquired a reputation for its handicraft work, whilst Miss Mabel Shaw pioneered women's education at Mbereshi, where she established a girls' village, each hut being in charge of a house-mother, the pupils living as far as possible like ordinary villagers, making their own fires, cooking their own cassava, whilst at the same time absorbing a simple literary education. At Kambole J. A. Ross tried to supplement mission work by promoting local industries and agriculture in order to stop the outward flow of labour which was seriously interfering with evangelical prospects. Ross himself founded 'Kambole Industries' which absorbed all his savings, and which attempted to grow cotton and later coffee, make soap, run stores and encourage crafts. Capital, however, proved inadequate, markets were insufficient, and only the stores made money, with the result that profits from trade had to subsidize the remainder of the enterprise. In addition the Mission found Government suspicious of native coffee cultivation, fearing that inefficient African methods would lead to the spread of pests, a further difficulty being found in the fact that the maturing period of the plant proved too long for poverty-stricken villagers who could not afford to wait a long time for a return on their labour. In 1934 Kambole Industries had to be wound up, and an interesting experiment collapsed.[1] The reputation of the Paris Evangelical Mission also stood high, and the Barotse continued to remain one of the Territory's educationally privileged tribes. French, Swiss and Italian Protestants went on producing men of the very highest calibre who impressed even a very critical Government Inspector by their 'simplicity, sincerity, genuine interest in the welfare of the people and scrupulous honesty in the use of grants'. Many of

[1] London Missionary Society. *Deputation reports, 1924* and *1931*; and R. H. Sabin to London Missionary Society: 25 Sep 1934 (L.M.S. Arch)

the missionaries were related by marriage and followed the mission career in their fathers' footsteps, which gave them a feeling of comradeship and cohesion that went far to make up for their perennial lack of funds. The Methodists gained added strength when the Primitive Methodists and the Wesleyan branches united into the Northern Rhodesia Synod in 1932. The Methodists enjoyed the advantage of working in a compact area, their organization was good, and their educational views enlightened. Their Training Institute at Kafue, first begun in 1918 by the Rev. John R. Fell, pioneered higher education for Africans and provided the model for later training schemes, its success doing much to persuade the Government to back education for Africans on a comprehensive scale. The Kafue institute probably became more widely known than any other school in Northern Rhodesia. Good work was also done by the Brethren in Christ, an American Group, particularly active in the Choma district. The Dutch Reformed Church[1] for their part mainly aimed primarily at evangelization, education being regarded merely as a means of enabling Africans to read the Bible. The Mission maintained a very large number of stations, but though the Afrikaners knew how to get on with their Africans, and proved excellent farmers into the bargain, the quality of their numerous stations proved inadequate from the schooling point of view. The Nsenga and Chewa admittedly made some progress, but the Ngoni learned little, the erstwhile conquerors, like the Bemba to the north, now finding themselves at a grave disadvantage on the labour market. The Anglican U.M.C.A. also maintained a number of priests of high individual quality in the field, but work suffered from lack of money, and also from an almost neurotic suspicion of Government and the Native Education Department. The Christian Missions in Many Lands exercized much influence over the Lunda and Lovale, who were impressed by the Brethren's evangelistic and fundamentalist approach, but the Mission's efficiency depended too much on the man on the spot, whilst progress was greatly impeded by the absence of a regular source of income. In addition a number of smaller Protestant societies operated in Northern Rhodesia, but they were generally poorly staffed, inadequately financed, and despite some great personal idealism, remained incapable of making an effective contribution to African education.

In the meantime the Catholics likewise expanded their activities, Northern Rhodesia's increasing importance in the mission field being recognized in 1927 when the Northern Rhodesian Jesuits separated from the parent mission in Southern Rhodesia, and the prefecture of Broken Hill was founded.[2] The region remained in charge of the Jesuits who retained their old spirit of discipline and learning, remaining an ecclesiastical elite of great cohesion, but ran into many difficulties when French priests were replaced by Polish fathers who at first

[1] The Church in question was the Nederduitse Gereformeerde Kerk. A separate European congregation was formed at Lusaka, where a clergyman began to work in 1913 in order to look after the local Afrikaans-speaking community.

[2] In 1946 it was changed into that of Lusaka, and in 1950 it was raised to the status of a Vicariate. In 1959 it was made into an Archdiocese, Northern Rhodesia becoming an Ecclesiastical Province with a fully established Ecclesiastical Hierarchy.

knew little English and were unfamiliar with the country. Poland in the 'thirties moreover was a poor country, which could not afford to send much money abroad, the position being made worse by severe exchange restrictions imposed by the Warsaw Government. Poland nevertheless produced a number of able men, who made a name for themselves in Northern Rhodesia. The most outstanding of these later turned out to be Adam Kozlowiecki, a Jesuit who during the War languished for six years in Nazi concentration camps, and in 1959 became the country's first Catholic Archbishop, though his name has not become widely known overseas, his co-religionists disdaining to make him the object of a publicity campaign of the type which popularized some clergymen of other denominations in Britain. A second foreign-born group were Italian Franciscan Fathers who began work on the Copper Belt in 1931, their difficult task being made no easier towards the end of the 'thirties when relations between Great Britain and Mussolini's Italy got steadily worse. The Catholics received a further access of strength from the Irish Capuchins who took over the area now comprised within the Livingstone Diocese. The Capuchins were distinguished for their push and initiative and their members specially trained for educational work, though one indignant official complained that their expansion into Barotse-land from 1931 destroyed the happy atmosphere of old, leading to a spirit of educational competition which resulted in 'all hating each other for the love of God!'

In North-Eastern Rhodesia the Catholic Church continued to rely on the White Fathers, whose special devotion to Africa formed a particularly note-worthy feature of their evangelical campaign.[1] At the same time the Catholics made various internal changes designed to cope with the increase in administra-tive and other work. In 1933 the Vicariate of Bangweulu—first formed in 1913 —was split into two; and in 1937 the Eastern Province—hitherto part of the Vicariate of Nyasaland—became the Prefecture of Fort Jameson. Particularly outstanding work was done by Father François Tanguy, a noted Bemba linguist, who translated many primers and other books for use in African schools; but the Fathers as a whole were more interested in evangelization than educa-tion, and work suffered further from quarrels with the Afrikaners.

However much they might differ amongst themselves, all societies laboured under a number of similar difficulties, for their efforts depended on the ability of well-wishers overseas to contribute to their funds. In days of prosperity Christian people would still give gladly but the Slump ruined many supporters, with disastrous results to mission finance. Nevertheless paganism gradually diminished; spirit-huts became rarer in the bush, and there were still sudden religious revivals, such as in the Tonga country, where evangelistic work made so much progress by 1930 that the Churches could no longer cope with the demand.[2] Africans became familiar with Bible stories, which devoted mission-

---

[1] Father François Tanguy came to Northern Rhodesia in 1913 and died there in 1961, having only twice during this period departed for leave. For his obituary see *Rhodesia herald*, 12 July 1961

[2] Wesleyan mission. *Annual report, 1930*, p. 75–86

aries translated into the local tongues, and the villagers grasped the Holy Book more clearly than in the pioneering days, when a story went round of a missionary who showed to his converts coloured slides of Jesus bearing the crown of thorns and the Cross. The villagers, who regarded white men as marvellously clever but lazy dogs with a knack for getting other people to do their hard work, apparently concluded that this was the European's special method for making an idle carrier work; if the wretch did not do as he was told, the soldiers would push thorns on his forehead, and if that did not help, they would nail the laggard to his burden! Now incidents from the Bible, Christian hymns and Biblical names became part of the cultural heritage which enriched the lives of many Africans; the Bible became the one and only great literary work to make a deep impact on the African people; and black men could often identify their contemporaries with folk mentioned in the Gospel, such as the townsmen of Corinth, a motley collection of Christians and pagans from many lands, who practised all kinds of sin, and whom St Paul warned against the evils of fornication.[1] The wider impact made by this kind of teaching on native thought is difficult to gauge; and while critics of the missionaries often forgot how many centuries passed in Northern Europe until, say, Saxon or Norwegian tribesmen truly accepted the Gospel. But whatever impression the missionaries may have made, there seems little doubt that European forms of systematic theology did not greatly influence Africans, so that a keen secular observer could criticize the way in which pupils at Mbereshi were imbibing what he called a 'rarified symbolism, strangely blended with esoteric forms of theism', the kind of ideas that would hardly have appealed to a serious-minded 'Foreign Secretary' of a Mission overseas.

At the same time the missions had to face the question of industrialization which burst upon them with such speed that they had no time to prepare themselves for its implications. The white preachers naturally began their work in the countryside, where they trained black teachers and artisans to help them in the work of evangelization and to create Christian villages where life would be superior to the old-time tribal communities. But black clerks and craftsmen had few opportunities of earning a living in backward rural areas, and when employers in the townships offered them higher wages, they emigrated in droves, much to the consternation of missionaries, who feared the baneful influence of irreligious mining camps where their ex-pupils were removed from church influence. Industrialization in fact depreciated the value of the missions' spiritual 'investment' in the reserves, and various European clergymen accordingly saw the solution of their problem in terms of something like territorial *apartheid*, a view which was later quietly abandoned by English-speaking churches and left to heretics at Stellenbosch! The case for segregation was thus forcefully put by the Rev. Edwin W. Smith. 'Some phil-Africans', he wrote, 'oppose a segregation policy on the ground that it implied a disbelief in the African's equality with

[1] Report of a sermon by the Rev. M. J. Rusike, an African, in minutes of the Methodist synod, 1933 (Methodist Mission Arch)

Europeans and endangers his participation in European civilization. On the contrary, we claim that the principle of equality demands that each people have an opportunity of developing its own character, and we are confident that Africans have a great contribution to make to the enrichment of humanity. Cut off from their land and social tradition, they are in a very serious danger of sinking to be a proletariat—mere subservient imitators and servants of the dominant Europeans, under Segregation they have a home of their own. . . .'[1] Smith in fact was thinking of a kind of 'Indirect Rule' in the ecclesiastical sphere, where Africans would slowly build up their own independent institutions under the guidance of sympathetic expatriates, though the ultimate hand-over of power would of course only come in the distant and nebulous future. Indigenous churches, however, needed indigenous funds which could not be collected from poverty stricken congregations in the back-veld, which meant that the mission churches, with their relatively high standards, remained desperately dependent on monetary assistance from overseas. Worse still was their staff problem, for though the Churches produced a number of able African pastors, like the Rev. Leonard W. Shapela, an African Methodist who did excellent work at Broken Hill, the general level of African teachers and evangelists remained low. Evangelists were poorly trained, they usually lacked permanent churches, and only spent about half the year on clerical or educational work, the remainder of their time being taken up in cultivating their crops or supplementing their meagre knowledge of the Bible at central training institutions,[2] specialization of African labour proceeding as slowly in the clerical as in the industrial and administrative fields.

In the evangelical field the Churches similarly began to adopt a new attitude, though there was often a considerable time lag until the changed concepts made themselves felt in remote outstations away in the bush. From the 'twenties onwards many more missionary writers argued that Africans also possessed cultural values of their own which should be preserved rather than destroyed by missionary teaching. Edwin W. Smith, Northern Rhodesia's most distinguished clerical scholar, thus firmly believed that the religion brought to Africa in the early days was really an amalgam of many different elements; that missionaries should distinguish between 'essential Christianity'—the pure teachings of the New Testament—and other, more secular aspects of Western civilization, which should be disentangled from the Gospel's greater message. A whole generation of learned Christians, men like Henri Junod and Dietrich Westermann, shared Smith's outlook, and helped to change the prevailing older missionary view which generally regarded African villagers as a people without either history or culture, empty vessels at best, that should be filled with the white man's truth.[3] Catholic clergymen argued along similar lines, stressing that their Church

---

[1] Smith, E. W. *The way of the white fields in Rhodesia.* . . . World dominion press, 1928, p. 136–137

[2] See for instance London Missionary Society. *Deputation reports, 1924,* p. 123; and 1931, p. 9

[3] Sundkler, B. *The Christian ministry in Africa.* Uppsala, Swedish institute of missionary research, 1960, p. 88–93

never identified itself with one particular culture, not even the Western variety with which it had been associated so closely in its history, that the Church could always draw new strength from other streams of thought, and that even pagan thought should neither be scorned nor completely rejected, but should be purified of its dross and perfected by Christian wisdom.[1]

At the same time Christian leaders began to appreciate the importance of bringing the Bible to the mining compound as well as to the kraal, the new town-orientated approach owing much to the initiative of John Merle Davis, a scholar of distinction. Davis belonged to the new generation of American churchmen who were filled with that post-war idealism which persuaded so many of his countrymen that they ought to make the world a better place after the bloody slaughter on the Western front. Davis moreover possessed a considerable knowledge of sociology, having made a name for himself earlier on by a survey of multi-racial problems on the Pacific Coast, and later as Secretary of the Institute of Pacific Relations. Davis's work made a considerable impression on the International Missionary Council which placed him in charge of its newly organized Department of Social and Industrial Research; this creation itself stood out as a sign of the times.[2] Davis worked at Geneva from where he investigated the problems of Africa south of the Sahara, his labours resulting in a major enquiry into the effects of the Northern Rhodesian copper mines on African life and evangelical problems.[3] In writing his report, he co-operated with a number of distinguished academic men and others, the new approach resulting in an attitude of mind very different from the old-fashioned, simple, unquestioning fire-and-brimstone faith of old. Davis and his collaborators recommended, amongst other things, a better anthropological training for missionaries, and the churches were urged to pay more attention to social welfare problems on the mines, and to acquire a better understanding of the implications of Indirect Rule. More important still, Davis suggested the formation of an inter-denominational Protestant Church on the Copper Belt which would tackle the evangelical problems raised by the new mining economy, which the Churches had hitherto neglected. In the meantime African workers on the Copper Belt had begun to form Christian groups of their own, governed by Elders, and from 1936 various Protestant churches co-operated in the creation of a United Mission on the Copper Belt, which was run on Presbyterian lines, and achieved so much success that the Government in 1937 asked the Mission to collaborate in the field of education.[4]

The same more sophisticated spirit of enquiry also began to effect Government officials who now gradually ceased to think of Africans as simple-minded

---

[1] See *Encyclical letter of ... John XXIII, by Divine Providence Pope, on the missions, known as Princeps pastorum, the prince of shepherds,* 28 Nov 1960

[2] Goodsell, F. F. 'Serenity amid Labour ... the life and work of John Merle Davis 1875–1960' (in *International review of missions,* v. 49, Oct 1960, p. 443–445)

[3] Davis, J. Merle, and others. *Modern industry and the African.* Macmillan, 1933

[4] For a detailed account see Taylor, J. V., and Lehmann, D. *Christians of the Copperbelt.* SCM Press ltd, 1961

savages who needed a good dose of discipline, the sort of outlook common during 'Chartered' days. Civil servants now began to discover the real or supposed virtues of indigenous institutions, particularly as the whole theory of Indirect Rule depended on 'finding the chief', or knowing who the legitimate rule of any given tribal area should be. Indirect Rule itself stimulated research on the part of intelligent District Commissioners, some of whom produced anthropological memoranda of considerable interest. At the same time anthropology became a flourishing science overseas, where scholars ceased to piece together secondhand reports of sea-captains, explorers and missionaries about the outlandish customs of savages, in order to construct preconceived schemes of social evolution; the 'scissors-and-paste' men disappeared; under the impact of great scholars like Bronislaw Malinowski, anthropologists devoted long periods to 'field work' amongst the tribes whom they wished to study, the value of their work being further enhanced by increasing academic specialization, so that anthropology became a field for professionals rather than for literary minded missionaries or civil servants. What is more, anthropologists, nearly all of them the spiritual children of the Age of Enlightenment with its optimistic rationalism, now generally professed to be scientifically 'objective'. They no longer wrote of ignorant, idle and immoral savages—like their missionary predecessors—but of 'preliterate man'; they no longer described a society as being 'good', but as 'existing in a state of social equilibrium'; they spoke of 'pre-marital intercourse' instead of 'fornication', without always realizing that this kind of cultural relativism itself involved value judgements as passionate as those of old-fashioned preachers whose work they intellectually demolished. Until comparatively recently, moreover, many British anthropologists lacked a sense of history, and a brilliant scholar like Bronislaw Malinowski could in all seriousness embark on a social analysis of a maritime South Sea island people, without ever once mentioning the little grey British gunboats, beyond the horizon and out of the anthropologist's sight, which prevented inter-island raiding, and thereby completely modified the significance of the institutions evolved by these brown-skinned Vikings, whose way of life Malinowski was trying to interpret.

Anthropologists, like other scientists, now attempted to divide their field of study into 'pure' and 'applied' branches. Many now became convinced that applied anthropology might help rulers to solve their colonial problems, and 'do good' in a world of slumps and crises, of unemployment and injustice, where the Fascist peril loomed threatening on the horizon; social scientists in the Anglo-Saxon countries devoted most of their attention to the 'odd men out' of Western society, to poverty-stricken immigrants, delinquent youngsters, and also to people like backward colonial tribesmen, their work helping to reshape the conventional social value judgements of the West, in much the same way as psychologists were likewise altering the moral climate of opinion. Anthropologists in fact acquired a missionary fervour of their own, at a time when many white clergymen in the colonies, burdened down with administrative problems, were losing theirs; whilst field work in the village and lengthy sessions round the

African camp-fire provided a kind of romantic satisfaction, which officials, now increasingly tied to their desks, began to miss. During the same period research was better organized, a major step forward being the creation of the International Institute of African Languages and Cultures, later known as the International African Institute. The new organization was first conceived by Oldham in 1924, just after the setting up of the Advisory Committee on Education at the Colonial Office, Lugard becoming its Chairman, and Oldham its Administrative Director,[1] the two between them making a considerable impact on prevailing opinion with regard to African problems.

Gradually the new trends of thought made themselves felt in the distant Northern Rhodesian backwater, where anthropological writing was previously largely the preserve of missionaries, ex-missionaries and civil servants. Earliest clerical attitudes were reflected in works like H. Masters' and Dr W. E. Masters' account of their work amongst the Lamba, telling of the Gospel's victories amongst lying, loathsome savages, whose customs were vile, and whose morals atrocious.[2] The Masters' book appeared in 1920 but by this time their views were already going out of fashion, the same year seeing the first major anthropological account published on a Northern Rhodesian tribe, a scholarly work produced by the Rev. E. W. Smith and by Andrew Murray Dale, a civil servant in the Chartered Company's administration.[3] This book was followed in 1931 by another account of the Lamba, produced by Clement Martyn Doke, a former Baptist missionary who took up an academic career and obtained a Chair at the University of the Witwatersrand, now feeling convinced that missionaries would have been spared many grievous mistakes if they had only possessed a better knowledge of the meaning of Lamba customs.[4] Next on the scene was Dr Audrey Richards, who wrote a work significantly called *Land, Labour and Diet* . . . the first anthropological account by a student without either an administrative or missionary background ever to have been published on a Northern Rhodesian people.[5]

This kind of research now met with strong official approval, Sir Hubert Young putting all the weight of his gubernatorial authority behind the project of creating a research institute to study the impact of European industry on the Africans. Young's earliest scheme was turned down, but the Governor persisted, and in 1937 the Rhodes-Livingstone Institute was established at Livingstone. The new body at first also incorporated the Rhodes-Livingstone Museum which was given its first permanent home by Young, who in 1934 set aside quarters in the Old Magistrate's Court in Livingstone to house a small ethnological collection. The museum was at first in charge of a part-time curator, but now archaeology ceased to be the preserve of literary minded district officers who—like

---

[1] Perham, M. *Lugard: the years of authority 1898–1945*. Collins, 1960, p. 699
[2] Masters, H., and Masters, W. E. *In wild Rhodesia*. Griffiths, 1920
[3] Smith, E. W., and Dale, A. M. *The Ila-speaking peoples of Northern Rhodesia*. Macmillan, 1920
[4] Doke, C. M. *The Lambas of Northern Rhodesia*. Harrap, 1931, p. 9
[5] Richards, A. I. *Land, labour and diet in Northern Rhodesia: an economic study of the Bemba tribe*. Oxford university press, 1939

Codrington in the old days—collected native curios in much the same way as English country gentlemen and parsons took up the study of antiquities as an interesting and profitable hobby. Archeology in Northern Rhodesia instead became a full-time, specialist study, employing the latest techniques of field-work and scientific investigation, major progress being made in the expansion of knowledge by John Desmond Clark, a Cambridge scholar, who was appointed Curator in 1938. In addition of course the Museum played an important part in the related tasks incumbent on such institutions—the acquisition and preservation of historical, ethnographic as well as archaeological material, and the diffusion of knowledge to scholars and laymen alike.

Anthropological work in Northern Rhodesia developed along similar lines. The new science passed out of the hands of gifted amateurs into those of specialists, who did academic work for a living, employing rigorous techniques of field work, and showing far more interest in understanding society as a whole than gathering information about picturesque, outlandish or revolting 'native customs'. In 1938 Godfrey Baldwin Wilson, a high-minded though over-sensitive scholar, a pupil of Malinowski's at the London School of Economics and Political Science, was appointed Director of the new Institute. Wilson was influenced by Marxist thought, and believed that the country was suffering from a grave social disequilibrium which was occasioned by the rapid but extremely uneven rate of change, brought about by the sudden impact of a capitalist mining economy on small-scale and backward tribal societies. He also felt that a large part of the contemporary crisis in Africa was due to mistaken attempts to maintain social organization on nothing more than a slender base of personal relations, instead of promoting the emergence of great impersonal organizations which would help to integrate small tribal communities into a world society. Wilson, a Christian and a pacifist, did not, however, envisage any revolutionary means to change the globe. Instead he set out with truly missionary enthusiasm to increase man's understanding of society, convinced that social anthropology constituted one of the most useful pursuits any man or woman might take up. In his view a wise and enduring native policy might only be built on the basis of accurate information; knowledge should be obtained slowly, step by step, true understanding only being reached in piecemeal fashion.[1] The local Europeans welcomed the foundation of the Institute, though Moore worried that the accursed parsons might get hold of it and use it to spread Christianity, as they used the B.B.C., a fear which proved quite unjustified in practice![2] Nevertheless, the creation of the Institute itself formed part of a much wider intellectual movement which gradually put the settler on the defensive. Anthropologists were not anti-white, but they conceived their task to be the study of Africans, not of Europeans, despite the fact that the problems of white and black labour migrants in fact bore a considerable resemblance to each other. Scholars would identify

---

[1] Wilson, G., and Hunter, M. *The study of African society*. (Rhodes-Livingstone papers, no. 2, 1939)
[2] *Livingstone mail*, 30 June 1937

themselves with 'their' people, as against white back-veld farmers, railwaymen or shopkeepers who rarely read a book, and could make nothing of the complicated new terminology of matrikin and siblings which anthropologists now used. The new science as an academic discipline produced some outstanding scholars and the Institute soon acquired a fine reputation, whilst from the anthropological point of view Northern Rhodesia became one of the best covered territories in Africa. In the field of 'public relations' however the new discipline proved a complete failure. In one of his early papers Wilson expressed the hope that 'the missionary, the compound manager, the farmer and the housewife' would find the new knowledge as useful as the District Commissioner,[1] but anthropology produced no popularizers capable of putting its conclusions into simple little handbooks which ordinary Europeans could either understand or apply in their working lives, whilst many settlers would have agreed with Dr Johnson, who, on learning about Rousseau's newly fashionable ideas, just snorted 'Sir, don't cant about savages!' In the field of Government the impact of the new science proved greater, as Colonial Service cadets began to study the subject, whilst some more senior men undertook studies of their own, though many hardworked district officers remained convinced, like Dr Huggins in Salisbury, that—generally speaking—anthropologists were too theoretical in their approach to help them in day-to-day work, where so much depended on humdrum problems of pounds, shillings and pence, and on administrative priorities, rather than on analytical interpretation; there were some even who laughingly saw special significance in the fact that 'intellectual' rhymed with 'ineffectual'!

Nevertheless the academic's influence on colonial government increased, a sign of the times being an advertisement published in the *Northern Rhodesia Gazette* in 1937[2] asking for local applicants for a University Summer School on Colonial Administration. The course was organized at Oxford by Professor Coupland and Margery Perham, who got university teachers and senior administrators wedded to Indirect Rule, men like Sir David Cameron, to lecture on native administration within the general setting of recent political economic and anthropological developments. This kind of undertaking would have met with snorts from a man like Codrington, who got his first leadership training in the Bechuanaland Border Police; but the new trend became more marked in the 'thirties, when Government seemed a much more complicated affair and senior officials themselves began to undertake large-scale research.[3]

The new approach in turn helped to affect the officials' general outlook on African questions. Speakers like Lugard or Coupland did not of course start off with a deliberate bias against the white settlers; they simply took certain assumptions about them for granted, the colonists themselves possessing neither train-

---

[1] Wilson, G., and Hunter, M., *op. cit.*

[2] Northern Rhodesia government gazette, 22 Jan 1937

[3] See for instance the masterly investigation carried out by A. W. Pim and S. Milligan into the economic, financial and administrative problems of Northern Rhodesia between 1937 and 1938, published as *Report of the commission appointed to enquire into the financial and economic position of Northern Rhodesia.* 1938 (Colonial no. 145)

ing nor aptitude to put *their* case in an academic fashion. As far as overseas opinion in general was concerned, the colonists as a whole were losing their old reputation as defenders of Queen, Empire and middle-class values in Darkest Africa, becoming instead associated in the minds of some reformers with imperialism, oppression and bourgeois exploitation, a movement of thought quickened by the growing antipathy felt by many British intellectuals towards *entrepreneurs* in general. 'The British Broadcasting Corporation' angrily wrote a colonial journal in the 'thirites 'has on various occasions devoted time on the wireless to talk on matters concerning Africa. It is a great pity that a wider variety of speakers has not been obtained, for invariably those chosen represent a school of thought . . . which is definitely hostile to the European settlers in British Africa. They are irritatingly impartial and broad-minded. There is no reason why some spokesmen on the other side—that is, of the people that have to live their days making a living in Africa—should not also have their say. . . .'[1] Other colonists used blunter language and complained alike of intellectuals and civil servants who only turned out 'bits of paper with writing on it' and turned up their noses at settlers who came to make money and produced solid goods, the gulf between the groups concerned widening as time went on.

[1] *The African observer*, v. 1, no. 5, Sep 1934, p. 2

Chapter Eleven

Northern Rhodesia in World War II

I

The Protectorate takes the field

When Britain declared war on Nazi Germany in September 1939, Northern Rhodesia found herself even less prepared for battle than did the mother country. Throughout the 'thirties, the Protectorate, like all British East African territories, remained responsible for its own defence, and the legislators at Lusaka refused to spend money on askaris. In 1932 the Administration wisely separated the civil and military branches of the Northern Rhodesia Police, the military unit becoming known in 1933 as the Northern Rhodesia Regiment. For the time being, however, administrative reform achieved little, both army and police remaining in a poor state, the Northern Rhodesia Regiment amounting to no more than a weak and ill-equipped battalion of colonial infantry which lacked both motor transport and modern arms. In 1936 Gore-Browne tried to draw public attention to the need for more effective defence, but met with little success, even though the Government admitted that the Northern Rhodesia Regiment was unfit to take the field. Government at first did little more than to recruit a senior officer from the British Regular Army to command the troops, fearing that the compulsory training of white men would interfere with business. The majority of Elected Members displayed even less interest, Moore arguing that the copper-lords should defend their own mines, whilst Knight warned against pessimists who continually cried 'wolf' and cheerfully predicted that 'this mad fetish of armaments would soon break down under its own weight'.[1] The Munich mood lay heavily over the country, re-armament being kept down to the irreducible minimum, though the Administration managed to effect a few minor reforms. In 1938 the Northern Rhodesia Regiment European Reserve was formed which attracted volunteers from all walks of life, on whose public spirit depended the subsequent expansion of the country's defence force. In the following year an African Reserve was formed, as well as the Northern Rhodesia Defence Force, a poorly equipped European Home Guard. But these efforts amounted to little, and when the Germans mobilized, the Protectorate still depended in the main on a single black battalion, numbering only 401 Africans, commanded by 20 European officers and N.C.O.'s. Northern Rhodesia was, however, fortunate in the quality of its fighting men. More than one third of the troops in the Northern Rhodesia Regiment consisted of Bemba; next on the list

[1] Northern Rhodesia. *Legislative Council debates*, 27 Oct 1936 ,p. 211-2

were the Ila, who continued their old fighting tradition in khaki, followed by Angoni and Chewa, recruited like the Swiss mercenaries of old from a bleak country where life was hard and where there was not much alternate employment.[1] The position improved in 1940 when a Compulsory Military Service Ordinance passed on to the Statute Book conscripting British subjects between 18 and 45, local Africans being exempt from the draft in their capacity as 'British Protected Persons'. By the end of 1940 already the Northern Rhodesia Defence Force numbered a total of 1,400, whilst 550 Europeans had joined various regular units, and the Northern Rhodesia Regiment was up to strength.

In 1940 the 1st Battalion of the Northern Rhodesia Regiment departed for British Somaliland which was threatened by Italian forces. In August the Italians, realizing that the British would get no support from Jibuti in French Somaliland held by a Vichy-French garrison, decided to advance into British Somaliland. The Regiment took part in the defence of the Tug Argan Gap where machine gunners and snipers attempted to hold up the enemy in rocky terrain. But the Italians outnumbered the British forces by 10 to 1, the Italians being further supported by aircraft and armour. Northern Rhodesian Africans were now subjected for the first time to modern mechanized warfare, but under white leadership stood up to the test, their prestige rapidly rising amongst Europeans in the Protectorate who originally expected little of local black troops. The British could not, however, hold out long, and after the capitulation of 'Observation Hill', the scene of a bitter struggle, the remainder of the Regiment retreated to Berbera, from where they were evacuated with the other units which defended Somaliland. The battalion rested at Aden and was then sent to Mombasa from where it was despatched to the Malindi front, being subsequently attached to the 21st East African Infantry Brigade. The Northern Rhodesians then took part in the invasion of Ethiopia where they fought several sharp actions and kept open lines of communications. In the meantime the Regiment was expanded, its total strength reaching eight battalions and one independent garrison company, each battalion being in charge of its own commanding officer and attached to the various branches of the East Africa Command, so that the Northern Rhodesians never fought as one division. The 5th Battalion garrisoned Italian Somaliland where Italian officers and Somali warriors organized anti-British risings, further trouble being caused by local cattle raiders. They subsequently went to the Middle East, mostly serving in Palestine where the African soldiers were apparently much more highly impressed by the Jews than the Arabs. The 2nd, 3rd and 4th Battalions were formed into the 27th (Northern Rhodesia) Infantry Brigade which in 1942 took part in the occupation of Madagascar, then in possession of the Vichy French and regarded as a potential threat to allied communications in the Indian Ocean. The island quickly

[1] Within the ranks of the Northern Rhodesia Regiment in 1938 the Bemba numbered 37·5 per cent, Angoni 12 per cent, Ila 18·5 per cent, Chewa 7 per cent. The remainder was made up of various other Northern Rhodesian tribes. In relation to their total population, the Ila and recruits from the Eastern Province were more highly represented than other tribes.

capitulated and the question then arose whether the Brigade should be sent to the Far East as one fighting formation. The authorities decided against such a policy, arguing that a unit drawn from a single, comparatively under-populated territory might suffer heavy casualties in one operation, with the result that Northern Rhodesia might incur a disproportionately great loss of life in one action. The Brigade therefore broke up to 'spread the risk', a similar policy being adopted with regard to white troops from Southern Rhodesia. The 1st Battalion left for Ceylon from where the men departed in July 1944 for Chitta-gong, an Indian base for the reconquest of Burma from the Japanese. The Nor-thern Rhodesians joined in a hard and difficult campaign which took them into northern Burma, and then down south, across the Chindwin River and beyond Kalewa, north west of Mandalay, fighting under the most appalling conditions, in mud and jungle, dirt and rain, where tropical downpours often caused trans-port to bog down in sodden ground whilst swollen rivers would sweep away bridges, life being made even more miserable by the ever-present threat of disease. The battalion took part in a number of savage clashes, plodding through jungle, swamp and mountain country and relying on the Allied Air Forces for supplies dropped by parachutes. The going was as tough as any Bri-tish troops had to face in the war, the Northern Rhodesians having to contend against an enemy adept at sniping and night fighting, who used to crawl up closely to the British positions and suddenly break into blood-curdling yells, firing at close range in the hope of panicking the askari. The Northern Rhode-sians, however, soon adapted themselves to this kind of warfare, and it was not long till they themselves employed 'jitter tactics' at night, sometimes getting to close quarters with hand grenades and machine carbines. In addition, useful work was done in constructing telephone lines, air-strips and roads, the troops finally leaving Burma in October 1945. Whilst the 1st Battalion was engaged in the last stages of these operations, the 3rd Battalion disembarked at Chittagong in December 1944, subsequently moving down the Arakan, crossing the Irra-wady, sweeping south towards Rangoon, and then turning north again in pur-suit of the retreating Japanese, till news of the Emperor's surrender reached the troops when they were less than 100 miles away from the Thailand border. Once again African soldiers, under European officers and senior N.C.O.s, displayed their customary courage, physical stamina, capacity for bushcraft and their skills in the arts of ambush and jungle-fighting.[1] A grand total of about 15,000 men joined East Africa Command from Northern Rhodesia, the majority being used on essential garrison duties, so that only a relatively small proportion of veterans were engaged in action, 98 men being killed, 171 suffering wounds, whilst 300 Africans died of various other causes.[2] In the Second World War, Northern Rhodesian Africans still mainly served as infantry, though they now handled more complicated arms—mortars, machine-carbines, P.I.A.T.s and

[1] See Anthony, L. F. G. 'The Second World War' (in Brelsford, W. V. *The story of the Northern Rhodesia Regiment*. Lusaka, Government printer, 1954, p. 75–102)

[2] Northern Rhodesia. *Legislative Council debates*, 24 Nov 1945, p. 13–14

Brens—than in the Great War when they relied on simpler weapons. Special mention should also be made of the relatively large number of African lorry drivers who took the field, the first training school for black recruits being started in May 1940, so that African soldiers now rose into 'semi-skilled' military occupations, just as they were rising into corresponding jobs in civilian life. In the Second World War moreover African troops travelled widely, to India, Burma, Madagascar and Palestine, with the result that their outlook became a great deal wider than in the Great War, when Northern Rhodesian askaris merely fought in their own country or in the adjoining East African countries where they met with conditions much the same as those at home. In the meantime the 'supervisory' tasks, and all the technical war jobs, like flying aircraft and handling armoured cars, were carried out by better educated and more highly qualified Europeans, Northern Rhodesian whites, like their countrymen south of the Zambezi, giving an excellent account of themselves on many fronts. Between 1939 and 1945 about 700 to 800 Europeans from the Protectorate served abroad, of whom 40 lost their lives, the number of men sent overseas forming a considerable percentage in relation to the territory's white population.[1]

II

Mining, farming and land settlement

The first of the Great Wars was fought with steam-power. Steam-engines transported the mass armies mobilized against one another, and steam-power in the main propelled the navies that fought for command of the world's trade routes. The Second World War, however, was waged with internal combustion engines and highly specialized equipment, copper becoming more important as a vital raw material than ever before; almost half the copper production for military purposes went into shells and cartridges, but the bulk of the remainder was now fashioned into electrical equipment and mechanical parts capable of resisting corrosion. The demands made on the mines became enormous, for a single battleship used up as much as 2,000,000 lb of the red metal. Great Britain now found itself fortunate in controlling a major supply of copper within the Sterling Area, and when rearmament was getting under way in 1937, the Protectorate turned out 210,000 tons per annum out of a world production of some 2,240,000 tons, the Territory coming fourth amongst the world's producers, the U.S.A. still easily retaining its lead. The Allies thus had access to most of the world's copper, but nevertheless their demands grew so insatiable that materials had to

---

[1] The number of white people in the territory during the Second World War amounted to between 14 to 15,000, so that something like 5 per cent served overseas. The corresponding figure for the Africans was about 15,000 out of a population of about 1,300,000, giving a percentage of 1·1.

be rationed. In Great Britain a Ministry of Supply was set up in 1939 and many important goods were excluded from the sphere of private purchasers. The Ministry acquired copper by bulk agreements with Canadian and Northern Rhodesian producers; and two years later the American Government followed suit, with the result that the free working of the copper market disappeared. Prices now depended on compacts between Government departments and powerful private concerns working in close co-operation, but the big companies did not fare too badly under the new regime. It is true that they could no longer drive up prices to the high levels attained in the First World War, and in addition they had to meet the heavy burden of Excess Profits Tax, whilst dividends fell.[1] But on the other hand they acquired a secure market and sheltered prices, and Government aided their expansion. Soon after the outbreak of war prices rose considerably, and in 1942 *The Economist* calculated that copper producers operated at a cost not much higher than half the prices they received, so that the companies could further expand production, the Northern Rhodesian output reaching its war-time peak in 1942, when it amounted to some 250,000 tons. The British Government gladly supported the Rhodesian expansion programme for it was not until the second half of 1943 that the Allies considered available copper supplies to be roughly equal to their needs. Britain moreover had to resume cash payments for a number of American raw materials, copper and zinc being made ineligible for Lend Lease supplies when the Americans began to worry about their own needs. In 1943 the Ministry of Supply advanced £750,000, half the cost of a big development programme for Nchanga mine, whilst private subscribers accounted for the remainder.[2] The position in fact improved so much that in 1944 the Colonial Office announced that Government purchases of

---

[1] Prices per long ton of electrolytically refined copper stood as follows in the period from the First to the aftermath of the Second World War:

Year	Price	Year	Price
1914	62·6	1932	25·6
1915	79·6	1933	32·4
1916	125·2	1934	38·8
1917	125·0	1935	40·2
1918	113·5	1936	43·6
1919	86·0	1937	60·7
1920	80·4	1938	46·1
1921	57·6	1939	50·6
1922	61·6	1940	63·6
1923	66·5	1941	66·1
1924	60·0	1942	66·1
1925	64·7	1943	66·1
1926	63·6	1944	66·1
1927	59·5	1945	66·1
1928	67·1	1946	77·5
1929	83·5	1947	117·5
1930	59·8	1948	123·5
1931	37·4	1949 Jan	131·3
		1950 Jan	148·4

[2] See Gann, L. H. 'The Northern Rhodesian copper industry and the world of copper: 1923–1952' (in *Rhodes-Livingstone journal*, no. 18, 1955, p. 1–18) for details and references. For the six years ended 30. 6. 1945 the territory produced a total of 1,424,289 long tons of copper

Rhodesian copper would be cut by about 20 to 25 per cent of the aggregate amount produced in 1943, the Government's decision deriving from an increase in the shipping tonnage available, reduction of losses, the expansion of alternate metals like aluminium, greater experience and economy in the use of materials, the completion of a large part of the American war-plant programme, and the fact that allied military successes gave them control over the battlefields and the 'battle-scrap' scattered over the scenes of these bloody encounters.[1] Economists, copper magnates and government officials all in fact foresaw a post-war slump arising from the large copper stocks in hand, their mood of pessimism communicating itself to the white workers on the Copper Belt who worried right through the war that a post-war depression would put them out of their jobs, a fear which seemed reasonable enough when the Governor himself explained in 1940 that Northern Rhodesia might have to face a sharp drop in production at the end of hostilities.[2] Fortunately the prophets of woe proved mistaken; the experts foresaw the past rather than the future. Production continued, the surplus being made available to the U.S.A. and the Soviet Union, though the workers' mood of uncertainty remained to bedevil labour relations on the Copper Belt.

In addition Northern Rhodesia expanded production of other minerals, Broken Hill producing zinc and lead, and also vanadium, a metal used in the manufacture of steel for armoured plating. In addition a substantial amount of cobalt was turned out, and in 1943 two small mica mines opened in the Territory, producing mica of high quality which came to be in great demand for the manufacture of valves in oxygen masks used in bombers. War lastly stimulated the country's incipient secondary industries, small components for ammunition being produced in mine and railway workshops by skilled white men and women, working round the clock to the limits of their strength. Thousands of parts for tanks, and bombs were turned out which reached the military workshops in North Africa, packed and labelled 'Urgent Fighting Stores'. Rhodesian Railwaymen at the same time solved the difficult task of coping with vastly increased traffic on a single line from the Congo to Bulawayo and beyond, without adequate replacements of rolling stocks, moving men, metals and machinery, material for aerodromes and camps, as well as civilian supplies over enormous distances, their job being made even more difficult by the diversion of many Congolese and Angolan products from Lobito to the safer Cape route.

The war effort in turn depended on food, fighting abroad proving a boon to the farmer at home. In 1937 Northern Rhodesia managed to produce 437,000 bags of maize of which 242,000 derived from European farms. But in the years following production fell, slumping to no more than 152,000 bags of which 120,000 were European grown, with the result that in 1941 the Territory found itself with a deficit of some 400,000 bags. The reasons for this disastrous state of affairs were manifold. Farmers suffered from a run of bad seasons; and once war

[1] *Economist*, 29 Jan 1944
[2] Northern Rhodesia. *Legislative Council debates*, 30 Nov 1947, p. 7–9

broke out, implements became expensive and hard to get. A Food Production Committee was set up to improve matters which advised farmers to expand their maize acreage, but no similar suggestions were at first made to African cultivators so as not to increase erosion. The white farming population moreover was small, the pre-war mood of economic pessimism having inhibited an active immigration policy at a time when Northern Rhodesia might have vastly increased the number of its people, thus expanding both its agricultural and industrial potential. The mines, Maybin argued in 1940, had nearly reached the limit of expansion, a conclusion which seemed perfectly reasonable in view of the companies' own views on the subject. The country could not afford to attract many more farmers because of transport and marketing difficulties, whilst the climate might prevent Europeans from permanently retaining their racial characteristics (a view earlier put forward by Maxwell, though resting on little scientific evidence). Admittedly, said the Governor, European immigration brought many benefits to the country, accelerating industrial and agricultural development, improving communications, and bringing in capital and brains, whilst Africans were introduced to new crops, finding more markets for their labour, and benefiting from the increased revenue available for social services. (Immigration, moreover, though Maybin did not make the point, also constituted a kind of economic subsidy paid by the settler's homeland to the 'receiving' territory which got the newcomer's skill, training and muscles free of charge at the 'exporting' country's expense). But nevertheless white immigration, the Governor felt, also brought many new problems; land would be alienated to Europeans; the sudden introduction of new ideas would lead to social disintegration and the disappearance of village crafts, whilst a people with a high standard of living would suddenly come into contact with a very backward people, with far-reaching consequences to the country's social stability, whilst markets were limited and did not appear to justify a vast increase in the number of producers. The settlers shared the officials' pessimism, fearing competition for their limited markets and anticipating that newcomers might take their jobs. Some Socialist critics of Imperialism arrived at similar conclusions, though for very different reasons. Europeans, argued a contributor to *Empire*, should no longer come to Africa in order to make money, to take away the black man's land, or enjoy the higher standard of living and social privileges of a *Herrenvolk*; Africa admittedly still needed technically qualified white men, but the new style pioneers should journey abroad in a spirit of humility, devotion and self sacrifice for the purpose of helping black men to better themselves. These views depended, however, on two unrecognized assumptions. The first was that the West still possessed a great 'reserve army' of highly skilled white labour which could be deployed abroad at small cost, a view perfectly true during the Slump, but no longer in accordance with the facts in the late 'thirties when prosperity and rearmament gradually did away with unemployment. Secondly, some Fabian theorists imagined that the British skilled workers or the liberal and socialist intelligentsia could as yet produce secular equivalents of 'lay-brothers' and 'artisan missionaries' of old, a fanciful belief, which bore no relationship to reality. Nevertheless, these views continued to be advocated with growing conviction and made a contribution to the anti-colonization mood now gaining ground both in Britain and the colonies themselves. Right-wing theorists, on the other hand, whilst theoretically approving of British settlement in Africa, envisaged grave dangers from unselective immigration of aliens which would rob British territories of their characteristic features, and strongly objected to the mass settlement of European foreigners. The pessimists thus carried the day on the immigration question, and whilst black settlers continued to drift into Northern Rhodesia from Angola and Mozambique, white colonization received little encouragement.

In 1939, for instance, when many German Jews were seeking to escape from Nazi persecution, Young privately suggested to a friend that refugees might settle in North-Western Rhodesia. Palestine could not absorb these people for political reasons, but Northern Rhodesia might; for Jews were not unpopular in Northern Rhodesia where some of the local Hebrew traders were amongst the best in the community; Jews moreover would be adaptable and would be grateful to the Imperial Government for allowing them to come. Young's ideas made some impression in London on the grounds that such a scheme might divert immigration from Palestine and thus reduce tension in the Holy Land, that the project was desirable for humanitarian reasons, that it might improve relations with the U.S.A., and be welcome at a time when Britain was engaging in intergovernmental discussions at Evian to solve the refugee problem. The question was then discussed with the Elected Members in Northern Rhodesia, but local opposition proved insuperable. The local Europeans worried over the country's shaky and ill-balanced economy; they also feared competition from outside, arguing that aliens would undercut them, a belief not altogether unjustified at a time when some homeless Jews, excluded from coming to South Africa and Southern Rhodesia, were trying to find work north of the Zambezi in return for merely board and lodging. In addition, Elected Members argued that Northern Rhodesia already contained between 800 to 1,000 aliens, that the proportion of foreigners to Britons should not be further raised, that the strangers might not identify themselves politically with white Rhodesians, and that Hebrew immigration might lead to increased anti-semitism, whilst imposing a financial burden on the existing Jewish community.[1]

Not all Northern Rhodesians agreed with these views. In 1938 a senior police officer for instance presented a very different case, arguing that aliens numbered only ten per cent of the population, but that the Central Europeans numbered amongst them doctors, manufacturers, lawyers and merchants, men of good standing and sometimes possessed of capital who would form a stable part of the population. The British population was fluctuating in character, two thirds of the British immigrants entering the country to replace other British nationals who had since left the country. But the alien refugees had no other country to go

[1] Northern Rhodesia. *Legislative Council debates*, 5 June 1939, p. 405–419

back to, with the result that of 148 foreigners who entered between January and September 1938, only one had left. In fact, the Commissioner argued, it was difficult to justify a restrictive policy in a territory covering some 300,000 square miles with only 15,000 whites. A year later an official Commission further investigated the question; the Commissioners agreed that the white population as a whole lacked stability, the mines in particular having an annual turnover of 35 per cent of their white labour force. Aliens on the other hand stayed on, becoming Northern Rhodesians in the true sense of the word, whilst standards of Central European craftsmanship were high.[1] But all the same, the Commissioners thought that there could be no question of mass immigration; Northern Rhodesia's economic prospects were far from rosy; and the Territory should handpick its white population by Immigrants' Selection Boards, which would screen the newcomers before they came in, the Commissioners never considering how far Rhodes and Beit themselves would have fared under such a system! Experts did get as far as discussing a scheme of settling some 500 German-speaking Jews as smallholders in the isolated Mwinilunga district where they would be more or less self sufficient and not compete with established farmers on the Railway Belt. But even this rather unrealistic project proved too much for local opinion, the *Livingstone Mail* arguing that the newcomers would soon need expensive services, that their settlement might become a reservoir of cheap labour, that the Jews would not stay in their 'reserves' permanently, but drift out to set up banks and businesses as far afield as Southern Rhodesia, and that the country ought to retain its British character instead of being turned into an annexe of Palestine.[2] The original project was thus whittled down to negligible proportions, but even this could not be carried out as war supervened, and the trickle of immigration dried up.

No special steps having been taken to promote land settlement during the War, the white farming population turned out to be pitifully small when hostilities started. Nevertheless, farmers responded magnificently to the new demands, and when Government in 1942 provided guaranteed minimum prices for wheat and maize over a period for three years, production rose dramatically. Loans now became available to cultivators, and inspectors went round the countryside with a right of entry to all European farms, enforcing better methods. In addition, oxen or machinery which were not being used to their full capacity had to be handed over to people who needed them most. The Administration in 1942 also began temporarily to conscript African labour, Northern Rhodesia adopting measures similar to those being used in Kenya and Tanganyika. Draftees were compelled to serve for two months at normal rates of pay, but the system worked badly, and the European farmers themselves expressed thorough dissatisfaction with a method of recruitment which dumped on them all the undesirables of whom local chiefs wanted to get rid, and conscription was abolished, a voluntary labour corps being set up instead. Even this solution

[1] *Report on immigration into Northern Rhodesia*. Lusaka, Government printer, 1939
[2] *Livingstone mail*, 3 Aug and 3 Sep 1938

proved unsatisfactory, and Geoffrey Bernard Beckett, a far-sighted spokesman for the farming industry later explained in the Legislative Council that the real remedy lay in improving pay, conditions and African labour efficiency, that mechanization could not be achieved with casual drifters; that the agricultural work force should be stabilized and that Government should assist the farm labourers' families to move to the breadwinners' place of work.[1]

Despite these weaknesses on the labour front, the forward policy in farming met with success, and production quickly expanded. Northern Rhodesian agriculture of course could never be organized as tightly as in the United Kingdom, and the authorities—for administrative reasons—found themselves unable to subsidize specific operations like clearing new land or buying more implements; the Administration instead relied more on the farmers' good sense and their desire for a cash return, a sound approach which results justified up to the hilt. In 1945 the Railway Belt as a whole grew 475,000 bags of maize (exclusive of what was being turned out for African inter-village trade), white farmers accounting for 268,000 bags, a dramatic increase on the figures of 1942 when Europeans only grew 146,000 and Africans 51,000 bags. The farmers thus won a major, though little publicized victory, which in turn helped to keep the wheels of industry turning.

African cultivators also played a major part in the food campaign, and throughout the War white farmers—relieved of the fear of African competition—supported the drive for greater productivity. The Government encouraged the utilization of scarce resources like natural rubber.[2] Agricultural officers as well as white farmers themselves worried about the bad shape of much of the native land, and Thomas Spurgeon Page, Member for the Eastern District, in particular impressed on the House the serious situation in the Eastern Province, where more and more Africans were drifting in from Portuguese territory on to already overcrowded lands. Page considered that white farmers possessed a most immediate and personal interest in native improvement schemes, for Europeans were now asked to plant maize as a rotation crop, the reserves being unable to meet their own demand for food, with the result that farmers could no longer purchase enough grain from the African villagers and had to grow their own, thus cutting down the acreage available for more valuable crops. Gore-Browne agreed that Africans must be taught better methods, and bitterly denounced 'the dead hand of vested interest', which, in the shape of the North Charterland Company, was locking up vast unused areas in the Eastern Province.[3] Captain Richard Ernest Campbell, a 'Railway Belt' Member, took a similar line about his part of the country, explaining that Africans were overploughing their land, indigenous cattle owners preferring to use their beasts as draft oxen instead of selling them for their meat: African cultivators required

---

[1] Northern Rhodesia. *Legislative Council debates*, 28 Nov 1945, p. 72–75

[2] See Hobson, R. H. *Rubber: a footnote to Northern Rhodesian history*, (Rhodes-Livingstone Museum occasional papers, no. 13, 1960) which provides an excellent account of the varying fortunes of this little industry.

[3] Northern Rhodesia. *Legislative Council debates*, 24 Jan 1940, p. 379–399

much more tuition, for at the moment they were still overstocking their reserves, ploughing up vleis and destroying trees and sponge areas, with the result that vlei lands were drying out and the water level dropping. Government was partly responsible for this state of affairs, having done much too little in the past to assist black peasants, unlike Southern Rhodesia which started 'contouring' the land as early as 1928, and was taking effective steps to divide blocs of native grazing from arable land. North of the Zambezi the position was much worse; Africans were spreading from their own areas into Forest Reserve and Crown Land, where they ploughed up and down the slopes with disastrous consequences for the soil. The Government's inspectorate was totally inadequate, Campbell himself having seen many an expensive dam destroyed by ignorant villagers, who cut the earthworks and let out the water to catch fish.[1]

The administrators' task of course was considerably more difficult than 'Unofficial' critics were apt to assume. The Agricultural Department, like the district staff, was over-worked and under-staffed, recruits being almost impossible to get at a time when every available man was put in khaki. The men who remained in the Service did what they could, a total of just under 50,000 acres of cultivated land being protected against erosion in the native areas during wartime. In addition Government was forced to engage in a bitter and long-drawn out struggle with the North Charterland Company for its land, the matter going to arbitration in 1941. The Company finally sold its land for the sum of £153,986, more than twice the sum which Northern Rhodesia originally offered, 3,776,741 acres now becoming available for European and African settlement. The North Charterland Company did not fare badly under the bargain, its shilling shares reaching 1/7½d before arbitration was announced, and settling at 1/3d after the award became known.[2] In the Legislative Council, on the other hand, the decision met with strong opposition, Gore-Browne denouncing the former Reserve Commission for not taking enough land in the first place, and causing unnecessary suffering to Africans.[3] Administrators, moreover, had to contend with major technical difficulties, the position with regard to African agriculture being particularly bad in the Fort Jameson area. William Allan, the Territory's able Assistant Director of Agriculture, thus explained to a land commission in 1942 that the Fort Jameson area formed one of his greatest headaches. Much had been achieved by agricultural 'demonstrators' on the Railway Belt where African tribal communities had largely broken down, and much of native farming in effect was based on peasant proprietorship. In the Fort Jameson area, on the other hand, tribal institutions still retained a strong hold on the people, discouraging local enterprise; land moreover was inadequate and no more Europeans should settle locally. The soil was threatened by an insidious process of slow deterioration, and no solution seemed in sight. Permanent agriculture on a 'maize standard' needed either green manure with the addition

[1] Northern Rhodesia. *Legislative Council debates*, 18 Mar 1941, p. 318–326
[2] *Financial times*, 18 Nov 1941
[3] Northern Rhodesia. *Legislative Council debates*, 9 Dec 1941, p. 34

of artificial fertilizers or cow-dung, but chemical fertilizers were unobtainable, and Africans in many areas just did not have enough beasts to manure their land, the herds being too unevenly distributed, and often threatened by the dreaded 'fly'. Besides African cultivators had no means of taking dung to their fields, and without adequate cash incentives they would shy from the additional labour involved. All the department could do was to resettle the surplus population elsewhere, improve methods, and test means of increasing the carrying capacity of the land, Fundamentally of course the question was linked to a vast demographic revolution; the population was no longer held in check by war and famine, pestilence and drought, with the result that Africans were doubling their numbers every 25 years, so that major local land problems remained to trouble the future.

III

Strikes and commotions

Mobilization led to a severe white labour shortage which greatly strengthened the bargaining position of the Mine Workers' Union. The Europeans, many of them young men fresh from the Rand, argued that now was the time to stand out for their pay, convinced that they would lose their chance if they waited for the expected days of peace, slump and unemployment. Besides the mine workers suffered from the war-time rise in the cost of living, and some complained that under existing emergency regulations they could not leave the country without a permit, though Management could still dismiss men who were no longer wanted. The position was perhaps aggravated further by lack of contact between Government officials and white labour migrants, tough Copper Belt miners showing scant respect for Englishmen from Eton and Balliol, whilst some officials in turn envisaged the miners as a brutal and lawless lot, an impression not borne out by the low crime figures characteristic of the Copper Belt. Trouble sparked off at Mufulira, and in March 1940 the white miners there held an angry meeting during the course of which they voted the Vice Chairman of their Union out of office, and set up a Committee of Action. The new Committee felt convinced that the companies were making a good thing out of the war, and demanded that white wages and overtime should be increased, that housing should be improved, and that the authorities should undertake an enquiry into the question of silicosis, a dreaded occupational disease. Government attempted to mediate between the mines and their men, but the workers would not accept conciliation and Mufulira came out on strike, Nkana following suit, though Chingola and Luanshya stayed at work. The whites gained most of their wage demands, and Managements also agreed to deduct monthly subscriptions to the Union from their members' pay packets at the unionists' voluntary request.

The European strike made a deep impression on the African workers, some of whom were apparently upbraided by their white supervisors for lacking guts in standing up for their rights. A story went about the compounds of a father who had two children, who were both hungry. One of them received food and then went to his brother and told him 'My father has given me food to eat because I refused to work for him'; then the second brother said to himself 'If I do as my brother, my father will assuredly feed me too', the moral being that Africans should likewise strike. The Africans never clearly formulated their demands which varied widely, but they did understand that their lot was not getting any better. A subsequent Commission of Enquiry found that black workers in 1940 were actually drawing smaller wage packets than during the roaring days of the construction boom when labour was short, subsequent wage reductions made after the Slump never having been made good, even when the mine owners began to earn substantial profits from the end of the 'thirties.[1] Africans also had other grievances. They resented the rise in the cost of living as much as the Europeans, and they disliked the wide disparity between their pay and the Europeans, arguing that black men might do some of the jobs done by white men for less pay, but still at a higher remuneration than was being received by Africans. Africans also objected to the insulting behaviour which some Europeans adopted towards them, one lout being able to undo the good work of dozens of fair minded foremen. A British labour expert who studied the question of race relations before the War, found that there was a small number of both English and Afrikaans-speaking workers who laboured under an obsessive hatred of Africans, their sinister preoccupation with the 'Black Peril' being comparable to war-time spy manias. But when trouble came, it did not break out between white and black workers, but between workers and mining companies. The expert was, however, quite right in fearing violence, for the compounds contained a number of workless or workshy youngsters with nothing better to do than look for a quarrel. The first sparks flew when an African woman at Chingola started to argue with a native food issuing clerk who hit her, the European Assistant Manager also getting in a few blows. The two culprits were punished, but the Africans in the Chingola compound were furious, and there was rioting before the men went back to work. By now the whole atmosphere was electrically charged, and at Nkana unknown Africans put up strike notices. 'In what respect do we differ from the police' read one of them 'because we are working men and the police are very overbearing towards us. This annoys me greatly and I say—all who feel like me should attack the police. Moreover this fact embitters my mind—the Europeans left their work without any trouble falling upon them.

---

[1] See *Report of the commission appointed to inquire into the disturbances in the copperbelt, Northern Rhodesia.* Lusaka, Government printer, 1940. Appendix 11 of this document gives detailed accounts of African wages.

In 1929 surface workers got an average of about 17/6 and underground workers 30/– a month. In 1942, after the companies had agreed to increases, the respective figures were 15/– and 28/–, even though the cost of living was higher. Workers also got rations. As far as the companies' profits were concerned, investors began to receive substantial returns from about 1937 onwards. In the year ended 30 June 1939 Mufulira earned £1,041,431, Roan Antelope £1,372,204, Rhokana £2,116,398 and Nchanga none.

z

Cannot a slave, too, speak to his master. . . .'[1] The mine management offered another 2/6 a month, but there was no recognized machinery to negotiate with the workers, management relying on the boss boys to make its offer known. These meetings broke up inconclusively and the Africans later went on strike, receiving letters of encouragement from Mufulira where trouble was also breaking out. The strikers were originally quite peaceable, but then the violent element gained control, Baushi and other Africans from the Fort Rosebery and Kawambwa districts taking a prominent part in disturbances throughout the strike. The position quickly deteriorated, and when on 3 April Nkana mine unwisely tried to hold a pay parade, a threatening crowd of several thousand strikers assembled and began to hurl stones, sticks and pieces of iron at the African troops and police who assembled to protect the office. The security forces first tried tear gas, but hotheads urged the mob on, shouting that the soldiers would only shoot with paper bullets. In the end the troops opened fire, having been forced back on the office buildings, and thirteen Africans were killed, and 69 wounded, of whom 4 died later on, whilst 21 black soldiers were put out of action by injuries.

At Mufulira the strike passed off without firing, though there was some rioting, as well as fights between Africans themselves, Mgumbo natives clashing with Bemba workers. The position at one time looked ugly when a truculent crowd of three or four thousand people assembled at the compound offices, all asking to be paid off, but the men were persuaded to disperse. The strike leaders later prevented a meeting between the Bemba and their Tribal Elders, the Bemba apparently taking a less prominent part in the outbreak than in 1935. The remaining miners disowned their Tribal Elders, who were accused of having accepted the extra 2/6 a month offered by the mines without consulting their followers. The workers also showed much hostility against the companies' African compound police who had to move out of their quarters, leadership of the strikes passing to a Council of Seventeen, as the District Commissioner had advised the men that they should select representatives to negotiate on their behalf. The men held out for a few more days, the Seventeen undertaking that further intimidation should cease, but in the end the strike collapsed, and the miners went back to work, with a slight increase in pay.

The Copper Belt riot ended with a Commission of Enquiry, which considered that Africans on the Copper Belt were not yet ready for trade unionism, but that the negotiating machinery should be improved. The Commissioners were favourably impressed by the Elder system, despite the fact that Elders proved incapable of controlling events at Mufulira, arguing that the fault lay with management for badly timing their offer of an increase in pay. The Elder system was described as analogous to that under which African village communities managed their own affairs, a view not in accordance with the facts, but in tune with the local climate of opinion which continued to regard unskilled miners as peasants temporarily resident in towns. The mines accepted this view

[1] See *Report of the commission appointed to inquire into the disturbances in the copperbelt, Northern Rhodesia.* Lusaka, Government printer, 1940, p. 63–64

and all subsequently worked through tribal representatives to deal with general complaints, matters of individual concern being taken up by Government Labour Officers. The Commission also suggested small increases in wages and improvements in general conditions, African workers gaining various minor benefits from these proposals. In addition the Commission recommended further advancement of Africans in industry, and proposed that talks should be held between Government and the European workers to promote black men to better jobs.

Rioting in the Copper Belt never constituted a serious security problem, for the African troops remained stoutly loyal, whilst even the most militant strike leaders do not appear to have thought in terms of setting up permanent organizations, but merely getting more pay here and now, as well as showing a bold front to the Europeans. African workers remained unorganized, though boss boys and clerks formed temporary associations, compound managers agreeing in 1942 to meet boss boys, both surface and underground, to discuss grievances relating to the black sub-foremen's grievances. But overseas the impact of the riot was considerable; Northern Rhodesia moved into the limelight and 'got a bad Press;' convinced Socialists like Arthur Creech Jones asked questions in the House; liberal minded scholars like Margery Perham wrote letters to *The Times*, and the Fabian Colonial Bureau, founded in 1940, began to concern itself specifically with Northern Rhodesia; Rhodesian mining companies and white workers alike came under attack at a time when Britain's desperate struggle for survival was making even the most conservative-minded impatient of both property rights and long established trade union privileges. The mining companies of course also had defenders like the *Economist*, which argued that mining profits were necessarily higher than those of other industries, because money had to be spent for lengthy periods without a return, and because ores constituted a wasting asset. The companies, the *Economist* pointed out, earned nothing at all until 1932, the full profit-earning stage not being reached until 1937; up to 1941 some £22,000,000 were invested in the copper mines, but gross trading profits over the last 18 years only amounted to £25,000,000 of which £7,000,000 had gone into taxes, shareholders having got less than £7,000,000 in dividends. Even so, the Journal agreed, much remained to be done: stabilization of labour now seemed desirable, the present system making the worst of both worlds; and black workers should be allowed to advance—if necessary at the whites expense.[1]

The Europeans, however, were in no mood to make concessions. Underground work in a tropical climate was a hard and dangerous job and—the whites argued—Copper Belt miners were far from being the world's best paid workers, as their critics asserted, some American workers drawing considerably larger pay packets. Deserving Africans, the miners continued, should of course be promoted to better posts, but if they did white men's jobs, they should get white men's wages, the trade union principle of 'equal pay for equal work'

[1] *Economist*, 22 Mar 1941

applying in Rhodesia as much as in Britain or the U.S.A. The miners should not allow greedy magnates to cut wages, however much pink pen pushers and pulpit pounding parsons might complain! As a matter of fact, the miners were probably exaggerating the extent by which they were liable to be thrown out of work by lower paid Africans; senior Labour Officers who investigated the position found that Europeans were still vastly more efficient in every respect than Africans, and quoted an experienced witness who estimated that even on ordinary manual labour, the average European could do four times as much work as an African, whilst on more advanced tasks the white man's yield was six times the African's. Black workers admittedly could carry out most of the underground jobs, but timbering, shaft-sinking and electrical installations all required Europeans. On the surface, Africans were able to drive engines and cranes, fit pipes, and perform various other tasks, but African advancement would not deprive many white men of their livelihood, except the most inefficient of daily paid hands, whilst the remainder would get better positions as supervisors or instructors. The position on the Copper Belt was often being compared to that in the Katanga, but contrary to prevailing impressions, Africans in the Congo were not much ahead of their brothers on the Copper Belt, though race relations were better in Belgian territories, where the Europeans were picked men, enjoying the added security of four-year contracts.

These arguments did not, however, impress suspicious Europeans, and their attitude placed the Government in a difficult position; 'N.R.G.' disliked both colour bar and 'closed shop', but the Allies desperately needed copper, and the authorities had few troops available to maintain order, if strikes broke out and led to violence. The Imperial Government was likewise impressed by the importance of maintaining production at all costs, at a time when the military outlook seemed grim, the United Kingdom Government's attitude being further affected by the fact that in Britain itself coal-mine owners were now expected to bring pressure on recalcitrant men to join the Union to prevent strikes. The white miners demanded the 'closed shop' and lengthy discussions took place between the Colonial Office and the mining companies, the Imperial authorities refusing to be brought directly into the dispute. After a final interview at the Colonial Office the Selection Trust reported that Government still would not commit itself, but that if a strike was occasioned by management's refusal to yield, Government might force the mines to give way in order to safeguard indispensable copper supplies. The Selection Trust then advised its local manager to make one more attempt, but to submit, if there was no other way out, and in the end the 'closed shop' principle prevailed, the mines agreeing in 1941 to employ no more recruits who did not join the Union, and to dismiss all those who refused to become members. 'Closed shop' placed the Union in a strong position, and the miners further safeguarded themselves by insisting that any 'dilution' of labour by Africans in war-time should only be effected after consultation between the Union and management. Once the fighting ended and the white miners now in uniform came home, each mine would revert to the practice existing at the time of the discussions. This meant that the white miners thus gained a secure position for themselves, though questions were asked in the Commons and Creech Jones continued to oppose the settlement. The *Manchester Guardian* and *New Statesman* strongly opposed the agreement, the *Statesman* arguing that the promise made to white settlers that they would be reinstated in their jobs on demobilization should not be made a reason to hold up African advancement,[1] whilst the white Rhodesian's case, that is to say the orthodox trade unionists', went by default in the British Press.

In Northern Rhodesia, however, the Mine Workers' Union continued to occupy a strong position which was exploited to the utmost by the Union's General Secretary, Frank Stanley Maybank. Maybank was a completely single-minded man, moody and difficult, but absorbed by his work and unshakeable in his convictions that only threats would serve in dealing with capitalists, an attitude which aroused strong personal hostility on the mine managers' part. His strategy was thus entirely opposed to Welensky's who believed in friendly negotiations, the railwaymen forming a much more moderate group than the miners, the difference possibly due to the fact that their leaders had been associated with Rhodesia over a much longer period of time, and were not influenced either by left-wing socialism or militant Afrikaner nationalism of the *Ossewabrandwag* variety. But the railwaymen failed to attain the closed shop principle, and Maybank for his part thought that only the mailed fist would get results, his views apparently being further coloured by personal admiration for Stalin and the Soviet Union, which he once visited with *Intourist*. Maybank was no believer in equality for its own sake, and at a time when some left-wing intellectuals were becoming disillusioned with the Soviet leadership which derided what it called 'petty bourgeois egalitarianism', Maybank reacted in exactly the opposite fashion, accepting the Russian view that equal pay for all workers could not yet be brought about for a long time. From this he concluded that Africa was in a similar position, and that the natives would still need several generations to advance to the European level. As far as the War was concerned, Maybank did not want a German victory, but would not support the Allies either, holding that the clash arose from an attempt to shore up a tottering Capitalist system, and therefore saw no reason why he should help the Allies; instead he preferred to get the best terms for his white miners and to work on real grievances, his demand to increase the basic wages of artisans being privately admitted by some managers to be perfectly reasonable. Maybank persisted with his strategy even after the Germans had begun their onslaught on the Soviet Union, and in April 1942 his Union launched a general attack against Government for its supposedly antagonistic attitude, threatening that the miners might take direct action unless Government speeded up the investigation of industrial diseases, and demanding that Government should meet the Executive of the Union on the Copper Belt to discuss matters like workers' compensation, apprenticeship, old age pensions, widows' pensions, price control, land settle-

[1] *Manchester guardian*, 18 Feb 1941; and *New statesman and nation*, 22 Feb 1941

ment and so forth. But Maybank's intransigent strategy lost him public sympathy, the European public favouring a vigorous prosecution of the War. The Administration refused to meet the miners' leaders on the Copper Belt, and whilst agreeing to give 'sympathetic consideration' to their demands, threatened to deal with actions prejudicial to the war effort under existing Emergency Regulations. Early in 1942 Governor Waddington expressed the view that Maybank should be deported, but the Managing Director of Roan Antelope Mine thought that this would be a mistake, unless Maybank actually broke the law. The miners then presented various new demands which Government agreed to investigate, but the calm was broken when trouble broke out on the Congo mines in August. The President and Secretary of the white Katanga Mine Workers' Union were prosecuted for defeatist talk, and dismissed from their jobs. The Mine Workers' Union who were in touch with Belgian workers in Katanga, then cabled to prominent labour leaders in the United Kingdom, urging that international trade unionism was vital to the war effort, and asking that trade unionism be recognized in the Congo, despite the fact that the Association des Agents de l'Union Minière du Haut Katanga et Filiales had been recognized *de facto*, though not as a legal entity. A strike broke out in Jadotville, but the Belgian authorities took strong action, and the strike collapsed. The Northern Rhodesian Mine Workers' Union then launched a series of virulent attacks on the Congolese authorities, and the position further deteriorated from the authorities' point of view, the miners naming various new demands, which included a request from Mufulira that the mine should stop Africans from doing work ordinarily done by white men. The Northern Rhodesian miners were further confirmed in their intransigent attitude by the fact that the Belgian miners got less pay than the Rhodesians, and they feared that after the war the Belgian mines might accordingly get the lion's share in a contracting copper market. Maybank tried to get in touch with the Rhodesian Railway Workers' Union, and in September threatened the Governor of the Congo that unless a satisfactory settlement was reached in the Katanga, he would negotiate for a rail strike. Government appealed for calm in the Legislative Council, but Maybank continued on his course, receiving support both from British miners with left-wing sympathies, and from Afrikaans-speaking miners, some of whom shared the semi-Fascist views of the *Ossewabrandwag*, a militant Nationalist organization. Some hotheads threatened violence and the mining companies got so alarmed that they thought they might completely lose control of the situation. Government worried even more, some officials fearing that the Copper Belt might become the scene of another outbreak like the desperate rising on the Witwatersrand of 1922, when white foremen and skilled workers took arms to prevent the mine magnates from cheapening labour costs by the employment of Africans, the white miners' 'commandos' shaking the country to its foundations. The Northern Rhodesian Government considered its position to be all the more difficult since few troops were available, the Northern Rhodesia Defence Force containing many miners who might sympathize with their former workmates, whilst black soldiers could not be used against white workers for reasons of policy. Waddington thus requested Huggins for armed help, arguing that local European units should be used rather than a battalion from the Middle East, the employment of British troops against miners (many of them Afrikaners) being liable to cause major difficulties in South Africa. The despatch of a battalion from the Near East would in any case have constituted an unnecessary drain of man-power from a vital theatre of war, and raised serious transport difficulties, all of which were avoided by the deployment of the Southern Rhodesia Armoured Car Regiment, then stationed at Moshi, and about to proceed to the Union of South Africa. Huggins agreed; Southern Rhodesian armoured vehicles moved to the Copper Belt, and the Administration struck. Maybank was arrested, and so were two of his assistants, Christian Schalk Willem Maeyer, and Jacobus Petrus Theunissen, apparently a militant Afrikaner Nationalist and a supporter of the *Ossewabrandwag*. These arrests broke the radical wing of the Mine Workers' Union which in any case never seriously considered an armed rising, for which they lacked alike will, arms and organization. The Radicals' position was further weakened by their complete isolation from the public at large, Welensky taking a particularly strong stand against their policies, and forcefully supporting the war effort. Maybank proved unable to establish a common front with the railway workers, and wielded no influence with Africans, who were not at that time taken very seriously as an industrial factor. By the early 'forties moreover, about forty per cent of the Union members consisted of Staff Employ-ees, hired on conditions different from those of ordinary white workers, possess-ing greater security of employment; these men became discontented with the way the Union was handling their affairs, and later split off to form their own organization. The arrests accordingly met with no resistance, and the remaining embers of discontent were extinguished by a visit on the part of the General Secretary of the Rand Mine Workers' Union, who told the workers to concen-trate on industrial matters and avoid Communism, the moderates' victory being confirmed by the election in 1943 of Marthinus Stephanus Visagie, a temperate and pro-British Afrikaner, to the post of General Secretary of the Union, the moderate wing receiving further strong support from Dave Welensky, Roy's brother, the Union's Senior Vice President and the head of the Broken Hill branch. There was some further trouble on the mines in 1944, discontent being particularly strong amongst artisans who considered their wages too low in comparison with relatively unskilled miners, and had lost in overtime when copper production was reduced in 1944. A temporary stoppage occurred at Nchanga in 1944, but no further disputes occurred on a really serious scale, the mine workers retaining their 'closed shop' and other industrial privileges which they gained between 1941 and 1942.

IV

War-time politics

The Europeans' increased bargaining power in the industrial sphere was reflected in the political field. The Copper Belt now became a key area, its growing influence being recognized in 1941, when the residential qualification for voters was reduced from eighteen months to six, a provision which primarily benefited white labour migrants. At the same time the existing Ndola and Nkana constituencies were replaced by three new seats, though a further nominated Official Member joined the Council in order to balance this addition to the Unofficials' ranks.[1] Welensky, Labour's only representative in the House at the beginning of the War, now formed a separate Northern Rhodesian Labour Party, not so much for the purpose of fighting for the workers' sectional interests, but in order to get away from the political individualism of Moore's days, and to provide a greater measure of political cohesion for the settlers, the Party's call for amalgamation and for the return of the Chartered Company's mineral rights to the Territory making a strong appeal to nearly all white Northern Rhodesians. The Labour Party backed the war effort and bitterly opposed extreme left-wingers and Afrikaner Nationalists who expressed neutralist sentiments on the Copper Belt. The Party, a rather loosely organized association, gained the allegiance of most European artisans, miners, clerks and foremen, but remained strictly independent of the Northern Rhodesian Mine Workers' Union. The latter body comprised a large number of daily paid workers who usually showed little interest in local politics, putting their faith rather in strike action, whilst the more senior technicians and staff workers, recruited on contracts and with relatively secure positions in the industry, tended to take a much more active part in the Party's affairs. Welensky himself sympathized in some ways with British socialists like Clement Richard Attlee and Herbert Stanley Morrison, whose lead he accepted in matters such as the direction of labour,[2] and like his British colleagues, Welensky also took a reformist line in the field of social policy, concentrating on immediate practical issues like education, pensions and workmen's compensation. The Unofficials' efforts helped to bring about some very worthwhile legislation in this respect; in 1941 schooling at last became compulsory for all European children between the ages of seven and fifteen living within reach of Government schools,[3] whilst a Workmen's Compensation Ordinance passed on to the Statute Book three years later. But as far as the country's political future was concerned, the Northern Rhodesian Labour Party

[1] Legislative council (amendment) ordinance, 1941

[2] Northern Rhodesia. *Legislative Council debates*, 7 July 1941, p. 43–46

[3] Northern Rhodesia. *Legislative Council debates*, 10 July 1941, p. 139–143, and European education ordinance, 1941

sharply disagreed with their British comrades, the amalgamation question becoming the main plank in Welensky's platform, whilst opposition to Downing Street rule and fear of 'native paramountcy' remained the most lively issues with an otherwise fairly apathetic electorate. In 1941 new elections took place and Welensky won a major success; his Party gained a majority, and of the independents only Page, Campbell and McKee returned to the House where they continued to represent the farmers' cause. No candidate could be found to fight Welensky in his stronghold at Broken Hill, Moore explaining this absence of public interest by the Elected Members' own lack of enthusiasm, which he put down to the fact that Legislative Councillors at Lusaka drew only £140. o. o. a year, and had no hope of promotion to Cabinet rank like their opposite numbers in Salisbury.[1] In the remaining four constituencies Labour swept the board. In Livingstone, Francis John Sinclair defeated Moore, who was driven out of politics, and died four years later—a disappointed man. Visagie won at Nkana, whilst Frederick Stanley Roberts, a former Railways employee, and now Mayor of Ndola, beat Colonel Arthur Stephenson at Ndola, Roberts receiving the support of many traders and shop assistants who objected to Import Control. At Luanshya, Michael Padraig McGann, another Welensky man, romped home on a 'win-the-war' ticket, a radical-minded mine workers' leader who also contested the seat coming last in the poll. Many people in authority viewed Welensky's victory with much satisfaction, anticipating little change, and feeling impressed by Welensky's 'scrupulously fair and broadminded' record with regard to Africans. Nevertheless, Welensky's project of giving the local Europeans a firm organizational backbone by means of his Labour Party did not entirely succeed. The Party never operated as a cohesive force; it remained small and financially weak; there were internal quarrels, Sinclair attacked Welensky in the Press, whilst the Party's Livingstone Committee apparently remained so apathetic that it would not even meet.[2] When further elections took place in 1944, the Northern Rhodesian Labour Party did badly; several of its candidates were beaten, Brian Goodwin, now President of the Northern Rhodesian Mine Workers' Union, entering the House as an Independent Labour member against the official candidate. But Welensky was returned unopposed for Broken Hill, and his personal influence grew, even though he refrained from taking over Unofficial leadership himself—as he might have done—preferring to support Gore-Browne for the purpose of achieving a united Unofficial front. Towards the end of the War, he managed to put up £400 to buy a near derelict newspaper, the *Northern News*, which was combined with a small printing business. Welensky and his partner made a tidy sum of money out of the paper, which developed into a prosperous provincial journal and was sold in 1950 to the Rhodesian Printing and Publishing Company, a Salisbury concern which was itself linked to the powerful South African Argus group of newspapers. From the political point of view, Welensky found a convenient organ for his opinions, and—

[1] *Livingstone mail*, 8 Aug 1941
[2] Letter by F. J. Sinclair in *Livingstone mail*, 1 Sep 1944

what was perhaps even more important—he learned a great deal about the working of the Press, the problems of moulding public opinion, and the way to deal with journalists, making many fruitful contacts with influential newspapermen both in Africa and overseas, which stood him in good stead during subsequent struggles.[1]

War also strengthened the settlers' general political position, for the Europeans' willing co-operation became essential for the successful mobilization of the country's resources. Major McKee was appointed Director of Civil Supplies charged with the task of producing and distributing scarce materials; Page accepted the unpopular post of Price Controller, whilst Gore-Browne was made Director of War Evacuees, saddled with the difficult task of constructing and administering camps for several thousand Polish refugees who sought a temporary home in Northern Rhodesia during the War. Welensky in 1941 took on himself the key appointment of Director of Manpower, a courageous decision whereby he made himself responsible for a host of unpalatable decisions concerned with the direction of labour and conscription, instead of confining himself to the easier and politically more profitable task of criticising Government from outside. The Elected Members' increasing share in administrative work was paralleled by their gaining a foothold on the Executive Council, a statutory body charged with assisting the Governor on policy matters, and hitherto an 'Official' stronghold. Just before the outbreak of the War, Maybin agreed that some Elected Members should sit on the Council, as previously suggested by the Bledisloe Commission, arguing that existing methods of consultation with Unofficials were too cumbrous, that the Official view on controversial matters was already tentatively formed by the time the Unofficials were brought in, and that Unofficial experience was valuable. In 1939 three Elected Members were called to join the Executive Council, their ranks being subsequently joined by Welensky. In 1940 three Elected Members moreover took their seats on a newly formed Budget Committee, the Governor obtaining the assistance of Elected Members in the actual drafting of the budget, instead of merely submitting proposals to the Finance Committee afterwards. Gore-Browne, who took a major share in bringing about these changes, considered that this concession in fact made Elected Members responsible for the country's financial policy, without their being over-ruled by Officials, though Members now became bound to defend the Committee's decisions against outside criticism.[2]

The Europeans, however, remained dissatisfied with these concessions and in 1941 the Elected Members demanded a majority in the Legislative Council; they admitted that ultimate responsibility should remain with the Colonial Office, the Governor being able to over-rule an adverse vote in the House on the 'reserved subjects' of finance and native affairs; the Executive Council was to contain three Nominated Unofficial Members out of seven, and these Unofficials should be placed in charge of departments; the new Ministers were to support the

[1] Taylor, D. *The Rhodesian: the life of Sir Roy Welensky.* Museum press, 1955, p. 152–153
[2] Northern Rhodesia. *Legislative Council debates,* 16 Jan 1940, p. 34–35

Government on all major issues, but should be allowed to resign over major differences regarding reserved subjects, the resignation of all Unofficials at the same time entailing a General Election. The Colonial Office would not, however, agree to these proposals on the grounds that they were not likely to work well constitutionally, that they would affect the amalgamation issue, on which the Imperial Government would not budge, that they would be followed by similar demands in Kenya, and would further tilt the balance against Africans, a serious matter, especially in view of the Northern Rhodesian Labour Party's successes. One senior official in fact hazarded the guess that the Europeans' demands would form an extension of the 'closed shop' principle from the industrial to the political field, an assessment not wholly in accordance with the facts, since the Elected Members at the same time also demanded the annexation of Northern Rhodesia to the Crown, a demand which would have automatically given the vote to qualified Africans. The Unofficials in fact were then not so much thinking in terms of consolidating themselves against African political opposition—then still in an embryonic stage—but of achieving greater administrative efficiency, and a tighter hold in the Executive. Gore-Browne thus pointed out in the House that the Executive Council, as at present consituted, formed too large and cumbrous a body, that its meetings only took place irregularly, that it could only decide on matters which the Governor put before it, apart from a few subjects which had to be considered by the Council under the existing law. Gore-Browne also complained that Unofficial Members could not see confidential despatches, and thus suggested a smaller War Committee which would deal with all major issues of Government and become responsible for their execution. Waddington went some way towards meeting these demands and in 1942 set up the War Committee, an inner ring of the Executive Council, consisting of the Governor, the Chief Secretary and Financial Secretary, as well as Gore-Browne and Welensky, who met frequently to deal with the more urgent business.[1] This tightening of links between Unofficials and Administration aroused some left-wing criticism from overseas, but resulted in real gains, not only to the Unofficial cause, but also to Government itself; the Administration was sometimes spared embarrassing questions in the House by the fact that Unofficial leaders were acquainted with the full reasons for disputed decisions, whilst the new responsibilities assumed by the Unofficials led to their adopting a more moderate and well informed attitude towards political questions than was customary in the heyday of Moore's agitation.[2] European pressure for an Unofficial majority continued during the latter part of the War, and Waddington— pleased with the co-operation obtained from Unofficials in the war effort— agreed with the idea of an Unofficial majority. Conversations took place in London in 1944, and the Colonial Office agreed to relinquish its majority in the Council, the change to be achieved by bringing two more Nominated Members into the House to represent Africans, as well as two further Nominated Members

---

[1] Northern Rhodesia. *Legislative Council debates*, 30 Mar 1942, p. 21–23; and 19 Sep 1942, p. 2
[2] See Davidson, J. W. *The Northern Rhodesian Legislative Council*. Faber and Faber, 1948, p. 59

to speak for special economic interest groups. The new concessions were designed to meet in some way the settlers' demands, whilst safeguarding Africans,
and also to provide some kind of a 'consolation prize' for amalgamationists who
remained bitterly disappointed with the Imperial Government's negative attitude. The new arrangement came into effect in 1945, shortly after the end of the
War, when Dr Alfred Charles Fisher and Robert Selby Taylor, the Anglican
bishop of Northern Rhodesia, joined the House as Unofficial Nominated
Members, the new appointments greatly strengthening the missionary element
in the country, which now for the first time achieved representation in the local
Legislature. Alfred Royden Harrison, the Managing Director of Rhokana
Corporation, was brought in to speak for the mining companies, much to
Chester Beatty's disgust, the veteran magnate at first objecting to the idea that
an employee from either of the big mining groups should represent the industry.
The fifth Nominated Member was Geoffrey Bernard Beckett, an English
rancher, educated at Reading University, who stood for the most progressive
section of the country's changing farming industry, the House as a whole now
containing the Governor as President, nine officials, five Nominated and eight
Elected Unofficial Members.

The change benefited the settlers only to a limited extent, only one of the four
newly appointed Members being directly associated with the white residents'
interests, and Welensky expressed his disappointment that the new Constitution
involved so many Nominated Members.[1] But from the constitutional point of
view, the reform represented a dramatic new departure. The Government lost
its automatic majority in the House, and could no longer steam-roller its measures through the Legislature against Unofficial opposition, though the Governor retained certain reserved powers which enabled him to validate an emergency measure, even though the Council might disapprove. But all such action
had to be reported to the Secretary of State, whilst public opinion would prevent
the use of such powers except in the most desperate circumstances. The balance
of power in fact now depended on the ability of a rather heterogenous body of
Unofficials to co-operate, and in 1945 an Unofficial Members' Organization was
formed under Gore-Browne's chairmanship for the purpose of achieving this aim.[2]

War and white politics in turn affected the Africans who were slowly becoming more interested in affairs outside their tribal areas. Government itself helped
to make Africans more conscious of wider issues by launching an extensive
propaganda campaign to fight indifference and apathy with regard to the War,
which remained widespread amongst black peasants and unskilled workers, who
regarded the conflict as a white man's affair, and widely listened to the pacifist
sermons of Watch Tower preachers. African politics in the main remained
confined to the local level, where competing groups attempted to manipulate the
Native Authorities for their own purposes. In many areas, like the poverty
stricken Northern Province, a dark undercurrent of fear continued beneath the

[1] Northern Rhodesia. *Legislative Council debates*, 16 Jan 1945, p. 188-196
[2] Northern Rhodesia. *Legislative Council debates*, 7 Feb 1945, p. 550-551

surface, and it was reported in 1944 that tribesmen continued to believe in the 'Banyama', criminals who supposedly killed others in order to sell their blood to the Europeans for the preparation of magical concoctions, some chiefs being regarded as being implicated in this nefarious traffic, whilst all Europeans were thought to be 'in the know'. The Banyama psychosis was stimulated by articles in the European press deploring the lack of native donors for the purpose of blood transfusions, Banyama scares always coinciding with the visits of strange Europeans. In addition the District Commissioner reported on the 'Bafyeka', indigenous Africans who kidnapped and murdered people, subsequently using their bodies for rain-making and other ceremonies.[1] The exact extent of these activities remains difficult to gauge, but in the same year two men were sentenced for attempted murder, the Provincial Commissioner for the Northern Province feeling certain that human sacrifices for rain-making and seed-blooding had taken place from time to time.

Government tried to influence African public opinion by means of a propaganda campaign involving leaflets, talks by District Commissioners, broadcasts and cinema shows, which were designed to explain the War to the Africans, account for the economic strains brought about by hostilities, and encourage recruitment to the Army. Distress of course was rife, for as a European speaker pointed out in the Legislature, the Africans too were suffering from the sharp rise in the cost of living, and native cultivators found that whereas they only got 6d more for their maize, they now had to pay 10/– for a blanket which sold at 5/– before the war, when the quality of the product was superior.[2] Feeling rose further by the white storekeepers' practice of refusing to sell goods in short supply to casual African buyers, preferring—quite naturally—to 'keep in' with their regular European customers.

Discontent, however, found at first few means of political expression, and African political representation at first remained confined to small Urban Advisory Councils, which were first established on the Copper Belt in 1938. These bodies generally consisted of about five members drawn from tribal representatives on the mines, who were themselves chosen by ballot, and five members from the public townships, appointed by District Commissioners from the ranks of the more educated. The African Welfare Societies were also permitted to elect delegates, but though Government tried to make these bodies more representative, the elective principle could not be wholly applied to the public townships because of the difficulties experienced in organizing a ballot; the Provincial Commissioner at the Copper Belt for instance found urban Africans scattered on private stands, in contractors' compounds, African townships and Management Board compounds, so that rosters of potential electors could not be kept. The vast majority of Africans moreover displayed little interest in these bodies which remained the prerogative of a small elite which

[1] For traditional human sacrifices, see Gouldsbury, G., and Sheane, H. *The great plateau of Northern Rhodesia.* Edward Arnold, 1911

[2] Northern Rhodesia. *Legislative Council debates,* 16 Dec 1941, p. 353-354

thereby gained convenient access to the 'D.C.'s' office. In the countryside, Government continued to uphold the principle of Indirect Rule, though the development of local institutions greatly suffered from lack of qualified white staff at a time when so many civil servants were joining the Forces. The whole system continued to rest on the assumption that the system of migrant labour could continue; the local authorities still felt that the bulk of the Copper Belt labour force should not become a permanent industrial community on the grounds that the benefits of the industry should not be confined to a small industrial population on the mines, and that a stabilized working force would only become the helpless victims of unemployment in times of slumps, the position being further affected by the copper magnates' own pessimism with regard to the copper outlook. In 1943 Ronald Lindsay Prain, (later knighted) a senior executive in the powerful Rhodesian Selection Trust, who saw distinguished war-time service in the British Ministry of Supply, thus explained to the Colonial Office that copper production could not continue on the same scale as before, and that mining might even cease altogether to be profitable in another fifty years' time, because of transport and other difficulties.

This economic reasoning continued to find expression in the Administration's approach to political problems. If the African was to remain a temporary townsman, politics must centre in the countryside, and a divorce between the intelligentsia and the villagers must at all costs be prevented. Maybin produced a lengthy memorandum in 1940 in which he explained that native policy should continue to rest on the country's indigenous institutions which should, however, be adapted to modern life. The Governor himself did not believe in the system of a common voters' roll, as practised in Southern Rhodesia and in the Cape, arguing that this singled out a small group of educated Africans and gave them an importance denied to unschooled African leaders. Africans must advance by slow stages; conferences between the different Native Authorities should be followed by the setting up of Provincial Councils, representation on a national scale being ultimately achieved either by a National Council, or by placing nominees from the Provincial Councils on the Legislature itself. The settlers thought on similar lines, the lead being taken by Gore-Browne. In 1941 the Colonel explained in Council that Africans were not as yet fit for political responsibility as understood by white men; but unless the Europeans were willing to sit on the safety valve, native opinion must be given a legitimate means of expression. The system of having a Nominated Member like himself to represent Africans—which was itself introduced originally at the settlers' behest —could only serve as a stop gap, for one man alone could hardly represent a still inarticulate people, or get round the whole of an enormous country like Northern Rhodesia. The answer consisted in some form of parallel representation: Africans should have their own councils, leading up to some supreme body which would instruct its representatives in the Legislative Council, which for many years to come would consist of Europeans.[1] Only Moore disagreed with

[1] Northern Rhodesia. *Legislative Council debates,* 12 Mar 1941, p. 64–67

the Colonel, arguing that the office of Nominated Member for African interests should be abolished, a view motivated not so much by dislike of African representation, but by resentment of Gore-Browne who displaced Moore as Unofficial leader. In 1942 Gore-Browne returned to the attack and moved that Native Advisory Councils should be extended from the Copper Belt to all urban areas, and that Regional Councils should be set up, which would advise on African affairs, embracing both representatives from the Native Authorities and the Advisory Councils. Much better, argued the Colonel, to make concessions now, rather than to make them later under duress, as in India and Ireland; Gore-Browne also disagreed with Maybin's views that qualified Africans should not be put on the ordinary voters' roll. Welensky and the other Elected Members backed Gore-Browne's motion, though the Government speakers were somewhat divided. Sandford, the Secretary for Native Affairs and a convinced advocate of the migrant labour system, thus argued that Indirect Rule still formed a plant of tender growth, and that nothing should be done to destroy the feeling of responsibility that was gradually being acquired by the Native Authorities; many people of course were saying that Native Authorities represented no one but themselves; this was true to some extent, but the situation was gradually changing; under these circumstances Sandford felt doubtful about introducing the elective principle to people who would probably neither understand nor make use of it. Sandford also stressed the practical administrative difficulties found in getting the Councils together, a point often overlooked by theoretical advocates of the system; and in the end a modified motion passed the House which gave added authority to the Provincial Commissioner's Conferences in determining the constitutions and functions of the Councils.[1] African representation by means of Regional Councils thus came about as the result of a settler initiative and owed nothing to pressure from Africans, who at first took little interest in the scheme.[2] By the end of 1943 the Administration completed its arrangements for the setting up of Regional Councils, except in Barotseland where public opinion continued to be expressed through the *khotla*. The new representative device for a time encountered considerable hostility from various chiefs, so much so that Copper Belt tribal dignitaries at first refused to sit in the same room with educated Africans, whilst the Fort Jameson chiefs would have nothing to do with the local Council. The Colonial Office, however, backed the project, prevailing opinion at Downing Street agreeing that conciliar representation would prevent the divorce of the wealthier and better educated Africans from ordinary tribesmen, thus facilitating a synthesis between the various elements, which was much preferable to allowing rich Africans to enter a non-native aristocracy. The new Council Members consisted of representatives from Native Authorities, Urban Advisory Councils and African Welfare Societies, who met under the Chairmanship of the Provincial Commissioners. The Councils were expected not to interfere with the actual working of the Native Authori-

---

[1] Northern Rhodesia. *Legislative Council debates*, 17 Sep 1942, p. 148–168
[2] From 1944 the Regional Councils became known officially as Provincial Councils.

ties, but to express public opinion, and advise both the Provincial Commissioner and the Member Nominated to represent Native Interests, the Councillors quickly learning European methods of their procedure from their official chairmen. In addition to getting conciliar representation for Africans, some settler representatives also demanded that British Protected Persons, no matter whether black or Coloured, should receive the vote whenever they met the ordinary qualifications. Page, in 1944, thus moved to amend the Legislative Council Ordinance, receiving support from Gore-Browne and from Godfrey Pelletier, the member for Ndola. The Colonial Office, however, remained opposed to the scheme; some thus argued at Downing Street that the project would give double representation to Africans and cut across the policy of placing representative Africans on a Central Council via Regional Assemblies; that the scheme would not make much numerical difference, anyway, and would simply annoy the Europeans, whilst another high-ranking civil servant pointed to the alleged dangers of splitting advanced Africans from their more backward brethren. In the final voting at Lusaka, the Northern Rhodesian Labour Party lined up with Government against Page, Gore-Browne and Pelletier, and the motion was defeated.[1] Downing Street preferred to assure African representation through the three Nominated Unofficial Members to represent African interests, though Waddington would not accept Gore-Browne's suggestion that the Members should be selected by the Regional Councils, arguing that the best people would not stand for election, that few Europeans were known to Africans, and that elections would be unreal, or else would involve canvassing which the Governor deprecated. The Colonial Office did agree that there should ultimately be an African Representative Council for the Territory as a whole, but the project was held up for the time being, as the Administration believed that Provincial Councils were as yet insufficiently representative of African opinion.[2]

V

'Closer Union' in war-time

When Huggins departed from London in 1939, he left empty-handed, and any kind of closer association seemed out of the question. Nevertheless white Rhodesians loyally supported the Imperial war effort, and never fully used their bargaining strength, which increased as the German panzer divisions smashed their way across Europe, and Britain's financial position rapidly deteriorated, with the result that the United Kingdom became even more dependent on raw materials from the Sterling area, including copper, chrome, tobacco and asbestos

[1] Northern Rhodesia. *Legislative Council debates*, 9 Aug 1944, p. 178–196. For the Aborigines' Protection Society's views, see *Anti-slavery reporter*, Jan 1945, p. 3–4
[2] Northern Rhodesia. *Legislative Council debates*, 22 Jan 1945, p. 339–340

from Rhodesia. Britain moreover could not afford to alienate South Africa at a time when the Union controlled the vital Cape route to India, a strategic key position, all the more important when the Allies lost the use of the Mediterranean; South Africa also remained essential as a supplier of raw materials and as a great industrial reservoir for the British armies in Africa, whilst Smuts mobilized an efficient white army which took a vital part in the war against the Italians in Africa, and greatly added to the General's political strength. 'Pan-Africanism' was in the air, but Pan-Africanism in Southern Africa was then mainly used to denote a white man's cause, involving the extension of the Union's influence beyond its borders, and the creation of larger territorial units, concepts which were put forward especially by Smuts's adherents in their Afrikaans propaganda. More important still was the need for co-ordination of the Imperial war effort in Africa; and the first effective impetus towards administrative collaboration between the three Central African territories came from officials north of the Zambezi, where the local authorities were anxious to secure Salisbury's co-operation in their local problems. In 1940 an East African Governors' Conference took place at Nairobi, and both Northern Rhodesia and Nyasaland decided that they could not become members of a proposed East African Economic Council. The meeting decided instead that a local wartime conference with a permanent Secretariat would prove a more workable arrangement for the purpose of co-ordinating the war effort of the three Central African territories. Maybin and Sir Donald Mackenzie-Kennedy, the Governor of Nyasaland and a former Chief Secretary of Northern Rhodesia, both agreed that the new arrangement should not prejudice political issues, but Kennedy felt convinced that the project was essential for economic reasons. The proposal received support from the Dominions Office which stressed Southern Rhodesia's fine war effort, and the need not to alienate Huggins, and also from Sir Henry Moore, the Governor of Kenya, who was perturbed about the growth of Union influence in East Africa. The Colonial Office at first resisted the scheme, regarding it as a possible step on the road to amalgamation, but Kennedy stuck to his guns. Southern Rhodesia he argued, was going to establish a War Supplies Committee, and Nyasaland should be associated with this body. There was no point in linking Nyasaland with the Northern territories with which the Protectorate possessed no common economic ties. The existing Inter-Territorial Labour Conference did not work very well, and neither did the Inter-Territorial Communications Board in Central Africa. The provision of agricultural implements, transport, import control, exports, shipping through Beira and other matters must be co-ordinated, and if Nyasaland did not take part in some joint scheme now, it might find itself left out in the cold; existing 'cumbersome triangular exchanges' between Lusaka, Zomba and Salisbury constituted no substitute for effective collaboration, which became all the more essential as Southern Rhodesia began to expand its infant secondary industries. Huggins was prepared to fall in with the scheme, and even professed himself willing to accept a Colonial Office man as Secretary, though he could certainly have used his country's bargaining

2A

strength to much greater effect. The Colonial Office finally agreed to the Secretariat, though stipulating that the office should be used only for the limited purpose of securing more effective co-ordination of the war effort; that it should be regarded as experimental, and that it should be reviewed when present conditions had disappeared. In 1941 a permanent Secretariat was thus set up at Salisbury, and Kenneth Lambert Hall, the Chief Secretary for Nyasaland, assumed charge. The older Inter-Territorial Communications Board and the Standing Committee on Labour were dissolved, their place being taken by permanent and more effective machinery. Lambert Hall then organized numerous meetings, dealing with all manner of subjects, from fertilizers to aviation, and the Secretariat took a major share in the co-ordination of the economic war effort. The establishment of the new office also went hand in hand with a more vigorous mobilization of Northern Rhodesia's resources, the old ways of *laissez faire* giving way to more strictly controlled economy. At the end of 1940 the Financial Secretary announced the institution of import control for the purpose of preventing the purchase of non-essential goods and of channeling trade into the Sterling area, whilst Royden Harrison undertook a general survey of workshops for the manufacture of war supplies.[1] In addition Northern Rhodesia imposed special war taxation, designed to help the mother country in its difficulties, and began to operate a system of exchange and export control, which also necessitated effective co-ordination with Southern Rhodesian policies. The creation of the Salisbury Secretariat of course did nothing to satisfy amalgamationists inside Central Africa, who continued to receive support from Nyasaland planters, hoping for lower transport charges, from Northern Rhodesian farmers, from many traders, and also from Copper Belt miners who would have liked Southern Rhodesia's Industrial Conciliation law to be enforced north of the Zambezi, and who were acquiring a more permanent stake in the country. In addition, war itself gave an impetus to amalgamationist feelings; the need for a co-ordinated economic and defence effort seemed ever more obvious and the delays incurred by the Downing Street Government ever more galling; many speakers now also stressed the need for secondary industries as goods from overseas were so hard to get. Welensky, who well remembered the days when barefooted, hungry, white youngsters were playing in Salisbury's Pioneer Street, also argued that the United Kingdom, for all its pious professions, never met its trusteeship obligations towards the natives who continued to live in poverty, that British investors skimmed off the country's wealth, and that the British were perhaps frightened to see rival industries established within their Protectorates.[2] Welensky further justified his stand by condemning the Chartered Company's mineral rights, by denouncing the way income tax from the copper mines mainly benefited the United Kingdom Treasury, and by calling—with

[1] Northern Rhodesia. *Legislative Council debates*, 9 Dec 1940, p. 193–195
[2] Northern Rhodesia. *Legislative Council debates*, 25 Nov 1943, p. 152–163. Welensky calculated that in 1939 the country's total revenue from the copper mines was about £492,000 which amounted to about 70 per cent of its income. During the same period the Chartered Company was getting something like £400,000 to £500,000 p.a.

Unofficial applause—for greater control over the mines, which never again should be allowed to close down in times of slump.[1] Anti-colonialism of a kind, suspicious of big business overseas, and comparable in some ways to American 'Populist' thought of a bye-gone age, thus continued to influence European thought in Northern Rhodesia at a time when Africans largely remained politically apathetic, the colonists' hostility to what they regarded as financial exploitation from overseas playing an important part in shaping the amalgamationists' case.

In the meantime Huggins took up the cudgels once more in the cause of Greater Rhodesia. By 1941 the Southern Rhodesian Prime Minister was likewise thinking in terms of bigger and better factories for Rhodesia, investors being more likely to put their money into a larger country with a wider internal market. In addition he felt that a united Rhodesia would attract more recruits to man the country's badly understaffed civil service. This argument carried considerable weight at a time when Huggins was moving leftwards, becoming convinced that Southern Rhodesia should develop its basic industries through public utilities, a policy which in 1942 resulted in the setting up of a state-controlled Iron and Steel Commission. In addition Huggins also argued that Smuts would not last for ever, and predicted—with a considerable degree of accuracy—that South Africa would become a Republic some ten years after Smuts's departure. Unless Southern Rhodesia consolidated its position now, the Colony would not last, but ultimately find itself part of an Afrikaner-dominated state. Privately the Southern Rhodesian Prime Minister also made much play of the Northern Rhodesian Labour Party's victory in the 1941 elections, putting forward the arguments that a locally based administration would be able to cope more easily with the situation than Downing Street, and that the Northern Rhodesian Labour Party's majority would be much less decisive in a Greater Rhodesian Parliament. During the same period Huggins was also swinging away from his former *apartheid* policy, which he found to be administratively unworkable, putting out in 1941 a new Statement on Native Affairs, in which he predicted that the two parallel lines of Southern Rhodesia's separate development policy would ultimately have to converge, and that Africans would in the end become like Europeans, though their advancement should not be at the white man's expense. During the same year Huggins invited various Unofficial Members from the Northern Territories to discuss the amalgamation issue once more, a move which met with bitter opposition from the British Labour Party, and also from the *Economist* which warned against 'a Munich in the Colonial Empire'. Welensky himself could not get support from Attlee over the amalgamation issue, the Labour Party subsequently issuing a new statement on post-war policy which demanded that Northern Rhodesia and Nyasaland should not be released from Colonial Office control until Africans obtained complete social and political equality with the settlers, and themselves wished for a handover.[2]

[1] Northern Rhodesia. *Legislature Council debates*, 3 Dec 1942, p. 154–155
[2] *The Times*, 3 Apr 1943

The Anti-Slavery Society likewise maintained its stand and strongly condemned Southern Rhodesia's native policy, whilst putting forward the additional argument that Southern Rhodesia's greater development was simply the result of good fortune in that the country possessed greater natural resources, a statement which bore no relation to the facts, but which revealed the underlying attitude of some British intellectuals who viewed economic process as something like an automatic process, the product of impersonal forces, and underplayed the vital contribution made by 'money-grubbing' *entrepreneurs*. Downing Street likewise persisted in its opposition to the amalgamationist cause which was now further weakened by splits within the Northern Rhodesians' own ranks. At Lusaka, Gore-Browne still held a key position, but the Colonel began to waver, not only towards the Greater Rhodesia cause but also towards Imperialism as a whole, his change of attitude being motivated by military rather than economic factors. All his life, Gore-Browne said, he used to believe in the 'Imperial mission of the Anglo-Saxon race', which was drummed into him from his school days—but now look at what happened in Malaya and Singapore! The British suffered a disastrous defeat and let down the people who trusted them, their subjects' indifference in face of the Japanese onslaught constituting a terrible indictment of Imperial rule, which made one wonder whether everything was all right in Northern Rhodesia itself.[1] Everyone was talking about a better future once the fighting stopped, but the country's real underdogs were the natives, and the whites should include them in their plans for a brave new world. There must be equal opportunity for all,[2] and whatever merits amalgamation might possess from the administrative and economic point of view, he could not support the cause in the face of bitter African opposition. In 1943 Gore-Browne thus sided against his colleagues in the course of a further amalgamation debate, and voted together with the Government members against a motion brought in by Welensky, so that the European cause suffered another defeat.[3] Whilst the amalgamationist cause could make no further progress, and even Welensky was privately becoming less optimistic, the case for a looser association was gaining in strength. In 1942 Baron Moyne, a firm advocate for 'making a stand on the Zambezi' lost his job as Secretary of State for the Colonies to Viscount Cranborne, another distinguished Conservative peer. Cranborne showed far more sympathy towards the cause of Central African co-operation, and in 1943 a meeting at the Colonial Office agreed that the three territories formed a natural economic unit, that His Majesty's Government should snatch the initative from local hands, and that the policy of confining the Salisbury Secretariat's machinery to wartime purposes, was becoming out of date, now that post-war problems were becoming more prominent. The Secretary of State accordingly asked for a memorandum outlining a scheme which would satisfy both black and white Rhodesians whilst providing for some-

---

[1] See Northern Rhodesia. *Legislative Council debates*, 30 Mar 1942, p. 19–20
[2] Northern Rhodesia. *Legislative Council debates*, 30 Nov 1942, p. 29–30
[3] Northern Rhodesia. *Legislative Council debates*, 25 Nov 1943, p. 152–182

thing more acceptable from Southern Rhodesia than a policy of parallel development. Senior officials then prepared a paper which aimed at safeguarding Imperial control north of the Zambezi, at preventing amalgamation, but at the same time assuring more effective co-ordination between the three territories. The advocates of the scheme pressed home the need for maintaining the present co-operation between the Northern Rhodesian Government and Elected Members, essential both for the Territory's general development and the expansion of its native services; they also stressed the way Southern Rhodesia co-operated in arresting subversive Europeans on the Copper Belt and pointed to the policy of encouraging larger regional groupings which was being pursued elsewhere in the colonial empire. A strong Central Africa was essential to stop the northward extension of Union influence. Amalgamation of course remained out of the question; Southern Rhodesia admittedly went much further than Northern Rhodesia and Nyasaland in the provision of various social and economic services for Africans—a point strongly made by Lord Hailey during the course of a previous, confidential investigation. But the Imperial Government remained fundamentally divided from Southern Rhodesia over the industrial colour bar which, though it existed unofficially on the Copper Belt, was not legally entrenched north of the Zambezi. Amalgamation—the officials thought —would extend Southern Rhodesia's colour policy to the north, the reservation of bills affecting natives' interests not in practice forming an effective safeguard for Africans. Handing over the Northern territories would be inconsistent with British policy and would meet much hostility in Parliament, whilst a Federation between the three territories would turn out to be unworkable for constitutional reasons. As an alternative solution the officials suggested that the Governor of Southern Rhodesia should be made High Commissioner for the two Northern Territories as well—a proposal not subsequently accepted. In addition, they also put up a case for an Inter-Territorial Council under the Chairmanship of the Governor of Southern Rhodesia, their project following closely previous suggestions made in the 'thirties; the new Council would co-ordinate policies between the three Governments, whilst an Inter-Territorial Development Commission would draw up development and welfare programmes and advise on the allocation of Colonial Development Funds to the Northern Territories, though no attempt should be made to define a common native policy. Sir Edmund Charles Richards, the new Governor of Nyasaland, showed little enthusiasm for the scheme, but Waddington favoured the suggestion. The Governor agreed that Southern Rhodesia's economic colour bar would prevent amalgamation, but argued that closer association was inevitable because of the need for concerted economic policies in the postwar period, and because Northern Rhodesia could not go in with East Africa. The local settlers—he continued—wanted amalgamation mainly because of the native question, and because they feared a British Labour victory after the War, but the proposed scheme might provide a workable compromise. Argument continued in high circles, where opposition against amalgamation remained unanimous. But went the official argument, Southern Rhodesia ought not to be allowed to drift into the Union, which would involve the Colony with South Africa's inter-white struggles, saddle the Territory with a 'poor white' question, aggravate the problem of urbanized Africans, delay the development of local secondary industries, close immigration from overseas, and possibly endanger African land tenure for the benefit of Europeans. Besides, Great Britain would lose control over an important source of raw materials, whilst Union would strengthen all those who opposed African advancement on the one hand and Southern Rhodesia's budding liberalism on the other. The suggested Inter-Territorial Council was regarded as the best possible alternative, and also as being consistent with Britain's responsibility; Downing Street should not just keep saying 'no'; Southern Rhodesia's wartime loyalty had stood every test; the existing co-operation between Unofficials and Government at Lusaka must at all costs be preserved, and a purely negative approach was in any case quite inconsistent with the policy which led to the setting up of the Bledisloe Commission. The proposed Council could do good work with regard to communications, economic relations, labour education, agriculture, veterinary, matters of currency and research, and it could be further strengthened both by standing committees and *ad hoc* conferences in all of which Unofficials should participate. The Colonial and Dominions Offices both agreed, and in 1944 the matter went to the Cabinet. Huggins was then informed that under existing circumstances amalgamation was 'out', but was offered a permanent Inter-Territorial Council, which rather disappointed the Southern Rhodesian Premier, who privately regarded the Council as a sop, but at first was willing to make it work. The scheme received 'a very mixed blessing' from the Southern Rhodesian Cabinet, which finally decided to co-operate on the grounds that if they did not adopt a positive attitude, they might soon find Northern Rhodesia and Nyasaland being absorbed by East Africa, whilst Southern Rhodesia might drift towards South Africa. Huggins continued to stress the advisory nature of the Council, whilst emphasizing that his country would still prefer early amalgamation, but all the same Southern Rhodesia's collaboration was assured; and at the end of 1944, Waddington announced the creation of the new Central African Council over the radio, giving news at the same time of the proposed Legislative Council Reform whereby the Unofficials were to get a majority through the creation of a new bloc of Unofficial Nominated Members. Welensky expressed his strong disappointment at the constitutional settlement which got a rather cool reception in the House where Gore-Browne once more joined the Unofficials in voting against the Government;[1] but the Unofficials approved of the Central African Council, which Welensky still regarded as a stepping stone towards subsequent amalgamation, though he now came round to the view that Africans too must be persuaded of the advantages of linking the two Rhodesias, arguing that a great mistake had been made in the past by neglecting to influence black opinion.[2]

[1] Northern Rhodesia. *Legislative Council debates*, 16 Jan 1945, p. 94–96; and 18 Jan 1945, p. 246–360
[2] Speech at Broken Hill, *Northern news*, 15 Feb 1945

Both Gore-Browne and Welensky took their seats on the new body, which first met at Salisbury in 1945, and set up its own permanent administrative machinery, as well as a number of Standing Committees to deal with specialized matters.

Both Gore-Browne and Welensky took their seats on the new body, which first met at Salisbury in 1945 to set up its own permanent administrative machinery, as well as a number of standing committees to deal with specialized matters.

Chapter Twelve

The aftermath of fighting: 1945–1948

I

Mining, labour and trade unions

When the guns stopped firing, and Germany's New Order collapsed in Europe, there was rejoicing all over Northern Rhodesia. But the copper magnates still viewed the future with pessimism, and there seemed ample reason for their caution. In 1944 the British Government decided to cut its purchases from the Copper Belt, expecting that the demand for arms would now diminish. A little later the Ministry of Supply ended its programme of bulk purchase, little realizing that it was failing to provide for adequate stocks during the lean years of post-war shortage. Experts feared over-production, calculating that the change-over from a two front conflict to the expected one front war against Japan alone would reduce copper consumption for military purposes by about 264,000 tons per annum. Besides, large supplies would be available and the demand from the Axis countries would temporarily disappear at a time when overseas supplies had vastly expanded their capacity.[1] The mines also reckoned with the menace of aluminium, which was beginning to challenge the red metal in many fields, with the result that the Rhodesian industry reduced its output, which fell from about 250,000 long tons in 1942 to 183,000 tons in 1946. Worse still, expenses were going up. Labour, for one thing, was getting dearer; the white workers at Roan Antelope for instance, managed to push up their earnings by about 30 per cent during the war, whilst African miners were taking home about 25 per cent more than in 1939. In addition, the companies faced new technical problems. As long as hostilities were going on, the mines expanded output as fast as possible and worked high-grade ores in easily accessible spots, development work being confined to a minimum. But soon mining had to be continued at greater depth, which meant that risk from rock-fall increased; and more was spent on timbering, ventilation and various safety devices, whilst the cost of transporting the ore also rose. Besides the companies had to meet heavy royalty charges to the British South Africa Company, and as prices increased, so did these payments, since they were linked to price and output, rather than profit.[2] The mines also had to cope with serious logistical problems for the railways were overburdened, the country having outstripped its transport capacity at a time when rolling stock was scarce, and more Rhodesian factory owners and farmers were clamouring

[1] *Economist*, 23 June 1945
[2] For a more detailed breakdown, see *Economist*, 8 Dec 1945

for space on railway trucks to move their products. Industrial development in Southern Rhodesia also increased the demand for coal from Wankie, and fuel accordingly became difficult to obtain, the mines being forced to use timber on a big scale. Mining machinery was likewise scarce and expensive and deliveries remained uncertain as firms overseas were snowed under with reconstruction orders; expenses thus rocketed, and Rhokana alone calculated that between the years 1938/9 and 1944/5 the cost per long ton of copper f.o.b. at the port of Beira went up from £20. 17. 5 to £33. 12. 0., amounting to an increase of 61 per cent, with the result that Northern Rhodesia ceased to be a low-cost producer.[1]

Nevertheless the Copper Belt soon pulled ahead, for developments abroad confounded all prophets. The world was starved of goods; devastated towns and cities needed rebuilding; and industry overseas soon required more copper than was ever thought possible. The United States became a net importer, whilst Britain—forced to 'export or die'—likewise increased its copper purchases, about 50 per cent of which now went into her expanding electrical industries. Prices thus continued to go up, jumping from £62. 10. 0. per ton to £137. 0. 0. in March 1947[2] and even Britain's belated return to bulk buying proving incapable of stopping the rush. Two years later, in 1949, the United Kingdom Government was forced to devalue the sterling currency and the exchange rate as between the pound and the dollar changed from $4.02 to $2.80 to the £, with the result that sterling prices for copper increased overnight by 44 per cent, devaluation setting off a period of unparalleled prosperity for the copper companies.[3]

All the same, expenses also kept rising, and the companies recognized that their halcyon days were past as far as costs were concerned. Technical problems continued to become more difficult, and an outstanding expert like Prain soon concluded that an increase in African labour charges amounting to 316 per cent during a quarter of a century could only be justified by greater personal efficiency, which in turn was not likely to be attained, unless black workers could be promoted into more responsible jobs. Another way of reducing labour costs was to increase mechanization, which again was expected to come as a corollary of African advancement and higher pay.[4] The new policy required a settled rather than a migrant work force, and in 1946 the mining companies agreed that —whilst 'detribalization and urbanization should not be encouraged in any

[1] By 1958 Sir Ronald Prain thus estimated that more than half of the copper produced in the non-Communist world was turned out at a lower cost than in the Copper Belt. See Prain, Sir R. L. 'Copper Pricing Systems: Address to the organization for European economic co-operation, Paris, June 25th 1958' printed in Prain, Sir R. L. *Selected papers*, v. 2, 1958–1960. Rhodesian Selection Trust, 1961, p. 34–35

[2] *Economist*, 2 Aug 1947

[3] Prain, R. L. 'The Northern Rhodesian Copperbelt' (in *New Commonwealth*, 7 Dec 1953). According to the Northern Rhodesia *Blue book for the year ended 31st December 1948* the country exported blister copper to the value of £17,553,357, electrolytic copper (wire bars) worth £5,615,648, electrolytic copper (cathode form) worth £845,744, cobalt alloy worth £193,879, lead worth £1,154,605 and zinc worth £1,522,335

[4] Prain, R. L. 'The Northern Rhodesian Copperbelt' (in *New Commonwealth*, 7 Dec 1953)

manner'—the mines should promote the 'stabilization of labour'. Prain later explained that this trend began with the provision of more married quarters, the encouragement of men to bring their families with them from home, the payment of holiday, travel and long service bonuses, favourable experiences with stabilized labour on the Katanga mines giving further encouragement for the new approach. Prain foresaw that a tradition of long service would emerge on the mines, work being interspersed with periods of furlough, ending with an honoured retirement on pension in the workers' village, there being no reason why mine employees should behave differently in this respect from African soldiers and messengers.[1] This policy possessed outstanding merits from the mining companies' point of view, giving them the best of both worlds. Native labour would now become more efficient, whilst the cost of full urbanization would still be avoided, the old age pensioner drawing his allowance in the villages where the cost of living was cheaper; this solution also being in tune with current ideas on white labour which was likewise regarded as mobile in character, European workers being expected to leave the Copper Belt and retire to their 'reserves' in South Africa or Britain at the end of their working lives, as did most government officials themselves. All the same Prain's views did constitute a striking departure from earlier theories, and as the companies were beginning to change their views on the native labour question, the Administration was modifying its outlook, the new attitude being linked to some extent to changes in the most senior ranks. In 1944 Sandford left the Service and was succeeded as Secretary for Native Affairs by Harold Francis Cartmel-Robinson (later knighted) who previously acquired a considerable knowledge of industrial problems on the Copper Belt. A year later Cartmel-Robinson was promoted to the key office of Chief Secretary, whilst Rowland Skeffington Hudson, another enlightened administrator and an advocate of stabilized labour, took over Cartmel-Robinson's job. At the same time anthropologists criticized the migrant labour system from the sociological point of view, the Rhodes-Livingstone Institute under the guidance of Dr Max Gluckman, a distinguished South African anthropologist with a marked interest in history, greatly expanding its staff and widening the field of research after the War. Besides the local Europeans were becoming much more conscious of the problem of African housing, a key question in the dispute, and Gore-Browne especially denounced the disgraceful conditions to be found in many townships, the Railways and municipalities being the worst offenders, whilst the mines maintained a much better record than anybody else. Gore-Browne thought that divided control in housing matters aggravated the problem and strongly criticized Government for its alleged shortcomings. At the same time the Colonel demolished the Railways' defence that housing was being delayed because white trade unionists denied progress; this was not the case, for the Northern Rhodesian branch of the Railway Workers' Union agreed that African labour might be used both on African

[1] Prain, R. L. 'The stabilization of labour in the Rhodesian copperbelt' (in Prain, Sir R. L. *Selected papers, 1953–1957*. Rhodesian Selection Trust, 1958, p. 99–109)

and European housing projects. The Chief Secretary's reply stressed administrative difficulties; pointed out that the mine companies obtained top priority over everyone else in wartime—including Government—and added that the housing shortage was a world-wide phenomenon.[1] But Government took the problem seriously enough and in 1946 set up an African Housing Department, whose subsequent recommendations in favour of 'balanced stabilization' were accepted by an official Adminstrative Conference in 1948, the Legislative Council having agreed on a big African housing programme to remedy a desperate situation.

The new departure still did not settle the question whether urbanization in itself was to be regarded as a good thing, the experts as yet differentiating between 'urbanization' and 'stabilization of labour'. Some argued that the Copper Belt already contained many black townees who would never go back to the village anyway, and that these people should be helped to strike new roots by means of home ownership and organized communal life. The capital outlay required of employers to house a rapidly growing African population was frightening, and might tend to make the Copper Belt into a high cost producer, whilst actually inhibiting the development of secondary industries. Africans both expected and deserved a higher standard of living, and black men should be able to rent or buy their own homes, which in turn would both foster an African middle class, and do away with the waste of manpower and the inefficiency involved in moving people from the countryside to the towns and back again. Critics of this policy, on the other hand, continued to point to the experiences of the Witwatersrand, arguing that the development of big cities produced slums, vice and crime; and that the quality of the local workers deteriorated so much on the Reef that the gold-mining industry could not employ local labour, and found itself chronically short of manpower. Urbanization might perhaps be inevitable—like drink and fornication—but this was no reason for pushing it! Urbanization moreover would result in serious political problems; each family which permanently settled in a town would produce many more children for whom there might be neither schools nor jobs, unemployment in turn saddling the country with a serious security problem. Argument between the opposing schools of thought continued; but as they went on, more and more Africans drifted into the townships, without heeding the debate, whilst mineworkers continued to sign on for ever lengthening periods, the average length of service going up from 35 months in January 1945 to 50 months in December 1954.[2] Permanent urbanization at last became established government policy, and by 1951 the Colony's review of its Ten-Year Plan recognized that in future the rural African would stay put as much as the now emerging African working class in the towns.[3]

[1] Northern Rhodesia. *Legislative Council debates*, 8 Dec 1945, p. 396–430

[2] For an excellent summary of the arguments see Prain, R. L. 'The stabilization of labour in the Rhodesian copperbelt' (in Prain, Sir R. L. *Selected papers, 1953–1957*. Rhodesian Selection Trust, 1958, p. 99–109)

[3] Northern Rhodesia. *Second (1951) review of the ten year development plan of Northern Rhodesia*. Lusaka, Government printer, 1951, p. 6

Stabilization of labour formed one leg of the companies' new policy—African advancement constituted the other, and the question of promoting Africans into European jobs soon led to a head-on clash with the European miners. The white workers of course approved of higher wages and better conditions for Africans, but argued that such improvements should not be made at the white's expense. In any case the Copper Belt was no paradise for a European miner, and Brian Goodwin, a Mine Workers' spokesman, thus pointed out in the Legislative Council that some Americans from the Congress of Industrial Organizations, and Australians at Broken Hill, 'down under', were taking home much bigger pay packets than Northern Rhodesians; white artisans in his view thus had every justification for a strike called in 1946, and the companies should be condemned for using black against white workers. The mine owners on the other hand argued that in the past Europeans had to be brought in at great expense to start the industry, but this did not mean that these original conditions should now be passed on to the indigenous people. The white miners' cry 'equal pay for equal work' meant in reality not just equal wages, but also equal leave, equal housing, equal cash bonuses and what have you, which—if accepted—would mean the end of all African aspirations, for no one would employ black men on such terms.[1] A further school of thought considered that whites on the Copper Belt should eventually be confined to supervisory jobs only, a view which found expression particularly within the Selection Trust Group of companies where American influence was strong. From the companies' point of view, this approach seemed sound enough, especially at a time when production costs were rising, but the Northern Rhodesian Mine Workers for a time successfully resisted all encroachments. In 1945 the European miners recalled Maybank, who once more became General Secretary of their Union and stuck to his old line of no compromise. The miners further strengthened their hand by joining the World Federation of Trade Unions, whose colonial members all accepted the principle of equal pay for equal work, a programme to this effect being agreed upon in 1945 by fifteen different organizations at Paris, where trade unionists from Nigeria, Sierra Leone, Gambia, the Gold Coast, Northern Rhodesia, the French Cameroons, Trinidad, British Guiana, Jamaica, Ceylon, India and from different Jewish and Arab labour organizations in Palestine all joined in the same demands.[2] Goodwin, now the white mineworkers' President, himself took his place on the Executive of the World Federation of Trade Unions representing Africa, so that the white miners found themselves in a strong position from the international point of view. They further benefited from the way in which demands for sterling copper went up again, making the mining companies even less willing to countenance strikes than they might have

[1] Prain, R. L. 'The problem of African advancement on the copperbelt of Northern Rhodesia' (in Prain, Sir R. L. *Selected papers, 1953–1957*. Rhodesian Selection Trust, 1958, p. 19–34)

[2] See speech by B. Goodwin in Northern Rhodesia. *Legislative Council debates*, 6 May 1946, p. 58–61. The organization also advocated recognition of trade unions, which should be organized regardless of colour or creed, guaranteed annual holidays, unemployment and social insurance, prohibition of child labour, and special protection for women in various industries.

been otherwise. The companies did successfully insist in 1945 that the Northern Rhodesian Mine Workers' Union should only represent Europeans, so that control over Africans should not pass into white hands, but on the other hand management had to agree that jobs handled by white workers at the time should not be given to persons 'to whom the terms and conditions of this agreement do not apply' which meant that Africans could not be promoted.[1] A further Conference, called by Government in 1947, proved abortive and the Administration then set up a Commission of Enquiry under the Chairmanship of Andrew Dalgleish who took recommendations from all interested parties, except the European Union which would not co-operate.[2] The Commission found that Africans were still backward in many respects, but that they could fill a number of specified jobs either right away or in the near future, whilst certain other positions should be opened to them after further training, a recommendation which induced the Administration to set up additional training facilities, though some officials complained that the mines were trying to 'pass the baby' to Government. Arthur Creech Jones—Colonial Secretary in the British Labour Government since 1946—strongly opposed Maybank and Goodwin, thus indirectly siding with the mining companies, on the grounds that serious trouble would break out if Africans were not allowed to make further progress. Creech Jones advised the Northern Rhodesian mine workers to arrive at an agreement with the Africans, and in 1950 a meeting took place between white and black miners. The conference stated that Africans should be allowed to progress, but the delegates completely disconcerted their employers by concluding that black men should not advance at the Europeans' expense, and that African progress should not take place at lower wages than those paid to white men; both white and black workers moreover joined in the same demand for a forty-hour week, whilst Maybank rejoiced that the delegates had made history.[3] The European miners maintained their unbroken stand, and the job position remained essentially unchanged throughout pre-Federation days.

'Stabilization' and African advancement between them implied a better-paid and more knowledgeable labour force, raising in turn the question of African trade unionism. In the early 'forties the mining companies still tried to solve the question by elected Tribal Representatives, who also dealt with the black miners' personal quarrels; 'Boss Boys' were consulted on technical matters, these sub-

[1] See Prain, R. L. 'The problem of African advancement on the copperbelt of Northern Rhodesia' (in Prain, Sir R. L. *Selected papers, 1953–1957*. Rhodesian Selection Trust, 1958, p. 19–34)

[2] *Report of the commission appointed to enquire into the advancement of Africans in industry.* Lusaka, Government printer, 1948

[3] The miners' claim was then investigated by a commission which rejected the forty-hour week. See Northern Rhodesia. *Report of the board of inquiry to consider the proposed 40-hour week in the copper mining industry.* Lusaka, Government printer, 1950. E. Moore, a member of the Commission, alone dissented on the grounds that the mines could afford this concession, that the miners' demands were in tune with those made in other parts of the world, that the 40-hour week would compensate Africans for their low wages, and that beneficial results would accrue to the health of miners doing an 8 hour day for six days in the week. During the same period the British Labour Government reduced working hours in the United Kingdom itself.

foremen, the most advanced and stable African workers, soon achieving separate representation for themselves on several mines. But the great majority of Africans remained migrant labourers from backward provinces like the Bemba country, who lacked contact with the more developed lands south of the Zambezi, where emissaries from the Industrial and Commercial Workers' Union (I.C.U.) a black South African body, tried to organize workers in Bulawayo and Salisbury from the early 'twenties. Northern Rhodesian Africans would of course also have liked to get more money, and during the War Gore-Browne found that wages were brought up at every meeting he held.[1] But the mining companies objected to black trade unions, arguing that the time was not yet ripe for their formation, and permanent organizations could not of course be established against their will in communities where the compound manager ruled like a little king, and where the men always went home to their villages after their contract expired. The African workers themselves at first displayed little initiative in the matter; and besides many black men did not see their problem so much in terms of getting more money from their employers, but rather as one of getting shopkeepers to lower their prices. Indian traders who did most of their business with Africans thus became a popular target of criticism, even though the Asian merchants themselves often had little choice in the matter, being forced by economic circumstances to pass the wholesalers' higher prices on to their customers. In 1942 Africans at Broken Hill organized an orderly boycott of all Indian stores, accusing the brown traders of extortion, sharp practices, and objectionable attitudes of racial superiority towards their customers. The boycott was supported by the whole African population, despite the absence of active picketing, and the traders subsequently reduced some articles in price. Many European workers sympathized with African wage demands, and Brian Goodwin later explained in the House that in 1943 four out of five branches of the Mine Workers' Union instructed their executives to examine the question of forming African unions, adding that if some unpleasant individual or other called an African a 'stinking kaffir', he did not represent white working class opinion, and that the publicity given to such abuses was distorting the facts.[2] Gore-Browne to some extent agreed with this estimate, pointing out that European railway workers were supporting the Africans' demand for overtime, and that European stewards put up their own money to help their black workmates.[3] Welensky thought Africans were as yet too backward to form trade unions most black workers still being illiterate, but in 1943 put up a motion to establish Advisory Boards under an existing Minimum Wage Ordinance (passed as early as 1932). Government carried out Welensky's suggestion, though for the time being nothing more was done about African trade unions. The European workers remained divided over this issue, and whereas Goodwin favoured a policy of organizing black workers, Dave Welensky, Roy's brother and Vice

[1] Northern Rhodesia. *Legislative Council debates*, 1 June 1943, p. 234–250
[2] Northern Rhodesia. *Legislative Council debates*, 6 May 1946, p. 53–54
[3] Northern Rhodesia. *Legislative Council debates*, 1 June 1943, p. 239

President of the Mine Workers Union, thought that the scheme was not really honest, that someone else should handle the job of organizing black workers, that the whites should be content to fight for their own interests and that, for his part, he would not accept natives either living or working side by side with him as equals.[1] Goodwin stuck to his views and accused Dave of dividing the workers,[2] but gained little popularity when he told a meeting at Broken Hill in connexion with another matter that it was like throwing pearls to swine to tell the members of the Broken Hill branch anything![3] Roy Welensky himself still stood out against African trade unionism in 1945, arguing that Africans were still too backward, and that their interests would best be served by a central organization comprising elected African representatives, white trade unionists from Northern Rhodesia and other unionists representing the Government, and not necessarily drawn from inside the territory.[4] A year later, however, Roy Welensky came round to the view that Africans too must have their organizations, his change of front being motivated by a previous African railway strike and also by the responsible way in which black workers negotiated with the Master Millers' Association at Bulawayo.[5] Discussions then took place in 1946 between Welensky, Gore-Browne and the Colonial Office, which agreed in principle that collective bargaining must be developed amongst Africans. The position became even more acute when shortly afterwards white Copper Belt artisans came out on strike, asking for more money, resentful of the way in which their wages were losing in purchasing power, as well as objecting to the way in which mining contractors and underground workers were making more than they themselves, even though artisans were required to know far more than in the past when working processes were less complicated. The companies threatened to disperse their African workers if work ceased, and white miners then distributed pamphlets amongst their black comrades, urging them not to go home if they were paid off. At the same time Goodwin and Maybank again announced their intention of organizing Africans, and a very senior government official urged at Lusaka that the decision to form trade unions amongst Africans should be implemented lest the position developed too far for effective action. But Downing Street did not take the white workers' threat very seriously, and in any case Africans themselves were now becoming interested in forming their own unions, so much so that in 1946 a big meeting held by Gore-Browne and Fisher on the Copper Belt, asked that an expert should come out from England to help them.[6] The position now completely passed out of the European workers' control, and in 1947 William M. Comrie arrived in the Territory as Government Labour Officer to promote African unions, his appointment forming part of the British Labour Government's wider policy of promoting trade unionism

[1] *Northern news*, 10 May 1945, and letter by D. Welensky in *Northern news*, 24 May 1945
[2] Letter by B. Goodwin in *Northern news*, 17 May 1945. For D. Welensky's views, see *Northern news*, 24 May 1945
[3] *Northern news*, 10 May 1945
[4] Northern Rhodesia. *Legislative Council debates*, 28 Nov 1945 p. 60–61
[5] *Northern news*, 1 Aug 1946   [6] *Northern news*, 14 Mar 1946

throughout the colonial empire, and guiding it into reformist rather than revolutionary channels. Comrie displayed great personal ability, and avoided the mistake of alienating white trade unionists whose confidence he gained by the quality of his advice on various technical matters. Like an old-time missionary, Comrie then gathered round him a small team of men who became known amongst local Africans as 'the Disciples', and spread the new gospel of unionism all round the Copper Belt. The shop assistants, a relatively well educated group, were the first to form an African union in 1947, and later on a General Workers' Union came into existence, whilst African drivers joined into a Drivers' Union, the nearest approach to an African craft organization in the territory. As far as the miners were concerned, Comrie met with some difficulty; their numbers were large; the rank and file lacked education, and some of the miners remained suspicious. After all—said the men—Comrie was a European and why should he be so keen to organize them when his 'brothers' only aimed at screwing money out of black men. Comrie also encountered some opposition from white-collar workers who talked of forming a Salaried Staff Organization like their European colleagues; whilst others thought that priority should be given to co-operatives, or that Africans were as yet too backward for a union. But Comrie found that, though Africans drifted around a good deal, their 'leadership core' remained fairly constant, and once their confidence was gained, the task of organizing Africans became much simpler. At Luanshya for instance, certain of the Tribal Representatives became Members of a Boss Boys' Committee, and later of a local Works' Committee which was formed of African representatives from each of the mine departments.[1] Similarly, members of the local Clerks' Association held office in the Welfare Society or sat on the Works Committee, this 'overlapping' of offices being paralleled to some extent on the European side where men like Goodwin and Welensky held their own both in trade unionism and politics.

Now that black trade unionism seemed imminent, the European Mine Workers' Union at last agreed to organize Africans, and Goodwin held various meetings where he told black miners that the Government and the Mines simply wanted to divide the workers by forming a 'yellow' union, that they wished to force down white wages to the black level, and that Comrie was 'a Government man'. But the Africans by now were thoroughly suspicious of the Europeans and a meeting at Kitwe told Goodwin that if he wanted to help them, he should help Comrie. The African leaders later stated that at the time they were not rejecting the idea of a merger with the white union out of hand, but wished to postpone this until they had achieved a strong bargaining position.[2] In any case, they were anxious to prove their ability to run their own organization, which would demonstrate that they could also take part in governing the country whilst if they joined the white union—all effective power would remain with the much more experienced European leaders. Besides, many Africans argued,

[1] Based on Epstein, A. L. *Politics in an urban African community*. Manchester university press, 1958
[2] Epstein, A. L. *op. cit.*

the Northern Rhodesian Mine Workers' Union had plenty of time in the past to organize Africans—yet they never did so; the reason was obvious; the whites were just scared of Africans getting better jobs, and their call for equal work for equal pay formed a mere blind to prevent African competition![1] The Africans thus went ahead with their own organizations, and in 1948 black miners, with Comrie's help, organized four separate unions, most leading positions being taken up by mine clerks and hospital orderlies who possessed more education than the rank and file. In 1949 these various bodies joined to form the Northern Rhodesian African Mine Workers' Trade Union which comprised both white-collar workers and ordinary labourers, Lawrence Charles Katilungu becoming the Union's first President. Katilungu, a Bemba, began his career as a Catholic mission teacher, but later made his way to Broken Hill where the Katilungu family had several relatives. From there he went to the Copper Belt, and failing to secure employment as a clerk, he began to work underground as a 'spanner boy', drawing the grand total of 9d a day plus rations for his work. The young teacher then worked his way up to become a 'bossboy' and when the 1940 strike broke out on the Copper Belt, he urged the men not to go back to work without getting a pay increase. After the shooting, he left for the Congo and for a time worked for a fish transport firm, finally returning to Nkana in 1941.[2] Katilungu now at last secured a job in the office and rose to be a senior interpreter, one of the few Bemba to have attained such a coveted position at a time when most office jobs were held by Nyasalanders who were often accused of unfairly favouring their own countrymen. Katilungu moreover was the grandson of a minor Bemba chief, and was commonly regarded by his compatriots as a member of the Bemba Royal House, his prestige rising further as he became well known to the local workers who passed through his hands on joining the company. Simon A. Kaluwa, a brother of George Kaluwa, a prominent Congress supporter and a farmer of Nyasaland origins, rose to be General Secretary of the Union, and between them, the two quickly built up a mass following which by 1949 numbered 10,0␣␣. The mine workers followed Comrie's advice to keep away from politics for the time being, and successfully negotiated with the mining companies who completely reversed their former stand, and in 1949 signed a procedural agreement with the union, a subsequent wage dispute going to arbitration which netted the Africans a small wage increase.

In the meantime African railway workers were also getting interested in trade unionism. In 1945 a serious African strike broke out at Bulawayo and spread to most of the railway line in Northern Rhodesia, but the Europeans kept aloof, accusing the Africans of irresponsibility, Northern Rhodesians becoming particularly worried at the way in which the strikers held up supplies of coal to the copper mines, which nearly closed down, with the possibility of their getting

[1] Letter by G. A. M. Lewanika in Northern news, 25 Mar 1948. For an African view opposed to Lewanika's, see letter in Northern news, 8 Apr 1948
[2] See Central African examiner, 4 July 1959, for a fuller biographical sketch. See also Epstein, A. L. Politics in an urban African community. Manchester university press, 1958

2B

flooded.[1] The European railway workers neither enforced a 'closed shop' nor maintained a colour bar clause in their constitution, the union actually counting some Coloured members within its ranks. But in Southern Rhodesia the Industrial Conciliation Act restricted blacks, and as far as the 'rate for the job' concept was concerned, white railwaymen would no more shift from their principle than the white miners. The African workers therefore struck out on their own, an African Railway Workers' Union being formed in 1950 with its headquarters at Broken Hill. Later on in the same year all these various African organizations joined to form a Northern Rhodesian African Trade Union Congress, of which Katilungu became President.

II

Agriculture and land settlement

The farmers benefited from the post-war boom, and production increased dramatically, the tobacco growers doing particularly well at a time when the British were short of dollars and relied on the Sterling Area to keep economically afloat. Mechanization went ahead, and by the end of 1949 white farmers between them owned about 650 tractors, interest in machinery being stimulated by the prevailing shortage of African labour which was now becoming the most important limiting factor to the further expansion of the industry.[2] Nevertheless, demand continued to outpace supply; the country remained short of maize, dairy products, wheat, bacon, and various other kinds of produce. Government tried to attract immigrants by giving loans of up to £3,000 at 4 per cent interest to suitable applicants who themselves owned at least £1,500, special conditions being made for ex-servicemen, but land settlement continued to encounter numerous difficulties. The earliest settlers usually took up the most accessible and best-watered farms, their choice rarely being dictated by the price of land which only constituted a small item in their total expenditure, so that newcomers sometimes found the most desirable areas already occupied. Government services remained limited, and many settlers thought that surveys were inadequate and that they got too little accurate information about soil and water, whilst the applicants' personal and financial credentials were not always adequately checked. Besides, standards of living overseas were rising, and new immigrants were apt to demand more of life than in the pioneering days. In 1948 a big

[1] Speech by S. Gore-Browne in Northern Rhodesia. *Legislative Council debates*, 6 Apr 1946, p. 448–449

[2] Northern Rhodesia. Department of agriculture. *Annual report for the year 1949.* Lusaka, Government printer, 1950. Between 1945 and 1949 the production of flue-cured Virginia type tobacco expanded from 2,207,000 lb to 4,076,000 lb. The production of maize increased from 273,000 bags (of 200 lb each) in 1945 to 343,000 bags in 1948, though the following year saw a sharp reduction, dropping to 283,000 bags. African production for the same years amounted to 202,000; 296,000; 61,000.

British firm submitted an interesting group settlement scheme whereby a Planning Committee would clear the land, make roads and instal central facilities; farm houses were to be built round specified centres provided with a club, tennis courts, a petrol engine plant for electricity, and running water from boreholes. Experienced farmers would come out from Britain, requiring only a little further training, used to marketing boards, co-operatives, fixed prices and wages, and all the complex administrative problems of modern farming. But—the firm argued—applicants of such a kind would want adequate facilities before they arrived, for English farmers' wives now had a big say with their husbands in the running of their joint enterprise, and wished for electric lights, water-flushed toilets, recreational facilities and such like amenities. British farmers moreover wanted freehold title, and Government should satisfy this very natural demand. The authorities concluded however that the established leasehold policy must continue, that no large blocs were available which would be suitable for the proposed group settlements of 50 to 60 farms, and that the country did not want pioneers who wanted their entertainment laid on in advance.

Besides, the wider question of land relationship between white and black still plagued the planners, disputes having dragged on and on from the 'thirties without reaching a final settlement. The old reserves system was designed to encourage white land colonization, but worked badly—even from the Euro-peans' point of view—and soon complaints were heard all over the country. Africans grimly gazed across the borders of the 'silent lands' which they had to leave, even though no white farmers would settle there and provide jobs or market for locally-grown grain; whilst Gore-Browne, a big landowner himself, stigmatized the Imperial land policy in Northern Rhodesia as worse than South Africa's, Southern Rhodesia's or Kenya's. In the latter countries, he thought, white men unfairly helped themselves to big slices at the Africans' expense, but at least they occupied the land. In Northern Rhodesia, on the other hand, hun-dreds of thousands of Africans were pushed into areas which were palpably too small—not because selfish settlers wanted the soil, but just for reasons of admini-strative convenience.[1] No European, on the other hand, could make a permanent home in an African reserve where his presence might act as an example of better farming, or provide jobs locally, like Shiwa Ngandu in the lonely north. The system of freehold tenure was applied over a purely arbitrary distance of 20 to 25 miles from the railway line, just because this happened to make things easier for the administrator, whilst African reserves mostly had inadequate access to the line of rail. In the 'thirties Young thought that this situation could best be remedied by introducing the Nyasaland practice. The Governor disliked the reserves system, and thought that all land should be divided into unalienated Crown land—available to all purchasers—and native trust land. The latter should comprise all country unsuited for white farmers or for mining development, but Europeans should be allowed to acquire farms on temporary leases, provided their presence conferred some obvious benefit on the indigenous people, the Native

[1] Northern Rhodesia. *Legislative Council debates*, 21 Sep 1942, p. 156

Treasuries receiving half the proceeds derived from such contracts. All Provincial Commissioners at the time agreed with Young's scheme, except the Commissioner in charge of Barotseland, but the Colonial Office considered the Governor's solution as too favourable to the settlers. The Imperial authorities thought that both the old Kasempa Province and North-Eastern Rhodesia must be regarded as African areas, and that the status of the existing native reserves should not be changed, Young being blamed for favouring whites at African expense, and for 'rationalizing' his policy as being in the Africans' best interest. The question dragged on and on, as the Colonial Office first awaited the report of the Financial Commissioners, and then the Report of the Royal Commission on Closer Union, further delay being caused by the outbreak of the War. In the meantime the position became so bad that Africans were permitted to leave various congested areas and settle outside the reserves, subject to various kinds of control, though no provision was made to encourage Africans to buy land on individual tenure in special areas—as in Southern Rhodesia—the Administration arguing that the most advanced Africans should not be artificially separated from their own people, a concept that also dominated official thought with regard to African politics. Europeans remained excluded from the native reserves on the grounds that white and black lands should not mingle, that Europeans would take up the best soil, that their farms would constitute a drain on local labour, that there were few areas suitable for Europeans anyway, and that the presence of settlers might create difficulties with regard to African political development. Discussions continued during the early 'forties, and in 1942 Government at last issued a statement with regard to African land. This established the general principle that all land not alienated to Europeans or set aside for native reserves should be divided into two categories. The first consisted of Crown Land, suitable for European settlement on an economic basis and also for mining development, Government now possessing much more information about the country's ecological and geological structure than in the past. In addition Native Trust Land would be set aside for the exclusive occupation of Africans, in these areas no alienations would be allowed, except for Africans wishing to farm on individual tenure, for townships, and for a few 'non-natives', whose work was considered beneficial to Africans, but who could only acquire land on leasehold, such purchases being restricted to 6,000 acres for each province. A Commission was appointed in 1943, but its report only reached the Colonial Office in 1945.[1]

Further discussion followed in Northern Rhodesia where many farmers rightly feared that the project would hold up development, exception being taken to the fact that white settlement would be limited to the small remaining areas of Crown land that remained, whilst only 30,000 acres would be left open in Trust Lands as a whole. Gore-Browne, however, managed to talk round the opponents of the scheme; the 6,000 acre limit disappeared, and after a private meeting between Gore-Browne, Beckett and various other members of the Council a new formula was adopted which appeased the critics. Leases were to

[1] Northern Rhodesia. *Report of the land commission.* Lusaka, Government printer, 1946

be permitted to Europeans in Native Trust Land, provided the Governor and the Secretary of State agreed—after consultation with the Native Authority concerned—that such contacts were in the best interest of both races; and the Colonial Office was finally brought round to accept this modification of previous policy. Some Europeans admittedly still had their doubts and even Gore-Browne remained disappointed that Crown land could still only be acquired on leasehold tenure,[1] a provision particularly galling to applicants who wished to acquire small holdings or township plots, obtainable only on 99 year leases, an unattractive proposition for purchasers of virgin land requiring a great deal of initial capital, and also for industrialists who much preferred freehold before they started putting up money to build a factory. Government officials in the Provincial Administration usually remained unsympathetic to the idea of Europeans settling in 'their' native district, so much so that a very senior man in the North could subsequently record how 'surprised, in fact shocked' he was when the African Local Government at Kasempa came along with the 'unbelievable request' that Europeans might start farming in their area, the Africans' move perhaps being motivated by the fear of Luchazi or Lovale immigrants, the local Kaonde appreciating that their country was only sparsely populated, and preferring whites to Angolan Africans. The Europeans nevertheless accepted the project without any further struggle, preferring to make their stand on the political rather than the land front. There was, after all, no apparent lack of land at a time when 3,407 square miles still remained available around Livingstone, Lusaka, Mazabuka and Broken Hill alone;[2] only a relatively small number of settlers were coming into the country, and the planners did not wish to be saddled with a situation of the kind which arose in the early 'thirties when many farms were left derelict; the farmers moreover were well represented on the Commission, and there seemed no point in quarrelling over a settlement which still remained flexible in character, and which did not prevent future mining activities or other forms of beneficial enterprise in Native Trust areas. But from the long term point of view the Northern Rhodesia (Native Trust Land) Order in Council, 1947, became perhaps one of the most significant documents in the country's history. Northern Rhodesia, to all intents and purposes, was in the main recognized as a native territory, with a tongue of 'open' land in the middle and a few more 'open' (and often little used) spots scattered about elsewhere; white land colonization remained confined to strictly circumscribed limits at a time when the northward push of the South African farmer's frontier had exhausted its impetus; and the majority in the Protectorate regarded the area as a black man's country.[3]

Post-war prosperity also gave an impetus to African farming, development

---

[1] Northern Rhodesia. *Legislative Council debates*, 11 Feb 1947, p. 808–834

[2] Northern Rhodesia. Land Board. *Information for intending settlers.* Lusaka, Government printer, 1949

[3] By 1950 20,030 square miles remained open for settlement out of the country's total area of 287,640 square miles; by then 11,644 square miles were occupied and 8,366 square miles of unalienated land remained, the freehold values rising steadily as Crown land became scarcer.

being encouraged by the Agricultural Department through agricultural stations and extensive services, which aimed at increasing the productivity of the soil and popularizing new methods. In 1947 the Department introduced an Improved African Farmers Scheme which was financed from an African Farming Improvement Fund, maintained from the annual cash balances of the Native Maize Pool operated by the Maize Control Board. Money was spent on providing permanent storage sheds, supplying platform scales and balances at rural depots, subsidizing people who wished to buy ox-carts, purchasing machinery and tractors, and so on. In addition bonuses were paid to farmers prepared to conform with methods approved by the Department, the Scheme aiming at improving agricultural practice all round, rather than getting a few individual farmers to adopt high standards. In 1948 the Administration began the first of several Peasant Farming Schemes, a start being made at Kawaza in the Eastern Province in 1948; groups of planned African farms were established on a form of leasehold tenancy from the Native Authority: farmers received help through a newly appointed Commissioner for Native Development, supervision and training being provided by the Agricultural Department; a District Officer organized the land clearing; the farms were contoured and divided into plots for crop rotation; the peasants used cattle for draught purposes and spread the kraal manure out on the fields, the average size of farms in the Eastern Province scheme ranging from eighteen to thirty acres, of which about half was kept under the plough at a time.[1] A small number of African farmers managed to do extremely well, a characteristic success story being the career of one Sylvester Chitimpa, who used to work as a small boy on the farm of John Clarke, an early pioneer in the country. Clarke helped to get Chitimpa a little education, and when the First World War started, Chitimpa joined a group of people who used to buy provisions for the soldiers, and later rose to be their *capitao*. In 1921, when the post-war boom broke, Chitimpa's former employer got a job with the Rhodesian Broken Hill Development Company and invited Chitimpa to join him at Broken Hill. The African accepted and stayed at the mine from 1921 right on to 1939, managing to save £50 from his wages, which he supplemented by working as a spare-time photographer with his own camera. In 1939 Chitimpa at last was able to satisfy his life ambition and buy a little farm in the Broken Hill area, containing sixteen head of cattle and a few primitive farming implements. In 1945 he moved over to Chibombo, the Lenje Native Authority headquarters, where—in 1949—he became the first Lenje 'Building Councillor' in charge of local construction. At the same time he continued to work on the land, graduated as an 'Improved Farmer', and as an 'Individual Farmer', and finally managed to buy a tractor on the hire purchase system, as well as a mill, which enabled him to grind maize for the people in the neighbourhood.

But people like Chitimpa still remained the exception. By the end of the War

[1] Northern Rhodesia. Department of agriculture. *Annual report for the year 1951.* Lusaka, Government printer, 1952, p. 16–17

some 85 per cent of the families inhabiting the Tonga maize growing area in the Mazabuka District, one of Northern Rhodesia's most progressive regions, still consisted of subsistence cultivators, who mainly confined themselves to producing for their own needs, not because they were short of land, but because they lacked other material necessities, or because they had so many dependents to look after, or because they lacked the initiative to improve themselves. About 14 per cent of the people were composed of smallholders who cultivated about twice as much land as they would have done under subsistence agriculture, most of these people acquiring their larger crops by taking their resting land under cultivation. Less than 1 per cent were described as 'farmers', wealthy native proprietors who kept up to about 90 acres under cultivation, and acquired their land either in accordance with Tonga customary law, or with the help of modern chiefs and Government officials. The 'farmers' ' total area of land remained quite insignificant, so that there was as yet no question of a solid class of African landowners displacing poorer men from their ancestral acres. The Tonga suffered from a general land shortage, but this was occasioned not by the growth of an indigenous class of *kulaks*, but by the limited amount of fertile maize soil available, by alienation of former tribal land to Europeans, by a vast and comparatively recent increase in the number of their cattle (which added much to Tonga prosperity), by the concentration of people along certain particularly favoured spots, by soil degeneration, and by wastage of land occasioned by the haphazard manner employed in laying out fields.[1] Some farmers did improve their methods, though the prosperous man with a nicely built brick house was not necessarily the best husbandman, his fine crops sometimes being simply due to the fact that his land only recently came under cultivation, and therefore showed as yet no signs of exhaustion. Many other peasants held back, because they felt that Government could simply restore the land situation by handing over European owned farms to the Tonga; or because they remained satisfied with low crop yields and a traditionally low standard of living. Most cultivators moreover lacked capital to buy implements, cattle or wagons; and those who purchased equipment often did not know how to maintain their machinery in proper working order. Others found that their kinship obligations prevented them from accumulating capital, the smallholders generally marrying more wives than subsistence farmers, and thus becoming saddled with a great many children dependent on their meagre income. Worse still, many Africans remained so suspicious of Government that they would not readily take up suggestions coming from the white man, thus making the Agricultural Officer's task much more difficult than it might have been otherwise. Government tried to improve the position by various administrative reforms, and by changes in the system of native land tenure. But no attempt was made to provide the more advanced farmers with holdings on an individual tenure outside the reserves,

[1] Allan, W., and others. 'Report on a reconnaissance survey' (Appendix 5 in Northern Rhodesia. Native land tenure committee. *Report . . . part II, Mazabuka district.* Lusaka, Government printer, 1946)

various experts agreeing that such a policy would be unsound, that it would not be practicable to provide land outside the reserves; the most advanced African farmers should not be 'culled' from their districts where they provided a valuable object lesson to others; and where many lesser men depended on their wealthier neighbours for the use of stock and implements, so that an exodus of better-off people would deprive the whole community of valuable capital resources like wagons, carts and trained oxen. Government also tried to help the more advanced African in other ways, for instance by doing away in 1945 with an old rule by which each village was obliged to contain at least ten tax-payers, an attempt being made to introduce a more flexible 'parish system' under which Africans would be registered as belonging to specific areas. The reasoning behind this new reform was rather complicated. Gore-Browne explained to his fellow Members of the Legislative Council that villages used to be large in the olden days, but that Africans now preferred to live in scattered family groups; Government should give way to the Africans' desire to live in more dispersed communities, the 'taxpayer rule' having become a burden on the most advanced members of the tribe. Progressive farmers, Gore-Browne felt, preferred to build permanent brick houses for themselves, with an orchard nearby, and people of that kind should not be expected to leave their homesteads whenever their fellow villagers shifted their village in accordance with the rules of *chitimene* agriculture. Government in 1945 accordingly permitted advanced Africans to break away from their villages, subject to certain kinds of control, and attempted to set up 'parishes' containing groups of villages with centralized schools and dispensaries. These recommendations were well meant, but met with expert criticism on the grounds that Government's approach was altogether too theoretical. The parish system did not by itself produce markets or schools, whilst the abolition of the ten taxpayer rule would simply scatter the people, making permanent improvements more difficult. Neither did the committee responsible for these proposals distinguish properly between areas of more or less fixed habitation, such as the Luapula Valley, and regions of shifting cultivation, like the Tonga country. The assumption that African villages would naturally split into family groups rested on a serious over-simplification, whilst the size of a settlement depended on economic and ecological factors; the parish system could only work in a hierarchical system, like that of the Bemba, but not amongst the Tonga, whose headmen were often independent of each other, and whose villages possessed no recognized boundaries. The new system moreover could not check wasteful use of land, any more than it would prevent movement from one parish to another or occasion any major improvements.

The parish system accordingly proved of but limited value and was only adopted sporadically; but more progress was made in other directions, a major step forward being made in the development of rural trade. European and Indian dealers, many of whom employed African 'store-boys', accounted for much of the business done in the villages, but side by side with these immigrant merchants, a new group of African businessmen was slowly coming into existence.

An outstanding black pioneer in this field was one Luka Mumba who was born the son of a village African near Fort Rosebery. At the age of about eight young Luka was sent by his relatives to a mission school in the Belgian Congo where he learnt French and drifted around to Uganda, Tanganyika and Rhodesia, doing all kinds of jobs and proving as versatile as white pioneers. Most important of all, he learned how to drive, and by 1942 he saved enough money to buy an old truck and set himself up as a transport contractor; the lorry kept breaking down, but Mumba kept going and expanded his business, transporting fish from Lake Bangweulu to the Copper Belt, until he acquired a whole fleet of buses and trucks, as well as stores and even a hotel. Other traders managed to accumulate their initial capital by working down the mines, as employees of European firms, in Government or as hawkers, until they were able to set up a little grocery store or butchery, or buy up a secondhand motor vehicle which in time enabled a few enterprising men to expand their sphere of operations. Trade also opened up new opportunities for women, and a characteristic pioneering story was that of Anne Lengalenga, the daughter of an African pastor. After leaving the mission school, Anne became a homecraft teacher, but soon left the job and returned to her family; her father later bought her a bicycle which gave her a start. She began to collect eggs from the villages and sold them in Lusaka, making up her earnings by baking scones and selling them in the streets, but life was so hard that for a time she gave up trade and became a nurse, working as far afield as Dar-es-Salaam. By means of stinting and scraping she finally managed to save £60 and bought a small grocery business some eighteen miles from Lusaka. Then began a time of toil and drudgery; she had to bring in goods from Lusaka twice a day on her bicycle, grimly struggling on until she managed to buy an old car and build a bigger and better shop which at last set her on the road to a modest fortune.[1]

The new African traders, like English, Scottish, Jewish and Indian pioneers before them, met with many difficulties. Capital was short, and their customers poor; many dealers took up too much credit from their wholesalers, without being able to meet their debts, and then found that they had stocked their stores with too many articles of one particular kind, which remained unsold in the shelves, until the European wholesaler stopped their credit, and their little business went to pieces. Others tried to make a profit too quickly, charging high prices instead of relying on a big turnover and smaller profits on each individual article, with the result that their customers preferred to go elsewhere. Many fell down on their book-keeping, and besides there was competition from European and Indian traders, as well as from Government itself which set up buying depots and encouraged co-operatives. A few African co-operatives started in the 'thirties and 'forties, much support being given by individual government officers. In 1943 the 'D.C.' at Mporokoso for instance began a little society, consisting of clerks and a head messenger who pooled their resources to buy fish from

[1] Samakai, J. B. 'Ambitious Anne . . .' (in Northern Rhodesia. Information department. *Success in Northern Rhodesia*. Lusaka, Information department, 1960, p. 10–11)

African fishermen in the Mweru swamps. Within a year, the Society's initial capital rose from £3. 10. 0. in 10/– shares to £60; a consumers' store came into existence which extended its activities from buying fish to purchasing salt, mats, baskets, brooms, grain, sweet potatoes and honey, as well as European goods like razor blades, soap, writing paper, envelopes, tea, coffee, sugar, paraffin, nails, cigarettes, matches, cycle spares, fish hooks, cotton piece goods, and so on. The Society was run by a Committee, elected by a General Meeting, and dividends were paid at 1d per shilling on purchases and sales to the society, which received no outside help except for the building of two stores by prison labour. The D.C. at the same time organized a 'Thrift and Loan Bank' which provided loans at 10 per cent interest, the absence of credit facilities constituting one of the major bars in the expansion of African enterprise. None of these organizations how-ever met with much permanent success, owing to lack of trained staff, and the fact that they were usually sponsored by well-intentioned outsiders like mis-sionaries or district officers, whose successors might not share the founder's interest. In 1945 an expert investigated the position, and a year later the Labour Government in London sent a Circular Despatch which stressed the value of co-operative methods. The Imperial Government's views met with considerable sympathy amongst Unofficials in the Legislature, and Gore-Browne moved the appointment of a Registrar of Co-operative Societies. In 1947 a separate de-partment came into being, which took over from the Registrar of the High Court, who used to deal with co-operative societies under an old ordinance promulgated in 1914.[1] The department actively encouraged the formation of new societies, both European and African, which rapidly increased in member-ship and turnover.[2] African Consumer and Supply Societies started up in many parts of the Territory, though their development was gravely hampered by the lack of good and reliable managers. The real backbone of the movement turned out to be the Producer Marketing Societies, and within a few years, the Eastern Province—the first in the field of African producer co-operatives—was completely covered by co-operative organizations which collected and disposed of African crops like groundnuts and Burley tobacco under adequate super-vision. Village trade of course still remained limited in extent, but by 1949 a Government investigation found that a buying organization of some sort now existed in practically every part of Northern Rhodesia, and that there were only a few Africans left who did not regularly sell any portion of their crop, about 85 per cent of the food sold by black cultivators being estimated to have been pro-duced specifically for the market. The basis of rural life thus gradually became transformed, and in time a creeping revolution profoundly altered the accus-tomed ways of the village.

[1] Northern Rhodesia. Registrar of co-operative societies. *Annual report for the year 1947.* Lusaka, Government printer, 1948

[2] Between 1948 and 1950 the membership of European Societies rose from 2,422 to 4,438 and their turnover from £693,000 to £1,163,048. The respective figures for African membership were 5,583 and 10,364; the turnover rose from £50,703 to £112,214.

III

African administration and politics

The rise of the 'new men' in African trade and agriculture found a parallel in the field of local administration, where tribal chiefs gradually became more dependent on village 'progressives'. In the early 'forties the process had not gone very far, and in 1943 the Provincial Commissioner for the Northern Province for instance still bitterly complained of the large number of petty, ineffective and jealous chiefs, who were rapidly losing the respect and obedience of the younger generation, a further weakness of the existing system being found in the fact that some of the Superior Native Authorities were not created in accordance with native customs, and that councillors and clerks were so inadequately paid that well educated people would not enter the chiefs' service. A Provincial Commissioner's Conference, held in the same year, arrived at similar conclusions, and agreed that Government in future should vest power in the Chief-in-Council rather than the chiefs in person, that more 'progressives' should be appointed to the Native Authorities; which ought to meet regularly, and should be paid in a more adequate fashion. The Native Authorities gradually ought to take over social services like primary education, sanitation and roads, whilst the number of petty rulers must be reduced; at the same time the demarcation between Native Authorities, that is to say Chiefs and Councillors on the one hand, and Native Courts, Chiefs and Assessors on the other, should be emphasized; the importance of Superior Native Authorities as law-making bodies must be stressed, and Native Authorities in time should collect all taxes, returning a proportion to the Central Government, whose share should be progressively decreased. A year later the Legislature voted an extra £25,000 to improve salaries, the remainder being paid into Native Treasury Funds as the Provincial Commissioner might advise, whilst the Secretary for Native Affairs had to busy himself more with political duties occasioned by his membership of the Legislative Council. In 1945 the Administration thus announced the abolition of 79 redundant Native Authorities, mostly in the Kaonde-Lunda and Eastern Provinces.[1] In 1948 the Government went one step further, and began to build up stronger African tribal councils on which existing chiefs and traditional councillors were joined by more progressive Africans; in addition departmental councillors began to be elected, each responsible for one particular function of government, reorganization of government proceeding so quickly that by the end of the following year the great majority of Native Authorities were operating in the new fashion.[2]

[1] Northern Rhodesia. *Legislative Council debates*, 9 Jan 1945, p. 33

[2] Northern Rhodesia. *African affairs annual report, 1948*. Lusaka, Government printer, 1949, p. 3; and *African affairs annual report*, 1949. Government printer, 1950, p. 3

At the same time the Administration attempted to provide a better education for chiefs who were now forced to deal with problems of ever-growing complexity. A beginning was made in 1939, when courses started at the Jeanes Training School, Chalimbana, under the auspices of the African Education Department. In 1943 these courses were extended, but it was only in 1946 that Government first began to give a specific training in local government, as opposed to more general subjects like history, geography, civics, agriculture hygiene and village improvement which used to form the bulk of the curriculum. In 1948 the Administration agreed that a separate African Local Government School should be established at Chalimbana and the first course opened in 1951, lectures being given on all kinds of administrative questions, native courts, elementary accounting and so forth.[1] Finally Government tried to tighten up the financial supervision of the Native Authorities, where peculation was rife, administrative integrity as understood by Western civil servants not perhaps being easily compatible with far-flung kinship obligations of a traditional kind, and in any case difficult to enforce amongst poorly paid officials to whom even small sums presented a great temptation.

Whatever the merits of administrative devolution, the process was inherent in the whole theory of Indirect Rule, and soon speeded up under its own momentum, even though some district officers disliked the rate of change. 'Formerly we did things ourselves' said a disgusted 'D.C.' 'and then we told them [the Africans] what we did. Now we tell them what to do, and we still do it!' But senior civil servants soon found that in fact they could no longer do it all themselves; they became more and more concerned with technical questions, with war and post-war problems, and supervision of native courts; whilst the Secretary for Native Affairs found more and more of his working hours taken up with political duties which were inescapably linked to membership of the Legislative Council. At the same time more educated Africans were leaving the Mission schools, and demanding new kinds of services which could only be supplied by a more efficient type of local government. Indirect rule was therefore bound to expand, and from 1945 the process met with even stronger encouragement from the British Labour Government, which regarded local bodies as a means—not only of administrative, but also of social and economic change—as instruments peculiarly well suited to its own mood of cautious reform. In 1947 Creech Jones sent round an important circular despatch in which he urged that local authorities must become 'efficient, democratic and local'—sufficiently close to the common people to command their confidence, but also sufficiently effective so as to manage local services and raise the general standard of living. The Labour Government was thinking both in terms of its own democratic ideals, and of promoting long-term development plans for the colonies, arguing that Africans would not derive full benefit from the monies voted for their benefit from the Imperial Parliament and the local Legislature, unless local government

[1] See North, A. C. 'Rural local government training in Northern Rhodesia' (in *Journal of African administration*, v. 13, no. 2, Apr 1961, p. 67–77)

developed in a more adequate fashion. The building up of local authorities was also considered important for political reasons, as a step towards giving the African masses a greater say in the running of their country. At the moment— Creech Jones felt—the more responsible jobs were largely filled by members of an educated black minority. This was inevitable for the time being; but Government did not want a class of professional African politicians absorbed in work at the centre, but out of touch with the people. The answer was a chain of councils, rising from local institutions to the Legislative Council, the rate of progress being bound to be rapid because of the force of world opinion, local pressures and the stimulus provided by the Government's own development programme. Creech Jones thought that conditions in the various African territories differed too widely to lay down hard and fast rules, but that there should be a common objective and a common manner of approach. The Colonial Secretary therefore proposed to hold a Summer School at Cambridge—itself a move characteristic of post-war England, where Summer Schools were becoming an important cultural institution, taking over in some ways the functions of intellectual upper-class *salons* and the great Whig Houses of old. The Summer School would study the various questions involved in local government, the view of African Governors being subsequently obtained on the subject. Under the new dispensation 'D.C.s' were to become primarily agents for putting the new policy into effect, the development of African local Government being regarded as the District Commissioner's primary task, whilst their routine work should be made easier by the installation of more mechanical office aids and by professional office managers. The Summer School recommended that Native Authorities should receive a sufficiently large share of direct revenue to defray recurrent administrative expenditure and expand existing services, whilst Central Government grants should be provided mainly for specific local developments, particular stress being placed on the importance of local taxes to develop local services. The Northern Rhodesian Administration professed itself in fundamental agreement with these principles, but urged a somewhat more cautious approach. Traditional chiefs were still highly respected by all classes, including the intelligentsia, and their authority should not be undermined, even if their rule involved some departure from democratic principles as understood in Western Europe. The Administration was already strengthening Native Authorities by amalgamating smaller units, pensioning off redundant chiefs, and building up councils containing both progressives and tribal elders. Reform was of course essential, but was impeded by the fact that the best men were leaving the countryside for the towns, and that the Native Authorities often depended on part-time workers who preferred easy work with little supervision and low pay, provided they could work near their homes. The answer was to build up larger Native Authorities; and Government therefore made a determined effort to get rid of smaller Native Authorities and accept them, where possible, as members of the Council of Superior Native Authorities, the new administrative units becoming economically stronger, and better able to afford a full time staff. At the same time the Administration encouraged specialization by pushing for the appointment of 'Departmental Councillors' in charge of particular functions. From 1949 administrative differentiation became more widespread, the resultant division of labour further encouraging the recruitment of 'new men' to the local authorities, with the result that chiefs became more dependent on their 'progressives' whom they could soon no longer afford to alienate.

The Administration promoted similar changes in Barotseland, where the old order continued with the greatest vigour, and where British Administrators were probably exaggerating the extent of the abuses believed to exist under the traditional system. Reform began on the *katengo* council, a body which at one time used to give representation to minor chiefs, headmen, stewards and lesser members of the royal family, who between them wielded considerable power by their numbers, though they might not possess much influence as individuals. British officials used to regard the *katengo* as Barotseland's 'House of Commons', and the *katengo* thus seemed to lend itself naturally to 'Parliamentary reform'. In 1946 the Barotse—under persuasion from above—agreed to make a number of important innovations, which were subsequently defended as forming a return to traditional ways. In future, members from each district *kuta (Khotla)* would combine with older members of the *katengo* to meet twice a year, subsequently joining the full National Council, a special stipulation providing that none of the *katengo* members should be office-holders under the Barotse Native Government. In 1947 the Provincial Commissioner received instructions to choose members from each district for the new *katengo*, the new members being selected after consultation between the District Commissioners and district *kutas*. The new appointees were to consist of commoners, and also comprised members of the subject tribes who thus achieved a greater say in government.

In 1948 the Administration followed up its success by introducing the elective principle, even though the new procedure was not at first always fully understood. In Mongu-Lealui and Senanga literate people wrote the names of their candidate on a piece of paper, whilst voters who could neither read nor write, told the Cadet-in-charge of their choice, some stating that they did not know the candidates and would leave the decision to the returning officer! In the Kalabo district the headmen voted for their villages, a procedure well adapted to a backward area, but in Sesheke the electors used ballot boxes according to the approved Western fashion. The reform movement also affected the native administration, which 'N.R.G.' considered to be cluttered up with obsolete posts and sinecures, as the functions of government continued to alter and many of the older posts became obsolete. During the War Dr Max Gluckman investigated the problem, and in a closely reasoned paper argued that the territorial division had come to stay on the grounds that the modern functions of government could be exercized on no other basis. But at the same time Gluckman stressed the need for historical continuity, and stressed the value of the older non-territorial divisions, recommending, amongst other things, that the old system of storehouses should be revived, so as to provide travellers with food.[1] The Administration, however, remained wedded solely to the territorial concept of government, and put all its trust into the *silalo indunas* whom it regarded as 'the backbone of government'. These dignitaries now received direct access to the *kuta*, even though they could not fully share in its deliberations. At the same time the number of indunas was reduced, some losing their posts though being compensated by a gratuity, whilst the remaining dignitaries received better salaries, reorganization aiming at a more rational system, so that the Barotse system became more assimilated to the patterns of a European bureaucracy. The Secretary for Native Affairs expressed thorough satisfaction with these reforms, which, in his view, introduced a democratic element into the stronghold of a well-entrenched aristocracy.

Nevertheless there was some discontent, opposition being aroused in several ways. A number of indunas in the neighbourhood of Lealui supported a 'back to Lewanika' movement, and there was an outbreak of arson directed against the house and person of the Ngambela, discontent apparently being made worse by a food shortage. In addition, the constitutional changes provided a new mouthpiece for dissatisfied people, including some younger members of the intelligentsia.[2] The position was made worse by the death of Imwiko, the Paramount chief, whose demise in 1948 temporarily unsettled the country. Imwiko's successor, Mwanawina III (later knighted as Sir Mwanawina Lewanika), was himself anything but a radical. An elderly man, some sixty years old at the time of his accession, he was educated at Lovedale, and professed the Christian faith. During the Great War he made a name for himself by personally leading 2,000 carriers and taking them as far as the Luapula, his loyalty to the Imperial cause never remaining in doubt. In 1937 he was appointed to head the Mankoya district; when hostilities broke out against the Germans, Mwanawina again did his share towards the Imperial war effort by collecting funds, encouraging the collection of wild rubber, and assisting with the recruiting campaign. But conservative as he might be, the Paramount shared the intelligentsia's fears of the European Unofficials' growing power. The Barotse Native Government moreover regarded the African Representative Council with some suspicion, and whilst not actually boycotting the Council, their delegates confined themselves to a watching brief, the Barotse remaining determined not to integrate their interests too closely with those of the remainder, even in such important measures as the control of natural resources. Isolationism derived further strength from literate and articulate Barotse who disliked the influx of educated strangers from the east, especially members of other tribes who belonged to the African Civil Service or were employed as Government artisans. The chiefs also complained that the Barotse Native Authority and Barotse Native Courts legislation, issued after the signing of new agreements, conflicted with the spirit

[1] See Gluckman, A. *Administrative organization of the Barotse native authorities with a plan for reforming them.* (Rhodes-Livingstone *communications*, no. 1, v. 2, 1943)

[2] Northern Rhodesia. *African affairs annual report, 1949.* Lusaka, Government printer, 1950, p. 82

—if not the letter—of the Lewanika treaties which guaranteed the Barotse against interference in their internal affairs, an additional source of discontent being found in the vast loss of territory by the Barotse since they put themselves under British protection. The Government, however, refused to give way, and explained that Barotseland should not cut adrift from the rest of Northern Rhodesia, at a time when the Territory was entering a period of unparalleled prosperity, an argument sufficiently well founded to carry conviction.

In the townships, power remained with the Europeans, and African progress remained confined to a limited number of institutions. First of all there were African townships which owed their origin to settlements of self-employed Africans; these people included carpenters, bicycle repairers, hawkers and the like, who did not fit into the locations run by local authorities, and who faced housing problems of particular severity, having no claim against any employer for accommodation. In addition the better paid Africans wished in some cases to avoid the disciplined atmosphere of locations, and Government therefore decided to institute African townships near the bigger centres. By 1943 sites were chosen near all the Copper Belt settlements, and three years later African Townships came into being at Ndola, Mufulira, Kitwe, Chingola and Luanshya. Houses in these townships were built either by the owners themselves according to approved standards, or by Government for disposal to Africans. In 1947 all these five settlements were gazetted as such, and Management Boards consisting of African householders were set up under the chairmanship of District Commissioners, the Central Government making *bloc* grants available to these new local authorities, which could also raise local rates. Africans also gained a greater measure of control over their own affairs through the setting up of Urban Courts whose members were drawn from the tribes having the largest number of followers in the area, the members of the Urban Courts being appointed after consultation with the Native Authorities and receiving their pay from Government. The new courts tried civil cases between Africans in the first instance, as well as some minor criminal offences, the urban councillors facing a vast range of new problems in the exacting task of trying cases between members of different tribes, with different customs, coming together in the new environment of a city.

Africans lastly achieved some measure of representation through Urban Advisory Councils. Once again Government began to propagate the elective principle, even though its efforts at first met with only limited success. In Fort Jameson, for instance, the District Commissioner divided the township into six wards, one for independent traders and artisans, others for employees of general dealers, for skilled and semi-skilled workers, for personal servants, for unskilled labourers, and for housewives—both inside and outside the location. The 'D.C.' then proudly reported that 756 persons registered their votes, though he failed to add that Fort Jameson township during this period comprised some 2,812 Africans in employment, so that representation remained a minority affair. All the same, election results provided a good indication of the way in which political consciousness was spreading through the various layers of African society. The unskilled labourers showed so little interest in the affair, that only six people turned up to vote, and elections had to be abandoned. The clerks and storemen, on the other hand, took a more active part, and so did personal servants. But astonishingly enough, the housewives turned out to be the most numerous voting group of all, making up more than half of the registered voters, a remarkable new departure in the field of African politics.[1]

Urban Advisory Councils of the type elected at Fort Jameson, rural Native Authorities, and Welfare Societies between them made up the African Provincial Councils, which joined in 1946 to form the African Representative Council, Northern Rhodesia's first instrument of black representation on a national scale. The Council owed its existence to Government which was anxious to channel the intelligentsia's political ambitions away from Welfare Societies, and to create a common link between the 'new men' and chiefs. The Council consisted of 29 members, of whom the four members from Barotseland owed their appointment to the Paramount Chief, whilst the remainder were elected from the African Provincial Councils. The new body met under the chairmanship of the Secretary for Native Affairs, procedure being modelled as far as possible on that of the Legislative Council. Government undertook to submit to the Council all Bills affecting black people, and the standard of debate was fairly high, the Council at first confining itself to proposals for specific reform, particularly those affecting the 'new men'. One motion demanded that Africans be allowed to sell their maize anywhere they wished; another proposed the establishment of a War Memorial College; a third asked that trading by Indians and white men should be restricted to townships. A further important move dealt with the question of wills, an overwhelming majority voting in favour of a motion that Africans should be able to make wills like Europeans, enabling them to dispose freely of their property to their immediate descendants, a practice not possible under the customary law of the matrilineal tribes, where the absence of legal wills most probably prevented the accumulation of rural capital. The Rev. Henry Kasokolo, a Bemba, thus urged that people with money, anxious to leave their property to their wife and children, should put their funds into a Savings Bank in their child's name. Otherwise the tribesmen would insist on the traditional manner of disposing of his inheritance, and the dead man's wife and children would be subjected to so many threats from their numerous relatives that the beneficiaries would be forced to hand over all they had.[2] In addition the more advanced Africans were becoming resentful of the wide disparity between their own wages and the white man's; and whilst there was widespread agreement that 'equal pay for equal work' would simply cut out the skilled African from

---

[1] The total number of Africans in employment according to the 1946 census was 2,821. The independent traders and artisans had a turnout of 55, employees of general dealers 105, skilled and semi-skilled 15, personal servants 152, unskilled labourers nil, housewives in locations 282, housewives outside locations 147. The new council consisted of an artisan, a literate head capitao of a firm, a head clerk, a cook, a rubbish-disposal worker, the wife of a clerk and a medical orderly's wife.

[2] Northern Rhodesia. African representative council. *Proceedings*, 15 Nov 1946, p. 67-72

the labour market, all felt convinced that black incomes should approximate more closely to those received by Europeans.

Right from the start the African Representative Council thus became the mouthpiece of 'progressive' Africans, an outcome not specifically intended by Government, but perhaps inherent in the whole structure of an assembly which was wholly based on the European model. But in addition to the Council the new men acquired an even more effective organ of expression through a Federation of Welfare Societies which in time developed into an African nationalist movement of great power. The origins of the movement were extremely modest. In 1946 Dauti Lawton Yamba, a schoolmaster born at Mbereshi mission, George Kaluwa, a trader and farmer from Mazabuka, and a veteran politician, as well as various other sympathizers, mostly with a background of elementary teaching, managed to combine various traders', shop assistants' and farmers' associations, as well as Welfare Societies and a body known as the African Christian Council. The new Federation specifically expressed the objects of the new African petty bourgeoisie and minor 'salariat' which was still unsure of itself, and groping for Government support. The Society thus began with an extremely moderate programme and asked for administrative backing to strengthen its position. In 1946 a deputation called on the Assistant Chief Secretary, asking that Government should officially recognize the new body, that the Secretary for Native Affairs should preside over its meetings, and that the Federation should be authorized to raise the sum of £1,000. In addition the delegates demanded that the Society should be allotted five members on the African Representative Council, stressing the wide support which they enjoyed amongst African traders, shop assistants, 'boss boys', and the more advanced farmers, the Society having branches in the Copper Belt as well as at Broken Hill and the Tonga country. Government made no attempt to interfere with the new body, though some officials regarded the new society as nothing more than a bunch of disgruntled intellectuals, but the Administration refused to be in any way officially associated with the movement, and denied them any special representation on the African Representative Council.

The Federation soon became more radical in temper, as its members worried increasingly about European agitation for self-government and amalgamation with Southern Rhodesia. Apart from that, a much vaster tide of anticolonialism was gathering momentum abroad. In the Metropolitan countries anti-Imperial sentiments became linked with demands for reforms at home; at the same time European working class movements often identified their own cause with that of the colonial races. Many intellectuals moreover were deeply influenced by the mechanized carnage of Auschwitz and the nuclear holocaust of Hiroshima, which led many Europeans to question the values of a civilization which, they thought, had produced such horrors, and which some began to contrast with the real and supposed virtues of 'pre-literate' man, untouched by the soul-destroying influence of advertising, mass entertainment and militarism. Britain's social conscience moreover became much more alive to African issues, though local Rhodesians like Welensky argued that all British Progressives were doing, was to shift the blame for past British exploitation on to the shoulders of the local white settlers who profited least from colonialism! In Asia the tide of independence seemed irresistible; Indonesia cast off Dutch rule; the British voluntarily handed over power in India, and subsequently evacuated Palestine, where they had been unable to solve the Jewish-Arab problem. The Western colonial powers moreover could not agree amongst themselves, with regard to their Imperial policies, and the French were forced out of the Middle East where their influence had been strong for centuries. In Africa itself the process of decolonization began with the collapse of Mussolini's East African Empire under the blows of white South African and British multi-racial forces; and later on the Italians lost Libya to the valour of the British 8th Army. On the West Coast the British began to make concessions to local nationalists, and in 1946 a more liberal constitution came into force on the Gold Coast. Besides the Allies' own war propaganda affected their subject races, and even in faraway Northern Rhodesia, Welfare Societies began to speak of freedom from want, freedom from fear, and the peoples' right of self-government. The Indian Congress Party in particular acquired particular prestige in the eyes of politically conscious Africans, who as yet put their trust in peaceful persuasion rather than violence, and in 1948 an Annual General Meeting, held by the Federation of Welfare Societies, decided to form the Northern Rhodesia African Congress. The new organization aimed at breaking down tribal barriers, fostering African unity and promoting African advancement in co-operation with Government. Congress was financed by small annual subscriptions from its members, and run by an Executive Committee, composed of a President, Secretary, Treasurer and four other members, who were all annually elected. Godwin A. M. Lewanika, an aristocrat from Barotseland who led the Kitwe African Society, and took an active part in founding the Federation, became the first President. The new movement retained a strong Protestant and missionary flavour, so much so that its General Meeting at Munali in 1948 opened with prayers by the Rev. Edward G. Nightingale, one of the Specially Nominated Members for African Interests in the Legislative Council. Nevertheless, Congress now aimed at much wider political objectives. The immigration of Afrikaners was to be restricted, whilst any kind of association with Southern Rhodesia was to be prevented at all costs. African interests should remain paramount—a reversion to the older Passfield doctrine—and the Colonial Office ought to carry out past promises for African self-government until Northern Rhodesia would join UNO. Congress argued that African interests clearly ought to over-ride all others because Africans predominated in numbers, because they were the sons of the soil, because of Imperial trusteeship obligations, and because Northern Rhodesia had never been conquered. Any policy not designed from the start to promote the interests and welfare of Africans ought to be rejected, never mind how much they might benefit the Europeans. In order to differentiate the Protectorate from Southern Rhodesia—the detested white-occupied country beyond the Zambezi—a further resolution suggested that Northern Rhodesia should become known as the 'Queen Victoria Protectorate'. Congress speakers, in other words, now turned round older trusteeship doctrines, originally designed to justify British Imperial rule to white critics, and reshaped this ideology into a weapon to serve the aims of African nationalism. In addition, Congress came out with a number of limited constitutional demands. Two African Members of the Legislative Council ought to join the Executive Council to balance the Unofficials' growing influence in Government. Congress also reiterated the former request for special representation on the African Representative Council on the grounds that, at the moment, elections depended on the number of friends a man could muster, instead of personal ability! The Society's economic objects at first largely confined themselves to the needs of the 'new men', particularly the schoolmasters, and Congress thus put forward suggestions for improved secondary education, a more generous programme of scholarships for bright youngsters, reduced fees for school children, and also demanded more pay for educated men serving on the chiefs' councils, as well as better railway facilities for African farmers.

IV

Taxes, royalties and white demands

Way back in 1907 Moore produced a cheerful Christmas number of his newspaper which in a lighter vein glimpsed into the country's future a hundred years hence. By A.D. 2007 Livingstone would have grown into a big city, and the Gorge below the Falls would be lined with mills, factories and workshops where a teeming black population would be at work. But the Africans, continued Moore's imaginary Asian correspondent, 'demanded and obtained equal rights in '42 and now return a solid majority of the legislature'. The upper chamber still consisted almost wholly of Europeans, chiefly manufacturers and professional men, 'but the qualification is being challenged in the lower house and another general election may see the last of the white regime'![1] Moore was joking, but his jest clearly illustrated the white man's dilemma. The settlers hoped for development; they wanted to make money and attain political rights, but many were left with the uneasy feeling that their pioneering would change the country to such an extent that black men would attain power over them. These fears never quite disappeared, but during the war years politics quietened down somewhat, as Officials and Unofficials alike devoted their energies to beating the enemy. But when the Germans and the Japanese surrendered, the political floodgate opened, and past resentments burst through. The new constitution, prepared in 1944, came into operation a year later, giving additional power to the Unofficials. But at the same time the British Labour Party obtained a land-

---

[1] 'A peep into the future . . . extract from the "Yokohama times", December 25, 2007' (in *Livingstone mail*, Christmas number, 1907)

slide victory, and power passed to a group of people who in the past consistently opposed Northern Rhodesian self-government, the union of the two Rhodesias and to whom the entire political and social structure of settler Africa was anathema, many Labour men feeling weighed down by a sense of guilt for the white man's real or alleged failings in the colonies. During the same period moreover relations between the Officials and Unofficials deteriorated in the Legislature. The Unofficials now possessed a majority and expected to control legislation and thereby Government policy. But the Officials still dominated the Executive Council and civil servants supervised all departments of government, as in the past, so that real power at Lusaka remained centred in the Secretariat and Government House. Tension could only have been lessened, if Officials and Unofficials had agreed; if planning could swiftly have been translated into action; and if white Rhodesians had trusted Downing Street, none of which seemed likely. Instead the settlers bitterly resented Labour's common assumption that only the Colonial Office was promoting African welfare. Had not African council representation come about as the result of an Unofficial Motion? Did not black men derive great benefits from the monies voted for the Askaris' Benefit Fund, from Silicosis and Workmen's Compensation laws, and similar measures introduced as the result of Unofficial legislation? Were not Elected Members always willing to vote massive funds to African development, a proposition frequently acknowledged by Government officials? But the settlers' efforts seemed to be disregarded, and there were delays with regard to future developments. The Labour Government was anxious to push on with development projects which would herald a new era of planning by which economic expansion would no longer be left solely to individual enterprise and chance. Some of this idealism seeped through to the Colonial Office where new bodies, designed to promote research and development, began to proliferate.[1] The new policy raised great hopes, but advance was hindered by a system of colonial government by which all important decisions necessarily had to be referred to London, whilst senior officials were moved around like chessmen. Northern Rhodesia's own Development Plan was not published until 1947, a good record when compared with that of other African territories, but a poor one in the eyes of local settlers. The Plan itself, which was later greatly expanded, provided for an expenditure of £13,000,000 over a period of ten years, to be financed to the tune of

[1] In 1942 the Imperial Government set up the Colonial Labour Advisory Committee, the Advisory Committee on the Welfare of Colonial People in the United Kingdom, and the Inter-departmental Committee on Locust Control. In 1943 the Secretary of State established a Colonial Products Research Council, the Colonial Social Welfare Advisory Committee and the Colonial Fisheries Advisory Committee. In 1944 the Colonial Social Science Research Council and the Tsetse Fly and Trypanosomiasis Committee were formed. In 1945 there followed the Colonial Medical Research Committee and the Committee for Colonial Agriculture, Animal Health and Forestry Research. These were followed in 1946 by the Colonial Economic and Development Council, the Inter-University Council for Higher Education in the Colonies, and the Colonial University Grants Advisory Committee. In 1947 a Director of Colonial Geological Surveys was appointed, as well as a Colonial Economic Research Committee, an Advisory Committee on Co-operation in the Colonies, and a Joint Standing Committee on Colonial Civil Aviation. In addition the vitally important Colonial Development Corporation was established.

£5,000,000 from Northern Rhodesian reserve funds and surpluses, £5,000,000 from loan funds whilst the British taxpayer would contribute £2,500,000 from the Colonial Development and Welfare Fund.[1] Labour felt that the Imperial contribution was generous, but white Rhodesians thought just the opposite. At the African Governors' Conference Sir Stafford Cripps, the Chancellor of the Exchequer, gave a talk in which he explained that the Sterling Group's financial future depended on a quick and extensive development of its African resources, and that the Colonies should make their contribution by reducing unnecessary current consumption, by devoting some of their own earnings to capital purposes, and by pushing ahead with their own schemes. Britain was exhausted by the war, she needed to accumulate new capital for future investment, and she was left with the pressing problem of the 'dollar gap', all of which necessitated colonial development. This sounded convincing enough in London, but many Rhodesians, like African and Asian anti-colonialists, were left with the impression that the British were using the Sterling Area, with its South African gold, Malayan tin, Rhodesian copper and other products, as an instrument for tiding themselves over their own difficulties, which in part at least, were brought about by their unsound policies at home. Welensky himself argued that Northern Rhodesia should forego the British contribution under the Colonial Development and Welfare Act, if the country in return could get the full tax levied by the British Treasury on companies in Northern Rhodesia, as well as the huge royalties which went into the British South Africa Company's coffers. He estimated that between 1938 and 1943 alone the British Treasury received a clear £6,000,000 from Northern Rhodesian company taxes, whilst the Chartered Company royalties were estimated to bring in £2,000,000 a year by 1948. Under these circumstances—the settlers argued—trusteeship doctrines, whether enunciated from the Left or from the Right, were just 'eye-wash', and the conflict of opinions became more bitter. Whilst many of the more radical Labour supporters overseas now saw in Rhodesian settlers nothing more than an overpaid and under-brained pigmentocracy, who would cling on to their outworn privileges even at the sound of the Last Trump, many settlers envisaged their opponents as a motley crew of headline hunters, society ladies with bored B.B.C. accents who sat on committees for this, that and the other, itinerant parsons with bees in their bonnets, and Research Fellows in barbarology with grants to count the cats in Kuala Lumpur! Anti-colonialists in their view were just helping to perpetuate a myth, and the sooner Downing Street control was ended, the better things would turn out for the country!

The local Europeans' second economic grievance, like that of other critics of

---

[1] *Northern Rhodesia ten year development plan . . . as approved by Legislative council on 11 February, 1947.* Lusaka, Government printer, 1947. The Plan provided that £3,384,000 should be spent on social services, including £1,598,000 on African and £250,000 on European education. £2,108,000 was earmarked for agricultural, veterinary, game, tsetse and fishery services, £1,820,000 for communications, £1,500,000 for rural development, £970,000 for water development, £500,000 for agricultural marketing development and secondary industries, £1,000,000 for African housing, £1,300,000 for a general public building programme, and £250,000 for loans to local authorities.

Empire elsewhere, dealt with the question of secondary industries. The War gave a slight stimulus to the manufacture of locally made goods, especially ammunitions of war, but Southern Rhodesia attracted most of what industries there were going, and manufacturing remained Northern Rhodesia's economic Cinderella, despite the country's vast potential wealth in timber, copper, lead, coal, limestone and other resources. Development of course was held up by such general factors as lack of markets and vast distances, Rhodesians finding them-selves in the unenviable position of having to 'service' vast areas with roads, railways and other amenities, though their population remained much smaller than those of more developed countries overseas, where industrialists found all kinds of facilities already 'laid on' for their use before they ever even built a factory. Markets were scarce, and so were skilled workers and people with entre-preneurial ability. But all the same more could have been done; and Northern Rhodesian businessmen pointed out that a settler government in Salisbury was making a much better job of things south of the Zambezi, that Northern Rho-desian development was held up by the high cost of services like water and roads, and by the Administration's inept land policy, whilst the senior government official's whole training and outlook, with his background of 'P.A.', of Provin-cial Administration, and his heavily rural bias, ill fitted him for the task of encouraging industry. White Northern Rhodesians also complained of the absence of special tariffs to protect infant industries, and of existing transport policies, which—they said—failed to use the railways as an instrument of economic expansion, but concentrated on making profits, whilst grossly favour-ing Bulawayo and Salisbury through its rate policies. Welensky also argued that Northern Rhodesia's coal-mining potentialities were not developed because of Davis's interests in Wankie, and quoted a statement from Sir Edmund designed to give substance to his case. African politicians for the time being remained quite indifferent to these issues, their lack of interest in these questions further contributing to the settlers' prevailing contempt for their abilities.

Manufacturing of course did make some progress, and in addition to the Zambezi Sawmills at Livingstone, the country's largest single industrial enter-prise, various firms began to manufacture articles like ferro-concrete pipes, bricks, and chemicals. In addition consumer goods were manufactured such as soap, mineral water and sweets, as well as furniture and veneer, clothing and blankets. Later on an iron foundry and a motor-body building workshop opened up, but enterprise remained small in scale, and confined to one or two localities like Ndola and Livingstone. The Administration tried to deal with the problem by commissioning an outside expert, Dr J. W. Busschau, to investigate the problem, but the Doctor's cautious conclusions[1] made no appeal to the settlers. Welensky harshly censured the report for assuming that 'non-economic' industries should not be encouraged, that Northern Rhodesian whites were just temporary residents; and he resented the investigator's implied criticism of the

[1] Busschau, J. W. *Report on the development of secondary industries in Northern Rhodesia....* Lusaka, Government printer, 1945

relatively high wages paid to Europeans. Busschau—Welensky added—assumed the profit motive, and had few positive suggestions to make, except to set up an Advisory Committee on Secondary Industries.[1] This was established, the mining industry acquiring a dominant voice on the new body, which generally endorsed Busschau's views. The Committee argued that until the country's white population had increased to over 35,000 and the Africans' standard considerably raised, the internal market would remain too small to support manufacturing industries of a size sufficiently large to warrant financial assistance from Government. Only the cement industry merited official sponsorship, and after heavy pressure from Welensky a cement plant with a capacity of 50,000 long tons a year was ordered in 1947 from Britain to assist Northern Rhodesia's over-worked construction industry.[2]

As far as the question of mineral royalties and taxes was concerned the settlers found themselves with a stiff fight on their hands. In 1938 the Colonial Office committed itself to a despatch with explained that the validity of the Company's claims could not be challenged, a view endorsed by the best legal brains in London. From 1941 Northern Rhodesia made some progress by taking a sizeable share of the mining profits under British and local legislation, securing for itself about half the income tax and half of the Excess Profits tax derived from Northern Rhodesian mining companies incorporated in London, gaining an income tax of 5/- in the £.[3] The Northern Rhodesians, however, remained dissatisfied, and Gore-Browne in the House effectively quoted Sir Alan Pim's devastating conclusion of 1938 that just under 60 per cent of the total levy on the copper industry, Northern Rhodesia's only major asset, went into the coffers of the United Kingdom Government and the British South Africa Company; the Imperial 'Trustee' had received from its 'ward' no less than £24,000,000 in the shape of taxes, whilst Northern Rhodesia got no more than £136,000 from Colonial Development Funds during the ten years prior to 1940.[4] In 1944 the Colonial Office under the more liberal-minded Oliver Frederick George Stanley began to consider the question of buying out the mineral rights both of the British South Africa Company in Northern Rhodesia and of the United Africa Company in Northern Nigeria, the Secretary of State considering that these rights were inconsistent with modern ideas. There followed a lengthy and bitter debate, affecting not only the Colonial Office but also the Treasury. One school of thought argued that, though the Chartered Company was never reimbursed for its original administrative deficit of £1,500,000 in Northern Rhodesia, it subsequently reaped a golden harvest of about £2,573,696 from its mineral royalties, so that the Company certainly managed to make Empire pay! The local administration was never consulted when the imperial Government concluded its former agreement with the Chartered Company, whilst the old Nor-

---

[1] Northern Rhodesia. *Legislative Council debates*, 31 May 1945, p. 179–197
[2] Northern Rhodesia. Advisory committee on industrial development. *Third report*. Lusaka, Government printer, 1948, p. 7
[3] Northern Rhodesia. *Legislative Council debates*, 29 Nov 1943, p. 273
[4] Northern Rhodesia. *Legislative Council debates*, 27 Nov 1943, p. 253–254

thern Rhodesian Advisory Council had already questioned the Company's mineral and land rights; the original concessions moreover were obtained from a Paramount Chief whose jurisdiction certainly never extended over the whole of the Copper Belt, whilst the native chiefs derived very little benefit from putting their marks to the original treaties. In approving these agreements, His Majesty's Government did not effectively safeguard the future of the territories concerned; later on, in 1923, an enquiry into the mineral rights was avoided on broad Imperial grounds, the Colonial Office aiming at a rapid solution of the problem, Government at the time being unwilling to ask Parliament for a lump sum for mineral rights which then appeared of very doubtful value. But now, the bargain could clearly be seen to have been as unsatisfactory in character as it was inconsistent with all modern ideas about Colonial policy. The opposition, represented by doughty champions of orthodox Conservatism like Sir John Anderson, the Chancellor of the Exchequer, presented a very different case. The mineral rights in Nigeria and Northern Rhodesia were not the only ones originally bought up at a low price; the chiefs and original inhabitants of the territories contributed nothing to the values that subsequently emerged, and the companies deserved a reward for their enterprise, the original settlements not having been unduly favourable to them at the time they were made. In any case it was nonsense to say that the present duties of the Imperial Government towards the natives should be conditioned by what its predecessors did, or did not do, in the past; Britain's financial resources were limited, and the Imperial government should rather spend money on Burma and Newfoundland. Others argued that it was difficult to see who should get the benefits, the local tribes, the people of Northern Rhodesia, or the world at large. Northern Rhodesia was after all a purely artificial unit, and if it got the mineral rights, the Elected Members might just use the income derived therefrom to reduce their own taxes, a proposition which was strongly attacked by another expert who pointed out that the settlers in fact never attempted anything of the kind. The Treasury refused to agree to an outright purchase of the mineral rights and the question dragged on until 1946, when Welensky and Gore-Browne called on the Colonial Office in 1946. The Colonial Secretary, now a Labour man, agreed that the purchase of the mineral rights would be in the public interest, but thought that the resultant commitments might lead to various financial risks. He added that legal advice would have to be taken with regard to the question of compulsory acquisition, but argued that compulsory acquisition of mineral rights held by one company by virtue of an agreement was not at all the same thing as nationalization of an industry in the United Kingdom. The Secretary of State's line appeared somewhat peculiar, coming from a member of an avowedly Socialist Government, but—ideological issues apart—the argument made some sense at a time when the British feared confiscatory legislation against British capital in other parts of the world, and were afraid of discouraging future investment in Northern Rhodesia. Purchase of the rights by the Northern Rhodesia Government was officially considered, but the Unofficials still questioned the Company's rights, and besides—copper prices continued to soar, to such an extent that experts calculated the value of the royalties for 1948 to amount to over £2,000,000 a year. Welensky at one time threatened a vote of non-confidence, but the Governor told him later that the country would have to pay over £10,000,000, that the purchase would throw a heavy load of debt on the country, that the deal would be speculative, and that the money could be used for a more worthwhile purpose. Welensky then modified his Motion and asked that the Secretary of State should reconsider the validity of the claims, and that the mineral rights should be vested in the people of Northern Rhodesia,[1] and Government associated itself with the second part of this Motion. In November 1948 Welensky drew up his heaviest artillery, and warned the Administration that in the coming Session he would introduce a royalties tax.[2] According to the legal experts there seemed no reason why this should not be done, provided the new impost was fiscal and not confiscatory in nature, a tax of up to 50 per cent not being regarded as punitive in character. Welensky—had the Chartered Company but known—was in fact playing an extremely difficult game, for the general could not rely on his little army, and if a show-down had occurred some Elected Members would have failed to support him, one of them expressing privately fears for the security of the farmers' land titles, if the case went to law.[3] But Welensky kept his nerve; and after some hard bargaining the Secretary of State in 1949 was able to announce agreement between the disputing parties. The British South Africa Company's mineral rights would continue for another 37 years, but the Company would assign 20 per cent of its revenue from these rights to the Northern Rhodesian Government. In 1986 the Company would transfer its mineral rights to the Northern Rhodesian Government; and in the meantime the company would be exempt from any special tax on mineral royalties during the 37 year period, His Majesty's Government promising to secure as far as possible that any future Government in Northern Rhodesia would be bound by this bargain. Dougal O. Malcolm then presented this agreement to his shareholders, urging them to accept on the grounds that the Company should rather make concessions now than hang on to rights which would only come under increasingly heavy attack, and which the Imperial Government would find more and more difficult to defend.[4] The new agreement was estimated to put an additional £250,000 to £270,000 per annum into the Territory's coffers, but at the same time the Company acquired security, its share-holders preferring a certainty to a speculative investment. The conservatively-minded *Economist* regarded the deal as a reasonable bargain, especially since the threatened royalties tax might have been higher than 20 per cent,[5] and the Company's shares rose by 2/3 to

[1] Northern Rhodesia. *Legislative Council debates*, 22 Mar 1948, p. 366–376; and 24 Mar 1948, p. 431

[2] Northern Rhodesia. *Legislative Council debates*, 25 Nov 1948, p. 263.

[3] Based partly on personal information. For a published, though rather incomplete account of the Welensky bluff see Lawman, M. *The long grass*. Hale ltd, 1958, p. 94–97

[4] The British South Africa Company. *Directors' report and accounts for the year ended 30 September 1949. . . .*

[5] *Economist*, 13 Aug 1949. Before the signing of the agreement the Company declared a dividend of

49/- once the news of the agreement became known. For Welensky the deal marked a great personal victory and also the highwater mark of his political and social radicalism, which henceforth lost some of its former impetus, Welensky becoming more and more a believer in the virtues of private enterprise, a cause in which he was encouraged by what he regarded as numerous examples of governmental ineptitude in economic matters, the Jewish trade unionist from Broken Hill ending as one of the last advocates of Empire in the grand Churchillian tradition.

In the meantime the Unofficials also continued their pressure both with regard to the responsible government and the amalgamation issues. In 1946 Gore-Browne and Welensky during their visit to London pressed for further constitutional reform on the Colonial Secretary, and George Hall—personally impressed by Welensky—agreed to make some concessions. A new constitution came into force in 1948, when the life of the Legislative Council was extended from three to five years, thus considerably strengthening the position of sitting members. The Governor ceased to be President of the Council, which henceforth was headed by a Speaker, the new job falling to Page, now an honoured political veteran. The Elected Members achieved a further increase in numbers from eight to ten, providing a numerical superiority over the nine Officials in the House. But at the same time a further Member was added to the little bloc of Unofficials representing African interests, which now rose to four, and continued to hold the balance of power in the House. Welensky, after considerable resistance, also agreed to a further provision by which two of the Members representing African interests had to be Africans, selected by the African Representative Council, so that black politicians for the first time achieved representation on a hitherto exclusively white assembly.[1]

The majority of settlers remained disappointed, the *Northern News* complaining that African representation since 1938 had rocketed by four hundred per cent, and that it was difficult to see where the handover would stop. But the Europeans nevertheless had done well, and in addition they managed to improve their position on the Executive Council, though at some cost with respect to their own political cohesion. A crack opened when Gore-Browne found his leadership of the Elected Members increasingly difficult to reconcile with his position as chief African representative in the House. In 1945 he decided to oppose his Unofficial colleagues over the amalgamation issue and a year later in Welensky's absence he resigned from the Chairmanship of the Unofficial Members Organization. The Colonel's place was taken by Welensky, with Beckett as his chief political lieutenant, and all the Elected Members rallied behind Welensky's undisputed leadership. For a time, Gore-Browne, still as keen and ambitious as ever, tried to take over direction once again, and in 1948 became the settlers' principal spokesman in an all-out offensive for responsible

26 2/8 per cent for the year ended September 1948, so that the buying public was not unduly worried about the threats made against the Company. See *Financial times*, 22 Apr 1949

[1] Northern Rhodesia. *Legislative Council debates*, 10 Nov 1948, p. 4

government. Gore-Browne imagined that on this issue at any rate, a common front might be established between white and black against the Colonial Office, and ended a dramatic speech in favour of self-government on what was perhaps the most menacing note yet heard from Unofficial benches, threatening that the Unofficials would if necessary paralyze the Government.[1] But the Colonel completely miscalculated native political feelings, and his speech sparked off violent reaction amongst politically conscious Africans who—far from being reconciled to Responsible Government—became even more bitterly suspicious by what they took to be the Colonel's desertion. The African Representative Council abandoned its mild manner of old, and passed a strong motion condemning the grant of self-government whilst urging that Northern Rhodesia was a black country.[2] The Africans then exacted a promise from Gore-Browne that he would faithfully stick to their line during the coming discussions in London, and Gore-Browne—for all his ability—thus fell between two stools, neither pleasing the Europeans nor fully regaining the Africans' confidence, and ended a potentially brilliant career in Central African politics by resigning from the House in 1951.

There followed a complicated tangle which was ably handled by Sir Gilbert Rennie, who succeeded Waddington at Government House in 1948. Rennie, a tough, determined little Scotsman, was very different in temper and appearance from his tall, aristocratic and somewhat vague looking predecessor. With his extensive previous experience in Kenya as Chief Secretary he proved himself the right kind of man to deal with the situation in a manner acceptable to Downing Street. The Governor went ahead with his own proposals to make the Standing Finance Committee more effective, and suggested that more Unofficials should be appointed to the Executive Council; he also agreed that their advice should be taken, except in unusual circumstances. Further discussions took place in London in 1948, and in the end a compromise was reached. The Unofficials gained four seats in the Executive Council, though one of them had to be nominated to represent African interests. The new arrangement still left the Unofficials in a majority, but the Governor promised that from henceforth their view would carry the same weight as on the Legislative Council, subject only to the Governor's reserved powers. In addition, Government agreed to give one or two Unofficials executive responsibility for a group of departments each. In 1949 Beckett thus became Member for Agriculture, Veterinary Services, Forestry, Game and Tsetse Control, Water Development and Irrigation, whilst Lieutenant-Colonel Ewain Murray Wilson, the new member for Ndola, an engineer, and a man personally acceptable to Welensky, took over Health and Local Government. The Leader of the Elected Members himself kept aloof from executive responsibility for tactical reasons, but his two colleagues now controlled a group of services vital both to white townsmen and farmers. Admittedly, in matters of administration, senior civil servants still normally would get

[1] Northern Rhodesia. *Legislative Council debates*, 12 Jan 1948, p. 829–831
[2] Northern Rhodesia. African representative council. *Proceedings*, 5 July 1948, p. 8–66

their way, even if only after lengthy and time-consuming discussions with Unofficials, but the civil servants' accustomed hold on departmental direction now began to weaken, never to be fully restored in future.

V

Closer Union: The Federal switch-over

In struggling for their political objectives, the Europeans never forgot the amalgamation issue, but here they met with their greatest obstacles. In 1945 the Legislative Council once more debated a motion in favour of amalgamation but Government held firm, and Gore-Browne abandoned his colleagues on this issue.[1] The case for closer union suffered a further setback in 1946 when a new general election was fought in Southern Rhodesia. Ever since 1933 Huggins had been running his country almost like a dictator, kindly, but quite firm, and not brooking the slightest interference with his decisions. Now after a lengthy period of governance, the electoral pendulum was swinging against the United Party, and though Huggins managed to scrape home, he was forced to form a minority government, in which Labour held the balance of power in the House. The conservative opposition, misnamed the Liberal Party, and representing the smaller farmers and businessmen, as well as many artisans, was strongly entrenched in opposition, and the Liberals strongly opposed any talk of linking up with the north, some of their supporters looking rather towards Pretoria for their salvation.

Huggins, however, managed to hold on, and the chances for closer union quickly improved. From the world wide economic point of view, the post-war years were a time of shortages; the 'Dollar Gap' became the British planners' constant headache; and as long as raw materials were in short supply the settlers' bargaining power improved—both locally as far as the Copper Belt workers were concerned and from a wider Central African point of view. Industrially, Southern Rhodesia shot ahead with staggering speed, the total gross value of her manufactures rising from £5,107,000 in 1938 to £31,316,000 in 1949, and the Northern territories were able to buy all kinds of goods from Bulawayo and Salisbury that proved difficult to obtain from overseas. Southern Rhodesia became a valued dollar saver, and what was even more important, an important dollar earner, whose economic co-operation proved essential for the prosperity of Northern Rhodesia's copper industry. The Southern Rhodesian Government acquired a commanding position in the Central African economy by a fine stroke of business, when in 1947 it bought the Rhodesia Railways, issuing £32,000,000 at $2\frac{1}{2}$ per cent of redeemable stock to finance this operation. In 1949 a Rhodesia Railways Higher Authority was established as well as a board of control which dealt with railway questions in the two Rhodesias and Bechuana-

[1] Northern Rhodesia. *Legislative Council debates*, 16 Jan 1945, p. 188-196; 18 Jan 1945, p. 246-279; and 22 Jan 1945, p. 336-360

land, the Southern Rhodesians being strongly entrenched to make their point of view heard. Rolling stock was short, and the transport system was over-worked; Southern Rhodesian farmers were clamouring for space to transport their maize and tobacco; Southern Rhodesian mine-owners demanded priority for their asbestos, and industrialists thought their own need for trucks should come first. But the Northern Rhodesian mining magnates also wanted room on the trucks, the Imperial government giving strong support to their needs which had to be met if Britain's vital copper imports were to continue. Huggins adopted a co-operative attitude, and even showed himself willing to subordinate the immediate needs of his own chrome producers to those of the northern copper mines; but all the same, a more effective and permanent means of co-operation seemed desirable. The position was frankly explained by Sir Miles Thomas, an out-standing British industrialist, a Managing Director of Morris Motors and many subsidiary companies, who in 1947 advised the Government of Southern Rho-desia on its economic problems, before becoming a Director of the Colonial Development Corporation a year later. In a published newspaper article Thomas showed that the two Rhodesias had now reached a stage of industrial develop-ment where they must either combine commercially, or become competitors for the limited capacity of an overloaded transport system. Nyasaland's problems were similar, for it depended on Beira with its overloaded port facilities, Nyasa-land's needs again competing with Southern Rhodesia's. Then there was the question of future mineral production; the world was threatened with a shortage of iron ore which was getting worse, as the demand for steel was rising. Southern Rhodesia was fortunate in possessing a vast body of iron ore with a content of 50 per cent as compared with only 38 per cent characteristic of good European and American deposits, and production should be encouraged. Salisbury's co-operation was, however, essential and this applied with particular force to Copper Belt producers who depended on rolling stock and coal from the south with return freights of copper to Beira. Southern Rhodesia possessed Central Africa's only great coal mine at Wankie, but from the Territory's own limited point of view, it was preferable to use her coal and her railway wagons to export her chrome and asbestos to earn dollars; a common policy was essential, especially if the three territories were to increase their railway facilities, an ex-pensive business at a time when construction costs had shot up to £20,000 a mile. In addition the three territories should have a common labour policy, especially in view of the fact that Nyasaland migration to South Africa was being increas-ingly restricted, partly as the result of currency difficulties, partly owing to the unsettled state of Natal and the growing stringency of labour conditions.[1] Apart from that Southern Rhodesia was of some importance to the Sterling Area as a dollar earner in her own right. After the War chrome production shot ahead; Southern Rhodesian gold helped to fill the Sterling Group's depleted resources in a modest way; whilst Rhodesian tobacco proved a great asset to the United Kingdom which could no longer afford to buy so much American

[1] Thomas, Sir M. 'Dominion of Capricornia' (in *Sunday times*, 6 Mar 1949)

Virginia tobacco. Southern Rhodesia's prestige accordingly stood high with the British Labour Government, which fully understood the Colony's dollar earning potential, and which was willing, if necessary, to assist financially, whilst a Government loan of £5,000,000 floated in London at 3 per cent in 1948, was oversubscribed fourteen times.

There were also other economic arguments in favour of closer association. As copper production and secondary industries expanded, so did the need for hydro-electric power. The Central African Council set up an Inter-Territorial Hydro-Electric Power Commission, but the selection of sites, the financing of new enterprises, the problems of construction and distributing supplies would all be much simpler under a single executive. Finally there was the vital question of obtaining capital from overseas. Only industrialization, the argument went, could absorb the rapidly rising native population unable to find an adequate living on the land, but industrialization and the expansion of primary industries alike required funds from overseas. Lenders traditionally feared the effects of a slump on debtors dependent on only the sale of a few commodities to meet their obligations, and from that point of view the three territories on their own were not particularly good risks as long as their economics remained unbalanced and over-specialized in character. But if they were joined under one political authority, investors would be able to negotiate with a Government that could rely on a revenue from a much larger range of products than any individual territory to meet its obligations; and a joint Central African state would also be better placed to overcome the effects of a recession, an argument particularly attractive in view of the sharp fluctuations of copper prices in the past. Federation finally would simplify the more efficient pooling of scarce capital resources, an important consideration during a world-wide reconstruction boom.

In addition of course South African politics vitally affected the question. In 1948 the British Imperial cause suffered a crushing defeat when General Smuts was defeated at the polls. The United Party, supported by the mining industry, the majority of the Press, most of the English speaking urban voters and a minority of the Afrikaner bourgeoisie, lost power; and Huggins's United Rhodesia Party Government, which sympathized with Smuts's general views, found itself politically isolated in Southern Africa. The new South African Government, lead by Dr Daniel François Malan, determined to uphold the cause of Afrikaner nationalism in politics, to defend in particular the cause of white farmers and artisans in the economic sphere, and to put its views of territorial *apartheid* between white and black into practice. South Africa's political revolution made a profound impact alike in London, Salisbury and Lusaka. For the first time in history a very large English-speaking community found itself in the unaccustomed position of being a political minority group; and whilst Englishmen with left-wing sympathies rallied against the Boers for their native policy, right-wingers opposed the "Nats" for their economic policies and their past anti-Imperial record, both groups being united in their condemnation of the Nationalists' neutralist and sometimes pro-German attitude during the Second World

War. The Nationalist victory moreover inspired fears with regard to Afrikaner plans concerning territories outside the Union's borders, both in the High Commission territories and the Rhodesias. In Salisbury and Lusaka these apprehensions increased as the result of Afrikaner emigration beyond the Limpopo. Rumours went round that Afrikaans settlement was being secretly promoted for political reasons, an interpretation not actually in accordance with the facts, as the emigrants simply crossed the border in search of greater economic opportunities. But the authorities in the Rhodesias took this question very seriously, and many Northern Rhodesian Elected Members feared that they might be voted out of office, if their small constituencies came to be dominated by Afrikaans speaking voters. Discrimination against British subjects on linguistic grounds alone proved unacceptable, but in 1953 the Northern Rhodesian Legislative Council finally passed an Ordinance which once more raised the residential qualifying period for the vote from 6 months to 2 years, thus excluding from the franchise all short-term immigrants—many of them Afrikaans-speaking miners.

The Nationalists' victory south of the Limpopo made the question of establishing the strong British bloc beyond their borders much more acute. Huggins at first showed himself willing to make the Central African Council machinery work, arguing that a co-operative attitude would convince the Imperial authorities of the need for closer political association; and a good deal of work was in fact accomplished. In October 1945 a permanent Secretariat came into being;[1] In 1946 the Central African Airways were set up; agreement was reached on migrant labour questions and on broadcasting; a joint film unit came into existence, as well as an Inter-Territorial Hydro-Electric Power Commission; the Rhodesian Court of Appeal extended its jurisdiction to Nyasaland; joint statistical, meteorological and archival services came into being, as well as the Joint Committee on Development Planning. The Council of course engendered some friction, Governor Richards of Nyasaland remaining particularly suspicious that joint services might in the end form milestones on the detested road to amalgamation. Opinion in the Colonial Office, however, backed the Council, stressing the way in which the Northern territories would stand to gain economically from their association with the more highly developed economy in Southern Rhodesia, pointing out the desirability of Central African co-operation as a counterweight to the Union, a further argument being that closer association with the North would encourage liberalism in Southern Rhodesia itself. The latter argument seemed particularly important since the Northern Rhodesian colour bar could not be effectively removed until Southern Rhodesia adopted a different attitude. The Colonial Office view had some substance. Though public criticism of Southern Rhodesia was becoming more outspoken overseas, Southern Rhodesia was in fact cautiously modifying some of her former policies. For

[1] The Council was run by the Governor of Southern Rhodesia as Chairman. The Prime Minister of Southern Rhodesia and the Governors of Northern Rhodesia and Nyasaland were *ex-officio* members. In addition each territory had 3 ordinary members. Funds were contributed in the proportion of 10, 7 and 3 by Southern Rhodesia, Northern Rhodesia and Nyasaland respectively.

one thing, the country was rapidly becoming wealthier; the Colony's estimated national income rose from £47,900,000 in 1946 to £76,800,000 in 1949; the grim backveld poverty of old largely disappeared, and the 'poor white' became a figure of the past like the 'remittance man' before him. Salisbury was now a trim little capital, very different from the dusty dorp of old where the roads were unpaved, malaria was rife, traders and civil servants split into exclusive cliques, and where—as one old-timer scathingly put it—'Mrs Twopenny would rather be dead than seen talking to Mrs Pennyhalfpenny!' Many Europeans moved up the social scale; artisans rose to be foremen; foremen were promoted to sub-managerial jobs, and some of the places vacated by white men at the lower level were filled by Africans, with the result that the social 'water-level' steadily rose. The changed situation was reflected in Southern Rhodesia's native policy which in some ways began to approximate more to the position in the North. Huggins dropped *apartheid* as an electoral slogan, now convinced that territorial segregation would become unworkable, and that the country needed a stable class of African farmers, as well as a permanent black labour force in the towns. In addition Southern Rhodesia began to give a little more power to its chiefs, and embarked on a policy of developing local councils, whilst a tentative project of removing African electors from the common voters roll was dropped.

In 1948 Huggins's new policy was at last put to the test, the electoral battle being sparked off in the first place through the Central African Council. The three territories came to an understanding on currency questions, and the Southern Rhodesian Government introduced a Coinage and Currency Bill. But the Southern Rhodesian Parliament, jealous of its own powers, rejected a clause in the Bill, which Huggins insisted must go on the Statute Book. The Opposition would not give way, and Huggins then dissolved Parliament. The Liberals now walked straight into the political quicksands; Malan's victory in South Africa may have helped to produce a startling British national reaction north of the Limpopo where even Smit's, the Opposition leader's, very name told against him.[1] The electors flocked to the poll, including thousands of immigrants with more than six months' residence, and Huggins gained a landslide victory. The United Party gained 24 out of 30 seats, Smit even lost in his own constituency, whilst Labour was reduced to political impotence. The election was an overwhelming personal victory for Huggins, whose rule was never again disputed as long as remained in office. More important still, Southern Rhodesian isolationism, the white artisans' and poorer farmers' cause, suffered a crushing defeat;[2] and Bulawayo and Salisbury businessmen now looked to the north for additional trade and industrial outlets, an important consideration at a time when the local

[1] Smit was in fact a Hollander and an early settler.

[2] A further argument used by anti-federationists to explain the trend towards Federation concerned Southern Rhodesia's Public Debt. Mass immigration strained the country's administrative and industrial resources, thus leading to heavier public expenditure and a bigger debt burden. Federation was therefore supposedly demanded in order to reduce the cost of servicing the debt. This argument is not, however, borne out by the statistics concerning the Public Debt. These show that the percentage of revenue required to meet the expenditure for service of loans actually dropped after 1943 when the

Southern Rhodesian bourgeoisie was rapidly growing in financial strength.[1]

Lastly some strategic arguments were advanced in favour of closer union. In Europe the temporary anti-Nazi alliance between the Western powers and Soviet Russia collapsed; a bitter dispute broke out in 1948 over Berlin, and the international position steadily deteriorated. Some advisers thus urged the desirability of a British stronghold in Central Africa which could by-pass the vital Cape route, should South Africa ever adopt a policy of right-wing neutralism, these speculations gaining some substance from various projects of linking Southern Rhodesia to the Atlantic by means of a route through South-West Africa.

The tide was thus beginning to run in favour of establishing some kind of Central African state, but the question remained of how this should be achieved. Huggins for a time remained an unrepentant amalgamationist, but Welensky, whose own political position was infinitely weaker than the Southern Rhodesian Prime Minister's, began to waver. In 1948 before leaving for a visit to London, he told a meeting at Broken Hill that the United Kingdom Government would insist on protecting the Africans, and that it was essential to obtain Imperial support. The solution might be found in some kind of Federation with Southern Rhodesia with a central legislature, whilst the territories would deal with local matters. Northern Rhodesians could not possibly go back on matters like African land rights, the power of the chiefs, pass laws and African representation, whilst the question of Indian immigration should be dealt with on a planned quota basis, the Asians at present in Northern Rhodesia being assured of a fair deal.[2] In the meantime a propaganda organization was formed with Huggins's blessing in Southern Rhodesia, which was headed in the early days by Stanley Charles Frank Cooke, a well-known Bulawayo industrialist. The new body was called the United Central Africa Association, and whilst Welensky was away overseas, a deputation headed by Cooke and his Vice-Chairman, Colonel Cyril Mainwaring Newman, met the other Elected Members of the Northern Rho-

amalgamation issue was once again raised. The percentage sharply increased between 1948 and 1950, but again dropped in 1951.

Year ending 31 March	Public Debt Liability in £	Percentage of Revenue Expenditure
1943	20,324,218	11·9
1944	22,747,582	9·2
1945	24,501,579	9·8
1946	24,684,264	8·8
1947	26,797,647	10·3
1948	61,707,740	12·4
1949	74,414,330	18·4
1950	82,407,840	20·2
1951	90,230,059	8·9

[1] Between 1946 and 1950 home investment in Southern Rhodesia rose from £6,200,000 to £34,900,000. The proportion of home investment as related to 'total available resources' rose from 12 per cent to 31 per cent. For figures see Southern Rhodesia. Central African statistical office. *Official yearbook of Southern Rhodesia.* Salisbury, Rhodesian printing and publishing company, limited, 1952, p. 625

Northern news, 22 Apr 1948

desian Legislative Council, as well as the three Members representing African interests who subsequently withdrew from the discussions. The Conference decided that only Federation was practicable and that African rights should be protected. A central government should control defence, external affairs, social and economic development as well as transport, civil aviation, customs, immigration and the postal services, the Federal Government itself attaining Dominion status in its own right.[1] The Colonial Office, now faced with a decision of some kind, found the current of thought going more strongly in the direction of a federal solution, which seemed all the more acceptable at a time when colonial theorists were envisaging a much wider policy of creating self-governing federal states out of the remaining parts of the British Empire, such as Malaya and the West Indies, which would be both friendly towards Great Britain, and sufficiently viable both from the economic and military point of view to guard their independence. As far as Central Africa was concerned, encouraging reports were coming in from senior British officials on the Central African Council, who were impressed by the increasing liberality of Southern Rhodesian politics, as well as the efficiency of the Southern Rhodesian civil service, which was taking the lead in most technical spheres. In June 1948 a closely reasoned memorandum from the Colonial Office argued in favour of a new course; Welensky had come round to Federation; in the past, the writer thought Federation should be delayed until the Northern Africans had made more political progress; but now he wondered whether Imperial authorities should not work for Federation now, possibly on the lines of the East African High Commission. A meeting took place between the Colonial Office and Commonwealth Relations Office, and again some strong pro-federal arguments were heard. United Kingdom native policies ought to be pushed southwards as much as possible, and this might be achieved by Federation; the European agitation for amalgamation derived from a sense of frustration, which would disappear if the local whites could play a useful part in a local Assembly. The Secretary of State and some of his officials, Rennie, Welensky, Beckett as well as two African delegates from Northern Rhodesia, then met at the Colonial Office. Welensky explained his conversion to federalism, and agreed that African interests must be safeguarded and that the United Kingdom would retain special responsibilities for the black people. M. Mubitana, an African delegate, reiterated black opposition, but the Colonial Secretary still would not fully commit himself beyond saying that amalgamation was impossible, but that the Imperial Government might consider some kind of central machinery, as in East Africa, and that native rights must be protected. The Federation of African Welfare Societies angrily protested, basing their stand on African paramountcy, but could make no headway, as the Administration explained once more that the operative doctrine was no longer the Devonshire White Paper of 1923, but the interpretation supplied by the Parliamentary Committee of 1931 which simply stated that the interests of the indigenous people should not be subordinated to those of the immigrants.

[1] *Northern news*, 10 June 1948

Welensky returned to Northern Rhodesia and reported to his constituents, concluding hopefully in a speech at Broken Hill that Federation could be brought about if African rights were guaranteed, and if the three territories presented a united front.[1] The Africans' stand was further weakened by the unimpressive stature of their two representatives on the Legislative Council, neither the Rev. Henry Kasokolo nor N. Nalumango being invited to take a place on the Northern Rhodesian delegation to the African Conference held in London later on in 1948. The new gathering, a kind of Continental Durbar, full of colour and speech making, opened under a blaze of publicity, and Welensky once more travelled to London. Welensky again had private discussions with both Creech Jones and Oliver Stanley, but neither of them would 'give an inch' on amalgamation, and Welensky realized that the Huggins line was no longer practical politics. He then went to see the Southern Rhodesian Prime Minister at an hotel in London, where Huggins was staying at the time. 'Amalgamation is out', he told the older man; no one in London would support it, and it was essential to achieve something before the sands ran out. If Federation could be achieved now, there was always a chance of improving on the Federal structure later on, but a start must be made.[2] Huggins came round to the Northern Rhodesian's point of view, and in the meantime Colonial Office opinion was becoming more malleable still; another weighty memorandum passed into the ministerial in-tray, explaining that Federation was desirable, provided African participation in the Central Assembly was assured and that African rights were safeguarded, but that the task of persuading black people should in the first place fall to local diplomacy. Nyasaland would have to join in order to justify the new structure, and Barotseland's position would have to be specially safeguarded. The territories should retain their separate Legislative Councils and control the Central Assembly through the power of the purse, the final machinery resembling the East African scheme. The best way to bring about a solution would be —not by setting up yet another Royal Commission—but by a local committee, the task of hammering out an initial scheme and of winning over the Africans best being left to the settlers. The Secretary of State then told Welensky that it was up to him and his colleagues to produce a solution. In addition the Colonial Office advised the leading Unofficial Member in Nyasaland, Malcolm Palliser Barrow (later knighted), an influential tea-planter and company director as well as a member of the Executive Council at Zomba, that Welensky had dropped amalgamation, and that Barrow should discuss the matter with the Northern Rhodesian leader. Welensky and Huggins then returned to Rhodesia to make preparations for a Conference where delegates from the three territories would discuss a common scheme to be placed before the Imperial Government. Amalgamation disappeared from the vocabulary of politics, and by the end of 1948 the stage was set for the Federation campaign.

[1] Northern news, 19 Aug 1948
[2] Taylor, D. The Rhodesian. Museum press limited, p. 103–107; and personal information from Sir Roy Welensky and Lord Malvern.

Chapter Thirteen

Progress and closer union: 1949–1953

I

Federation in the balance: 1949–1951

Early in 1949 an Unofficial Conference assembled at the Victoria Falls, now the traditional meeting place for such discussions. Sir Miles Thomas sat in the Chair; and the other delegates included Huggins and Welensky, as well as several Southern Rhodesian Cabinet Ministers and Members of Parliament, and leading Unofficials from the two Northern Territories. No Africans were invited, though Gore-Browne represented the black community in Northern Rhodesia. The Conference passed a motion in favour of Federation and then set up a committee to consider details. The Southern Rhodesians took the lead, and a draft was produced which took the Australian constitution as its model and put forward something approximating to an amalgamationist solution in federal dress; the central legislature would consist of a Senate, with five members from each state, chosen in a manner which each constituent territory might see fit; all real power rested with a House of Representatives, from which the Southern Rhodesians at first wished to exclude Africans, and which would wield effective powers over the national purse; the states would control African affairs, but the Federal Parliament would handle most other functions, and even exercise general supervision over native policies. The Conference, however, failed to make any formal proposals to the Imperial Government, and its only achievement was thoroughly to frighten educated Africans in the Northern territories, a disastrous mistake from the federalists' point of view. Overseas reactions were mixed, and whilst the *Daily Mail* and *Sunday Times* were friendly, prestige-worthy weeklies like the *Spectator* and the *New Statesman*[1] remained hostile, the *Statesman* arguing that the federalists only wanted cheap native labour; this was an economic interpretation gone badly awry, and did not take account of the white anti-federalists south of the Zambezi, who were often the poorer employers who could not so easily pay higher wages, whilst the wealthier *entrepreneurs* tended to back the cause of United Central Africa.

The Federation proposals also met with bitter hostility from the growing number of Africans expatriates in Britain who were now beginning to play a much more important part in Central African politics—comparable in some ways with that of Latin American and Eastern European exiles during the last century. In the 'twenties and 'thirties a number of Northern Rhodesian

[1] *New statesman*, 9 Dec 1949; and *Spectator*, 8 Mar 1949

Africans acquired some schooling in Southern Rhodesia and South Africa. After the Second World War the Central African expatriate became a more familiar figure abroad, as local standards of education improved, the demand for teachers increased, and the Administration became convinced that standards must be raised. Two African teachers received bursaries from the London School of Oriental and African Studies, and three Africans left for Makerere in East Africa, whilst in 1946 a Bursaries Committee was set up to deal with the question of awarding grants. By now there was a tremendous thirst for higher education in the country, and a year later Gore-Browne reported that there were three hundred applications for twelve vacancies, whilst only a few years ago, a selection board would hardly have found three.[1] But colonial students overseas often found themselves in a difficult position, wandering between two worlds, and exposed to a good deal of colour prejudice which became perhaps all the more wounding, because discrimination did not derive from some impersonal law, but from individual white people. There was the eternal hunt for accommodation, enlivened by the landlady who either advertised openly that she did not want blacks, or who whispered shamefacedly that she was terribly sorry but that her vacant room had just been taken! At long last the visitor from overseas would manage to find 'digs', settling down perhaps in a cold shabby North London house, where the milk bottles stood outside the door, the entrance hall smelt of cats, and where enthusiastic reformers would warm their feet on a poky little gas fire, and discuss politics till late at night over endless cups of Nescafé, the very dinginess of the surroundings foiling the splendour of their visions. An attempt was made to cope with the students' accommodation problem by setting up hostels, but a Northern Rhodesian official who visited black students in a London hostel was unfavourably impressed by the place he saw; the food was poor, the house was gloomy, and the men were thrown too much on each other's company, and apt to compare grievances, the Northern Rhodesians' position being made more difficult by the fact that their allowances did not cover travelling or visiting. One Northern Rhodesian student thought indeed that hostels themselves constituted some kind of colour discrimination, an interpretation not in accordance with the facts, but one easy to be believed by sensitive people suspicious of insults. African undergraduates moreover met colonial students from other territories, and many of them became bitter critics of the existing social order. Moreover their experiences with colour prejudiced European people may have helped to make them more sympathetic to ideas current at the time, which postulated that the world was divided into 'have' and 'have not' nations, whose conflicts cut across conventional class struggles, thus unwittingly repeating ideas already previously worked out by Fascist writers in Mussolini's days.

One of the politically-minded students overseas was Harry Nkumbula, a young schoolmaster. Nkumbula was educated by the Methodists with whom he quarrelled; for a time he became a protégé of Gore-Browne's, and later went to the London School of Economics where he studied without taking a degree. In

[1] In 1951 the first Northern Rhodesian African to gain a degree, John Mwanakatwe, took his B.A.

the British capital he met Dr Hastings Kamuzu Banda, a Nyasalander, who had gone as far afield as South Africa and the United States, and after qualifying as a physician in Scotland, later set himself up in practice in North London. Banda remained in touch with the Nyasaland African Congress as well as the politically minded 'West Coasters'; he joined the Fabian Colonial Bureau as well as the socially more highly placed Aborigines Protection Society; and became acquainted with Labour theoreticians like Dr Rita Hinden, a South African supporter of the Fabian movement, who was later appointed to the now influential Colonial Labour Advisory Bureau. In 1949 when the Federation struggle began in earnest, Banda and Nkumbula between them produced a lengthy memorandum on behalf of Northern Rhodesian and Nyasaland Africans in the United Kingdom, outlining the now familiar reasons for opposition. Federation would dissolve all political and cultural ties with the United Kingdom; it would mean domination by Southern Rhodesia, which would soon be able to acquire dominion status and push her own colour bars beyond the Zambezi; Federation would entail the end of political and economic advancement for Africans, who would be deprived of all rights. Politicians might talk about constitutional guarantees, but the South African precedent had shown just how utterly worthless such scraps of paper became in practice, the supposed South African parallel now playing a major part in shaping opinion in this matter. In Northern Rhodesia African opposition likewise increased, the decisive argument being the land question, an issue on which both the educated and the illiterate could unite. 'Without land we shall be like wild pigs, driven from place to place', they said, and no arguments would convince the doubters; land rights might be entrenched, but the whites were so clever, they would get around these clauses somehow; white promises were just words for children; the European was like a man who called his dog, but held a stick behind his back.[1] The land-fear in fact became a real obsession with many Africans, despite the fact that there was little land hunger, apart from a few areas like the Tonga country, whilst only a small proportion of the territory's surface had been alienated to white men. Land became a symbol for African rights and hopes, a symbol all the more powerful because so many industrial and white-collar workers too were still relying on the security of their tribal land rights for the dreaded days of old age and unemployment. African fears were not allayed by European utterances threatening the black men with the fate of the Red Indians if they did not keep in step with civilization, or demanding massive white immigration in future, though the advocates of increased settlement did not in fact wish to do away with any native land rights. Apart from that, many Africans felt that they were not yet ready to compete with the white man on even terms, and that the Colonial Office should remain in charge, until Africans could take over. Once upon a time there was a tortoise and two pigeons, ran a story. The pigeons asked the tortoise to fly with them into the air; the stupid tortoise consented, and the

[1] Quoted from Fraenkel, P. *Wayaleshi*. Weidenfeld and Nicholson, 1959, p. 169, which is an interesting source for moods and personalities during the Federation campaign.

pigeons got hold of a little stick, which the tortoise held in its mouth, whilst the pigeons held on to both ends. Off they went, flying all over the country, but when the strange trio passed over a village, the people started laughing at the funny sight. The tortoise opened its mouth to rebuke them, and miserably crashed to its death. The moral was obvious. The white men were the pigeons, and the black man was the tortoise, and the black tortoise should stay safely on the ground until it too could fly without the pigeons' help!—a conviction shared by a few local Europeans like Gore-Browne who wrote that the Victoria Falls proposals should be dropped.[1]

But events did not stand still, and the federationist campaign continued. In Northern Rhodesia many whites became alarmed at events in the Gold Coast, where black government was more firmly entrenched—whatever else might happen, the Europeans said, they were not going to step into the place of a politically powerless national minority in their own country, the kind of argument which particularly appealed to a man like Welensky, who with his own mixed national background possessed a better appreciation of the realities of minority-status than most upper middle class British liberals with their easy-going optimism. In the meantime pressure on the Imperial Government continued. The United Kingdom's desperate balance of payments problems remained unsolved; there was a big rise in the dollar deficit, and in September 1949 Cripps broadcast the news that his Government had decided on a very drastic devaluation of the pound. At the same time British experts began to devise plans for curtailing capital and current expenditure, for checking renewed inflationary tendencies, and increasing production available for dollar markets. The dollar crisis emphasized Rhodesia's value to the Sterling Group, as well as the need for Salisbury's co-operation at a time when Southern Rhodesian industrialists and miners continued to clamour for coal and trucks, and the Imperial Government did all in its power to assure priority for the Northern copper mines. But the Central African Council machinery was now creaking heavily, and Thomas Hugh William Beadle, the Southern Rhodesian Minister for Internal Affairs, gave public expression to its unpopularity, whilst other politicians used it as a political scapegoat for all kinds of ills. At the end of 1949 Huggins made another speech in Salisbury, attacking both the Council and the suggested alternative of an East African High Commission, a sort of mongrel institution, a 'Senate without a Lower House', whilst Welensky put forward a motion in the Legislative Council, asking that His Majesty's Government should take the lead in setting up Federation.[2] The outcome of the debate made a disturbed situation worse, for the Government members abstained, whilst all Members representing African interests opposed the motion, with the result that educated Africans became even more suspicious, concluding that the white officials themselves would not oppose such a dreadful measure.

In Southern Rhodesia the Federation campaign meanwhile continued, backed

---

[1] Letter to *Manchester guardian*, 2 Nov 1948
[2] Northern Rhodesia. *Legislative Council debates*, 24 Nov 1949, p. 322–425

by the powerful Argus group, which controlled all the main newspapers. In addition the United Central Africa Association was greatly strengthened when Sir Thomas Ellis Robins, (later Baron Robins of Rhodesia and of Chelsea), the British South Africa Company's Resident Director in Africa, joined the Association's National Executive as well as its Policy Committee. Welensky also managed to secure some financial support both from Rhodesia Selection Trust interests and from Sir Ernest Oppenheimer whose views on the Central African question were now changing. According to one unpublished source, Oppenheimer previously thought that South Africa's most important objective should be to get financial support in London, so that new goldfields might open up in South Africa, and the Union could then finance its industrial development by importing more capital plant and machinery in return for gold. At that time Oppenheimer also felt that Rhodesia's future was likewise linked for the time being to the expansion of the South African gold industry, and that the limited amount of capital available in London should not be tapped to finance independent industrial development in Rhodesia, unless such investments could be directly related to the immediate improvement of the country's external trade balances. From 1947, however, the position began to change; new resources were exploited in the Rhodesias, and London lenders became increasingly willing to invest directly in the two Rhodesias, instead of routing their funds via Johannesburg. This movement found a political parallel in the Union, where the Nationalist victory in 1948 profoundly disconcerted the mine-owners; and many mine magnates and industrialists began to favour a British northern bloc. Soon moreover strategic issues began to move into the foreground, when in 1950 Communist and Western forces openly clashed in a major war over Korea. War also placed a new premium on Rhodesian raw materials, the shortage of various primary products becoming so serious that an International Raw Materials Conference had to be set up in Washington in 1951 to reorganize the share-out, and protect weaker countries like Britain, copper, lead and zinc all becoming the subject of control.[1]

The country's political future was also concerned to some extent with the question of where the big copper companies should reside, a point on which the two giant groups did not at first quite agree. The American-controlled Rhodesia Selection Trust at first still looked to London, and in 1950 Prain explained that Roan's headquarters would not move from the British metropolis, though the question might have to be reconsidered if Rhodesia became a Dominion.[2] Oppenheimer, whose main interests lay in South Africa, and who long since regarded a fusion of the territories as inevitable, adopted a more 'African' outlook, and in 1950 the Rho-Anglo Group moved to Rhodesia on the grounds that the shift would increase administrative efficiency, and avoid the heavy burden of Income and Excess Profits Tax in the United Kingdom.[3] The tax

[1] *Economist*, 29 Dec 1951   [2] *Economist*, 16 Dec 1960
[3] The shift involved Rhokana Corporation, Nchanga Consolidated Mines, Rhodesia Copper Refineries, Rhodesian Anglo American, and Rhodesia Broken Hill Development Company.

argument was a strong one, for in 1947 the Labour Government sharply increased the Profits Tax to reduce inflation at home, and prevent concerns from declaring increased dividends. For the time being, Rhodesia Selection Trust Group remained cautious, as Prain argued that the existing differential between taxes might not always continue, and that there might still be a chance of bringing home to the British tax authorities the danger of their policy; whilst a move to Rhodesia would prevent a majority of their shareholders from attending a general meeting. But later on Rhodesia Selection Trust's policy changed, and Prain summed up the new situation at an Extraordinary General Meeting of Roan Antelope Copper Mines held in London. He explained that the Board could certainly have effected a substantial saving in taxes by moving its domicile in 1947, when the disparity between Rhodesian and British taxes became a major factor. But a question of such magnitude could not be determined merely by tax considerations; London remained a focus of much of the Company's business, and the Board subscribed to the traditional rule that mining could best be undertaken by a strong group located in one of the world's big financial centres. By May 1952, however, the Board realized that the political centre of gravity had in fact shifted to Rhodesia, and that future working efficiency would be impaired if they did not move. In addition Welensky was pressing them for a transfer of headquarters, whilst the need to maintain satisfactory relations with the local trade unions likewise called for closer contacts than could be obtained by occasional visits. Apart from that, the Company was anxious to maintain better liaison, both with the Northern Rhodesian Government and with the Rho-Anglo Group, whilst recurrent difficulties over coal, transport and hydro-electrical developments could all be settled more easily on the spot. In 1953 the Rhodesia Selection Trust Group finally left London, and Rhodesia itself became the focus of local mining policy.[1]

The general economic outlook favoured the federalists, who further improved their position by a skilful shift in tactics. In 1950 the British held another General Election, and Creech Jones lost his seat at Shipley, his defeat being part of a general swing against Labour which now lost its earlier impetus, James Griffiths, formerly Minister for National Insurance, took over at the Colonial Office, and Griffiths accepted a suggestion by Huggins, first made apparently by George Herbert Baxter, then Assistant Under-Secretary for Commonwealth Relations, that the whole question should be reconsidered by a committee of officials. This was a sound move, for civil servants could hardly be accused of prejudice in favour of the local Europeans, whilst official advice would help to shift the burden of responsibility from a wavering Government which still shied from making a decision. The conference assembled in 1951 under Baxter's chairmanship, its proceedings being assisted by a comparative survey of native policies which had previously been carried out by the territories. The Southern Rhodesians at first pressed for the unification of every possible department,

---

[1] The group now included Roan Antelope, Rhodesian Selection Trust, Mufulira Copper Mines, Chibuluma Mines, and Rhodesian Selection Trust Services.

whilst the Northern Rhodesians fought for a looser structure, and at first even insisted on controlling their own economic policy, arguing that all services affecting Africans must be ruled out, and stressing possible opposition from Northern Rhodesian Europeans whose own development plans might be prejudiced, and who would insist on greater powers for the Lusaka Legislature. But in the end the officials produced a unanimous report.[1] The civil servants stressed the economic interdependence of the three territories, as well as their need for unity in view of developments south of the Limpopo; they emphasized the similarities in the native policies of the three territories and noted Southern Rhodesia's achievements in this sphere. The alternatives of a Central African League or of an amalgamated Rhodesia were both rejected in favour of a federal solution with a strictly defined division of function between the territorial and federal governments, designed to leave African affairs in local hands. The federal legislature was to consist of a single chamber of 35 members, and three members from each territory would represent African interests. In addition there was to be an African Affairs Board and a Minister for African Interests who would be appointed by the Governor-General from the members representing African interests, an innovation which became known to white Rhodesians as the 'cuckoo in the nest'. The world press was favourable, and Griffiths gave a good reception to the report, subsequently touring the Protectorates extensively to explain the proposals to Africans. African dislike of Federation grew, the opposition receiving much encouragement from the absence of an official lead, whilst the coming and going of ministers and the prevailing air of uncertainty added to their distrust. Many Southern Rhodesians likewise continued to be sceptical of the scheme, on the grounds that the United Kingdom yielded nothing, whilst the nominated members in the Federal Parliament might become a party of their own, able to hold the balance of power, much hostility also being expressed to the 'cuckoo minister'.

Later on in 1951 a second Conference met at the Victoria Falls under the Chairmanship of Sir John Kennedy, the Governor of Southern Rhodesia. The Northern Rhodesian delegation included Rennie and Welensky as well as two Africans, whilst the Nyasalanders contained three black delegates. Welensky and Huggins saw eye to eye on most questions, and the Southern Rhodesian delegation formed a fairly solid bloc, but white Nyasalanders were prepared if necessary to side with their own Africans, the settler representatives thus being far from presenting a united front. At one point future prospects looked so bleak that Huggins suggested there was no point in continuing, in view of the Nyasaland Africans' rigid opposition. The Labour Ministers, with an impending General Election on their hands, would not however sanction either Nyasaland's exclusion, or commit themselves as yet to an official campaign in favour of Federation without Cabinet or possibly Parliamentary approval.

[1] *Central African territories: report of conference on closer association*, London, March *1951* (Cmd. 8233: 1951). See also *Central African territories: geographical, historical and economic survey* (Cmd. 8234: 1951) and *Central African territories: comparative survey of native policy* (Cmd. 8235: 1951)

Imperial opinion firmly held that Nyasaland must go in to get its due share of revenue, to promote its economic development and also to balance 'white' interests south of the Zambezi. In the end a compromise was found. The Protectorate status of Northern Rhodesia and Nyasaland would be enshrined, whilst land questions and African political advancement in the Protectorates would remain the territorial governments' preserve. Subject to these reservations, the representatives of all four Governments endorsed the principle of Federation, adding as a corollary that this entailed a policy of political and economic partnership between the races, whilst the Northern Rhodesian Africans explained that they might be willing to consider Federation, once partnership had been defined and put into progressive operation. The Labour Ministers were now committed to Federation, and reported favourably on the scheme. The economic advantages of Federation seemed indisputable, and the Labour men attached much importance to the argument that the population of the three territories would double itself every twenty five years, and that economic planning on a Central African basis would be required to increase food supplies, raise living standards, and provide effective machinery for the settling of priorities regarding transport and supply; the existing units of government were too small to sustain the expenditure needed for hydro-electrical development and large-scale water control schemes, and the Zambezi should become a centre of economic activity rather than a frontier; the three territories were also interdependent regarding coal, railway transport, the use of Beira and manpower, whilst some means had to be found to counter political pressure from the south, some experts fearing that Afrikaners might get half the European seats on the Northern Rhodesian Legislative Council. To give up Federation now would simply worsen relations between Europeans and Africans, and create a political vacuum, which would facilitate Afrikaner penetration. Admittedly, African opposition to Federation was widespread, but black people might be won over by further discussions, especially since the Northern Rhodesian African delegates were now ready to consider proposals, if their political future was safeguarded. The Labour Ministers were moreover favourably impressed by the way white Southern Rhodesians for the first time sat round the table with black men to discuss Central Africa's political destiny, whilst the Northern Africans were apparently quite pleasantly surprised by Huggins whom they first imagined to be another Malan. The old 'Railway Belt solution' was shelved, as Welensky explained publicly that the dismemberment of Northern Rhodesia was a counsel of despair which he could not consider until Federation's fate was known.[1] Labour of course still faced opposition within its own ranks, but Griffiths did not think very highly of the quality of the arguments put by Africans against Federation in the North, his sympathies being further alienated by the way in which Simon Ber Zukas, a local European left-winger in Northern Rhodesia, assisted in the anti-Federation campaign, whilst Nyasaland opposition was seen as being largely directed by Banda from London. Griffiths and Patrick Chrestien

[1] Speech at Broken Hill, *Rhodesia herald*, 20 Nov 1951

Gordon Walker, the Secretary of State for Commonwealth Relations, thus put their weight of authority behind the federal cause, and only Labour's left wing kept aloof. The Conservatives proved equally co-operative and when a Tory Government was voted into office at the end of 1951, the Imperial authorities after two years' of delay, at last made up their minds. In November 1951 Oliver Lyttelton, Churchill's Colonial Secretary, announced his Government's agreement with the scheme, and Federation carried the day.[1]

II

The campaign continues: political and missionary cleavages in Britain

The new Conservative Government quickly assembled an informal Conference in London, where Imperial and local delegates prepared the way for a more formal gathering later on in the year. The United Kingdom once more rejected amalgamation, and Rhodesians were told that Nyasaland could not possibly be excluded from the scheme which would be abandoned, unless the Protectorate became part of the Federation. The 'cuckoo' minister on the other hand disappeared, agreement being reached that it would be impossible to have a Minister for African Interests in the Cabinet who would not be responsible to his colleagues. The African Affairs Board was re-designed, partly to meet Southern Rhodesian objections and partly to enable the United Kingdom better to fulfil its obligations towards Africans now that the Minister of African Interests had been dropped. As far as the composition of the Federal Legislature was concerned, the United Kingdom would not consent to a reduction in the number of Africans. The Conference agreed that provision for the federal franchise should be written into the constitution; amendments would need the support of a two-thirds majority and be reserved for Her Majesty's approval. Delegates also agreed that the constitution should include a declaration of rights of all races inhabiting Central Africa, which would form part of the preamble but have no binding legal force. As far as the question of a unified civil service was concerned, opinions differed considerably; the Southern Rhodesians favoured a single service for the Federation as well as the three territories; the question being held over for subsequent discussions. The Imperial Government would not accept any proposals whereby the Federal Government would have the power to veto any state legislation which conflicted with the proposed multi-racial declaration. On the question of whether the Federal Government should be able to stop state legislation which it considered prejudicial to the Federation as a whole, the delegates thought that the remedy lay in the careful division of functions between the Federation and the State. Immigration from outside the Federation was to constitute a federal responsibility, but the territories retained the right to

[1] *Closer association in Central Africa: statement by His Majesty's government in the United Kingdom, 21st November 1951* (Cmd. 8411: 1951)

control movement within the Federation itself, thus enabling Southern Rhodesians to control the influx of Indians from the North. The delegates also agreed that there should be a concurrent list of subjects, in addition to an exclusively federal list, other conclusions dealing with matters like finance and future procedure. Later on in 1952 a full ministerial conference under the chairmanship of the Marquess of Salisbury, the Secretary of State for Commonwealth Relations, hammered out a draft constitution, the delegates receiving technical advice from Professor Kenneth Clinton Wheare, one of the foremost British experts on constitutional law. The conference was again headed by Salisbury, and attended by large delegations, including Lyttelton, several other British and Southern Rhodesian Ministers, by Rennie, Welensky, Beckett and Barrow, as well as strong contingents of senior civil servants from the United Kingdom and the three Central African territories. Africans from the two Northern Territories were invited, but would not make an appearance, on the grounds that they opposed the principle of Federation itself. Hard bargaining continued as the Southern Rhodesians still tried to establish a strong central authority, which would control a unified civil service for all the territories; in addition the Southern Rhodesians once more submitted a proposal for a bi-cameral legislature. The Imperial authorities on the other hand strove for a more decentralized government, and opposed a bi-cameral legislature, Welensky being unwilling to press the point unless the United Kingdom would consent; Huggins and Welensky also favoured a unified police, on the grounds that the new force would have to enforce many federal laws, that the scheme would make for both greater efficiency and economy, and that security was closely linked to the question of defence which was a federal responsibility. The United Kingdom on the other hand argued that even in the United Kingdom itself local authorities maintained their own police, and that territorial laws should not be enforced by a federal force. Discussion also took place on various other subjects such as the franchise, the African Affairs Board, the right of secession, the latter being advocated by a member of the Southern Rhodesian opposition, but resisted both by Huggins and Imperial opinion itself. The delegates also went into the question of naming the new state, some Southern Rhodesians suggesting the title 'Kingdom of Rhodesia and Nyasaland' on the grounds that this would both reassure Africans and gain popularity amongst the Europeans by emphasizing the British connexion, the argument against the title of kingdom emphasizing the anomalous nature of the word in view of the Federation's constitutional status.

In the end the conference published an agreed communiqué, and recommended that three Commissions should be appointed to investigate the financial consequences of Federation, the establishment of a federal civil service, and of a Federal Supreme Court.[1] These Commissions duly produced their reports,[2]

[1] *Southern Rhodesia, Northern Rhodesia and Nyasaland: draft federal scheme* . . . (Cmd. 8573: 1952)
[2] *Southern Rhodesia, Northern Rhodesia and Nyasaland: draft federal scheme: report of the judicial commission* (Cmd. 8671: 1952) *Southern Rhodesia, Northern Rhodesia and Nyasaland: draft federal scheme: report of the fiscal commission* (Cmd. 8672: 1952) *Southern Rhodesia, Northern Rhodesia and Nyasaland: draft federal scheme: report of the civil service preparatory commission* (Cmd. 8673: 1952)

and in the beginning of 1953 the Imperial Government convened a final conference to produce a White Paper embodying all previous modifications, as well as the additional points arising out of the specialist commissions.

By now, however, the Federation issue ceased to be a matter for experts, and opened up a major political cleavage in British politics. Before 1950 an undergraduate could spend three years at Oxford without ever hearing the word 'Rhodesia', whilst a popular history of British politics published at the time did not even list terms like 'Africa', 'Central Africa or 'Federation' in its index.[1] In the late 'forties the British were occupied with pressing problems like the Dollar Gap; relations between the Labour Government and South Africa, the Sterling Group's main gold producer, were perfectly friendly; and the British placed much stress on Southern Rhodesian and South African co-operation in their financial policies. Abroad, British public opinion was preoccupied with such pressing matters as the Communist seizure of power in Prague, the temporary Soviet blockade of Berlin or the British withdrawal from India and Palestine. In the early 'fifties, however, Britain suddenly became Africa-conscious. Britain's Asian Empire was largely a thing of the past, and anti-colonialists turned their attention to the Dark Continent, sympathy with African nationalism becoming comparable in strength with the Philhellenes' enthusiasm during the War of Greek Independence, or with Gladstonian commitment for the cause of Bulgaria against the 'Unspeakable Turk'. To some, the anti-colonial crusade in Africa acquired the character of a great moral cause, something to fight for, at a time when enthusiasm for Labour's 'brave new world' was evaporating. The very decline of Empire itself heightened a feeling of intense urgency over African affairs amongst left-wingers and right-wingers, who both sensed that the sands were running out, that Britain's last chance had come in the Dark Continent, and that she must either act now, or forever after lose all chance of shaping Africa in the British image. At the same time British intellectuals effected a major transvaluation in the colonial prestige scale. Late Victorians used to idealize white settlers in Africa, the supposed representatives of Queen, Empire, and middle class values, clean-shaven, sunburnt young Englishmen who built a new Britain in the bush. Africans at the same time were often endowed with all the supposed vices of the proletariat; they were described as a thriftless, lustful, idle crew who needed a good dose of discipline. But now the African's reputation went up, and many of the supposed qualities which used to disgust Victorian missionaries became virtues in the eyes of British progressives in revolt against their grandfathers' standards. The identification of white colonists with middle class standards and empire became, on the other hand, a positive disadvantage to Rhodesians or Kenyans, so much so that the very word 'white settler' became to some a term of reproach, heavily laden with emotion,[2] some of the clerical and left-wing critics of white settlerdom drawing on a rich vein of Evangelical and abolitionist tradition that had never disappeared from British

---

[1] See Somervell, D. C. *British politics since 1900.* Andrew Dakers, 1950
[2] Gann, L. H. 'The white settler: a changing image' (in *Race*, v. 2, no. 2, May 1961, p. 28–40)

thought, and sometimes attaching to themselves an aura of martyrdom, which capitalized on every local reaction to their point of view.[1] At the same time international opinion underwent a striking change which was expressed in the United Nations pronouncements relating to trust territories, and non-self-governing territories,[2] the new attitude being strongly influenced by the genuine idealism engendered by the struggle against Nazi racialism, but often accompanied by a lack of historical perspective which led to the assumption that two generations or so of European rule had obliterated all those features of African life which made European rule inevitable in the first place; colonialism now became at best an inevitable expedient, which could only be justified by the speed with which it would abolish itself, and the white-skinned élite in Africa became identified with the very Imperial powers which they often opposed. On the other side of the Atlantic the position of the Negro, a depressed community until the late 'thirties, began to change rapidly under the impact of war and of the new industrial upsurge, which both accompanied and followed the great conflict. By 1953 'gradualism' had ceased to be a respectable term in Negro parlance, giving place to the demand for speedy integration, which was in time being conceded, as restrictive covenants in housing and segregated military units disappeared and Negro incomes were rapidly rising. At the same time the growing military and economic strength of the Soviet Union gave a new emphasis to the Leninist critique of Imperialism, even though the orthodox Marxist approach made only a relatively limited impact in Britain itself. But all the same—complained the settlers—many non-Communist intellectuals on the Left began to be moved by a selective kind of indignation; mass expulsions, or liquidations east of the Iron Curtain became excusable in their eyes because of the Communists' indisputably great achievements; but similar excuses were never accepted for the settlers' failings, despite the speed and comparative humanity with which they helped to transform their own underdeveloped country within two generations, and assisted in that primary accumulation of capital which was being effected by much harsher means elsewhere. Some white Rhodesians also argued that their motives were being misunderstood, and that left-wing journalists and 'pink parsons' regarded them as expatriate lowbrows, on whom the intelligentsia could project their civilizational guilt-complexes and dislike of suburbia, whilst the African village, with its poverty, disease, its lack of opportunity, its bitter personal feuds and witchcraft accusations, was being plunged into a golden haze of glamour. Whatever the merits of these disputes, Central and Southern Africa in fact became looked upon to some extent as a new kind of 'Spain', the last place on earth where Communists, Socialists and Liberals might stand together in a common front to defend what they regarded as the cause of freedom, the attractiveness of their crusade being heightened by the fact that involvement

---

[1] For comparative purposes, see Wolf, H. C. *On freedom's altar: the martyr complex in the abolitionist movement*. University of Wisconsin press, 1952

[2] Robinson, K. 'Colonial issues and policies with special reference to tropical Africa' (in *Annals of the American academy of political and social science*, v. 298, Mar 1955, p. 84–94)

in Africa—unlike class struggles at home—demanded no sacrifice of any kind from its British adherents. The division over the Federation issue of course did not entirely coincide with party political divisions. Some conservatively minded people also opposed Federation, continuing in the traditions of the Milner policy, putting their trust in the Imperial Factor and an extended spell of Colonial Office rule to enforce reforms from above with a strong hand; others stressed the military aspect, and argued that the Imperial Government should not pursue policies requiring the despatch of British battalions, who would uselessly chase native guerillas through the bush, whilst leaving the NATO lines in Europe desperately undermanned. Moderate anti-federationists predicted that Federation would fail, because it was imposed against the will of the African majority, because the scheme only accorded minority representation to Africans, and because of the scarcity of political talent amongst the Europeans on the spot. Colonial government—they argued—should rest on the consent of the governed, rather than on superior administrative or technical skill, a view which sometimes committed them to the 'treaty fallacy', and led them to under-estimate the part played by superior military strength in the occupation of Central Africa. The moderate liberals were strongly influenced by South African experience; some, like Kenneth Kirkwood, later Professor of Race Relations at Oxford and himself a South African, argued that Britain should avoid the mistakes of the past, and instead use her vast fund of colonial knowledge to better effect, that the decisive problem was political and that Britain should work towards partnership, Kirkwood's avowed aim being an 'assimilationist' solution which would integrate African leaders into the Western political and legal tradition.[1] Kirkwood, like other liberal reformers, did not face fully the question whether Africans in fact *wanted* the kind of liberal state which their white tutors thought best for them, the resulting contradiction between assimilationist ideals and a theory of government by consent not always being fully resolved in their minds. From the organizational point of view, the anti-federationist cause was poorly co-ordinated, but received support from a broad spectrum of political opinion, ranging from Communists to upper middle class liberals, including many academic men. Their case was argued forcefully by the Fabians, who by now were hardly even aware of their founders' concept of Empire as a powerful force for social improvement and the rational exploitation of natural resources, even if this involved comparative indifference towards native rights—a concept now almost monopolized by the right wing in British politics. In addition vigorous efforts were made by various other organizations, many of them reformist, pacifist or clerical in character, specially noteworthy being Michael Scott's Africa Bureau, and Canon Collins' Christian Action.

The supporters of Federation, for their part, also included people of varying political opinions. Some liberals argued that devolution of power was inevitable, and that white and black Africans should settle their own problems on the spot.

[1] See for instance Kirkwood, K. 'British Central Africa: politics under federation' (in *Annals of the American academy of political and social science*, v. 298, Mar 1955, p. 130–141)

A number of right-wing Labour men agreed with the Conservatives that the Africans, Britain's wards, should not contradict their more experienced guardian, that Federation was best for Africans for economic reasons, and that simple-minded tribesmen who believed that white villains would steal their land by anti-soil erosion campaigns, or deprive them of their virility through poisoned sugar, were unfit to decide. Attlee himself was personally impressed by Welensky, and even favoured a yet wider British Federation in East and Central Africa, a concept which also appealed to Huggins. But as far as politics in general were concerned, Federation now became a Tory cause, whilst the Labour Party renounced responsibility for the new state on the ground that Africans were inadequately consulted, and that the Conservatives were simply bulldozing the required legislation through Parliament, without heeding the black men's opposition, Labour now deriving considerable tactical advantages from the fact of being in opposition. From the propaganda point of view, much work was done by the London Committee of the Central Africa Association, which counted amongst its Vice Presidents various prominent men in public life like Baron Altrincham, Leopold Stennet Amery, Sir Alfred Beit, General Sir Bernard Paget, Sir Shenton Thomas, a former colonial Governor, Professor Frank Debenham, a well-known geographer, and others. The Committee made some progress but wound up in 1953, a serious mistake from the federalists' point of view, who failed to consolidate their gains in the field of public relations, an omission motivated by the ever-pressing lack of funds. The federal propagandists moreover limited their appeal to persons of moderate or right-wing sympathies, making no attempt to adjust their phraseology for left-wing consumption, and arguing their case in terms of, say 'the historically progressive role of the local Rhodesian bourgeoisie in effecting a revolutionary transformation from tribalism to industrial capitalism'. Neither did they adopt the language of neo-Hegelian thought with its self-fulfilling prophecies, which postulated that whatever was predicted was inevitable, and whatever was inevitable ought not to be resisted, a philosophy which was becoming one of the most powerful ideological weapons in the anti-colonialist armoury. The federalists' appeal thus remained very one-sided, and the British Press remained about evenly divided, *The Times* itself maintaining a very critical attitude, and the cleavage running through the daily Press roughly reflecting the divided state of British public opinion as a whole.[1]

The Federation issue also profoundly affected missionary opinion, the issue raising the much wider question of how far the Churches should intervene in

[1] The pro-federation daily newspapers included *The Sunday times, Daily telegraph, Financial times, Daily mail, Daily express,* and a number of big provincials such as the *Yorkshire post, Nottingham guardian, Birmingham post, Newcastle journal.* The *News chronicle* supported Federation, subject to very considerable reservations, whilst *The Times, Manchester guardian, Daily mirror, Daily herald, Observer, The Daily worker, Western mail, Scotsman,* and *Glasgow herald* ranged from moderate criticism to hostile condemnation. A public relations analyst who investigated the position in 1953 on behalf of the United Central Africa Association, estimated that the readership of the pro-Federation newspapers amounted to 8,317,500; the readership of the critical or hostile papers amounted to 7,645,700, whilst the *News chronicle* held the balance with 1,390,000.

politics. In the 'thirties and early 'forties, the British missions in Northern Rhodesia used to oppose amalgamation, but otherwise largely declined to be drawn into politics, even though one or two local clergymen, like the Rev. J. G. Soulsby, for many years Chairman of the Methodist Synod in Northern Rhodesia, tended to sympathize with left-wing causes overseas. At the end of the War, however, the Churches came under much heavier pressure than ever before. Christians became deeply disturbed at the *débacle* in China, where ideological resistance against the Communists in the minds of most intellectuals collapsed with the same speed as resistance by the Kuomintang's military forces on the battlefield. Protestant missionary opinion, as mirrored in the *International Review of Missions*, now became convinced that never again must the Church ally herself to an outworn régime like Chiang Kai Chek's, and that she should take an active part in the political and social emancipation of her charges, if she was to survive as an active force amongst the more progressive Africans. In Rhodesia this view met with some resistance, and some clergymen argued like the Rev. E. G. Nightingale, himself a keen believer in African advancement, that the Church would never be able to compete with local nationalists on the basis of issuing expurgated versions of their programmes. Others felt that the Church should completely abstain from politics on the grounds that Jesus of Nazareth was never an activist, and that the Sermon on the Mount made no mention of either 'one man one vote,' 'Home Rule for Judaea', or Palestinian representation in the Roman Senate! This point of view was particularly popular in Rhodesia amongst small revivalist sects working amongst European artisans, but aroused considerable criticism from other clergymen loth to accept a politically passive role.[1] Others argued in a more sophisticated fashion that the Churches, by concerning themselves with the political distribution of power, were in fact adopting a double standard of political morality; east of the Iron Curtain Christian clergymen publicly proclaimed that they did not wish to overthrow the existing régimes or later the structure of one-party rule; they simply demanded freedom of worship, freedom of conscience, whilst even their maximum demands only amounted to their adherents' right to public employment, or to limited concessions regarding their educational and charitable work. But in 'colonialist' countries west of the Iron Curtain, where all these objectives were perfectly secure, 'political parsons' were accused of adopting a completely contrary line. In Southern Africa—the settlers said—no clergymen languished in concentration camps; none was brainwashed; none was put up against a wall; one or two might suffer a well publicized martyrdom in homeopathic doses by getting themselves deported from a British Colony or by a short spell in jail. But these risks were strictly of the 'limited liability' variety, involving no serious personal danger, whilst resulting in the maximum public acclaim for the parson involved. What did the difference imply? Did the right to interference depend on geographical location? Or did it depend on the size of the stick which Caesar was willing to use on his critics? Churchmen replied that they could not remain

[1] See for instance Scott, M. *A time to speak*. Faber and Faber, 1958

indifferent to political matters in as far as moral issues were involved; even if they temporarily had to keep silent in Communist countries. The critics then retorted that 'political parsons' and 'post-Protestant Progressives' did not always adopt the same absolute standards for their protégés which they required of colonialists and such like? Were they not always finding excuses for the former whilst denouncing the latter? Were they not steering straight towards a novel doctrine of 'Selective Pre-destination', which accounted for the sins of their friends by showing that the Good could not help it—that their misdeeds were determined by psychological or sociological factors beyond their control, whilst leaving Imperialists, settlers, policemen and other objectionable members of the Establishment in full possession of Free Will, and thus personally responsible for their evil actions? In any case what about the Churches' own political record in the past? Was not much of their criticism based on ignorance of their own history? Was it not true that roughly speaking all Churchmen in the 'nineties supported the cause of Imperial expansion in Rhodesia, that a generation later the Churches helped to shape those very segregationist views which they later condemned, and that their recent conversion to the cause of colonial nationalism was simply motivated by tactical expediency in a threadbare theological dress? Churchmen for their part replied that the Church must adjust her tactics to a changing world, and unless she adopted herself to altered conditions, her influences with the masses would break down.

But whatever the merits of such arguments, political neutrality was in fact a difficult object to pursue in Africa. A new generation of mission educated Africans was growing up in Northern Rhodesia, who occupied key positions in African society as teachers, storemen, and civil servants. These people had to be wooed, a difficult task, as many of the 'new men' regarded Church membership as a purely nominal affair, deriving from the accident of having been educated by one Society or another, whilst some just looked at the Church as an agency to further their political and economic aims. The Protestants moreover suffered from a shortage of ordinands, their Churches being unable to provide the salaries or the prestige that could be acquired in other careers.[1] The 'new men' moreover often inclined towards scepticism or agnosticism, sometimes strangely blended with magical beliefs of an older vintage, the position being made worse from the Churches' point of view by the suspicion shown by many students towards all things European, which led a Methodist minister to argue that the teachers trained at his institution might become instruments of Satan, unless they could become dedicated to truly Christian leadership.[2] Even in the villages the Faith was still meeting resistance, and though the Gospel now permeated the life of the people to a greater or lesser extent, comparatively few people were as yet ready to accept Christ as their personal saviour. Generalizations of course are dangerous. Some Churches, especially the Catholics, secured African clergymen

[1] See for instance London Missionary Society. *Deputation report, 1953*, p. 29–31
[2] Report by J. L. Matthews on Kafue training institute, to Northern Rhodesia Methodist synod, 1952 (Methodist Missionary Arch)

of high calibre, the Catholics making a slower but more thorough job than their rivals of training indigenous priests.[1] In addition many, often elderly, evangelists continued to plough their spiritual acres with accustomed devotion and inadequate tools, often working for a small wage on a part-time basis. But the ill-lettered evangelist of old was now often becoming as inadequate for his spiritual duties as the chief's part-time clerk was becoming inadequate in the administrative sphere, and if the Churches wanted to expand, they were bound to reform their methods. The answer lay in a more aggressive mission policy that would absorb the lessons of China, make the mission church more self-governing, self-supporting and self-propagating.[2] For the Methodists, Nightingale put forward a sound and well reasoned plan for abandoning the existing policy of maintaining large and burdensom mission stations, which formed a drain on the Church's time and energy. Instead, he argued, the Church should concentrate on its evangelical and pastoral work, whilst laymen should take over the upkeep of farms and building, as well as the work of education.[3] The missionaries' position was also made more difficult by increasing economic pressure on the churches who suffered from the sharply increasing cost of living, which raised their expenditure on labour and materials at a time when their revenue did not expand in the same proportion. Clerical devolution of power thus became the order of the day. But the new policy required the support of the 'new men' of Africa, whose co-operation became essential, both as far as the leadership and economic backing for the Church was concerned.[4] The Church needed a new start in order to do away with its dependence on European missionaries and provide a new impetus. The London Missionary Society thus concluded that the congregations should themselves take a more active part, that Church members should know more about their faith, and that the missionaries should simply concentrate on leadership training. By this means only could the existing weaknesses of the Church be cured and the danger of a self-perpetuating routine concerned solely with the examination of catechumens, Church discipline, questions of schools and building be removed.[5] But an active Church relying on the emergent African intelligentsia, could not easily detach itself from political questions, which occupied the minds of emergent Africans in such far-reaching fashion. Besides, there were the Churches' commitments in other parts of the world. In the 'forties for instance the Anglicans possessed one Province only in Africa, the Province of South Africa which attained the ecclesiastical equivalent

[1] The process of devolving local ecclesiastical power to Afro-Asian clergymen was therefore slower too within the Catholic Church. Within the territories entrusted to the Sacred College for the Propagation of the Faith, not including those at present subject to persecution, the first bishop of Asiatic origin was consecrated in 1923 and the first Apostolic Vicars of African origin were named in 1939. From then onwards there was a swift expansion in numbers.

[2] Letter from Northern Rhodesian district synod to Methodist Missionary Society, London, 1952 (Methodist Missionary Arch)

[3] E. G. Nightingale to Methodist Missionary Society, London. Annual letter of the Northern Rhodesia missionary meeting of the Methodists, Jan 1947 (Methodist Missionary Arch)

[4] London Missionary Society. *Deputation report, 1953*

[5] London Missionary Society. *Deputation report, 1948*, p. 35–38

of 'Dominion status' in the nineteenth century. In 1951 West Africa became a new Province, subsequently followed by several others in Africa, and only the Roman Catholic Church preserved its time-honoured, rigidly centralized structure which made it much less dependent on local pressures than its Protestant rivals. Try as they might to keep aloof, the Churches were drawn into the political maelstrom, and forced to strike a balance between the interests of their white and black adherents in matters affecting the common weal.

The Churches thus became involved in the Federation issue, their own reaction differing in various ways. The Dutch Reformed Church adopted a favourable outlook, whilst the Catholics remained neutral on what they considered as a question open to legitimate political dispute, arguing that the Church would not interfere in political matters provided Natural or Revealed Law were not being violated. Nevertheless *The Shield,* the diocesan magazine for Salisbury,[1] cautiously backed the project; so did the majority of the Anglican Church, including Archbishop Geoffrey Francis Fisher, though a radical wing, including Canon Lewis John Collins, the Chancellor of St Paul's Cathedral and Chairman of Christian Action, as well as Rev. Guthrie Michael Scott, a co-founder of the Africa Bureau, strongly opposed the scheme, giving expression to a mood of social radicalism in a part of the Anglican Church, whose lower clergy were facing a serious decline of both social and financial status, and who sought to extend their failing influence by more forceful social action. The main opposition, however, came from the Church of Scotland, which abandoned its mission work in Manchuria and China between 1950 and 1951, but which maintained large native congregations in the Gold Coast and also in Nyasaland, where its members now formed part of the 'Church of Central Africa Presbyterian',[2] enjoying extensive powers of self-government. From 1951 the Blantyre Mission Council began to devolve its extensive administrative functions on the indigenous Church, a policy which culminated in the Council's ultimate abolition. The Church's policy was influenced by various factors, including its own democratic tradition, a deeply felt belief in the need for African ecclesiastical autonomy, and also by the need to rely more on local funds, as well as by the desire for wider popular appeal in the competitive struggle against the White Fathers who were also making headway in the battle for African minds. In 1952 the Foreign Mission Committee of the Church of Scotland thus issued a statement that the Federation should not be imposed without the Africans' assent, and that a Royal Commission should go to Africa to discuss what steps should be taken to ensure the undoubted advantages of closer union without calling a halt to

---

[1] *The Shield,* no. 85, Jan 1953, p. 1–3

[2] In 1945 the Commissioners from the Churches in the care of the L.M.S. in Northern Rhodesia, the Union Church of the Copper Belt, and the congregations of the North Eastern Presbytery in Rhodesia of the Church of Central Africa (Presbyterian) met to establish a union. They adopted as basis for union the Apostles' Creed, government of the Church by elders, but agreed that the constituent congregations should retain their own traditions of Church government. The new united group called itself the Church of Central Africa in Rhodesia, but the union remained a product of mission rather than Church activity, and the Missions remained organizationally separate.

African advancement. At the same time clerical and secular publicists ransacked history for arguments, making a great deal of the fact that Northern Rhodesia had supposedly never been conquered, without however going into the question of how in fact Kazembe's and Mpeseni's kingdoms fell to the British. They stressed Imperial trusteeship obligations, but studiously avoided any reference as to the way these treaties had been carried out in the past, or how they were applied to questions like the mineral royalties. They likewise emphasized that the consent of the African people should be obtained for any change of their political status, though did not discuss why this assent had not been previously insisted upon when the Chartered Company joined up North-Eastern Rhodesia, largely a native territory, to North-Western Rhodesia with its white settler element, or when the Colonial Office took over from the Chartered Company.

In the end British Protestants arrived at an agreed communique, designed to reconcile various opposing views. In 1952 the British Council of Churches, including representatives of the conference of British Missionary societies issued a cautious statement, which maintained a precarious balance. Central Africa differed from Nigeria or the Gold Coast in that two main races had made their homes there, and both communities had their contribution to make. The future lay, neither by way of domination of either race, or by segregation, but by way of partnership, a solution which apparently excluded either African rule by right of their majority, or rule by the European colonists, leaving power uneasily balanced between the two. The Council argued that partnership depended not only on European, but also on African confidence. Africans valued freedom above economic or administrative advantages, and Federation should not therefore be imposed against their unanimous opposition; their co-operation should be won instead by sympathetic understanding of their misgivings and by clear demonstrations of good faith,[1] a decision which by implication cut the ground from beneath the federalists' feet.

III

Federation: the campaign in Northern Rhodesia

In advocating closer union, the whites in Northern Rhodesia hoped to secure their political position, but their very campaign itself helped to make Africans more politically conscious. The general air of uncertainty, the coming and going of ministers, the speech-making, the lengthy letters in the white newspapers, as well as the long-drawn out period of official neutrality all helped to convince Africans that trouble was afoot. African nationalists gradually built up their forces, and slowly improved their organization. In 1951 Kasokolo and Nalumango were displaced on the Legislative Council by two African headmasters, Dauti Lawton Yamba and Paskale Sokata, both convinced supporters of Con-

[1] Printed in *Chronicle: a magazine of world enterprise*, July 1952, p. 139–140

gress; the African Representative Council stepped up its constitutional demands for more African representation on the Legislative Council. Within Congress itself, Nkumbula in 1951 wrested the Presidency from the more moderate Lewanika, and general organization improved. In 1952 the constitution was altered so that the office bearers and branch delegates to the Annual Conference were re-elected every three years, instead of annually, a reform which gave greater continuity to Congress leadership. Later on in 1952 a new clause was introduced which allowed for the disciplining of members, and a Congress Youth League was formed, which steered a yet more radical course. Congress also acquired greater administrative stability when in 1951 National Head-quarters was set up in Chilenje township of Lusaka in a rented two-roomed hut, and a full-time clerk-bookkeeper was appointed to deal with correspondence and run administrative matters during Nkumbula's absence. Office work im-proved and files no longer got lost, as they did in the early days when many records disappeared. In 1951 Congress for the first time began to appoint field officers, one for each province, and branches opened up in various parts of the territory,[1] the regional organization being subsequently strengthened by the creation of Provincial Headquarters with their own Presidents, and Secretaries and Financial Secretaries, with District and Branch Organizing Secretaries lower down the hierarchy. Congress thus modelled its organization on the 'boma', and gradually extended its influence. Organizers toured their areas on foot or on bicycle, like pioneering District Commissioners in the Chartered days, and membership quickly increased. The Northern Province, the Copper Belt's poverty-stricken labour reservoir, acquired the largest number of bran-ches; the Copper Belt itself was also well represented, most of the remainder being found on the railway belt, the Tonga country—weighed down by serious agrarian problems—becoming a particularly loyal stronghold of Nkumbula's. In addition, expatriate branches were established in Southern Rhodesia, and even as far afield as Johannesburg.[2] Nkumbula, like an early colonial Governor, spent an enormous amount of time 'on tour', thus maintaining active contact with his supporters, whilst neglecting the equally important work of central administration; which remained the Party's major weakness. Money was ob-tained by subscriptions, donations, collections run by friendly chiefs or organiz-ing secretaries, through entertainments like dances. But incomes, like Congress membership, fluctuated considerably, with the result that the organization had to rely much more on donations and collections than on regular revenue, a serious weakness from the organizers' point of view. Congress nevertheless managed to collect fairly large sums, something like £7,000 being gathered in the course of 1952. This was spent on objects as varied as legal defence fees, costs of sending delegates to Britain, touring fees and salaries. But though the Cong-

[1] Northern Rhodesia African national congress. *Historical extract of the African national congress—its activities and growth 1951–1960.* Lusaka, The Congress, 1960.

[2] According to Government sources, known Congress branches in 1952 in the Provinces were distributed as follows: Northern—24; Western—11; Central—9; Southern—13; Eastern—4; Barotse—nil; Southern Rhodesia—13; Johannesburg—1; branches numbered up to 50 persons.

gress organization worked on low overheads, its Treasury failed to build up reserves, head office accounts being overdrawn at the end of the year. Cash was wasted; there was misuse of funds, further distrust being aroused by African spivs who collected money ostensibly for Congress purposes, and pocketed the proceeds.[1] Lack of financial integrity in its cadres thus formed one of the Party's main weaknesses, and led to a number of resignations among highly placed functionaries, though wide-spread peculation was not sufficiently serious to paralyze Congress from the organizational point of view. Congress had more-over a number of trump cards which were played for all they were worth. In the publicity field, the land question remained the Party's most powerful talking point. Congress tried to appeal to all social sections, illiterate peasants, hawkers, chiefs and clerks, whose interests did not always coincide. But all Africans still feared for their land at a time when most black men looked to the tribal areas for security in old age or unemployment, and African feelings over land ran strong. Some chiefs also worried about what would happen to their political and ad-ministrative powers, if Southern Rhodesians managed to impose 'Direct Rule' north of the Zambezi, and accordingly opposed Federation. In addition, many tribal dignitaries nursed grievances, resulting from their difficult 'buffer' posi-tion between 'boma' and people, and all these now came to the forefront. In 1951 a group of chiefs addressed a memorandum to the Secretary for Native Affairs, complaining of small salaries, and of the rising cost of living. Native Authority employees, they added, should not get more pay than their superiors, and it was wrong that clerks, with smaller commitments, should live better than chiefs. They also asked that tribal dignitaries should no longer be deposed, except by popular consent, and that District Commissioners should confine their work to giving advice. A year later some 70 chiefs attended a Congress Conference at Lusaka, and many Tonga chiefs, as well as Chitimukulu, supported Nkumbula's politics, even though many other tribal heads retained strong misgivings with regard to Congress which they considered to be a potential rival, the Barotse remaining specially averse to any kind of political penetration from the east. Nkumbula himself took a fairly moderate line, placing special emphasis on legal and constitutional issues, though again the land question was brought in. He attacked the proposed division of powers between the Federal and Territorial Legislatures which supposedly would enable the whites to take away African lands. He also argued that the proposed African Affairs Board would degenerate into the Governor-General's instrument for achieving domination over Africans with a minimum amount of interference from Britain, these views being held with all sincerity by a man who, like so many African students, had come to regard 'them', the 'Establishment', with intense suspicion. The composition of the Federal House was unacceptable because it would be dominated by whites, who would be able to attain both amalgamation and dominion status by their two thirds majority in the Assembly. Nkumbula also played on white class

[1] See Epstein, A. L. *Politics in an urban African community.* Manchester university press, 1958, p. 163–164

snobbery and British nationalism by describing Welensky as 'a Pole of humble education', a shrewd move in a country to which Poles came as penniless and little honoured refugees; Poland, Nkumbula added, had never been a stable country in the past; Polish leaders always made trouble, and Welensky would bring his national heritage to Central Africa, where Huggins's British Imperialism and Welensky's continental habits would make the worst of both worlds. Northern Rhodesia should not be thrown open to foreign immigration, and the country should strive for African government 'fully manned and run by the black people of Africa'.[1] Kenneth Kaunda, the Party's general secretary from 1953 onwards, took a similar line. Kaunda was the son of a Nyasaland evangelist who first preached the Gospel amongst the Bemba on behalf of the Livingstonia Mission, and grew up on a mission station, subsequently becoming a teacher. In 1947 he went to the Copper Belt where for the first time he felt the full shock of the colour bar and joined the local African Welfare Association, founded by Yamba. Later on he went back to teaching but soon became involved with African politics and joined Congress, his political work soon making so many demands on him that he resigned from his teaching job and returned to his mother's farm near Lubwa to set himself up in business and carry on with his political work. Kaunda started trading in secondhand clothes which at the time could be bought cheaply in the Belgian Congo, his work involving a cycle ride of three hundred miles to buy up bales of garments, a training which physically stood him in very good stead when it came to organizing Congress branches scattered over the length and breadth of the Northern Province. During this period he came into conflict with the missionaries at his old station at Lubwa over the Federation proposals, and fervently quoted Bernard Shaw at his erstwhile teachers.[2] Kaunda who, like Moore and Welensky before him, 'came up the hard way', possessed real organizing ability, and appealed to the illiterate through fiery Congress songs which pictured the whites as vultures hovering over the land to pounce on their victims,[3] though he objected to physical violence against the hated cause of Federation. In the villages other Congress speakers denounced the proposals on the lines that joining with the white man in a Federation was like trying to sit on a small stool with a person possessed of an over-large backside, or more seriously, that the Europeans wished to seize the people's land and use the game and forestry reserves for the purpose of settling more white immigrants. Huggins and Welensky were said to have their eyes specially on the Mwinilunga country where a mysterious mineral was buried in the soil which enabled aircraft to fly. Africans ought not to work for whites, who treated them like slaves. Admittedly, there were some good Europeans; anthropologists for instance might be trusted, for they advised the people against Federation and served as informers for Congress—an assertion not quite in accordance with the

[1] African national congress. *The general president's statement at a public meeting held at Mapoloto African township, Lusaka, 26 June 1952.* Lusaka, African national congress, 1952
[2] Temple, M. F. 'Profile of Kenneth Kaunda' (in Morris, C., and Kaunda, K. *Black government: a discussion.* . . . Lusaka, United society for Christian literature, 1960, p. 3–22)
[3] See Fraenkel, P. *Wayaleshi.* Weidenfeld and Nicholson, 1959

facts, but shrewdly assessing the private views of the small white intelligentsia! In Britain, the speakers added, Michael Scott and Creech Jones were standing up for Africans, but Creech Jones was now languishing in jail at Churchill's orders —a characteristic interpretation of the 'in' and 'out' involved in a Parliamentary two-party system. Lastly, bloodstained Banyama myths arose in new dress, and Federation was linked to dark terrors. Stories went round of vampire men who abducted Africans to suck their blood, a modern version of the creed asserting that the vampires' unfortunate victims lost their will power and supported Federation. Unusual events became the subject of fear ridden rumours, and when a soap company gave away free samples, Africans would throw their soap away, fearing that it would make them support Federation. Other tales asserted that Welensky had ordered the Africans' sugar to be poisoned, so that African women might miscarry and African men became impotent. From sugar the rumours turned to meat, and certain tins became suspected of containing human flesh, poisoned to break the African opposition to Federation. A District Commissioner on the Copper Belt then held a public meat eating demonstration in which he and his senior African clerk sampled some of the suspected food, but the audience merely concluded that the 'D.C.' possessed some strong medicine to resist the poison, and their fears continued unabated. Other frightening rumours concerned the broadcasting staff; and when Lusaka Station supported Federation, the station's green van became suspected of serving as the vampire men's motor transport. Real or supposed opponents of Federation were threatened; two African broadcasters received menacing letters telling them they would be poisoned; and an African headmaster who wrote a paper defending Federation had to be given police protection. Suspicion stalked the land; and Federation to many became a magical word of evil, which embodied the white man's supposed iniquities.

In the meantime, however, the Conservative Government in Britain decided to go ahead. From 1952 onwards the Administration tried to persuade Africans of the advantages of the Federation, and the district officers' efforts were supported by Henry Lennox D'Aubignee Hopkinson, Minister of State at the Colonial Office, who visited Northern Rhodesia. In the struggle for African public opinion, official counter-propaganda, thin-blooded, tight-lipped and dull, was quite ineffective. Some civil servants like Sir Geoffrey Colby, the Governor of Nyasaland, showed little enthusiasm for the new scheme; and in any case District Commissioners using polite understatements were hardly the kind of people to rouse African town workers or villagers, even had they been allowed to employ genuinely popular demagogy of the hot-dog selling and Billingsgate variety! Some of the European broadcasting staff opposed Federation, whilst the settlers lacked any kind of machinery to put their views across to Africans, the Provincial Administration remaining the officials' undisputed stronghold, whatever inroads the Europeans might make on the central agencies at Lusaka. The federalists moreover lacked imagination and allowed themselves to be driven on the propagandist defensive. What they needed was a simple and convincing slogan, embodying a genuine concession to the masses, perhaps something like 'Federation ends the native tax', but the abolition of direct African imposts as a possible *quid pro quo* for Federation would have raised serious political and financial questions, awkward to face at a critical period. The federalists moreover required an army of well-paid African agents, ready to oppose Congress speakers at village meetings, and harangue the people in their own language, using terms which they understood. They needed wagonloads of cheap and attractive reading material, in order to appeal to a semi-literate people, thirsting for the written word, but though Welensky himself had some inkling of the problem, the federalists as a whole lacked alike the minds, the men and the means for a propagandistic onslaught of such magnitude. The Conservative Government in Britain failed to understand the importance of the publicity aspect, and Hopkinson concluded that the great majority of Africans neither knew nor cared about Federation. Of those who were interested, the majority were under the influence of Congress and had not studied the details, their reasons for rejection often having no connexion with the scheme, a perfectly correct assessment, but one quite irrelevant to the problem in hand.

In the face of local opposition the Conservatives decided that the scheme was nevertheless satisfactory, and that the growth of aggressive African nationalism simply increased the urgency of obtaining a decision. They believed that the safeguards were adequate, whilst the Central Government would retain effective powers to deal with the major economic problems of the area. The Conservatives also considered possible objections from Africans in other parts of the Continent, but concluded that these were not worth worrying about. In West Africa the politically passive majority were not interested. The active minority would probably denounce the scheme, but the security situation would not be seriously affected. In East Africa the bulk of African opinion would likewise remain indifferent to events outside their own area, though a minority would oppose the project. If the Imperial Government went ahead, it would provide proof of its determination to carry out its stated intentions and do the best for the people in its charge, regardless of politically immature opposition. Such a policy would have a stabilizing effect, whereas African nationalists would only gather new courage if the scheme were dropped. South African repercussions might be of a different kind. A decision not to proceed would certainly be looked upon as weakness. South Africans might of course clamour that if the British over-rode African opposition north of the Zambezi, they should also do so in the case of the High Commission territories, and hand these over to the Union. But Britain could always point out that under Federation her control over Northern Rhodesia and Nyasaland would continue, which would not be true, if Swaziland, Basutoland or Bechuanaland passed under Pretoria's control. In Britain itself organizations like the Church of Scotland, the Fabian Society and the Africa Bureau were carrying out a hostile campaign, but these bodies were said to be scarcely open to argument, and could only be won over by the success of the scheme. Finally there was the security problem in Central Africa itself. The country might see some organized resistance in the shape of strikes in Government and other services, non-co-operation, passive resistance or threats of Mau Mau type of activity. But if trouble came, there was a good chance that it would only be of short duration. Once Africans understood that the Government could not be intimidated, respect for the authorities would grow, and Africans would be won over. The chiefs were expected to abstain from disorders, particularly if the situation were firmly handled. But if the project were dropped at this stage, Congress would gain prestige; the whites would be disheartened, race relations would deteriorate, and the eventual conflict would be greater than if Federation were imposed. Admittedly there was virtually no African support for the scheme, but the Federation offered the last chance in Africa for a policy of co-operation between the races. If the Government retreated now, the days of British administration in Africa would surely be numbered, and Southern Rhodesia would probably join South Africa.

In January 1953 a final Conference took place between the four Governments, and a number of last-minute changes were made in the constitution.[1] Then the legal machine rolled into action. In Southern Rhodesia the matter was decided by a referendum from a predominantly white electorate. The isolationists, supported by a large bloc of European artisans, minor employees and small farmers, rallied in considerable strength, the Referendum reproducing an inter-white class cleavage similar to the split which divided the Colony in 1922, at the time of the Union referendum. The poorer strata once more tended to vote for Southern Rhodesian autonomy, whilst the wealthier groups, which supported Smuts and Union in the early 'twenties, now cast their votes for Federation and a limited measure of African advancement. Huggins himself threw all his great personal abilities behind the Federation campaign, arguing that, whilst the original danger arose from the possibility of an Afrikaner majority on the Northern Rhodesian Legislative Council, matters now became even more urgent owing to the rise of African nationalism in the north which in a few years' time would make the scheme impossible. To some extent the Referendum also showed the division between the mass of recent immigrants from the United Kingdom and the older Rhodesians, most of the newcomers voting in favour, whilst old established Rhodesians were split. Another political cleavage followed linguistic lines, a large proportion of Afrikaans-speaking Rhodesians opposing Federation in the south, whereas they generally supported the scheme on the other side of the Zambezi. European liberals, including many Churchmen, gave their support to the project on the grounds that it would liberalize Southern Rhodesian native policies and assist the cause of African advancement, echoing Colonial Office views which envisaged Federation as a means of carrying Northern policies south of the Zambezi. In addition a certain proportion of European workers and clerks voted for the scheme, feeling confident of their

[1] *Southern Rhodesia, Northern Rhodesia and Nyasaland: Report by the conference on federation held in London in January, 1953.* (Cmd. 8753: 1953) and *Southern Rhodesia, Northern Rhodesia and Nyasaland. The federal scheme . . .* (Cmd. 8754: 1953)

abilities to withstand African competition in an expanding economy, the country no longer being weighed down by a great bloc of 'poor whites' anxious to prevent African encroachments into the lower ranks of industry. Finally Huggins appealed to businessmen and industrialists; Southern Rhodesia was admittedly pulling ahead very fast, but now the very speed of its development was creating difficulties. The Dollar crisis caused a general shortage of investment funds; credit facilities were scarce; confidence was waning; profits were falling in relation to turnover, and merchants found that they bought too much stock at exaggeratedly high prices; Federation was expected to give a boost to public confidence and provide new capital, a hope which proved justified in practice. The Southern Rhodesians approved of the proposals by 25,570 votes to 14,729, and the ball rolled into the northern pitch. The Nyasaland Legislature adopted the scheme against African and Asian opposition, whilst the Northern Rhodesian Legislative Council voted in favour by 17 votes to 4, both the African and the European Members representing African Interests remaining in opposition.[1]

Whilst the pros and cons of Federation were being argued in the Council Chamber the campaign continued in mine compounds and little villages, where Congress and their supporters made a last minute attempt to prevent the scheme. Government made no attempt to smash the Congress cadres, though Simon Ber Zukas, a European Congress supporter of extreme left-wing views was deported, the Attorney General arguing that this step was necessary, not because Zukas was a Communist, but because he threatened the public peace.[2] The anti-Federation campaign, however, proved a complete failure, African opposition actually turning out to be smaller in scale than the authorities envisaged. As far as left-wing European opposition to the scheme was concerned, both Zukas and Commander Thomas Stanley Lane Fox-Pitt, an anti-federationist of more moderate views, showed little grasp of political strategy. Their open adherence to the Congress cause simply helped to persuade the authorities that African opposition was to some extent inspired from without, and senior civil servants never tired of showing that many Congress memoranda presented against Federation were obviously 'ghosted', and that African speakers presenting their case to Government did not always understand the meaning of the terms or the arguments used. Zukas and Fox-Pitt would have played their cards better by keeping their Congress contacts underground; and Zukas made the additional mistake of committing his views on revolutionary socialism to paper; both could probably have wielded much more influence by confining their overt activities to missionary circles, and to the powerful white settler community, organizing their campaign on ostensibly 'loyalist' lines, appealing to white Northern Rhodesians on grounds of economic self-interest, and following Moore's original line that their country should not tie itself to Salisbury's apron strings. On the African side Congress was able to wield a considerable influence

---

[1] Northern Rhodesia. *Legislative Council debates*, 17 and 18 Apr 1953, p. 27–142
[2] For details of the deportation proceedings and the officials' arguments, see *Northern news*, 5 Apr 1952

on black public opinion, Congress propaganda making some impact even on people who did not agree with its views in any other respects. But Congress showed little capacity for effective action, a weakness which in part arose from its loose and decentralized system of administration. Throughout Northern Rhodesia the various branches retained a good deal of independence, the Provincial Executives owing their election to meetings of District Organizing Secretaries, Branch Organizing Secretaries and Branch officials, with the result that central control remained limited.[1] Congress was divided over the question of tactics, and its general strategy remained ineffective. Threats were made that the movement would organize a general exodus of black workers from the towns back to the reserves to paralyze the economy, but a move of that magnitude was beyond the party's limited capacity. Even if Congress had been able to organize such a migration the reserves could no longer have stood the strain; and the move would have made impossible demands on African workers, who complained that Congress asked them to leave their jobs, but could not pay their wages. Congress moreover failed to consolidate its influence over the industrial labourers, especially the miners, Congress hold remaining strongest in the general municipal compounds, with their floating population of general workers, hawkers and odd-job men, whilst the miners supported their own trade union.[2] In 1953 Nkumbula tried to organize a 'Two Day National Prayer', a kind of political general strike, but the 'prayer' was a resounding failure. Katilungu, the black miners' leader, stated that he privately supported the move, but that the Union machinery should not be used in its support, with the result that only Mufulira was affected, work continuing quite normally at Kitwe, Chingola, Luanshya, Ndola and Broken Hill. The Secretary of the African General Workers' Union advised members not to work, and so did the President of the Railway Workers' Union, but the railways continued normally, and most of the African civil servants stayed at work. Federation accordingly went through without serious opposition, and none of its expected dire consequences materialized. There was no rapid influx of white farmers; tribal lands stayed in African ownership; the routine of district administration continued; and Congress for a time suffered a severe loss of prestige, remaining at loggerheads with the Mine Workers' Union, whilst existing differences between Congress organizers and chiefs flared up once more.

The Federation issue as a whole was closely interlocked with the question of partnership, which became the federationists main slogan, and which merits a short digression. In the 'thirties Gore-Browne used the term to justify a semi-segregationist solution. Matters remained in abeyance for a time, but after the

[1] In 1953 a Provincial Conference was held in the vital Tonga area. Members included 21 chiefs, 4 officials from the Central organization, 13 invited members, including Native Authority Councillors and heads of farmers' and traders' organizations, as well as 23 Provincial officials and 58 branch delegates—two from each branch. Subsequently the District Organizing Secretaries, Branch Organizing Secretaries and Branch officials met privately, the other delegates and chiefs leaving. The meeting then elected the Provincial Executive Committee.

[2] See Epstein, A. L. *Politics in an urban African community.* Manchester university press, 1958

War the issue once more came to the forefront, when a meeting of educated Africans at Kitwe denounced white Responsible Government proposals on the grounds that African interests would cease to be paramount. Welensky quickly asked for a clarification, and in 1945 Government accepted a Motion in the Council which stated that the interests of whites and blacks were interlocked, and that a policy of subordinating the interests of one section of the community to those of another would be fatal to the country.[1] The local authorities stuck to this interpretation, whilst the Labour Government gave a public assurance that it would adhere to the views of the Joint Select Committee of Parliament which in 1931 abandoned the 'native paramountcy' doctrine. The Imperial authorities accepted in full a Statement made by the Secretary for Native Affairs to the African Representative Council in 1948, reiterating Government's determination not to subordinate the interests of one community to those of another.[2] Creech Jones instead advocated the merits of partnership, with the result that the Northern Rhodesian Unofficials asked for a definition, complaining that intelligent Africans still believed that the whites would only stay in the country until the blacks attained a majority, whereupon the Europeans would gracefully retire.[3] The Secretary of State's reply rather hedged the issue, but agreed that the Governor should work out a statement on partnership in co-operation with European and African Unofficials. A concerted definition however, was difficult to get, for Welensky now spoke in terms of 'senior' and 'junior' partners, whilst many Africans mistakenly asserted that Government had surreptitiously introduced a major policy change, and brought in partnership by some sleight of hand to speed on Federation and subvert black paramountcy. In 1951 the position began to look a little more hopeful when the representative for African Interests at the Victoria Falls Conference stated that Africans would be willing to consider Federation, once the policy of partnership was defined and put into progressive operation. The African representatives thought they acquired a bargaining counter for domestic reform, but their pronouncement produced a bitter reaction from other black politicians, and a joint conference of Members of the African Urban Advisory Councils of the Copper Belt, as well as delegates from trade unions and from the African National Congress, strongly denounced both partnership and the Victoria Falls statement. The delegates held that partnership was incompatible with Protectorate status, that it would endanger African rights, that it was just a sop to Africans to get them to accept Federation, that it implied racial representation incompatible with majority rule, that it would lessen control over immigration, and stand in the way of independence within the Commonwealth. The African Representative Council took a similar line and declared itself unwilling to take part in preliminary discussions to define partnership, but asked for a Government statement to be referred for discussion

[1] Northern Rhodesia. *Legislative Council debates*, 4 July 1945, p. 230–247
[2] Northern Rhodesia. *Legislative Council debates*, 22 June 1949, p. 1–2
[3] Northern Rhodesia. *Legislative Council debates*, 19 June 1950, p. 366–401; and 22 June 1950, p. 532–538

to various African bodies, the Council remaining irreconciliably opposed to Federation—convinced apparently that participation in talks would commit them to the scheme. In 1952 the Government then issued a draft policy which tried to please everybody. Partnership implied mutual regard for the other's outlook, beliefs, customs and legitimate aspirations and anxieties. In the economic sphere every individual should be able to rise to the level which qualifications, abilities and character permitted; Africans must be helped to advance, and discriminatory practices were incompatible with partnership. But no attempt was made to define standards, the only 'hard' promise of any kind appearing in the political sphere, where Government aimed at ultimate parity; Africans would increase their representation until they had reached the same number as Europeans, both in the Legislative and Executive Councils, this arrangement being designed to last until representation on racial grounds disappeared.[1]

The federal constitution likewise contained a vaguely worded preamble, put in under Imperial pressure, which asserted that the new state should foster partnership and co-operation between the two races, but no one agreed on how exactly this should be done. Welensky put forward an 'assimilationist' pro- gramme which demanded that Africans should rise to the European level, a considerable change from his earlier views in his engine-driving days, but completely unacceptable to most African nationalists who believed in African domination without strings. Throughout the Federation campaign Africans in the Northern territories thus steered well clear of 'partnership' which to many became a bone of contention more than an unifying bond, 'a woolly term . . . interpreted in an astonishing number of different ways',[2] which most Europeans regarded as a confirmation of their status, whilst their opponents soon interpreted it either as 'eyewash', or else as a broken promise of black majority rule and full integration.

[1] *East Africa and Rhodesia*, v. 28, no. 1436, 17 Apr 1952

[2] J. S. Moffat in Northern Rhodesia. *Legislative Council debates*, 29 July 1954, p. 617. In 1954 a further attempt was made to paper over the cracks by a resolution which stated that Northern Rhodesia should not be dominated by either one race or the other; that ultimately a racial franchise should disappear, that special arrangements should remain during the interim period to prevent racial predominance, that the Secretary of State should hold the balance during this transition period, and that every lawful inhabitant should be allowed to progress in accordance with his abilities, a definition which was as acceptable to the advocate of universal franchise, as well as to the advocate of the most highly 'loaded' property and income qualification franchise on the European side. See Northern Rhodesia. *Legislative Council debates*, 29 July 1954, p. 616–668

IV

Federation accomplished

Whilst partnership controversies continued, the new ship of state was finally launched. In 1953 the British Parliament passed an Act permitting the Queen-in-Council to provide for a Federal Constitution; and in August the required Order-in-Council passed on to the Statute Book, and was progressively put into operation later on in the year.[1] As far as Northern Rhodesia was concerned, Government now rested on a triangle of power whose three points rested on Salisbury, London and Lusaka. The architects of Federation regarded their handiwork as a permanent feature on the African political scene. The Constitution made no provision for the right of secession on the part of individual territories, an arrangement which would only have undermined the confidence of investors willing to loan money to the new state, or of civil servants intent on joining the new administration, Imperial negotiators themselves stressing that no federal constitution in any Western country permitted of its own dissolution. The Federal Government controlled the main economic functions including most kinds of banking, a large range of commercial matters, customs, currency and company legislation, immigration and citizenship, as well as transport and communications, including railways, aviation, posts, telegraphs and telephones. Subject to certain reservations, the Federal Government held the powers of the purse; taxes on income and profits appearing on the 'Federal Legislative List', though the territories retained certain financial rights, remaining entitled to a territorial surcharge, and to specified deductions from income and profit taxes. More important still, the Federation controlled its own defence, so that all local military and air forces were now commanded from Salisbury. But police, much to Huggins's disgust, remained a territorial matter, so that effective control of public security remained with the Territories. As a compromise, the Federal authorities received the right to set up an additional police force which could, however, only be used at the request of the territories and under their governors' operational control; this force in fact was never raised. Native affairs, and various related services like African education and agriculture, remained with the territories, a division of powers which assumed that matters affecting black people could be neatly parcelled off from other administrative functions, a point of view fundamentally segregationist in concept, and productive of many administrative anomalies. The Federal authorities controlled higher education, as well as schools for Europeans, Coloureds and Asians, whilst the territories

---

[1] The Federation of Rhodesia and Nyasaland (constitution) order in council, 1953; the Federation of Rhodesia and Nyasaland (commencement) order in council, 1953. See also Royal instructions to the Governor-general and commander in chief of the Federation of Rhodesia and Nyasaland: 1 Aug 1953

continued to be responsible for African pupils. The Federal Ministry of Agriculture soon took over various technical services, but native agriculture remained a territorial matter. Labour and trade union affairs stayed with the territories, though the Federal Government remained responsible for subjects like railways whose running was intimately affected by labour questions. The Federal authorities, on the other hand, controlled a fairly large range of specialist services, considered to be 'harmless' from the political point of view, including health, and functions like meteorology, archives and statistics. Legally, this division was embodied in two separate Legislative Lists, one of which comprised matters on which the Federal Legislature alone could make laws, whilst a 'Concurrent Legislative List' dealt with subjects like development of industries and co-operatives, road traffic, electricity, research, prisons and deportations, security information, surveys and other subjects, on which both the Federal Assembly and the Territorial Legislatures might pass laws.[1]

The composition of the Federal Legislature was likewise an elaborate compromise, uneasily combining the British tradition of Cabinet government and the elective principle with special representation, the system being weighted to keep power within the hands of the propertied and educated strata, whilst at the same time providing some special safeguards for Africans. The Federal House consisted of a Speaker and thirty-five members. The main body consisted of 26 ordinary elected members, comprising 14 from Southern Rhodesia, 8 from Northern Rhodesia and 4 from Nyasaland. The Federal Assembly was empowered to define voting qualifications by a two thirds majority and subject to reservation for the Queen's pleasure. But the first elections were held on the existing franchise laws in Northern Rhodesia and Southern Rhodesia, special provisions obtaining in the case of Nyasaland. This meant that voting qualifications would be on non-racial lines, though in practice the overwhelming majority of voters would consist of Europeans, since the high territorial qualifications excluded most Africans, though they enfranchised the Indian minority. In addition the Constitution provided for six African members, two from each territory, the four Northern Members in practice being elected by the African Representative Council of Northern Rhodesia and the African Protectorate Council in Nyasaland, the two Southern Rhodesians being elected from the common roll. Lastly three European members charged with special responsibilities for Africans took their seat in the Assembly. The Federal Assembly could legislate on a constitutionally limited range of subjects, but Bills had to receive the approval of the Governor General, who alternatively might reserve them for the signification of Her Majesty's pleasure. The Queen remained in a position to disallow any law of the Federal Legislature assented to by the Governor-General, within twelve months of its having passed. In addition the Constitution contained special safeguards with regard to constitutional amend-

---

[1] For the full distribution of administrative powers, see the Constitution of the Federation of Rhodesia and Nyasaland, annex. to the Federation of Rhodesia and Nyasaland (constitution) order in council, 1953, second schedule parts I and II

ments, which required a two-thirds majority as well as the Queen's assent. Her Majesty's consent to a constitutional Bill had furthermore to be signified by Order-in-Council if one of the Territorial Legislatures objected to a Bill, or if requested by the African Affairs Board on the grounds that it was a racially differentiating measure. The African Affairs Board, as finally provided for under the Constitution, was a Standing Committee of the House, and was designed to scrutinize legislation for any differentiating measures, though the Board could not itself veto such legislation. The Constitution moreover set up a Federal Supreme Court, as well as making provision for a Federal Civil Service which was designed to be locally based, and distinct from the existing administrative machinery in the three territories.

The Federal Constitution, with its checks and balances, thus turned out to be a complicated instrument, so difficult to understand that few European electors— not to speak of Africans—would have been able to describe it in reasonably accurate fashion. This turned out to be a serious, though a rarely recognized weakness for an instrument designed to ensure parliamentary government through an instructed electorate. Internally the Constitution in some ways mirrored the position in Northern Rhodesia.[1] The Federal Assembly was responsible for a large range of subjects which either directly concerned the Europeans or were of an economic nature; in Northern Rhodesia European elected members wielded responsibility for groups of departments on a roughly similar basis. Elected members dominated the Federal Assembly, as did the Unofficials in the Northern Rhodesian Legislature, with the difference that the voting strength of the Federal elected members was much greater than the strength of Elected Members in the Northern Rhodesian Legislative Council. African Affairs remained with the Imperial authorities, though Federation shattered the Northern Rhodesian Africans' hope that Northern Rhodesia would become a black state, like the Gold Coast. But neither did the Europeans gain all they wanted. The elected members were returned on a non-racial basis, so that the growth of an African bourgeoisie or a black 'labour aristocracy' was bound slowly to reverse the political balance of power. In addition the distribution of functions was so complicated, that any really serious conflicts between Territories and Federation was liable to bring the whole machinery grinding to a halt, a possibility not apparently foreseen at the time. The new Federal Government found itself largely excluded from legislating on African subjects, a restriction on its powers designed to prevent oppression, but also one that made it difficult for the federal authorities to expand services for Africans and thus gain their confidence, the federal authorities frequently receiving blame for sins of omission or commission for which they were not constitutionally responsible. Federation lastly disappointed the hopes of such white Southern Rhodesians as believed that their country should attain Dominion status, the new state thus resting on an uneasy equilibrium of opposing forces, and a

[1] Clegg, E. *Race and politics: partnership in the Federation of Rhodesia and Nyasaland.* Oxford university press, 1960, p. 182

somewhat artificial distribution of functions which might make sense to political men, but not necessarily to administrators charged with working the machine in practice. But though many problems remained, the constitution-makers believed that these might be solved in time; and the Constitution thus provided for subsequent review conference, to be convened between seven or nine years of the Constitution's coming into force. Both white and black political men thus put their hopes in a future revision, to be negotiated with the Imperial Government in London, which meant that an extra element of instability was built into the very foundations of government.

Political organization in the new state now operated on two levels, the federal and the territorial. The United Central Africa Association dissolved, and a Committee was set up, containing Huggins, Welensky, Barrow and several others who built up the Federal Party. Huggins formed the Federation's first government in which Welensky assumed the key post of Minister for Transport, Communications and Posts, Welensky shying away from the Ministry of Finance on the grounds that this might worry 'the City' whom he had given such a fright over the Chartered royalties question. The new Party agreed on a compromise statement concerning racial partnership which asserted that Europeans and Africans had distinctive and complementary roles to play, that each should be rewarded according to his contributions to partnership, that the races naturally wished to develop on traditional lines, and that this would have to be borne in mind in the provision of facilities and amenities, as long as existing wide differences in the cultural levels of the mass of the people continued. At the same time the statement foresaw the gradual extension of political rights and privileges to those who conformed to civilized standards of behaviour and culture. As more Africans would reach full political privileges, special political representation would disappear, the ultimate idea of the federals being a society in which the emergent African middle class would be fully 'built into' the European structure. In the first federal elections in 1953, the new Party won a sweeping victory.[1] The segregationist Confederate Party obtained only a single seat in the new Federal Assembly, the Confederates securing just under one-third of all the votes cast over the Federation as a whole, though attracting very few votes north of the Zambezi.

The Federal Constitution still left major powers in the hands of the territories, and the struggle for local control thus continued with undiminished heat. The Europeans pressed for further constitutional advances, with the result that the Africans also stepped up their demands at a time when the federal talks were still going on. The Imperial authorities then postponed further discussions until

---

[1] Out of a total number of registered voters of 67,039, 48,719 voters went to the polls, giving a percentage of 73·83, the Nyasaland votes not being included in the overall figures. In Southern Rhodesia 39,934 cast their votes out of 50,474. In Northern Rhodesia there were 15,507 voters, but only 9,795 cast their votes. In the two Rhodesias the Federal Party obtained 32,582 votes and the Confederates 15,234. Independents polled 1,658. In Southern Rhodesia the Federals' vote amounted to 25,527 and the Confederates 13,376. In Northern Rhodesia the Federals polled 7,055 and the Confederates 1,858.

A HISTORY OF NORTHERN RHODESIA

that vexed question was settled, but later the Europeans returned to the attack. In September 1953 Welensky and Beckett demanded two more Elected Seats on the Legislature, as well as an additional portfolio, but in return they were willing to concede a portfolio for the European Member nominated to represent African Interests. They were prepared to accept two more African members in the Legislature, provided that one of the Nominated European Members representing African Interests was withdrawn, so that in fact the Africans would only gain one member as compared to the Europeans' two. They also proposed a reduction of Official Members on the Legislature, as well as parity for the Unofficials on the Executive Council. The Africans then in turn put up their price, and held out at first for an African majority on the Legislature, and three African Members on the Executive Council, where the Europeans should only retain one member and lose their two portfolios, the Africans' strategy in white opinion following the line that in order to get a minnow it was best to ask for a whale! Subsequently they agreed to scale down their demand to parity with the Europeans, whilst also asking that qualified British Protected Persons should be allowed to vote, a move designed to bring them on the common voters roll. In the end the Secretary of State put up a compromise solution which would increase the number of Elected Members from ten to twelve and the number of African members from two to four. In the Executive Council, all members were to hold portfolios, including the Member Representing African Interests as well as the third European member who hitherto lacked executive responsibilities.

Welensky and Beckett, however, regarded this proposal as appeasement and determined to resist. Welensky at first thought of resigning from federal politics and waging an all-out political campaign, even envisaging political strikes, a serious threat in view of the white mineworkers' and railwaymen's strategic key position in the country. The Secretary of State, however, would not yield, and subsequently Welensky was persuaded to abstain from leaving the Interim Government, a course of action which might have endangered the federal state from the start, Welensky's personal loyalty to Huggins and to Federation as a whole playing a major part in his decision. European opposition, hampered by Welensky's federal commitment, thus took a relatively mild form. The European Elected Members resigned from all official bodies, including the Executive Council, but Lyttelton managed to pour oil on troubled waters by promising to visit the territory in person, and not to make any changes in the franchise for the next five years. In the end a temporary solution was effected by means of a new Order in Council. The Legislative Council now consisted of a Speaker, eight official, and eighteen Unofficial Members. The Unofficials in turn were split into twelve Elected Members and six Unofficial Members to Represent African Interests, of whom four were selected for appointment by the African Representative Council. The Northern Rhodesian whites failed to control the Legislature where the balance of power remained in official hands. The Executive Council likewise remained a Government stronghold, the officials holding five seats as against the Unofficials' four, one of the Unofficials being a Nominated Member to Represent African Interests.

In 1954 the first elections took place under the new constitution. The divisional Congress of the Federal Party decided to fight the campaign itself, and a committee was set up for the purpose under Beckett, the Party's territorial leader. Beckett originally favoured a 'best man' team and a non-party election, but he now explained that conditions had altered, whilst Guillaume François Marais van Eeden, an Afrikaans-speaking farmer and an influential supporter of the Federal party, argued that the party should fight as a solid phalanx to keep out the Confederates and form a cohesive force on the Legislative Council, able to hold its own against the Officials. The Federals demanded the maintenance of franchise rights for all British subjects irrespective of colour, provided they conformed to 'civilized standards', the placing of European agriculture under the federal authority, the convertibility of Crown leasehold title into freehold title, the admission of more Rhodesians to the public service, and they also suggested the appointment of an impartial commission to investigate African claims to industrial advancement. The elections were held early in 1954 and resulted in a resounding victory for the Federals who gained ten out of twelve seats, Welensky's name playing a decisive part, whilst the Federals managed to hold the loyalty both of the urban voters and of the farmers, including most Afrikaners. On the Copper Belt independent white trade unionists put up their own candidates, pledged to prevent the dilution of labour, but they were all beaten, the elections thus marking a swing towards the political centre, and away from the Rhodesian 'right'. Beckett did not get into the Council again, and Herbert John Roberts, a progressive farmer of English descent, assumed leadership of the Elected Members, acting as Welensky's principal lieutenant in the Northern Rhodesian field. The Africans, for their part, now commanded a small bloc of their own, their debating strength being greatly reinforced by Henry Franklin, a former Director of Information with wide experience, and by John Smith Moffat (later knighted), a descendant of a Rhodesian missionary family with liberal views, who reached high office in the Northern Rhodesian administration before settling down to farming, and who previously played a major part in fighting for African interests on the Legislative Council. The Barotse finally received further specific recognition of their special status through a separate Order in Council which officially styled their country the 'Barotseland Protectorate':[1] and whilst the territory continued to remain part of Northern Rhodesia, the change in nomenclature at any rate went some way towards meeting the Barotse's misgivings with regard to the drift of events in Central Africa.

[1] Northern Rhodesia (Barotseland) order in council, 1953

V

Northern Rhodesia in the early 'fifties

A septuagenarian Ngoni looking back to the tribal past from the early 'fifties would have seen changes within his own lifetime that would have seemed childish fairy tales to the warriors that rallied to fight the white men in the Ngoni war of 1898. A veteran from those days would probably have found himself reasonably at ease amongst the ancient Teutons, as described in somewhat rosy colours by Tacitus. True enough, horses and iron helmets were never used by the Ngoni, but Mpeseni's people would have looked down upon the Aestyans, of whom Tacitus wrote that they knew no iron, and only had clubs to batter their enemies' skulls. An old Ngoni would have seen nothing peculiar in a people who 'in cultivating the soil . . . do not settle on one spot, but shift from place to place. The state or community takes possession of certain tracts proportioned to its numbers; allotments are afterwards made to individuals according to their rank and dignity. In so extensive a country where there is no want of land, the partition is easily made. The ground is tilled one year, lies fallow the next, and a sufficient quantity remains . . .' An Ngoni warrior would likewise have approved of a people who liked their beer as much as the Germans and would have been perfectly happy to stay in one of their huts, built without mortar or tiles in such a fashion that 'particular parts are covered with a kind of earth so smooth and shining that the natural veins have some resemblance to the lights and shades of painting'. In Teutonic, as in ancient Ngoni society, 'the field of danger is the field of glory. Without violence and rapine, a train of dependents cannot be maintained. The chief must show his liberality, and the follower expects it. . . . The prince's table, however inelegant, must always be plentiful: it is the only pay of his followers . . .', Teuton, like Bantu tribesmen having no alternative way of investing their wealth. The Ngoni would similarly see nothing wrong in a way of life where the men concentrated on politics, war and hunting and where 'the management of his house and land he leaves to the women, to the old men, and to the infirm part of his family', though Tacitus, like later missionary writers in Africa, may perhaps have overestimated the barbarians' sloth. The Ngoni method of fighting would have recommended itself to Germanic warriors, whilst an Ngoni visitor to the lands of the Teutons would not have been surprised by the Northerners' marriage customs, of which Tacitus wrote with astonishment that 'the bride brings no portion; she receives a dowry from her husband'; neither would an Ngoni have found anything noteworthy in the Teutonic idea that 'a numerous train of relatives is the comfort and honour of old age'. Admittedly these parallels should not be pushed too far; the Ngoni would not have shared the Teutons' characteristically 'Western' kinship system, whereby a man rarely had more than one wife, whilst the

Teutonic law of inheritance did not correspond to Ngoni concepts in that either maternal or paternal uncles would stand next in line of succession, if a man had no sons or brothers to succeed him.[1] But by and large an Ngoni born about 1870, whose son might have become perhaps a factory worker in Bulawayo, a Congress organizer on the Copper Belt, a sergeant in the Northern Rhodesia Regiment or a teacher at Munali, had in his own lifetime been catapulted right from the days of Tacitus to an era of mass democracy, and of great industrial, political and social, military and ideological revolutions that had taken Europeans hundreds of years to produce and digest.

The new society was created in the first place by European immigrants who leavened the lump. White men at the same time occupied the top of the social pyramid. By 1951 there were 37,097 Europeans in the country, whose rapid but erratic growth of numbers was mainly attributable to immigration, with the result that European society displayed the characteristics typical of settler communities in other parts of the world.[2] For long Northern Rhodesia remained a man's country, where women were in short supply, and government doctors complained that bringing out nurses to work in local hospitals was almost like running a marriage bureau! All the same, the number of women was rising;[3] and many children were born. As the youngsters got older, many of them left the territory to go to school elsewhere; but above their age group there was a 'bulge' of people in their prime of life, the age-pyramid sharply narrowing at the top, though the number of old people increased considerably from earlier days, when Rhodesia was a land without grandparents.[4]

[1] See Tacitus 'A Treatise on the Situation, Manners and People of Germany' (in Blakeney, E. H., ed. *The history, Germania and Agricola*, translated by A. Murray. Dent & Sons, p. 321–328)

[2] Between 1921 and 1931, during a period of general prosperity, the excess of births over deaths amounted to about 790 people, whilst net immigration added about 9,420 to the recorded increase. Then came the depression, and later on the War, with the result that between 1931 and 1946 the white population only grew by 8,061 persons, the natural increase of the population was 4,788, the remaining growth being largely accounted for by the temporary influx of some 3,000 Polish refugees. Between 1931 and 1946 over 27,000 immigrants were admitted to the territory, but these were offset by an almost equally large number of emigrants. During the boom years, between 1946 and 1951, the European population increased by approximately 15,200. Nearly 3,300 of these reflected the excess of births over deaths and the remaining 12,000 the net migration movement. Gross European immigration was about 26,300 persons so that emigration must have amounted to about 14,300, including some 3,000 Poles. These and other figures are drawn from Northern Rhodesia. *Report on the census of population, 1951.* Lusaka, Government printer, 1954, and previous census reports.

[3] The proportion of European women per thousand men rose as follows: 1911—335; 1921—605; 1931—580; 1946—943; 1951—847; the slight drop between 1946 and 1951 being partly attributable to the presence of Polish evacuees who mostly consisted of women and girls.

[4] The following provides comparative figures of age distribution. The figures refer to proportion per 1,000 persons:

	1931	1946	1951
0– 4	91	120	137
5– 9	72	99	107
10–14	50	73	71
15–19	54	61	44
20–24	119	77	79
25–29	159	87	113
30–34	112	105	109

Most of the whites in the country were townsmen, living on the Copper Belt, the country's urban population having risen much more quickly than the people living in scattered small villages, in isolated farms, government or mission stations.[1] Many immigrants brought their wives with them; others married on the spot, with the result that the country's relatively youthful population could boast of one of the highest proportion of wedded people in the world.[2] The typical Northern Rhodesian was now a family man, the country's birth rate remained high; cots, highchairs and prams rarely found their way into the lumber room, but quickly changed hands, as some other couple about to start a family picked them up secondhand from people whose children had got beyond the 'nappy' stage, the high birth rate sharply differentiating Northern Rhodesia's European community from older countries overseas with their much slighter rates of increase, and influencing perhaps the whole psychological outlook of the European community.[3] At the same time Northern Rhodesia was faced with a serious divorce problem, the high rate of marriage casualties probably being linked to the young immigrants' loss of home and family ties.

As far as the residential stability of the European population was concerned, generalizations are difficult. White Northern Rhodesia still possessed an air of impermanence lacking south of the Zambezi, where the majority of immigrants came to stay, and where most civil servants looked on their country as 'home' like their white fellow citizens. On the other side of the river, however, most government officials, miners, managers and missionaries still regarded the territory only as a place to work; and even some of the farmers and shopkeepers, the most stable part of the community, looked towards Southern Rhodesia or further afield for a place to retire. But all the same the number of whites expecting to live in the Protectorate till their dying days appears to have been on the increase, even on the Copper Belt, where the proportion of houses owned by

	1931	1946	1951
35–39	95	105	104
40–44	73	84	84
45–49	64	58	55
50–54	53	45	33
55–59	31	32	22
60 and over	26	53	40

[1] The following are comparative figures for the Copper Belt and the remainder of the territory for the years 1931, 1946 and 1951 respectively;

Total for Copper Belt: 9,763; 16,053; 28,936;

Remainder of territory: 4,083; 5,854; 8,143;

The 1946 figures include 3,181 Polish evacuees

[2] In 1951 the proportions per thousand men were as follows, married men—478; widowed men 11; divorced 10. The comparative figures for England and Wales were 444; 37 and 1. The figures for women were as follows: 513 married women, 41 widowed women, 9 divorced women; the comparative figures for England and Wales were 413, 86 and 1.

[3] Between 1931 and 1951 the average Net Reproduction Rate, that is to say the rate at which the female population was growing in a generation, rose from 1·28 to 1·58. These figures assumed a constant rate of mortality, though in fact mortality dropped considerably, with the result that the natural rate of growth was even faster than suggested by these figures.

their occupier rose from only 5·4 per cent in 1946 to 8·2 per cent in 1951.[1] The settlers' national ancestry changed somewhat in character; there was a sharp rise in the number of people born in the two Rhodesias which in 1951 comprised a little under one fifth of the population, whilst not much less than half of the people were born in South Africa, and about a quarter came from the United Kingdom.[2] More than nine tenths of the people were born in British possessions and the percentage of foreigners was small, having further declined since the early pioneering days.[3] These figures however are a little deceptive; Rhodesia was certainly not becoming more 'English' in character; the proportion of people born in the United Kingdom actually dropped, whilst the proportion of Afrikaans-speaking people went up, the proportion of members of the Dutch Reformed Church, as good an index as any, rising from 15·4 in 1931 to 20·1 per thousand in 1951. If the foreign born are added to their number, one would probably be right in saying that about a quarter of the European whites did not speak English as their native language, the most substantial foreign born groups coming from Poland and Germany.

Most of these people were immigrants of comparitively recent standing, some three quarters of the white population in 1951 having lived in Northern Rhodesia for only five years or less. As far as the immigrants' religions were concerned, statisticians calculated that the Anglican Church was still the most numerous, though a decline had set in since earlier days, which was shared to a lesser extent by the Presbyterians, and also by the Jews, whose proportion of the population went down by nearly half from the early days, when many pioneers from Lithuania on the Baltic fled from Tsarist rule to seek new homes for themselves in South Africa and elsewhere, a trickle finding their way to the north,[4] where they set themselves up as traders. At the same time the Catholics maintained their proportion of about ten per cent of the population, whilst the Dutch

[1] See Northern Rhodesia. *Report on the census of population, 1951*, p. 29. The highest proportion of houses owned by their occupiers was to be found in Ndola Suburbs where 56·9 per cent of all houses were owned by the occupier, followed by Lusaka Suburbs with 54 per cent and Luanshya Government Township with 30 per cent. Some people of course just bought their houses as an investment, but the majority probably wanted them for their own permanent use.

[2] The comparative figures per thousand people for the years 1931 and 1951 respectively were as follows:

Northern Rhodesia	93	177
United Kingdom & Ireland	305	249
Union of South Africa	417	436
Southern Rhodesia	66	49
Total British possessions	919	943

[3] The following are comparative figures for 1931 and 1951 per thousand of the population:

Germany	8	8
Poland	4	11
U.S.A.	14	4
Other foreign countries	54	31
Total foreign countries	80	54

[4] Between 1911 and 1951 the proportion of Anglicans decreased from 408 per thousand to 372 per thousand; of Presbyterians, most of them probably of Scottish origins, from 127 to 101 and of Jews from 46 to 21. The Dutch Reformed Church went up from 168 to 201 per thousand.

Reformed, the Greek Orthodox and smaller sects registered a substantial increase in their proportions.

From the occupational point of view the largest proportion of white Northern Rhodesians continued to make their living in the mining industry, which attracted recruits from all walks of life, people as varied as local government officers or butchers joining the companies as gangers. All the same mining and quarrying dropped a little as a source of income since 1931, when more than one third of the 'economically active persons' were dependent for their living on the mines. Next on the list came services of various kinds, followed by manufacturing and construction, both of which expanded their proportion of people employed in their ranks. Agriculture employed less than one tenth of the white population, though the two decades between 1931 and 1951 saw a slight increase in the percentage of farmers.[1] Northern Rhodesia's white community thus comprised a large proportion of skilled workers in industry, mining and transport, who between them numbered 6,850 out of 16,694 'economically active' people; they were followed by a substantial bloc of white-collar workers numbering 4,643 persons, and a relatively strong contingent of professional men and technicians, numbering 2,548. The people who made their living in the open veld or bush as farmers, hunters and lumbermen only amounted to 1,244. The typical Northern Rhodesian thus earned his living in a town, and whereas his predecessor in the early days probably lived in a rough native-type hut or a tin shack, most likely with malaria parasites in his blood stream, but at home on the open veld, and accustomed to shooting 'for the pot', the new Rhodesian lived in a reasonably well built house with a radio; he could drive a car and probably knew all about repairing it, though he was generally ignorant of veld lore, knew little or nothing about African customs, and could not speak any indigenous tongue. This of course did not mean that he knew nothing about soldiering; he might have seen fighting of the fiercest kind in the Western Desert, on the beaches of Normandy and the jungles of Burma and he would probably have looked upon the Matabele War as a sideshow of little importance, but even his military experience was gained overseas rather than in the African bush. There was of course nothing surprising in all this. In the old days men used to cross the Zambezi in search of cheap land or cheap cattle, the traditional incentives on the South African frontier; but now high wages and salaries formed the magnet that drew immigrants to the Far North; and even in remote

[1] The following are the respective figures for economically active persons for 1921, 1931 and 1951 respectively per thousand:

	1921	1931	1951
Agriculture and forestry	338	73	80
Mining and quarrying	63	351	293
Manufacturing, construction, water and electricity, sanitary services	54	134	175
Transport and communications	145	100	92
Commerce and finance	122	110	127
Government, community and recreational services	232	141	209
Personal services	26	30	19
Other activities	20	61	5

little dorps in South Africa the Copper Belt was spoken of as a fabulous land where people might make a great deal of money. The Copper Belt in fact was now the 'Second Rand' of which Rhodes dreamt but never found, and Northern Rhodesia largely remained part of Southern Africa's mining frontier which had created Kimberly and Johannesburg, a large proportion of its immigrants being townsmen who went to new settlements, rather than displaced countrymen like the Afrikaners of an earlier generation, who glimpsed the city lights for the first time in Johannesburg. The Protectorate as a whole was now a major producer of wealth; copper shares formed an excellent investment, in a characteristically colonial economy, where prosperity depended largely on a single commodity, and a very high proportion of the country's national income went into the coffers of a few companies,[1] on whose prosperity in turn rested the whole of the country's financial and fiscal structure. Some of the white workers drew good wages, and some specialists had almost princely salaries. In addition the miners received a considerable copper bonus, which fluctuated a good deal from year to year. But nevertheless rumour, as spread across the bar at Klerksdorp, or in the leader pages of some British left wing journals, exaggerated the position, and Northern Rhodesia was certainly not a place where white settlers might pick up golden ducats in the streets. In 1951 only 69 people in the Protectorate earned more than £5,000 p.a., whilst the great majority of white Northern Rhodesians took home less than £1,000.[2] White Northern Rhodesia in fact still possessed a submerged group, though the number of people who somehow managed to keep alive on an income of less than £250 per annum dropped from 9·8 per cent in 1946 to 5·1 per cent in 1951, when prosperity was gradually doing away with the 'poor white'.

[1] In 1949 wages and salaries represented 43 per cent and company incomes 48 per cent of the 'net geographical income' of the territory. The breakdown was as follows: (figures in £ millions)

Wages and Mining	Salaries Other	Company Mining	incomes Other
7·908	9·116	14·600	4·400

Northern Rhodesia. *Report of the board of inquiry to consider the proposed 40 hour week in the copper mining industry.* . . . Lusaka, Government printer, 1950, p. 24

[2] In 1951 out of 37,079 Europeans, 22,279 either had no income or drew less than £50; these comprised mainly women and children, religious workers receiving no remuneration, or very recent immigrants. The following are the figures for known percentages in 1946 and 1951 respectively:

	1946	1951
nil and under £50	60·2	61·8
£50–£249	9·8	5·1
£250–£499	10·9	7·6
£500–£999	16·0	17·3
£1,000–£4,999	3·0	8·0
£5,000–£7,499		
£7,500–£9,999		
£10,000–£14,999	0·1	0·1
£15,000 and over		

In the mining industry which employed 4,608 out of a total Northern Rhodesian labour force of 13,094 men, 356 earned nothing; 217 earned less than £249, 298 earned between £250 and £499; 496 earned between £500 and £699; 1,583 earned between £700 and £999; 930 earned between £1,000 and £1,249; 272 earned between £1,250 and £1,499; 141 earned between £1,500 and £1,999; 48 between £2,000 and £4,999; only 4 earned more than £5,000.

On the face of it, Northern Rhodesian white society possessed little unity. The missionaries formed a world of their own, overlapping to some extent with that of their more worldly countrymen, but distinct in interest and approach, and internally divided along sectarian lines. The expatriate Government official tended to look towards Government House, though the stereotype of the 'fly-by-night', whose interests centred on Britain, no longer quite corresponded to the facts, at a time when many civil servants put their children into local schools finding this cheaper and more satisfactory than sending them to England, whilst some elderly men were beginning to retire in Rhodesia, where they got used to the climate, made friends, and could often more easily get a job to eke out their pensions. The professional people in turn were divided from the workers, the farmers forming a separate community with interests and ambitions of their own, though they were themselves split once more along lines of wealth, the agricultural community containing a small bloc of extremely prosperous men who played a major part in the country's social and political life.[1] Of the whites living in the Protectorate at the time, only a comparatively limited number would have described themselves as 'Rhodesians' pure and simple, most of them had a 'hyphen' somewhere; many spoke of England or Scotland as 'home'; many others intended going back to South Africa when their contract on the mines expired, and others looked as far afield as Greece or Israel, the Greek community remaining tightly knit, whilst Zionism remained a major force amongst the Jews. But all the same, Rhodesia in time gave a common stamp to most of its citizens; their children went to the same schools where many of them picked up a characteristically Rhodesian accent, a variant of South African English, which blended various phonetic elements from Cockney, Scottish and Afrikaans, and which from early days onwards distinguished the local-born person, the 'Ridgeback'. 'You have undoubtedly realized', wrote the Director of Education in a warning circular to the parents of Salisbury High School children more than a generation ago 'that the youth in this country are at a disadvantage in the matter of learning the correct pronunciation of the English language. More often than not their ears are accustomed to variants of the English language far from pleasant to hear and, which, if acquired, would in later years betray a lack of cultured training. . . .'[2] But Education Department circulars did not stop the development of a new kind of accent, which was spoken on both sides of the Zambezi, and adopted by children of whatever national ancestry, who went to school in Rhodesia, the new speech acting as a social bond and sometimes a

[1] In 1951 of the 65 people in Northern Rhodesia earning £5,000 or more 24 were engaged in agriculture, 16 in commerce, 9 in construction, 6 in community and business services, 4 in mining, 2 in manufacturing, 2 in recreational and personal services, 1 in Government, and 1 in transport and communications.

Within the farming industry itself, out of 1,248 persons, 213 earned nothing, 177 earned between £1 and £249; 194 earned between £250 and £499; 163 between £500 and £699; 122 between £700 and £999; 73 between £1,000 and £1,249; 23 between £1,250 and £1,499; 45 between £1,500 and £1,999; 90 between £2,000 and £4,999; 24 over £5,000.

[2] Circular of the Director of Education to parents and guardians attending the Salisbury High Schools: 10 May 1912 (in E 5/2/3, Nat Arch SR)

means of recognizing who was or was not a genuine 'Ridgeback' (though of course many Rhodesian-born children also continued to speak English in other fashions). Another element in the new white Rhodesian 'pro-nationalism' was a common feeling of resentment against what the Europeans regarded as unjustified or prejudiced criticism from overseas, and even a feeling of isolation. Many Rhodesians would have heartily shared the feelings of a Jamaican planter, who complained in 1823 that he was here 'in a state of banishment and gliding fast into ruin; and while thus weighed down with misery, without one ray of hope to illuminate the dreary prospect before me, I am with the rest of the colonists, depicted by the Saints, the Methodists, the Quakers and the Man of Beer, and at their instigation by three-fourths of the people of Great Britain, as a hard-hearted, inhuman monster . . .'[1], this strong feeling against the outsider forming part, not only of the country's colour complex, but also of an incipient sense of feeling 'separate' from other parts of the world. In addition white Rhodesia, a youthful community, then displayed a general feeling of optimism; the country possessed great resources; its economy was expanding at an unparalleled rate, the immigrants hoped to better themselves more quickly than at home, the mere act of moving to a new country often providing a new psychological incentive. The story went round in a bar of a woodpecker who decided to look for another place to live in, having got tired of his accustomed haunts; off he flew to another forest and settled down in a huge tree; then he gave a hard peck at the bark, and as he did so, lightning struck the forest giant and split it asunder; but undaunted, the little bird got up, preened his feathers and said to himself 'Well, this just shows what a chap can do, once he has got away from home!' Many immigrants in fact were bettering themselves; and even if they were not, the mere sight of an expanding community was likely to prove an exhilarating experience. Apart from that, the Europeans, however much they might differ amongst themselves on lines of class and religion, all possessed similar cultural traditions; they shared the same kinship system, and only married among themselves, weddings outside their colour group being prohibited by social custom, though not by law, with the result that the Europeans rigidly kept their identity.

Below the white community came the Asians and Coloureds, both small communities without political influence, and both equally apt to marry only amongst themselves. The Indians in 1951 numbered some 2,524 people, their numbers having doubled since 1946, when business began to pick up, and many more Asians entered the country, though men still heavily preponderated, with the result that many Indians had to look outside the country for a wife.[2] Almost two thirds professed the Hindu religion, most of the remainder practising Islam, whilst nearly three fourths of the Asians were born in India or Pakistan. The

[1] Extract from a quotation taken from the short but excellent work by Burn L. *The British Wes Indies.* Hutchinson's university library, 1951, p. 113

[2] Between the years 1931, 1946 and 1951, the proportion of Indian women per thousand persons rose from 182, to 257 and then to 338.

overwhelming majority of all Indians engaged in wholesale or retail trading; the money-lender, an important and even indispensable person in any peasant economy devoid of state run rural credit schemes, was absent from the Rhodesian scene. The Indians were popularly supposed to be able to 'live on the smell of an oil rag', and salt away thousands of pounds which were sent to India; but Northern Rhodesia was no more a brown man's Eldorado than a white man's, and nearly all the 'traders' in fact had to earn their living as salesmen, shop assistants or managers; the Indians almost entirely lacked a professional or technically skilled stratum,[1] whilst their children had very little chance of better-ing themselves socially by entering the civil service or other professions, with the result that they were mostly pushed back again into trading. Like the whites, the Indians were mostly town dwellers, Lusaka, Livingstone and Ndola forming the main communities, whilst they found themselves excluded from the 'closed' townships of Nkana, Nchanga and Mufulira. Nevertheless Northern Rhodesia retained many attractions for Asian newcomers, 'who voted with their legs' to get into the country so that in the days following the Second World War the Asians could boast of by far the highest rate of increase.[2]

If the Asians formed a typical immigrants' community, the Coloureds stood out as the Northern Rhodesian *par excellence* amongst the country's non-African population. The Coloureds like the Asians rarely emigrated, and by 1951 nearly three quarters of the country's 1,112 Coloured people were born within the territory, where intermingling across the colour line was continuing, with the result that statisticians calculated that over half the Coloured population growth between 1946 and 1951 arose from miscegenation between the different races, many Northern Rhodesian Coloureds bearing the surnames of highly respected European families, a minority having Asian fathers.[3] Most Coloured people made their living as semi-skilled or skilled workers, as sub-foremen, or in the service industries, but only a handful managed to become white-collar workers or rise to be their own masters.[4] Socially the Coloureds found themselves in an even more difficult position than the Indians; the taint of illegitimacy hung heavily over many of them, and a good deal of nonsense was still being talked about half-breeds inheriting the worst characteristics of both parents, a stereo-type without any basis in genetics. Unlike the Indians, the Coloureds had no recognizable culture of their own; most of them lived like poor Europeans

---

[1] In 1951 out of 1,251 economically active Asians, 6 were professionally or technically employed; 1,090 worked in various forms of trade and contracting, these including 465 retail managers and 585 salesmen and shop assistants. 82 worked in farming, mining, as craftsmen or other occupations of that type, including 49 tailors.

[2] Between 1946 and 1951 the Asian population increased by 1,410 persons, of whom 1,168 consisted of immigrants, the annual geometric (compound interest) rate of increase amounting to 17·5 per cent for the Asians, 11·1 for the Europeans and 6·7 for the Coloureds, 2·6 for Africans.

[3] See Northern Rhodesia. *Report on the census of population, 1951*, p. 35 for details of the Coloureds' maternal and paternal ancestry.

[4] In 1951 out of 344 'economically active' Coloureds 16 had professional jobs as nurses, hospital orderlies, teachers and so on; 17 made a living as contractors, managers or proprietors outside farming, and only 3 were clerks, and 11 were employed as sales workers. 52 were employed in farming or hunting, 11 as workers in various industries and trades, and 42 as service workers.

rather than Africans, speaking English amongst themselves and practising a European religion, Catholicism making remarkable progress amongst their community, nearly one third of whom looked to Rome for their salvation.[1] As a community the Coloureds were of course deeply concerned with the question of status, which in turn affected their economic position. The Coloureds in fact constituted a separate and distinct community, though Government in some ways still resisted the emergence of yet another recognized racial group, a policy regarded as unsound both from the political and economic point of view, and one apt needlessly to alienate the emergent African intelligentsia. The Europeans on the other hand were quite ready to concede to the Coloureds a distinct position, though unlike the Portuguese they would not grant them social equality and much less accept them as brothers-in-law.

Between them the European, Asian and Coloured communities still only made up a small percentage of the country's population; in the backveld a man might travel for hundreds of miles and see very few whites, the vast majority of the people remaining Africans. By 1951 statisticians reckoned that there were 1,920,000 black people in the country, their numbers having doubled themselves in about a generation.[2] The experts of course differed on the exact rate of growth, but there is no doubt that the Bantu speakers of Northern Rhodesia multiplied mightily since the Chartered Company first established its rule beyond the Zambezi, white governance possessing a considerable biological survival value for its subjects, though a Southern Rhodesian African still possessed a considerably higher expectation of life than his brother beyond the Zambezi. The Europeans by pacifying the country, prevented internecine warfare, whilst at the same time stabilizing the existing tribes. Large scale treks, where whole peoples would seek new land for themselves, became a thing of the past, just as they were now a matter of historical memory for the Afrikaners. Equally important was the railway engine and the lorry, which did away with some of the former isolation of the countryside and helped to distribute food more equally through the territory. The impact of medical services proper was slower, the pioneering work was left to the missions, which received government subsidies, a large-scale expansion of health services only beginning after the Second World War and progress in Northern Rhodesia lagging far behind the more advanced sister colony south of the Zambezi where 'rural dispensaries'

[1] In 1951 out of 1,000 Coloured persons Roman Catholicism had 379 adherents, the Anglican Church 224, the Methodists 95, Islam 74, Presbyterianism 69.

[2] According to figures worked out in the early 'fifties Northern Rhodesia had one of the world's highest birthrates with 59 per thousand. But both infant mortality and death rates were much higher than in Southern Rhodesia. In spite of the high birth rate the net reproduction rate of the Northern Rhodesian African was 1·7, of the Southern Rhodesian African 2·0 and of the Ghanaian 1·5; see Gelfand, M. *Proud record*. Salisbury, Federal information department, 1960, p. 52–53. Northern Rhodesia's African population is stated by the official figures to have been as follows: 820,000 in 1911, 980,000 for 1921, 1,350,000 for 1931, 1,530,000 for 1941, and 1,880,000 for 1951, though these must be treated with considerable reserve, the erratic rate of growth indicated probably being due to the inaccuracies of the estimates.

opened their doors in the reserves as early as 1911. In the field of preventive medicine, however, the Protectorate achieved a good deal since a sanitary branch was set up in 1931, and Africans benefited from the stamping out of yaws, by successful attacks on plague, as well as assaults on scourges like venereal disease, penicillin being first introduced in the territory in 1946. In addition Northern Rhodesia was the scene of some interesting medical research, the most interesting experiments of all deriving from a German expedition under F. K. Kleine and Dr R. D. Fischer which in 1921 discovered that a German drug called Bayer 205 could kill the deadly sleeping sickness in its early stages.

Under the white man's dispensation the population rose and the labour force vastly increased, the African villager becoming a great traveller, with the difference that he now left the village as an individual in search of wages, and no longer as a member of a raiding army in search of women, cattle or land. Labour migration was of course nothing new in the world's history; the so-called *Sachsengänger* or *Pendler* were as familiar to oldtime Germany as the *golondrinas*, Italian-speaking 'swallows' were to the Argentine, whilst an African labour migrant would probably have found nothing very peculiar in the set-up of a company town like Schefferville in Canada's frozen north, where the bulk of the workers came as unmarried men who lived in a 'bunk house' and took their meals in a cafeteria, and returned home after their six months' contracts expired.[1] At the same time many white Rhodesians remained labour migrants as much as the people whom they supervised, but amongst the Africans the system reached much larger proportions with the result that the villages were drained of their menfolk, who laboured in the towns or on European farms, whilst continuing to hold customary rights in their tribal land. To some extent the system acted as a buffer; no one was likely to starve in old age, as long as tribal bonds retained their strength, whilst women and children to some extent remained sheltered from the worst effects of industrialization as experienced in 18th century Britain, when young girls worked down the pits, and small children crowded together in insanitary workshops to earn their pitiful mite.[2] At the same time working hours were never as long for Africans as for Englishmen in the early days of the industrial revolution in Britain, when the labourers often toiled to the very limits of their endurance; and by the early 'fifties few Northern Rhodesian employers asked for more than a forty-eight hour week, some contenting themselves with forty, the African worker considerably benefiting from the strong bargaining position which the white unions had established for themselves in the past.

But if Africans never paid the same price for the Industrial Revolution, which English villagers did 100 or 150 years ago in the new manufacturing towns,

[1] See Derbyshire, E. 'Notes on the social structure of a Canadian pioneer town' (in *The Sociologicae review*, v. 8, July 1960, p. 63–75), which provided a most striking parallel to the Copper Belt.

[2] In 1951 the total female labour force only amounted to 8,320, or 3·6 per cent of the total labour force, and a considerable increase from 1931 when women only amounted to 1·9 of the total labour force.

neither did they garner the same benefits, for wages mostly remained attuned to the needs of a single man rather than those of a family, and once a man brought his wife and children into a town, he usually found it hard to make both ends meet, a large proportion of the labour migrants living in poverty, so that few Africans could accumulate capital to any appreciable extent, and temporary spells of unemployment presented a serious hazard to African families. As far as the general structure of the towns along the railway line was concerned, they retained many of the characteristics of a 'gold-rush' settlement. Africans flocked to the cities from many different parts of the country, speaking different languages and practising diverse customs, and there was a constant coming and going of people. Africans moved from one town to the other, for responsibility for housing generally rested with the employers, so that if a man gave up or lost his job, he also lost his house and had to move elsewhere. Besides the rapid growth of the towns itself speeded up circulation, for as new housing areas opened up, new residents would often move in from the older parts of the location, and their vacated houses would be taken over by people coming from dwellings marked for demolition. Again Africans left for other townships or returned to their villages, the whole system resting to some extent on the Africans' ability to adapt traditional tribal and kinship links to an urban setting, so that black people could usually discover relatives or friends, who would tide them over an evil day or put them up for a night.

In the African, as in the European townships, most people were in their prime of life. Men moreover heavily outnumbered women and few old people were to be seen in the streets.[1] The average black town dweller remained an unskilled or at best a semi-skilled labourer, though a small class of more specialized workers, traders, and 'white collar' men were beginning to emerge.[2] This incipient economic cleavage within the African community did not, however, as yet go very deep, the black-white division remaining a much more important source of potential friction. Financially a black artisan who knew his job was often doing better than an office worker; but clerical or the more senior supervisory jobs most closely approximating positions held by white men carried a very much higher status than others, African clergymen, education officers and suchlike people being on the whole more highly regarded by Africans, since thire way

[1] See for details Mitchell, J. C. *African urbanization in Ndola and Luanshya* (Rhodes-Livingstone communications, no. 6, 1954) and McCulloch, M. *A Social survey of the African population of Livingstone* (Rhodes-Livingstone papers, no. 26, 1956)

[2] By 1956 for instance a research worker in Livingstone working from a selected sample, calculated that 18·4 per cent were employed as domestic servants; 48·2 as labourers; 6·7 as foremen, night watchmen and policemen; 2·5 as traders and hawkers who were mostly self-employed men, though including a few others; 19·3 working as skilled men including tailors, drivers, painters, bricklayers, plumbers and carpenters; and 4·4 per cent as white collar workers such as clerks, typists, hospital orderlies, teachers, urban court assessors, welfare assistants and shop assistants. See McCulloch, M. *A social survey of the African population of Livingstone* (Rhodes-Livingstone papers, no. 26, 1956) p. 37–39. African wages ranged from 25/– to 60/– per month for unskilled men, 40/– to 100/– for semi-skilled workers, and up to about £17. o. o. for trade-tested transport drivers, bricklayers, carpenters and typists, all—excepting the latter—receiving free food and housing or cash in lieu.

of life most nearly resembled that of the envied white man.[1] These educated Africans for their part generally took more interest in politics than their less well-lettered countrymen, and at the same time suffered more psychologically from the various kinds of social discrimination which they still encountered in shops, hotels and other public places. Numerically, however, these 'white collar groups' as yet remained small; over the Protectorate as a whole agriculture stood out as the most important employer of black labour, followed by the construction industry; mining and quarrying only came third on the list, whilst little more than one tenth of the employed made their living from a great variety of posts like school teaching, hospital and church work, administration, hotels, laundries and so forth, the 'service industries' still playing a relatively small part in the African economy.[2]

Once the traveller got off the beaten track and left the farms and townships on the railway line and the Copper Belt for the open veld, he came into a world which, superficially at any rate, would have seemed far more familiar to the old-time Ngoni visitor mentioned at the beginning of this chapter. Only a few Europeans lived out in the 'bundu', still the place of residence of nearly nine tenths of all the Africans in the country, and though a visitor from the past might have been surprised by an occasional road, or a motor lorry passing by, he would have found the sights of village life familiar enough. Nevertheless life was no longer the same as in the past, even though the rate of change was very uneven. The Lovale for instance, once renowned as great hunters, had turned to trade on a considerable scale and brought about considerable changes in their agricultural methods, which were unusual in that they resulted largely from the initiative of the people concerned without any prodding from the Agricultural Department; bullrush millet lost much of its popularity as a staple crop and in place of the older kinds of shifting cultivation there emerged a semi-stable kind of agriculture based on cassava and intermittent resting, groundnuts sometimes also being alternated in the resting periods, with the result that the Lovale had more and better food to eat than most Africans in the backwoods.[3] Mention has

[1] See for instance Epstein, A. L. 'The Network and urban social organization' (in *Rhodes-Livingstone journal*, no. 29, June 1961, p. 29–62) for a study of Ndola.

[2] In 1951 the African labour force in employment was deployed as follows:

Agriculture and forestry	57,025
Mining and quarrying	37,749
Manufacturing	19,375
Construction	46,424
Electrical, water and sanitary services	717
Commerce and finance	9,305
Transport and communications	6,158
Private domestic service	20,528
Others (schools, hospitals, churches, Government, hotels, laundries etc)	31,345

In addition 50,336 Northern Rhodesian Africans worked in Southern Rhodesia. See Northern Rhodesia. *Report on the census of population, 1951*, p. 37 for their industrial classification, the figures given differing somewhat from Colonial Office. *Report on Northern Rhodesia for . . . 1951*, p. 13

[3] White, C. M. N. *A preliminary survey of Luvale rural economy*. Rhodes-Livingstone papers, no. 29, 1959)

already been made of the emergent farmers in the Tonga country, and of improvements in the Eastern Province, where peasants learned much from agricultural officers and considerably changed their methods. The village traders' little shacks were now a familiar sight, and in addition Government was intensifying its efforts to develop the countryside, the secular gospel of 'development' largely replacing the older missionary approach which regarded 'commerce' as nothing but the handmaiden of the Gospel.

As copper revenue rapidly rose from the late 'forties, Government development plans were repeatedly expanded, and in 1951 a revised project provided for the expenditure of £19,000,000 of which £7,500,000 came from Territorial funds, £2,500,000 from Colonial Development and Welfare Funds, and £9,000,000 from Loans. Admittedly the plan had certain weaknesses; there were no production targets of the kind involved in other plans of that sort; and as money started pouring in, and the needs of the railway belt became more urgent, the original bias towards rural development gave way to a more urban orientation, whilst more money was spent for capital purposes of the orthodox kind.[1] Lack of men proved an even more serious obstacle than money, for the Provincial and Area Teams charged with the task of development required highly skilled personnel, who could not easily be secured in a hurry, with the result that the original concept of general territorial development had to give way to a more cautious scheme involving regional priorities. Work was concentrated in 'Intensive Development Areas' where the natural advantages of soil, water, access to markets and such like seemed likely to yield the highest return. In addition 'Development Areas' were scheduled, to be developed as manpower and funds became available, whilst the less fortunate 'Other Areas' were neglected on the grounds that they were too poor in quality to maintain many people making a reasonable living from the land. Within these limits, however, a good deal was accomplished; capital works went up, and various schemes began for the promotion of peasant farming, fisheries, drainage works and suchlike, progress also involving various kinds of sociological, hydrological and other kinds of research, whilst some good work was done by development area schools which were set up in various villages; the services provided by the Health Department and the Department of African Education rapidly expanded, as more money poured into government coffers.[2]

[1] See Northern Rhodesia. *Review of the ten-year development plan of Northern Rhodesia . . . 1951.* Lusaka, Government printer, 1951. As on 1 January 1951 the allocation from the Development Plan stood as follows (in £s): Health 1,700,000; African Education 1,463,363; European Education 981,550; Publications Bureau 16,130; Agriculture 731,007; Forestry 287,925; Veterinary 485,929; Game and Tsetse 497,940; Tourist Development 20,000; Rural Development 1,498,813; Roads, air and inland water transport 2,066,188; Aerodromes 867,000; Posts, telegraphs and telephones 400,000; Water Supplies 650,825; Irrigation 293,789; Agricultural Development, Marketing and Co-operative Societies 520,000; Urban African Housing 1,000,000; Loans to Local Authorities 500,000; Building— general 3,792,312; P.W.D. Staff 150,000; Public Works and Utilities 745,000; reserve for research schemes etc. 68,200; Unallocated 299,064.

[2] For details see Northern Rhodesia. *Community development in Northern Rhodesia: correspondence between the Secretary of State for the Colonies and the Governor of Northern Rhodesia.* Lusaka Government printer 1952

As far as the training of African children was concerned, Government educationalists now hoped that the Ten Year Development Plan would ultimately provide elementary school education for all youngsters between the ages of eight and twelve, in the course of which they would learn reading and writing in one of the main vernaculars. A much smaller number became fitted for subordinate jobs in the social services, industry, trade, and government, the educational pyramid rapidly narrowing at the top, providing for only a small number of pupils with secondary training and very few graduates.[1] Development also received a real impetus from broadcasting, especially through the so-called 'Saucepan Special', a small and cheap shortwave battery set which was sold in Northern Rhodesia from 1949. At last Africans could switch on the radio in their huts where there were no electrical mains, and by a turn of the knob brought the world to the kraal. The poor man's radio was designed not only to amuse, but also to instruct; now that more money and equipment became available, Lusaka Broadcasting Station, first set up in 1941 to help the war effort, ceased to be a kind of 'Heath Robinson' affair, and became an efficient means of spreading news and views. Even people who could neither read nor write could understand the voices from the air, with the result that propaganda for hygiene and better agricultural methods spread much more easily. In addition Africans learned something about the wider world, and broadcasting proved an enormous success, as say, a Bemba villager could settle down after work to listen to a news bulletin, a choir, a talk on land development, a play or a sketch, 'World News and News from Cape to Cairo', the wireless at home proving much more effective than sets in overcrowded beer halls, where most of the visitors would drink and argue, where the women shouted gossip to one another, whilst a few earnest listners tried to catch what was being said on the air, and would gladly have thrown out everybody else by the ear.[2] In addition Africans liked to tune in to the new music which was becoming extremely popular, and which blended traditional with 'white' elements derived from American jazz, Church music and military bands, whilst machine-made Western instruments, especially the guitar, further influenced the structure of popular African music, in the same way as factory produced concertinas and mouth-

[1] By about 1950 there were 1,284 aided and maintained African schools with 142,009 enrolled pupils. Of these about 126,000 were in elementary schools with four year courses, 12,300 were in middle schools with two year courses, and 3,700 were in upper schools with three year courses. In addition there were 331 unaided schools, attended by 19,300 pupils, all elementary. The enrolment for the 1949 to 1950 session for secondary schools was 209 in junior secondary schools and 39 in senior secondary schools. Vocational trade training for pupils was given in building and carpentry at Munali Training Centre and in junior trade schools. In addition a Medical School turned out hospital and dispensary assistants, a survey school provided elementary training, and there were some agricultural schools. Besides, African Veterinary Assistants were being trained, whilst various other government departments, such as the Posts and Telegraphs Department, provided specialist courses. In addition 392 men teachers and 81 women teachers were trained in 1950, whilst a number of post-secondary students were educated outside Northern Rhodesia.

[2] See Franklin, H. *Northern Rhodesia: report on the development of broadcasting to Africans in Northern Rhodesia.* Lusaka, Government printer, 1949; and Franklin, H. *Report on the saucepan special.* . . . Lusaka, Government printer, 1950

organs deeply affected European folksongs in the 19th century, to the extent of the 'concertina' becoming regarded as a traditional instrument. The villagers also benefited from the services of a government film unit which sent cinema vans into the countryside, whilst the Northern Rhodesia and Nyasaland Joint Publications Bureau, set up in 1948, tried to spread the written word amongst the country's scattered African population.

Nevertheless as far as the Territory as a whole was concerned, development remained extremely uneven, and much of the country's potential wealth stayed unused or even unexplored. At the same time the different peoples of the Protectorate went along their different ways, sharply divided into highly exclusive racial groups, almost devoid of social contacts, and without a common ideology.[1] Even the African community itself was broken into many different groups, speaking different languages, practising different customs, and containing within its ranks the whole range of mankind, from a westernized university graduate to a simple shepherd, who would not have found himself out of place in the days of the Old Testament. Christianity had made considerable progress, even in the towns, where a statistical survey made later on in 1960 calculated the Catholics to be by far the strongest congregation, followed by the Free Church, Watch Tower and Dutch Reformed Church in that order, whilst Anglicans and other groups commanded fewer followers. Many Africans now knew their Bible; and Christian names were widely used even by people who otherwise had no religious affiliation. Churchgoing often acquired considerable prestige, as Christianity was associated with western values as a whole; and the churches also created many new social bonds which cut right across tribal affiliations. Some of the faithful acquired a new spiritual dignity; and the austere standards of many of the missions may well have encouraged the true believers to save rather than gamble their money away or spend it on loose women or beer. But for all the missionaries' devoted labours, their Faith did not as yet give any religious or cultural uniformity to the mixed black, white and brown peoples that made their living in the Protectorate. Perhaps even more important was the fact that by 1960 almost a quarter of urban Africans seem to have professed no religion of any sort, the 'denomination of the spiritually uncommitted' forming the biggest of all in the townships of the Protectorate, a great bloc of people who one day might follow a new Messiah.[2]

The different groups that made up Northern Rhodesia's plural society thus had little in common except that, in the last instance, they were more or less tied to a single market economy dominated by the copper mines. Politically the country was held together by the scaffolding of a European administration which

[1] In 1948 the so-called 'Fortyeight Club' was founded in Lusaka to promote inter-racial contacts, the Rev. E. G. Nightingale being a leading member. The Club wound up in 1953 and its assets were made over to the United Northern Rhodesia Association. Membership, however, remained limited, and inter-racial clubs of this kind made no impact on the Colony's social pattern.

[2] Adequate comparative religious statistics for the Territory as a whole are extremely difficult to obtain. The most reliable figures for the urban areas are given in Central African Statistical Office. *Second report on urban African budget survey held in Northern Rhodesia, May to August 1960.* Salisbury

relied on prestige, on a reputation for personal honesty and on technical skill rather than on military might;[1] the physical force at the Government's disposal remained strictly limited, the British never having militarized any of their subject peoples. Much was achieved physically—in mortar, brick and steel; something was also done in the realms of faith and culture; but the worlds of white men, brown men and black men stayed apart. The infinitely harder task of forging a new nation remains with the future.

1961. This covers the eight main towns in the Territory. The Survey calculates that a total of 24 per cent of family adults and 23 per cent of single men had no religion. Numerically the most important religions of adults in families and of single men were:

	Adults in families	Single men
Roman Catholic	27 per cent	21 per cent
Free Church	13 „	18 „
Watch Tower	10 „	7 „
Dutch Reformed Church	7 „	11 „
Anglican	3 „	3 „
Methodist	3 „	3 „
Seventh Day Adventist	2 „	4 „
Apostolic Faith	2 „	2 „

[1] In 1951 the budget only provided for the Northern Rhodesia Police a total of 1720 African policemen and 248 officers from the rank of Assistant Inspector upwards, the police forming less than one *per mille* of the total population. The territory's military defence depended on one regular infantry battalion, the 1st battalion of the Northern Rhodesia Regiment.

Note on sources and treatment

ACCESS

The bulk of Colonial Office archives in the Public Record Office, London, are open to the public fifty years after their creation. The same period applies to the public archives of Northern Rhodesia which are preserved in the Regional Archives at Lusaka, a branch of the National Archives of Rhodesia and Nyasaland. Southern Rhodesia, on the other hand, permits access to nearly all its files thirty years after their creation.

The author received special permission to use 'closed' Northern Rhodesian and Colonial Office sources, subject to certain conditions. The publication in any form, direct or indirect, of material in such records was made subject to the approval of the Secretary of State. Direct quotation from official records has been avoided as far as possible; differences of opinion between individual members of the British Cabinet, and also the authorship of minutes and despatches in the 'closed' period have not been revealed. Source references to documents not open to the public have been omitted. Reference to 'open' sources has been given, though these were not necessarily the only ones used to illustrate any particular point.

UNPUBLISHED SOURCES OF OFFICIAL PROVENANCE

Imperial Records

The author used material belonging to the Colonial Office in London. In addition some records of Imperial provenance are to be found at the headquarters of the National Archives of Rhodesia and Nyasaland at Salisbury. These include correspondence of the High Commissioner for South Africa (HC) and material produced in the office of the Resident Commissioner (RC), an Imperial officer stationed at Salisbury between 1898 and 1923. The rules of access for these files are those which apply to Colonial Office material overseas. Further, the author has used Foreign Office material, including series FO 2 (Africa-General correspondence) and FO 84 (Slave Trade) of which microfilm copies are held in the National Archives.

Northern Rhodesian Public Archives

The material created before the unification of the territory in 1911 dividds into the public archives of North-Western Rhodesia (symbolized by 'Nat. Arch. NWR') and those of North Eastern Rhodesia ('Nat. Arch. NER'). The most important material in both territories was produced by their respective Administrator's Department (A). In addition other departmental records are worth consulting. The North-Western Rhodesian Archives, for instance, include interesting judicial records (H), the files of local magistrates (IMA and IMF) and those of the Secretary for Native Affairs (IN), as well as those of individual District Commissioners (IND, INH). The remaining records of North-Eastern Rhodesia include High Court records (F) and those of the Consular Court at Fort Jameson (IMA) and those of local Magistrates and Civil Commissioners (INA, INH).

The most important records for the period 1911 to 1924 are contained in the files of the Administrator of Northern Rhodesia (A), the Northern Rhodesian records as a whole for the period after the unification in 1911 being symbolized by 'Nat. Arch. NR.' The key-post of Administrator disappeared after the Colonial Office took over and the most important records were those produced by the Secretariat (B). In addition there is an extensive body of departmental records. Records of the District Administration are identified by three-letter symbols (KDA to KDG for the provinces, KSA to KTD for districts).

Southern Rhodesian Public Archives

The Southern Rhodesian public archives are housed at the headquarters of the National Archives of Rhodesia and Nyasaland at Salisbury. The National Archives have issued a detailed description of this material in a *Guide to the public records of Southern Rhodesia under the regime of the British South Africa Company, 1890–1923*, Cape Town, Longmans, 1956. The Southern Rhodesian public archives include much material derived from the British South Africa Company's London office which is of special value in view of the destruction of the Company's London archives by enemy action in 1941. The London office material (LO), contains copies of minutes and agenda, with annexures for the Director's meetings dating from 1898, which are of special importance to the study of Central African history. Material relating to Northern Rhodesia is also found in other archives groups, particularly in the correspondence of the Administrator (A) and the Company's Cape Town office (CT). References to Southern Rhodesia public archives are designated 'Nat. Arch. SR'.

SOURCES OF PRIVATE PROVENANCE

The Historical Manuscripts Collection of the National Archives contains a considerable body of material of relevance to Northern Rhodesia. References to this collection are marked 'Nat. Arch. MS'.

The Collection includes the papers concerned with or derived from: Carruthers, J., prospector (CA 4); Clarke, F. J. ('Mopani'), rancher (CL 3); Coillard, Rev. F. and Mrs L., pioneer missionaries (CO 5); Copeman, E. A., civil servant and farmer (CO 3); Cuninghame, B. A., soldier and farmer (CU 1); Deare, G. R., soldier and prospector (DE 1); Fisher, W., doctor and missionary, and Fisher, Mrs S. E. (FI 2); Fisher, W. S. missionary (FI 4); '48' Club, an inter-racial association in Northern Rhodesia (FO 1); German consular files, Cape Town, copies (GE 1); Harrington, H. T., civil servant, soldier and legal employee (HA 5); Helmore, H. W., missionary (HE 3); Hoste, C., prospector (HO 9); Livingstone, D., missionary, explorer (LI 1, LI 2); Livingstone public library (LI 4); Mackintosh, Miss C. W., writer (MA 18); Northern Rhodesia European Civil Servants, Association (NO 2); Northern Rhodesian Record Society (NO 4); Pia, J., capitao and clerk (MISC/PI 3); Poole, E. H. L., civil servant (MISC/PO 6); Price, R., missionary (PR 2); Quicke, F. C., explorer (QU 1); Rangeley, H., civil servant (RA 1); Robins, H. G., prospector and farmer (RO 1); Stevenson-Hamilton, J., soldier and explorer (HA 6); Waddell, W. T., artisan missionary (WA 1); Westbeech, G., trader (WE 1); Worthington, F. V., civil servant (WO 3).

In addition the Historical Manuscripts Collection in the National Archives includes a valuable collection of the papers of various Southern Rhodesian political men containing reference to Northern Rhodesia. These include the papers of: Chaplin, Sir F. D. P., Administrator (CH 8, access restricted); Coghlan, Sir C. P. J., Southern Rhodesian Premier (CO 8); Downie, J. W. Southern Rhodesian Minister and later High Commissioner (DO 1); Fynn, Sir P. D. L., Southern Rhodesian Treasurer, later Minister (FY 1); Leggate, W. M., Southern Rhodesian Minister (LE 3); Moffat, H. U., Southern Rhodesian Minister, later Premier (MO 13).

The writer was also given access to some of the papers belonging to Sir Roy Welensky and to those of Lord Malvern in Salisbury, but the same restrictions have been observed as in the case of material of Colonial Office provenance.

In addition there is a good deal of valuable manuscript material to be found outside the Federation. Rhodes House, Oxford, has a splendid collection of Rhodes papers. Unfortunately this material contains relatively little with regard to Northern Rhodesia. British missionary collections include the Central African correspondence of the London Missionary Society and the archives of the Methodist Missionary Society, London. References to these are marked 'L.M.S. Arch.' and 'Methodist Missionary Arch.' respectively.

PUBLISHED SOURCES

The library of the National Archives, Salisbury, has fairly complete files of all Central African newspapers, with only a few gaps here and there. These papers include the *Northern news*, the *Livingstone mail*, the *Central African post* and others, as well as Southern Rhodesian newspapers, particularly the *Bulawayo chronicle*, the *Rhodesia herald* and the official Government Gazettes. The Library also keeps Northern Rhodesian and Colonial Office printed departmental and commission reports and similar material. It also owns a set of Colonial Office Confidential Prints. Access to the latter series is on the same conditions as to unpublished Colonial Office correspondence. The Library has also collected a vast body of secondary literature.

SELECT BIBLIOGRAPHY

1. Books, Pamphlets and Periodical Articles (including Official Publications by Individual Authors)

'Africanus' (i.e. Melland, F. H.) 'A Central African confederation' (in *Journal of the African society*, v. 17, 1918, p. 276–306)

Allan, W. 'African land usage' (in *Rhodes-Livingstone journal*, no. 3, June 1945, p. 13–20)

Allan, W. and others. *Land holding and land usage among the plateau Tonga of Mazabuka district: a reconnaissance survey, 1945*. Cape Town, Oxford university press for the Rhodes-Livingstone institute, 1948

Altham, E. A. *Some notes on the life of Major Patrick William Forbes*. Printed for private circulation, 1928

Anderson, W. H. *On the trail of Livingstone*. Mountain View, Pacific press publishing association, 1919

Arnot, F. S. *Bihé and Garenganze: or, Four years' further work and travel in Central Africa*. Hawkins, 1893

Arnot, F.S. *Garenganze: or, Seven years pioneer mission work in Central Africa*. Hawkins, 1889

Arnot, F.S. *Missionary travels in Central Africa*. Bath, Office of 'Echoes of service', 1914

Axelson, E. 'Gold mining in Mashonaland in the 16th and 17th centuries' (in *Optima*, v. 9, no. 3, Sep 1959, p. 164–170)

Axelson, E. *South-East Africa 1488–1530*. Longmans, Green and co., 1940

Baião, A. (ed.) *O manuscrito Valentim Fernandes*. Lisbon, Academia Portuguesa da Historia, 1940

Baker, E. *Arnot: a knight of Africa*. Seeley Service & co., limited, 1925

Barnes, J. *Politics in a changing society: a political history of the Fort Jameson Ngoni*. Cape Town, Oxford university press, 1954

Baxter, T. W. 'The discovery and historical associations' (in Clark, J. D. ed. *The Victoria Falls* ... Lusaka, Commission for the preservation of natural and historical monuments and relics, 1952, p. 21–48)

Bennett, G. 'Paramountcy to partnership: J. H. Oldham and Africa' (in *Africa*, v. 30, no. 4, Oct 1960, p. 356–360)

Bocarro, A. 'Extracts from the decade ... of the performances of the Portuguese in the East'. (in Theal, G. M., ed. *Records of south-eastern Africa* ... Cape Town, the Government of the Cape Colony, 1896–1905, v. 3, p. 342–435)

Boiteux, E. 'Rapport sur le mission du Zambèze pendant l'année 1905' (in *Journal des missions évangéliques*, 1906, p. 254)

Bradley, K. G. *Copper venture: the discovery and development of* [*the*] *Roan Antelope and Mufulira* [*copper mines*]. Selection trust ltd, 1952

Bradley, K. G. 'The turn of the tide' (in *African observer*, v. 5, no. 2, June 1936, p. 28–39)

Brelsford, W. V. (ed.) *Handbook to the Federation of Rhodesia and Nyasaland*. Cassell and company ltd, 1960

Brelsford, W. V. *The succession of Bemba chiefs*. Lusaka, Government printer, 1944

Brelsford, W. V. (ed.) *The story of the Northern Rhodesia regiment*. Lusaka, Government printer, 1954

Brooks, R. 'How the Northern Rhodesia coppers were found' (in *Northern Rhodesia journal*, v. 1, no. 1, June 1950, p. 42–48; no. 2, Dec 1950, p. 29–34; and no. 3, June 1951, p. 32–38)

Browne, G. St. J. O. *Labour conditions in Northern Rhodesia*. H.M. Stationery office, 1938 (Colonial no. 150)

Burnham, F. R. *Scouting on two continents*. Los Angeles, Ivan Deach, 1934

Burnham, F. R. *Taking chances*. Los Angeles, Haynes Corporation, 1944

Busschau, W. J. *Report on the development of secondary industries in Northern Rhodesia*. ... Lusaka, Government printer, 1945

Campbell, D. *Blazing trails in Bantuland*. Pickering and Inglis, 1930

Capello, H., and Ivens, R. *De Angola à contra-costa*. ... Lisboa, Emprensa nacional, 1886. 2 v.

Clark, J. D. 'A note on the pre-Bantu inhabitants of Northern Rhodesia and Nyasaland'. (in *Northern Rhodesia journal*, v. 1, no. 2, Dec 1950, p. 42–52)

Clark, J. D. *The prehistory of southern Africa*. Penguin books ltd, 1959

Clark, J. D. *The stone age cultures of Northern Rhodesia*. . . . Claremont, South African archaeological society, 1950

Clark, P. M. *Autobiography of an old drifter*. George G. Harrap, 1936

Clarke, R. F. *Cardinal Lavigerie and the African slave trade*. Longmans, Green and co., 1889

Clay, G. F. . . . *Memorandum on post war development planning in Northern Rhodesia*. Lusaka, Government printer, 1945

Clegg, E. *Race and politics: partnership in the Federation of Rhodesia and Nyasaland*. Oxford university press, 1960

Coillard, F. *On the threshold of Central Africa: a record of twenty years' pioneering among the Barotse of the upper Zambesi*. . . . Hodder and Stoughton, 1897

Colson, E. 'Modern political organisation of the plateau Tonga' (in *African studies*, v. 10, 1948, p. 85–98)

Colson, E. 'A note on Tonga and Ndebele' (in *Northern Rhodesia journal*, no. 2, 1950, p. 35–41)

Colson, E. *Social organization of the Gwembe Tonga*. Manchester university press, 1960

Colson, E., and Gluckman, M. (ed.) *Seven tribes of British central Africa*. Oxford university press, 1951. Reprinted Manchester university press, 1959

Cornet, R. J. *Katanga: le Katanga avant les Belges et l'expédition Bia-Francqui-Cornet*. Bruxelles, Edition L. Cuypers, 1946

Coxhead, J. C. C. *The native tribes of North-Eastern Rhodesia: their laws and customs*. Royal anthropological institute, 1914. (Royal anthropological institute. Occasional paper no. 5)

Cripps, A. S. *An Africa for Africans*. Longmans Green, 1927

Cronje, J. M. *En daar was lig, die sending van die Ned. Geref. Kerk in die O.V.S. in Noord en Suid Rhodesië gedurende die jare 1899–1947*. Bloemfontein, Algemene sendingskommissie van die Ned. Geref. Kerk in die O.V.S., 1948

Cunnison, I. 'A watch tower assembly in central Africa' (in *International review of missions*, v. 40, no. 160, Oct 1951, p. 456–469)

Cunnison, I. G. 'Kazembe and the Portuguese 1798–1832' (in *Journal of African history*, v. 2, 1961, p. 61–76)

Cunnison, I. G. *The Luapula peoples of Northern Rhodesia*. Manchester university press, 1959

Dann, H. C. *The romance of the posts of Rhodesia*. F. Gooden ltd, 1940

Davidson, J. W. *The Northern Rhodesian legislative council*. Faber and Faber, 1948

Davis, J. Merle, (ed.) *Modern industry and the African*. . . . Macmillan and co. limited, 1933

Debenham, F. *The way to Ilala: David Livingstone's pilgrimage*. Longmans, Green and co., 1955

Depelchin, H., and Croonenberghs, C. *Trois ans dans l'Afrique australe*. . . . *débuts de la mission du Zambèse*. . . . Bruxelles, Kiessling et cie., 1882–1883. 2 v.

[D'Erlanger, E. B.] *The history of the construction and finance of the Rhodesian transport system*. Printed by Burrup, Mathieson and co., ltd, 1939

Doke, A. M. *The Lambas of Northern Rhodesia*. George G. Harrap and co. ltd, 1931

Dougall, J. W. C. 'Thomas Jesse Jones: crusader for Africa' (in *International review of missions*, v. 39, 1950, p. 311–317)

Epstein, A. L. *Politics in an urban African community*. Manchester university press, 1958

Epstein, A. L. 'The network and urban social organisation' (in *Rhodes-Livingstone journal*, no. 29, June 1961, p. 29–62)

Favre, E. *François Coillard, 1834–1904*. 2nd ed. Paris, Société des missions évangéliques, 1946

Fisher, W. S., and Hoyte, J. *Africa looks ahead*. Pickering and Inglis, ltd, 1948

Fox, H. W. *Memorandum . . . containing notes and information concerning land policy*. British South Africa company, 1912

Fox, H. W. *Memorandum containing notes concerning the development of estates and industries by the company*. British South Africa company, 1914

Fox, H. W. *Memorandum on constitutional, political, financial and other questions concerning Rhodesia*. British South Africa company, 1912

Fox, H. W. *Memorandum . . . on problems of development and policy*. British South Africa company, 1910

Fraenkel, P. *Wayaleshi*. Weidenfeld and Nicholson, 1959

Frankel, S. H. *Capital investment in Africa*. Oxford university press, 1938

Franklin, H. . . . *Report on 'the saucepan special', the poor man's radio for rural populations.* Lusaka, the Government printer, 1950

Franklin, H. . . . *Report on the development of broadcasting to Africans in Central Africa.* Lusaka, the Government printer, 1949

Frisby, A. W. . . . *African education development plans, 1945–1955.* Lusaka, the Government printer, 1945

Gallagher, J., and Robinson, R. 'The imperialism of free trade' (in *Economic history review*, v. 6, no. 1, Jan 1953, p. 1–15)

Gallagher, J., and Robinson, R. *Africa and the Victorians: the official mind of imperialism.* Macmillan and co., 1961

Gamitto, A. C. P. (ed.) *O muata Cazembe e os povos Maraves, Chevas, Muizas, Muembas, Lundas e outros da Africa australe.* . . . Lisboa, Imprensa nacional, 1854

Gann, L. H. 'The end of the slave trade in British Central Africa 1889–1912' (in *Rhodes-Livingstone journal*, no. 16, 1954, p. 27–51)

Gann, L. H. 'The Northern Rhodesian copper industry and the world of copper, 1923–1952' (in *Rhodes-Livingstone journal*, no. 18, 1955, p. 1–18)

Gann, L. H. *The birth of a plural society: the development of Northern Rhodesia under the British South Africa company 1894–1914.* Manchester university press, 1958

Gann, L. H. 'The white settler: a changing image' (in *Race*, vol. 2, no. 2, May 1961 p. 28–40)

Gelfand, M. *Proud record: an account of the health services provided for Africans in the Federation of Rhodesia and Nyasaland.* Salisbury, Federal information department, 1960

Gelfand, M. *Tropical victory.* . . . Cape Town, Juta & co. ltd, 1953

Gelfand, M. *Livingstone the doctor: his life and travels.* Oxford, Basil Blackwell, 1957

Gelfand, M. *Northern Rhodesia in the days of the charter: a medical and social study 1878–1924.* Oxford, Basil Blackwell, 1961

'The ghost mines of Mumbwa' (in *Horizon*, v. 3, no. 3, Mar 1961, p. 18–19)

Giraud, V. *Les lacs de l'Afrique équatoriale: voyage d'exploration éxecuté de 1883 à 1885.* Paris, Librarie Hachette et cie, 1890

Gluckman, M. *The economy of the central Barotse plain.* Livingstone, Rhodes-Livingstone institute, 1941 (Paper no. 7)

Gluckman, M. *Essays on Lozi land and royal property.* Livingstone, Rhodes-Livingstone institute, 1941 (Paper no. 10)

Gluckman, M. *Administrative organization of the Barotse native authorities with a plan for reforming them.* Livingstone, Rhodes-Livingstone institute, 1943 (Communication no. 1)

Gluckman, M. *The judicial process among the Barotse of Northern Rhodesia.* Manchester university press, 1955

Gluckman, M. 'As men are everywhere else' (in *Rhodes-Livingstone journal*, no. 20, 1956, p. 68–73)

Goffin, L. 'Histoire du Congo' (in *Encyclopédie du Congo Belge.* Bruxelles, Editions Bierleveld, n.d., v. 1, p. 1–44)

Goodsell, F. F. 'Serenity amid labour . . . the life and work of John Merle Davis 1875–1960' (in *International review of missions*, v. 49, Oct 1960, p. 443–445)

Gouldsbury, C., and Sheane, H. *The great plateau of Northern Rhodesia.* . . . Edward Arnold, 1911

Gregory, Sir T. *Ernest Oppenheimer and the economic development of southern Africa.* Cape Town, Oxford university press, 1962

Hailey, Lord. *Note on the bearing of native policy on the proposed amalgamation of the Rhodesias and Nyasaland.* H.M. Stationery office, 1941

Hamilton, J. Stevenson. *The Barotseland journal of James Stevenson-Hamilton 1898–1899*: ed. by J. P. R. Wallis. Chatto and Windus, 1953 (Oppenheimer series, no. 7)

Hammond, F. D. *Report . . . on the railway system of Southern Rhodesia.* Salisbury, the Government printer, 1926

Hanna, A. J. *The beginnings of Nyasaland and North-Eastern Rhodesia, 1859–95.* Oxford, at the Clarendon press, 1956

Harding, C. *Frontier patrols: a history of the British South Africa police and other Rhodesian forces.* G. Bell and sons, ltd, 1937

Harding, C. *Far bugles.* Simpkin Marshall ltd, 1933

Harding, C. *In remotest Barotseland.* . . . Hurst and Blackett, ltd, 1905

Harrington, H. T. 'The taming of North-Eastern Rhodesia' (in *Northern Rhodesia journal*, v. 2, no. 3, 1954, p. 3–20)

Harris, *Sir* J. H. *The chartered millions: Rhodesia and the challenge to the British commonwealth.* The Swarthmore press ltd, 1920

Hertslet, E. *The map of Africa by treaty.* Harrison, 1909. 3 v.

Hine, E. J. *Days gone by, being some account of past years chiefly in Central Africa.* John Murray, 1924

Hobson, R. H. *Rubber: a footnote to Northern Rhodesian history.* Livingstone, Rhodes-Livingstone Museum, 1960 (Occasional paper no. 13)

Hofmeyr, A. L. *Het land langs het Meer.* Stellenbosch, Christen studenten vereniging van Zuid Afrika, 1910

Hole, H. M. *The making of Rhodesia.* Macmillan and co., ltd, 1926

Holub, E. *Seven years in South Africa: travels, researches and hunting adventures between the diamond fields and the Zambesi 1872–79.* Trans. by E. E. Frewer. Sampson Low, Marston, Searle and Rivington, 1881. 2 v.

Holub, E. *Von der Capstadt ins Land der Maschukulumbwe: Reisen im südlichen Afrika in den Jahren 1883–1887.* Vienna, Alfred Hölder, 1890, 2 v.

Holzhausen, R. 'Deutschland und die Gebiete nördlich des Limpopo in den Gründungsjahren Südrhodesiens' (in *Afrikanischer Heimatkalender*, Windhoek, Kirchenbundesrat des Deutschen Kirchenbundes für Süd-und-Südwestafrika, 1955, p. 58–70)

Hore, E. C. *Tanganyika: eleven years in Central Africa.* Edward Stanford, 1892

Jalla, A. *Pionniers parmi les Ma-Rotse.* Florence, Imprimerie Claudienne, 1903

Jalla, A. *The story of the Barotse nation.* Lusaka, Publications bureau of Northern Rhodesia and Nyasaland, 1961

Jenkins, E. E. *Report of enquiry into the causes of a disturbance at Nkana on 4th and 5th November 1937.* Lusaka, the Government printer, 1937

John XXIII, *pope. Encyclical letter . . . on the missions, known as Princeps pastorum, the prince of shepherds,* 28 Nov 1960

Johnston, *Sir* H. H. *A history of the colonization of Africa by alien races.* 2nd ed. Cambridge university press, 1930

Keller, J. W. 'Responsible government or Union' (in *Rhodesian railway review*, Oct 1921, p. 1–5)

Kirkwood, K. 'British Central Africa: politics under Federation' (in *Annals of the American academy of political and social science*, v. 298, Mar 1955, p. 130–141)

Lacerda e Almeida, F. J. de. *Lacerda's journey to Cazembe in 1798: translated and annotated by R. F. Burton. Also journey of the pombeiros, P. J. Baptista and A. José, across Africa from Angola to Tette on the Zambeze: translated by B. A. Beadle, and a résumé of the journey by M. M. Monteiro and Gamitto by C. T. Beke.* Royal geographical society, 1873

Lane Poole, E. H. 'An early Portuguese settlement in Northern Rhodesia' (in *Journal of the African society*, v. 30, no. 119, April 1931, p. 164–168)

Lane Poole, E. H. *Native tribes of the eastern province of Northern Rhodesia.* 3rd ed. Lusaka, Government printer, 1949

Lawman, M. *The long grass.* Robert Hale ltd, 1958

Laws, R. *Reminiscences of Livingstonia.* Edinburgh, Oliver and Boyd, 1934

Letcher, O. *South central Africa: an outline of the history, geography, commerce and transportation systems of the Congo-Zambesi watershed, with special reference to the mineral industry.* Johannesburg, African publications, ltd, 1932

Livingstone, D. *Missionary travels and researches in South Africa.* John Murray, 1857

Livingstone, D. *The last journals of David Livingstone in central Africa from 1865 to his death. . . .* John Murray, 1874

Livingstone, D. *The Zambesi expedition of David Livingstone, 1858–1863;* ed. by J. P. R. Wallis. Chatto and Windus ltd, 1956 (Oppenheimer series, no. 9)

London missionary society. *Report of . . . deputation to South and Central Africa January-July 1924.* London missionary society, 1924

Long, B. K. *Drummond Chaplin: his life and times in Africa.* Oxford university press, 1941

Lucas, *Sir* C. 'The Lake Tanganyika expedition' (in Lucas, *Sir* C., ed. *The Empire at war, v. 4.* Oxford university press, 1925, p. 243–247)

Lugard, F. D. 'Treaty-making in Africa' (in *Geographical journal*, v. 1, no. 1, Jan 1893, p. 53–55)

Lugard, F. D. *The dual mandate in British tropical Africa.* Blackwood, 1922

MacConnachie, J. *An artisan missionary on the Zambesi, being the life story of William Thomson Waddell. . . .* Edinburgh, Oliphant, Anderson and Ferrier, 1910

McCulloch, M. *A social survey of the African population of Livingstone*. Lusaka, Rhodes-Livingstone institute, 1956 (Paper no. 26)

Macdonald, R. A. S. *Further memorandum on the economics of the cattle industry in Northern Rhodesia, with special reference to the native cattle industry.* . . . Lusaka, the Government printer, 1937

Mackintosh, C. W. *Coillard of the Zambesi: the lives of François and Christina Coillard, of the Paris missionary society, in South and Central Africa, 1858–1904.* T. Fisher Unwin, 1907

Mackintosh, C. W. *Some pioneer missions of Northern Rhodesia and Nyasaland.* Livingstone, Rhodes-Livingstone museum, 1950 (Occasional paper no. 8)

Mackintosh, C. W. *Yeta III, paramount chief of the Barotse, Northern Rhodesia: a sketch of his life.* Pickering and Inglis, 1937

Masters, H., and Masters, W. E. *In wild Rhodesia: a story of missionary enterprise and adventure in the land where Livingstone lived, laboured and died.* Francis Griffiths, 1920

Maugham, R. C. F. *Zambezia.* . . . John Murray, 1910

Maxwell, J. C. 'Some aspects of native policy in Northern Rhodesia' (in *Journal of the African society*, v. 29, 1930, p. 471–477)

Melland, F. H. *In Witchbound Africa*. Seeley service and co, ltd, 1923

Milligan, S. *Report on the present position of the agricultural industry and the necessity, or otherwise, of encouraging further European settlement in agricultural areas.* Livingstone, the Government printer, 1931

Miracle, M. P. 'Plateau Tonga entrepreneurs in historical inter-regional trade' (in *Rhodes-Lvingstone journal*, no. 26, Dec 1959, p. 34–50)

Mitchell, J. C. *African urbanization in Ndola and Luanshya.* Lusaka, Rhodes-Livingstone institute, 1954 (Communication no. 6)

Mitchell, J. C. *The Kalela dance.* Lusaka, Rhodes-Livingstone institute, 1957 (Paper no. 27)

Moloney, J. A. *With Captain Stairs to Katanga.* Sampson Low, Marston and co. 1893

Monclaro, Fr. 'Account of the journey made . . . with Francisco Barreto in the conquest of Mono-motapa in the year 1569' (in Theal, G. M., ed. *Records of south-eastern Africa.* . . . Cape Town, the Government of the Cape Colony, 1896–1905, v. 3, p. 202–253)

Moore, L. F. *Rhodesia's problem: a series of three articles . . . entitled For the company: For the settlers: The next step.* Livingstone, L. F. Moore, 1912

Morris, C., and Kaunda, K. *Black government: a discussion.* . . . Lusaka, United society for Christian literature, 1960

North, A. C. 'Rural local government training in Northern Rhodesia' (in *Journal of African administration*, v. 13, no. 2, April 1961, p. 67–77)

Northern Rhodesia African national congress. *The general president's statement at a public meeting held at Mapololo African township, Lusaka: 26 June 1952.* Lusaka, The Congress, 1952

Northern Rhodesia African national congress. *Historical extract of the African national congress — its activities and growth 1951–1960.* Lusaka, The Congress, 1960

Northern Rhodesia mineworkers' union. *Constitution.* Bulawayo, The Union, 1936

Oliver, R. *The missionary factor in East Africa.* Longmans, Green and co., 1952

Oliver, R. *Sir Harry Johnston and the scramble for Africa.* Chatto and Windus, 1957

Olivier, S. *1st Baron Olivier. White capital and coloured labour.* Independent labour party, 1906

Perham, M. *Lugard: the years of adventure 1858–1898.* Collins, 1956

Perham, M. *Lugard: the years of authority 1898–1945.* Collins, 1960

Petermann, A. 'Die Reisen von Ladislaus Magyar in Süd Afrika' (in *Petermann's Geographische Mittheilungen*, 1857, p. 182–183)

Petermann, A. 'Ladislaus Magyar's Enforschungen von Inner-Afrika' (in *Petermann's Geographische Mittheilungen*, 1860, p. 227–237)

Pineau, H. *Evêque roi des brigands: Monseigneur Dupont des pères blancs, premier vicaire apostolique du Nyassa (1850–1930).* 3rd ed. Quebec, Province du Canada des pères blancs, 1944

Pinto, A. de Serpa. *How I crossed Africa from the Atlantic to the Indian Ocean.* 2v. Sampson Low, Searle and Rivington, 1881

Pôrto, A. F. da S. *Viagaem e apontementos de um Portuense em África.* Lisbon, Agência Geral das Colônias, 1942

Prain, Sir R. L. 'The Copperbelt of Northern Rhodesia' (in *Journal of the Royal society of arts*, 18 Feb 1955, p. 196–216)

Prain, R. L. 'The Northern Rhodesian copperbelt' (in *New Commonwealth*, 7 Dec 1953)

Prain, R. L. *Selected papers, 1953–1957.* Rhodesian selection trust, 1959

2H

Prain, R. L. *Selected papers, volume II, 1958–1960.* Rhodesian selection trust, 1961

Quick, G. 'Some Aspects of the African watch tower movement in Northern Rhodesia' (in *International review of missions*, v. 29, no. 114, April 1940, p. 216–226)

Rhodesian Anglo American ltd. *Mining developments in Northern Rhodesia.* Johannesburg, Anglo American corporation, 1929

Richards, A. I. *Land, labour and diet in Northern Rhodesia: an economic study of the Bemba tribe.* Oxford university press, 1939

Robinson, K. 'Colonial issues and policies with special reference to tropical Africa' (in *Annals of the American academy of political and social science*, v. 298, Mar 1955, p. 84–94)

Robinson, R. E. 'Imperial problems in British politics, 1880–1895' (in Benians, E. A. and others *ed. The Cambridge history of the British empire.* v. 3, Cambridge university press, 1959, p. 127–180)

Rolin, H. *Les lois et l'administration de la Rhodésie.* Bruxelles, Etablissements Emile Bruyant, 1913

Saffrey, A. L. *A report on some aspects of African living conditions on the copperbelt of Northern Rhodesia.* Lusaka, the Government printer, 1943

Sampson, R. *So this was Lusaakas. . . .* Lusaka, Lusaka publicity association, 1959

Scannell, D. T. 'Aviation in Central Africa' (in *Horizon*, v. 2, no. 11, Nov 1960, p. 18–22)

Schultz, A., and Hammar, A. *The new Africa: a journey up the Chobe and down the Okovango rivers. . . .* William Heinemann, 1897

Scott, M. *A time to speak.* Faber and Faber, 1958

Seaver, G. *David Livingstone: his life and letters.* Lutterworth press, 1957

Selous, F. C. *Travel and adventure in south-east Africa. . . .* Rowland Ward and co., ltd, 1893

Sharp, R. R. *Early days in Katanga.* Bulawayo, R. R. Sharp, 1956

Shaul, J. R. H. *Report on the enquiry into the cost of living in Northern Rhodesia.* Salisbury, Department of statistics, 1941

Shaw, J. R. 'The first European settlement on the Kafue and the first copper mine' (in *Northern Rhodesia journal*, v. 1, no. 6, Dec 1952, p. 49–51)

Shepperson, G., and Price, T. *Independent African. . . .* Edinburgh university press, 1958

Shepperson, G. 'The literature of British Central Africa' (in *Rhodes-Livingstone journal*, no. 23, June 1958, p. 42–43)

Shepperson, G. 'Notes on the Negro American influences on the emergence of African nationalism' (in *Journal of African history*, v. 1, no. 2, 1960, p. 299–312)

Silva Rego, A. da *Portuguese colonisation in the sixteenth century: a study of the royal ordinances.* Johannesburg, Witwatersrand university press, 1959

Smith, E. W. *The way of the white fields in Rhodesia.* World dominion press, 1928

Smith, E. W., and Dale, A. M. *The Illa-speaking peoples of Northern Rhodesia.* Macmillan and co. ltd, 1920

Smith, E. W. 'Sebetwane and the Makololo' (in *African studies*, v. 15, 1956, p. 49–74)

Some account of George Grey and his work in Africa. Privately printed at the Chiswick press, 1914

Stephenson, J. E. *Chirupula's tale. . . .* Geoffrey Bles, 1937

Storrs, *Sir* R. *Orientations.* Readers' Union ltd, 1939

Summers, R. *Inyanga: prehistoric settlements in Southern Rhodesia.* Cambridge university press, 1958

Sundkler, B. *The Christian ministry in Africa.* Uppsala, Swedish institute of missionary research, 1960

Tabler, E. C. *The far interior: chronicles of pioneering in the Matabele and Mashona countries, 1847–1879.* Cape Town, A. A. Balkema, 1955

Tanganyika concessions ltd. *Reports on the discoveries made by Mr George Grey's expedition in Northern Rhodesia and Congo Free State.* Tanganyika concessions ltd, 1903

Taylor, D. *The Rhodesian: the life of Sir Roy Welensky.* Museum press, 1955

Taylor, J. V., and Lehman, D. A. *Christians of the copperbelt: the growth of the church in Northern Rhodesia.* S.C.M. press, 1961

Thomas, *Sir* M. 'Dominion of Capricornia' (*Sunday times*, 6 Mar 1949)

Thomson, J. 'To Lake Bangweolo and the unexplored region of British Central Africa' (in *Geographical journal*, v. 1, 1893, p. 97–121)

Trapnell, C. G. *Interim report on methods of extraction of Landolphia rubber.* Lusaka, the Government printer, 1942

Trapnell, C. G. *The soils, vegetation and agriculture of North-Eastern Rhodesia: report of the ecological survey.* Lusaka, the Government printer, 1943

Trapnell, C. G., and Clothier, J. N. *The soils, vegetation and agricultural systems of North-Western Rhodesia: report of the ecological survey.* Lusaka, the Government printer, 1937

Turner, V. W. *Schism and continuity in an African society: a study of Ndembu village life.* Manchester university press, 1957

Van Ortroy, J. *Conventions internationales définissant les limites actuelles des possessions, protectorats et spheres d' influence en Afrique.* Bruxelles, Société Belge de librairie, 1898

Varian, H. F. *Some African milestones.* Oxford, George Ronald, 1953

Von Wissmann, H. *Meine zweite Durchquerung Äquatorial-Afrikas.* Berlin, Globus Verlag, 1907

Wallace, L. A. 'The beginning of native administration in Northern Rhodesia' (in *Journal of the African society,* v. 21, 1922, p. 165–176)

Wallace, L. A. 'North eastern Rhodesia' (in *Geographical journal,* v. 29, no. 4, April 1907, p. 369–400)

Wallace, L. A. 'The Nyasa-Tanganyika plateau' (in *Geographical journal,* v. 13, no. 6, June 1899, p. 595–621)

Watson, Sir M. *African highway: the battle for health in Central Africa.* John Murray, 1953

Watson, W. *Tribal cohesion in a money economy. . . .* Manchester university press, 1958

Weinthal, L. (ed) *The story of the Cape to Cairo railway and river route 1887–1922.* Pioneer publishing co. ltd, 1923, 4 v.

Welensky, R. 'Trade unions in Northern Rhodesia' (in *United empire,* v. 37, 1946, p. 236–240)

White, C. M. N. 'A preliminary survey of Luvale rural economy'. (Lusaka, Rhodes–Livingstone institute, 1959 (Paper no. 29)

White, C. M. N. . . . *Witchcraft, divination and magic.* Lusaka, the Government printer, 1947

Wills, W. A., and Collingridge, L. T. *The downfall of Lobengula. . . .* 'The African review', 1894

Wills, W. H., and Hall, J. (ed.) *Bulawayo up-to-date. . . .* Simpkin, Marshall, Hamilton, Kent & co. ltd, 1899

Wilson, G. *An essay on the economics of detribalization in Northern Rhodesia.* Livingstone, Rhodes-Livingstone institute, 1941–42. 2 v. (Papers nos. 5–6)

Wilson, G., and Hunter, M. *The study of African society.* Livingstone, Rhodes-Livingstone institute, 1939 (Paper no. 2)

2. Official Publications

British South Africa Company

Administration of North-Western Rhodesia: instructions to native commissioners. Livingstone, Native affairs dept, 1908

Directors' reports and accounts [for the period 29 Oct 1889–]. British South Africa company, 1889–

Draft scheme of administration. . . . Salisbury, Government printer, 1916

Information as to the conditions on which land will be sold or leased to bona fide settlers in North-Western Rhodesia, together with notes on North-Western Rhodesia as a farming country. Waterlow and sons, 1906

Instructions for native commissioners. Fort Jameson, Administration press, 1903

Reports on the administration of Rhodesia, 1889/92–1900/02. British South Africa company, 1892–1902. 9 v.

Statute law of North-Eastern Rhodesia 1908–1911, of North-Western Rhodesia 1910–1911 and Northern Rhodesia 1911–1916. Livingstone, Government printer, 1916

Statute law of North-Western Rhodesia 1899–1909. . . . Livingstone, Government printer, 1910

Government of the Federation of Rhodesia & Nyasaland

Central African statistical office. *Northern Rhodesia: report on the census of population, 1951.* Lusaka, Government printer, 1954

Central African statistical office. *Second report on urban African budget survey held in Northern Rhodesia, May to August, 1960.* Salisbury, the office, 1960

Northern Rhodesia Government

Advisory committee on industrial development. *First report, March 1946.* Lusaka, the Government printer, 1946

Advisory committee on industrial development. . . . *Second report, January 1947.* Lusaka, the Government printer, 1947

Advisory committee on industrial development. . . . *Third report, May 1948.* Lusaka, the Government printer, 1948

Board of inquiry to consider the proposed 40 hour week in the copper mining industry of Northern Rhodesia. *Report.* . . . Lusaka, the Government printer, 1950

Commission appointed to enquire into the advancement of Africans in industry. *Report.* . . . Lusaka, the Government printer, 1948

Central advisory board on native education. *Report of the proceedings of the central advisory board on native education, 1937.* Lusaka, The Board, 1937

Commission appointed to inquire into the administration and finances of native locations in urban areas. *Report.* . . . Lusaka, the Government printer, 1944.

Community development in Northern Rhodesia: correspondence between the Secretary of state for the colonies and the Governor of Northern Rhodesia, 1952. Lusaka, the Government printer, 1953

Commission appointed to enquire into the disturbances in the copperbelt, Northern Rhodesia. *Report . . . together with the Governor's despatch to the Secretary of State on the report, November 1935.* Lusaka, the Government printer, 1935

Commission appointed to inquire into the disturbances in the Copperbelt, Northern Rhodesia, July 1940. *Report.* . . . Lusaka, the Government printer, 1941

Commission on silicosis legislation. *Report.* . . . Lusaka, the Government printer, 1949

Commissioner for unemployment. *Report by the Commissioner for unemployment, 1934.* Lusaka, the Government printer, 1935

Committee appointed to enquire into the development of the European farming industry. *Report.* . . . Lusaka, the Government printer, 1946

Committee appointed to investigate European education in Northern Rhodesia. *Report . . . May-July 1948.* Lusaka, the Government printer, 1948

Committee on further secondary education for European children. *Report.* . . . Lusaka, the Government printer, 1944

Committee on immigration. *Report on immigration into Northern Rhodesia.* Lusaka, the Government printer, 1939

Committee on the status and welfare of coloured persons in Northern Rhodesia. *Report.* . . . Lusaka, the Government printer, 1950

Committee to inquire into the African and Eurafrican housing position in Lusaka. *Report.* . . . Lusaka, the Government printer, 1953

Committee to review native taxation. *Report.* . . . Lusaka, the Government printer, 1948

Community development in Northern Rhodesia: correspondence between the Secretary of state for the colonies and the Governor of Northern Rhodesia. Lusaka, the Government printer, 1952

Department of animal health. *Memorandum on the economics of the cattle industry in Northern Rhodesia.* Livingstone, the Government printer, 1935

Development authority. *Review of the ten-year development plan of Northern Rhodesia: submitted by the Development authority and approved by the Legislative council, June 1948.* Lusaka, the Government printer, 1948

Development authority. *Second (1951) review of the ten-year development plan of Northern Rhodesia: submitted by the Development authority and approved by the Legislative council, November 1951.* Lusaka, the Government printer, 1951

Development of social services for Africans: development centres. Lusaka, the Government printer, 1945.

European education commission. *Report of the European education commission.* Lusaka, the Government printer, 1929

Government unemployment committee. *Report of the Government unemployment committee 1932.* Livingstone, the Government printer, 1933

Information department. *Success in Northern Rhodesia.* Lusaka, Information department, 1960

Land board. *Information for intending settlers.* Lusaka, the Government printer, 1949

Land commission. *Report of the Land commission.* Lusaka, the Government printer, 1946

Land commission. *Report of the Land commission on the area acquired by Government from the North Charterland exploration company.* Lusaka, the Government printer, 1944

Land tenure committee. *Report. . . .* Lusaka, the Government printer, 1943

Native land tenure committee. *Report. . . .* Lusaka, the Government printer, 1945

Legislative council. Select committee on land settlement on Northern Rhodesia for ex-servicemen and others. *Interim report. . . .* Lusaka, the Government printer, 1945

Local government committee. *Report . . . September 1936.* Lusaka, the committee, 1936

Local committee on refugee settlement. *Report. . . .* Lusaka, the Government printer, 1940

Northern Rhodesia ten year development plan . . . as approved by Legislative council on 11 February 1947. Lusaka, the Government printer, 1947

Native development board. Sub-committee to review the facilities for the employment of children leaving school. *Interim report of the sub-committee of the Native development board appointed to review the facilities for the employment of children leaving school and in the light of this review to consider to what extent the present native education policy is suitable to the present economic system.* Lusaka, The Board, 1941

Native industrial labour advisory board. *Report of sub-committee of the Native industrial labour advisory board: administrative control of industrial population.* Lusaka, the Government printer, 1936

Native land tenure committee. *Report . . . Part II Maʒabuka district.* Lusaka, the Government printer, 1946

Native taxation committee. *Report on native taxation by a committee consisting of C. R. Lockhart . . . T. F. Sandford . . . S. Gore-Browne.* Lusaka, the Government printer, 1938

Northern Rhodesia blue book. Livingstone and Lusaka, the Government printer, 1924–38

Northern Rhodesia regiment. 1st battalion. *Ceylon to the Chindwin, Burma 1944.* Lusaka, the Government printer, 1946

Report of investigation into the grievances which gave rise to the strike amongst the African employees of the Rhodesia railways and the conditions of employment incidental to such grievances, and to make recommendations for the elimination of any grievances proved to be well-founded. Lusaka, the Government printer, 1945

Statement by the government of Northern Rhodesia on the recommendations of the report of the Copperbelt commission, 1940, issued at Lusaka, 18th February, 1941. Lusaka, the Government printer, 1941

Taxation committee. *Report . . . April, 1934.* Livingstone, the Government printer, 1934

Southern Rhodesia Government

Customs agreement entered into between the governments of Southern and Northern Rhodesia, 1930. Salisbury, the Government printer, 1930

Draft scheme of administration under the proposals for amalgamation of the territories of Southern and Northern Rhodesia. Salisbury, the Government printer, 1916

Central African statistical office. *Report on Northern Rhodesia family expenditure survey, 1951.* Salisbury, the office, 1953

United Kingdom Government

C. 4739 (1886) *General act of the conference of Berlin*

C. 6046 (1890) *Correspondence respecting the Anglo-German agreement relative to Africa and Heligoland*

C. 6048 (1890) *General act of the Brussels conference, 1889–90; with annexed declaration*

C. 6049–1 (1890) *Translations and protocols and general act of the slave trade conference held at Brussels, 1889–90; with annexed declaration*

C. 6212 (1890) *Correspondence respecting the Anglo-Portuguese convention of August 20, 1890, and the subsequent agreement of November 14, 1890*

C. 6370 (1891) *Papers relating to the Anglo-Portuguese convention signed at Lisbon, June 11, 1891*

C. 6375 (1891) *Treaty between Her Majesty and His Majesty the King of Portugal defining their respective spheres of influence in Africa*

C. 7032 (1893) *Agreement between Great Britain and Portugal relative to spheres of influence north of the Zambesi*

C. 7358 (1894) *Agreement between Great Britain and His Majesty King Leopold II, Sovereign of the Independent state of the Congo, relating to the spheres of influence of Great Britain and the Independent state of the Congo, in East and Central Africa, signed at Brussels, May 12, 1894*

C. 7360 (1894) *Papers relating to the agreement between Great Britain and His Majesty the King of the Belgians, Sovereign of the Independent state of the Congo, signed at Brussels, May 12, 1894*

C. 7637 (1895) *Papers respecting the British sphere north of the Zambesi, and agreements with British South Africa company*

C. 7971 (1896) *Agreement between Great Britain and Portugal prolonging the 'modus vivendi' of 1893, respecting the boundaries of their respective spheres of influence to the north of the Zambesi, London, January 20, 1896*

Cd. 7645 (1914) *British South Africa company: correspondence relating to the continuance of the administrative provisions of the charter of the British South Africa company*

Cd. 2584 (1905) *Award of His Majesty the King of Italy respecting the western boundaries of the Barotse kingdom*

Cd. 6265 (1912) *Agreement between the United Kingdom and Portugal respecting the boundary between British and Portuguese possessions north and south of the Zambesi, October 21-November 20, 1911*

Cmd. 1273 (1921) *South Africa: first report of a committee appointed by the Secretary of state for the colonies to consider certain questions relating to Rhodesia*

Cmd. 1471 (1921) *South Africa: second report of the Committee appointed by the Secretary of state for the colonies to consider certain questions relating to Rhodesia*

Cmd. 1914 (1923) *Rhodesia: correspondence regarding a proposed settlement of various outstanding questions relating to the British South Africa company's position in Southern and Northern Rhodesia*

Cmd. 1922 (1923) *Memorandum relating to Indians in Kenya*

Cmd. 1984 (1923) *Rhodesia: agreement between the Secretary of state for the colonies and the British South Africa company for the settlement of outstanding questions relating to Southern and Northern Rhodesia, dated 29th September 1923*

Cmd. 2904 (1927) *Future policy in regard to eastern Africa*

Cmd. 3234 (1929) *Report of the commission on closer union of the dependencies in eastern and central Africa*

Cmd. 3574 (1930) *Statement of the conclusions of His Majesty's government in the United Kingdom as regards closer union in East Africa*

Cmd. 4141 (1932) *Correspondence (1931–1932) arising from the report of the joint select committee on closer union in East Africa*

Cmd. 5949 (1939) *Rhodesia-Nyasaland Royal commission report*

Cmd. 8233 (1951) *Central African territories: report of conference on closer association: London, March 1951*

Cmd. 8234 (1951) *Central African territories: geographical, historical and economic survey*

Cmd. 8235 (1951) *Central African territories: comparative survey of native policy*

Cmd. 8411 (1951) *Closer association in Central Africa: statement by His Majesty's government in the United Kingdom, 21st November 1951*

Cmd. 8573 (1952) *Southern Rhodesia, Northern Rhodesia and Nyasaland: draft federal scheme ... prepared by a conference held in London in April and May 1952*

Cmd. 8671 (1952) *Southern Rhodesia, Northern Rhodesia and Nyasaland: draft federal scheme: report of the judicial commission*

Cmd. 8672 (1952) *Southern Rhodesia, Northern Rhodesia and Nyasaland: draft federal scheme: report of the fiscal commission*

Cmd. 8673 (1952) *Southern Rhodesia, Northern Rhodesia and Nyasaland: draft federal scheme: report of the civil service preparatory commission*

Cmd. 8753 (1953) *Southern Rhodesia, Northern Rhodesia and Nyasaland: report by the conference on federation, held in London in January, 1953*

Cmd. 8754 (1953) *Southern Rhodesia, Northern Rhodesia and Nyasaland: the federal scheme, prepared by a conference held in London in January, 1953*

North Charterland concession inquiry: report to the Governor of Northern Rhodesia by the commissioner, Mr. Justice Maugham, July 1932. (Colonial no. 73)

*North Charterland concession inquiry: report to the Governor of Northern Rhodesia by the Commissioner,
Mr. Justice Maugham, 30th May 1933.* (Colonial no. 85)

*Report of the commission appointed to enquire into the financial and economic position of Northern
Rhodesia,* 1938. (Colonial no. 145)

Commission appointed to enquire into the disturbances in the copperbelt, Northern Rhodesia.
Evidence taken. . . . 1935. 2 v.

INDEX